I0759816

THE CHICAGO WAY

THE CHICAGO WAY

AN ORAL HISTORY OF CHICAGO DINING

MICHAEL GEBERT

A MIDWAY BOOK
AGATE
CHICAGO

First printed in February 2026

Printed in the United States

10 9 8 7 6 5 4 3 2 1 26 27 28 29 30

Library of Congress Cataloging-in-Publication Data
Names: Gebert, Michael author
Title: The Chicago way / Michael Gebert.
Description: Chicago : A Midway Book : Agate, [2026] | Includes index. |
Identifiers: LCCN 2025034611 (print) | LCCN 2025034612 (ebook) | ISBN 9781572843608 hardback | ISBN 9781572849044 ebook
Subjects: LCSH: Restaurants--Illinois--Chicago--History | Ethnic restaurants--Illinois--Chicago--History | Ethnic neighborhoods--Illinois--Chicago--History
Classification: LCC TX907.3.I32 G434 2026 (print) | LCC TX907.3.I32 (ebook) | DDC 647.95773/11--dc23/eng/20250829
LC record available at https://lccn.loc.gov/2025034611
LC ebook record available at https://lccn.loc.gov/2025034612

Cover photo by tunart, iStock

Midway Books is an imprint of Agate Publishing. Agate books are available in bulk at discount prices. For more information, visit agatepublishing.com.

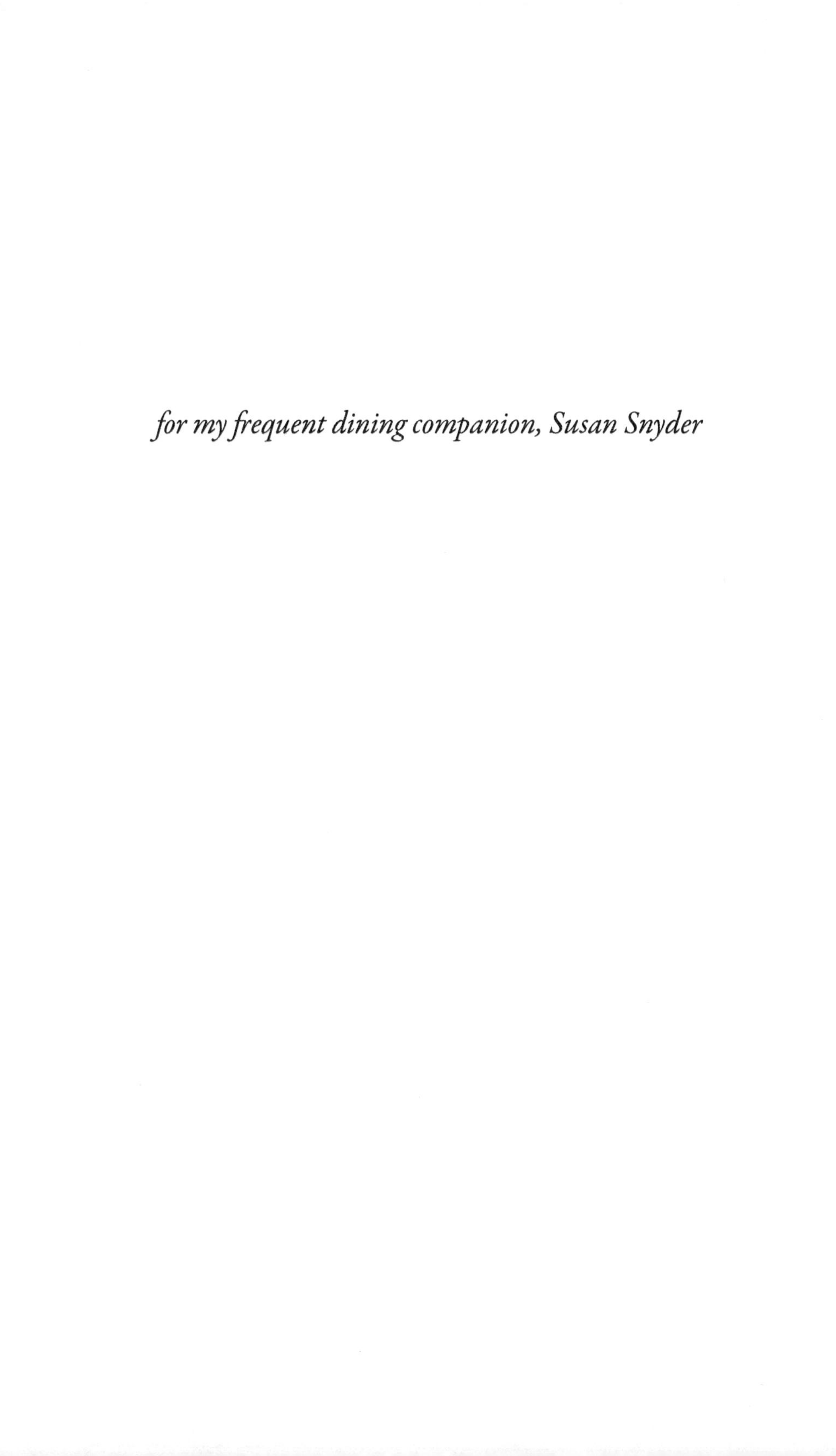

for my frequent dining companion, Susan Snyder

We're a great city, aren't we? We don't do anything right, but we're the best of the best. We have our own nature, our own personality. Say what you want and watch all the media, see all the unrest. Not in Chicago restaurants. Not in Chicago restaurants. We all eat and live and love together.

—TOM CORNILLE, third-generation Chicago produce purveyor

TABLE OF CONTENTS

INTRODUCTION

By the mid-twentieth century, America's list of great restaurant cities ran to, perhaps, three: New York, San Francisco and New Orleans. But beginning in the 1960s and 1970s, Chicago muscled its way onto that list—not because we copied other places, but because we were so much ourselves.

At a time when Chicago was synonymous with the stockyards and steak, Chicago chefs turned that around and became world-famous figures, known for their creativity and innovation in devising inventive dishes and theatrical dining experiences. Trends that began in Chicago swept the world; diners came from all over the globe to experience what was happening here. And all that innovation was built on the foundation of one of America and the world's great regular-people dining cultures, rooted in blue-collar eats like Chicago hot dogs, pizza and a local specialty called Italian beef. Those parallel food worlds complemented and fed off each other; it's not for nothing that when foie gras was temporarily outlawed here, the only restaurant to actually get busted for serving it was a hot dog stand.

So is Chicago the best dining city in America, or even the world? Publications love to serve that question up as clickbait, and both answers—"Chicago is the best" and "Chicago is *so* overrated"—are good for traffic and can be counted on to come around as regularly as the seasons (or the James Beard Awards). Honestly, I don't care one way or the other; it's certainly the best and only dining city I've lived in for more than thirty years, and written about food in for much of that time. This book is the opposite of the kind of feature piece where a well-connected writer parachutes into a city for a weekend and comes out confidently announcing the five restaurants that *matter* right now. It's a book for sinking deeply into one place, about being at home here, and eating what the people who lived here ate over the course of half a century. *That* Chicago has more than enough fascinating stories to justify spending the length of this book exploring it.

A word about what this book sets out to do. It's an oral history, told in the words of the people who worked in the restaurant industry (or interacted with it in some way, as diners, farmers, media figures, or real estate professionals), rather than in my own words as any kind of critic. It doesn't talk about every well-remembered restaurant—which would be impossible in any case, but there are lots of very good restaurants that had a nice run and made people happy, but don't really have a story to tell. The focus here is on the restaurants that *changed our world*—as women entered professional kitchens, neighborhoods evolved into destinations, chefs became celebrities, cooking became the subject of competitive TV shows, and what we in America did for fun became increasingly centered on food over the past half century.

It's about how the city itself changed—how restaurants created hot neighborhoods via the familiar process of artists and bohemians moving in where rent is cheap, with funky coffeehouses and eclectic restaurants popping up to serve (and employ) them. Those spots in turn attract new visitors to the neighborhood, spawning more and more restaurants—and eventually not only the bohemians but their restaurants get priced out of the neighborhoods they created.

Gentrification, it's called, and for many it's a dirty word. But cities aren't static—they're always going to change with economics, and immigration patterns, and how fashionable or not it is to live in the city. The alternative to Chicago's continuous reinvention of the last half-century was what preceded it—a blighted and declining urban landscape of fading prewar factories, surrounded by prosperous, deeply segregated suburbs. As ruthless on individuals as the process of gentrification can be, as dull as the cookie-cutter condos and generic commercial strips that clear-cut old ethnic neighborhoods can seem, this is the story of a city that reinvented itself—that came back to creative and economic life, in no small part because restaurants made new communities. They are, mostly, the heroes of that story and the markers of its change.

Who am I to tell this story? Well, I came to Chicago in the late 1980s from my hometown, Wichita, Kansas, known to this day as a place so perfectly middle-American that new food products and restaurant concepts are often tested there—if Wichitans will eat it, Americans anywhere will, the thinking goes.

Nothing against the place I grew up in, but I wanted to live somewhere where food existed as a *culture*—even if it was also home to big food marketers like Kraft and McDonald's (whose advertising account I would eventually work on). Eating in my new home was the key to exploring it—going into a restaurant or a corner tavern was the easiest way to get to know a neighborhood and my fellow citizens. My essential skill for this book, listening in as others talk, was no doubt honed in these places.

For my first decade here I explored things I was often clueless about, and occasionally sampled the higher end—I never went to Gordon or Le Francais, alas, but I did eat (when I could scarcely afford to) at Le Perroquet, Charlie Trotter's, Spiaggia, Topolobampo and Trio. The millennium had just changed when I read an article by Calvin Trillin in *The New Yorker* about a site called Chowhound, which introduced me to a new world of talking about food with strangers online.

Suddenly the array of dishes on Mexican menus, or in steam pans on Indian buffets, or the little plates of *panchan* at Korean restaurants, were no longer impenetrable mysteries—I could ask for help and quickly get up to speed on them, know what to eat before I went. The democratization of food opinions is one of the things that shaped this new world, and I lived that as much as anybody. (See Chapter 14.)

****

Food media in the early 2000s was a new world of online snarkiness and inside baseball, for which I was a perfect fit. I became the editor of the Chicago edition of *New York* magazine's food column Grub Street, covering the who-went-wheres and tempests-in-sous-vide of Chicago's restaurant scene. And I started shooting a chef challenge video series for the alt-weekly

Chicago Reader, which introduced me to dozens of prominent chefs. That was a huge boost that opened many doors for me, as did winning a James Beard Award for that *Reader* series the next year.

For me, that has meant becoming a chronicler of how chefs try to turn their passions into successful businesses; over the last decade I've set up shop for a morning in dozens of restaurants as chefs poured out their dreams to me, and I've come to love their industry and the commitment of people who work long hours and drive themselves kind of nuts to satisfy a basic human need—with creativity that's anything but basic.

And then that world ended. Or so it seemed.

I had just signed the contract for this book when a coronavirus shuttered Chicago's world-famous restaurant scene and kept home the travelers who were drawn to Chicago to dine; canceled the James Beard Awards that had been resident here for half a decade; and put on hold the Michelin Guides that we loved-hated for considering us worthy of their exquisite Gallic condescension.

Our tasting menu chefs pivoted desperately to takeout short rib dinners, Nashville hot chicken sandwiches and Detroit-style pan pizza in a quest to survive. I never doubted I could still do the book—but I did think, with dark humor, that my ending had just been written for me. Chicago's hot restaurant scene, 1960-something to March 2020.

But watching restaurant people adapt and survive in this terrible situation made me more determined than ever to tell the story of their roots and earlier triumphs. As the chefs of the post-lockdown era rebuilt our food scene from the wreckage of COVID-19, it seemed like the best thing I could do to help was to capture the history and the legends of how they had already, once, built up from nothing a restaurant culture that changed the world.

****

The majority of this book is taken from new interviews I conducted between 2020 and 2024, but it also draws on my journalism from the last couple of decades for my site Fooditor and other places. In each chapter, interviewees are introduced in the way that is relevant to the period being discussed (e.g., "busboy"), with fuller career bios at the end of the book.

Literal speech transcription, of course, makes for hard reading, so I've tried to edit and adapt these free-flowing conversations into what I hope is coherent prose. But I've tried to preserve every voice that contributed and never materially altered the intentions of the people I interviewed. Across sixty-plus years of Chicago's restaurant scene, these are their stories, the way they told them to me.

MICHAEL GEBERT
August 2025

1: FIRST DATE: THE BAKERY

Round as Santa Claus and with an extravagant flowing mustache, Louis Szathmary looked the part of a chef as surely as the Marlboro Man looked the part of a cowboy—and it was just as much a self-created image as any ad man could have concocted. Born in Hungary in 1919, Szathmary earned a doctorate in psychology, but learned to cook in the Hungarian army and wound up in a succession of refugee camps at the end of World War II.

In 1951 he emigrated to the US, finding what work he could as a short order cook in New York City. Through the 1950s he worked as a chef and food scientist for major brands like Armour, developing Stouffer's frozen food line. With his third wife Sadako (Sada) Tanino, who had also been interned during World War II as a Japanese resident in the US, he reinvented himself in the image of a classic European chef. Louis and Sada opened The Bakery in 1963 in a neighborhood called Lincoln Park, best known at that time for its gang activity. The Szathmarys bought the building and filled its upper floors with Louis's massive collection of culinary books.

The shabby-genteel restaurant quickly became a hard-to-get reservation frequented by celebrities and Chicago society. And Chef Louis himself became Chicago's first modern celebrity chef, through his newspaper columns and appearances with TV hosts from Mike Douglas and Dinah Shore to Phil Donahue and Oprah Winfrey. Within a couple of decades after The Bakery opened, Lincoln

Park would be Chicago's most popular neighborhood among yuppies (a term which first appeared in print anywhere in Chicago *magazine in 1980), and Chef Louis was the man who first taught them how to eat.*

SCOTT WARNER (journalist, and busboy at The Bakery): Sada was going to the University of Chicago before she was forced to go to the Japanese internment camp during World War II. And she ended up opening the most prestigious hair salon in Chicago at the time, the '50s. It was called Kay Sada. She would have all the Gold Coast women come in there. Where they did the hair was in the back. The women would come in, and they would have to walk past all the women who are waiting, so everybody could show off their fur coats.

MIKLOS SIMON (busboy and waiter): Louis worked for Armour & Co. So he went to visit Chicago for some meetings. He ended up staying at the Drake, and Sada owned a beauty salon next to the Drake. Eventually he was working more in Chicago than anywhere else, even though he was from Connecticut, his second wife was from Connecticut. He and Sada met somehow, and eventually they got married. They opened The Bakery to bake for airlines, little snacks, basically finger foods—*pogácsa* in Hungarian. And so because there were two Hungarian workers who were mostly drunk every day, they only made about eight hundred of these little biscuits a day. Sada said, we are going to go bankrupt. So they started to open for little dinners. Just four or five tables.

It was a difficult start, but obviously they took off and then they bought the building and expanded, expanded, expanded. Both of them were extremely savvy, hardworking business people and cooks.

SCOTT WARNER: Sada was very, very smart, and she was a tough little cookie in a very good sense. She told me she was Louis's "editor" in that he had tons of creative ideas for The Bakery that he would run by her, and she would guide him into which ones to use and which ones to toss.

He had three wives, I think. And the first one the Nazis killed, she was Jewish, I understand he had a kid with her. He went down to ninety pounds during World War II, almost starved to death between the Nazis and the Communist takeover. Talk about a survivor coming here not speaking English, and literally with hardly any money in his pockets. And I think he faked his way into the restaurant business.

FRANÇOIS DE MÉLOGUE (executive chef, 1980s): When Louis first came to the US, his brother Géza was here first, and got him a job cooking for Jesuits. He could barely speak English at the time. And one day, the Jesuits wanted dessert afterwards. They asked Louis, can you make dessert? and Louis didn't understand what they were asking for. He walked in the back, and he's looking in the storeroom for a can that said "dessert" on it.

He opened The Bakery in what was a funky neighborhood at that time, Lincoln Park. Louis smartly picked it and bought the building because he could afford it. A fifty-seat restaurant, and it immediately gained a reputation, you know, as being *the* spot to eat out in Chicago at the time. He used to do six hundred covers a night, he had a line a full block long of people wanting to get in, into the '70s.

SCOTT WARNER: He had three rooms where you would dine, because that was how whatever had been in the building before him was designed. He just made it work. And one of the rooms had a sink in it, and we would scoop up the dirty dishes, and we were rinsing stuff right in the dining room. And another with a refrigerator case in there, where he kept his cakes.

He had shadow boxes hanging high up on one wall. And they had lobsters in them and one was Amazonian, I mean it's the biggest lobster I'd ever seen. It was from a monster movie. And when they were about to put it in the pot Louis had his back to it, and it was trying to grab Louis like a dinosaur. And somebody screamed, because it could have killed him. Louis turned around and shoved a broom handle at it and the lobster cut the broom handle with its pincer. But they killed it, and so that was the lobster hanging there.

His furniture was secondhand Salvation Army, literally. He'd buy stuff from thrift stores for the restaurant. I saw this happen, the chairs kept breaking when Louis came downstairs and sat. The silverware was all mismatched—it was all secondhand, but nice silverware. And everything was covered with white tablecloths. There was an air of elegance—it really wasn't elegant, but there was something about it. This old building, his personality shone through like something you'd see in Europe. It wasn't pretentious, it was real.

FRANÇOIS DE MÉLOGUE: One day, I made a comment because we sat and had family meal, breakfast, lunch and dinner together every day. And I said God, these chairs are uncomfortable, and he goes, François, that is not a chair. And I'm like, okay? He said, it's a ninety-minute moneymaker. He had figured out that the chairs after ninety minutes would hurt your butt so much that you would want to leave. In the old days, before my time, they used to just straight up walk up to tables, and be like, okay, your time's up. Here's your check. Thank you and kick you out. But when you have a line out the door and you're the cat's meow, nobody fights it, everybody understands.

GARY ALAN FINE (diner): It represented a kind of creative, but also traditional gourmet dining, that was then popular at the high-end restaurants. It was not the kind of French restaurant where there is this quite limited tradition and a lot of frou-frou—decorations, wallpapers and wall sconces. It was a more sedate experience, a more serious experience. It was the restaurant in Chicago that *Gourmet* magazine would have known about.

PAT DAILEY (*Chicago Tribune* writer): For the most part, chefs didn't have personality. They were surly at best. They stayed in the kitchen. And here comes Louis, he's got the iconic look. He's got the belly of a baker. He's got this mustache that you'll never forget. He was jovial, he was a presence. He was friendly. He was fun. He was a great self-promoter, before most people were. And that certainly set him apart.

He was in a cool space in an unexpected area. Again, Lincoln Avenue down at Webster at that point, I mean, who was going out to dinner there at a really nice restaurant? Nice restaurants were downtown. You have to put it in the time frame, understand what Lincoln Avenue was at that time, seedy and dumpy, not a nice place at all. But again, such a wonderful personality, and that, in its own way, was a precursor of chefs becoming more than just somebody who stayed in the kitchen and cooked French-inflected meals or European-influenced meals.

MICHAEL CURTIN (waiter): There was no written menu of any sort. But the waiters would come around to the tables and recite the entire menu to the guests. And then we would go back and take the order.

Everything was French service, all the food would come out on platters and the waiters would silver-serve the food to the guests. We didn't have the luxury of having food runners in those days. The waiter went to the kitchen, you took your order in—there were no computers, of course. Each waiter had like four or five tables. We used to be very, very busy during the restaurant show,[1] we'd do four or five or six hundred people a night. And we'd have maybe two or three seatings.

All chefs are strict, and some of them do not like waiters at all. But he was very good with the guests, he would come out and greet the guests when they'd arrive. He'd let them enjoy their dinner and then he'd come out halfway through to review, see how they were doing, and he would make several trips through the room.

FRANÇOIS DE MÉLOGUE: It was a five-course meal. Everybody started out with the pâté. Then it went to soup and salad. Then it went to the main course. And then dessert. Dishes that were on the main stage were the beef Wellington, of course. The roast duck with a cherry sauce—you can't get more classic than that. On Fridays he did his version of bouillabaisse, and then he had roast pork that was stuffed with a Hungarian sausage. Those are the dishes that really stick out the most.

Louis made the pâté, and the pâté was kind of like his little joke with the richer clientele that we had. Because 50 percent of the ingredients were pork snouts—this super humble, peasant ingredient that he'd use. And I've never again worked in a restaurant where I was roasting, like a hundred pounds or braising a hundred pounds of pork snouts that we pureed, and used as the primary ingredient in the pâté.

A five-course meal at The Bakery when I was there was twenty-three dollars. Louis would always tell me, I'm not here to make money. This is a school for people that work here. He almost felt like it was a community service. You know, for the people that came and ate there. You know you're coming to this

1 The National Restaurant Association show, held every May in Chicago.

institution. And you know you're going to have this experience. Here's the admission fee.

SCOTT WARNER: I don't even know if I should admit this, but I did not like his beef Wellington. People loved it, so it might have been just my taste, but I didn't like whatever ground meat he put on top of it. But in spite of me he went all the way to the bank.

MIKLOS SIMON: We had a very nice wine selection, limited, very limited cocktails. I don't think we had space for it. We had Charles Krug Cabernet Sauvignon, which is my favorite wine from '85 and '86. You could buy that in the restaurant for eighteen bucks. If you look it up now, it's probably $300. But people didn't know what to do with those wines. Sometimes they had a sip and they left half a bottle on the table. Happy for the waiters, because Uncle Louis was very liberal. He said, okay, at the end of the night, you know, if you guys want to have it, you can have it if they don't take it. And he also had a brown bag policy. It was not legal 100 percent, but he said if they paid for it and they want to take it, I'm happy. They are grownups to be responsible.

Again, I was new to the country. I was very surprised that people drink coffee with dinner. Instead of wine or anything, they were asking for coffee with entrees. So that was the general American approach to dining then, into the '80s.

JUAN BOLDIZSAR (employee): He served beef stroganoff because he needed to do something with the part of the tenderloin that he couldn't make into Wellington. Some people might give those scraps to their employees or something like that. But everything went someplace. The trimmings from the chicken were in the goose and the duck, while he rendered that fat and used that to make the pâté that he served, some of which also went into the Wellington with some ground beef on the top. But then the cracklings from when he rendered it got served to the employees as a treat with breakfast. And yeah, that was another tax deduction.

I'm sure part of it came from his Hungarian cleverness, but part of it came from the fact that he spent some time at Armour & Co. where the old saying goes, we use everything but the squeal.

FRANÇOIS DE MÉLOGUE: I think it was United Airlines—I could be wrong about which airline—but they wanted Louis to design airplane food. We had all the little teeny trays that you have on an airplane. We had like twelve execs or twenty execs from the airline fly in, for a tasting. So we made twenty trays of like ten different dishes for them to try. He always was doing stuff like that, you know, he did the food for the first space shot—the food in the tubes. All kinds of cool stuff.

SCOTT WARNER: He used all these canned sauces from Sexton. These large industrial cans of sauces. But of course he was a food scientist who had worked for different food companies. He used some really commercial methods in his food—whatever worked. He brought it all together and made it his.

SHERMAN KAPLAN (reviewer, WBBM radio): Almost everything in that five-course menu had something sweet to it. There was a salad with a sweetened vinegar. The main course was the beef Wellington, which came in a very sweet currant Cumberland sauce. And then of course the desserts. And I thought, here was Louis, his background originally was as an industrial psychologist, he understood what made restaurants tick. And what people like, the flavors that we perceive—sweet, sour, salt and bitter. Well, sweet is the one that we initially all gravitate to, isn't it?

MIKLOS SIMON: I think he was more of a librarian researcher than a cook. He never grew up with an apprenticeship. So he complimented or embellished his knowledge by researching and trying to understand different dishes. Going back to his desk, he created recipes based on recipes that he read. And he figured out creatively how to combine these recipes to make the best result.

SCOTT WARNER: I never saw him cooking in the kitchen. He developed every single recipe and he trained everybody how to do it. He'd be upstairs, developing and testing recipes for all kinds of things, reading his cookbooks.

One night Harry Truman's daughter Margaret came for dinner. She knew him because he'd catered for her in New York. The story was that he didn't really know who she was at first. She placed the order and he told her what he was going to do. And then while he's cooking in her ritzy apartment, at the last minute, she said, oh, my father's going to join us for dinner. Can you make one more serving? It's like an assembly line, but he started making one more, and he's all flustered and this little man comes into the kitchen. "Oh, could I get a glass of water?" He said, sir, I'm very busy, could you get your water out there? And the guy said, I was president of the United States, I'd think I could ask for a glass of water.

FRANÇOIS DE MÉLOGUE: One of the waiters, Miklos Simon, his father Szandor was the head chef for the Communist Party in Hungary. And he came to spend a month with us in the kitchen. Szandor was older, but built like a bull. Another guy like Louis that could outwork any of us young guys.

Szandor didn't speak any English at all. And we had a big party, where a lot of the regulars of The Bakery, the who's who of Chicago culture were there. Szandor's walking around, he couldn't speak a lick of English and everybody's just congratulating them and saying hi to him. Szandor's shaking everybody's hands and saying the one English word he knew. And he was like, thank you. Thank you. Thank you.

And so I see Szandor in the dining room and I pull him aside and I was looking really horrified. I'm like pantomiming half of this—Szandor, you can't say that, thank you, that's a bad word. You say "fuck you." So the rest of the night, he's walking around the dining room, socialites on the level of the Wrigleys or something are walking up and they're saying, oh, thank you so much for cooking this wonderful meal. And he's like, fuck you. Fuck you very much.

MICHAEL CURTIN: A personal friend of Chef Louis who came in on a regular basis was Sir Georg Solti, music conductor of the Chicago Symphony. He was Hungarian, and he was a true gentleman.

JUAN BOLDIZSAR: He had some notebooks from some of the celebrity parties that he hosted. One of the people who had Louis cater a party for him was Frank Zappa. And in this notebook, there was a picture of this marzipan cake in the form of a naked lady that we made, with Zappa's head between her legs.

FRANÇOIS DE MÉLOGUE: Zappa and Louis were friends. Whenever he came into town, we would get backstage passes, and he would come and have this crazy party at The Bakery. It was the stuff of legend when you worked in the kitchen. One time Louis baked a blackbird pie that had fifty live blackbirds inside of it, when they cut the crust the birds just went flying all over the place through the restaurant. They totally trashed the restaurant, I mean, not breaking furniture, but he had to repaint it for the next morning.

I was thinking about two days in a row back in '85. One was, when the Lyric Opera had their opening for an opera, everybody would come to The Bakery afterwards, and we'd always have a private party. So Pavarotti is there, all these super famous people. I forget what, but one course was like something very fingery and messy, so Louis put down Wet-Naps. And the people there were kind of looking at him. It was like they'd never seen one before. I think some people actually thought they were mints or something.

The next day, Louis did another party—I forget what law school was having a graduation, but they had their graduation meal at The Bakery. So here's all these young lawyer wannabes, coming to The Bakery. And Louis served a silver finger bowl with a slice of lemon, and a little water in there to rinse your fingers. I can't tell you how many people drank it, like lemonade. Just the contrast between opera stars one night with the finger wipes and silver finger bowls the next day was ironic, like the shifting of the guard, so to speak.

****

MIKLOS SIMON: Lincoln Park was still a shitshow then. It was not what you know now. It was still dangerous. I remember looking out one time and a car was crossing Oz Park with two police cars chasing it. During the day. So I imagine that at night, it was not much different.

DEB MAJIC (chef and co-owner of Cafe Figaro): Our friend who invested the first $25,000 which started our restaurant, he wanted something on Clark Street. I walked Clark Street and I just didn't feel comfortable. So I took a walk down Lincoln Avenue and spotted this house—oh my God, look at this. It has a little front yard and a patio. Just looking at it drew us. And The Bakery was there on the same block. Chef Szathmary was there. This has to be a great place. Sterch's Bar was there, it was a big bar next to us. The block had a lot of energy.

There was also a pizza place where a lot of the Mob hung out. Well, we didn't realize that until one fellow got shot in the head. They did not like us opening up an outside patio, being able to watch them. We were fighting in City Hall [to get a patio] and we knew it was them trying to stop us from seeing what they're up to.

JUAN BOLDIZSAR: I want to say there was a Yugoslavian fellow who worked at The Bakery for a while. And you know if you've ever been to the restaurant or you know where it was, the alley opened onto Webster there, right on the other side of Oz Park. And you know there's a rat problem in Lincoln Park. There always has been, and Louis's building had those three buildings together. They were all interconnected.

Don't get me wrong, he was a stickler for sanitation. Everything that was kept in the basement was kept up on racks and what have you, but you have to actively take measures. So the bathrooms for the employees were right near the back entrances. And there was a patio right off the back that led to the alley. So everybody's in that back room behind the office, where people set up tables there for the diners. And this fellow from Yugoslavia comes marching into the dining room, you know holding up an enormous rat that had crawled out of the toilet when he was in that back bathroom. And he holds it up and goes, look, Louis, look, Louis, I killed the rat. And he was very disappointed when instead of praising him Louis said basically, get that thing out of here! But yeah, in one hand, he held it. And the guy was an amputee, and he holds up this stump. He smashed the thing with his stump.

MIKLOS SIMON: He was always inviting Hungarian literary people who also gave lectures there. And he basically hosted them for a week or two weeks. Every summer we had Hungarian summer students. Some of them were already in America, but they came to do some research work on food psychology. I lived there probably from '81 to '87, six years.

JUAN BOLDIZSAR: When Louis bought the place, I think he paid fifty dollars per storefront in rent, and then relatively early on, he bought the place. Which was the smartest thing he could have ever done. No permits for any kind of work were ever pulled for as long as he was there, so the taxes didn't go crazy on him. And yeah, he didn't have anybody to pay rent to. If he put up an employee, at the same time he'd reduce their wages in cash, and get a tax deduction. He got a kick out of collecting cookbooks, they were his personal collection. But, also a big tax write-off. Research. So everything was there for a reason and played a part. Everything fit together like a Jenga puzzle.

SCOTT WARNER: He was very caring about people. In 1970, he had health benefits for his employees. He would have his apartment building complex filled with refugees he brought over to give them jobs and help them find work. They were all these educated people who had fled Eastern European countries, they'd been teachers and accountants and stuff. These refugees would come with nothing. And he would put them up in his apartment giving them a job working in the restaurant. The work ethic of these Europeans—I mean, these teachers and accountants, they didn't think anything of cleaning the tables and mopping the floors. It was just what you do. You work hard. And then he would help get them settled in better jobs.

He took care of his employees. He told me to come in the morning, even though that wasn't my shift. He said, you can have breakfast with us. He had somebody cooking for the staff, and it was delicious. It was like earthy, peasant food. Or lunch, we could have breakfast or lunch, you know, depending on which shift we were on. But he said even if you're not on that shift, come on in. The chicken soup was the best I'd ever had in my life. I can still taste it. I mean, you could taste chicken in it, it was just heaven. And I said, how did you make that? He said, "Gott demn that dish! This old lady come in and make it from bones and everythink every day. I don't know how she make it, Gott demn it, but it's so good!"

JUAN BOLDIZSAR: Louis had employee breakfast at a quarter of nine every day. And you had your choice of scrambled or fried eggs. I think it was either Fridays or Saturdays they made French toast with the leftover bread from earlier in the week. It was a treat. Sometimes they put out duck cracklings at breakfast, duck and goose cracklings. And for the Mexican staff, jalapeño peppers. A cook named Rafael would get his eggs. And then he would take a jalapeño pepper and cut it down its length into a star pattern. And then you know depending on whether it was a medium or a large one, he'd either take the entire jalapeño or maybe half if it was a bigger one, and sprinkle it all over his eggs. Followed by what seemed to be almost two tablespoons of Tabasco sauce. Well, that's probably what woke him up.

MICHAEL CURTIN: We'd have dinner, Chef Louis and his wife, and whoever worked the office, the accountant, or whatever, and the chefs and waiters, we would all sit down as a family and have dinner at four o'clock. We all had dinner together like a family. It was really the most tight-knit family operation that I ever worked in in my life, to be honest with you.

JUAN BOLDIZSAR: There was relatively little turnover. It was like many of the other old school high-end restaurants where these guys just went and stayed. Franz, Rudy, a guy named Szandor, Hungarian guy. Omer, who was a captain at the Drake Hotel as well, he was there for a long time. These guys were making fifty grand, then, and that was before anybody had the forced tip declaration.

FRANÇOIS DE MÉLOGUE: Louis was that kind of guy, you know, like on one hand, you'd be crouching in the corner fearing for your life, ripping you a new asshole for something. But in the second moment, the most compassionate person you'd ever want like in your corner—your advocate when you're really in trouble.

We had a Hungarian cleaner named Podor who didn't speak a word of English despite having worked at The Bakery for like, twenty years. But he was the guy that did all the cleaning of the whole building. Louis totally took care of him, fed him three meals a day, gave him a place to live in one of the apartments above the restaurant. Every time he got paid, Podor would go out and get a hooker. He'd put on his best suit, go out, find some woman, have a great hour or whatever, and then he was back to being broke, drinking beers and eating the food at the restaurant.

So one night, he goes out, he's got on his best outfit. He's walking out on the street, and there's a woman. And what he didn't realize was that she was an undercover police officer, busting a prostitution ring. And in the unmarked car not too far away from her were two Dick Butkus-sized plainclothes officers. So Podor in his broken English makes the deal with her and grabs her hand and he's leading her back, all set to go for the night. And the two cops hop out of the car and go up to Podor and try to arrest him. But he doesn't understand what they're saying. He thinks they're trying to take her from him. And he's already like, scheduled her, so he kicks both of their asses, knocks them both out and grabs the undercover cop woman, dragging her into the building until she can pull out her gun and badge. And that took Louis all kinds of stuff to get him out.

****

JUAN BOLDIZSAR: My father was Hungarian. My folks came to the US in 1961 from Montevideo, and they were friends with Louis and Sada. When I was a kid, they wanted to get rid of me on Saturdays 'cause I was just bored. Let's see if Louis can do something with him! So I spent my Saturday mornings hanging around The Bakery, from about '79 to '89, when he closed.

I was twelve years old. I would cut Louis's newspaper column out, because he would clip them from the *Sun-Times* and before that the *Daily News*, and file them away so that he had copies to give to people. So that was one project. And then in his cookbook library, he had a lady who was helping him catalog and sell all of his seconds, his extra copies of this or that. And, you know, I helped type up the cards for the books and pack them up into boxes so that when somebody ordered something from the sale, we'd know where to find it.

If I was left unsupervised for a couple of minutes, I might sneak into the rare book room. Which is where he had all of these fourteenth and fifteenth century illuminated manuscripts, wow. And then I graduated to answering the phone taking reservations. Helping the staff accountant take inventory of what was sold the night before. After that, yeah, I worked as a busboy—I helped out as a server, but that was pretty much towards the very end because you needed to be old enough.

SCOTT WARNER: When I was twenty, I started contributing articles to the Lerner newspapers. That was 1966. They hired me to work part time while I was in school, and they used to give me Louis's columns to edit. What did I know about editing, I just took the Hungarian-ness of them and made them sound like English. He had colorful stuff to say, so it was like polishing a diamond.

And then I decided I wanted to meet him. So I ate at his restaurant. The Hungarian goulash, we thought it was expensive. I think it was less than ten dollars for the whole dinner.

He became like family to me. And he had me over for all kinds of media events, and I'd go to events in his home on Wellington, and then I ended up working for him as a busboy. I had him over a couple of times to my place to eat. How many people have the top chef in Chicago to your place to eat? And I just thought, well, nobody invites him because they're too scared. I served him lox and bagels and cream cheese and I bought a dessert from Kenessey [Hungarian restaurant and bakery in the Chicago neighborhood of Lakeview]. And he loved it. And he said to me, he said, you know, I know lots of people, but I don't have many friends. You're my friend.

FRANÇOIS DE MÉLOGUE: I went to the New England Culinary Institute. And the second year Louis Szathmary came and spoke at the school. He was a really, really intense person. And everything he said in that speech, just totally solidified that I wanted to be a chef. So I struck up a friendship with Louis through letters. And we stayed in touch and I ate at The Bakery a few times.

I was going to go work for Jovan Trboyevic at Les Nomades. He was close friends with my father. And I also happened to be calling The Bakery for a reservation. And whoever answered the phone was like, no, hold on, Louis has been looking for you. And Louis offered me the executive chef job, which was ridiculous—I was fresh out of school, and other than working for my family I'd only worked at one restaurant. But I was completely headstrong. I thought I knew everything, just like everybody starting out in the restaurant business.

Louis was a hard guy to work for. Very intense person, and nothing against Hungarians but in my experience, they're forceful people. Even when they say "I love you," it kind of sounds like they want to rip your head off.

He was a character straight out of the old school. To me, he was one of America's bridges to the past, in much the same way that Paul Bocuse was in France. I ate at Bocuse a month after Paul Bocuse passed away. And eating at his restaurant was kind of like going back in time in France—dishes that were on his menu were dishes from the 1800s that his mentor's mentor learned on her internship. And here it still is on a menu, completely irrelevant in this time and day, but one of those iconic dishes. Working for Louis was the same kind of thing.

He had a volatile character about him. Barbara [Kuck] was his assistant, she worked with him in the test kitchen, she was his right hand—but I remember a time when I came out of the walk-in during a party, Louis was sitting on the stool in the kitchen, and all of a sudden he picks up a knife. And Louis is a huge guy, he's ambling after her. "Barbara, I will keel you." He got mad at me one time, I forget for what, he cornered me in the kitchen saying, you are not my chef. You are my *shit.* Lines you're like half laughing at. I don't mean it to sound as abusive as it sounds. I never felt like Louis was abusing me. It always felt like your grandfather scolding you for screwing something up.

On the other side, Louis was also just one of the most incredible people. He had a memory, I mean, he just knew something about everything and liked to go on for hours talking about food. That kind of knowledge, I think, is not as prevalent in today's chefs as it was back then. He was definitely a well-read person. He was just such an intense guy, and when he saw you took an interest in something, he would give you anything in the world to help you out.

SCOTT WARNER: Louis would sometimes erupt at Sada, as he did with just about everyone. And after one eruption, Sada bluntly told him, Louis, if you want I can leave, right now. Do you want me to leave? Louis shut up and immediately ordered flowers for her and apologetically took her out to dinner.

MIKLOS SIMON: My father came to America in 1970, he had a brother who lived in Chicago. And so a good friend of Louis who was also Hungarian said, you can maybe work in his restaurant and make a little extra money and enhance your life in Hungary. So he met Louis and Géza, and they just totally embraced him. He was known in The Bakery as the *gombó király,* which means the dumpling king. He made the best traditional bread dumplings, like they make in Austria.

So I came and we both moved into The Bakery building. I became a dishwasher. Wash glasses, every night six, eight hundred dishes. And then I started at the School of the Art Institute, well, you need to make money as a student. So Louis promoted me to be a waiter. I also cooked with him, many times. Eventually, he fired me. And this is my favorite story. So I became a citizen in '87. And, well, he's like my uncle. I know his temperament. So I said, Uncle, I'd like to visit my family. And I'd like to take a month of vacation. What, how do you dare to, I'm firing you right now. He called Sada and said, I fired Miklos. She said, and why did you fire him? Because he wanted to take vacation.

She says, we only have eight waiters including him, usually we have ten, we are short of staff, you cannot fire him. He asks, well, when will the other staff be back? Two weeks from now. Okay, Miklos, you're fired two weeks from now.

****

SCOTT WARNER: I don't ever recall him having a PR person. He was his own best PR person. He was a master. And I guess the reason for the success of The Bakery was because he was such a showman and such a PR person and knew how to promote himself in a very meaningful way to the press. He was a showman with substance behind him. But I guess it wouldn't have been anything without showmanship. And then, you know, he ended up writing a column for the *Sun-Times* for years, right? It was syndicated. One media luncheon, he had me over for lunch, and he had somebody else there. I think it was just the two of us because he wanted me to meet him: Allen Kelson, who had just started reviewing at *Chicago* magazine.

FRANÇOIS DE MÉLOGUE: Louis wielded immense power on the restaurant scene in Chicago. I remember when I was there, we got a negative review. And I can't remember if was the *Sun-Times* or the *Tribune*. But the writer went on about how shitty the food was, it was completely dated. It was crap. And he made this huge point about talking about the tomato bisque soup, that was godawful. Well, Louis had never served tomato bisque soup in the history of the restaurant. And so he was just completely livid. You know, not about getting a bad review, but that, obviously, this guy had fabricated and had some axe to grind with him. Louis pretty much got the guy fired over it.

JUAN BOLDIZSAR: When he opened he was considered novel, revolutionary, something new, something cool. He was an early ham-it-up kind of guy, an early promoter of himself and his business. He had his column, he had his radio show. But people's tastes changed. Later on, I think he might have even conceded that.

FRANÇOIS DE MÉLOGUE: When I worked there in the '80s, it had become the faded gem, because the next crop of big restaurants were popping up. Louis never adapted. He served beef Wellington from day one. I think he really thought that style was going to come back.

I think in a way, Louis became a caricature of himself in his later days, almost became a joke for the stuff that made him famous, the fact that he stuck to it. But so many people still looked to The Bakery as that special spot because a lot of people ate there as kids. And it became very formative in a lot of people's education.

SCOTT WARNER: Louis was the reason Charlie Trotter became a chef. Because he ate there on his prom night. And when he saw Louis coming out of the kitchen into the dining room, he said, that's what I want to do.

MIKLOS SIMON: They showed up all well dressed, they were having good food. And Uncle Louis, kind of looked around. And I said, well, guys, you are so well dressed, and I understand it's the prom, but where is your wine with the meal? Charlie Trotter says, we are not twenty-one. And then Louis said, you know what, it's my restaurant. Everybody can have a sip of wine with a meal. And you have to. So he basically offered them a modest portion of wine with their meal. That's why Charlie Trotter at some point decided to be a chef, because of the power that a chef has in the kitchen, or in the dining room. That was one of the motivations, there were many, many others but that was a motivation to him.

FRANÇOIS DE MÉLOGUE: People like that just aren't made anymore. I think a lot of people look at the image of Jean Banchet as more high-end and premium, but people like Louis were really important steps in our country's culinary development. A lot of people don't realize all the things that he did. When I grew up my mom used to buy this spinach soufflé. Little Stouffer's things that I would bake and get the crust like really brown and kinda almost slightly burnt on the top and eat. That was Louis's grandmother's recipe. Louis did like five of the early, really successful dishes for Stouffer's. Louis did all kinds of things like this.

SCOTT WARNER: He was a benevolent dictator. Looking back, I just wish environments were that nice today. Because here's an entrepreneur who went through hell, and built a business himself, he knew what it was like to almost starve to death. He knew what it was like to suffer.

JUAN BOLDIZSAR: If somebody was there for any period of time and didn't learn something from Louis, they were trying not to.

The Bakery closed in 1989, and Chef Louis died in 1996; Sada died in 2016. His collection of culinary books went to Johnson & Wales University in Rhode Island and the University of Iowa, which publishes a series of culinary arts scholarly works named for Chef Szathmary. In 1991, the city of Chicago designated a stretch in Lincoln Park "Honorary Szathmary Lane."

2: FRENCH LESSONS

There had always been French restaurants in Chicago, since at least the time of the 1893 Columbian Exposition, which set off a local fad for eating snails at De Jonghe's. John Drury's 1931 guidebook Dining in Chicago *cites a number of French establishments in the 1920s and 1930s—at least some, it is hinted, still offering the fruits of serious wine cellars during Prohibition. In the 1940s Henri Charpentier, inventor of crêpes Suzette, served authentic French dishes in the Cafe de Paris in the Park Dearborn hotel, before heading for Hollywood in 1948 and ending his career as French chef to the stars. And before Julia Child, Antoinette and François Pope taught French cooking to upper-middle-class housewives at the Antoinette Pope School of Fancy Cookery and via their 1950s TV show, produced in Chicago and syndicated around the country.*

But French was just one European cuisine among many, and what was served in Chicago in the 1950s and 1960s was often so-called "Continental" cuisine, a mix of European cuisines and dishes adapted to American tastes (and product availability). But beginning in the 1960s, real French chefs and restaurateurs started being lured to Chicago, some of them trained in the nouvelle cuisine style of lighter French cooking coming out of restaurants like Paul Bocuse's in Lyon and Frédy Girardet's in Crissier, Switzerland—meaning that French food in Chicago sometimes actually resembled cooking in Europe at that moment, not a world war or two before. These French chefs—and their young American protégés—would transform restaurant dining to the point where, by the late 1970s, a French restaurant in the steak-and-potato town would be declared by a major critic to be the best restaurant in America.

Alain Maes is a Frenchman who came to Chicago in the 1960s, eventually working as a French trade representative; he has a site devoted to the history of French restaurants in Chicago, French Virtual Cafe.[2] *He recalls "French" dining at the time:*

ALAIN MAES: The first time I came to the US was in August of 1968, during the famous Democratic Convention, which was so violent. I had met a young American lady, who would become my wife, when I was in college; she was in Provence on a Fulbright scholarship. She was from Racine, Wisconsin, and not really knowledgeable in the field of eating good dishes and drinking wine. So the first thing I did was to take her to a few restaurants and introduce her to Provençal cuisine and good wine. And she became very rapidly addicted.

So then I spent two weeks in Racine. My mother-in-law, she was doing okay as far as cooking. But she was very intimidated by the fact that I knew a lot about food. She did what she could, but the kind of food they served in 1968 in Racine, Wisconsin was not exactly the type of food we were used to. And not only that, but my wife told her that we were used in France to having wine with lunch and dinner. So she went to the pharmacy, because in those days in Racine, the closest place where you could find some wine was at the pharmacy. And she bought some wine, which was either Paul Masson Cabernet, or Christian Brothers. And there was a terrible wine from Portugal, which was sort of a rosé in an earthenware bottle—Mateus or Lancers, I don't remember which it was, but it was terrible. And so that was my first contact with American food and American wine.

His brother-in-law invited him to dine at a real French restaurant in downtown Chicago:

He took me to lunch to what was called Jacques French Restaurant. I was very impressed by the decor and the environment, we were sitting at a table

2 Frenchvirtualcafe.blogspot.com

next to a little inner garden. I was sort of celebrating in advance about having a French lunch.

So the waiter came, and my brother-in-law tells him that I was French. And he says, oh, *très bien, très bien,* with a *terrible* accent. He said that he was half French, but I don't know where from. The entree was an omelet which was totally overcooked, with fries which were soggy. Before that, I think it was some sort of salad. The waiter asked me, of course you want French dressing? I said, sure. And what he brought was half wilted leaves of iceberg lettuce, totally submerged in this very sweet, white sauce. And I was told this is the finest dressing. And after that, he brought me some pudding—I think it was based on rhubarb.

So my brother-in-law was embarrassed because he could see that I was not eating much. And the waiter came back and said, you want some coffee? He first tried to serve me coffee with the appetizer. In France, we drink coffee after dinner. And I said, well, I wouldn't mind having a glass of wine. And the waiter brought me a glass of a Sauvignon, which was so sweet that I couldn't touch it. So I ended that meal by discovering what was considered in those days one of the finest beers—called Michelob.

JOVAN TRBOYEVIC

You wouldn't know it from Alain Maes's dire experiences, but Chicago was then in the early days of a French revolution that would change dining culture. One of the restaurateurs who would lead Chicagoans there was a Serb from Yugoslavia, Jovan Trboyevic. Like Louis Szathmary, he had a long and tumultuous path through the mid-twentieth century on his way to becoming a Chicago restaurateur.

Philip Hess and his late wife Margaret were young law students whose journey to becoming sophisticated diners might be typical for the period (of course it involved Julia Child)—but also unusual in how close they would become with Jovan Trboyevic and his wife Maggie.

PHILIP HESS: Margaret had been cooking for her family, just basic, Betty Crocker-type meals, all through her childhood. And when we got together, she asked me what my favorite food was. I was raised in a very different background, and I said, well, my favorite food is chocolate soufflé. And she thought for a minute and said, well, I've never made one of those. But if you give me the right equipment and the right book, I'll give it a try. So we looked in our neighborhood, which was Hyde Park because we were both going to the University of Chicago. And we found a couple of very good Le Creuset cookware items, and we found volume one of Julia Child. And Margaret made a chocolate soufflé, and never looked back.

When she turned twenty-one in 1971, we wanted to have a special dinner, because of the two of us, she was the first one legally allowed to drink alcohol. Back then the main restaurant resource was what became *Chicago* magazine, the WFMT [classical radio station] program guide. And Allen Kelson was the restaurant reviewer, and we relied on his encyclopedic listings—at least to us they looked encyclopedic. So one of the restaurants that intrigued us was a place called Jovan, which was downtown or Near North Side—we didn't know much about the area, but it sounded nice.

We had a wonderful time with a bottle of champagne, which they didn't question, just served it. And it was a very, very memorable evening. I remember the waiter or the captain came over after we finished the champagne and said, more wine, sir? I said, uh, no. He said, no, I think not. Anyway, we had a wonderful evening.

We started going there for lunch occasionally. It was not crowded and it wasn't at all charged with the atmosphere of a fancy dinner. Right around the time we started law school, we got a mailing saying Jovan Trboyevic proudly announces the opening of his new restaurant Le Perroquet, and you're invited to opening night.

It was quite the occasion. Everybody was having champagne cocktails. Jovan, who had pulled out all the stops for this place, had nothing but Val Saint Lambert crystal for his wine glasses. And I would see these waiters, bringing trays of six or eight of them, and they had to walk like they were on eggshells because they were full to the brim.

After about six or eight visits, we began saying to ourselves, I wonder who Jovan is. Which one do you think he is? So we began to identify different people, and finally settled on this one person who *must* be Jovan, because he didn't seem to have a particular function, he just sort of wandered around.

Margaret decided one day that Le Perroquet was just such a wonderful inspiration for us, she sat down and wrote a letter. Just sent it to Jovan Trboyevic, Le Perroquet. By then we had traveled to Europe once or twice, and we'd been to a couple of very fancy restaurants. But her letter said we just want you to know, we have never had a more wonderful restaurant experience, not in Paris, not in France, not in New York. She got a very nice letter back from Jovan saying, thank you so much for your kind words, and next time you come to the restaurant, please let the staff know, I want to come say hello to you. The next time we went there, we told them and a few minutes later, Jovan came out and of course, we'd *never* seen him on the floor. We were completely stunned. *That's* Jovan?

But he was extremely nice. He told us how much he loved our letter. And then as he left after a brief conversation, he said, you have to tell us what you want us to cook for you. You can't just eat off the menu every time. So Margaret got to work and planned out an amazing menu, which the next time we went, we gave to Jean-Pierre, the maître d', to give to Jovan. The main course was *poulet demi-deuil,* which is chicken with black truffles inserted under the skin and roasted. And then dessert was going to be Pithiviers, which was a wonderful French apple-almond puff pastry dessert. So we picked a night and we invited I think two other friends. And we had this unbelievable dinner and the staff were just as happy to serve it as we were to eat it. It was an amazing experience.

Margaret decided to write him a letter inviting him to dinner. I said, are you crazy? She said, I want to cook for him. That's what I do. And to our astonishment, he wrote back and said he'd love to come to dinner. Margaret said, would you like to bring someone, and so we met [his wife] Maggie. Some time later they invited us over to their place and we had an equally wonderful time. So a real friendship developed.

We just loved listening to him talk about what he was planning to cook and how he was getting more and more adventurous in terms of his raw materials. He was one of the first people we knew of who was going all over the country for ingredients. He was getting diver scallops from Maine, he was getting Smithfield hams, he was getting stuff from all over the place. He and I used to have endless debates about wine because I was getting more interested in wine, especially California wine. And he kept scoffing at California wine because, he said, the problem with these California wineries is yes, they can make some very good wines, but they don't make enough of them for a restaurant, I can find a wine that I really like. And they'll sell me three bottles of it, or six. I'm not going to put a wine on my wine list, which the day after I put it on wine list, it's gone, and I can't reorder it.

Anyway, 1975 came and I was graduating law school and we were leaving Chicago, moving to New York. And we had a wonderful farewell lunch for the last day of law school and said goodbye and drove off to New York. But for the next two years, we made a point, because we were kind of homesick, that every few months, we would fly back to Chicago and go to Le Perroquet. Margaret and I both were absolutely certain that Jovan taught us, both of us, everything we knew about great food and wine. I mean, without him we never would have developed the tastes and the curiosity and the enthusiasm that we did. So he really was the source of all of our education and our early experience, and you couldn't have asked for a better teacher.

****

MAGGIE TRBOYEVIC (artist, interior designer; wife of Jovan Trboyevic): When Jovan was 19 or so, he was living in Yugoslavia. He went to engineering school in Kotor Bay, where they had a lot of ships and shipping areas on the Adriatic. So he was in school when Yugoslavia was invaded by the Germans. He went down to the port, and there was a submarine there. And he asked the captain if he could come with them. He wanted to get out of Yugoslavia, join them. He was in engineering school and he worked with motors and so on and he knew a lot about electricity. So they took him on, and they in effect stole this boat, called the Nebojša.

They ended up going to Crete. They would recognize them as fellow Orthodox, friendly. He got off, he wanted to stay. At that point, the Italians were bombing the harbor there. They hooked themselves up with the English fleet, they became part of the British navy. They went to Alexandria, where he stayed. He was being trained to take radios back into Yugoslavia, so they could give them to a general who was in the mountains of Bosnia, Mihailović. He stayed up there, I think, close to two years.

The Allies switched allegiance from Draža Mihailović's Chetniks to Tito's Communist partisans in 1944. Mihailović's forces had to disperse.

Jovan made his way through the mountains and came down on the other side. And because it was raining, he waited and waited until there was a storm, so that the Germans wouldn't be out. He went across and he got to the other side, and he was in Switzerland. The sun came out, he dried off his clothes and everything on the stones there. And then he went down into the village, and he turned himself into the British delegation there. And they interned him at the Palace Hotel.

There was a British woman, Lady something, and she was a widow. And he was very handsome and charming. She told him, with your knowledge of food, you could go to the Lausanne cooking school. I'll send you there. You really should get a trade because you can't go back to your country. There's nothing else you can do. So that's how he learned about service.

He liked Americans. He liked their energy, their attitude. The Americans asked him if he would work in Frankfurt, to debrief German prisoners there. And he was doing that. They were all his age. They got along very well. He got a lot of information from them. They all drank and he was a great drinker and they'd drink together. And then the Americans asked him if he wanted to come and work in Washington. So he immediately became an American citizen.

Trboyevic came to America with his first wife, whom he married in Switzerland, and they opened a restaurant in New York City. It was successful, but the marriage wasn't. While in New York, Trboyevic met Burton Browne, who owned the Chicago-based Gaslight Clubs, inspiration for the Playboy Clubs. After helping open one in Los Angeles and working in Washington, DC, he came to Chicago, and opened his first restaurant, eventually having three: Jovan, Le Perroquet and Les Nomades. He met his second wife, Maggie Abbott, when she was hired to paint murals at Jovan, around 1967.

Jovan was the first of his restaurants. As you walked in, you went down a few steps—it was an old Chicago brownstone. We had a bar downstairs, an area where you could sit and drink but it was a very low ceiling. The menu was a fixed menu. I mean, you had everything that you wanted on it, but it was $9.50 for dinner, and lunch was like $5.75 or something. This is about 1966, 1967.

I started to do paintings for him. And then we'd sit and we'd talk. And we loved to talk. I mean, it was just great. I loved talking to him. He liked talking to me. And we had really a good time. He asked me out and I said, oh, you know, he's too old. And I had heard about his reputation. No, I don't think so. But then eventually I did go out with him. And that was that.

****

Spanish-born Gabino Sotelino was the chef at Le Perroquet in the mid-seventies; the first time he came to Le Perroquet, he had already crossed paths with Trboyevic in Washington, DC, where Trboyevic had managed a private club.

GABINO SOTELINO: I come to Chicago in the spring of 1974. I come to see a friend, who worked in Wheeling for Jean Banchet, and we go to eat at the restaurant that was supposed to be the best in the city, Le Perroquet.

I never knew that Jovan was the owner. But I hear, hey, Basque, what are you doing here? I said I had a lunch, what are *you* doing here? He say, well, I'm the boss, I'm the big big boss over here. One thing led to another, and the conversation after lunch ended up to be until seven in the evening. He was telling me that he was in trouble because he needed a chef, he had an older French chef but he had some problems. So he ask if I can help him, work for him for a couple of weeks. I end up there for three and a half years.

I was introducing the nouvelle cuisine that I was doing from my friends at Paul Bocuse and Michel Guérard and all of those people in Europe. In fact, two years later, we did a dinner for Michel Guérard and Paul Bocuse in Le Perroquet, which was a fantastic event. I think it was one of the biggest events that ever happen in Chicago because 1973, 1974, you can count them on your fingers of your hands how many white tablecloth restaurants there were. Chicago was basically meat and potatoes, is what it was.

MAGGIE TRBOYEVIC: The food at Jovan was kind of a classic French cuisine, where at Le Perroquet, he wanted to do a lighter cuisine. He knew a number of friends in France who were fiddling around with what became nouvelle cuisine. One of his closest friends was Frédy Girardet, who had his restaurant in Crissier [Switzerland]. That was fabulous, and it was very light, very interesting cuisine. So Frédy and he would talk a lot about food, and he patterned a lot of his thinking on this food.

BERNARD GUINAND (cook at Le Perroquet): I was working at the Claridge Hotel in Paris. And Mr. Jovan was there for vacation. And he asked the chef, do you have cooks? I'm going to open a fancy restaurant. So I came here and worked at Jovan restaurant.

If you do your job, he was very good to work for, like Jean Banchet. Everything was top notch—cooking, service. You expected the best. All the captains, they used to be maître d's somewhere.

FRANK LEE (cook at Le Perroquet and Les Nomades): I got into this crazy business by starting a militant hippie vegetarian restaurant in Columbia, South Carolina in 1972. I thought I was going to do it for a year and then go back to college, and I look up and six years have gone by. And so I started to get serious about cooking. I wrote a bunch of letters and Jovan was one of the few that called me. And I jumped in the car and got there in twenty hours, and he was kind enough to hire me to be a morning line cook at Le Perroquet, just as green as could be.

MARY SUE MILLIKEN (cook at Le Perroquet): I went to Washburne trade school on the South Side of Chicago. My first job was at the Conrad Hilton Hotel in the banquet department, and then after that, I got a job at Maxim's [in Chicago], which had a very, very French brigade. I came in as the shallot peeler. I was very low man on the totem pole at Maxim's, I would turn potatoes and peel asparagus. And then they gave me one job of cooking, which was to take the live trout, and knock it on the head and kill it, and then hand it to the chef on the fish station, to put in their *truite au bleu* court bouillon. That was the worst job, they gave it to me because I was a woman.

I had eaten at Le Francais, and at Le Perroquet, because my boyfriend at the time was a big foodie. Otherwise, I would have never been able to afford to eat at those places. I got my heart set on getting a job at Le Perroquet, because the food was so different from all the other French restaurants that I've eaten in—so much better and more creative. It just had its own flair and its own simplicity and attention to the ingredients and where they come from, which I wasn't feeling at some of these other stodgy kinds of places.

So, I told the director of my school that I wanted to work there, and he said, oh, well, I'm a Yugoslav, he's one of my countrymen. I'll call Jovan and I'll get you an interview. I thought, oh, good, I'm going to land a job right away. I went to the interview, and Jovan was just like, oh, I don't think that could possibly work. You couldn't work in my kitchen, you're far too beautiful. And, you know, all those men in there, they wouldn't be able to handle it. And I was like, but this is the only place I want to work. He said, well, if you want to come and be a hat check girl . . . I remember I cried on the way home in the car. I'd sort of been set up to think that the director of the school had like a relationship with this guy and I was gonna get this job. So I just didn't know what to do.

I wrote him a couple of letters. I sent them and I called [him] a few times. And finally, he picked up the phone and said, look, are you gonna sue me? I said, no, I just want a job. I'd already been through two years of chef school. I'd work at nighttime throughout chef school, I just graduated with like, the highest honors in the whole class. So he said, all right, come in tomorrow. $3.25 an hour, you can peel shallots.

Jean Banchet was doing, like, chicken liver mousse in a pâte à choux that looks like a swan. That's like from the '40s or something, or Escoffier. It was stodgy and old-fashioned French, whereas Jovan was doing all new ideas. *Beurre blancs* were really the thing. We also made pâtés there, we made some very old rustic pâtés. We did like, a suckling pig, braised in milk and stuffed with seared collard greens. And it was delicious. Nobody was doing things like that. We'd do really traditional beautiful confits and *pot-au-feu.* He was experimenting with really interesting ingredients in a more nouvelle style, like Roger Vergé and the guys in France that were doing the newer stuff. Whereas I felt like Le Francais, L'Escargot, they were more like the Ritz-Carlton in Paris or La Tour d'Argent. Really, not very innovative.

MAGGIE TRBOYEVIC: He also brought in dishes that were Eastern European—like he made a *burek* [savory pastry] which was very light and very good. At Le Perroquet he made coulibiac, which is a Russian salmon and pastry thing which is also excellent. At Les Nomades we made a cassoulet, which he called lean cassoulet, but it didn't taste lean. It tasted the same, but you didn't have that feeling of great heaviness.

FRANK LEE: I was privileged to work under Michael Beck [executive chef]. I learned how the waitstaff can knock out, you know, fifty, sixty, seventy covers, because we'd make the coulibiac of salmon or a veal roast and all the little vegetables that accompany it, and they would do Russian service where they wheel out the cart, and they had the puree of green peas and the *macédoine* of vegetables and their sauces, so they can carve or cut the salmon and pastry or the leg of lamb and really take the heat off the kitchen.

I learned just how the brigade system worked and how cooperative everybody was. I never saw abuse in the brigade system, I never saw that in the kitchens that we visited in France and I've been back to France probably fifteen times. You gotta drink the Kool-Aid, you gotta buy into the game—and if you do it's just like the military. If you do, you know the guy beside you has your back. You want somebody who'll tell you, don't roll out the dough this way, roll it out that way, don't do the *gaufrettes* yet, wait till you can see the whites of their eyes. Training in the brigade system is one of the best things you can ever have.

MARY SUE MILLIKEN: He had this young guy, Mike Beck, as chef, and once I got in, I was just rabid to learn everything I could. Mike was a great teacher. I learned a ton from him. Mike had worked under Gabino, who was a Spanish chef—I think he really laid out the food plan there. So a lot of the things that Mike was teaching me were Gabino's.

I was also an overachiever and, and, you know, really good at proving myself and working circles around everybody else and not complaining. I think Jovan was kind of surprised. He thought, wow, she works twice as hard as the boys and she's half the price. And then another woman came in applied for a job, and he hired her on the spot. And she, it turns out, was Susan Feniger. We've been business partners for forty years. We both worked there for over a year, and we both would say that we learned more in that kitchen than we learned in chef school. It was just the best training of anywhere we ever worked.

The whole plan was very specific. Every day we had a different vegetable mousse. And it was made out of the stems of watercress or broccoli or cauliflower. We'd always have a mousse, and it was always garnished with sea scallops, and a *beurre blanc* or some kind of a sauce. Also the colors were really important to Jovan; he would be like, we can't have two sauces on the same day that are the same color. They had to be different.

Jovan wasn't scary, if you were a good worker. He was scary if you weren't good, but he never scared me. Susan was newly out as a lesbian, and Mike Beck was *so* mean to her. It was just like, shocking. Everything I did was fine but everything Susan did was wrong. I would witness him telling her one way to do something one day and the next day she'd be doing it exactly the way he told her and he'd yell at her, really meanly. She had a much harder time. I would coach her, like, look, you've got to stay here, this is such a good place to learn. Jovan never yelled that I remember at all. We were close until he died. He was just a really good friend and mentor and role model and helped me in a million ways.

****

MAGGIE TRBOYEVIC: He insisted on fresh fish. He brought in things from all over the country—we brought the crayfish up live from New Orleans, and lobster and clams from Boston, mussels from the West Coast. Our cheese we got from a purveyor in New York, a wonderful cheese man who brought his cheese in from San Francisco, which had come from France, because they didn't have the restrictions that New York had. We could get all kinds of unpasteurized cheese, and we told people that it was direct from France, so they could have it or not have it—but everyone loved it.

We had the first espresso machine in Chicago, that we knew of. We brought in interesting things that we learned about through the restaurant show—one year we found a Belgian man who was selling endive, no one in Chicago could sell you endive, but you could get it in New York City. So we had it shipped from Belgium, and we used it fast—we put it into salads and under the appetizers.

We bought geese and ducks—not live, but, you know, the whole animal—and then we would take the breast and we would wrap it in fat and we would have it smoked by a fellow who had a German smoke house on the west side somewhere. And one day he told Jovan he didn't want to do it anymore because he just about burned his place down because of all the fat that came out of the geese.

He had a farmer up in Wisconsin who had calves. We had an old Ford station wagon in those days. So he arranged for this farmer to come down from somewhere in the inlands of farmland there. And he brought the calf in the back of his truck. And it's the whole calf in a bucket, its liver and its brains and I don't know what else you put in there. All that was transferred in our car, you're not supposed to bring it across the state line but he said, well, you know, it's *my* animal. So we brought it down to the restaurant, we bring it in and lay it out on the preparation table, and our chef was just brilliant. He carved it all up into various parts and pieces and, and we used every bit of it for something. And it was fresh. I mean, it was within days of slaughter, and it was just fantastic.

FRANK LEE: We worked with top-notch ingredients—out of my station we did the navarin and the cassoulet and the sweetbreads, we did this puree of calves' brains. We did it because Jovan was bringing home calves and goats from somewhere in Wisconsin. Crack the goat head and a calf's head and gently scoop out the brains and do dishes with that.

ALLEN KELSON (dining editor, *Chicago* magazine, 1970s–80s): He was the first guy to serve fresh vegetables in restaurants. Every place was serving canned or frozen vegetables, he would always have fresh vegetables. And sometimes it would be a puree. He would have a different puree of vegetables every day.

One time he invited me over. And he and I and James Beard had lunch.

MICHAEL FOLEY (future owner of Printer's Row and, ultimately, Le Perroquet): I had my first French watercress soup at Jovan, while I was still in college. And it just changed my life. I was sitting there across from my date in a banquette and in front of this fantastic wall mural of a chef whimsically inflating a soufflé, the work of Maggie Trboyevic whose brilliant creative talent continued into Le Perroquet. I put one spoon of the soup in my mouth and was shocked! It was lustrously green from the cooking technique. It tasted so richly of the velouté watercress. My reaction was, oh my God. My date says, what's the problem? And all I could say was, this is incredible. This is like being in France. So amazing. This is so delicious.

Jovan came over and asked, is something wrong? I said, you know what? This is phenomenal. This is delicious. And he was so surprised. I think he was used to people saying bad things. And he looked at me and said, thank you, and he gave me this very severe bow. That was our first meeting and after Le Perroquet opened, whenever I could I had lunch or dinner at one or the other. In the years to come, Jovan introduced me to Frédy Girardet; I visited and spent a week at Girardet's talking about food styles and technique. Like Jean Banchet who opened many doors for me throughout France, Jovan was a master and helped people he knew were in earnest. As with others, he became a solid mentor in expanding my life and pressing me to live up to my own talents and what I could be.

As a few years passed I stayed in touch with him. I wrote to him, and asked, can you tell me how to make this or that? No! he'd say. But if you want to come to the kitchen, they'll show you. This is the guy who would sit with Bill Rice [*Tribune* dining editor] and they would argue back and forth about how to roast a good chicken.

MAGGIE TRBOYEVIC: He wanted to use local products and local help working for us. But that never worked out very well. I don't know why, but they weren't interested in going and learning in the French restaurant. In hindsight, I think it could have been the European employees, who could have given them a very hard time. And they're not going to complain to the owner, and they're not going to complain to me. So you don't know what's happening sometimes.

MARY SUE MILLIKEN: At Maxim's they were *so* cheap. This is not even a joke. They made staff meal out of like, boiled salt pork, and water. Literally the staff meal would be inedible. Or like after they clarify a consommé, they'd take out the wrap, which is like the vegetables mixed together with egg whites and meat that has no flavor whatsoever, and they'd serve that as staff meal.

At Le Perroquet, on the other hand, we had really nice staff meals. And we would all sit down together at this skinny little table. And we would be literally like a foot away from each other and a foot across the table from each other. And we'd always be together every single afternoon. I learned some great things about managing a kitchen there.

You felt valued at Le Perroquet. I was so shy, I often didn't sit down with everybody else, and I'd also want to be an overachiever and work harder than everybody else. So it seemed like it was a strike against me if I took a break, but they would force me to come and sit down. So they valued people and they served us good food.

FRANK LEE: Jovan was a wild man, but like a father figure to me. He could get adamant, and he could get demonstrative, but never unkind. He had a wonderful, dry wit about him, and a great sense of humor. And he was extremely well read and intelligent, so he could discuss many things with authority and confidence. He would definitely take up oxygen in the room. But for me, he was always very generous. I just wish I had more of him.

At Les Nomades, after the customers would go, it was not uncommon for Jovan to get the staff, whoever wanted to stay and who wants a cocktail, and sit in the little bar there and have a tête-à-tête for an hour or so to unwind. And I asked him one time why they didn't have bread and butter plates, or bread plates; the bread was just put on the tablecloth. And he said, well, the tablecloth is clean. It's yours. It's yours for the night—we don't reuse the tablecloth. We can just put the bread right on the tablecloth. It was just little spots of quality like that showed through. But the main thing I wanted to get across is how generous and kind and loving he really was. He didn't suffer fools but for me, he was a kind and thoughtful person. I laugh at people who said he was such a grump.

Here's my quintessential Jovan tale. My wife and I had been married about a year and a half, and I was getting a big head, I was going to open a restaurant in Columbia, South Carolina. I asked Mike Beck how much time I should give Jovan when I quit. And he said, just give two weeks. Because if you give him longer than that, he'll just get pissed and fire you.

Well, that didn't align with the guy I knew, but I took his advice. So I told Jovan I was going to South Carolina, and he says, how much notice will you give me? Well, two weeks. And he looked at me up and down. And I had that shrinking feeling. And he said to me, I thought you were different. Is that what you think of yourself? That I can replace you in two weeks? I never forgot that.

****

MARY SUE MILLIKEN: Maggie's artistic vision really set the tone for the dining room at both Le Perroquet and Les Nomades. And I think she was a really wonderful partner for Jovan in the restaurant. She was there a lot. She didn't work that much at night. She was there in the daytime though, quite often. And her artistic vision was definitely felt throughout Le Perroquet. She's really an amazing artist.

MARGARET SHERIDAN [*Tribune* writer]: I asked him, Jovan, what was the magic? Why was Le Perroquet sexy even at lunch? He said, what did you notice? He said that it's all about lighting. A lamp about this big, with a little shade over it. When the light is [placed in the middle], two people come together—look at their bodies. It's all about lighting and making intimacy.

MAGGIE TRBOYEVIC: At Le Perroquet, we had these wonderful lamps that we had made out of millefiori vases. We had the marble guy make the base, and then we had another person do the nine-volt wiring, so that the wire had to be on the table, and if you tripped on it, you wouldn't cause a fire or an accident. And then we had a little shade made out of silk. And it was a wonderful light, very flattering light. It looked like a little mushroom cap.

It had a wonderful glow to it, it made the guests look great. It wasn't dim. Some places were very dim, and they had red shades and so on—but these just made women look beautiful. You didn't see a wrinkle on anybody.

Inevitably, we'd have people come in and pick [the lampshade] up and put it on their head when they'd had a few drinks. Oldest joke in the world. They would take the flowers. I'd do these arrangements on every table, and they'd give the flowers to their girlfriend, or the woman they were with. So I'd have to come back and redo all the stuff because by after lunch, it was all picked over. But people think that's perfectly normal, like stealing things out of a hotel. You think, you paid for the room, so you paid for everything in it.

STEPHEN ANDERSON (bookkeeper at Le Perroquet and Les Nomades): I remember getting a bomb threat one day during lunch service at Le Perroquet. I think it was a woman who was checking on her husband, who was out to lunch with his mistress.

MAGGIE TRBOYEVIC: Les Nomades came about because he wanted a restaurant where he didn't have to deal with conventioneers. The problem was always that secretaries in those days, they'd book a lot of restaurants. The boss is coming into town for whatever reason, and they would give him a list—there's six restaurants that you can choose from, where would you like to go tonight? And he would make his choices, and she would never cancel anything. This was infuriating to Jovan.

BERNARD GUINAND: He always knew if they were convention people, because they were [parties of] six, seven, eight.

MAGGIE TRBOYEVIC: He was the first person that I know of in this city that ever took phone numbers. When they booked a big table, he would ask for a name and phone number. We'd call them that morning, or maybe the day before, and we'd call and say, are you coming for your reservation? And usually it was, oh no, you know, we're not coming—then we could release the table and book someone else because we always had a little waiting list.

STEPHEN ANDERSON: It was a tiny little office, I sat at one end of the desk and the other bookkeeper—his secretary, Betty—sat at the other. I don't know if she was Serb or Czech, but she and Jovan had this kind of Old World connection thing.

Basically, my job was to reconfirm all the reservations for that evening. I answered the phones, took reservations. And, during that time when he started talking about Les Nomades, I started compiling membership lists of the potential clientele for the place.

MAGGIE TRBOYEVIC: What happened was people were getting annoyed that we asked for phone numbers because nobody ever used to do that. What do you want my phone number for? They'd give phony names, which were usually obscene. And the woman who worked in the office was Czech, and she didn't realize it. So she would pronounce these names, and some of them in the office spoke English well enough to say, oh my God, if you pronounce this name, it sounds like. . . . That was really bad because then if you saw a name that was dicey, then you call up and say, you've been canceled or whatever, that was a problem.

****

MAGGIE TRBOYEVIC: There were some real characters that just wanted to be miserable, and make your life as miserable as they could and make the waiters' lives miserable. It's amazing how these people define themselves very early on, they're unhappy, and they want everyone else to be unhappy.

He said, I don't want to do that anymore. He really loved to make people happy with food. That was his biggest pleasure, to see them happy and have him talk to him and thank him for what he had done. So he said, I'm going to open a club, and it's not going to be expensive—because Le Perroquet was very expensive, when we opened dinner was $15.95 a person and lunch was $9.50 a person. That was a lot in those days. But he sold Le Perroquet when he opened Les Nomades. He said it was being semi-retired, because we didn't have lunch, just dinner, Tuesday through Saturday. Sunday we were closed, and Monday we were closed—that to him was like a vacation. It was a holiday.

Charging a dollar made it a club. And then he could just simply say to someone who was really miserable—you know, you're not happy here, you're always complaining about everything, and we want you to be happy. And we're not happy with you, either. So we're just going to remove your name from our list, and you don't have to come here anymore. Just go somewhere else where you'll be happy.

SKIP FOX (attorney, Les Nomades member): It was an annual fee, but he enforced it. If you misbehaved, didn't do what he expected, you didn't get your membership renewed.

There was a partner at Jenner & Block who was a member of the club, and one night he was at Les Nomades with his wife or some friends, and he was loud and obnoxious. And Jovan came over and stood next to him and said, I hope you're enjoying your dinner tonight. He said, yes, I'm very much enjoying it, it's a wonderful dinner. And Jovan said, can I see your membership card? He said of course, and pulled the membership card out of his wallet. Jovan looked at the membership card, and in front of the guy and his friends, he tore up the card and said, I hope you enjoy your last meal at Les Nomades. And he was never let back in.

STEPHEN ANDERSON: I would get calls from people pleading for memberships. Like secretaries telling me their boss was in the $100 million bracket. With Jovan, that might keep somebody out! Because he was whimsical in a way, but it had its purposes.

I pretty much had the membership in my head, and who referred who. So more than once he'd call me at home and ask, who *is* that at table such and such? Sometimes it would just be this flash of anger at something and he'd get over it, but sometimes I'm sure people didn't get invited back.

One time, I was sitting with Maggie, and we overheard the people at the next table saying how much they liked Ambria [a new restaurant at that time]. She whispered that to Jovan, in confidence, and of course he turns to them and says, so you'd rather be at Ambria? Maggie was mortified. I was mortified. She turned to me and said, it's going to be really awkward the next time I see them—they live in our building.

There was a woman who dined at Les Nomades, like, the first Wednesday of every month. Her secretary would call every month to get her usual table. And one time she was dining with her mother, I think. And as they were leaving, Jovan was at the door, wishing everyone good night. I was probably eating at the bar, and this party of fat cats came in with their wives. The men were a little behind, and one of them says, look at the ass on that one—speaking about this woman with her mother.

I mentioned this to Jovan, and those guys did *not* get their membership renewed. He kept score, and he said he did not want to run a place where a woman would not feel comfortable dining alone, or with her mother.

PHILIP HESS: By then there were private club disputes breaking all over the country, because a lot of the really famous traditional ones were being sued for their admission policies. They were not being terribly strict about their membership restrictions, it was all very gentlemen's agreement handshake. The ones that excluded women, the women who sued them were able to prove quite easily that the clubs had become almost entirely business associations. And everybody went there for business to network and keep the old boy networks going.

Jovan researched it carefully, and he discovered that as long as he was completely dictatorial, and kept total control over who could get in, only allowed members in and only allowed others in if brought by members and approved by him, he could get away with it. And that's what he did. We used to get these annual letters saying here is your annual membership card, the dues are one dollar. And you never paid it, and you never had to show your card. And he was very happy with his new system, and even happier with the publicity he got. Because after a while, the *Chicago Tribune* and others began writing story after story about this mysterious club and who can get in and who can't get in and how there are taxi drivers who are members, but members of Chicago society couldn't get in. And he just loved that.

STEPHEN ANDERSON: The dress code was enforced, suit and ties for everyone. But there was a New York artist, Dan Flavin, he had work in major museums all over the world. And he would come in there in jeans. Jovan said, well, that was his business attire.

MAGGIE TRBOYEVIC: We had a lovely clientele. A lot of artists, a lot of architects, we had museum people, they came from all over the world. A lot of musicians would come before performances or after performances, conductors, or performers who were in from out of town, they'd book there because they loved it and was quiet. He once had the idea of having this great big ball of cotton, way up in the ceiling above every table. And when people started getting noisy, he'd lower it to absorb the sound until it got right down to the plate to shut them up completely.

He didn't want people table hopping. That's something that you will always hear about. People say oh, yeah, I know someone who got thrown out because they table hopped, and it wasn't just table hopping. It was, we had these tables fairly close together. And they'd be talking to these people and you know, the people sitting there at the other table, it was not nice to have someone standing right nearby, especially looking at their butt.

PHILIP HESS: By the time he opened Les Nomades, his dream of Le Perroquet had been severely compromised. All sorts of things drove him up a wall. His whole dream of having a restaurant without numbers failed, because he had an amazing percentage of people who just stiffed him, he'd send them statements, they'd sign the check and they wouldn't pay. So he finally had to cave in and start taking credit cards. And he limited the house accounts to people he knew and trusted. And that was a huge compromise that he only went into very unwillingly.

He also was beset with the kinds of problems that were getting more and more frequent in the industry, where customers will complain. He started getting formal complaints being written to newspapers and government agencies. What really drove him up the wall was a couple who came with their three-year-old. I think the staff had told them this was not appropriate, but they brought the kid anyway. And the kid is of course, howling and very disturbing to the other customers. And finally, they tried to suggest gently these people might want to, you know, wrap up things and leave. And they turned around and sued the restaurant for discrimination and he had to hire lawyers to fight it in court. I don't know how it ended up.

GORDON SINCLAIR (owner, Gordon): When I went to Les Nomades I escorted Aleka Armour—she lived in Lake Forest and picked me up in her car, chauffeured. And we arrived somewhat late. So I go into the restaurant and nobody's there. Except Jovan was standing against the wall, with his hands behind his back. He didn't say hello, or welcome, Gordon, he just pointed to the ceiling. So when we came down from the private party and lovely dinner, and I said, Jovan, this has really been a wonderful dinner. And *that* chandelier up where we had cocktails. Where did you ever get that? And he turns and looks down at me and says, I tell you *nothing*. You steal *everything*.

I didn't steal anything, he was flattering himself. It *was* a fabulous chandelier, though. I wonder what ever happened to it.

SKIP FOX: The food was always changing. But for the first fifteen years that we went there, I think there were basically the same four or five waiters.

Beth and I still talk about a dish that was the Portuguese equivalent of cioppino. They only had it on the menu once when we went there. And we still think that is probably the best soup we've ever had in our life. And that's thirty years ago, right?

They had the best cheese courses in Chicago. Just a wide selection of different cheeses and we always went and would have both cheese course and a dessert. And that's just because my grandfather served in an American unit attached to the French Army in World War I and he learned to appreciate cheese and passed it on to my father. You never felt hurried at Les Nomades. But the service was always timed to how quickly your conversation was moving, and how you were doing in the middle. But you were never pushed out.

It wasn't over the top like Le Francais. Trotter's was like a show, but Les Nomades was a place where you were there to enjoy each other and not ooh and ahh over the food. You knew you'd have good food but it was really a place where you could have good conversation, enjoy good wine, enjoy good food, but really talk about other things.

Having been the first woman in the kitchen at Le Perroquet, Mary Sue Milliken took it upon herself to get women into the front of house staff at Les Nomades.

MARY SUE MILLIKEN: I think I always forgave him for, you know, growing up in a time and a place, Yugoslavia, a long time ago, where his mother, his grandparents, all the women in his life didn't fit this modern woman kind of idea. It was a thing he had to really adjust his brain to. And so rather than be upset about it or angry, I decided I would just force him to change. I was very proud of getting the first woman on the floor at Les Nomades, and my friend Marge worked there for a long time.

****

Michael Foley—more on him in Chapter 4—wound up acquiring Le Perroquet in tribute to what he'd learned from Jovan:

MICHAEL FOLEY: I went back to Jovan every single time I came back to Chicago, [from] college. And I would just sit there and have dinner alone and enjoy the most incredible meals and service. Years later I returned to Chicago and ended up working like a dog in my first Chicago chef's position. I was uncomfortable with the volume and style of food, but grateful for the position. I wrote Jovan. He responded, I gave three weeks' notice, and off to Le Perroquet I went to be a cook.

Le Perroquet was my home away from home. Discussing the finer details of a dish prep and presentation with Jovan was inspiring. My time there was abruptly shortened with a call from my family to help my dad close a business. Jovan expectedly was furious. I left two weeks later he did not talk to me for years. Finally, after writing to him when I got to travel almost half a decade later, I saw him on a Chicago street alone walking. He saw me first and started to cross the street. I felt bad and ran to catch up with him. He said, well? I had just opened Printer's Row and he made a comment that restaurants were a lot easier to work in than to own, and hoped I would be okay. All I wanted to say was, I am sorry I left Le Perroquet. I really am.

Jovan softened and said, ok, ok. Some night tell me about all your travels, Mr. Marco Polo! And every once and a while when we could over the next years, we would go out for a late evening cocktail after service, Jovan would share stories of his life and we would spend an hour or two talking global politics, food, travel and, occasionally but not often, about restaurants. Jovan was a very special person in my life whose acquaintance I highly valued and still do.

When I heard that Le Perroquet had closed, I felt terrible. It was my favorite spot for privacy and full appreciation of a great restaurant. I decided then I wanted to get it reopened.

My brother Mark came to work with me and we cleaned, refreshed, repaired, refitted and repainted the details where we could. Gerard Nespoux, former captain and maître d', returned. Didier Durand from Bergerac, who later opened Cyrano's Bistrot, became the chef. Some press ridiculed me for trying to recreate a dinosaur or emulate and copy Jovan. However, the truth is that Le Perroquet for me and many others was all that we loved in restaurants from quiet elegance to precision in a style of food and service.

I was drawn to Le Perroquet as a lifestyle. My goal in reopening Le Perroquet was to make sure this beautiful life I had experienced did not simply exit the world so suddenly. The learning and takeaway has stayed with me in so many ways that never would have happened if I had not done it. Regardless of the criticism, we all worked hard for what we loved and believed to be part of our inner soul and spirit. The restaurant drew close to the end of its lease. Michigan Avenue rents were skyrocketing. I had reached my goal. The French bird sleeps with dignity.

STEPHEN ANDERSON: When I quit, it took me months to work up the courage. Because he was pretty volatile. But when I finally did it, no one has ever said kinder things to me. You're irreplaceable, I will never find anyone with your tact and sensitivity, and so on.

After I left, I would go to Les Nomades, sometimes just to have dinner with Maggie, and he would join us when he could. If I brought my friends, or visitors from other parts of the country, he was always perfect with us.

FRANK LEE: Les Nomades was where Jovan was, and Maggie was, and that's where a lot of artists and writers and the strange people were, that would show up in the back door in these long trenchcoat-looking things. I heard rumors that Jovan would go down to some section of town where they'd play balalaikas and drink vodka and stuff. He had an interesting path that few were privy to—definitely a man of mystery. He was royalty in exile. You had to stand up—royalty in your presence.

MAGGIE TRBOYEVIC: He called it Les Nomades because he was a nomad. And he knew so many nomads and so many experiences he had were in other places that he lived. He felt like a nomad until we finally settled down and made a home here.

Jovan Trboyevic sold Les Nomades to Mary Beth Liccioni in 1993, and retired. He died in 2010.

THE VATEL CLUB

By the mid-1970s Chicago had such a strong community of French chefs that they formed their own club—a Midwest chapter of the Vatel Club, named for a seventeenth century French chef, one of the membership requirements of which was that you spoke French. So not all the young Americans who worked for them qualified to be in their club, but many would learn how to run restaurants the Old World way under these French chefs.

Born in Normandy, Pierre Pollin was for many years, with his wife Judith, the chef-owner of Le Titi de Paris, which got its start in northwest suburban Palatine but ultimately spent much of its forty-year run in nearby Arlington Heights.

PIERRE POLLIN: I was part of the Vatel Club. We created it as a French-speaking club. Some people were not French, like Gabino Sotelino who was Spanish, but he was part of it. We started the Bocuse d'Or in Chicago, which is a competition where we select the best chef in America to compete in France. So mostly it was functional. We would meet once a month for some talk about what's going on.

The point was to promote French cooking, to keep it alive. We had an inferiority complex in the Chicago cooking scene. Also to promote the Bocuse d'Or. We would choose the best chef from around the country in Chicago, and then twenty people from Chicago would be there for the competition, to promote cooking in Chicago. You know, when I came to this country Chicago was not known as a very good eating place. Then it became one of the best eating places in America, right? The best restaurants hired French chefs, because American chefs were not ready yet. It was a job, but not yet a profession.

People understood French food at that time, more or less. Le Francais opened [in the suburb of Wheeling], and Le Vichyssois opened [in McHenry county, north and west of Chicago]. There were a few restaurants where the food was very good, so we had competition. One thing I noticed, when I came to this country, was that people didn't eat much fish. There were one or two fish on the menu. I say I want to sell more fish. I want to educate people that fish is good. That was the thing that shocked me a little bit at the beginning.

Nouvelle cuisine was coming, no use of flour and everything. But I was doing that in France before I came to this country, where we would do the *beurre blanc* and the reduction sauce. That was coming slowly in this country, but that's normal—some younger chef comes and tries it. That was the case with Jean Banchet. That was a baby step but it was still lighter, on the lighter side. Jean Joho came with cooking from Alsace.

[By the 1980s and 1990s] you could see that things were changing because the diners didn't talk about steak places, they talked about good French restaurants—they will say we ate at Tru, we ate at Everest Room, we ate at Ambria. You had to give them the best you could do, to please them. Also the same people were looking at wine, better wine, more expensive wine. Different areas. It was from France, and then Italy, and South America, and then California. The wines of California became really, really good. It was a big thing.

[By the 2000s] the work was getting old, so that's why we dissolved the club [Chicago's Vatel Club, like those in other cities, merged into the local chapter of the American Culinary Federation]. We still meet for lunch once in a while, at Shaw's Crab House or Le Bouchon.

Two of the young chefs Pollin mentored were Michael and Susan Maddox, who worked at Le Titi de Paris and bought it from him in the early 2000s, running it until closing it in 2012. Today Michael teaches the next generation of chefs at the College of DuPage.

MICHAEL MADDOX: When I came up to culinary school at Kendall College, it was interesting because there really weren't too many people that came from the country. And I always thought that was kind of unique when they talked about farm-to-table—for me as a kid growing up, we didn't really buy too much from the store between canning and preserving and butchering. It was a lot of hard work as a kid, but I appreciated that as well, and I tried to instill that into people I worked with as a cook.

SUSAN MADDOX: It wasn't a glamorous career to go into when we were doing this. The French chefs, they weren't going to culinary school—they learned it by working their way up.

MICHAEL MADDOX: Pierre and Judith Pollin, who I worked under for twelve years, had a garden when we bought the restaurant. And we continued that as well, we had grape vines, we had two apple trees there on the property, and we grew all kinds of other vegetables. And I think it's kind of neat that the customers would come and see us out there in the garden, sometimes pulling weeds, but a lot of times it was picking those tomatoes, or taking chives or whatever out of the garden.

Julia Child had a huge impact, and then you had Jean Banchet and Pierre Pollin and Patrick Chabert [Le Francais] and Roland Liccioni [Carlos', Les Nomades] and Bernard Cretier [Maxim's, Le Vichyssois]. When they came to this country, that was the heyday for French cuisine, refined cuisine. They grew products here that they grew in their country, barley and those kinds of things. And I don't think it's a surprise to anyone, but the closer you are to pulling it from the ground to cooking it or having a raw application, the better it is. I think it's great now that even restaurants in the city have rooftop gardens.

SUSAN MADDOX: French cuisine was the game—Ambria and the Everest Room and Le Titi and Le Francais. People would come in, they'd be in a sport coat. It was fine dining, people could spend four to six hours sitting having dinner, or a three-martini lunch.

MICHAEL MADDOX: We were in competition but also professional courtesy, I can't tell you how many times we went back and forth with Banchet, or Bernard from Le Vichyssois would come and borrow the slicer, we'd borrow stuff back and forth because we were always food-front, but also customer-front as well. Because you go to a place for your favorite item, you know, you hate to tell the customer you don't have it, we can't do it. I think that is French cuisine as well, or just good hospitality—it doesn't matter what cuisine it is. If you can make the magic happen, do it.

MAXIM'S

One of the first Chicago restaurants with an all-French staff was literally a franchise of the famous Maxim's de Paris, opened in the Gold Coast in 1963 by Florsheim Shoes heiress Nancy Goldberg, in a building built by her architect husband Bertrand Goldberg. He lavishly reproduced the Art Nouveau look of Maxim's, even as the rest of the building was modernist, and provided Chicago with a posh hangout for celebrities (John Lennon held an apologetic press event there after he said the Beatles were bigger than Jesus). Seven chefs, led by Alex Humbert, were sent from the Paris original to help open the Chicago outpost; one of them was Christian Gaborit.

CHRISTIAN GABORIT: I came here in December 1963. At the time I was a chef de partie. You had the British invasion, this was the French invasion. I don't want to come to this country but in France when the boss says something, you have to do it. Maxim's in Paris was like a school, it was one of the places where you had to work if someday you want to become a chef.

Nancy Goldberg was a wonderful, wonderful lady. At that time in Chicago, all the show business people used to perform at Mister Kelly's, from Sinatra to Count Basie. Everyone came to Maxim's, from the Kennedys to Sammy Davis Jr. to Zsa Zsa Gabor. Nancy was a fascinating person—a grande dame. Very generous—when my daughter was born, she paid for everything.

ALLEN KELSON: You'd walk down a set of spiral stairs, and you were transported into the nineteenth century. When it first opened you had to have a tuxedo, and the captains and the maître d's had tails. They always had a violinist who would work the tables.

CHRISTIAN GABORIT: Typically the menu was a copy of the menu of Maxim's in Paris. No change. People ate beef, rack of lamb, veal. At that time there was not a lot of fish. Fish was trout. Kiki, Georges Cuisance [later owner of Kiki's Bistro], was a sommelier then, and he had to educate people about other kinds of fish. Some of the fish came from France—other things came from France, too. The pastry was made by Maurice Ferre, who spent twenty years at Maxim's.

It was an absolutely fabulous experience. I was there for almost six years and then I came back to France to open a restaurant. Nancy Goldberg came one day to my restaurant and said to me, pack everything and come back to Chicago with me, I can't find a chef for Maxim's. Three times she tried to get me back. I said sweetie, I can't do it, but we always stay in touch.

Goldberg closed Maxim's in 1982; but in 1983 the space was taken over by a music producer, George Badonsky, who owned other buzzy Chicago French restaurants (Tango, Le Bastille) and was known for popularizing Beaujolais Nouveau in Chicago. His right to use the Maxim's name would eventually be disputed in court by the brand's owner, Pierre Cardin. (The story—possibly too good to check—was that Badonsky won when his lawyer showed pictures he'd taken of places called "Maxim's" all around the globe.) Badonsky's Maxim's was short-lived, closing in 1986, but the young chef Badonsky brought from Alsace would last longer on the Chicago scene: Jean Joho.

PAULA CAMP (*Tribune* reviewer, 1980s): George was a yeller, the old school. He was well hated in the restaurant industry, for being kind of a bull in a china shop. He was also a terrific friend of mine later in life—I actually have his dining room table in my home, because we ate so many wonderful, wonderful meals there. So I'm not disparaging George at all. He came up in a rough and tumble restaurant world that was changing.

Le Bastille—you talk about a party. He would fly in Beaujolais Nouveau when it was released, on a Concorde jet. With big tents in the middle of the parking lot. He really did do French food for the common man.

JOE SPELLMAN (bartender and sommelier): George palled around with artists and dancers and photographers and had interesting art in Tango, [his place] in the Belmont Hotel. It was among the gayest places I've ever worked. I mean, I'd say 80 percent of the front of house staff were gay men. Maybe a couple gay women, too. And I was the oddball straight. It was a real see-and-be-seen place, a lot of suburbanites came in. There were some very famous waiters there who had great reputations there, like Appy Moll. A lot of them passed away because, you know, it was the AIDS crisis.

JEAN JOHO: I came to reopen Maxim's in 1983. George Badonsky was pretty advanced for a restaurateur in his time. We did very upscale dining in the Gold Coast, on Goethe [Street] and Astor [Street]. And it was really elegant.

I came to bring some new blood to Chicago, and a new way to do fine dining. In the '80s Chicago was still a bit on the conservative side when it came to fine dining. I came up with a new approach—there was a tasting menu right away. At the time there used to be a kind of tasting menu in restaurants, but you had to order a day ahead, for a minimum of four people. At the same time I did right away a vegetarian menu. So that's what I started and it was very successful. But Rich Melman came many times to eat at the restaurant, and soon we became partners.

Joho and Melman opened the Everest Room, later simply Everest, in 1986—but that's a story for another chapter. Maxim's never reopened after Badonsky's short run, but Nancy Goldberg reacquired the room and gave it to the city as a cultural event space under the name Maxim's: The Nancy Goldberg International Center, until COVID closed it. In 2022 the space was restored to its original Art Nouveau splendor and reopened as Astor Club, a private club. Nancy Goldberg died in 2006; George Badonsky died in 2016.

CHEZ PAUL AND L'ESCARGOT

If there's one vintage Chicago restaurant you've seen the interior of, it's Chez Paul—though what you saw in both The Blues Brothers *and* Ferris Bueller's Day Off *was a replica built on a soundstage. Located in an 1875 McCormick family mansion on the Gold Coast, it was opened in 1945 by Paul Contos, and lasted fifty years under his son Bill, one of the great old-school Chicago restaurateurs and hosts, and then under Bill's fourth wife and widow, Regina.*

REGINA CONTOS: The height of Chez Paul was in the '60s and '70s, when French cuisine became popular and Bill imported French chefs like Lucien Verge, who later had L'Escargot. It was easier in those days than it is now, so Bill did that a lot.

Bill and I actually met at Chez Paul. I had dinner with a girlfriend, we were celebrating, and I knew of the place at the time. That was '77, '78. We didn't have reservations, but we were two girls, and I guess we were good looking. I was from Europe, and I was always intrigued with good food and wine. I demanded the wine list, and kind of whispered to my girlfriend, how much should we spend? And Bill was intrigued by us, and he wasn't happy in his marriage then, and we got to know each other. We got married in '83.

Bill was very gregarious. He was a Zorba the Greek, he lived life to the fullest—like I told you, I'm wife number four. He was at the restaurant all the time, he would greet everybody, it was his life. He knew his people—in those days you weren't just a menu dropper, you bought people drinks, you cultivated a clientele. He had a maître d', but he still made the rounds. He knew everybody, and he brought French cuisine to Chicago. It's fun to own a restaurant, but it's a lot of work, and if you do it the way Bill did, eventually you need a new liver. We always marveled how people could have dinner with just one glass of wine.

Bill passed away in '93, and I sort of ran it then for three years at the end, then we lost the lease. It belonged to the College of Surgeons, and it was a triple net lease, at that time the taxes were less than $10,000. By the time that I quit [in 1995], the taxes were $100,000. You can't run a restaurant that way.

Lucien Verge came to Chicago in 1965 to work at Chez Paul, but in 1968 he and a partner, Alan Tutzer, opened the restaurant credited with bringing French provincial cuisine to Chicago, L'Escargot. L'Escargot started on Halsted Street in Lincoln Park, but that location burned in 1979; it was followed by two locations, one further north on Halsted in Lakeview and the other in the Allerton Hotel on Michigan Avenue. L'Escargot was noted for its informality—which in those days meant not requiring jackets for men.

Camille Stagg was the food editor at the Sun-Times *for much of the seventies.*

CAMILLE STAGG: Lucien Verge just shows how Chicago was a provincial place then—he couldn't even find French mustard, meaning Dijon mustard, when he moved to Chicago in '65. So he had to send to New York for it, because he came to New York via Paris. First of all Lyon, which is a wonderful eating mecca. And from there he went to Plaza Athenée in Paris. Then he went to New York and then Chicago.

I'm so glad he did, because he was not going to do nouvelle cuisine, he was going to do what you call *cuisine du terroir*, cuisine of the earth. He did things like a wonderful cassoulet, he did lamb, and snails, of course. He prided himself on the ability to communicate the foods from which other chefs were basing their innovations. And he was teaching people how to eat properly. He said at first he couldn't get people to try some of the dishes. But after a while they trusted him. He really elevated Chicago's taste in food.

Carlos Nieto, who would later have Carlos' for many years on the North Shore, got his start at L'Escargot.

CARLOS NIETO: I trained in Mexico as a silversmith, but I came here and started as a busboy at L'Escargot, for Lucien Verge. And then I helped him in the kitchen. Doris Banchet used to work there as a waitress, and then they opened Le Francais in Wheeling.

I really didn't have experience and when my friend took me to work there the owner said, you ever work in the restaurant business? No. Okay, so he showed me where the coffee cups are, where you get the silver, how you put the setups and everything. And at the end of the night, he said, I thought you never worked in the restaurant industry, you did a great job. Thank you. And then the next day, I come in early, like two o'clock. Lucien said to me, why are you here so early? You're not supposed to be here until four o'clock. Well, my friend dropped me here. So I went and set up everything up, clean the silver, clean the glasses. When the waiters come in, they say, who cleaned up everything? Well, Carlos did. Being a silversmith is being an artist. But when I finished doing this, I loved being in the restaurant business the same way.

Lucien was a great guy and a great teacher. His cuisine was more casual, but good flavors because they'd do cassoulet, coq au vin, things you wouldn't see in many restaurants now—*blanquette de veau*, onion soup, crispy duck. From him I learned flavors. And a lot of the seasoning, and a lot of the French style—I never really cooked French food myself. I came early every day and worked with him in the kitchen. I learned a lot of the little things.

He was a little different from Jean Banchet. Banchet used to scream at the cooks. Lucien was a hard worker, his kitchen was pretty small, he had only himself and two other guys and a dishwasher. As I said, when I came earlier I used to help him clean potatoes, clean onions and chop things around. It was an art form to me, I loved it.

JOHN HOGAN (cook): You sat down, and you got the ratatouille as a gift. And then you ordered a three-course prix fixe. That was the menu. He was doing veal kidneys and sweetbreads and frog legs and just all the unique items that come from French bistro cooking or whatever—bourgeois cooking, I guess.

I liked the fact that he was doing really kind of unique items on the menu because I guess he had to keep his costs down because it was a three-course prepaid, but he was using all kinds of off cuts, you know, a lot of braised meats.

Lucien was amazing. He was very kind and gentle. I barely knew him—I really got interviewed by him twice and maybe worked one or two days in the kitchen with him. And I don't know if he hired me knowing that he wasn't going to be around long, thinking I was a guy that was going to take L'Escargot to the next spot. I don't know.

In 1983 I had decided to go to France. I went there with the intention, either this is what I'm going to do for the rest of my life, or find something else. Well, I was able to land a stage at Roger Vergé at Moulin de Mougins on the Riviera. And it changed my life. I saw how it was done in the motherland and when I came back, I decided I needed to be in the city. So I got a job at L'Escargot on Michigan Avenue. Lucien hired me and then died three months later. So they kind of threw me into the chef role, which I was definitely not ready for. They hired me as a sous chef, and it was my first sous chef job. And I didn't even know how to break down a fish. I needed a lot of help from the subordinates in the restaurant, you know, which were mostly Latinos, even back then.

Jason Chan's parents owned restaurants and bars, but didn't want him to follow them into the business—advice he's ignored for 40 years at literally dozens of iconic Chicago nightspots. When he got his first job as a cook at L'Escargot, he kept it a secret from his parents.

JASON CHAN: They forbade me to be in the restaurant business. They were pushing really hard for me to become a doctor. They made me clean our whole restaurant every morning on Saturday and Sunday. So when everybody else is going to the movies, playing baseball and doing kid stuff on weekends, I had to get up at seven in the morning. And it took me six hours to clean the entire bar and restaurant. And they paid me five dollars a day. So I made ten dollars a weekend. But after three months of hating it, I would pretend I was a bartender, I would pretend I was a chef, I would pretend I was the manager. They saw I loved it—and so they said, that's it, we're selling the bar.

I got the job at L'Escargot working for Lucien and his wife Lucette and their partner Alan Tutzer. I was lying to my parents, I told them I was doing gymnastics after school and in math club, any excuse I could think of. I worked, of course, fourteen to sixteen hours, we only got paid for eight. That was the times then.

I went to a Christmas party with one of the busboys who I was friends with, we smoked pot before and after. We went to this Christmas party, one of the waiters who lived in Boystown, and when I walked into the apartment, I was gobsmacked. I looked at my friend busboy and said, is his husband wealthy? And he's like, no, he's in the business too. He's a waiter at another restaurant. And I looked at their house, I looked at this spread. They had a rack of lamb and a big beef roast and then they had a table with like, all this wine and spirits, and then they had a dessert table, a sweet table and on the sweet table they had this tray with what looked like sugar on the tray. I said, well, how much do these waiters make, how much cocaine is that? He said it's about $3,000. He told me, back in 1985, that they made close to $200 a night on Friday and Saturday.

I started to cry. My eyes literally teared up, because I was living on a back porch that I paid $75 a month for on Irving and Sheridan. It was like a tenement building. It was illegal. I didn't have a kitchen. It was just a room basically. And I thought, I'm suffering, there's no air conditioning, I live like a dog, and waiters make as much in a weekend as I make in a month.

So I walked in the next day. And I told Lucien that I quit. Of course they didn't want me to quit. You're on track to become a chef, I'm gonna teach you how to break down fish and beef and you're going to work each station there, you're gonna be a sous chef, and this will take three, four years and then you can work anywhere. I told them I want to be a waiter. And, of course, they were very opposed to it. Lucette said, I can't make you a server. It's impossible. You've never done it before. You're nineteen years old. These waiters are grown men who've been here for years. So I'll make you a busboy and we'll train you to be a waiter. And I said, fine. She said, well, you keep one or two shifts in the kitchen until we can replace you—which, I was easily replaced, but they just wanted to keep me in the kitchen, right? Eventually I stopped doing my one or two shifts. I was a full-time busboy and I made $60 to $80 a night. And I was so happy, because my income just quadrupled. And then I decided, well, I can try to make this a career for myself.

Lucien Verge had just filmed an episode of the PBS series Great Chefs of Chicago, *an early example of Chicago getting national attention as a culinary destination, when he died at age fifty-two in 1985. Both locations of L'Escargot were closed by 1993.*

THE DINING ROOM AT THE RITZ-CARLTON

Carrie Nahabedian won a James Beard Award for Best Chef: Great Lakes in 2008 for her restaurant Naha. That journey started for her in the '70s in the kitchen of the Ritz-Carlton's Dining Room under Dijon-born chef Fernand Gutierrez, who would open the world of French cooking to her.

CARRIE NAHABEDIAN: I was in high school, Maine East in Park Ridge [Illinois]. I was always a very creative person. And I really didn't know what I wanted to do, but I knew I wasn't going to go to college. And my father was very strict that every one of his kids was going to college, because back when he grew up, they chose one person to go to college. So my dad said, everybody's going to college.

My mother had to have surgery that was two weeks in the hospital and eight weeks at home. So my father and I were alone, and I just got tired of my dad and me going out to eat every single night. And I said to my dad, how hard can it be? I got the Time-Life *Foods of the World* book on provincial France,[3] and I just read the whole thing. I used to watch Julia Child all the time, like run home from school to watch her, I watched my mother cook. I was always in the kitchen.

So by the time my mother was completely back to normal I had taken over the kitchen, so we were eating, you know, tournedos Rossini for dinner. We're eating Greek chicken, artichokes, you name it, we were doing it. And that's when I looked at my dad and I said, I think I'm going to be a chef. And I applied to the CIA [Culinary Institute of America], and I got in.

3 *The Cooking of Provincial France,* M.F.K. Fisher et al., 1968.

A teacher suggested that she could make up a missing high school credit with a work program in foodservice. She knew where she wanted to work.

My dad worked for Marshall Field's, he did carpeting. My dad was doing the intricate carpeting at the Ritz-Carlton Chicago. It was in the newspaper all the time, because the only other luxury hotel was the Drake, and here's the Ritz coming. And I said, Dad, you gotta get me a job there. I can't work at a hospital or country club. I was sixteen, almost seventeen, but I knew already which direction I was going.

And he said, okay, I'll try. I'll talk French to the chef—my dad was in Normandy, he was part of the liberation of Paris. He was wounded and hidden by the French Resistance, so he knew French. He went to the chefs and started speaking French to them and told him that he was in Normandy, was at the liberation of Paris. And you know, for the French there's nothing greater than someone who saved their country, right? So the chefs said to my dad, here's an application. And we'll see what we can do.

I brought it to my school counselor and she gave me the okay, so I was hired at the Ritz. And it was like, every day was Willy Wonka, I was getting paid to do what I loved to do. I was working forty hours a week, full time, in high school. Every day, I would go to my counselor and say, I need to get out of school and finally, I was going to school at eight o'clock in the morning, I was getting out of school at eleven thirty because I needed to get downtown and start working.

I had to start in room service because I wasn't of age to work in the kitchen. I organized all the room service orders, and I got the food. But I was constantly hanging out with all the chefs because remember, I'm like, seventeen, these guys are all from France and looking at me like wow, who is this girl? And I'd go and talk with them about Bocuse and Antonin Carême and Fernand Point.

Fernand Gutierrez was the chef, and Jacques Abadie was the chef de cuisine. Fernand scooped me up and became my mentor—and also George Bumbaris's and Sarah Stegner's [Prairie Grass Cafe], Susan Weaver [Lettuce Entertain You], a lot more people than you actually know.

I went from room service, to banquets, to the dining room line—the dining room is where it was at. We were doing 270 covers a night, all silver service. Veal with morels, lobster Thermidor, chateaubriand—I mean the stuff we did, I don't even know how we got our work done. I'd come into work at two thirty, and we'd start serving at five thirty. I was just in heaven, and one day I came home and told my dad that I wasn't going to go to the CIA for college, because why blow fifty grand? That's how I got him, why blow fifty grand when I'm learning more, I've met enough people. I knew Banchet because he used to come to the Ritz all the time and sit at the chef's table. All those chefs in Chicago used to come to the Ritz kitchen chef's table.

Jacques Abadie was an amazing chef. He'd worked for Raymond Oliver [Le Grand Véfour, Paris], and he actually had me set up to go work there. But instead I just went to Europe and traveled all around. To work anywhere you had to have a letter. So Banchet wrote me a letter, Jovan wrote me a letter, Jacques, Fernand—that's how I got to see the kitchens at La Pyramide, and Raymond Oliver, and Lucas Carton. I mean, Fernand was the god. These guys were on speed dial with Bocuse, the fact that Fernand could pick up the phone and make a reservation and talk to the chef at Taillevent—with Charlie [Trotter] gone, there's nobody like that left.

Fernand Gutierrez had two stints at the Ritz-Carlton in Chicago, in the '70s and again in the '80s, along with working in Atlantic City and Houston. He was the chef-owner of Bistrot La Bourgogne in Mexico City when he died in 2006. He was succeeded by Sarah Stegner, who won two James Beard awards at the Ritz-Carlton; we'll hear more from her in chapter 8.

THE COTTAGE

The most unlikely place for fine French food to turn up was in south suburban Calumet City, known at the time as a wide-open town for gambling and other vices near the steel mills. Gerald and Carolyn Buster were a local couple who decided to open a French countryside restaurant called The Cottage in 1974—him in the front of the house and her in the kitchen. In 1985, when the PBS series Great Chefs *came to Chicago, Carolyn Buster was one of only two women chefs featured—an impressive feat for someone whose culinary training consisted of a ten-week Sears course for housewives.*

GERALD BUSTER: I had been in the army, and they sent me to Orleans, the town of Joan of Arc, south of Paris. We went to Paris a lot. I wasn't particularly interested in food or anything—we went to Paris to be with the young ladies.

As far as food, even at our little bistro, by our army base, the cooking was damn good. The French, they're into that. And I learned a little bit of the language there. And then I got out and met my wife. We were both working in the steel mills, which were booming, actually. She worked for one company and I worked for another and we got together and started dating, and we always went out to restaurants. Some people go dancing, some go roller-skating, we went to restaurants. We were always kind of interested in upscale places as well.

So we got married and then she was working at a steel mill, in the office, and she didn't like that. So she got a job working for Louis Szathmary at The Bakery. She worked upstairs, Louis had a test kitchen up there. She helped him write *The Chef's Secret Cookbook* [1971]. And interestingly, he would dictate recipes to her and she would take them down, and she would go to the store and get all the ingredients and make the dish and see if it needed anything. It was a test kitchen away from his restaurant. And the dishes were all just great. I mean, very rarely did he have to make any changes to these recipes.

I had a degree in psychology and I was working in a factory as assistant personnel manager. And I had been there five years and they started to slow down, they were actually getting ready to close the plant. My number came up and they let me go. And I said, well, what am I going to do now? My wife consulted with Louis and she said, well, you know what, while he's in between these office jobs, why doesn't he come down here and work a little bit as a waiter? And I said, I've never worked in the restaurant before in my life. So I did. And first they made me a busboy. And that restaurant had a superb cast of waiters from all over Europe. Well trained in the old European tradition, which you don't see too much around America these days. I worked my way up from busboy to waiter and I worked between two of the best waiters in town.

One day, one of the guys came to me and he said, you know, I'm looking at you and your wife, you're getting pretty good here. Why don't you open your own restaurant? And I said, okay. We'll think about it. It literally had not occurred to me. Maybe it occurred to her because she had her own plans or her own agenda. But I didn't think about that. Of course, from our background, we're both blue collar, nobody in her family or my family had ever been to college or owned a business.

We made one last trip to France. And we went from Paris, down all the way to the Riviera, and ate at all these two- and three-star restaurants. I mean, it cost us a fortune, we really went in debt, but we wanted to see what they were doing over there. Because that was really the only cuisine that we were interested in and wanted to get involved in. So we did that and I made a business plan. We built a building from scratch—before we did that, we made another trip, to England, and I photographed all these little cottages over there. The thatched roofs and everything

The restaurant was ready, but we weren't ready. The first night that we were open was October 30 [1974]. I think we served thirty people—that was okay, we could handle that. All new staff, new equipment, the whole thing. The second night, we served thirty-five people, I was fine. Third night was a Saturday. And apparently the word got around that people were waiting for us to open. We served 103 people on the third night we were open. And half of those people I'm sure walked away from that experience thinking, oh, shit, I'm never going back *there* again. We just couldn't handle it, it was too much for us. But we did it and from there on, it was pretty smooth sailing. We lasted until the restaurant closed on July 1, 1996. Twenty-one years and eight months later.

One of the things I think made us successful is, there was nothing else like that in the south quadrant. People were amazed that we even had the balls to open out there. There were the steel mills, but there wasn't much else happening culturally out there. When we started, everybody was in full tux for service, and that really set the tone for the whole experience for guests. We had some windows that let you look in as you're walking up the walkway, and more than once I saw some people peek in that window and see us all in tuxedos and turn around and leave. They didn't want no part of that tuxedo place!

How we ended up in Calumet City was, we lived in that town, and we wanted to go to one of the more upscale towns in the south area, like Flossmoor, which was richer. We appealed to the village fathers to give us a liquor license so we could open and they say, oh, no, no, no, no way, you can come here as BYOB. But I didn't want to do that for obvious reasons. So we went to the mayor of Calumet City, Bob Stefaniak, and as soon as he saw the business plan, his eyes lit up like a Christmas tree. And he said, well, we don't have any more liquor licenses available, but I'll pass another law that will allow you to have a liquor license. So he just snapped his fingers and the village fathers came through with a liquor license, which was kind of surprising to us at the time because we thought it would be more of a hassle than that.

It was really a rough town. But we were on the west side of town, as opposed to the east side, which was State Street, which was the dividing line between Illinois and Indiana. And that's where all these joints were, prostitution and everything. There were murders over there.

His thinking I'm sure was that he wanted us pretty badly to come there and be successful because it would raise Calumet City a little bit in people's eyes from where it had been. And, you know, a lot of people came to us because we got a lot of good press, we got awards, too. We got four stars from the Mobil travel guide—we didn't have Michelin in those days, the Mobil travel guide was the thing that everybody aspired to. And when we got the four stars, we were very happy about that.

We used some of Louis's ideas—we had white tablecloths and fresh flowers on the table and real silverware. And the menu was five courses, no choices, except the entree—so it was appetizer of the day, soup of the day, salad of the day and a choice of desserts. That was also a shock to the people out there because everybody else was thinking à la carte. I found a couple of old blackboards at flea markets, and we wrote the entrees on the blackboard. And everything, except one item, was priced at $9.95. The only thing that was more expensive was a dish called steak Madagascar. It was a green peppercorn sauce, cream sauce on a sirloin steak, and that was $12.95.

We had the usual suspects—the duck, and our biggest seller was a dish called Cottage schnitzel, which was a pounded pork tenderloin served *a la Française,* finished with butter and lemon juice. Of course, in the '70s people smoked up a storm, they smoked like chimneys. It got so smoky in our place that I had to get one of those zappers and mount it on the ceiling. When I think back on it, Jesus Christ, that really affected the taste of the food, all that smoking.

Even being a French restaurant, it wasn't as gourmet in those days. We were quite successful with this menu that if you'd feature it today, people would laugh. One thing we did that was a little ahead of its time, we discovered a little restaurant in the city, at Irving Park and Western, called Thai Room. This is when there were maybe five Thai restaurants in the whole metro area. But we just loved that place—it was, of course, very different food from what we were serving. We'd go there on Sundays, damn near once a month. Because it was so good, and all these ingredients that we didn't know about—nobody did.

I saw an ad in one of these magazines, I think it was sponsored by American Express, a trip to Bangkok to go to a Thai cooking school. And I said to my wife, we gotta go there, see what ginger and galangal and all these ingredients are, we don't know anything about them. So we went to Bangkok, and it was very nicely done, and we learned about ginger, and lemongrass too, and we came back and Carolyn started using some of those ingredients in her cooking. So that was a little bit of a turning point, that brought us into that realm of gourmet.

But the swinging doors between the dining room and the kitchen were very well determined in our case. Because if I would try to go in there and try to do anything with the food, make any suggestions, she'd point to the door and say, stay out there, wouldja?

We burned out several times. And then we'd have her sister watch the place and we'd take off and we'd take the Orient Express or go to Paris or stay at the Ritz and recharge our batteries, so to speak. But at the seventeen-year mark, Carolyn says, you know, I don't want to be working this restaurant anymore, I don't want to be married to you anymore. I want a different life. So the judge gave her the house and gave me the restaurant and the cars. And I ran it for three years without her, with employee chefs. And that went okay, but then the neighborhood started changing. And now I guess if you and I drove out there, we'd be dodging gunshots from all the corners.

PAT DAILEY (*Tribune* writer): The house that the restaurant was in was beautiful—definitely something you would call a mansion. It was huge, kind of

English Tudor style. Their Christmas decor was just a very special experience. I went out there with a photographer, we shot the whole thing. Because of newspaper lead times, I wrote that story the year before it appeared, it was in the can until the next Christmas. And as soon as the story ran, they announced they were getting divorced. They didn't want to ruin the story, they wanted the story to run for the restaurant's business.

GERALD BUSTER: We had a wonderful run. I still think back how some of the people as they were leaving would give you a handshake and say, God bless you guys for being here and doing this birthday dinner. That's what makes you proud of what you did, you know you not only had a good life for yourself and made some money, but you made a lot of people happy.

Gerald Buster worked in catering after closing The Cottage. Carolyn remarried and moved to New Mexico, where she died in 2008.

3: JEAN BANCHET

The most celebrated French chef in Chicago, and perhaps in America in his time, Jean Banchet was born the eldest of triplets in Roanne, near Lyon. He started his career at La Pyramide in Vienne at age thirteen; stints followed in Monte Carlo and London, and then in 1968 he was recruited by Arnie Morton, executive vice president of Playboy Enterprises, for the Playboy Club in Lake Geneva, a summer getaway for wealthy Chicagoans just over the Wisconsin border.

In 1974 he opened Le Francais in Wheeling, a North Shore suburb known for its restaurant scene's liveliness—if not its sophistication. Le Francais put Wheeling on the national culinary map; a 1978 article in Esquire *by Mimi Sheraton ranked it ahead of anything in the city of Chicago and on par with the three best restaurants in New York at the time.*[4] *In 1980,* Bon Appétit *declared it the best restaurant in America.*

DORIS BANCHET (widow of Jean Banchet): We met in London. He was working as the chef in a casino. And I was across the street, in a Viennese restaurant—I'm from Germany. I was managing the restaurant, which was only breakfast and lunch. And he came in for breakfast all the time and wanted to take me out. And, well, you know the rest.

Arnie Morton and a few others, managers and directors from Playboy,

4 "Le Francais: A Gastronomic Miracle in the Midwest," November 21, 1978.

came over to London to look for chefs for the Lake Geneva resort. It was opening the end of '68. And Jean said, I would like to go to America just for one year just to see what it's like. I didn't want to go but in the end I said okay—for one year. That's it. I was happy where we were. Well, anyway, we went and this is, well, fifty-two years ago, and I'm still here, right? Unfortunately, he is gone.

The casino in London was the best. Oh my God yes, the best. In those days, they had all the money they wanted, they could do whatever they wanted. And definitely real French cuisine, upper class. And that's what he kept up in Playboy as well, because he was working in the VIP room. From there, he went to Chicago, to the Gaslight Clubs, they took him away from Playboy. I stayed on at Playboy for a little while until he got settled because he wasn't sure if he was going to stay where he went.

But first of all, we had to be here for five years. And then we took American citizenship. Okay, and we tried to find a place. And we couldn't afford anything in Chicago proper, or in an area where we wanted to be, so we went out to Wheeling. Everybody said, oh, you can't go there. Wheeling isn't even on the map. You're never going to make it. But on the weekends I worked at L'Escargot, and most of our customers came from the suburbs. Northbrook, Highland Park and all that area. And when I saw Wheeling, you know, it's so close to all the expressways—well, why not try because then they don't have to go to Chicago, they can come to us. Right. So that's what we did.

For the longest time, before the expressways came along, Milwaukee Avenue was it, it was the only route to go from Chicago to Milwaukee. So Wheeling, that whole strip, was road houses. And when we came, of course, everybody said, oh God, a French restaurant here. What's that going to be? Nothing.

We had $8,000 in the bank. Of course, we went to banks, and who was lending us money? Nobody. But the bank in Wheeling had just opened. It was a new bank. I went there and talked with the manager, director, whatever. And, well, he did it. He lent us the money. Wow. Jean had a partner at the time, too [Henri Coudrier]. He also had a few thousand dollars. But it was an old building where we went in. We had to nail the chairs together every night so they held for another day.

I remember the first day, we opened the door and we had like forty-nine people and there was only a busboy and myself. That was a bad day. And from then on, it just went up. We opened at like eleven thirty and by twelve o'clock, we locked the door. It was full. And by five o'clock we had to throw everybody out because we had to get ready for the night. Because in those days people stayed for these long business lunches, with cognac and cigars afterward and so on. We only stayed open for lunch for barely a year. It was too much for the kitchen. They couldn't do it and we couldn't do it in the front either. We just didn't have time for anything else.

From there it went, mouth to mouth everywhere. We never ever did advertising. The newspapers and magazines wrote about us—Bill Rice was writing about us all the time in the *Tribune,* and various others, of course. In time, of course, the mayor and everybody went shopping with our name. I remember one time Mayor [William] Hein came back from a meeting of mayors in Washington. He said, Doris, guess what happened? We were sitting there and they called the names for the mayors. I said, Mayor Hein, from Wheeling, Illinois. And everybody said, you are the mayor not of Wheeling, but of Le Francais!

****

CARLOS NIETO (head waiter): Working for Banchet was an experience because it was a different cuisine for myself. It was a more traditional cuisine—they'd use one hundred gallons of stock and reduce it to thirty gallons. And once you chilled it, it was like a rubber band. The food was very rich—if you asked for a plate of pâté, they'd give you twelve different pâtés. We had carts where we would carve salmon en croute. And we had a rack of lamb, and a number of items that we'd carve, so it was an experience.

MICHAEL LACHOWICZ (cook): They would do something called the grand show. They would have beautiful service carts that were lined with silver trays for everything, under aspic. So before they presented proper menus, everything was paraded through the dining room. And each tray is presented to each table and everything is explained in great details, which encouraged a terrific dialogue between the service staff and the guests. Things like veal en croute and roasted loin of lamb wrapped in eggplant mousse with spinach leaves. Everything was under jelly.

Their mouths were agape before they even got to put anything in their mouth. So it set their palate and their expectations at a level that nobody had really ever achieved before. It just wasn't like that anywhere else. It was really a cacophony of service and all this pomp and circumstance. It was absolutely beautiful. If there'd been the Internet back then everything would have gone viral.

SHERMAN KAPLAN (reviewer, WBBM radio): Their service was so impeccable. One of their jokes was, if it was somebody's birthday, they'd bring things under a silver dome, and for the person whose birthday was being celebrated, that dome would come out last. And they would with a flourish remove the dome, and a hamburger was sitting there.

It was not a nouvelle cuisine menu at all. This was classic French, a great deal of Escoffier influence. He was a very traditional guy.

PAULA CAMP: We all had to make the pilgrimage there. He was, at the time, by far the most famous chef in town and, interestingly, kind of uniquely Chicago. His cuisine was classically French, presented with the fanfare of the silver dome over your dish when it came out. And it was quite an elaborate display. But there was a sense of humor and trying to make serious French cuisine acceptable, I guess, or seamless, mystical. And I think that's a very Chicago trait. I think some of the early chefs were really working to make things more agreeable to the Midwest, steak and potatoes kind of mentality.

DORIS BANCHET: I don't think a lot of people in the beginning were that sophisticated. And well, once in a while, we got the steak and potato people. But I guess they didn't come back. We had lots of couples. And people came for special occasions. Even if they came only once every couple of months or so, that was a regular customer. I knew their families and where their kids went to school.

CARLOS NIETO: He was a pretty tough guy. He used to scream at me, why do these people want the meat well done? And I'd say well, that's what people want. They're paying. "Well, I don't want to serve it that way." Okay. He'd come back and see the people were happy. I'd say, of course they're happy. "Oh, okay."

DORIS BANCHET: I ran the whole front of the house and the office and everything. And Jean did the kitchen, the hiring, firing in the kitchen and ordering of food and everything. I did everything in the front, hiring, firing in the front, the office work. We talked about stuff but we left each other pretty much alone. We worked good together, I must say. There were times that I threw a pot at him, you know, but I guess that happens everywhere.

BERNARD GUINAND (cook): If you do your job, absolutely no problem. Well, he was screaming in the kitchen, whoo, my God. "You all don't know nothing, you know nothing, I gave you the best food and you ruined it!" Sometimes the customers, they are eating and he is screaming, and the waiter would say, ah, the food will be good tonight.

CARRIE NAHABEDIAN (cook): I walked in and it was all men, except Mary Beth [Hoey, the future Mary Beth Liccioni] in pastry. She was on the outs with Banchet. He said, she works in pastry. I said, well, that's the kitchen. "No, pastry's not the kitchen. You want to work here, this is how it is." And the guys were all looking at me like, "Oh great, now we're going to get a woman in the kitchen."

Banchet would take the whole month of January off, often to go to France. I came back from Europe around Thanksgiving, and he said, okay, you can start February 1. And I looked at him and said, Chef, it's really great. I'm very honored, but I have an American Express bill due and I ate a lot at La Pyramide. I have to pay that bill and I can't ask my parents for money, I gotta get a job now to last me till I can work for you. He said, okay, and he picked up the phone, and he called Michel Saragueta at Le Ciel Bleu in the Mayfair Regent and said, I got this girl here, this is how much money she needs to make. And I want you to pay it to her right now. And then she's going to work for you till the last week of January. And I don't care how much you like her. She's coming to work for me.

So he would come visit me in December during the holidays and stuff like that. And check up on me, give me a phone call—how's it going? Which, that shit does not happen. We had a very strong relationship.

I started in *garde manger*. Then I had to do pastry, people knew I knew pastry. I didn't advertise it, because once they know you know pastry, then you get locked in. So one day he heard me say to the guys, I'll never work pastry because he doesn't know I know pastry. I turned around and he was there. He looked at me and he said, tomorrow you're in pastry. And every day he said to me, you have to create something new. So I would rush home at the end of the night, and pore through my books and say like, okay, what am I going to do? Like, he leaves me ten mangoes and says, I need a dessert tomorrow.

Banchet beat us all up. But at the end of the day, we were the ones that he relied upon to make sure that we shared his vision. I remember making a lime tart. Because he was known for his *tarte au citron* which was so much work and so amazing. So one day I had this idea, and in my own spare time I came in and I made a layered orange, lime and lemon with lemon on the top. So when Banchet looked at it, he said oh, it's a beautiful lemon tart. So we put it under the broiler and then he cut into it. And he looked at me and goes, what's this in it? Oh, I just thought I'd change it up a little. And he looked at me like, are you kidding me? Like, who the hell are you? Then he tasted it and he goes, it's really nice. I like how one layer's baked, one layer's cold. But he was not one of those people that you were going to tell how to change things up.

MICHAEL LACHOWICZ: This is late '88, '89. I was working in Granite Springs, New York, and I was making too much money, so it was time for my chef to find another CIA student. He says, where do you want to go? I said, I miss Chicago, I want to go home. He says, okay, I got the guy. And he makes the call.

I load up everything in my Firebird, waterbed strapped to the top of the car, and two days later I show up at Banchet's house, next door to Le Francais. I knock on the door at ten in the morning and say, I'm here. And he goes, who are you? I tell him my chef called, and he says, I don't know, come back tomorrow. That happens three more times and finally I show up on Friday in my whites with my knives, and I say, Chef, I'm ready to do whatever you need me to do, I don't even care if you pay me. So then his eyes light up. He puts me on and I worked for free for three weeks. Finally I said, listen Chef, I love it here, this is an amazing experience, but I can't afford the gas to get back and forth. So he gave me a hundred dollars for gas money.

He was a crazy guy. I mean, he was exactly what he was portrayed to be. But I didn't give a shit. I was twenty-one years old, I was ten feet tall and bulletproof.

The gateau of crab, the navarin of lamb, we did a cannelloni of shellfish and crayfish, which was like an angel hair pasta that was wrapped in a turban around a mold that was filled with the mousse and steamed. And that was inverted and finished with whole crayfish and little butterflies that are fashioned out of Peruvian purple potato and lotus root chips and chives. If you look at back at it now it's like geez, that's kind of dated. But back then, it was fucking cool.

MARK GROSZ (cook): I was twenty-two years old and working at a country club in a nice suburb of Detroit. The chef got fired and I took over, but I thought—this is nice, I make good money, but there's so much more to learn. I sent Banchet my resume because I saw *Bon Appétit*, number one restaurant in America. He called me and said come on over. I went over there. He said, what took you so long? I said, I live in Detroit. He thought Detroit was a suburb of Chicago.

I spent the day in the kitchen with him. He showed me around, then he made dinner for me. At that point I threw all my recipes away. It was remarkable, the quality, the flavors, the teamwork—I was lucky to get in there. And they were *packed.* They did a buck twenty, a buck fifty [diners] every night, and there wasn't a slow day until maybe a few years later.

It was the best and worst three years of my life. We were the first batch of American guys that were there, and there were a few women too, but mostly it was French before us. So it was good to have the American guys with us, just complaining about everything. The French guys were already beaten down. One guy, a French guy, used to throw up every day before service. He had to work right next to Banchet, so he took the brunt of it every night.

DAVID JARVIS (cook): Banchet worked as hard as anybody I've ever seen. He was a chef, but what he really was, was a really great cook. He was incredibly good at teaching. You weren't really given much freedom, as opposed to robotics, where you were driven to the repetition of perfection.

The biggest thing I gained from him from was just, strive for the best and don't compromise. The customer can wait, if it means the food can be better. It was the equivalent of going to France and doing the stages—which, back at that time, Americans weren't doing stages [unpaid culinary internships]. We'd never even heard the word.

JOHN HOGAN: I started reading about Banchet in the late '70s. Here's this guy from France who's driving Ferraris, and people would fly into Palwaukee Airport [in Wheeling] from all over the world to eat his food, and I'm like, *this* guy has got somethin' going on.

I never worked for Jean. I interviewed with him a couple of times, but I had kids and he was offering 150 bucks a week for like, seventy-two hours, and it just didn't work out. But I always kept a relationship with him. When I opened Bistro Banlieue in Lombard with Emilio [Gervilla], he used to come in to see how the progress with the restaurant was going. I'd put food up for him to taste and a lot of times, he'd say, "John, thees taste like I make eet! You never work for me, how you know how I cook?" I said, I've worked for a few guys who've worked for you, and I picked their brains.

We became really good friends, I went to France with him and a lot of other French chefs for the Bocuse d'Or back in the '90s. We went two or three times, every other year for I think six years.

DORIS BANCHET: In France, he was pretty much known, especially because he was a close friend of Paul Bocuse. They'd worked in the same place, La Pyramide—not at the same time, because Bocuse was older than Jean. But they'd both worked for the chef, Fernand Point. Bocuse had his sixtieth birthday at Le Francais, and everybody from all the three-star restaurants flew in.

CARRIE NAHABEDIAN: He was extraordinarily generous. We were closed the entire month of January and three weeks in August. And we weren't paid—he paid us so well during the year, I mean, cooks nowadays don't even make the money that we were making, because we worked our asses off and a lot of it was cash. No one used a credit card in the restaurant.

When we'd come back from vacation, everybody would be kind of lined up outside his office, and he would just have a stack of money. And, you know, back then you only needed a couple hundred bucks, right? Everybody's rent was like two hundred bucks. You'd say I need $400, and he would take like twenty bucks a week out of your check for the whole year, and that was cool. And then the Christmas bonuses and the gifts—he was incredibly generous. I try to mimic him like that. I try to remember all my cooks that work for me, if it's their birthday. It means a lot for someone to remember you. He was a class act.

I mean, don't get me wrong. He was a bastard. He was hard. But at the end of the day, it was his restaurant. I mean, we were the number two restaurant in the country, sometimes number one.

BERNARD GUINAND: He was a crazy man. He was a teenager.

JEAN JOHO (chef, Maxim's, Everest): He knew how to sell himself, to be a marketing person. He had his sports cars, and his motorcycles, and his gold chains—he knew the best way to promote himself. He was generous—you never had one plate with a little thing on it. You got a lot. You want a pâté, you get four pieces of pâté. In the '70s or '80s, that's what people wanted. I think that's what his philosophy gave me.

MARY BETH LICCIONI (pastry cook): He loved to motorcycle. He was originally famous for his car collection, but then he switched to motorcycles. He would go to all these Harley-Davidson gatherings.

I had a good experience with him, because he didn't scream at me. I was the first female in his kitchen. So he didn't know quite what to do. He was actually very polite. But I could watch the circus when he was getting on everybody, go in the cooler and guys are crying in there.

But I learned a lot. I can remember everything I learned there. How to do things—I was just learning to cook, and I hadn't been to France yet. I was single, and so I was just kind of immersed in the whole thing.

DAVID JARVIS: The amount of screaming was amazing. It was like being in boot camp, with the drill sergeant screaming at you from a foot away. That was Mr. Banchet, to the point where, when I'd see it starting, I'd grab an empty pan and run into the walk-in and try to grab anything I was going to need over the next hour. So that I was bypassed by the screaming going around the kitchen. Because he'd go from person to person and just blast everybody.

MARK GROSZ: He always had a couple of guys who were kind of like the whipping boys, you know? It was rough, old school French. Verbally abusive, big time. This tastes like shit, that's not the way I show you, what is the matter with you? He told one guy, you're James Bond, except instead of double-oh seven, you're double zero.

But you couldn't just take it. You had to stand up to him and say, what do we really want here? How do we fix it? Then he'd take a step back and say oh, okay. People who stood up to him, he respected a little more, and they weren't beaten up that way. My brother Paul worked there, too, and one day he pushed my brother, he pushed him really hard. And Paul took off his apron and said no, you can't push me like that. He put up his fist. And after that, Banchet was totally cool with him.

SHERMAN KAPLAN: I found Banchet to be a very pleasant person. I know that he was a bear to work for. But that didn't take away from his greatness at all.

MICHAEL MADDOX: Every chef's demanding, he was a little on the screaming side of demanding. But we saw him evolve over the years.

****

One advantage the restaurant had versus restaurants in the city was that it was about a mile and a half north of Palwaukee Airport, popular with owners of private planes.

DORIS BANCHET: People were flying in from all over. We had customers from Germany, from France, from Japan. And they had meetings somewhere in the states, so they made a stopover. And we picked them up at the airport, took them back. By that time they were talking about us all over. We had a Rolls-Royce to pick them up. We even had one guest come in a helicopter, they parked it on our private side.

DON YAMAUCHI (chef of Le Francais, 2001-2): We had one doctor, I think he was from Boston, he did not fly. So every time he wanted to eat dinner, he took three limousines from Boston to La Francais. And he had three daughters. And each daughter had a nanny. And the nannies had like, a general manager-type nanny. And I said to one of the oldest daughters, I said, for kids coming in, we would make burgers or roasted chicken or whatever. And the oldest daughter goes, I only eat filet and lobster. I said, yes, ma'am. At the time I had a thirteen-year-old at home who was like, I'll take a burger at any time. Different caliber, for sure.

SHERMAN KAPLAN: We went to pick up our car after dinner. And the valet says your car, sir? I said, well, it's a silver Mercedes. And he said, sir, they're *all* silver Mercedes.

CARLOS NIETO: The customers were flying from all over the world, flying from New York—you know, we complain now that sometimes it's too hard. It's too cold. It's raining. It's snowing over there. Every day, we were booked up three months in advance. The first of June we open the reservations for July. In one hour we were sold out a month. So you have to wait until the next month. We were full every day, lunch and dinner.

MARK GROSZ: A lot of celebrities—Tom Jones would come after a show and then go back to his hotel. And I remember Seka, the porn star—Banchet took her into the walk in, and I don't know what was going on in there.

CELESTE ZACCARO (pastry cook at Carlos' and Le Francais): John Candy and John Hughes came in one night, right, you know, and Roland [Liccioni] wanted to meet them. So John Candy came back in the kitchen and bought us all beers.

MICHAEL LACHOWICZ: The customers at Le Francais tended to be in their forties or early fifties, because those were the people who could afford to eat that style of cooking, and be appreciative at the level that it needed to be appreciated at. Because if you didn't look like you were wildly enjoying your experience, the waiters would ask you, is something wrong?

It was a huge amount of business dining—foodies were not what foodies are today. There was no identity for a foodie back then—there was just people who appreciated the cuisine, and or people who wanted to eat it because they wanted to be able to say they did. So there was a tremendous amount of business dining, convention dining, and the busiest days of the week were not Friday and Saturday, they were Monday and Tuesday, when people were in town for business. We would do two full seatings of ninety people each seating. It was just a beating we'd take every week. Then we're closed on Sunday, and everybody would kind of lick our wounds.

CARLOS NIETO: It was two and a half to three hours dining. We had the first seating between five thirty and six o'clock and then we had the eight thirty to nine o'clock reservations. It would be one o'clock, one thirty by the time you go home.

Customers were spending money on wine. He had one of the big wine cellars in the country, and he used to sell $500, $1,000 bottles of wine. People used to pass out because it was so rich. When you're sitting there for that long and you're eating and drinking, and there was a twelve-inch plate with all this pâté, it was unbelievable.

DORIS BANCHET: In the beginning I did the wine list myself. I'm not that much of an expert, but I did this with the wine people, they helped me. We had a small wine list, and then it got bigger and bigger. Then we got wine stewards who were very knowledgeable, so I left it to them. Most customers didn't know wine that well when we started, but we had to get better, which we did—the big book, with many expensive and older wines.

Jean was always doing the real, old French food. His sauces were out of this world, the sauces that really taste of what you're eating. In those days, I went practically every day to the airport to pick up things from France. Fish, foie gras, even vegetables—you couldn't get the fine *haricots verts* in America, nobody knew what that was. We picked all those things up from the airport, so naturally, the price was up there, too.

DAVID JARVIS: They did a lot of things between Lutèce in New York and L'Ermitage in Los Angeles—basically the other two best French restaurants in the country at the time. They would exchange products. Lutèce got a lot of the illegal stuff from France, to get through customs. So you're working with products as an American cook that you've never really seen. The quality of it was the best, so what you did had to be the best.

CARRIE NAHABEDIAN: I would fillet the big turbots that came in—first of all, you never see a turbot over twenty pounds anymore, they're extinct. You get these little two-pound turbots. His fish would come from France, from seafood merchants, and those were his relationships. When I was *garde manger* I was in charge of the pâtés and terrines, and all the butchery of fish. And I open up the turbots and there's a whole foie gras shoved inside the turbots. Because you couldn't bring them into the US then.

I remember when I got hired there. He said, you start at twelve noon. So I pull up at like, twenty of twelve. And I walk in the kitchen, and everybody's already in the kitchen. And it looks like people have been there for a half hour, there's pots on the stove. And I'm like, oh, so this is how it is. I asked one of the cooks and he's like, yeah, we all come in at eleven thirty.

BERNARD GUINAND: Nine o'clock in the morning, he was already in the kitchen. There were twenty, twenty-four cooks in the kitchen. If you came at noon we'd have used all the pots and pans already.

CARRIE NAHABEDIAN: The *Chicago Tribune* magazine did a day in the life of Le Francais. And in it was how, the cooks are running the kitchen, and they're starting work at noon and they work six days a week. And evidently, a guy from the Labor Department was reading the magazine at home on a Sunday afternoon, and said, I wonder how these guys get paid, working six days a week, twelve hours a day. So sure enough, Banchet got popped because we got paid salary [rather than hourly], and that was against the law.

MICHAEL LACHOWICZ: It was just like being at Trotter's or any of the other restaurants of that ilk. You were expected to work sixty-five hours a week, and say nothing about it. We didn't feel like we were being abused. It just felt like we were being trained. And we were, and that was cool. And that worked to a detriment for me for some time, because I thought that okay, well, this is the way I learned, this is the way they learned, this is the way I'm going to teach. But times change, and you can't run around with a side towel hanging out of your mouth, growling at people, and expect them to respond to you in a positive fashion.

MARK GROSZ: I've mellowed a lot since those days. I wanted to do—obviously not the *same* type of cuisine because it was expensive, you know, truffles and foie gras. But certainly, having high quality and standards for what we want to serve. But trying to make it more human. Letting the guys play music in the kitchen. It took a few years to soften my stance in the kitchen. It's tough when you come from that level of intensity and scrutiny.

****

Carlos Nieto opened his own restaurant, Carlos', in 1981 in nearby Highwood, kicking off a thirty-year run that often saw it ranked as one of the top restaurants in the Chicago area. Its success alongside Le Francais was also an indicator of changing tastes in fine dining, and its future and that of Le Francais would be intertwined in the coming years, starting with the presence of Carlos' first chef, the Saigon-born, French-trained Roland Liccioni.

CARLOS NIETO: I thought I would have a restaurant that was a little bit lighter than Le Francais. A smaller menu, because we only have like six or seven items on the menu for entrees, and maybe four or five things for appetizers. And then we have four or five desserts on the menu. We only had sixty-five seats in the main dining room, then later on we took over the upstairs for private dining rooms.

It was rich, but not as rich as Le Francais. We still used a lot of butter, and we made sure that when they look at the plate, it looks beautiful. And then make sure when they eat it that they were going home comfortable. Back then I would buy ten cases of Dom Perignon, that maybe at the time cost $45, now it costs you about $125 a bottle. But the expense accounts started to be depleted at many companies. And there were more restrictions on drinking and driving. We'd often have five or six or seven limousines waiting outside. New Year's Eve, we used to sell so much wine and champagne, and people would just drive home.

When we were under construction and didn't have a chef yet, Roland Liccioni was working at Alouette in Highwood. And his sister used to date a friend of mine who worked at L'Escargot. So my friend calls me up and says, I've got this guy, he's Vietnamese-French, he worked in London.

ROLAND LICCIONI (chef, Carlos'): I worked in Paris, I worked in England. I have good basic French cooking. Carlos' was a very good experience for me. I came from traditional, classic French cooking, but what I was doing was more nouvelle cuisine. Because you know, it's a different way to approach how to cook the ingredients, to have a different thing in your mind of how to prepare the food for American people, because I never work in the US before. So, I learned a lot from that, and after two or three years we had a really good reputation.

MARY BETH LICCIONI: I was working at La Mer—that was Banchet's downtown restaurant, with Arnie Morton. I was weary of the tension in the kitchen [at Le Francais] and asked him if I could come downtown. And then I met Roland, because I also worked at Carlos'. Carlos and I used to work together, so I asked him, I'd love to be able to work with your chef on Sundays. The way Roland did things was so elegant, classical. He's a chef's chef. He doesn't just stand by the pass—"Pick up such and such." I learned a ton of stuff.

We became friends, and eventually got married. That's when I started going to France, in the summers. That was amazing, too. I've had a charmed life.

CELESTE ZACCARO: Working with Mary Beth was one of the best things that could have happened to me. She was one of the top pastry chefs of the time, if not *the* top pastry chef. And Roland knew a lot about pastry, too.

She went to France, she spent lots of time there. So she was like another font of knowledge. And she was a great teacher. So, for me, I think that's when I really started to have an interest in pastry. Learning from somebody like that.

Roland was very seasonal, in his cooking. And he was to me the original farm-to-table guy, even though it wasn't really labeled yet. He would go to the market every day, and he would bring back every seasonal fruit you could ever imagine.

DON YAMAUCHI (cook at Carlos'): Roland was a no-frills sort of a guy, there was no playing in his kitchen. It was very serious. It was driven by the quality of the food and presentation. We would go to the South Water market—I want to say it was Mondays and Thursdays or Mondays and Fridays. And he hand-picked every tomato, every potato, every onion, he would tell them when he wanted. And then when we got back, he was the hardest-working guy in the kitchen. Prepping, cooking. Every minute of the day, there was no rest for that guy.

One of the first times I met Banchet, he came through to talk to Roland about Roland taking over Carlos, and, you know, hindsight being twenty-twenty and knowing what I know now, it was about him taking over Le Francais.

MARY BETH LICCIONI: Carlos was horrified. Roland gave him two months' notice, because a job like that, you don't give two weeks' notice. But Carlos's father-in-law told him we should leave right away, because you never know. So we lost our jobs two months out.

MICHAEL LACHOWICZ: You had to sign an agreement to work for Banchet for two years. I signed it, everybody signed it. Otherwise he didn't give you a reference. And then five months after I signed, he made the announcement that Roland and Mary Beth were taking it over. Banchet transitioned out and was going to go do his thing in Atlanta, because the Olympics were coming. He started building restaurants in Atlanta. And I called him while still working for Mary Beth, and I talked to Patrick Chabert, who was chef de cuisine—amazing chef, I learned all my charcuterie from him. I said I want to go to France. I needed to work in France. So they set me up to go work at a restaurant in Lyon. They're all like a big French mafia, and they all were descendants of Bocuse in some way.

It was fascinating because it was like a culinary encyclopedia to be able to work at Le Francais. In that time that I was there, I got to see things that nobody else saw, except for other people who were there during that period of time. Because it went from classic with Banchet, to this modern Pacific Rim Asian influence, Thai style of high-end luxury French cuisine with Roland.

A lot of Asian flavors—there was cilantro and Thai chili peppers and lemongrass and ginger in a lot of his dishes. I'd never seen that before. It certainly wasn't Banchet. But I thought it was great.

Roland could carve ice and had exceptional pastry skills and just did beautiful, beautiful work, just very talented artistic work. Banchet was not as finesse driven—he was just hardcore French in your face, don't care if it's too rich. They were both extraordinary, but for two different reasons. Banchet was the last of that guard who really drove home—*this* is French cuisine, this is the way it's going to be, you want this French you come to me, and he was able to carry that off. Roland took it and he added finesse and nuance. And I got to benefit from both of them.

MARY BETH LICCIONI: When we came in the menu was shortened a little bit, because [Banchet] had a huge menu. It was a little lighter, a little fresher. We didn't do tableside things like he did. Presentation was a big deal for him, because when he opened people didn't know what cuisine was. So he had a show, and in the beginning that was terrific. People loved it. But as time went on, it got to be redundant.

CARLOS NIETO: Roland was at Carlos' for seven years, we have a nice combination of presentation, and wine combinations for food. Then he went to Le Francais, to be the chef and partner there. And then Banchet wanted to charge him more money for rent. So he and his wife Mary Beth went to Les Nomades.

Convinced by then that the city was a better prospect for fine dining than the suburbs, Mary Beth Liccioni bought Les Nomades from Jovan Trboyevic in 1993. The Liccionis divorced, and Roland left in 2004 to open other restaurants, but returned to Les Nomades in 2011. He worked there until retiring in 2024.

DORIS BANCHET: In '89, we leased the restaurant out to the Liccionis. Jean was ready to be out of it, and he also wasn't, because he went right to Atlanta and opened two restaurants. Then he just stopped. He came home and said, that's it.

JOHN HOGAN: He went to Atlanta and opened Ciboulette and he had a ten-year non-compete with Mary Beth and Roland. Ten years to the week he came back. He did a dinner with me at [Hogan's restaurant] Savarin, which I thought was really nice. I did little mini versions of a lot of his classics, like the pithivier of duck, and the snail strudel. He was floored. His relationship with me was of a young American guy who really wanted to be like him—"I want to be like Mike," you know. He was the best in the world as far as I was concerned. This country had so many chefs come out of that kitchen that were really good.

DORIS BANCHET: Then we opened Le Francais again and we closed that, we were so lucky, just before 9/11. I'm telling you, it never was the same. It just didn't hit it off.

MICHAEL LACHOWICZ: It became dated. It became no longer in vogue, and it was too long an experience for people.

CARLOS NIETO: Things started to change when the expense account went down. The pharmaceutical companies were not doing parties. So we change Carlos' to Nieto's to do those more casual things, but people still didn't want to go home early. They still wanted to spend three hours for dinner instead of an hour and a half.

DORIS BANCHET: Jean had to retire, he just couldn't do it anymore because he was very diabetic. But he never stopped being a chef. Never. Every young person who wanted to be a chef, he talked to them, and he helped them. Even here in Florida, you know, all over. Cooking was his life.

DON YAMAUCHI: Actually, the first time I ever sort of shook Chef Banchet's hand was, one of my cooks said to me, Chef, there's some old guy in the back, picking through your garbage. Like, let's get him some food if we need to. And I'm thinking, are there really bums in Highwood? So I walk outside, and it was Banchet, and he was looking for boxes, because he was moving to Florida. Like, oh, my God, Chef, come on in and out of the cold. And he's like, well, hey, if you've got some boxes . . .

When we took Le Francais over my partner was Phil Mott, and he signed the deal on March 2 of '01. And then I walked into the dining room of Le Francais. And in the dining room was Chef Banchet with Paul Bocuse, at a table just talking. I'm like, you've got to be kidding me. Who walks into a restaurant in Wheeling, Illinois, and finds Paul Bocuse? I cooked for Paul Bocuse at Carlos', he came with Bernard Cretier, Jean Joho, and a few others. I didn't know that Banchet and Paul Bocuse were like blood brothers.

So when our opening day came I was going to be as driven as you could be to make sure that the place wasn't going down under my watch. I wasn't sure if I could get cooks, I wasn't sure if I could get sous chefs or anything and Chef Banchet said, listen, if you need help, you could take this side of the kitchen and I'll take that side of the kitchen and we'll make it work. He was there whenever he was in town, he would be there stopping by to say hi asking me if I needed anything. I mean, you name it, the guy was generous, and also gracious. I'm sure in his heyday, he was a little nuts in the kitchen. But when I knew him, he was very humble and very giving.

I think fine dining in that area, it was going south after 9/11. I mean, we used to have planes flying from wherever into the Palwaukee airport. Have dinner and then fly back out. Which I thought was just the craziest thing I've ever heard. It wasn't an everyday occurrence, but three, four times a month people would tell us this, we're flying in on this day at this time, can we get a reservation and be able to fly out at such and such a time? We'd be like yeah, for sure. And after 9/11, that all stopped.

CARRIE NAHABEDIAN: He never wrote a cookbook, which is incredible. But he did do a lot of things for *Bon Appétit.* That's how journalism has changed. If you saw my scrapbooks you'd see Banchet on the cover of *Bon Appétit*—who's the last chef you can remember who was on the cover of a food magazine? Not happening.

MICHAEL LACHOWICZ: Banchet was very driven by his reputation and how he was being perceived, and what was being said about him. But he was very careful and cautious to manage the way he was being seen and perceived. He never had a publicist. There weren't any publicists back then, there were only a handful of restaurants that were worth writing about.

It was such a really interesting time because there was a pivot point. Roland is in the middle of running his tenure, and suddenly Charlie Trotter comes along. Now there's a new kid in town. And I swear to God, it was exactly for Banchet and Roland at that point, with Charlie Trotter coming around, as it was for Charlie when Grant Achatz came. Now the comfort level is gone, and that's how we felt.

Banchet was the same as Trotter, he was hard to get close to. But then he became my biggest fan when I opened Les Deux Gros in Glen Ellyn, because it was very much in the style of Banchet and his cooking. He embraced it, and all of a sudden it was like I had worked for him for ten years, not six months. He wanted to make sure he massaged it into a situation where he was helping me succeed. And I'm forever grateful for that, but he was also getting his name back out where he wanted it to be.

My brother and I went back to Le Francais with a partner. And we ran it for a year until we realized that there was no way to put lightning back in that bottle. We got great reviews and things were wonderful with the restaurant making money, but there was never going to be another heyday of Le Francais. And after my brother and I left Roland went back. And, again, Roland ran it to the highest regard, but he couldn't do anything with it either. So the property had run its course over thirty years. It was sad, but it was reality.

CELESTE ZACCARO: I didn't really know much about the restaurant world. I just was coming to do my silly little salads or whatever. But I started to learn little by little, like, oh, my gosh, this is the best stuff in the world, or at least in the country at the time. So I was always in awe of all that. But Banchet was just a friendly guy who would come and say hi and chat with everybody, even if he didn't know who you were. And years later, I worked with Roland, again at Le Francais and Banchet lived, you know, next door. But they were celebrities without really being celebrities. It wasn't like, oh, I've seen you on the Food Network.

SUSAN MADDOX: It was the best to us to see Jean Banchet come to Kendall College and be a guest speaker. And then to be sitting with him—actually

Jean and Michael [Maddox] were outside, walking around his garden, but I'm sitting across the table from Doris Banchet. And that was the a-ha moment, I'm at the grownup table. And Banchet comes around the corner of his restaurant on his Harley, and he's like, oh, hello Susan. And he kisses me on both cheeks, and I'm like, oh holy cow.

MICHAEL MADDOX: When we had Le Titi, Pierre [Pollin] would stop by, and then Jean would every couple of months, saying, I just want to shoot the breeze and see what's going on. His passion was still there. And to me, it meant a lot as one of the people that was a big influence on me, Jean and Pierre and the other French chefs, like Roland, I think it was neat to have them still want to come and visit. These chefs were all people you put on a shelf, and you wanted to be like them and have that pride and passion and elegance.

He was known for yelling and screaming and all kinds of things. I never worked with him personally, but I had friends that did and he was demanding like all chefs are. He wanted your best, just like we demand from our students. But to see him evolve as he got older, and Doris got older—it was interesting to see when Roland and Mary Beth took over the restaurant. It was wonderful, because he was able to do more things, enjoy life a little bit more. It was interesting to see him evolve, not that he ever had a mean personality, but into a more gentle personality. And I think as he evolved, he kind of saw, maybe as we all do on certain levels, the true meaning of life. And you look back on your life, and you say, wow, what did I do, what did I accomplish? He had great heights of accomplishment. He brought fine dining to Chicago.

CARRIE NAHABEDIAN: It was really rough when he came to Naha the last time and he died a few weeks later of pancreatic cancer. I recently gave Curtis Duffy something that he has in his kitchen at Ever. It was one of the soup bowls from Banchet, from the truffle en croute bowl that Bocuse did for the President of France, Giscard d'Estaing. When I went to see Curtis when they were building Ever, I gave it to him. And I said here, you know, you do so much work for the Cystic Fibrosis Foundation. And maybe it'll just bring you visions of Banchet in your life.

Le Francais reopened and closed multiple times before finally closing for good in 2007. Jean Banchet died in 2013; the leading awards show for Chicago restaurants, launched by the Cystic Fibrosis Foundation, is called The Banchet Awards.

4: LIVE FROM CHICAGO

A woman sitting at a lunch counter places her order. "I'll have a tuna salad sandwich, and an order of French fries, please."

"No tuna. Cheeseburger?" the owner, a doughy guy in a white shirt with rolled-up sleeves and a skinny black tie, says. Well, that's not exactly what he says—he pronounces it "chee-borger," with a thick, indeterminate accent.

This is, of course, the Saturday Night Live *sketch about a Greek lunch counter, with John Belushi as the owner of "The Olympia Restaurant." As every Chicagoan knows, it was inspired by the Billy Goat Tavern on Lower Wacker Drive, with Chicago native Belushi imitating Greek-accented owner Sam Sianis shouting "chee-borger" to the kitchen and telling customers "no fries, cheeps" and "no Coke, Pepsi" (*SNL *got that one backwards). The sketch, first aired in 1978, marked the ascendance of Chicago as a flavorful and distinctive local subculture on the American scene, a decade after Mayor Richard J. Daley made it best known for police beating up hippies at the Democratic convention. Now it was the city of John Hughes and Siskel and Ebert, Michael Jordan and Oprah.*

In the process, parts of the city that had been considered abandoned to crime and dereliction would revive in the coming decades—and restaurants would be one of the things that made it happen. The first and most visible example of this in the 1970s and 1980s was the area just north of the Loop, once known as Smokey Hollow for its foundries and small factories, now divided into the rough and tumble Tenderloin on the north end and the Clark Street flophouses closer to downtown.

But being in the shadow of the Merchandise Mart and its furniture showrooms, by the 1960s the Clark Street area was also becoming home to decorators and galleries—and to gay bars, like the legendary drag club The Baton Show Lounge. Developer Al Friedman—whose father had been The Baton's landlord—started buying up the rundown but historic Victorian buildings in the early '70s, and began advocating to call the area River North. Restaurants—one in particular—would be central to his plans for its revitalization.

GORDON

AL FRIEDMAN: My father owned an empty building, and his brother-in-law was employed with a hot dog company called David Berg's. And he felt that would be a good space [for a fast food stand]. So we had Italian beef and hot dogs. I was thirteen and I'd just started high school. And every day after school, I'd go down to work; every Saturday, every Sunday, I helped run the hot dog stand. So I learned all about food, and I made deliveries. In fact, I took it to a whole 'nother level because I started delivering food to all the harbors for people with boats.

I remember in the late '60s or early '70s, going with a friend of mine to pick up some food in Lincolnwood [northern suburb]. We're talking to the guy at the counter and he asks what I do. I tell him where I work and he says, I feel badly for you. That's the impression that people were escaping—not just Chicago but all the urban environments. They fled for safety, their family's wellbeing, to suburban areas.

My dad also had a gay bar that he had leased to—he didn't even know what they were doing. That was The Baton Show Lounge. So in 1970, my father passed away. I was twenty-one. And I look at this downtrodden neighborhood, and I see brand new cars coming in all the time, to the Baton and other places. People actually dressed up nice. I said, what the heck is this?

I had an epiphany. I said, you know, people will go out of their way for food. And that experience that people have when you break bread, it's almost a religious experience. When we have a business meeting, it's a lunch, right? If I have a social event, it's a dinner that we go to. So let's change the neighborhood with restaurants. Gordon was the start of the idea of people going out of the way for food and being willing to go to sketchy neighborhoods—if the food is good.

Gordon Sinclair had been a PR director for the military at the time that President Nixon eliminated the draft and established the all-volunteer army. His path to becoming a Chicago restaurateur began when he was lured away to the Chicago Tribune *in 1973—but the newspaper turned out to be less accepting than the Army had been.*

GORDON SINCLAIR: I got fired from the *Tribune* in 1974. They said for not knowing how to spell, which is pretty ridiculous. That wasn't why I was getting fired. It was because I wore a puff hanky in my tailored suit and they weren't into the gay scene, they were homophobic. So I got canned. That was the great upset in my life, that turned out to be a very wonderful thing.

I went to work for Gene Sage [restaurateur of Eugene's and Mon Petit in the Gold Coast]. I thought if I'm going to open up a restaurant, I should become a waiter. Well, that's *not* what you should do. In fact the story at Gordon was that if I went to a table to take a drink order because the waitress was in the weeds, and then their waitress went to take their order, they'd say, Gordon already took our order. And she'd say, oh, *he* won't remember it.

Instead I was made the sommelier—I didn't know anything about wine! I had that silver cup around my neck—which gives you authority, of course. I remember selling to a young couple, probably thirty-five, the Sauternes—I don't know what they were eating, but it was much too sweet. But eventually I started to learn something about it.

I took my business training at Michigan State and formed a corporation and sold shares. In 1975 I was selling shares for $600 a share. And I did raise the money, $44,000, to open Gordon, though I certainly didn't have anything extra.

I met two designers at a dinner party. They frequented this leather bar on the corner of Clark and Illinois [Streets]. And one of them said, there's only one place to open your restaurant and that's on Clark Street. I said, jeez, who's going to come to that location, that's so low in the heel. But they pushed it, and I opened up between a dirty bookstore and a currency exchange.

It was a charming, well, sort of coffee shop once, I guess, in a fairly nice hotel. It was only twelve feet wide, I think it was sixty feet long. But there was a floor in there, there were bathrooms, there was a sort of dilapidated kitchen. And there was a walk-in icebox, that used blocks of ice—it wasn't electric. So once we tore that out, that gave us more kitchen space, and we put in a real walk-in, not freezer, but walk-in cooler. And it had a long counter with a bar up the front. And so I thought, well, we'll just leave the counter there and you'd get your cocktails at the counter. And then you'd wait for one of the seven precious tables.

My two designers wanted to do tied-back drapes on the columns—we had beams going up and across the ceiling, and the ceiling was made of white Vitrolite glass that was cigarette-stained black. I thought it had been painted. One Saturday I was down there working on cleaning the wood—the dirt was so bad I couldn't see any wood grain or anything. But I ran across the street to the hardware store and got some paint stripper and I remember putting that toxic stuff on the wall. As I was talking on the phone, a Princess phone with a long cord, the sun came right in and hit that spot where I was cleaning and my god, it was rosewood and it had an inlay of black ebony wood of some sort and a crown molding on it. It was quite stunning. Well, once we saw that, we thought, we have to tear out the counter and make a real restaurant.

The designers, they talked it up that this restaurant was going to open and it was really great. And their friends were hairdressers, and hairdressers know everybody, so they talked it up to their clients. I hadn't even opened yet and their clients were anxious to check it out. I remember taxis coming down—the man would stay in the taxi while the woman got out and came in. "Hold the taxi, this doesn't look good." You couldn't see through the glass windows, because there were blinds. A glass door was painted out, milk chocolate brown, but "Gordon" was transparent and you could see in that way. Well, if you looked in it was spectacular with spotlights on the tie-back curtains, which were held by white ceramic fists, big fat fists that used to be bookends. So it was very avant-garde, and looked fabulous. And the business grew every month, and year after year.

Who were my customers? Well in a word, Jewish. They're the first-nighters, like hairdressers. One would talk to the other and so we had a lot of Jewish clientele, who continued to be my best customers. They appreciated the good food, the good value and the ambience.

Rich Melman and Arnie Morton came in. They sat in the fabulous new banquetted dining room at a two-top. And I remember Stanley Marcus [chairman of Neiman Marcus] came in early on, when I just had the one room. I didn't take credit cards and he said, Gordon, you have to take credit cards. So I started taking credit cards, but I remember being asked by the *Tribune*, what would you wish for, for the new year? I said one weekend, all cash.

AL FRIEDMAN: In his day anybody who was anybody went there. And Gordon was there to greet them. So he understood the business, you walked in, there's a piano player there. After dinner, there'd be dancing.

GORDON SINCLAIR: I got the space because it was what I could afford—it was only $235 a month. I had two five-year leases, a five-year and a five-year extension if I wanted it, which I did. The first thing I did was buy the dirty bookstore next door. That allowed us to add on a second room that was really quite unique. It had banquette seating around the walls, but in the corners we had a leatherette square box with lamps, that had white enamel bases and shades made of leaded white glass. There were three of them in that room and they became the icons of Gordon, and outside we began with potted shrubberies in a dark exterior. It looked like that blue blood private club behind the Hancock building [the Casino Club]. And there was a big parking lot beside the second building. We didn't have valet. And there was a guy who came in and said, my car's missing. I said, you gave it to the valet? I don't *have* valet.

I didn't take any tables for two. I'd say, do you have any friends? Well, get another couple and call me back! That's how I talked back then and didn't think anything of it. But hurry, because we're a busy restaurant. I think at one point we may have been the busiest per chair in the country.

The bathrooms were unisex. I think they said that was against the law, but I ignored it. Why would it be against the law? I had no idea. We had what women would need in both. But then my beautifully, semi-gloss painted white bathrooms began to get graffiti. And I thought, oh, I had to paint it out immediately. And then the next day graffiti again and on the weekend, a lot of graffiti. Everyone went in to write on the walls and so I let it go and we became the graffiti bathrooms that really kept people in there reading it. And the most memorable quote on there said, "I'm eight inches long, and three inches wide. Are you interested?" And under it was written, "How big is your cock?"

JOHN TERCZAK (chef at Gordon): It was just kind of a magical little place. There were no other restaurants in River North. There were a couple of gay bars, but that was it. So he kind of broke ground and I've got to give him credit for that, you know? Imagine going to River North right now, and not seeing a single restaurant.

TODD STEIN (cook): There was a moose head attached to a mirrored bar. There were drapes that were all throughout the restaurant being held up by a giant, closed fist. The bathrooms had copper sinks and were elaborate and spectacular. In the same way that Gordon could wear paisley, stripes and polka dots and make it look good.

PHIL VETTEL (*Tribune* reviewer): Gordon really brought people downtown. If you went to Charlie Trotter's you were having dinner in Lincoln Park—a beautiful tree-lined street, and Charlie even used his own money to improve the sidewalks because he couldn't wait for the city to do it. But Gordon brought people to River North when that was really a crappy part of town. My late mother-in-law worked at the original American Medical Association building, which was basically across the street from where Gordon was. Their parking lot was surrounded by eight-foot fencing, and they gave women security escorts to their car when they left for the day. So that was River North at five o'clock on a Wednesday. Now the only danger is that a bridal party might throw up on you.

AL FRIEDMAN: At one of Gordon's anniversary parties, he got up and said, if it wasn't for Al and myself, the neighborhood that we've made such a significant change to wouldn't exist. Couldn't have been a nicer speech. And right then some guy pulls up to the stop sign outside, gets out of his car and urinates in front of everyone.

****

The business side of the Tribune *may have fired Gordon Sinclair—but the food section quickly fell in love with his hot new restaurant, giving it the ultimate praise in 1976 Chicago: saying it was like something out of New York.*

GORDON SINCLAIR: There was only one food magazine when I opened Gordon, which was *Gourmet*. But the kickoff for me was the *Tribune*. They did a big feature in the Sunday edition. A full page of Sunday brunch, and Gordon was one along with the Pump Room above the fold. Before that, there appeared in the *Tribune* magazine, just text, two or three columns called "A Little Touch of New York City." I remember, we were opening for brunch and I went outside to open up the door and my God, there was a line out there. And, you know, we were already booked. So I went out and I said, oh, goodness, those of you who have reservations may remain in line, but we have no other reservations available. And once you can't get into something, then you *really* want to get in, right?

The food was very Continental, at first. It became more Californian with Jeremiah Tower's influence at the time. The menu was soup or salad, we didn't have any appetizers. And I think I had five entrees—fish, meat, pork, chicken, and I think I had a pasta, which was probably pretty revolutionary. I served a hamburger but not French fries—I didn't have a deep fryer. Macaroni salad was what I had in place of fries with the hamburger. That in itself was—nobody had ever had macaroni salad on their menu. But nobody criticized it, they all thought it was very novel. So I opened with that silly menu.

PAULA CAMP (*Tribune* reviewer): It was in contrast to what was fine dining at the time, which was very stuffy. Think the Cape Cod Room as our premiere seafood restaurant, supposedly. Not that I didn't like the Cape Cod Room, it was okay, but it was from a different era, the era of the big bands, and they never quite progressed beyond that. Gordon was a party, a different party nightly, and Gordon presided over the fun. Very few people left that restaurant unhappy.

GORDON SINCLAIR: At the first brunch or something somebody ordered rosé. Way back then, rosé was very popular, besides Mateus, you know, in that clay bottle? Well, I didn't have any rosé, so I poured white and added some red wine to it. This is very good, she said, how can I get that? I said, I don't know, we just tried a new supplier.

I introduced things at Gordon that others hadn't ever had before. Like Pineau des Charente. Nobody had had that, but I went to the Champagne area and that's where I had my first sip of it, and then we got someone to import it for us. And I introduced that instead of the overpriced, overrated Pouilly-Fuissé.

We started with a hundred bottles on the wine list. But we didn't have first growths, I didn't go for the high-end stuff. I went for the best wine at the best value. I enjoyed doing that. People didn't know much about wine. They would want a bottle of Pouilly-Fuissé, or a red Cabernet. They knew that, but I don't know if they knew Pinot noir, or—well, we'd never sell a Petite Sirah. No food out of our kitchen would ever be big enough for that.

I remember our first New Year's Eve, when I realized I'm giving everyone half a bottle of champagne and I don't have any buckets. I didn't realize you really don't need a bucket for half a bottle. But for a four-top, you got a whole bottle. Well, I could have just set it on the table. Instead, I ran to the hardware store and bought some of those little galvanized rails, and just a little ice and a bottle would fit in it. And I left the sticker on it. It really fit into the arrogance and the uniqueness and the tongue-in-cheek of Gordon. It was attitude.

The menu was so limited, but that in itself was somewhat of an advantage because you didn't have too much to decide from. Salad or soup, and we only had one dressing, oil and vinegar. Everything had a sauce, everything. Very pretentiously, I would go down the line before we opened with my handful of spoons—oh, very good, very good! Needs a little salt . . . I didn't know what I was talking about, but it seemed to be agreed upon by the chef.

The revolving door of Gordon's kitchen began even before I opened. The chef at Eugene's had heard that I was opening a restaurant and he said he would like to join me. Well, goodness, I don't know if it was ten days before I was ready to open, but he quit and went out to the suburbs at a country club. And it went on like that until after twenty-four years, I had had seventeen chefs. So that gave it the vitality, because each new chef had to be reviewed by the press.

Next I had my sous chef, who turned out to be crazy. I last saw him running down the alley chasing one of my waiters with a knife. So I did lunch that day with no chef, I think my omelet must have been from Bert Greene [food columnist for *Women's Wear Daily]* or maybe I invented it myself, but it was an omelet of refried beans, sour cream and avocado. Pretty good. I served thirty-six people that day, I don't know how but I guess the waitstaff figured it out. Oh, my *garde manger* didn't come in, either. So I called my maid to come in, she didn't know anything. It sounds funny now. But it was really stressful, yet we pulled it off. I remember making one of those omelets and it fell on the rubber mat in the kitchen. I just took it over to the hot water tap. Hosed it off and put it on the plate. Oh, this is delicious, Gordon. Well, I wondered because it *did* fall on the floor, madam.

The afternoon after that lunch, I met John Terczak. He walked in looking for a job and did dinner that night.

JOHN TERCZAK: I worked at sixteen places before I started at Gordon, when I was twenty-three. The most formative was all the French restaurant experience that I had and the French cooking school that I went to. I worked at Café Bernard, as a cook and a busboy, I worked at Biggs as a cook, and at the Gaslight Club.

I was helping out a friend at a country club out in the western suburbs, who called me up and said, hey, I got this buddy of mine named Gordon who opened this place about a week ago, he needs somebody really bad. The reason I went there was when I sat down and talked to Gordon initially, it was a place where I knew I could kind of do what I wanted.

Gordon and I were a very good, well-matched pair for Chicago's food scene in that time frame. We were the only New American cuisine restaurant in Chicago. For the most part we introduced, and definitely popularized, grilled fish. I mean, you can't even imagine living in a world where people aren't grilling fish, but that was 1972 and 1973 and 1974. You couldn't go into a restaurant anywhere and order a piece of grilled fish. The combination of the food we were cooking and the Gordon personality, it made people crazy.

We were sold out every day for lunch and dinner for a solid five years, non-stop. You couldn't get a seat for lunch during lunch for five years straight. And the same thing for dinner. Unless you had a reservation.

MICHAEL KORNICK (cook and later chef at Gordon): John and Dennis Terczak kind of came up through the ranks, Washburne trade school guys, and terrific enthusiasts for Chicago. John was a very innovative nouvelle cuisine guy. I remember eating there in the '70s, and having poached halibut. And it was written in French, and it said, *aux deux sauces.* And it was a tomato-based sauce on one side and hollandaise on the other underneath, like thick, and then this piece of poached halibut in the center, covered with herbs.

Gordon introduced me to everybody. In '85 I went to the symposium in American cuisine and later in '85 I went out to work with, you know, Wolfgang Puck and Jeremiah Tower and Jonathan Waxman and Alice Waters and Bradley Ogden.

JIM WYGONSKI (server at Gordon): Any guy who makes a smoked chicken soup with peas in it, and the artichoke fritters with Béarnaise sauce, you can't go wrong. Terczak was way ahead of his time, just so innovative.

Gordon was phenomenal to work with. He was just a cool restauranteur who knew exactly what he needed and wanted. I was working at the Pump Room and I went to Gordon restaurant when that was the hot place, because us waiters, we jumped restaurants, we'd hear a good one was starting up and making a lot of money.

GORDON SINCLAIR: Terczak worked seven and a half years for me. He's the one that brought me the flourless chocolate cake, which I guess was unheard of, and the artichoke fritters Béarnaise that became our classic. Everyone wanted the artichoke fritters, I couldn't make the price high enough to get people to stop buying it. Same with the flourless chocolate cake—you want people to eat *all* your desserts, right?

I think the menu was certainly agreeable. It was all swallowable, but I think it was the ambience in the area. That's what made it unlike any other restaurant. We were the first to do half portions. Oh, the staff hated it because they thought all their tips were going to be cut in half. But instead they ordered a half fish, and a half lamb, and the ticket averages actually went up. Then people thought I was a great prophet. But I like to eat that way—when I go out I only order off the appetizer list. I want a little of this and a little of that.

It was more matter of fact [than French or Continental cuisine]. Although we had sauces—when I was with Terczak, he was a wonderful chef, he made wonderful soups. I remember when Jean Troisgros [chef of Les Frères Troisgros in Roanne, France] was here, he commented on John's smoked chicken soup and talked to him about it, because he had never had that. But his sauces were lovely. The plates were very nice, but it's not like they were simple. They became more and more architectural or more designed, and dripped and splattered.

JOHN TERCZAK: The smoked chicken soup was very popular. Gordon's was the only place that had anything like that at that time. It was so difficult in terms of getting product. I had to have my meat guy deliver a case of chickens to my fish guy. My fish guy delivered the chickens to his fish smokehouse guy. And then the fish house delivered the smoked chickens to me. And then I only use them for soup.

I'll never forget the day I put on a poached stuffed rainbow trout, surrounded by creamed Brussels sprouts with bacon and mushrooms. Everybody started scratching their heads, saying nobody's gonna want to eat this. And I said, well, it's going on the menu anyway, and people did eat it. I mean, now, nobody can live without Brussels sprouts. But I used to put things on—I mean, I was putting uni, sea urchin, on fish for a garnish in 1975, 1976, 1977. That was unheard of. Because sushi wasn't even popular.

NORMAN VAN AKEN (chef, Sinclair's in Lake Forest, early '80s): Gordon was talking to a reporter. She said, so Gordon, how do you define New American cuisine? And Gordon crossed his arms and put his one of his hands up against his face and he goes, well, I think it's when you put the sauce under the food. I just loved it. I would have had to go on for paragraphs to describe what I thought New American cuisine was, and he pretty much nailed it, epigrammatically.

JOHN TERCZAK: I wasn't thinking to myself, oh, this is the new cuisine. We weren't thinking like that. The only reason the words "New American cuisine" came up is because they showed up in the media one day. They have a way of creating their own news. What happened was, nouvelle French cuisine began to flourish, the very same year that Gordon opened. So the food media got plugged into French nouns, nouvelle cuisine first. And they all turned and looked at each other and said, yo, we've got New American cuisine, right here at Gordon.

I'm not saying that it started at Gordon. I'm saying that in the Chicago metro area, it started at Gordon, but it was happening around the country. It's not like I was the only one that was doing it. There was a whole host of mainly guys at that point that were doing it. I think there was one or two women. But like for example, in '83, the year before I left Chicago, *Food & Wine* magazine published the first edition of the annual best chefs in America issue and the very first one that they published, me and Mike Foley were in it.

****

PAULA CAMP: Gordon was a PR person. And he understood taste, and his customers. I think that restaurants are self-organizing communities, and people are attracted to certain restaurants because of the community they feel there, more than the food, and I think Gordon was a wonderful example. The food was good. It was always tasty. The artichoke fritters, you know, everybody loved them. But it was not groundbreaking, on the food level precisely.

It was groundbreaking because Gordon understood that if he provided a certain environment, a group of people would be attracted to that environment if the food was good. So I think that he was unique in that sense of creating this community, and comfort level for people who might not have found a really good restaurant, bordering on fine dining, that was welcoming to their kind.

JOHN TERCZAK: Every single person, except for two people, maybe three in the front of the house was gay. Right. And everybody in the kitchen was straight. It was like that for years. It was kind of a weird place in that regard. It was in Gay Town, it was kind of like a gay restaurant in the front and a straight restaurant in the back. By today's standards there is no such thing. I had a lot of sex at that restaurant but for the record, it was all straight sex. I met my first wife there, she was a waitress.

JIM WYGONSKI: A lot of my colleagues were gay. Gordon would go through and he would just snap his fingers, inspecting as he walked in. Like, there's something wrong with that table, boom, boom, boom, boom, boom. I'm in the back, where he had this big moose by the two bathrooms, and all he said every time is, how are you doing today, Jim? Because he knew I was the only married guy in the whole place. They'd all be like, what are you doing? You doing things to him that we should be doing?

GORDON SINCLAIR: They would all go and unwind, even the straights would go to the gay leather bar.

JOHN TERCZAK: Me and my buddy Kevin, who was a cook there, we were at the bars on Rush Street with two female cooks, and the bars closed. So I said, let's go to Gordon and we can hit the bar there. So I unlocked the place and they went in and started drinking. And then we got in the kitchen, we were smoking weed and having a great time, and I think it was about three o'clock in the morning. And we get into this gigantic egg fight in the kitchen, we were throwing whole trays of thirty eggs on a tray at each other. The place was completely destroyed. And you know what dried egg is like. We kind of sat down, smoked a joint and opened a bottle of champagne, trying to figure out how that was all gonna get cleaned up, because we were beat. Four o'clock in the morning, knocking at the back door, two Mexican guys looking for a job. We looked at each other. Those guys worked until seven thirty in the morning, doing nothing but cleaning up eggs.

The same two female cooks, we're down on Halsted drinking martinis at an outdoor café. It was Monday so Gordon was closed. And we get so drunk we talk ourselves into believing that it's a good idea to go to San Francisco. So we ended up at O'Hare, getting on a flight to San Francisco. And eventually we realize that there's not going to be anybody there to open the restaurant on the following morning. We were all looking at each other. Obviously I was the chef so it landed on my ass to call Gordon. But before I did that, I called a couple of other cooks and told them what happened. And they said they'd cover for us until we got there. Tuesday at work, four of the top, most important cooks in the kitchen are out—we only had seven or eight cooks. We missed the entire day. And Gordon overlooked that. That's how busy we were, and that's how happy he was about it.

GORDON SINCLAIR: For the twenty-second anniversary, they had me doing four and a half minutes of Swan Lake with the London Symphonic Orchestra. A tutu for 2-2, with Gordon doing the swan and three dancers in their fabulous Nutcracker outfits.

Nobody wanted their picture taken with me as a swan, but the next year, the 23rd, I was Queen Elizabeth I, the hair salon did those little curls that she had, and I came out to knight Sir Gordon, this Scottish restaurateur. "She" knighted one of my waiters, who came up the back so you couldn't tell it wasn't me, and then it went from the trumpets to "Dancing Queen" by ABBA.

In 1983, Gordon moved to a new building at 500 N. Clark.

GORDON SINCLAIR: Al Friedman had the hot dog stand on the corner, across the street from the leather bar, and he built a four-story building, and encouraged me to move down there. Even with the expansion into the dirty bookstore, we were limited—I had ninety seats, and a music lounge where we served overflow on weekends. We needed more space—in fact, we had rented the back of where the dirty bookstore had moved, and we did all our prep in there.

I didn't want to have any entree over twenty dollars, but when we moved to the new Gordon in 1983, it became more expensive ingredients. We were doing milk-fed veal—we never would have done that in the original Gordon. All the suppliers and the ingredients were farm-to-table, back before that began. And I bought a farm. People didn't really know farm-to-table, but the *Tribune* ran multiple pictures of Gordon at the farm on his tractor. I had raised beds, I had a rototiller, eventually I had 235 tomato plants in seven or eight different colors and flavors. It was eight dollars to get Gordon's tomatoes. That was a lot! But you know what they tasted like, with a simple oil vinaigrette and maybe a splash of the dark aged balsamic? With maybe a chiffonade of fresh basil and some crusty French bread? Oh! Died and went to heaven. And no grated egg on them, either. You had to get that at The Bakery. They went out talking about the tomatoes at Gordon.

We dipped them in hot water to get they skins off. That was a Gordonesque touch.

JOHN TERCZAK: I have a contention with this whole concept of farm-to-table, because where does everybody think their food comes from? Of course it comes from a farm. There isn't that much difference between the tomato that's grown in somebody's backyard, and a tomato that's grown out in a California tomato farm.

I think there's something good to be said, about kitchens being in closer touch with the growing process, and possibly even the growing locations. But I think it's way oversold. Once they chewed up New American cuisine, they needed a new concept, and farm-to-table gave people something new to talk about and write about.

After John Terczak set the standard at Gordon, other chefs made their own mark there. One was Keith Korn.

TODD STEIN: Gordon was the very first restaurant I ever worked in. I was at Kendall College and the person who helped people find jobs came into the classroom and said, this place needs help, is anybody interested? I was the only one who raised my hand, because I had eaten there with my mom.

What I didn't know was that the chef who hired me was just filling in until the new chef from DC arrived. That was Keith Korn. Keith was incredibly kind, and took me under his wing and introduced me to a lot of people who became very influential in my career later on—David Burke, Michael Kornick, etc. He really opened up the world of what being a chef was like, to me, being a twenty- to twenty-three-year-old kid.

Keith was all about product. Whether it came from France, Virginia, here, whatever it was, he had to have it and he knew where to get it. We were buying snails that were raised in Arizona that were fed basil and porcini. I can remember this big pot of live snails, as we were soaking them, them trying to crawl out. We served fancy things, but things that people were familiar with. It was never weird for the sake of being weird. We weren't doing cocoa-crusted tuna. It was really French and Italian, simple ingredients that people would understand, done extremely well.

Cooks didn't get tickets, you didn't see what you were picking up. You responded to orders in a very militaristic way and either you survived or you didn't. Just learning how to cook and then learning how to do what a chef tells you to, creates a thing in your brain that helps your memory get really good, because you're responding to so much at once and having to do it.

I was fortunate I got to work for Keith. And then I went back later and worked with Don Yamauchi, and saw two very different Gordon restaurants. But I think Gordon was creating hospitality like it was a dinner party every night, and who was coming? I don't think anybody throws a party like Gordon did. And he wanted everybody that came there to experience him, and what his restaurant meant to him through the food and wine.

GORDON SINCLAIR: Keith was a lot of fun, he was very lively and didn't steal *too* much. His food was good—his chowders were excellent.

BERNIE LASKOWSKI (sous chef in Chicago): Keith was like Jimi Hendrix, like Jim Morrison. Here is this individual that got taught and made into the best cook on the planet. And as a cook, you want to be that person that chefs are like, come work for me. He was a guy that was touched by the gods. Gift of gab, can cook like a motherfucker, jump on any station, out-cook anybody in any type of environment, know everything.

But he had a demon. And if you can't control your demons, your demons kill you. I think he was out in Martha's Vineyard. We just saw him a little while earlier, and he seemed in a really good place. He was really happy. He handed me Alain Ducasse's corporate recipe book. And we were talking about different cooking techniques. And then he went back home to Martha's Vineyard and wrapped his car around a telephone pole.

GORDON SINCLAIR: One of the chefs I had at the new Gordon was Don Yamauchi, He did a fillet and it was boiled in olive oil. Well, you know, nobody else ever cooked a steak that way! Medium rare, and I was so uppity then. I remember when somebody wanted their steak well done. I went to the table, and I said we don't have any more of these steaks, what else would you like? Cooking steak well done. That's like Trump, he eats in that way, with ketchup.

Speaking of future presidents, one got engaged at Gordon.

GORDON SINCLAIR: Obama and Michelle sat at table 40, which was a show table—I didn't know who he was, because he *wasn't* who he became. He was a state senator in Illinois, but they were a very attractive couple. I don't think I even went to their table—not that I was intimidated, maybe just that every time I was free, their mouths were full.

Gordon had other restaurants—Alexander's in River North and Sinclair's Ocean Grill in Jupiter, Florida, where he first hired a Chicago suburban transplant to Florida named Norman Van Aken. Later Gordon and Marshall Field V opened Sinclair's on the North Shore with Van Aken, who gave a start in the restaurant industry to a high school kid named Chuck Trotter (more about him later).

GORDON SINCLAIR: I opened Sinclair's with Marshall Field and Norman Van Aken, in Lake Forest right next to a Marshall Field's, guess why. Norman was a very good chef and a gentleman, though difficult to make money with—high labor and high ingredients, he wasn't a good manager of the kitchen yet.

NORMAN VAN AKEN: I learned so much working with Gordon, he was such an interesting character. He came along at a point in my life when I only understood restaurants from a micro level, and he was much more able to understand restaurants from the breadth of the entirety of the United States when my wife and I came out of Key West to return home.

Gordon was definitely forward-thinking. I know he was very affected by the menus of the Four Seasons in New York. Somewhere in my mix of stuff I have his onion skin paper where he typed out his ideas for the menu for Sinclair's, and yet he let me weave my way into his thinking. So we kind of collaborated on that. And then when a review came out, not long after we opened, James Ward, who was a critic in Chicago, said if Hemingway was a chef, this might be the food he was cooking.

I don't know that he was specifically engineering a Key West vibe into the suburban restaurant. But he had a painting that was on the main back wall, in the style of the 1800s. And it was a woman, and there was one fairly large part of the painting that was a woman who was in a dress, but you could see her nipple. Oh my Lord. People went ballistic, they're like, that's outrageous! You cannot show a nipple on a woman. And so Gordon, very witty, he managed to create a lamp fixture that just essentially grew out of the nipple. No more nipple.

I made him a plate once, I did my best to make sure the presentation was incredibly put together. And I guess artful in a way. Gordon looked at it and he said, it looks delicious. But Norman, imagine the Mona Lisa. I want to see a little bit of spaghetti coming out of her lips. He wasn't a clown by any means. But he had a kind of panache that came through in his restaurants.

It was a very, very galvanizing time. We really felt a sense of obligation and freedom to do justice to American cuisine. Our scope was all of America.

CARRIE NAHABEDIAN (cook, Sinclair's): Everybody knew Gordon and John Terczak and the whole gang of chefs that worked there. I was at Le Francais at the time. I don't know what happened, but I went to Banchet and I said, I don't even know how to make a gumbo. And he said, what do you care? Who cares how to make a gumbo—*somebody* knows how. [French food] is *your* cuisine. I said, I'm American and I need to learn American cuisine. This is my heritage and I need to know it. He said, all right, you can make it for family meal. That was his answer, you want to make gumbo, you can make it for family meal.

But I was at a crossroads, I'd worked for Banchet for two years, and everything in my life was destroyed except work. And at the time, Leslee Reis had asked me to come work at Café Provençal [in Evanston], which I loved. I loved the kitchen. It was so Alice Waters, herbs grown in the window and shit like that.

I don't like when people play with foods—kitschy things like what Gordon would do for Valentine's Day, you cut into something and the heart would bleed, stuff like that. That wasn't my cup of tea. But I knew that he was opening an American restaurant in Lake Forest. I knew Lake Forest because I grew up on the North Shore.

So I went to see Gordon and that was my first time meeting him and Marshall Field. My father knew him, because he worked at Marshall Field's. And Gordon told me that he was bringing on this new chef, Norman Van Aken, who does Floridian cuisine. I'm looking at him like, I'm so gonna go to the library. Because all I knew was conch fritters and key lime pie and stuff like that. So I met Norman, we hit it off right away. I told Leslee, I can't cook French. I need to take a break from French to learn American cuisine. And Gordon was just so eccentric, he pushed the envelope all day long.

Norman and I hit it off immediately. We're very close personal friends to this day. Norman leaned on me to teach him, basically, the fundamentals of a strong kitchen and how to refine your cooking because Norman had been working at Louie's Backyard in Key West, which is a really killer place but a fun place that everybody hung out at. He wanted a little more refinement. So he thought, I'll bring Carrie in, she already knows how to do all of this, she can help me write menus. We were a great working team.

I was there for a year when I finally said to myself, okay, I know how to make a gumbo. I know everything about American cuisine now. You could learn American in a week.

NORMAN VAN AKEN: Carrie knew a lot more about cooking than I did. I've said it often that Carrie really should have been the chef and I should have been sous chef. She'd worked for Banchet and I'd worked at, basically, a barbecue place for the drunks of Key West. But she was cool with it—she just wanted to cook. And I think she liked the idea of some of the rusticity and regionalism that I brought to the party, so we collaborated pretty well.

CELESTE ZACCARO (cook, Sinclair's): I had a little bit of kitchen experience from some pizza places that I worked at in Minneapolis, just little mom and pop places. But I didn't really know what I was getting into, to be honest. And so I fell into something really awesome. It couldn't have worked out better because it was Carrie and Susie Crofton and Norman Van Aken—Charlie Trotter was there, too, but he was kind of a nobody at the time. Gordon, of course, he was a god in the restaurant world. John Terczak, he would come and kind of consult, every couple of days and work in the kitchen. So it was a really great place to learn, from all of these people.

I trusted them because Gordon already had two other restaurants that were successful. Carrie obviously had already been at Le Francais, she knew what was going on. And everybody else was a little bit older. So I just put myself in their hands. And they didn't steer me wrong.

DON YAMAUCHI (chef at Gordon, late '90s): At Carlos' a busy night was about 170 covers. I get to Gordon and a busy night there was 450-some odd covers. So it was eye-opening, to say the least, in terms of volume and organization and things like that. Gordon really taught me how to run a business. He taught me how to make sure that my food costs were in line, my labor costs. And again, also, his work ethic was amazing. He was there five, six nights or days a week and if my dishwashers needed help, he would take off his sport coat and his suit jacket and roll up the sleeves and wash dishes.

I loved working there because of all that and his energy on a Friday or Saturday. Tonight we're doing three to four hundred people, boy that restaurant just had the buzz. It was a lot of fun.

GORDON SINCLAIR: I was always nice to my staff, especially when I taught the Mexican dishwashers. I loved doing that because I loved dishwashing. It's just such a wonderful, zen experience of everything so dirty and grimy coming out so beautiful and clean. By the way, that guy who was the dishwasher and then we moved him up to the line ended up having his own restaurant. He has more than one Mexican restaurant, I don't know what suburb it is. It was wonderful, to have that happen.

DON YAMAUCHI: Gordon was quick-witted. We were in New York, going into the Monkey Bar at the time just for a drink. And out of nowhere. I mean, New York is huge, some guy honked his horn from nowhere. "Hey, Gordon, how are you? Gordon Sinclair, how are you?" I mean, who walks through New York and someone actually recognizes them? But that was Gordon, he was larger than life.

Every year, a couple of times a year, he would say, listen, I want you to go to New York, I want you to eat at however many restaurants and he paid for the whole thing, just to give me experience eating and dining. But he goes, when you spend the money, you've got to make sure that you come back with a report. So you would have to go and write an essay on your dining experience. Sure, if that's what it takes for you to send me to New York and eat at whatever restaurant I want, on your dime. And he put some of those things into effect here at the restaurant. I thought that was the smartest thing anyone's ever done. What a small investment to get some great ideas.

After nearly a quarter century, Gordon decided to close at the end of 1999.

GORDON SINCLAIR: I closed Gordon in '99. I was sixty-five, I had bought myself a Bulgari gold watch in New York, and I thought, am I going to go on saying, this way, please? And also because we had another recession and business had changed a lot—as much as it changed when Sears moved out [to the suburbs in 1992], we used to get all the Sears buyers in for lunch. So that made a big change, and there was competition, Rick Bayless was across the street. I had offers to sell it, but I didn't need that money and they all required my staying on for a year, and I didn't feel comfortable with that.

So I said we're going to close, and it was black tie, and a set menu, and it was dancing and a trio with a singer, and we really decorated for New Year's with gold lamé hanging from all those draperies, and white and silver balloons, hundreds of balloons, so the place just looked sparkling. It was a big night. I wore my kilt, I said goodbye to everyone, and everyone got a Gordon plate that said, "The last great meal of the century was eaten off this plate." So it was a wonderful and exhausting night.

DON YAMAUCHI: It was New Year's Eve, and it was out of control. And I do remember being in the weeds for a good hour or two. But what I remember the most, besides the energy, was just at the end. Gordon told everybody in October at the restaurant that he's shutting the doors, but if you stay till the end, whoever's here, plus their significant other, he'll take them to Vegas. So I want to say 99 percent of the staff stayed.

We made it through that last service. After the last ticket out, for at least the kitchen it was like the air going out of a hot air balloon, just huge relief that we didn't screw up that last service and it was successful. And knowing that everybody that ended up doing that last ticket would stay and clean up and we would go to Vegas in a week or two.

[Guests on the last night] had to order your champagne or your wine ahead of time, just because we wanted to make sure we had enough, but we wouldn't have *too* much on hand. And a handful of people didn't take their bottle or two or three or whatever. So there was without exaggeration, ten or fifteen bottles of great champagne that we were able to all partake in. As a chef, you really don't get to do that. So that was awesome. He's awesome. I love him.

KEVIN BOEHM (co-founder of the Boka Group): I opened up my first restaurant in Florida in 1982, with my girlfriend at the time. And I brought her to Springfield [Illinois] to meet my parents, and we had enough money to come to Chicago for one meal. So I thought we'll go to Gordon, and I had them fax me a wine list. I had it all planned out—I knew how much money I had on my credit card.

So we go there and at one point I go to the bathroom. And when I come back, Gordon is sitting talking to my girlfriend. It's a two-top, so I just sort of squeeze next to her on the banquette. Kevin, this is Gordon Sinclair, she says to me. I'm like, oh my God, so nice to meet you. And he just says, how about I join you for dessert? We said that'd be incredible. We had crème brûlée, we sat there and drank after dinner drinks and chitchatted for a half hour. It was December 30, and he says, I'd love for you guys to be my guests at my New Year's Eve party tomorrow night. And we're like, that'd be incredible. He says it's black tie.

He leaves and our server comes back, and we ask her, why would he come by our table and join us like that? She says, you know, he's interesting. He picks out people in the room, and we were probably noticeably out of place. We were probably the youngest people in there, we might have looked like we didn't belong there. But at the same time he asked who we were, and she said, oh, they're the nicest couple, they just opened a restaurant in Florida, and he's like, really? We're out in Florida too. So that's probably why he came by.

We woke up the next morning, and we're like, wait a second, it's black tie. I don't have a tuxedo. She didn't have a proper dress. What are we going to do? And we were embarrassed, and we just never showed up.

Jump ahead to 2004. Our PR person at the time was Jenn Galdes, and she was like, it's Gordon's seventieth birthday, and he's looking for somewhere to have his birthday, and I suggested maybe Boka. So you know, send him an email, if you want to throw your hat in the ring. So I sent him an email telling him that entire story of that evening and how much it meant to me. I said, I watched you and how personal you made our experience. And you made me, as a twenty-two-year-old kid, feel really important. It meant the world to me. And I would love to have the opportunity to return the favor and throw a party for the ultimate party thrower.

Within five minutes he sent me an email back. He said, I believe that in this world, everything is meant to be. And you were meant to throw my seventieth birthday. So we did. We brought in a grand piano, and all the piano players from Gordon. There were three different ones and people stood up and made toasts and everyone got up and danced in their seats. And it was this magical, beautiful little evening.

Al Friedman wanted to follow Gordon in the 500 N. Clark space with a restaurant worthy of its reputation. He found Carrie Nahabedian and her cousin Michael, who opened Naha in 2000. Eight years later Naha would win her the James Beard award for Best Chef Great Lakes.

CARRIE NAHABEDIAN: Gordon just left the space. Like okay, service is over and he just walked out the door. It took us a month to get all the shit out of there, like office files, oil in the fryer, there was food in the refrigerator. Like leaving your house and you just leave.

When you look at some of the things that Gordon did, the promotions—people had the money to advertise in *Chicago* magazine, full page ads that were really funny. I look at them now and say to myself, damn, I wish I had $18,000 to take a one-page ad in *Chicago* mag to say something funny, like, we're gonna have brunch and the waiters are gonna wear pajamas and they're not wearing anything underneath.

In the wake of Gordon's phenomenal success came other innovative, primarily American restaurants; you no longer had to make French food to draw a trendy crowd. Naha closed in 2018; Al Friedman's third tenant in almost 40 years in the 500 N. Clark space was José Andrés, with Jaleo.

JACKIE'S

In 1985, Chicago's restaurant scene made a national splash—a PBS series called Great Chefs *devoted its season to chefs of Chicago. Most were very French (Banchet, Liccioni, Lucien Verge) and, given the times, very male, but among them were two women chefs: Carolyn Buster of The Cottage, and Jackie Shen, born in Hong Kong but a veteran of Chicago restaurants including The Bakery (she says she lasted one week) and Le Francais (where her then-husband, Pierre Etcheber, was a wine steward). Jackie's French-Asian fusion cuisine was, it turned out, exactly what 1980s Americans were hungry for. It was one whimsical dessert in particular—a chocolate dessert in the shape of a paper bag—that made her a hot name and Jackie's the next hot restaurant on the same strip as The Bakery, Lincoln Avenue.*

JACKIE SHEN: I graduated from hotel school at the University of Houston, and then I came back to Chicago and took a job at the Ritz-Carlton. They had a semi-casual restaurant, where I was an assistant manager. But back in those days, they didn't really promote women to a management position. I couldn't get any higher up, so I went across the street to the Water Tower Hyatt.

I was the dining room manager for breakfast. But I didn't know how to cook. I only knew how to flip pancakes and burgers because that was what I'd cooked in college.

So I did that for about eighteen months, and Chef Banchet was looking for help in his downtown restaurant, La Mer. I became a salad prep cook, but they gave it a fancy title, *garde manger*. First day Chef says, go wash this head of lettuce. I look at it and say okay. Then I go to the dishwasher and I say, Florencio, how do you wash this head of lettuce? He says, you kidding me? He showed me many things, like how you clean the beard off the mussels. So I did *garde manger* for three months and then the fish cook quit, so I said, Chef, can I do that station? He said, yeah, you can do that station—plus your *garde manger* station.

So instead of coming to work at nine, I came at seven, and I knock off the *garde manger* so I can do the fish. The saucier quit and I said, can I do the saucier? He says, yeah, but you have to do this, this and this. I said okay.

After eighteen months I left and went to work at Le Ciel Bleu, and then that Lincoln Park location became available. At that time Lincoln Avenue was very bohemian—you had folksinging bars, and some of the old-fashioned bookstores and stuff like that. And when I took [the space] over it had been a vegetarian restaurant. I had, at that time, $60,000 saved. So I fixed it up and opened Jackie's on Lincoln.

Three months into opening Jackie's, one of the Pritzkers, who own Hyatt, said you need some publicity, and introduced me to the publicists Ruth Rashman and Penny Wasserman. They said the selling point was that I was a woman, I was Asian, and I was cooking French. And at that point I was tired of doing cream, butter, demiglace, veal stock reduction—all that kind of stuff. So I was fusing in a lot of Asian ingredients, Asian flavors, using things like star anise in the veal stock. So that's how they pitched me, and after a few articles came out, and the *Tribune* review came out, the phone was ringing off the hook.

By that time I had already created the chocolate bag, which made me famous. So on my day off, I watched Julia Child, which would usually air Monday on PBS—at that time you didn't have a VCR, you actually had to watch it when it's on. I was watching her prepare something, and she usually had a big long butcher block table that had all her prep. At the corner of the table, there was a grocery bag overflowing with vegetables. And I looked at the bag, and I thought, wouldn't it be cool if I could make it into a smaller bag, but make it out of chocolate. I had this idea, but I didn't know how to execute it. Because I was never a pastry chef. I was always a savory chef.

I got my hands on every kind of bag I could find, and either they were too heavy, or I didn't know how to work with chocolate. One day, I was downtown running errands, and I always loved Garrett Popcorn. And so I would line up, waiting for my caramel popcorn. I always like to watch the salespeople, and so I was watching the salesperson scooting the popcorn into the bag. And I saw this four-ounce bag and something rang in my head. And I said that might be the bag that I was looking for. So I went to the manager, I said, would it be possible to buy two hundred of these bags?

It's always made with Belgian semi-sweet chocolate. I use Callebaut semi-sweet, and I knew it had to be a white chocolate mousse inside, for the contrast with the dark chocolate, and berries. And it had to be a raspberry sauce for balancing the acidity.

First of all, you have to trim it to the right height. And then you flip the edges outward. You temper the chocolate to 91 degrees. And then you take a brush and you hand-paint it, inside of each crevice. Then you set it straight on the sheet pan and let it sit in the refrigerator to get hard. Then after you take it off the glassine bag, you fill it up with the mousse. I finally had to take a chocolate lesson from Elaine Gonzalez, she was at that time the master chocolatier in Chicago, I took a lesson from her in how to temper chocolate, how to work with chocolate.

I started putting the chocolate bag in the dessert items. The *Tribune* promoted it, and before I knew it I was in an article in *Chicago* magazine, I was in all kinds of things. So that's how my career took off.

The whole country was copying me. One time it was in Napa. They were showing it as a beverage, and filling it with a milkshake. And someone saw it in Atlanta. It was interesting how it traveled—but my name didn't travel with it.

I don't think that back then, we wanted to be known as a food city. I don't think it had crossed anyone's mind that they wanted us to be a food city like New York or [cities in] California. Eventually Chicago caught on, but I think that being Midwestern, we're probably a more humble city than New York, and less glamorous than California. We're hardworking chefs, nobody was looking for fame and fortune.

HEAVEN ON SEVEN

One of the hot trends of early '80s dining was Cajun food. You might think Chicago would be an unlikely place to find one of America's most-recognized Cajun restaurants—and the seventh floor of an office building on the Loop's "Jeweler's Row" an even more unlikely one. But Heaven on Seven, in the 1914 Garland Building, proved to be exactly that over its forty-year lifespan, bringing an authentic regional American cuisine to Chicago. It was run by a third-generation Greek American chef-owner named Jimmy Bannos—now mostly known as Jimmy Sr., as his son Jimmy Jr. ran an acclaimed second restaurant, the popular Michigan Avenue gastropub The Purple Pig.

JIMMY BANNOS SR.: I started in restaurants when I was nine years old. My dad had a restaurant at 35th and Western, called the Corner Grill. And to be honest I think it was love at first sight. It was love that I got to work side by side with my dad. My mom would be working, my brother would be working. I went to Triton College for a year, but I knew some guys who went to Washburne Trade School and said, you can make $20,000 a year, you'll be set for life. Even though it was a hundred years ago I knew $20,000 is not gonna work for me.

But I got into Washburne and it was the best thing I ever did in my life. Truly a great, great experience for me. It was five phases, first phase, introductory, second phase was soup, salads and appetizers, third was pastry, fourth entrees, and fifth was everything that you learned. Every day you'd be just doing cooking, cooking, cooking. They would teach you business and stuff like that, but I had a head start in that. My dad was a second-generation restaurateur, his parents both came from Greece and both were in the restaurant business. When I graduated, my dad and I opened up the New Garland Coffee Shop in 1980.

I got interested in Cajun food because I was trapped. I was working seven days a week. I got Paul Prudhomme's cookbook[5] and that changed my life. So I cold-called him. And he got back to me the next day. We had a two-hour conversation. He was magnificent. He was such a really nice guy. And I honestly I couldn't ask for anybody better than that to be a mentor. He invited me to come down [to New Orleans], this is probably about '85. My wife and I went down there for a four-day weekend. That truly opened my eyes and changed my life.

He was a family guy, and I'm a family guy, and as soon as he met my wife, I think he really felt that, and there was no turning back. I met Emeril [Lagasse], who had just started at Commander's Palace. The Brennans [owners of Commander's Palace] were just really nice to me. And then it just started. I would get any book I could on Louisiana and New Orleans. I was relentless. My wife and I, or my brother, would go down there and we would just eat, eat, eat. We would get there on Friday and leave Sunday, and we go to between twenty-five and thirty-five places—not full meals, we would go to a place that was famous for red beans, and we would try that and leave. We had a cab driver we knew, he would take us to all the different places that we probably wouldn't know to go to. He would take us all around, we would try everything.

5 *Chef Paul Prudhomme's Louisiana Kitchen,* 1984.

Bannos started putting a few Cajun dishes on the coffee shop's menu.

People didn't know much about it, but they were receptive to it. They saw the craze, and I was probably the first one to do blackened tuna in Chicago. You know as a chef when your customers trust you and mine really trusted me. Whatever I put on the plate, they would go crazy for it.

When we bought it, it had been a Jewish deli. So I trimmed that menu down, and people would say, hey, where's that gumbo you made the other day? It was insane, we would do eight hundred people from like eleven o'clock to two thirty. We eventually had five guys working in that tiny kitchen. And then the magazines started writing about it, *Food & Wine* was one of the first ones, James Ward [local TV reviewer] did a piece, Margaret Sheridan did one for the *Tribune.* We started doing our Mardi Gras celebration, which was huge.

But chefs are very, what are we going to do next? So we started opening up for dinner the first Friday of every month. We would do two, three hundred customers. I was doing a seven course "Let Jimmy Feed You" for thirty bucks. We've just had some tremendous customers over the years, I couldn't be any happier.

My dad and I working side by side, my mom passed away first. And my dad passed away, and my brother just a few years ago. So I'm the last person standing. It's kind of sad. But my two kids are tremendous restaurateurs, I mean, my son got a James Beard award for The Purple Pig.[6] I would never pressure any of them, you got to do this. But he likes what he's doing, and my daughter, she just became a mother so she's got her hands full with a baby.

Or, perhaps the start of a fifth generation in the restaurant business. Heaven on Seven closed during the COVID lockdown, but the Bannos family continues to open and operate restaurants.

PRINTER'S ROW

When Elwood Blues picks up his brother Jake upon his release from prison in Joliet, he takes him back to an SRO in the South Loop—and the dingy flophouse where Elwood lives offers a pretty accurate picture of the south end of Chicago's

6 Rising Star Chef of the Year, 2014.

business district in the late 1970s. Like River North, the South Loop was derelict, but it had vintage building stock that offered promise, particularly to young restaurant owners.

One such was the district of early twentieth century printing company buildings on South Dearborn; in 1981, a year after The Blues Brothers *came out, a young chef named Michael Foley gave it its start with a restaurant called Printer's Row, named at the suggestion of his restaurateur father. When Charlie Trotter was still a busboy at Sinclair's, Foley became the face of a new generation of young Chicago chefs, featured in the PBS series* Great Chefs of Chicago *and named to what became the James Beard Foundation's "Who's Who in Food and Beverage" in its inaugural year, 1984.*

MICHAEL FOLEY: I was third-generation in the hotel and restaurant business. My grandparents opened a restaurant named Ray Foley's in Oak Park before World War II, and my father and uncle partnered with the Pritzkers on the first Hyatt Hotel in Lincolnwood, Illinois. I grew up in restaurants ever since I was ten.

I went to Georgetown, but my goal was to become a professional golfer. By then, I wanted nothing to do with restaurants. But as luck has it, I ended up breaking my hand. I had three operations adding pins and bone grafts. I wore a cast for three and a half years. My dream of a golf career was over.

While at Georgetown I worked at night in some of the little varied ethnic restaurants—and I really got into it. I loved everything from Irish public houses with steak through Indian vegetable-based menus, to French cafés and fine dining. I also got into working on weekends at great men's clothing shops, precursors to Ralph Lauren. I learned to cut cloth, fit clothes and appreciate style. I grew to like the combined lifestyle built around food, clothing and the growing design industry.

When I first came back to Chicago, I went to work for Gordon. I did the day shift and John Terczak, who was the chef, did nights. I was at Gordon for two and a half years. I knew I wanted to open my own place eventually, so I worked two jobs, day at Gordon and night atop Lake Point Tower at their club, and I worked for Jovan Trboyevic at Le Perroquet. What I learned from Jovan was precision and mastering a task. Some people working with him might not have liked that. I loved it. I was very much into the detail, I was very much into learning how to make sauce, make confits, stuffed and flavored game birds and all the things he did.

While in high school, my grandparents had taken me to Europe. We visited countries throughout most of Europe, really wonderful places, each with their own style of cooking, café, brasserie, roadside stand up to the posh, like George V or Lasserre in Paris—you could just go through all the one-, two-, three-star cafés, restaurants and hotels. Because of that trip and others, I kind of had in my head what I was trying to do for myself—not a steak house, and not a French restaurant. I wanted to apply what I had seen in regional cooking to what I would consider to be upgraded American cooking. Pork with onions, citrus and mint, lamb shanks with fresh rosemary and thyme, vegetable pot pies—it was just well-balanced locally and nationally product-driven menus. About 20 percent of the dishes were vegetables.

Foley found his neighborhood in the strip of vintage buildings on south Dearborn, and his landlord in John Baird of Baird and Warner, who as president of the Metropolitan Housing and Planning Council in the 1960s had fought successfully to pass an open housing ordinance in the highly segregated city. His vision, however, did not extend at first to the idea of upscale restaurants in what the city officially termed a "condemned and blighted area."

I found Printer's Row late one afternoon driving back in a snowstorm from Michigan. I had been off to see Larry Bell of Bell's Brewery, in Kalamazoo. I got off the Skyway and snaked my way back to the Loop and suddenly, I'm like, wow, this is interesting. But it was a ghost town. All these old lithography buildings, empty. Stairs had fallen in, few had power, and no one was around—no cars, few street lamps. One building even had a tree growing right in the middle of it.

Next morning, I went to a corner Greek coffee shop, the Pontiac Grill, in the 1891 Pontiac building, which was almost completely empty above it for thirteen floors! I went and had coffee every day, until the owner said to me, whaddaya doin' here? I said, well, you know, I really like your place. I'd like to buy it. He goes *what?* All there was, was like a little griddle, an old dish machine and one half-working four-door refrigerator. A forty-year-old kitchen, short order, ten-foot line and passthrough for orders. That was it.

I went to see John Baird, who owned the building with five partners. My family and friends thought I was crazy. They said, it's *John Baird.* And I said I don't care who he is, he's still a landlord. So I sat there in his office until he would see me. And I said to him, I would like to lease the ground floor of the Pontiac building. He thought I was absolutely out of my mind. "You come from this great restaurant family. Why do you want an old, dilapidated coffee shop? That's got an eight-to-ten-foot kitchen that doesn't even work?" I said, because I'm gonna make it my place.

He pushes back, does your family know you're here?

And I said, I'm twenty-four years old, I make my own decisions. I kept coming back and coming back and finally met with his partners. I cut a twenty-five-year lease—you don't do those things anymore. I had a stepped lease, with renewable clauses. When you're a guy at twenty-four, and you sign a twenty-five-year lease with extensions, and personal limited guarantees tied to performance that roll over, it's scary—but I figured, as long as I hit certain objectives, the personal guarantees were dissolved. And I just worked like a crazy man. I had one other guy with me in the kitchen. The first year, I worked lunch and dinner, did lunch by myself, including the dish room. I was basically petrified of not paying my loan. Few people I meet are like that today—seems like few can work without having eight people in the kitchen, and a dishwasher on top of that payroll. I created the entire kitchen around me, I checked in the produce and made the bread and everything. That first year—it was terrible!

I had a certain number of pots and pans and that was it. I had a budget, and I didn't go over that. I bought Rosenthal China where I needed to make a statement. Believe me, since I did my own dishes, I never broke a plate! And that's how I paid my three-year note back in a year.

In the first three years, we had terrible staff turnover. I was difficult. I wasn't trying to be like some crazy chef, I was just nervous, and serious. You can be *very* serious about not wanting to go out of business—the right kind of fear creates its own kind of sauce. I came from a successful family, and failing was not an option. But it's like you're trying to play the piano and keep the keys in the keyboard at the same time. You're learning about legal issues and the city's challenges and regulations and landlords and at the same time you got to worry about your plumbing and a refrigerator breaking. And when the snow came and there was no one around to shovel it, you put a coat on and you went out and you shoveled the snow.

It was my first business, and I learned how to handle people. We had about 15 percent of the staff stay with me for over sixteen years. And at the end, when I finally closed Printer's Row, we had eight people there that were at Printer's from the original group, out of forty.

I think we all felt like we were doing something significant. We were getting past the commercial restaurants of the late '50s and '60s. It wasn't about prestige. I wanted to be affordable quality, not fancy. I wanted to develop my own ideas with others. I wanted full-service. I worked with great people to put us on the map in spite of all kinds of outside influences and obstacles. And we were elated to see others wanted the same, and being supported by individual small wineries and breweries and fishermen, all the purveyors. It was a very complete circle.

****

Again, before the term "farm-to-table" had been invented, Foley was one of the chefs pioneering it in Chicago. He would call it "the American cooking movement."

MICHAEL FOLEY: At that time, we didn't have the kinds of produce that I wanted. The distribution system developed over the next thirty years, it didn't exist yet. We closed on Saturday night, and I would get in my old Beemer on Sunday and head to Wisconsin or Indiana, even Minnesota. I put two hundred thousand miles on that Beemer looking for regional products. And then finally I realized one of the best things I could do was find purveyors of the things that I wanted, even if they were in Colorado or California. O'Hare was the greatest thing we ever had in seafood, because you can call over to Europe at times when the US had limited choices and they would pack whatever you wanted. We would broker it in, and that's how some of the seafood businesses really got into large scale distribution.

The other great thing that happened to me was Greyhound bus service. It was only four blocks away. If I found somebody who had terrific chicken, they could pack it in thermal bags or in shipping containers and put it on Greyhound for shipping. They would call me on the package arrival, and I would go down and pick it up. And that's how with overnight service we got a lot of our specialty produce, local fish and game until some of the purveyors developed over the next five years.

Developing the farmers, working with different people and creating a market for them was one of the things I really loved. Because once they start selling, they want to grow. And the best thing that can happen is to turn that grower on to someone else. We were connecting people who were not just local, but national and international. Monique Hooker [Monique's], Jackie Shen, Jennifer Newbury [Amérique], Dennis and John Terczak, Richard Knox [Park Hyatt], Jeff Jackson [Park Hyatt]—all these people got into the whole farmers market movement, and Abby Mandel and her friends developed the organic side.

I kept using this term "the American cooking movement" because to me, it wasn't about American cuisine. It was about the movement, it was about purveyors and wine and beer and the distribution market and all the chefs and sommeliers and beer gurus that came up and out of it. My job in running a restaurant was one thing, but my job and self-driven work to help to market the American cooking movement was a much bigger job.

I called it a movement because you had all these growers, doing everything from dairy to fish—such as Rushing Waters trout in Wisconsin. We had a lot of interest in just things like cleaning up the Great Lakes and riverways, so we could fish it better. Pike and whitefish and, who would have thought? *Petits gris*, tiny escargot from Illinois at one time, frog legs from Indiana. Great Lakes and Collins Caviars. In short, we had all these people who were interested in growing food and getting it into small restaurants.

If you remember, we had very little growth in wine then. I was lucky to find myself meeting guys like Peter Wilkins of Barrique Wine Company. Some of them had returned from the military and were able to access government loans to plant and grow out the industry in great locations in California, Washington State and Oregon as well as others. I started to get calls from people like David Lett, who had been an encyclopedia salesman turned wine grower building the Eyrie Vineyards [Oregon], while living in a trailer for years out there. Add in David Adelsheim [Adelsheim Vineyards, Oregon],

Dick Ponzi of Ponzi, Joy Sterling of Iron Horse. They put their plants in the ground and the American wine scene exploded, red, white and sparkling.

What was really kind of interesting was how other businesses took advantage of this. American Airlines had the Chef's Conclave, and United Airlines had theirs. They tried to bring what was happening in the restaurant scene into first and business class on their planes to take advantage of "the American movement."

Baby boomers were starting to be a little bit successful, and they were looking for places to go and spend their money. And it wasn't about expensive stuff. It was not about truffles, and expensive wine. It was about pike and smelts and sand dabs and growth in small craftsmanship, like making your own tofu, or handmade noodles, pulling noodles, stuffing noodles, the whole Italian scene. It was about doing something well, not charging a lot.

Up until, say, '95, the American cooking movement was just remarkable—Alice [Waters; Chez Panisse, Berkeley] was doing her thing, and Jeremiah [Tower; Stars, San Francisco], Louis Osteen [Louis's, Charleston] down south, Mark Miller [Coyote Cafe, Santa Fe] and adding his thing with Tex Mex, Stephan Pyles [Star Canyon, Dallas]—they all networked with everybody. Pushing good food, simple restaurants. It wasn't until years later that everything got to be very flamboyant, way more money was put into it. But during that period, say, '77 to '90, there were a lot of really terrific small chef-owned, self-funded restaurants.

My goal was never to be a Midwestern cook. My goal was always to bring some kind of great sensibility to Chicago and make it an international city.

PAULA CAMP: There's promoters who want their name in print every day. And then there are promoters who want to actually teach. And Michael was a teacher—if you do a search in the *Tribune*, he was often in there demonstrating an idea. Not overtly saying, come to my restaurant and try this. But trying to deconstruct it for people, so they understood what was going on. And he had the Southwest Michigan connection with the Tabor Hill winery [collaborating to make food-friendly wines for the Chicago market].

So he was in the forefront of saying, look, we've got wine from not far away, we've got great produce from one of the great produce-producing, especially fruit-producing regions in America. Let's use this. And I think it was a fresh approach for Chicago, even if it was a little bit later than these discoveries were taking place on either coast.

****

Printer's Row (the neighborhood) caught on, especially with architects—and it wasn't long before Foley would find the improvements in the area a threat to his business.

MICHAEL FOLEY: If you remember Judy Chicago, with The Dinner Party [art installation exhibited in the Printer's Row neighborhood for five months in 1981], during the day people would come to the South Loop for Judy Chicago and we were packed at lunch. That's when Printer's Row started to have bookstores and more retail. As long as Judy Chicago was there, it helped me at lunch. But when dinner time came, it was like slithering down the street, people were so worried about coming to the South Loop.

As the area developed, developers started to gut and repurpose the empty buildings. And after working so hard to build a following, my landlord wanted me to move out of my ground floor Pontiac Building location as it was being completely renovated, all fourteen stories. They were all about, well, we have to get you out of here because we can't renovate the building around you. I was not happy. My answer was, you're going to have to, because my lease doesn't call for any closing.

They offered me the Dearborn Station front first floor. I even drew up plans. But when none of them wanted to foot the bill to relocate the restaurant, I refused to move, and the lease had no foreseeable way to move me. The landlord boarded all my windows for almost two years. On the outside you saw only unfinished black-painted plywood, spray-painted "Still Open for Business." On the inside we had to make murals on all eight massive windows to soften the look. When people came in, they freaked out because they were not expecting not to see windows, but we smiled a lot and acted our part to serve high-quality with care. We did what we had to survive.

With his building boarded up, Foley thought more about the 1883 Romanesque Revival railroad station at the south end of Dearborn Street, now on the

National Register of Historic Places.

A friend, architect and well-known developer named Royal Fabian came to me and said, let's just buy the Dearborn Station, which was going up for grabs and was all covered in chain link fence. We designed a whole retail working village, but we found out that someone was going to try and undercut us. They did. They undercut us by $20,000. But we also found out, the guy who bought it was going to tear it all down and put up a huge housing development. We might have lost the bid, but the area people did not want to lose the station, and we made a big deal of the teardown and we stood around when the wrecking ball came. We called the various Chicago news crews and they started to film the wrecking ball making its way to the chain link fence. With the film running and all of us standing there, we ended up saving the station.

And that's kind of how it went then, not just Printer's Row, but the West Loop, Lincoln Park, all these areas of the city. Everybody had something going on, everyone had pride in trying to make something work. It wasn't just restaurants. It was a very dynamic time for everybody. Everyone was trying to work full speed making things happen again in the city. You didn't have enough hours in the day for it all.

Printer's Row Restaurant lasted until 2004. Foley has had a farm, interests in wineries, and other restaurants, including reviving Le Perroquet.

5: LETTUCE ENTERTAIN YOU

"Thick English mutton chops and plum pudding await you in delightful old St. Hubert's English Grill... Decorative beer steins, leaded windows bearing Teutonic coats of arms, wooden tabletops scoured to the point of whiteness, and fat waiters with a German accent as thick as one of Papa Gallauer's liver dumplings. . . . Out of the crowds, automobiles, street-cars, and shop windows of south Dearborn Street, you step into the cabin of the palatial yacht, 'S.S. 'Rainbo,' somewhere out, say, in mid-Atlantic."

That's a few scenes of dining from John Drury's 1931 Dining in Chicago, *offering a picture of themed dining since time immemorial—English chophouses evoking merry Olde England, German bierstubes conjuring up collegiate Heidelberg. They were fanciful echoes of the Old World, more theater than anthropology, but there was usually something real at the bottom of them. Even the guy who conjured up an imaginary yacht on Dearborn Street apparently knew something about the sea and seafood.*

But in the 1970s, there were suddenly places with names like R.J. Grunts, Lawrence of Oregano, The Great Gritzbe's Flying Food Show, and Cafe Ba-Ba-Reeba! Even when they had a theme connected to the real world, like tapas at Cafe Ba-Ba-Reeba!, other parts of the experience were pure fantasy—like the staff uniforms from a theatrical costume supplier.

These restaurants, with their cartoonish themes, were the product of Lettuce

Entertain You Enterprises, launched in 1971 by twenty-nine-year-old Rich Melman, who approached dining with a sense of humor out of stand-up comedy or Mad *magazine. As his empire grew, it would grow more serious—not least by revitalizing the legendary movie star hangout the Pump Room—but his underlying idea of dining as a form of showbiz would shape restaurants nationwide.*

RICH MELMAN: My dad did a whole bunch of different things—drug stores, he had a grocery store. And he and his brother found this place across from the Civic Opera House, I think it was a cafeteria. And they opened a place.

What I later found out was, they were bookies. Whatever [their legal business] was, it was a front for what they were really doing. They weren't so open about talking about their illegal stuff with me, but they said one day that the restaurant was so busy, they said, hey, let's pay attention to the restaurant. And that's really how they got in the restaurant business, by accident.

The bookmaking got a little bit more difficult; the Outfit was their partner and they wanted to take it over. They were low-level guys, they played cards, they booked horses. My uncle and my dad, they were sort of tough, wild guys, that's what they were like.

I don't like playing cards that much, and I certainly don't bet horses. I was a bad student, I didn't have anything I was good at. I was okay in sports, I played in high school. You know, when you're a kid you don't have all that much confidence. So the jobs I had would be working in fast food places—Henry's Drive-In [a 1960s hamburger chain], I don't know if you've ever heard of it.

And I worked for my dad. I started out working in the kitchen. One of the first jobs I had was on the fountain, and then I worked a sandwich board. I sort of worked my way up, but they didn't let me do the, to them the important things, the broiling of steaks or things like that. Then I sort of went into management and worked behind a deli counter and I just did whatever they needed, wherever they were short, I would do it. And eventually, I was really running the place.

Let's say it's '63, '64, something like that. And I read about a thing called Weight Watchers. I get ahold of this guy, Dick Cooper. He's the guy that was bringing the franchise to Chicago. And I was really interested in it. And I wound up being the first one in Chicago to put the Weight Watchers menu into my dad's restaurant. It was a big hit. I remember you could get shakes, Weight Watchers shakes. Like breakfast and lunch is a shake. Did I think the food was great? No, but I did it according to what people wanted.

I had saved up over a five-year period of time. Ten thousand dollars—it was like gigantic money to me in those days. And I was willing to put all the money in. I would have been happy if they offered me two and a half percent of the business. But they would never let me near anything that had to do with money. I mean, never. So who knows what they were doing? I don't.

I just said I'd like to buy in, I didn't say give it to me. And they said let us think about it. Four or five days go by and they say, we've thought it over and we don't think you're settled enough. You know, if you get married and have a family, we could talk about it. I'm not even dating anybody, I mean that was the farthest thing from my mind. I was just really focused on learning my profession.

I remember I went back to work right after that. And I absolutely within five minutes felt differently about what I was doing. I mean, it was strange to me how fast it took. And within a week or so I went and I said, no, I'm gonna leave. And so I took jobs. I had one particular job at this restaurant called Robbie's and I worked there, and I learned a lot—I learned a lot about what I didn't want to do, and the type of people I didn't want to be involved with.

I thought the big change in restaurants came about in the end of the '60s, beginning of the '70s. That's what it seemed to me. There was a place called Oxford Pub that I liked. It was on Lincoln Avenue, there were a number of places that popped up on Lincoln Avenue. They were hippie type of places, but they were cool! They were funky, I don't know how to describe it other than that. And the food sometimes, it'd be *okay.* But it was very unprofessional. If you had a date, and you wanted to go to a movie, the movie was eight o'clock, and you got in the restaurant at six, you weren't guaranteed that you'd be out by eight. I came from a restaurant where we were really knocking 'em out, really being very professional. So I brought that to the table. And so when we did R.J. Grunts [Lettuce's first restaurant] I wanted the feeling of those places, but I wanted to be professional.

Those hippie places were mostly drinking places. There'd be a hamburger.

They didn't have organic stuff or anything like that. You know, salads, it was maybe a step up from what the normal restaurants in those days were serving. I think the big thing was, they served things on planks. A lot of planks going on in those days.

No uniforms—the kids were in jeans. And that was different, because almost every restaurant had people in uniforms. But the kids were real casual, everything was casual. They'd get to you, they wouldn't get to you, but the music was good. They always had nice music.

In the spirit of the times, Melman and his original partner, Jerry Orzoff, launched Lettuce Entertain You with R.J. Grunts, across from the Lincoln Park Zoo in 1971 and claiming to be the inventor of a dining innovation—the salad bar.

My father thought it was the worst location ever—he said, who you gonna feed, the lions? My wife-to-be, Martha, she went with her then-boyfriend to Grunts, and she liked it. So she suggested to a girlfriend that they go back, and she couldn't quite remember where it was. They kind of wandered around, trying to find it.

I counted on Jerry for where to open. He was in real estate, so I just thought he had a good sense of these things.

CAROL MIGHTON HADDIX (*Tribune* food editor): It was entertainment. It was really fun to go to these places. And he knew how to do good service. You never had bad service at these places. And it wasn't the chefs who were important at all. You never knew who the chefs were at these places. But the food was pretty darn good, for a casual place. And so they just kept coming back.

PAT DAILEY (*Tribune* writer): My father worked in the liquor industry, so I ate dinners out at great restaurants all the time. But they were all pretty staid and predictable. My senior year in high school, I went to R.J. Grunts—and it was like, oh, my God, how can restaurants be so cool?

THE PUMP ROOM

More youth-oriented restaurants with zany names followed, but Melman soon had his eye on a higher caliber of dining—even if personally, he didn't know how to dress for a place like the Pump Room yet.

RICH MELMAN: I went on a date to the Pump Room with my future wife. I wanted to see it from the inside. I wore blue jeans, and Arturo Petterino [maître d'] stopped me. "We have a dress code, sir." He was very nice about it. But I noticed it was a quarter full, while my places were packed. So I started thinking about what I'd do with it.

I called the owner, but he never got back to me. Six months later Sheldon Good [commercial realtor] calls—we were pretty hot so we got a lot of calls. He told me about two places he had, I wasn't interested, and he said, well you definitely won't be interested in the third one, it's the Pump Room.

We redecorated it. It was nice—I really studied it, we had uniforms for the staff and everything. But the food was no good, we were losing our shirts. All the money made from the other restaurants went to the Pump Room. All the other restaurants were rockin' and rollin'. The public didn't know I wasn't making any money. I was living an interesting life, I never had more fun losing money. But it started teaching me about being a better businessman.

To fix the Pump Room, Melman turned to a French-trained chef he had met at Jovan Trboyevic's Le Perroquet—Gabino Sotelino.

GABINO SOTELINO: I told Jovan that I wanted to go and open my own restaurant. He say, I'll sell you my restaurant. But the way he wants to sell the restaurant was not how I wanted to buy the restaurant—he wants to still own the restaurant and I pay little by little to him. Which was not the way I want to do it.

I met Richard Melman and he started talking to me for about three months. Every time he got more intense in the conversation, and at one point he says I need your help [with the Pump Room]. I say, look, I don't know anything about hamburgers or ribs or anything. I did not have the time each day to water the Pump Room! It was a different kind of animal for them—first of all, it was a big restaurant, seating two hundred. And it had a big name, and they want to build them back to what it was in 1938 when the Pump Room was new and they were serving, like, partridge or venison or rack of lamb. I was supposed to bring it back to the day when Frank Sinatra had Booth One. But it was an old building and to make the changes you need to spend some money.

They had a team that they basically hired from the other restaurants they had. And I said, I need to change the kitchen to make it work for the food that we need to do. And when you do any change to the line, you have to change the prep process. I told him the only way for me to come in is to give me three or four months with a new team before you tell anybody I'm here.

RICH MELMAN: Gabino delivered an instant turnaround on the food. We had an old PR guy and a younger one, they filled the place with celebrities. Kup [Irv Kupcinet, *Sun-Times*] was *the* gossip columnist—you had East Coast, West Coast, he was the Midwest.

Gordon vet Jim Wygonski had gone to work for Brennan's and Commander's Palace in New Orleans, but when he returned to Chicago he saw Irv Kupcinet on TV saying that Lettuce was taking over the Pump Room.

JIM WYGONSKI (server): I looked at my mom and said, I'm going to go work there in a month. She looked at me like, ain't you a cocky little bastard. I said no, because working at Commander's and Brennan's, that was a whole great stepping stone for me to know what I'm doing.

So, I met Melman, showed him my resume, he looked at me and said, so when do you want to start? I said I can start tomorrow. Melman was smart, he made most of the girls the captains, the guys were just the backup to do the hard labor.

We were waiters in our twenties, you're going for it, jumping around to whatever was new and hot. It was the disco years, you had to have money, because you'd go out all night.

What was really cool to experience was all the celebrities. You met all these people, but they were just people. And that's what's cool about it, you know? Like Sinatra and the boys at the Pump Room. "How you doin', kid?"

Kevin Brown was the first person Lettuce ever interviewed on a college campus—the hospitality program at Michigan State—and the first one they hired. He started as a manager at R.J. Grunts; forty-plus years later, he's Lettuce's executive chairman.

KEVIN BROWN: They had six restaurants, they had just opened the Pump Room in the past year. I had been a line cook, so I didn't really have any front of house or a lot of managing people experience, and that was what the challenge was. You start to manage people, it's a whole different ballgame, right? I enjoyed it. I mean, I wasn't very good at it, it took me some time to figure out how to do it, but I still love the business.

I left [R.J. Grunts] and went to the Pump Room. I worked there for the summer, really training again, because it was a whole different thing, fine dining. Two weeks into it, I'm wearing a tuxedo, I'm on the floor, it's great. I mean, who wouldn't want this job?

The first five restaurants had good humor, really good entertainment value, but you knew the food you were getting. When we did the Pump Room, in the first year, we didn't do it great, because we didn't know how good we had to be. Rich took a lot of grief for signing the Pump Room. Like what the hell did these guys know, that have these cartoon restaurants? But what you have to understand is that these cartoon restaurants were damn busy.

DAVE LIGON (manager): I was the first manager of the Pump Room, early '77 until New Year's Eve of '80, when I moved over to Ambria. The Pump Room was busy. All the things that you expect to happen happened—big crowds, lots of single ladies, and that's aside from just people dining in the dining room. It seems like every day there was some noteworthy celebrity or near celebrity coming in to dine with this.

When it first reopened under Lettuce's control, every day was the same, the specials were baby back ribs and salmon, those were like the daily specials for the first six months I was there. And then Rich brought Gabino Sotelino on board, and good things started happening with the food. And so we went from, the first thing on a lot of people's minds at the Pump Room was the free hors d'oeuvre buffet in the afternoon, and a great bar and a chance to meet some attractive ladies, to a place that had serious food as well.

What was the movie about the nuclear reactor that had Jack Lemmon,

Jane Fonda, and Michael Douglas? *[The China Syndrome.]* They were here on a big presser for that, and they had Booth One for a party of four. But what started as a party of four became a part of twelve, and we had to scamper around to find tables. It looked like the seating on a jet.

Hume Cronyn and Jessica Tandy, when they were in town they stayed at the Ambassador, they were the most gracious people. One night they were joined by a relative unknown who had just been in *Alien*—Sigourney Weaver. One Sunday night, the great character actor John Carradine came into the bar—I recognized him immediately. He had rheumatoid arthritis, and his hands were gnarled to the point that he had to pick up his glass with his knuckles, almost, to take a drink. But he seemed so genuinely appreciative of the fact that I recognized him. Bob Hope, that was a thrill for me. He came in one Sunday evening. And I was able to tell him, I saw him in Da Nang on Christmas Eve, 1970.

We had a couple of back waiters that were Iranian, during the Iran hostage crisis. And immigration came in looking particularly for Middle Easterners and we had to hide them. In the back of the café area, there was an area called the green booths. And we put them underneath the table there and pulled the tablecloth down all the way to the floor. So they didn't find them even when they walked all through the restaurant on a Saturday evening.

AMBRIA

RICH MELMAN: I probably would not have gone into fine dining, except that I made Gabino a commitment. I promised him that if he bailed me out of the Pump Room, we'd do his idea, which was Ambria. The Pump Room was our first big financial success, turning that restaurant from the biggest loser to making the most money, and a lot of it had to do with Gabino. And then Ambria followed. That was his dream restaurant. I said fine. I'm gonna work with you. And we did it together and I learned a lot about fine dining. And so that's how I got into it.

Despite Melman's promise, Sotelino felt dubious about Lettuce as a partner for a fine dining concept.

GABINO SOTELINO: When the time came, he say, why you not coming to me, your partner? I say, Richard, the restaurant I want to do, is higher than [the Pump Room]. The restaurant I want to do, it needs to be the top, something you deliver once in your life. If we're going to do it together I need to show you what kind of restaurant I want to do, so we need to go to Europe. I find out later that he's never had a passport or hardly been on a plane, he's scared of planes.

But we go to France, to Switzerland, running from one place to another, I think it was about two weeks we spent between France and Switzerland. Me and Richard and his wife. Paris, Lyon, we go to Rennes and then to Lausanne, then to Crissier. We taught him two [phrases] in French while we were there—one, how to order still water, *sans gaz.* And the other was asking for the check, *l'addition, s'il vous plait.*

I think Richard was so impressed that he was totally changed. So in 1979 we open Ambria [in Lincoln Park], and we closed it twenty-seven years later.

RICH MELMAN: The press was a little unhappy with us doing the Pump Room early on—rightly so, foodwise. But my recollection is that they loved Ambria.

KEVIN BROWN: They didn't have much choice, when you're bringing in a chef like Gabino. It wasn't a requirement that [the press] came in—they *wanted* to come in. Gabino had a reputation. He was from Le Perroquet. But it started making all of us think differently, about food, and about being better.

JENNIFER SMITH DRILON (pastry chef, Ambria; chef, Cafe Ba-Ba-Reeba!): I was working at R.J. Grunts and waiting to go [to Washburne]. And their pastry chef backed out. And so because Lettuce Entertain You was a very progressive, figure-it-out kind of group, they said, maybe that little girl who works at Grunts and is going to chef school, maybe we can teach her. And I never went to school again.

They brought in George Bay, from Bays English Muffins, who had gone to Le Cordon Bleu in Paris, and he would come over and teach me a few pastries at night. I'd try to reproduce them the next day, and he'd come in, everybody would taste them and critique them and figure out if it was good or bad.

And so we went through and developed the first dessert menu for Ambria.

There I was, a young white girl, the only one in the kitchen. Everybody else was from other countries—France, Spain, Mexico. I was trying to make soufflés but there weren't even a lot of places back then to reference "soufflé," there was no internet. I think Julia Child was one of the only places I found some instruction. And one of the other guys said, oh, you just do this, blah blah blah. I would practice and work it out. We just did it, because there weren't a lot of pastry chefs to pick from then. It wasn't chic to be a chef yet.

GABINO SOTELINO: Ambria was a dream restaurant. People marry, celebrate their weddings there, they celebrate the news of their child, they even named their daughter Ambria. It was a success not only because of the cooking, but also the philosophy of great service. I remember one of the things we used to do was, no matter who we're celebrating coming to the restaurant, we don't allow people to come up to the table and ask for an autograph or something.

DAVE LIGON: I had a relationship with Gabino—a love-hate relationship, but I felt really good that he placed that kind of trust [as manager of Ambria] in me. Gabino was fake tough, but he had a heart of gold.

I went over to Ambria [from the Pump Room] and it was a culture shock. Because you went from a place that was just white-hot in terms of the business and in the energy in the room to a totally different type of energy. But we got off to a good start with some good press—though Mimi Sheraton took umbrage to the fact that we had a Midwestern openness. I didn't look at that as a bad thing.

The presentations of the food were so elegant, when they got to the table. The entrees would all go down and simultaneously all the silver dome covers would come off the plates. It might have been James Ward [TV food critic] said something about, heaven forbid, somebody would drop one of those silver domes, you would do somebody real harm. But it was just elegance all across the board.

KEVIN BROWN: Rich wanted the food to be serious, but not presented seriously, and certainly not served seriously. Most fine-dining restaurants are hushed, right? I think it was more important to us to make it approachable. I mean, the servers would talk to you, right. They would entertain you, they would have conversations with you. They weren't, we weren't afraid.

MICHAEL MUSER (server/sommelier at Ambria): Everybody went there for their anniversaries, their birthdays. It was an old-ass restaurant when I got there, but it was awesome. It was so Art Nouveau, you felt like you were walking on the deck of the Titanic. The waiters wore fucking tuxedos. It was classic fine dining with china with all the ornate stuff on it.

GABINO SOTELINO: The late Bob Bansberg, he was working for me in the Pump Room. I'm a connoisseur of wine, I'm collecting wines myself, I always have a wine and food connection emotionally. The list was a little bit of everything but at the time, there were not many good wines in Chicago per se. But when I opened up the restaurant I wanted to have a real collection, so I might have sixteen different vintages of a particular wine. I had to create the relationships with the importers in New York—because back then people were keeping the wines with no temperature control, so if you had two bottles one would be proper and the other one was trash.

JIM WYGONSKI: Bansberg was my buddy, God rest his soul. He said, Melman's looking for you to come into Ambria, but Gabino doesn't want you there because Gabino says you'll pack a roach, which I did back in the Pump Room days: "I don't like that Wygonski, he's crazier than me." He wanted it to be like his buddy Banchet's place, no messing around. But Melman said, he's starting next week. He accumulated all the goofballs from the Pump Room to run Ambria, because we knew how to be professionals—when I was teaching my waiters, I called it deadly but silent. I could stand right next to you and you won't even know that I'm there, but if you need water, I'll have it down in your glass before you can even think it.

I wouldn't see Bansberg on the floor. And I'm looking, looking, looking, I go behind the back bar and go, hey, Gus, You seen Bansberg? He goes, he's sitting over there. and I open up the door to the service bar. I go, Bob, what are you doing? He had a thick book and he goes, this wine thing is really interesting. I said well, son of a bitch. Not only am I doing my job, I'm doing *your* job, give me half your tips you bastard. Five years later he was the king of wines there, he was the man. He'd talk to the table for twenty minutes about wine, and I'm just thinking, you're costing me money again.

PHIL VETTEL (*Tribune* restaurant reviewer): The wine service was what always knocked me out there. I'd always get to try some bottle Bob Bansberg would recommend, it'd be something I never knew about. And, you know, this is at my budget. So we never got close to the *good* stuff, right? I'd be timorously going, okay, let's go eighty-five dollars. Nowhere near the upper reaches of the wine list, which the people who had *real* money would order.

I remember one time service was surprisingly slow and I had drained our wine glasses. So I reached and I poured a little wine myself and like three servers were mortified, like I touched something I wasn't supposed to touch. Oh my God, we screwed up. He had to reach for his own bottle of wine, I must kill myself now.

MICHAEL MUSER: The best job I will ever have was being Bob Bansberg's assistant sommelier at Ambria. Talk about a gig you could only have when you're not married and don't have a kid, we would play poker in the private dining room until like four in the morning, three nights a week. I mean, we lived at that restaurant. We would just get slammed, wasted, and run around in the park half naked at like three o'clock in the morning. We were animals back then. We went to tastings three, four days a week.

He was the sommelier for the entire time it was open—I went to dinner there on its last night and he was working it. The wine list was extraordinary because Bob just bought what he loved, and he loved these big, beautiful wines, but he also had a brilliant palate for structure. Everything was powerful, Bob loved big powerful wines.

Bob *was* Ambria. We didn't have Michelin yet, but I think Forbes or AAA, someone important, rated Ambria and they named Bob in the rating. Like, Bob Bansberg is a world class sommelier, and he *is* the experience at Ambria. And after that you couldn't get him out of there if you wanted to.

After Ambria closed in 2007, Bansberg taught at Kendall College. He was working there when he died in 2019.

MICHAEL MUSER: Bob taught at Kendall College. Bob didn't care. Bob didn't have an ego. He would do whatever needed to be done. And if it was teaching anywhere, nothing was too small for him. He was incredible.

Across the hall from Ambria, they opened a more casual bistro, originally called Un Grand Café.

GABINO SOTELINO: Un Grand Café was a replica of a restaurant in a hotel in the Plaza de l'Opéra in Paris.

RICH MELMAN: You know why we did Un Grand Café. I spent a lot of time in Ambria. Whatever we did that was new, I'd spend time with Gabino. And his sous chef made the best goddamn employee meals ever. It was like peasant French food. And I said, holy shit, this is great. I'd go eat coq au vin [at Ambria], and it would be great. But I liked the family meal better than eating at Ambria. And I said, maybe we should do a bistro. And this location across the hall from Ambria opened up and it was without question, I want to do it. And it's been a smash ever since.

After some years Un Grand Café evolved into Mon Ami Gabi, with locations in Vegas, Reston, Virginia and Bethesda, Maryland.

GABINO SOTELINO: We changed the name because of Jean Banchet. It had been open for nineteen years, so we were remodeling. And he said, you're changing so much of the restaurant, you need to change the name. So we have a couple of names that I think are very French. And you know, Banchet loved sports cars. Every time he buys a new sports car, he drives it to the city and parks in front of Ambria and says hey, Gabi. look what I have. And the PR people hear him—"Ehh, *mon ami* Gabi, *comment ça va*?"

We opened a bunch of restaurants in 1985. I wanted to do a Spanish restaurant. When I told Richard I wanted to open a tapas restaurant, he told me, you're crazy. Nobody will allow you to have a topless restaurant in Chicago. Not topless—ta-*pas* . . .

Cafe Ba-Ba-Reeba! opened in Lincoln Park in 1985, under Sotelino and one of his chefs, Emilio Gervilla, who would later own several tapas restaurants bearing his name.

PAUL VIRANT (cook): Ambria was more French than Spanish, but every once in a while Gabino would have a contingent of Spanish folks that would come in and eat, and he would cook on the line. And he would pull out, like, a boss dish—I remember he did some kind of braised fish, and he used a particular sherry, I don't remember if it was a fino or what. But it was super simple. He deglazed the pan with the sherry, garlic and sherry, and it was awesome. They went all Spanish when it was closing, which was cool.

RICH MELMAN: I didn't know anything about Spanish food. And Emilio and Gabino kept badgering me about doing a Spanish restaurant. And I said, well, let me try the food, which is what I always do. And I thought it was pretty interesting. We bought the building and then I said, well, let me do the decor. They kept saying, it's nothing like Spain, you know what you're doing? And I said, what's the difference? It'll work. It'll be cool. I just did crazy stuff. I remember we went to New York. And I found this place that was like a uniform shop. But not hotel uniforms—like crazy uniforms, a theatrical type of place. And I went crazy. I said, you know, nobody knows what the hell Spanish food is. Let's have fun, we'll dress the kids up in real funny ways. And so that's what we did.

JENNIFER SMITH DRILON: It was our first demo kitchen, that was really kind of out in the open. You could walk by and see all the tapas at the time. That was really new, and so were the bright colors and decorations that they did. It had a big bar in front because tapas is really about that, there's not a lot of sit-down in Spanish tapas bars, just a couple of little tables. You go from place to place in Spain. That obviously wasn't going to happen in Chicago, so they had some sit-down and that great patio. Who served sangria then? Nobody, but we had a whole refrigerated room upstairs that turned into gallons and gallons of sangria being prepped.

RICH MELMAN: We opened Cafe Ba-Ba-Reeba! in Vegas in the 2000s. It was a big place, probably five hundred seats. And we lost our ass. They didn't know what the hell it was. They knew steak houses, they didn't know Spanish food. You don't want to overshoot the receiver. You don't want to overshoot the customer.

I like doing something that I think excites the public or the public will be interested in and it's fun for me. It's sort of like why I don't like doing the same thing over and over and over again. It's probably a weakness as well as a strength.

JIM WYGONSKI: Years later, in early 2011, a lot of things had changed for me personally. I called Melman, and we're talking and I said Richard, I'm out of a job, I don't have anything going. He was mentioning Vegas back then. I said I'm too old for Vegas. And we're talking, we're talking, and he says, well, Jim, you know, things are different in the restaurant world. You have to go through all this training—I said, I'm aware of it. I understand. I said Richard, remember the day when I walked in the Pump Room, back in '76, and you just said, when can you start?

He looks at me and says, son of a bitch, I miss those days. Because now everything's got to go through HR. I spoke to Kevin Brown right after Melman, he was the waiter who trained me, and he was training to be a manager. And by then he was the CEO of Lettuce. I said no regrets—while you were working at two, three in the morning, I was out getting discoed.

GABINO SOTELINO: It's a fantastic thing to say that you bring new kinds of food to a city that deserves it. Chicago was always a great city but restaurants, it was difficult to bring them to Chicago because people always wanted to have the same stuff. There were [private] clubs that had wonderful food but the restaurants were very poor at the time. What I wanted to bring was a new gourmet culture of food. When I brought tapas to Chicago people thought I was crazy or something. But it worked, because one of the things is that young people want to try stuff. Older people are not the customers to change their habits, but young people are willing to try new food, new culture.

THE EVEREST ROOM

Another European chef lured by Melman was Alsace-born Jean Joho, who had come to Chicago to be chef at Maxim's. Together they opened The Everest Room (later just Everest), named for its scenic location on the fortieth floor of the Chicago Stock Exchange in the Loop, which earned acclaim for a lighter style of French food rooted in Alsatian cuisine and seasonality, and drawing from farmers, cheesemakers and winemakers in the upper Midwest.

RICH MELMAN: Joho was a great chef. I didn't bring him to Chicago—a friend of mine, George Badonsky, brought him to Chicago. I don't remember what happened that George got out of the business. He was a music producer, and he could have been a great restaurateur. But it took a turn the wrong way for him, I'm not sure why or how.

I was thrilled to do the Everest Room. It was hard to get to. But I wasn't worried about that, I thought his food was so special. We were there a long time—we'd still be there, but the building wanted to turn it into something else.

JEAN JOHO: We opened Everest in '84. The Chicago Stock Exchange wanted us to run it as their private club, but when we start we find out right from the beginning that we can't make this level of restaurant work as a private club. We said, let's be private for lunch, but open to the public for dinner. And from day one, I get the customers for the evening time, and after two years I close for lunch anyway. The Stock Exchange, when it's busy they're too busy for lunch, and when the market is slow, maybe they go home for lunch. I never focused on the business in the building, I always focused national, international. And then a year later we bought the restaurant from the building. Right away we were successful, and Paula Camp in the *Tribune* said it was the best place to eat in Chicago.

PAULA CAMP: The Everest Room was an eye opener. Here we are, suddenly eating little quail eggs with caviar on them in a potato carved into an egg-looking thing. He was doing really remarkable things. And it had a great view of the west side of the city from his restaurant windows, but it was a struggle to get there [on the fortieth floor].

LYNN BUZZA (cook): It was a tough, tough kitchen. But I saw things there that I never saw anywhere else. Like I can clean and cook a barnacle. I can dress tons of pounds of soft-shell crab and if you put one in front of me now, I could probably still de-bone a frog because I had to do thousands of them as a prep cook there. So it was fascinating. It was stressful. My badge of honor was it I made it a year there and I never cried in front of them. Because I saw grown men cry.

But being that young and that green then and looking back on it now, I can see that Chef Joho genuinely felt like he was doing his best to teach. It's how he came up. He didn't know a different way to run a kitchen. And so while I didn't really like it, it wound up being a very important year for me.

PAUL VIRANT: The Alsatian influence was kind of a full circle for me, back to my grandmother who was born in this very German town. It just was interesting to use, like, sauerkraut—I hadn't worked with that kind of stuff in a professional kitchen. And Joho had a place in Michigan for a long time. So it was cool to get exposed to Michigan produce, some of the wines—he was always an advocate, and still is, for all the products. That was pretty awesome.

JEAN JOHO: I never talked "farm-to-table" but what I did was source all the products, local ingredients, fresh, from the United States. At the time when you opened a French restaurant you had to bring the peaches from France, green beans from France. I set to work with a lot of farmers or a lot of producers or lots of fishermen and I use only fresh American products. In 1985, that was really avant-garde. I never talked about it but I always looked for the best that I could find.

At the same time I did a tasting menu every night, a seven- or eight-course meal, where two people didn't have to pre-order it—this was pretty new then. The menu was very diverse—I always had the risotto, I had lived in Italy and I was known for speaking pretty fluent Italian. Craig Claiborne in the *New*

York Times put our risotto on the best risottos in the country.

It was an evolution, to have a French restaurant with risotto on the menu—you could get risotto then but you had to order three days ahead for the whole table. You could come here and get it for one, that's where I was very different. I'd been to the best French restaurants in this country and they were very conservative—the pâtés and so on. I was interested in doing things my own way and putting lots of Alsatian touches in the food. And I had the largest wine list from Alsace—Robert Parker said I had the best [Alsatian] selection on the biggest wine list in the hemisphere.

I did a lot of simple food, the simple with the novel, that people had never seen. I did a cabbage soup with smoked sturgeon on caviar all the way at the beginning. It's the [food of the] poor with the novel, I always liked to mix that up together. Especially when it was food coming directly from the farmers. It's the end of the season? Well, then you have no tomatoes. Most people had strawberries all year. No. It's a season, you have it and when you have no season you don't. I think that was pretty avant-garde at the time—"You don't have it?" I'm sorry, we don't have it.

When I opened Everest I only used American cheeses, farmstead cheeses. Trust me, there were not many doing that in 1984. There were only two or three cheese makers in the United States who were what we called a farmstead [making cheese from milk produced on property]. And I cooked with them, we worked together on them, we made some tastings together, and we make some different cheeses. I was the first chef to buy from them. Same thing when I met the fishermen, and when I met the produce people. I find somebody who brings me the best blueberries. I find somebody who has the best apples. I have the person who finds the best seafood, the best scallops, the best mushrooms. I was hunting all the time. At the time, you can't make it local to Chicago, but I used American produce in season as much I can, and I still do today. Use the best of what you can find, and if it's not available, you don't have to use it.

Besides Everest in the Loop, Joho also had a mid-priced French restaurant in River North, Brasserie Jo (opened 1995), which won a James Beard award for best new restaurant in 1996.

I loved brasseries, and there were no brasseries in Chicago at the time. Remember, all the brasseries in Paris were opened by people from Alsace. Brasseries and Alsace were always connected together. A brasserie is just a big house, bustling with good food and reasonable prices, all very comfortable and unpretentious.

So we made it very French but you have to see what the American consumer wants. They don't want kidneys, or pig's feet, or brains—even in France that's not very popular any more. Once in a while I'd put liver on the menu, and that week we'd have it. But we made it very welcoming. A brasserie is always in a simple style, and I think we achieved that. You can have one course, you can have three courses, you can have something to eat with a drink at the bar. You can eat by yourself or have a party of ten.

I studied wine, I made wine. I grew up in Alsace, I know all the hills and everybody that makes wine. This means I have a really big knowledge in wine, I know so many winemakers and I was always involved with the wine. I also know the food world, like, I know what the wine would go with. I have to believe that the wine would go with my philosophy and what the food is that we're serving.

Alpana [Singh, sommelier] came later and was there for, I'm guessing, ten years. She came from Carmel, [where] I did a fundraiser with Jean-Louis Palladin and Michel Richard, and she came to me and said, my dream is some day to come work for you.

Another chef had ambitions of opening a brasserie at Lettuce—Michael Kornick. The end result was The Eccentric, with Oprah Winfrey as a partner.

MICHAEL KORNICK: They wanted a much bigger menu. And so we opened with forty-something items, and we couldn't keep up. Russell Bry came in, he was the corporate chef—there were lots of corporate chefs at the time. And he really helped engineer that restaurant to be able to do the volume properly. But it lost its soul for me.

Melman has built one of the great companies in our industry, period. And he was like a second father to me, I loved working for those guys. But I didn't love the restaurant, because it had gone away from my ability to kind of go out in the dining room and really talk about my cuisine because it had been shaped in a different way. I envisioned myself as kind of like a young American version of Joho and Gabino. And they envisioned me as sort of a manufacturer to compete with like the Scoozi!s [big, casual Italian restaurant] of the world. And those were two different things, you know?

LETTUCE EAT ITALIAN

Lettuce's rise in the 1980s and 1990s coincided with the evolution of Italian food in Chicago, toward lighter, fresher cooking. The result was that Lettuce became to a large degree an Italian restaurant company, with many different styles of Italian restaurants—from the chicly modern business-lunch spot, Avanzare (under chef Dennis Terczak, brother of John), to River North's boisterous Scoozi!, serving freshly-made risotto on the half hour in a warehouse-sized space, and Maggiano's Little Italy, built on big parties eating big portions of heartier Southern Italian-style cooking. The success of these established River North as a major center for Lettuce.

RICH MELMAN: I just love Italian food. It's as simple as that. And I think that some of my favorite places served Italian foods and pizzas. Jerry and I used to go to this place called Welcome Inn, and they had this thin pizza that I loved. I could think of ten different ways to do Italian restaurants—we could do an Italian ice place, we could do a place with Italian sandwiches. We could do a pizzeria. Because it's my favorite food, period. I could eat Italian food every day. It's fun for me to do things that I like.

KEVIN BROWN: It certainly is some of our guests' favorite food. [Focusing on] Italian food wasn't just us, but it's what the guests want. And especially that it's not just Chicago. I mean, the amount of Italian restaurants in New York City? There's a ton.

Scoozi! was an unbelievable space. If you remember what was going on around the country, there were a lot of big restaurants being built. So I think Rich thought, let's do a big Italian pizza, pasta place, a big party. Very New York City, like you're going to the warehouse district when there's only one restaurant there and you're like, where the hell are we? I think Rich has always been good at this—he makes people reach to get the concept, but not that far.

RICH MELMAN: Scoozi! was River North technically, as was Ed Debevic's, but with Debevic's it was mainly about being on a high visibility corner. It was really Maggiano's and Corner Bakery that brought us to River North, and we met Al Friedman then—it would have been about 1991, and we started talking then.

AL FRIEDMAN: One day, Rich Melman came to me. He said, I have an idea for an Italian restaurant. I said, okay, I happen to be half Italian. So, I know that when going to my grandparents' farm, I was ten years old, I'd walk in and my grandmother always had fresh baked goods going. She had a pizza being made, bread—the aromas were just overwhelming. You start salivating. And then when we ate, they all served everything family style. So it was all in the middle and everyone shared.

So I said, what do you plan to do? He says, I'm going to do these small plates. And you'll get like, appetizer portions. I said, you're *not* Italian! I said, I'm not doing this unless we do a bakery where you walk in, and it's all family style. So anyway, we open the Corner Bakery, and we open Maggiano's. At Maggiano's the whole concept was family style dining. And with the bakery, you walk in, you had to smell all the baked goods. I said, now we've got it.

His partners at the time were so dead set against this concept that they forced me to make sure that that corner could be given back to me so they could have the entrance for the restaurant when the bakery failed. So make a long story short, I think Oprah Winfrey was one of the first customers so she put it on national TV—"This is unbelievable, it's the greatest!"

But we got killed in the reviews. The first couple reviews were terrible. And I said to Rich at the time, maybe I was wrong. Maybe you were right. He said, well, let's go to the kitchen. And let's see what the plates look like. So we actually sat in the kitchen to watch the bussers bring the plates back. They were empty. In fact we did so well that people then said we want to have private events here. I didn't have a private event space figured into this, I had to dig out the basement to make a private events space while the restaurant was still open.

JEAN JOHO: When I opened Corner Bakery there were not many bread shops in Chicago. You had one who made Italian bread, one who made Jewish rye. And I went to Rich Melman and said, it is so difficult to find good bread, but I cannot make bread at the restaurant. You have to make bread seven nights a week, but the restaurant is only open five nights a week. We don't do enough volume in one restaurant for a bakery. Why don't we open a bakery [for the company]?

In the original Maggiano's we opened a Corner Bakery. And if we didn't sell the bread we'd give it to the people eating at the restaurant. We did lots of training, lots of tasting, and when we opened the bakery, I can tell you, it was something very very new in Chicago. You can have bread at the bakery but you can also have a croque monsieur, you can have a baguette with ham, you can have different sandwiches, soups. People were lining up for it. Although we set out to make a wholesale business, it was successful [serving diners] from the start.

JENNIFER SMITH DRILON: Wolfgang Puck came to Chicago to do something for Neiman-Marcus, but he didn't like the kitchen there, so he came to Ambria to work. So we're having family lunch and Gabino says to him, the girl, she wants to come to California. So I worked at Spago for a couple of years, and then I worked for Nancy Silverton at La Brea Bakery.

So I was the one who opened and ran Corner Bakery. We were trying to make the space work, we just had a little portion [of the total space]. The CEO wanted numbers from me, and I wasn't a numbers person. I can't tell you how many people are going to come in and buy a loaf of bread. But I can tell you, if they see this bread, they're gonna want it. It's coming right out of the restaurant right next to the bakery. We're going to sell some bread.

Corner Bakery, started in 1991, expanded rapidly; in 1995 Corner Bakery and Maggiano's were sold to Brinker International, parent company of Chili's and other casual restaurants.

ED DEBEVIC'S

For the average diner, though, the most visible flag Lettuce planted in River North was a throwback to its origins in loud, cartoonish concepts—the faux-fif-

ties diner Ed Debevic's, with sassy waiters cracking jokes at the customers' expense. The area near Ed Debevic's became Chicago's ground zero for such concepts in the '90s and '00s, like Planet Hollywood and Rainforest Cafe.

KEVIN BROWN: It was iconic. Crazy lines out the door on Saturday. Lines down the block. Gum-smacking servers, malts and burgers, and it wasn't very expensive.

RICH MELMAN: Ed Debevic's really came from the '50s, when I was a teenager. We hired a lot of actors and actresses. And that was the cool thing about [opening one in] Beverly Hills. I mean, we had the crème de la crème of actors. We had a lot of well-known people who became stars work there.

DAVE DRAVENACK (server at Ed Debevic's, late 1990s): When I was taking classes at Second City, my roommate told me, hey, I can get you a job at Ed Debevic's. I had never been, but I knew the lore of it. Like, my parents would come home and tell me about this magical place where the line was around the block, and everybody was just rude. And I was like, I gotta work there.

When you applied, the interview was actually an audition. They didn't care if you could serve food—they just wanted to see if you could jump up on the counter and dance. I don't think they even cared if you had any experience as a server, because customer service wasn't a big deal. Even if you were in the weeds, you could just go to your customers and go, Yeah, I fucked up. It's going to be a while.

We were all dressed as characters that were '50s-related. I was Ed Norton from *The Honeymooners.* You'd get there in the morning, and everybody would be in their costumes, and we'd all eat breakfast. We opened at 11 a.m. And by 10:30, you'd look out the door and there'd be a line of people just looking inside—we used to call them "hungry little minions." Because we knew like the second we open that door, it's gonna be nonstop from 11 a.m. till 10:30 p.m. You had to get used to serving food by walking through masses of humanity. But it was fun, because you could also yell at them to get out of the way.

Because of my improv training, I basically treated every interaction like it was a scene. Like a lot of times, parents were bringing teenagers in, and you could tell that the reason they were there was so that I could beat up their children. You guys won't listen to me? Well, this guy's gonna put you in your place. And you would just do that with stupid things, like—"Oh, you're getting a Diet Coke? Like that's gonna help with all the cheeseburgers." One time I got the complaint that I wasn't being rude enough. I guess they expected more from me.

It wasn't all about being rude—it was about the playfulness, like, you can do things that other waiters would never do. Like, I would push somebody out of their chair, or we had booths. So to take their order, I would just scoot them over and sit in the booth with them to take the order.

Dancing on the countertops was the big thing. There were about five songs that we had to learn the choreography to. You'd hear the song kick off, about once an hour, and if you were able to, you'd jump on the counter or a chair or whatever and do your little dance for a couple of minutes, and then go back to being a server. The other gimmick they had was birthdays—that was a huge part of it. The gimmick we had was the world's smallest sundae, which was literally like a thimble. But you got to keep the glass. And it was basically a parody of the T.G.I. Friday's birthday celebration. You'd get up on a chair and be like, hey everyone, I know you're eating, but Janet here thinks she's special because she was born, so let's sing her a song. *Ha-appy birth-daaaay*—okay, we're done.

Surprisingly, no fights ever broke out, which you would think—I mean, every other job I've had, fights broke out at some point. So I don't know if it was just that everyone was kind of docile, because *we* were beating them down or whatever.

I quit because I was moving to LA to be famous. But of all the jobs I had, that was my favorite. That was the only one where I looked forward to going, because I knew that it would be fun. It would be quick. Your shifts were lightning fast, because it was so busy. And you knew you could just have fun and be creative the whole time.

They had one in LA. But LA people could not deal with that concept. I was in LA when it opened and I talked to some people who worked there, and they were like, oh, these people do *not* like it, they do not like what we're doing to them. LA people are entitled, they don't want to be yelled at.

The original Ed Debevic's lasted in River North from 1984 to 2015; still cherished in memory by thousands of Chicagoans and tolerant tourists, it reopened in Streeterville in 2021.

****

Many more Lettuce restaurants have followed over the decades. Today, Rich Melman is doing with his kids what his father and uncle did not do with him—managing the transition to them taking over.

R.J. MELMAN (CEO of Lettuce Entertain You): When I was a little kid, I could go to work with my dad and often spent time at the restaurants. I have vivid memories of the opening of Shaw's Crab House, of Ed Debevic's. It wasn't like, let's eat out every night, but it was often, a new restaurant was opening, let's go support our dad. It's very cool to see a restaurant change over the first four or five, six days, so we'd often go many days in a row, eating there for practice events and seeing what was going on.

From the time I was in my mid-teens, I was working hourly roles. I started cooking at seventeen and all the way to becoming a sous chef at twenty-two. I loved it, from the time I started working as a teenager it was what I loved doing. My parents never pushed it, but they were definitely supportive—how could they not be? I think a lot of my dad's rejection from his parents shaped his life in terms of how he's picked partners, and how Lettuce has been set up with, now, seventy-five partners.

I came up through the management training program, I was actually the general manager of R.J. Grunts for quite a long time. Then my brother and I had this idea for what became Hub 51 [in River North]. We opened it in 2008, and we started running our own restaurants within the company, and my sister joined shortly before the opening of Hub 51.

You have to weigh that you have the best consultant in the world [in Rich Melman], people anywhere would pay for him. But there's also times that you don't want his opinion, and him not understanding what we're doing. Hub 51 was open late, and we were in our mid to late twenties when it opened. We were building the place for our friends, and he was talking to us about how we weren't busy at six o'clock. Don't worry, it's gonna be busy. And you know, eight thirty, the place is jammed, we have a line down the door at eleven and he's like, I don't understand this at all.

What excited us was going out to eat Mexican, and sushi. Hub 51 was kind of like everything we liked to eat at night, we would call it food that wasn't traditionally American, but was becoming American. We created Ramen-San, which we now have three of, and I don't think there was any dream of doing a ramen restaurant within the company. But it started with a chef at RPM Italian doing one dish, which was ramen for staff meal. It wasn't on the menu, it was a chef playing around and making something that led to a whole concept.

I'm CEO of the company now, so I certainly lead my own projects, but we always lean on him. We collaborate a lot. But we have five or six or seven projects going on that he's very little involved in. He's earned the right, I would say, to work on as little or as much as he wants to in this organization. And we're lucky to be able to get his ideas and his time when we can and he also is an amazing, amazing leader and mentor. He gives us a lot of space to work.

RICH MELMAN: I like having partners. Generally speaking, I stick with my partners. And if they're chefs, and they want to do other things, I do it. I trust them and I like their taste.

I remember how I felt when I was turned down. If I didn't think my two sons and daughter were good at what they are doing, I would tell them, go find something that you're really passionate about that you really love. They really are good at what they're doing. And I feel very good about them taking over. I don't want to ever sell this company. I don't want to take this company public. I'm not in it just for the money.

6: STEAK AND VIAGRA

The Gold Coast neighborhood north of where Michigan Avenue's "Magnificent Mile" terminates at Oak Street means different things to people in different places in life. If you are older and wealthier, it's home to top steak houses for business dinners. If you were younger and looking for action, it was "Rush Street," once home to nightclubs like the famous Mister Kelly's, and a land of busy singles bars in the '70s and '80s. And if you're a bit of both—older and wealthier but still on the prowl—it's the sardonically named Viagra Triangle, where many a fling and more than a few second and third marriages got their start.

Rush Street's transformation from a divey nightlife district in the '70s and '80s to an upscale dining neighborhood came about through the efforts of ambitious restaurant owners—but also through the City of Chicago recognizing that restaurants could be important allies in reversing decline in an area in which wealth and seediness, Gold Coast high-rises and crime-ridden public housing projects, existed side by side.

MORTON'S

Arnie Morton grew up in a restaurant family in Hyde Park on the South Side, but made his name in the restaurant industry when he helped Hugh Hefner create the Playboy Clubs—among other things, luring Jean Banchet to the Chicago area at the Playboy Club in Lake Geneva, Wisconsin. He opened his first Gold

Coast restaurant, Arnie's, in the 1970s, and followed it with the original Morton's next door on State Street in 1978, literally serving only steaks and potatoes.

His children mostly followed him into the business, including Peter with Hard Rock Cafe and Morton's in LA, Michael with the N9NE steak house chain in Chicago and Las Vegas, David with DMK Restaurants with chef Michael Kornick, and Amy with Mirador and the Blue Room beginning in 1989. After taking some years off, she returned in the 2010s with Found, La Tour and other restaurants in the suburbs.

AMY MORTON: The wave of restaurants that we now know as the industry in this city, as well as across the country and the world, I see as starting in the early to mid-seventies. And my dad doing Arnie's was probably the first see-and-be-seen restaurant that we think of as the modern era generation. He was the predecessor to Gordon as being kind of the great-grandfather of restaurants, Gordon the grandfather, and even Rich Melman came up at that same time, the early '70s. They took hospitality, and food and drink, which could have been served in a coffee mug fifty years before, and created what has become the hottest form of entertainment in the world today.

My dad had been around for years already as vice president of Playboy, he built all the Playboy clubs and hotels around the world. My parents met at a crazy party at the [Playboy] mansion. He'd done a couple of restaurants back in the '50s, with his brother. They did the Walton Walk, which was the first key club that Chicago had ever seen, which is how Victor Lownes [vice president of Playboy] and Hef met him. They came to my dad and said, we love your place here, and we want you to build us an empire on a global scale.

So my dad would open a club and we would go out there. We got the benefit of seeing Lake Geneva, Great Gorge [New Jersey], Miami, Jamaica, London. And we would often spend Christmas, or even three, four months at a time when we were much younger, where he was opening the places. I didn't feel it was out of the ordinary.

He was independent, creative, a concept guy. And once Playboy went public, he left, in '72, when I was ten. And the next year he opened Arnie's. My dad really was about the vibe.

Gordon created the first truly chef-driven kitchen, certainly in our city, and crafting food in that way that became a scratch kitchen. Michael Kornick, who is my very dearest childhood friend, was a chef for all three of those guys, and he went to Arnie's and he said he wanted to make it a scratch kitchen. And oh my god, my father thought he was insane. What's going to happen with my food cost? My dad had never heard of it. We were still, for brunch, going into the gigantic room of dry storage and opening up a can of Hormel corned beef hash. That all changed.

Morton's was just the cleanest, smartest, simplest concept, that had the very best product money could buy in a super relaxed space. He called them saloons for the rich, it was deco nouveau craziness. He was even bringing in the sides of beef, and Jimmy, our butcher, butchered every steak in house. There were less than ten items on the Morton's menu. And he did that so he could control the quality, nobody had ever had quality like that before.

I did not want to go into the restaurant business. My dad kept bringing over our friend Art Miner and drawing restaurants up, and calling them Amy's Place. I said no, I'm going to be an actor. I didn't want to be in the restaurant business. And lo and behold, I found myself going down that path.

In 1987 Arnie Morton sold Morton's, by then a chain of nine restaurants, to a venture capital group; at its height it had some seventy locations from Chicago to Beijing. He died in 2005; the city has named a stretch of Maple near State "Arnie Morton Way." The original Morton's on State Street closed during lockdown in 2020.

RUSH STREET

Today, chef Kevin Hickey owns a popular restaurant, The Duck Inn, in the Irish enclave of Bridgeport, where he grew up—a return home after decades working for the Ritz-Carlton and Four Seasons chains around the world. But when his parents divorced in the 1970s, he and his mom left their insular South Side neighborhood and settled in an apartment across from the Ambassador East hotel. More interested in restaurant work than schooling, he quickly found employment on Rush Street.

KEVIN HICKEY: My uncle Tom Hickey was one of the owners of the Snuggery, on Division. Our very first night in that apartment, we went there for dinner and my uncle said, do you want to work here? Sure, whatever—busboy, bar back, prep cook. I'd make burgers. I cut steaks, cut fish, and then I'd make shots in giant buckets. I would set up all the bars. And then they found out, because I was like fifteen or sixteen, that I was only supposed to be working fifteen hours a week. So they cut my hours, but I would just come in anyway, and the bartenders would pay me in cash.

I was six foot two, three, whatever I am now. So people would start streaming in on Sunday from a Bears game, and they put a Snuggery jacket on me and put me on the front door and told me to start checking IDs. I didn't have a driver's license. I had a fake ID from the currency exchange on Archer. I didn't even know where to look on an ID for a birthday. I just figured if somebody hands you their ID, they're probably twenty-one.

I was sixteen, I was mostly cooking during the day and on the weekends and then bouncing at night. The key to that was that I had my Snuggery jacket with my name on it, so that got me entrance into every other bar on Division. I was a regular at Mother's, BBC, Ginger Man, The Lodge—they all knew me.

The Back Room was a jazz joint that's gone now. I think it was left over from Prohibition days because it was literally just like a cutout between two buildings, a thirty-foot straight shot, like a gangway between two buildings on Rush. You'd go in the door, down some stairs, and then up a bunch of stairs. And if you went there after five, six o'clock at night, it was pitch black. You'd get a table, and the cocktail waitress would be like "What do you want?" and I'd say *[lowers voice]* "Scotch and soda," and you'd be cool. That's how I fell in love with jazz.

Rush Street was rough-and-tumble and seedy as shit. It was dirty bookstores and peep shows, literal peep shows, where you'd buy tokens and go in the booth and the glass would go up and there'd be a naked lady there. Chicago Avenue was so rough the moment you walked off Michigan Avenue and two feet past the Park Hyatt. I was sixteen and working in a restaurant and going to nightclubs and had cash and was drinking, my mom was fine with all that—but I was not allowed west of Clark Street. No way. That's how bad it was.

My first summer back from college, I got my first job at Gordon for Michael Kornick, who will deny to this day that I ever worked for him. Which in his defense, was only for about five or six days, because it was three something an hour and I just couldn't survive. I don't know how or why, I ended up going to Sweetwater, where I got hired as a morning prep cook for five bucks an hour.

So I go back to Kornick and say, hey, can I work nights? He says, you're not a fucking cook. I say, well, all you've had me do is chop carrots and onions, I can work sauté, I can make sauces. We argue back and forth for a little bit, and I say, well, I'm working at this other place and they pay me five bucks an hour in the morning and I was hoping maybe I could work here at night. And he says, well maybe you should just fucking work there, and threw me out the back door.

So now Sweetwater was the only job I had, and I wound up working twelve, thirteen hours a day in the summer. And I loved it. Sweetwater was an interesting place. It was one of the first places that had like celebrity ownership—Doug Buffone, who was a Bears player, was one of the owners, and they would use his name a lot to promote the fact that they were a celebrity place. And the owner, Steve Lombardo, had just broken with his partners, these guys he had grown up with in Park Ridge. They all split up and each took a place, and they all thought that Steve got the lemon. Because it was a white tablecloth restaurant, with a kickass bar. It was this giant oval bar in the middle of the restaurant, with a really high ceiling.

I worked there for four years, every chance I got, and I worked all summer long, Thanksgiving, Christmas, spring break and weekends. Any chance I got to come back to work. I worked mostly in the kitchen, but then started dabbling in the front of the house. And Steve Lombardo really took a shine to me. And my junior year, he called me up in school in my apartment and he's like, hey, we're going to close the restaurant at the end of the summer and do a new concept. And I don't have anybody to run it for the summer. You want to do it? I was nineteen.

I came in and they were on their last legs. They had no liquor or wine list menu, they would buy wine at the 7-11 across the street. So I got my dad to print up a menu, because he was in the paper business, and then I went to work trying to get liquor because we had no credit, the business had been just dying, slowly. Paterno Imports agreed to give me Corvo Red and Corvo White, but I had to take this white wine, Santa Margherita Pinot Grigio. Okay, whatever the fuck.

It was the summer of my life, I had the greatest time with a lot of fun and a lot of bad behavior. And at the end of the summer Steve Lombardo says to me, we're going to close it down and turn it into a steak house, and all the regulars at the bar, they're going to invest. I said fuck that, I'm going back to school. This has been too wild for me. And a year later they opened Gibsons.

GIBSONS

Gibsons, one of Chicago's busiest steak houses, was founded by Steve Lombardo Sr. and Hugo Ralli in 1989. This author spoke with Lombardo and Gibsons Restaurant Group managing partner John Colletti over—of course—an impeccably prepared steak lunch at the original Gibsons on Rush.

STEVE LOMBARDO: This building was Sweetwater, and prior to that it was Mister Kelly's. This area had developed more as an entertainment tavern area—but in the old days all the entertainment venues had restaurants. Mister Kelly's was one of the most popular venues, but there was the Gate of Horn, the Happy Medium down the street—

JOHN COLLETTI: Faces . . .

STEVE LOMBARDO: Trade Winds was a big early restaurant.

JOHN COLLETTI: Kon-Tiki Ports . . .

STEVE LOMBARDO: The famous Cape Cod Room. The Pump Room was, of course, big big. They had all the celebrities because they used to have to stop here on the way to New York. We had a restaurant called Hotspurs on Division, that was one of the first legitimate restaurants on Division. We had a nightclub upstairs, called BBC.

Mister Kelly's ended because it was too small to do well. They had Barbra Streisand here getting $5,000 a week. But all the entertainment ended up going to Vegas, where they could make big money.

Before we opened one day, about two in the afternoon, the door was open and a woman came in just in jeans and a sweater. Hi, can I help you?

Yes, I used to work here. She spent about fifteen minutes looking around, and I said a few words to her, had she been a waitress or something? Well, it was Bette Midler and she was performing at the United Center that night. Someone said that she mentioned in the concert that she had been here, she was very nice.

So we were here with Sweetwater, which had been very successful. And in the early '80s, this street—for whatever reason, almost everybody left. Morton's was here, we were here, but there were about fifty bars and nightclubs between Chicago and Division on Wabash and State. And they pretty much all closed.

I had sold out of this area to my partners, in the late '70s, and I didn't come back and take this over until the late '80s. Sweetwater was on its knees. Nobody wanted it, so I took it. I spent a lot of time in the area, and the most stable things were steak houses. And I'd been in the bar business, so I wanted to do a steak house with a real bar, not just a little someplace to wait before you sit down and eat.

JOHN COLLETTI: In '89 there was no retail, there was nothing like you see now. It was very difficult.

STEVE LOMBARDO: When we got here there was a lot of street crime. People would get rolled, a lot of prostitution. We came back in '86 and kind of limped along with Sweetwater, until Mayor [Richard M.] Daley got elected and we reconcepted it to this.

JOHN COLLETTI: But it wasn't an immediate success.

STEVE LOMBARDO: No, no, but in terms of the crime, it was immediate. As soon as the mayor was elected, the crime was gone. It took a couple of years, for people to start coming back. But they did and then restaurants started opening. Mayor Daley appointed a liquor commissioner and said, I want you to get together with all the restaurant guys, bar owners, whatever and clean it up. And everybody did and got rid of a lot of offending types, multiple offenders. Guys who stay open past their license or whatever. So they either shaped up or they're out.

He also told the police commanders in the 18th District, as soon as you take over the job, you go to Rush Street and you greet those people and work with them. Because they're an economic engine. This corner is probably $100 million worth of retail. So that's sales taxes, retail taxes. When we came here, the rent was $2,000 a month, and we didn't pay retail taxes. Now, last year, we paid about a million and a half in rent, plus the real estate taxes which were a couple of hundred [thousand].

Mayor Daley just wanted to improve the city. His whole philosophy was keep it clean, keep it safe, educate the kids, and try to help business do well, so they can help pay for the education and the safety. You couldn't get a building permit without planting trees. When we built the restaurant in Oak Brook [suburb], we had to buy trees from Canada, because Daley had bought every tree from the nurseries in Michigan, Wisconsin, Minnesota, Indiana and Ohio.

The neighborhood is all around us now, but in the beginning it was east of here. And the residents didn't come here, because this had been known as a nightclub street. But they got to feel safe. They can walk over and be safe. So locals—locals are a big deal.

JOHN COLLETTI: I think the key to the restaurant's success is the commitment to the locals. There's conventions that come in and go out. But we kept a promise to—like the way Steve walked up to that group over there. They're all locals and, and we keep committed to them. Locals can also be from New York or LA or Europe or wherever. You recognize them, and greet them.

****

STEVE LOMBARDO: When we opened, people used to have hearts on the menus, everything was heart-healthy. We were going to open a steak house and everybody was saying that steak houses are dead. So we're thinking, what can we put on the menu to put a little heart next to it? Nobody was drinking martinis then, that was kind of dead. So we decided we were going to be a steak house, and feature the martini. So we're looking in the glass catalog for an old-fashioned martini glass, and then we spot one. So we took down the number and we ordered them.

Well, they came in and they were really dessert glasses, eleven or twelve ounces. They were huge. And we were deciding on the name, Gibsons was one of the choices—it was a buddy of mine's name, and it was like an old-time saloon guy's name. So we thought about the Gibson [a variation on the martini], and my partner said, here's the plan. Let's give 'em this martini, which ends up being about six ounces, and we'll put an onion in it instead of an olive. And the heck with this heart-healthy stuff. Martinis, red wine and red-red steaks. Forge ahead, don't worry about the cholesterol and stuff like that. This will be the place to go *for* cholesterol, if you're light on cholesterol!

There were two things that we were concerned about, the heart-healthy stuff and that the place might be too masculine. So we ended up with Charles Dana Gibson, you know who he was? [Illustrator famous for the turn-of-the-century Gibson Girls, and one possible source for the cocktail's name.] So we got some Gibson illustrations—there's one of a bunch of women pushing some guys around with a knitting needle. So we promoted it at the time as being for women, and that the name comes from Charles Dana Gibson, who was a feminist.

There were different kinds of cliques that we attracted, that I really don't think exist anymore. Or if they do, I'm not aware of them. Like all of the media guys, ABC, CBS, NBC. They used to go to work and by lunchtime, whatever they did at the office was over with and they'd go out to lunch. And they were out until midnight, one, two o'clock in the morning. Then there were the traders, two, three in the afternoon, they're finished, and they had tons of money.

The name "Viagra Triangle" is really from the Sweetwater days. Harry's Cafe was across the street, Arnie's was next door. Arnie's was one of the most beautiful restaurants, so Sweetwater had to compete with that—crystal chandeliers and waterfalls and all kinds of stuff. Those were the first really expensive bars, where if you went to a tavern and something was one dollar, here it was two dollars. So those three formed the triangle, and there was a lot of meeting, matchmaking, and there were a few older guys who were dating younger girls, because there was a lot of money. But that was forty years ago, not now.

JOHN COLLETTI: We were growing in conjunction with the whole city. For our first seven years, the Bulls were hot. If they were traveling the next day, the majority of the team would be here for dinner. And what that did for us was, it put our late-night business on the market. The players were genuinely wonderful guys, no matter what you think about them, whether it was Jordan or Dennis Rodman, who was the wild guy—he was the nicest guy in the world, he would sit here with his people. They were gracious to our staff, which is very important. You know, they were just good customers.

But people got to know that they were here, and that we were open, and we cook till 1 a.m., last call for liquor and close the doors at 2. They made our late-night business, they put us on the map. And we're very appreciative. We wouldn't bother them. The big thing, no matter who it is, we've never asked for an autograph or a picture. If they ask us, we'll put their picture on the wall.

STEVE LOMBARDO: We've had everybody and their mother. Clinton, both Bushes, Obama. That corner was Frank Sinatra's when he was in town. And [Congressman] Danny Rostenkowski, the pictures are up there. But a lot of celebrities, and a lot of cute celebrity stories. Like Billy Joel's here one night. And like I said, we never asked for autographs, but our hostess, Cathy, went up to him and said, Mr. Joel, this is against the rules, I'm not supposed to do this, but I keep a picture of you on my desk, you're my favorite performer. And if you would sign it, that would be something. They'd been joking around, so he said, sure, no problem. And there was a record store across the street that had a life-sized picture, a cardboard cutout of Billy Joel, and she sends a busboy to go get it. He says, I'll sign it but only if I can smoke a cigar—at the time you could still smoke in the bar, but not in the restaurant. And she said, I'll get you a table in the bar. And I'll get it right next to the piano player. But I'm only getting that table if you play. So he signed it. He went in the bar, he didn't get rid of the piano player, but he sat down with him.

Johnny Depp spent a lot of time here, and Jack Nicholson, I think Depp was shooting a movie about Dillinger *[Public Enemies]* and Nicholson was shooting *Hoffa*. Clint Eastwood . . . Kiefer Sutherland met Julia Roberts here, they were staying at the hotel across the street when they were making, what was that movie, *Flatliners*. Depp was a big tipper, he tipped everybody in the place, about $40,000. We just had a guy give one of the biggest tips in our history—$100,000 in tips to the whole building, Everybody that worked—the night cleaners, the dishwashers, line cooks, everybody got a piece of the action.

JOHN COLLETTI: We've seen chains come and go. But I think the persistence in our company is quality of service. We're not bragging. This is just a fact of how we live every day.

Gibsons Restaurant Group operates a dozen restaurants in Chicago, the Chicago suburbs, and in Orlando; on Restaurant Business Online's 2024 list of the top-grossing independent restaurants in the country, they held three of the top ten slots.

7: CHARLIE TROTTER

In 1996, Chicago *magazine published a list of the fifty meanest Chicagoans. Number one was the most famous Chicagoan in the world, the sports star who that year led the Chicago Bulls to the fourth of their six championships in the '90s: Michael Jordan.*

The response was immediate from the second name on the list. Chef Charlie Trotter objected to his having been denied the top spot, saying, "I never like being number two."

If any moment in his career sums Charlie Trotter up, it's this one. Willfully embracing his image as an egotistical hard-ass, but doing so in a self-amused way (though the humor often seemed to fly over many heads). Thinking that a chef, serving two hundred covers a night, deserved to be in contention for a title with a sports figure who was watched by millions on television. And seeing something in the title that wasn't an insult, but a kind of recognition: "It was a story about Chicago's ten 'meanest' people—those who will do whatever it takes to be at the top of their field . . . I actually had CEOs come in to the restaurant who were upset at not making the top ten," he told an interviewer from a magazine devoted to one of his favorite authors—Ayn Rand.

Trotter, who put American cooking at the top of food culture globally and Chicago at the top of US food cities, remains a mysterious, mercurial figure after his death at fifty-four in 2013. Some remember his tyranny in the kitchen, others his generosity and how he inspired them to be their best. Here in their words is life in Charlie Trotter's world.

****

Charlie Trotter's father, Robert, was a top executive for IBM, and then started a recruitment firm for employees with computer experience, with offices around the country. The Trotters lived on Chicago's wealthy North Shore, but even so, the world of fine dining was something they had little experience of as "Chuck" Trotter was growing up.

DONA-LEE TROTTER (mother of Charlie Trotter): We were not into that kind of food. And there were four kids. We hardly ever went out, and we went through kind of a recession in the '70s. Everything was home cooking, but it was nothing like what he later did.

ANNE TROTTER HINKAMP (sister): My mother was just really doing very basic Midwest cooking like meatloaf, baked potatoes, chicken and rice, burgers. It really was very simple, and we didn't go out a lot. Our big night out was Hackney's [family restaurant chain on the North Shore]. And Charlie had been a busboy and a waiter, but it wasn't like, oh, I have to get in the food business. He just wanted a job.

DONA-LEE TROTTER: Charlie always had some kind of job since the time he was fourteen. He was a window washer. He did lawns. He worked at the restaurant in the plaza over here. Starting like when he was fourteen. When he was in high school, he'd get up and deliver the papers before he went to school in the morning. He was just always driven to be doing something.

Charlie was hyperactive. And we didn't realize it. They said they were going to hold him back in school, and I said, you can't hold him back. He has no self image. What are you going to do to his childhood? So we took him to this horrible creature in the city, who wanted to put him on Ritalin. And Charlie was smart enough to know what Ritalin was. And he'd pretend like he'd taken it, and he didn't. Because he felt he could fix himself.

Charlie gets to [the University of Wisconsin in] Madison, and he realizes he really can't read. He forced himself to read. It's really sad. These days, that wouldn't happen.

ANNE TROTTER HINKAMP: The one thing about him is he did jump into all kinds of different things. Usually with a great deal of conviction. He would believe in these things and do them. Cooking, though, wasn't anything that I would have guessed just because he really wasn't doing any cooking while we grew up.

DONA-LEE TROTTER: He started having an interest in cooking when he was at the University of Wisconsin, and he had a roommate that he went to high school with, and they both loved to cook. They would have Bob and me up for dinners. The first one was like, macaroni and cheese or something. But they moved up to some kind of salmon, you could see big changes.

ANNE TROTTER HINKAMP: They made it a competition and would try to outdo one another. The third time [their parents] came to visit he served them a soufflé, and our mother realized that this is something he's really interested in.

DONA-LEE TROTTER: He decided that the best restaurants and the best food was in San Francisco. So he took the train to Seattle, and then he rode his bicycle from Seattle to San Francisco. To start eating at these restaurants and testing them out and everything. He basically was a huge correspondent, not only with me, but everybody he knew got these postcards that followed him through the first few years.

ANNE TROTTER HINKAMP: Not having cell phones or other quick means of communication, he was big into writing postcards. My other brothers and I, we'd all communicate that way, we'd find weird artsy photographs, like you used to find all over in record stores or coffee shops. He wrote about wanting to do all these things and how interested he was. They became more elevated as he got more into it. Then he'd come home and cook. It was all-engulfing at that time.

DONA-LEE TROTTER: He decided that he wanted to go to France. He had read about all these chefs and knew everything about them. And he wanted to see what they were doing. So he went to France and spend a couple months over there, eating in fine restaurants and gathering all the information he could.

ANNE TROTTER HINKAMP: Lisa [Ehrlich], who wound up being his first wife, she had been a girlfriend, and then they kind of broke up—she was living there and going to the Sorbonne. He approached her and said, I'm going to be coming out there, I want to stay with you. She said, well, all right, but they were strictly friends at that point. She helped with the language, and it was nice for my parents, I guess, because he didn't have to pay for any lodging unless he went out of town.

DONA-LEE TROTTER: He got a lot from going to France. As I said, he had read their books, he knew about them. But unless you've tasted the food, really, you don't know. And then when he came back, he said he was ready to open his own restaurant.

****

Carrie Nahabedian met Trotter when he came to work at Gordon Sinclair and Marshall Field's Sinclair's in Lake Forest, under Chef Norman Van Aken.

CARRIE NAHABEDIAN: Charlie walks in one day. I interviewed him on the steps to the basement—it was a really nice basement because it was a brand-new restaurant, but it was the only place we could interview. And all I remember was saying to myself, this is a really thoughtful guy. He's really cool. He's got beautiful hands. He's from the North Shore. He's an intellect.

We kind of grew up similar in terms of our schools, he was at New Trier, I went to Maine East. I showed him my film study class film, you had to make a movie. So I show my movie which was about two beach balls with smiley faces that fall in love. Charlie shows me his, and it's basically Steven Spielberg's movie of the truck driver—*Duel.* I was like, are you kidding me? But that's how we all bonded.

I had to sell him to Norman, because we had a really strong kitchen crew.

And I said, don't worry, I'll take Charlie. Gordon must have seen the same thing in Charlie, or maybe it was that North Shore WASPy thing. He kept Charlie in the dining room, which would be like putting me in the dining room. So Charlie worked the front of the house, and he was constantly cutting himself on the bread station, and I was watching him from the kitchen and I'd be like, Norm, why the hell is he doing that? How did *he* become a back waiter? Norman didn't understand that term "back waiter," that was a Le Francais term, a Le Perroquet term. You weren't a busboy. Back waiter meant you did other things besides go to the table. You were servicing the guests but from the kitchen side as well as the front of house.

And then suddenly Charlie was in the kitchen. Because you couldn't go to the table with Band-Aids on your fingers.

NORMAN VAN AKEN (chef at Sinclair's): When he came into the kitchen and asked me for a job—I was the chef, so he had to ask me—my first impression of it was, he was incredibly pale. He was incredibly thin. He was nervous, he didn't look me in the eye when he spoke to me. He was really kind of, he really just seemed like a kid, you know. We were set, we didn't need anybody in the kitchen.

He came back almost every day, I think for two weeks. Hey, any openings yet, Chef, anything going on? I could see that after he got used to speaking to me, that he wasn't timid anymore. He was hopeful. And then he came in one day and we were short-handed in what we called the pantry back then, *garde manger*, and Carrie said, why don't we put him over there? What could be the harm, let's give him a try. So with that he joined the kitchen.

Around the same time, Charlie decided he wanted to go to cooking school in California. So he went out to the California Culinary Academy in San Francisco. But we'd begun to establish a little bit of a relationship with each other. Because he was surprised to see an American chef, a person who didn't look the part, who wore cowboy boots and blue jeans and was athletic. Also, in me talking to him about the dishes, I would pull out *The Encyclopedia of Fish Cookery* by A.J. McClane, who not only knew everything there was about seafood, but he could cite Roman history and quote the scholars of Greece and all of that.

So he saw in me a person who was an American, and an American that loves literature and music and had been living in Key West. He and I talked about literature and talked about music in the context of food. And so I think that seed got planted then.

ANNE TROTTER HINKAMP: He only lasted a year, or maybe just a semester, at the school in California. He felt these people are here as a last resort, they've tried other things and everything failed. And now they're taking this up with just half of the effort. He didn't like that they were teaching ice sculpting and all these things that he just didn't feel were applicable to what he wanted to do.

NORMAN VAN AKEN: He was dining, like, where Mark Miller was the chef, Fourth Street Cafe [in Berkeley]. And he talked about not only food, he talked about service, and design and setting and vibe, in such an articulate way. And he could jam more words onto a single postcard than anybody I've ever seen. He was soaking up everything, just madly soaking up the entire world of restaurants.

CARRIE NAHABEDIAN: He lived a life where he didn't want for anything, and yes, he liked living on the North Shore, but he loved living on Foster in some crappy walk-up apartment that had a thousand albums and 250 cookbooks and a futon. And a refrigerator filled with killer wine.

But that's what we were all like—we spent money on music, and food, and cookbooks and travel. And then throw in a few pairs of jeans and some knives. And that was our life.

After California, Trotter worked again for Van Aken, in Jupiter, Florida.

NORMAN VAN AKEN: Charlie had become my right hand, and his enthusiasm, my God, was one of a kind, We just fed off of each other. We were totally in love with Paula Wolfert's *The Cooking of Southwest France.* This was our bible at that time. When she makes cassoulet, it's eight pages in length. We were just enthralled with anything that made us dig that deep.

When he left to go to Illinois, he continued to write me and tell me of his progress with the restaurant. His initial name for the restaurant wasn't "Charlie Trotter's." It was "Zelda." Like Fitzgerald.

He was known as Chuck. He wasn't known as Charlie, we had to get used to calling him Charlie after he opened up the restaurant. He had no issues with it, it was his name. And his family called him Chuck. But that's when we saw Chuck turn into Charlie, as we saw him go through this process of change into a much more creative individual.

He said, Chef, I gotta go back to Illinois to open up a restaurant of my own with my father. And I said, but you've never been the chef of a restaurant. Though this was a point in time where the melding of *garde manger* and hot food began to become more of a thing—you could put some seared scallops next to the cold lettuces and it wouldn't be like that was breaking rules.

I said, are you sure? And he was like, yeah, I've got to do that. So he went back to Illinois and began to work on the project.

DONA-LEE TROTTER: My husband had retired and he didn't know what to do with himself. And so this came at exactly the right moment. He spent his time in the basement doing all the under work on it, or whatever. And he enjoyed—for the most part—setting up another business.

There was a chef in Evanston named Leslee Reis [at Café Provençal], she was so kind. Bob was on the phone almost every day asking her questions about the business. And she was very great in answering. Unfortunately, she was a diabetic, and she died very early in her life. But you know, people in the industry are not jealous, they're very happy to help somebody else along.

ANNE TROTTER HINKAMP: I'm sure my dad felt that, oh, he'll learn about business this way, which I think my dad felt was important. There weren't a lot of people going on to become chefs, necessarily, like it is now, but our parents were always really, really behind what he wanted to do. His work ethic was so solid, and he was reading cookbooks and reading up on people. It wasn't just a fly by night idea.

Even once they bought the building, none of us thought, oh, this thing's going to go twenty-five years. In fact, I made a sign for the window, hand-painted, that just made it so pedestrian: coming soon, Charlie Trotter's. We didn't even go to a professional sign company. It was just kind of, let's put it in the window and see what happens.

In the beginning the prices were super low, just to get people in there. And then they slowly raised them. But they really did have a great partnership, because Charlie had never run a business and, and my dad didn't really know much about cooking. Even once it was up and running, my dad would do guest surveys and analyze what Charlie was doing. I found a letter where he said, you've got to come out in the dining room, people are curious about you, your name's on the door. Charlie really didn't like that at all. He just wanted to make his food and serve it, he didn't want the accolades and the acknowledgement.

DONA-LEE TROTTER: At first, it was curiosity and neighbors. And then it got to be known. More people came in that wanted to try it. There was nothing in Chicago but French chefs, and the heaviest meals you've ever had in your life. He was the first one that came in with this idea of having it be very light.

Mostly I went around talking to people and giving them kitchen tours. I think the idea for the kitchen tours came from Europe. I'm not even sure, because I don't think the European chefs ask people into their restaurant kitchens, but I do know that he was very impressed with the French chefs, who would have a table in the kitchen, and they would sit down and have dinners with the farmers and others that brought them the food and stuff. I think that's where he got the idea of the kitchen table, from that chef's table in the kitchen.

It was so much fun. When my husband died, I was thinking that I'm not sitting home feeling sorry for myself. I'm busy all the time. And I loved going down there. Because we wanted to help him in any way we could. And I loved the staff. They were all my kids. I used to bring two one-pound boxes of Fannie Mae candy, one for the upstairs station and one for the downstairs station every Saturday night. And they would wait, patiently, for me.

****

Charlie Trotter's opened in 1987. The first employee that Trotter interviewed—and hired—was an African American cook named Reggie Watkins, who ran morning prep for much of the restaurant's run and would be for many who worked there the heart of the kitchen.

SARI ZERNICH WORSHAM (cook): Reggie was a character. He was tough as hell. He had been in the Navy or the Marines, I can't remember which. But he was regimented. He started as a dishwasher and then moved up and up. I believe his final level was sous chef, though that title didn't really matter at Trotter's—none of us really went by anything there.

But Reggie would train anyone who came in at any kind of level—you're trying out for the day, he would let Chef know if you had what it took to be there or not. He would teach you how to do everything from receiving produce from the back door, like going through a case of oranges you don't just say okay, oranges, check it off. You go through the case and if there's a moldy one, you're getting a credit for it. The whole kitchen was just afraid of Reggie, just feared him because vendors would deliver bad product, and he'd send it back, and the kitchen's like, we *need* this product. He was fearless, and he made decisions quickly.

Even though he grew up on the tough South Side, he had such a tender heart. If it got really tense in the kitchen, he'd help bring us all back up. But when it was serious, hard time, he took no prisoners. He trained everyone there how to do things the right way. Reggie had his way and if you were going to make it there, it was probably because you're under Reggie's tutelage for a good long while.

He had so many Reggie sayings. I mean, he would make boxing bets with Chef Trotter, big fights, and often Reggie would win. And so Trotter would come in and pay him in the kitchen. And then the next day, he'd point to his new shoes. He's like, Charlie Trotter dollars. He would just rub it in Chef Trotter's face that he was taking his money. He made a soft sweep and mop every thirty minutes. Like, if you dropped stuff on that kitchen floor, I had no problem eating it. That place was *clean*. There was a specific way to sweep and mop and I don't know if that came from his military days, but it was precise. He had a great impact on everyone that worked there, for sure. All the visiting chefs, Gordon Ramsay, Raymond Blanc, Ferran Adria—if they're going to remember anyone, they're going to remember Reggie.

GUILLERMO TELLEZ-CRUZ (cook): I met Charlie's mom and dad before I even met Charlie. I was going to culinary school and my ex-mother-in-law and Mrs. Trotter were friends. They said, he's opening a restaurant and you should go work for him. I said, maybe when I finish school. I did my internship at Carlos' in Highland Park, for Roland Liccioni, and I became interested in fine dining. So I just went to the back door and asked for Charlie. And he said, if you really want to do this, come in and spend a day and we'll see if you fit in.

At the end of the night he asked me, what do you think? I said, I really like it. And he said, I'll see you tomorrow.

I always came in early, because I wanted to learn, and I didn't want to get behind, and being the first Latino in that kitchen—I was very intimidated by everyone, everyone had experience somewhere. It was hard in the beginning, but it started making sense. I was always doing the extra mile and, you know, being hungry for knowledge. I wanted to learn everything. I worked on each of the stations and I said, I don't want you to move me until I can master each and every station, to the point where I can say, I'm ready for the next one.

MICHAEL TAUS (cook): I worked at Trotter's in the very beginning. There were only eight people in the kitchen at that time working, and he did three tasting menus and à la carte every night. So it was brutal. A hundred eighty people a day. When I tried out, I get home, and my dad said, what happened? How much do you make? I go, I don't know. How many hours you work? I'm like, I have no clue. What *do* you know? I go, I know I got the job. I don't even care about the rest of it, just to get in the door of that amazing place that changed my life.

It had been open about a year, and I knew that it was on its way to being one of the best restaurants in America. But other than great food and inventive and amazing ingredients, it was about service. I wanted to open a restaurant someday in my life, so I was thinking differently than most young cooks. I wanted to learn about service and wine and how it all came together.

BILL KIM (cook): I really, really wanted to work at Le Francais. I had the book called *Great Chefs of Chicago.* And I got to work with Pierre Pollin, I did my internship there. Then I wanted to work with Banchet, but he wasn't here, he'd gone to Atlanta. So I went to Atlanta to work for Banchet.

I got really homesick after a year and I came back up. I interviewed at Gordon and Carlos'. And you know, I was eager, young, and basically asked them if you were me, had no girlfriend, and just wanted to cook, where would you go work? They both pointed to Charlie Trotter's. I had no idea who he was.

I was just two years out of culinary school, and I was working there—like a mad person. I was just happy to be back in Chicago, and to have my head down and be working.

JOE CAMPAGNA (cook): I was working for a tech company, and I got laid off like everyone was getting laid off. So I went to culinary school, and then I started looking for work. I wrote to Charlie, and I got a call that said Charlie would like to have you stage for a day. And I was like, awesome, and I'm really thinking, I'm gonna throw up on my shoes the whole time.

But I liked it more than corporate life. Because in corporate life, there's the ability to hide, and people can get promoted because they've been there long enough. That's not the way in a kitchen. You can be there forever, but if you suck, I get promoted over you. They'll keep you around because you do your job, but you're not moving up.

PATRICK CRANE (cook): Colin Turner, who owned Tinfish in Tinley Park, got me a stage at Trotter's. And the night I went in there, one of the assistant sous chefs no-showed to work. So I worked the *amuse* station as a stage. And I kept my station clean and I got done with setting out my fifteen plates, and then I would go and help *garde manger* clean their plates while I was plating. And so he hired me on the spot. I was the only guy ever to get hired on the spot at Trotter's. Bill Kim gave me the nickname "the total package."

During the restaurant show, we would have guest chefs come in and they would all say, this place is so intense. And I'd say, yeah, with the restaurant show all week, it's like the Super Bowl every night.

JOHN WINTERMAN (food runner): I had worked for a nice couple who had a restaurant in Breckinridge, Colorado. And I started to think, if I was going to make a career of this, I didn't want to be a career waiter in a steak house. I'd read about Charlie, in the *Wine Spectator* and *Chicago* magazine, and it seemed like he was doing things in a different way than everybody else. I decided, kind of naively, oh, that's the place I should be working. It was like going from junior high into Harvard Law.

You start to learn how to not make excuses. We worked with a very competitive staff, both the kitchen and the front of the house. At the time, there were no side work manuals, no training manuals, no mini descriptions. You had to learn on the fly, you had to learn from the people ahead of you that had been there. And if you couldn't do that you weren't going to make it.

You learned what the guests might sense or see or hear. I think one time we stood in the hallway, right between the kitchen and the first-floor dining room. And Charlie just had us listen to the sounds of the dish machine. And I looked at him and about ten seconds later I said, yeah, we need to change the water dispersion. Because we had a kitchen table, so obviously, we want their experience to be as amazing as it could be, and having that funky aroma coming from the dispersing was not part of that experience.

So he taught people a way of looking at your world from a different angle than you might normally look at it. Always with the consideration to the guests in mind, what if the guest sees us? We sort of had to consider everywhere to be in the building, both buildings, in fact, to be what somebody might potentially see. He told us we should start acting as if we're at work within three blocks of the restaurant.

MINDY SEGAL (pastry chef): I didn't like the fact that they were slightly misogynistic, of course, at that time. But it was just a bunch of kids working in a kitchen trying to stroke the ego of Charlie. And it was just a cutthroat kitchen, it was dumb—it wasn't for me. I was also young, and I didn't want to work from seven in the morning until three thirty in the morning.

I didn't last there very long. Eight months, I hated it.

PAUL VIRANT (cook): I was there for about five months, March to September. I like to describe it as a growing season. It was a great experience, but I had a rough run with Guillermo. We've since made amends, but it was kind of like hazing. They had the kitchen door locked until two o'clock. You know, I wasn't looking to get paid, I wanted to get my shit done. We were always in the shit, because there wasn't enough time. The majority of the time I'd be doing *amuses* and canapés with the interns, trying to knock out all this stuff with people that maybe didn't have the experience they needed. Guillermo would be like, you probably need to think about a different career.

I did a couple of off-site events with Trotter. Obviously he was tough, and he was always there to expo in service. But he wasn't around in the kitchen. After one of the events he actually gave me Fernand Point's book, which had been out of print for a long time.

When I gave notice, he actually pulled me aside and was like, you're making a mistake, I'd like you to stay. I was pretty disenchanted with the industry, I was pretty beat up. I was thinking about the Peace Corps, I told him that. I regret not being honest with him. So I left Trotter's and got an associate job at Ambria. So five or six years later, I'm in New York, I was at one of the restaurants making hundreds of hors d'oeuvres. And I'm coming home, and I turn around in the line at LaGuardia and there's Charlie Trotter right behind me. And he looked at me, he didn't miss a beat. He said, how was the Peace Corps?

CURTIS DUFFY (cook): My only ambition for coming to Chicago was to work at Trotter's—I wanted to work at a handful of the great restaurants in the US, and Chicago was the closest [to Duffy's hometown of Columbus, Ohio]. But Charlie was also my favorite go-to chef—the internet was just popping around that time, the late '90s, so I was always Googling, searching "Charles Trotter" all the time trying to find menus, pictures, anything that I could find about the man. I really became obsessed with him and what he was doing at the restaurant, what he was doing for dining.

I don't think I even had an email yet, so it was just a cover letter and resume, or it might have been a cold call to the restaurant, but they put me through to Sari Zernich. And she was like, yeah, we can set up a stage. And I remember getting off that phone call with them, and running over to where one of my buddies was working and it was like I'd won the lottery. I was still in college, so I went there and worked two weeks, it had to have been winter or summer break. And I came back and I felt like I was a different person, a different cook. I felt it was where I was meant to be. Everything that I learned there, I tried to apply to everything that I was doing currently—not in the food sense, but just the discipline that I learned in the two weeks that I was there. Like, it just changed who I was. And because of that change, I craved it even more.

****

SARI ZERNICH WORSHAM: People would come in at ten in the morning. And then Trotter would get mad that people are there from ten in the morning till three in the morning. So he would lock the back door and not let any of us come in till like noon or one. So we're all pacing in the alley, stressed out. He'd unlock that door and we'd be running through the gates and changing our clothes, turning on ovens, putting pots on the fire. And we'd still all be ready by five o'clock.

I think he definitely enjoyed challenging us. And I'm not saying he enjoyed it when we broke, but it was a test. I mean, I saw grown men cry on the daily. People would come in and stage. And they'd say they were going to go put money in their meter, and they'd never come back, even to get their knives.

It actually had a really good result in strengthening the team to work together. You'd have to help out your fellow person because you know what's coming your way next. As much as Trotter did not want us to socialize outside of work, it resulted in us all becoming a really tight pack, like in the military. It was not what he wanted to happen, but it definitely happened.

PATRICK CRANE: People would come in earlier and earlier every day, because you wanted to secure your equipment for the day. One day, the team had been there for a while, and they were super tight. Charlie didn't like that. So he came in—your mise en place? Throw it away. Here's your menu, get busy. That was one of the worst days I ever worked, I was shucking the oysters to order because my *place* wasn't set. He would do that quite a bit, he'd say, you know what? I'm feeling good today. Patrick, extra course out of your station for everybody today. And you knew you had like an hour to set up a whole extra course.

MICHAEL TAUS: I worked with a lot of chefs that were kind of egomaniacs. Charlie was the first person I felt that showed us all off like a team, like we're family. Like this guy did this. This girl did that. So I felt, well, that was really nice.

GUILLERMO TELLEZ-CRUZ: Little by little, I think I gained his trust. And it got to the point where, I was his sous chef, his right hand and left. And then the other sous chef left. And so he's like, what I want is to give you an opportunity. He always used a football analogy—I'm gonna pass you the ball, and you need to figure out what you want to do. You can either run with the ball, or you can get crushed with the ball. Believe me, I was about to shit my pants when he said that.

He was never the guy that said no, but when I told him what I wanted to learn, he was like, prove to me that you can do this other thing, master that first. That was an encouragement, intimidating, but at the same time, hey, he's willing to give me a chance.

He was always about respect what you do and respect the products that you work with. A lot of the cooks used to burn a lot of stuff, so he eliminated the dishwasher position during the day. So all the cooks, all of us had to watch our dishes, pots and pans, because I knew that if I burned something, I'm gonna spend twenty minutes I don't have scrubbing the pot.

RICK TRAMONTO (daytime sous chef): Charlie preached excellence and he made you live excellence every day. All the good, bad and ugly of how he executed excellence is another conversation. But I think the message was, if it's not good enough, throw it away. If you dirty it, you clean it—we didn't have the luxury of having daytime dishwashers.

It was really demanding, and really chaotic. That was another Trotter trait, that I didn't want to take with me. I'm very controlled and methodical in the kitchen. Trotter loved to create chaos, because he felt it elevated your game, if he could walk up to you thirty minutes before service and throw a bunch of your shit away and make you go prep it again. Everybody had to swarm like bees to help you catch up, and that created teamwork.

I guess the question was, what did you take away? It was excellence and stopping at nothing, even putting your whole service in the shit to create it every day. But I also think some of it became, I don't know, a drug, a rush?

GIUSEPPE TENTORI (cook): The kitchen at Trotter's was not a culture shock for me [coming from Italy]. What was a culture shock was service, because we did multiple seatings. You start at five o'clock, packed, and you leave at two o'clock in the morning. Usually in Europe you start service at eight thirty, and it's one service, one turn, and you leave like eleven, twelve, one o'clock in the morning.

[At Trotter's] you walk into the kitchen and you know that you are doing exactly one, two dishes, you know the eight to ten ingredients, and within those dishes, you have to make 150-200 plates every night—that's a lot. And they have to be perfect every time. A lot of fine dining these days, they prepare food ahead. So you buy time with the first course for the fourth course, they're already started plating it. Charlie was more focused on the freshness of the ingredients, cooked to order. No walk-in cooler, so things came by FedEx every single day, from the fish to the onions. So you had to make everything fresh every day.

When service starts at five o'clock, you'll see one station is a wave that is going to come your way. Nobody will hold your hand, you had to make sure you know what you're doing. And then you have to help other people on different stations. At that time I was working on the hot line, and I was lucky enough to have Curtis Duffy on my station, Homaro Cantu on fish, Graham Elliot on *garde manger*. A lot of chefs came out of that kitchen.

CURTIS DUFFY: You could watch it snake around the kitchen, the movement of the courses. You knew you were getting royally fucked once pastry comes. You knew when last meat went out, it was go time.

You had three, sometimes four different seasonal menus. If you had a tomato menu, all tomatoes, then you had a couple of desserts for that. And then you had maybe a mushroom menu at the same time, with mushroom desserts. And then you had the grand menu, and the vegetable menu. These had different desserts, and then there was the kitchen table menu. So at any time you could have four or five menus, always a minimum of three.

JOE SPELLMAN (sommelier): The structure of the menu typically would be, you'd start with a few small *amuses*, even just little canapés. Then you go to either a vegetable course or a raw fish course or a lightly prepared fish course. Then there might be a terrine, then there'd be a more substantial shellfish or fish course. And then maybe a bird course. We never did sorbets or anything like that—that was old school. There was never really a salad.

The main course might be venison, from some special farm in Texas. Or some really interesting beef or bison, or we might have wild boar a lot, or we did a lot of duck breast. Those would be small, and we would have people grumbling about being there for three hours and leaving hungry. Because it was tweezer food, where every leaf of the herb would be perfectly placed. That was the normal menu of, I believe, eight courses, including dessert, you're getting basically five savory courses, then a palate cleanser, then other dessert things. Eight courses, but more than eight individual things. If you wanted a cheese course, you could get that for a slight extra charge.

When I started there was still an à la carte menu, but that was hardly even presented to people, you go to the table and say, this is Charlie's menu this evening. And what we really recommend is the grand degustation and it's $125 a person or whatever—it wasn't that high at the time.

I have really fond memories of so much of it. There was just that sort of energy, of being "Showtime!" We were all in the back of the house elbowing each other for spaces. It was so cramped in everything, to the point where my colleague, Patricia [Mowen-Ziegler], who was the dining room manager, and was a former dancer, she was actually giving servers dancing lessons on how to move. Elegant, very elegant.

GARY ALAN FINE (professor at Northwestern): I had a fish, which I thought was slightly overcooked, not send it back overcooked, but more overcooked than was the style. And so I mentioned it—but I had basically eaten the dinner. So that was that, until we left the restaurant. And Charlie was at the door to apologize for that dish, and to give me a set of three cookbooks and some food from the restaurant. I thought that was really quite special. I was very impressed.

MICHAEL TAUS: He would research a fish or whatever. And then it was just like, I want to make all these different components and then we're going to taste a couple of different ones together and see how it all comes together. Like Picasso and all those people in Paris, when they're sitting in a café, they're all talking art and things are changing. I feel like because Charlie was really into jazz, he talked about his cooking being like jazz, like a riff, it starts out one way and then kind of like, evolves. I never saw food evolving before. Like, through the week, it just got better.

There was a battle there. Everybody worked so hard to be the best. I feel like that was really exciting that everybody had the same goal.

GIUSEPPE TENTORI: Chef Trotter would come to me and say, hey, Giuseppe, maybe it's time to change this halibut. Why don't you get some scallop, fennel, maybe some salt cod, mustard, and something else, surprise me. That was the direction of the dish, and eventually it was a collaboration with Chef Trotter. I'm making multiple dishes and seeing what he thinks. Like, oh, maybe the mustard, now let's make a sauce. Let's make it cold, emulsified and let's try an oyster, and then we'll pair the wine. So you try a couple of times, and that's the evolution of dishes.

Nothing would go on the menu if he did not try it. So it was always a collaboration. You make the dish, you make sure Chef is in the house, he gives it feedback. If it was thumbs up, you put it on the menu the next day or next week. And after a dish was on the menu, by the time two, three months goes by, it was time to change it. Every season—yes, the ramps are coming up, the morels are coming up, but it was always a different presentation.

With Charlie it was like, never the same dish twice. So if you have a repeat customer, you have to change the menu. Also with so many ingredients at our disposal in the restaurant, so we can adjust for allergies, or for pairing to the right wine. We will have extra wagyu, squash, grouse, veal, bison. We knew that there was a gentleman coming with a $500 Or $1,000 bottle of wine. So for the next course, we'll come up with a dish and on the fly Chef will taste a spoon of something and say, okay, let's do it, and put them on the menu.

CURTIS DUFFY: They were very whimsical, or maybe not whimsical—spontaneous. Where they would take a dish and just change a few things out. So in a way, it's like, you're still cooking mushrooms for that dish, but it's a different mushroom.

I think their idea of never serving the same dish twice was not that they didn't serve, say, the rabbit course, night after night. But maybe they used, I don't know, cream cheese on the dish. And then next week, it was mascarpone. And then the following week, they changed the mushroom on the rabbit dish to morels instead of chanterelles. Then maybe hit it with red wine. Now it becomes a red wine friendly dish, as opposed to a white wine dish. So that's how they were always thinking it was never the same dish twice.

ROBERT HOUDE (wine steward): There was always this edge to everything that in the moment, may have been a little frustrating. But looking back at it, those were the best times that we ever had, because it was walking the tightrope with the highest level of clientele, including other chefs and *Wine Spectator* and other people like that all sitting in the same room. So that's what makes it really exciting.

He really let you go as far as you wanted to go. If you were the kind of person that needed to be pushed along, that's where you hear the horror stories. Because anybody who had to be told what to do or pushed along had a really bad time there—got run over, and not very nicely. But the difference was that if you showed that you had the initiative to try to do something better than it was already being done, or show him a different way of doing things that would be better than the way we were already doing it, that's what he was looking for. And he encouraged you to do that. For me, there was no other place that pushed you or gave me the opportunity to really do it to your best to the best of your ability. Most places were always holding you back.

LESLIE TELLEZ (cook): Yeah, we got yelled at. Did I cry? Yeah. But you know, he also cared a lot about every one of his employees. It took the right person to be able to survive that kitchen. And those who did, did, and those who didn't, they found out they couldn't. A lot of them, even though they didn't make it at Charlie Trotter's, they made it some place else.

I never had an issue with being a woman on the line. I mean, it was a dog-eat-dog world for everybody, but being a woman made no difference. The last thing I wanted to do was be a woman in the kitchen, I just wanted to be a chef in the kitchen. I didn't want a label on me. And Charlie was really good about that, and other people as well.

Look at some of those other chefs out there, you know, they too are hot-heads. It's all in the heat of the moment, there's that whole adrenaline rush going on. But he had a huge heart, no matter how many times he yelled or screamed at you and stuff like that. It was just trying to make everything as great as it could be and have everybody enjoy the experience that he wanted them to have. I don't regret a single moment with him.

PATRICK CRANE: Guillermo was a buffer. He helped calm things down. He was a guy that was so skillful and so aware of what everything that was going on that if he saw something going wrong, he was there helping that situation. He never let anything get too out of hand.

PAULA HOUDE (cook/office staff): I'm not gonna lie, there were some frustrating evenings when we thought we were doing this thing, and he'd be like, nope, do it different. You know, that's the thing that I think he gets chastised for more than he should, because it made everybody think out of the box. When he saw something becoming a cookie-cutter thing, he was like, no, we're not gonna do that. And so he taught you to think on your feet. There were eight hundred chefs that came in and out of that kitchen. Whether they liked it or not, they learned something.

We really did view each other as family. When you saw somebody sort of not having a great night, someone would chip in and help. And yeah, it wasn't always successful. Some nights we had really bad nights, really bad. And I spent the next day calling customers like so sorry, that sucked for you. But that didn't happen very often.

Trotter had a reputation for yelling in the kitchen—and yet, paradoxically, he put a table in the kitchen, so guests could watch how smoothly it ran while they were dining. But if they got a "mean Charlie" show, that was a bonus.

LARRY STONE (sommelier): The kitchen table came about basically by accident because Charlie ran out of seats for a wine dinner. And Bill Rice, the dining editor for the *Chicago Tribune*, he wanted to eat at that dinner. And Charlie said okay, we'll have a kitchen table for you. Very few restaurants had a kitchen table. In Europe there was one with a glass wall, and that was basically a walled-off area for the kitchen. So you could be in the kitchen, but you'd be walled off from the kitchen smells and the noise. So it was very elegant, and it was the most expensive table in the house.

But Charlie Trotter created a kitchen table and it was more like you're in the kitchen. And Bill Rice liked his experience so much, being in the thick of it, seeing the action, the screaming, the tension. He said, this is the best hot seat in Chicago. So after that people asked for the kitchen table.

GARY ALAN FINE: I had studied restaurant kitchens before. And a lot of restaurant kitchens are kind of chaotic places, there's a lot of yelling and banging and so forth. But at least when we were in Trotter's it was all very quiet, very sedate. We were able to watch these professionals preparing food in a very restrained, quiet fashion, which impressed me a lot. And they were very gracious to us. We were able to talk with them and, you know, Charlie Trotter was there. I don't remember all that we said, but it was probably about the restaurants we had been to.

LESLIE TELLEZ: At first, you felt like you were in the zoo, because people were watching you. They're watching you work, and they're pointing and stuff. But honestly, you get so busy after the first couple of days, you really don't notice them, until it's your turn to put up your plate. And then you watch the guest enjoy it. And I think as a chef, we don't always see our guests enjoy the food. Being in the kitchen, watching the guests get our plates and their reaction to it gives you that adrenaline rush to keep going.

To a lot of the chefs that were in the kitchen, it was a mystery what went on in the restaurant. Sometimes we never ate in the restaurant until like a year or so into it. So to have a kitchen table in our space, we had to be aware of how we moved around the guests and everything, which I think was just making it a life lesson, you should be aware of what's happening around you anyway.

You might be walking by them. And they might ask you a question, and then you just turn to answer that question. It was actually kind of nice.

JOHN WINTERMAN: He would sometimes actually go behind the dish machine just to make sure the captains and the waiters were separating their plates appropriately and scraping things off into the garbage. Also, you couldn't really hide when there was food coming back from a table, he'd want to know why. Is this something that we need to replace, that did not work with the wine, are they getting too full—whatever the story was, he wanted to know.

People who sat at the kitchen table, they wanted to see Charlie in action. So if there was a dispute or a problem, it was part of the show in a way. That's not to make excuses. There were people who left because of the aggression, but I didn't. It was really just busting your balls, trying to get you to think about doing a better job.

JOE CAMPAGNA: I was doing cleanup on Thursday and putting stuff in the cryovac. Table 86 is right behind us in the kitchen. I made a noise that I didn't register, it was just normal kitchen noise. And out of nowhere, I just feel his hand on my neck. And he's like, why don't we just bang everything in the kitchen, just make all the noise on the planet, just cause chaos. And I was just like, I'm so sorry, Chef. Like, I was literally, like, so frightened. And he wasn't wrong, right? It's like, when you're cleaning up, or you're cooking, it's that mentality of every detail matters.

MICHAEL TAUS: When you're expediting, it wasn't fun, because people would try to chitchat with you. And I'm like, please don't. Don't talk to me because Charlie will kill me and my whole family if I screw up.[7] Like some lady was trying to set me up with her niece. I'm like, no, please. First of all, I work a hundred hours a week. I have no time for that.

There was a show sometimes. He would just yell a little bit for fun. Like he didn't mean it, he was just, like, being silly, I felt, during the show. But people expected it.

7 Quoting a self-parodying tine delivered by Trotter in the movie *My Best Friend's Wedding.*

LARRY STONE: God forbid [a diner at the kitchen table] would look at their watch, because if Charlie noticed that they did, he'd take the clock off the wall and throw it in the garbage can. He'd say, you'll be done with this meal when I say you're done. And that made the night for those people. They were so thrilled.

BILL KIM: He was demanding. He was sometimes impossible, as in the details that he wanted you to have—sometimes he wanted us to have some kind of tape on our shoes. So when we go into the dining room that we would get the lint out. These are little things that to me is okay, if that's what you want me to do, I'll do it. But it made me who I am, and made me see different things and the level of detail that I have, that he has shown me. It's a skill that I take pride in knowing, and I think a lot of alumni say the same thing.

MICHAEL TAUS: "Don't do this for me. Do it for yourself." He said that a lot. Be the best you can be. I never worked with somebody that gave you so much insight all the time, inspiring you.

SARI ZERNICH WORSHAM: One night, I was on the fish station. Guillermo was the chef de cuisine at the time. And he said to me, he's coming for you today. Why? I don't know, but he's coming for you. Like, great.

So at one point in the night, he just started sending back all my food and you know, you work as a team. So my food has to time with another station's food coming up. So when he sends back something on your plate, it messes everybody else up.

And so he kept sending my food back and everyone's getting angry. And then he would just say Reggie, go help Sarah. And like, your station is so small. Reggie comes over into my station and he was trying to box me out, way up in my way. Well, first I stuck my head in the oven to get some space, and Trotter's yelling at me, like what are you doing down there? Honestly, I stuck my head in the oven to get myself together because I was like, he's not going to make me cry.

And then I come back up and Reggie's up on my station, like just trying to take it over. And I don't know what came out of me. I've never hit a person in my life. But my fists clenched, and I punched Reggie in the back. And he fell to his knees. And Trotter says Reggie, where'd you go? Reggie starts laughing. He's like, Mama punched me in the back, Chef, and the whole kitchen laughs at my nickname, which was Mama. Reggie gets back up, he gets off my station and Trotter left me alone after that. I've never hit another person since. But it was just one of those nights where he was doing it to people randomly.

Trust me, there were moments where, I mean, he was trying to break me for sure. And you know, he did at times. The first six months, I think I had a nauseous stomach every day before going in to work. And then the team would help you recover, and you'd get back in the game.

****

MICHAEL TAUS: We were just using amazing products flown in—abalone from Tasmania, all this amazing fish flown in from Hawaii or the East Coast. Tom Cornille, we would go down to his place on South Water Market and pick stuff out. All these things were just so inspiring, that nobody else was doing.

JOE CAMPAGNA: You would see matsutakes come in, and they would mound up this huge mountain on a sheet tray. And you're making 100 a day or 125 a day. That was the rate for cooks at the time, and this tray of mushrooms is worth eight hundred bucks. It's worth more than your week.

TOM CORNILLE (vegetable purveyor, George Cornille and Sons): I remember when he started. I didn't service them at the beginning because I serviced other accounts. A vendor told me, there's this kid trying to open a restaurant, and he wanted to use the best produce, and we asked him what his background was. Well, he didn't really have a background. They said, we were trying to kind of shoo him out the door, but he kept bugging us, he wouldn't leave. This guy was an older guy, he was established with a lot of the top older restaurants—Cafe Bohemia and everywhere. And he said he told Charlie, well, you gotta have references. He knew if he really didn't have a job before a restaurant, he can't have references. So bye bye, sorry, *arrivederci*.

And Charlie finally told the vendor, how about if I give you my dad's bank number? And the guy told me, I had a soft spot for his persistence, even though he had no qualifications. I owed it to him to call the bank. That was one of the bigger downtown banks. And he talked to the person who answered the phone and said, you know, I'm calling on a reference, on a Mr. Robert Trotter. The person that answered the phone said, one minute, sir, I will be right back. And within a minute, one of the top officials of the bank came back and said, our advice to you is that if Mr. Robert Trotter wants to take you in any business enterprise, go with him.

GUILLERMO TELLEZ-CRUZ: Tom Cornille was my savior, my hero, because he would bring in really exotic things that you didn't see in the manuals. I'd buy them to try to figure them out. Back then there was no internet, so it was all about reading, reading, reading and trying to come up with ideas. Back then you really had to read and work with the recipes.

The restaurant always kept changing. I started working with different farmers—I think that's one of the main reasons I stayed there such a long time, because it was always changing, there was always something different, there was always something new that we were doing. I would visit Farmer Lee Jones [of Chef's Garden in Ohio] when they were a very small farm.

FARMER LEE JONES: Charlie was a huge supporter, he loved vegetables and he did that *Raw* cookbook with Roxanne Klein.[8] He could tell our commitment and passion for trying to produce the best flavored vegetables that existed, and trying to do that naturally rather than chemically.

It was fun because Charlie was being invited to go all over the country as a special guest chef. And so we would always know where he was going, because he would have us send a box to whatever city and whatever restaurant he was at. At the time, our boxes weren't even marked—it wasn't because we were trying to be cagey, we just didn't have our name on the box yet. And we would get these kind of cryptic phone calls saying, I was in such and such kitchen and I saw this product, is there any way that you would sell to us?

Baby vegetables were the rage, early baby carrots, baby squash. Baby beets, baby kohlrabi. I think that it really became about unique textures and sizes, but always flavor was the first priority. It can be any size you want, but if it didn't

8 *Raw*, Charlie Trotter and Roxanne Klein, 2003.

taste good, then what's the point? They were tough on us. But we appreciated that. Because they demanded excellence, and they wanted things a specific way.

MICHAEL TAUS: The reason Chef's Garden in Ohio is the way it is because Charlie helped him out and told him what to grow. Like, all that stuff was Charlie's idea. He kept asking him to plant stuff, the smaller, the better. Interesting things.

RAY HARRIS (diner): Farmer Lee started tailoring some of his microgreens at the suggestion of Charlie. Charlie went into the growing room and there was a type of sprout that Farmer Lee typically sold at twenty-one days. Charlie said, ooh, can I try some of these? They were only seven days old, and he said, these are fine, and so Farmer Lee started selling them at seven days, fourteen days, and twenty-one days.

FARMER LEE JONES: One of the things that Charlie did with us on four different occasions was invite us to bring twenty people from the farm to the restaurant, and we rented up a bus. It was a big deal. We had a young man from Mexico that was working with us, and we took him over to JCPenney, and he got the first suit that he had ever owned in his life. We took a cross section of people from the farm, and it really helped propel us to the next level, because we were in that kitchen, and we saw the applications. And it was just mind-changing for our team to be able to see, to experience the level of service and quality, from when we got there and they greeted us at the bus with a handshake for every person. And then he had his team members presenting the dishes they had prepared. Everybody was learning. It was always about the learning.

And then when we got on the bus, he was there and handed every person a gift bag with two of his books and a printed menu from the day. And Charlie says, Farmer Jones has told you all you have to be on your best behavior. But after this bus gets moving, I want you to look under the back seat. There was a case—I don't remember the kind of champagne it was. But he says, I expect that champagne to be gone by the time this bus gets back to the farm. And the whole bus erupted and cheered.

One time I got a phone call—whenever he would call, it would say "number unknown." But I pick up and he says, this is your best friend Charlie Trotter, I'd like to ask you a hypothetical question. What would you think if I asked you about flying into the nearest airport on a private jet with Ferran Adria [el Bulli, Roses, Spain] and his wife and we get a farm tour? And I'll send six of my staff in the day before and we have a simple little twelve-course lunch at the end of the tour, and then we're flying back to Chicago for dinner. That was an epic day.

The way a chef and farmer can learn from each other in a symbiotic relationship is what has allowed us to grow over the years and helped the restaurants grow. Getting product direct from the farm really moved the food scene in Chicago to unprecedented levels.

GUILLERMO TELLEZ-CRUZ: In the beginning, we were doing an à la carte menu. And then one day Charlie's like, let's just get rid of this stupid menu and do all tasting. And we'll do a vegetable menu. Charlie Trotter's was the first restaurant to completely cut off the à la carte menu. So we had three menus, one for the kitchen table, and one that included vegetable items, and some fish and meats, and one that was all vegetables. We never wanted to call it "vegetarian," we called it vegetable-driven, because the stars were the vegetables and in some cases we used cheese. We used butter. Even I thought, who's going to buy this? But being the first restaurant to do this, people went crazy. It was a total success.

MICHAEL TAUS: I was really into Asian and Indian stuff. So I would go up to those markets and bring stuff in. And I did a lot of vegetarian cooking. I was dating a vegetarian at the time. So Charlie really let me go a little crazy with vegetarian stuff, because we had a vegetarian tasting menu, which no one was doing.

We were doing more and more vegetarian, but also, part of my style of cooking was a lot of vegetables. Like the meat was not always the star, it was part of the dish. And that was the first time I saw that the dish was all a little bit of its components.

DR. LEE SMITH (diner): I remember one time I had the vegetable degustation, and I had a beet dish with a Grand Cru red burgundy. I went, Jesus Christ,

Charlie, I got La Tache here. But the way he did the beet dish, it actually worked.

PHIL VETTEL (*Tribune* restaurant reviewer): People hadn't seen that kind of focus and attention and devotion to vegetables. Charlie represented a cleaner and more visually impressive way of dining, and he would blow people away just by the sheer quality of ingredients and how far away he had gone to get them and the kind of stuff he could get his hands on. And that was a big thing. Jean Banchet didn't tell you where he was getting his squab from. Charlie told you where he was getting his scallops from. And that resonated with a lot of diners, knowing more about their food and knowing just where it came from, being able to say, wow, this is really good stuff.

I don't think I ever got Charlie to tell me what the percentage was of sales [for the vegetarian menu]. But I think for one thing, if you're a table of two or four, at least one of you would have the vegetable menu, just to see what it was like, since you're probably swapping plates anyhow. It was kind of bold at the time, but he proved that there was a market for it—otherwise, he would have dropped the damn thing.

****

One of the things that set Trotter's apart was its focus on wine. In time Charlie Trotter's sommeliers, beginning with Larry Stone, would take wine culture in the city to a level unequalled before or since.

LARRY STONE: When I went to interview with Charlie, he said, I want to have the best restaurant in the world. I want to be the next Frédy Girardet, the next Marco Pierre White [Harveys, London]. These are chefs whose books he looked at every day and memorized. He wasn't trying to recreate their dishes, he was trying to create a new lexicon for American cuisine that was of the same caliber.

And frankly, no one believed he could do it, because he had such weird combinations for food and wine, according to what Americans were used to—even the, quote, gourmets from the wine clubs. "None of his dishes work with wine." That's why he recruited me, in a way.

There was a tasting group, called the Commanderie de Bordeaux. They focused on Bordeaux and they wanted to go to the best restaurants and hold these tastings. But the wines were all cooked. Frankly, none of the wines in America, nowhere in this country were wines shipped refrigerated from Europe, until the mid-nineties. And even in the mid-nineties, I had trouble getting refrigerated wines.

Stone was working for one of the top hotels in Chicago, and discovered other problems in the supply chain.

I made up a wine list based on quality available at the time, and the head of purchasing where I worked kept saying, no, they just don't ship. They're not reliable at all. I'd call the distributor and say, did you ship, and he'd say, we tried to ship, but he rejected it at the dock when we showed up. I called the distributor and said, bring it again, I'll wait for you in the dock. I came to the dock at the right time and I saw the head of purchasing telling him to go away. I said, I ordered this, it's on my list, I have a party tonight that's expecting this. If you reject this shipment I will go to the GM of the hotel. He says, you do that, I've been working for him a long time. We went to his office to talk about it, and under his desk there was a case of stuff from a competing distributor, including like six bottles of Cristal [champagne]. So condition at delivery was one thing, but the corruption all the way through—that's what I was fighting against.

When I came to Trotter's, I had a Master Sommelier degree from the English Court, for all the wines of the world. I inherited a very small list from his first wife, who basically focused on American wines from producers she liked, such as Randall Grahm [Bonny Doon], Jim Clendenen [Au Bon Climat] and Donald Patz [Patz & Hall]. She felt that if we do American wine, just do American wine, we can get all these producers that come in and do dinners here. And that'll be exciting. They hired me knowing I also had great experience with European wines—I had already won the title of best sommelier in the world in French wine in Paris, where I had been granted a master's in French wine, and I wrote a column for the *Chicago Tribune*. All the French wine producers who came through town wanted to meet me because I was already the best sommelier of French wine in the world. So that was a big impetus for them to come meet me and do dinners.

Charlie said, what do you need? I said, well, it would be nice to have a little of this and a little of that. Then it became, what would it take to get a Grand Award [from *Wine Spectator*] I said, well, they don't give it to you until you're so many years old, and you must have all the first growths from Bordeaux, you must have all the great estates, first growths, second growths, third growths, and multiple vintages going back forty years, or they don't give you any credibility. He said, okay. Pretty soon I realized he didn't care how much money he poured into the restaurant, he wanted to be recognized as a great restaurateur.

Once I received a release sheet of the first Domaine Leroy wines, vintage 1989, from Martine Saunier of Martine's Wines in Novato [California], along with her offering of Henri Jayer, I made a list of wines that I thought would be good to have for the prestige of the restaurant. And I knew it was also an historic opportunity. It was now around 2 a.m. in the restaurant and Charlie asked me what I was doing. I told him that the offering was way too big for the restaurant to handle even simply in terms of storage. I told Charlie, this is way too much. If I added this all up it would be like $70,000 or more, and we have no place to store it all. And he said, well, why don't we just buy it all? I'll find room. So that led to buying the house next door to store the wine. That's how he worked.

Charlie would create the food to match the wines they were drinking. If someone came in with a great bottle of wine or bought a great bottle of wine on the list, and it wasn't going to go with the menu that they had for the day, he would change the menu for them to match the wines, on the fly. That was the great collaboration between him and me. Say they were supposed to have three or four fish courses first, suitable for a white wine that was lightweight. And I'd say, Charlie, they're bringing Sassicaia '85 [Tuscan red wine], that won't go with the fish and the sauces. I was able to say, look, if you do the fish, you can do it this way, with these kinds of sauces. Because really, it's about the sauces and what you put on the plate, more than the protein.

It took a little time for the customers to understand it, but once they did, it was very exciting to be able to say, oh, I had this with that. David Rosengarten had written his book *Red Wine With Fish* [1989] around that time, so we did seared tuna with a red wine reduction.

In 1993, Stone left Charlie Trotter's to open Rubicon in San Francisco with Drew Nieporent (Tribeca Grill). Joe Spellman, who'd worked with Michael Foley and George Badonsky and at the Pump Room, succeeded him.

JOE SPELLMAN: I had interviewed with Charlie, back in '89, just a couple of years after the restaurant opened, because I kind of befriended his wife Lisa, who was then doing the wine buying. She told him you should interview Joe, he's great. But we didn't really click and he also was interviewing Larry, who was a legendary sommelier at the Four Seasons.

This time, '93, it worked out and I was there for about five years. The restaurant had really gained in reputation—Charlie was making more and more national news. Larry had built the cellar up quite a bit over the four years he was there. In fact, in the summer of '93, it was announced that it was going to be one of the *Wine Spectator* Grand Award winners, which usually go to the thousand-item or more wine lists with really great selections on depth, and verticals and all that stuff.

But keeping that up required that I continue to buy from a lot of those key producers, whether they're Burgundy, Rhone, you know, even some of the California high-quality stuff that was scarce because it was allocated or small production. I also grew the cellar in breadth, particularly in areas like Spanish wine, German wine, Austrian wine, Italian wine—there was some Italian, but I wanted to be a little more broad-based rather than being so French dominated. And I thought I was successful in doing that. Charlie kept expanding the cellar space, so what was originally the office space in the basement of the restaurant was converted to a very nice-looking cellar.

ROBERT HOUDE: That restaurant had four different cellars devoted to wines at all the right temperatures. There was several million dollars of wine sitting there at any time. It was a program that was far above almost anything that's being done today.

JOE SPELLMAN: Diners enjoyed the idea of Larry lecturing to them for half an hour at tableside. So he did that a lot more than I did. I mean, I have to say that the restaurant was bigger and busier many of the years I was there. I didn't want to spend too long at a table. And my teammates on the floor—hey, you should go to table 45. Hey, stop talking to table 13. I think as a sommelier you have to pick your spots where you can invest your time.

The more challenging ones would be the people who had dietary restrictions or special menus worked up for them, and then we'd come up with a pairing of wine for each course, for eight or ten courses with a small sip, two, three ounces of wine per course. And that was a lot of legwork and a lot of decision making and a lot of explaining of each wine.

Another thing that was a great opportunity for us was, Charlie was working on his books, and doing the photography, preparing the dish in the afternoon, and we would open several wines to determine what's the best pairing for that dish. So we'd have those wines to work with for the evening, too. And of course, there'd be three-quarters of a bottle. So not everybody got those wines, but there was a lot of wine floating around all the time.

I think people wanted to know that you're honest. What do you really like in this list? What's your favorite burgundy for $150? I enjoyed those interactions.

The era of mega wine lists is declining, for sure. For one thing, Bordeaux isn't so important anymore. And the dollar inventory weight is massive on a restaurant if you're not turning it. And generally you're not, so it's inefficient. And more and more, it has to do with natural wine, ancient methods, grapes that nobody ever heard of, the kind of wine only a sommelier can sell, if they're unknown varietals, or blends, or less-known techniques. To the point now where I think there is a current generation of drinkers who expect that and desire it. I roll my eyes a lot. But I understand where they're coming from, because there's been an article about vegan wine in *Food & Wine* magazine or something, then suddenly that's the thing.

LARRY STONE: There are still wine clubs, but they really need to recruit younger people. They didn't do a good job of that because the people who came after that generation of older wine buyers, they were more into competitive buying. They were after unicorn wines. Where with the old collectors, the wine wasn't worth that much. They had lots of money, and places to store it, and they enjoyed having dinner with these other guys or sharing it with younger colleagues, sitting together and talking about what was going on in the world.

People came to the restaurant to learn about things. So I'd tell them about wine from Oregon, but they're at Charlie Trotter's and they want to impress people, so it's not expensive enough for them—and they'd order a red Burgundy.

Countless guests dined at Charlie Trotter's over the years, but there was a handful of guests who dined there into the hundreds of times and established relationships with Chef Trotter—even to the extent of cooking in his kitchen.

RAY HARRIS (financial executive): I live in New York, but I commuted to Chicago for work for years, and I was kind of looking for that classic Parisian bistro on a Thursday night, and I couldn't find it. I called over to Trotter's. I said, I understand the economics of the restaurant business, I wouldn't come on a busy night, but do you ever seat a table of one? He said they did, and so I called the following Tuesday. That was August '94, and soon I went once a month, or every two weeks, and I had a standing reservation on Thursday at nine o'clock. I probably averaged thirty-five to forty Thursday nights a year for approximately five years, and another fifteen years of ten to fifteen times a year.

After three or four visits, I wrote Charlie a letter, comparing his cooking to the greats of France, Joël Robuchon and a bunch of other guys. And the next visit Charlie came to the table, and we had a nice chat. I think he thought I understood what he was trying to do with his food and his restaurant and his vision, and that just started, you know, just a lifetime, just a great friendship. Then over time, the team would kind of tease me with menus that come out. One night every dish had tomatoes in it, one night corn was an ingredient in every dish.

I would bring in a bottle of wine, nice wine, I would say, you know, Chef, I'm not going to drink the whole bottle, you can have a little taste, the somm can have a taste. And then Charlie told me quote, it is unseemly to carry wine in the front door, close quote. So I started shipping cases of wine to the restaurant. And then eventually I had my own personal section in his wine cellar. When I had friends come to the restaurant he would send over my list and tell people to pick something, and it took them a while to see the little "Ray" in the upper corner.

DR. LEE SMITH: Bipin Desai [wine collector], who was like Mr. Wine Tasting, said, I think the greatest chef in the world is in Chicago. I said that's big coming from you, because you're in France all the time. Would you give me an introduction?

I called Larry Stone, and said, can I bring some wines? I told him what I wanted to bring in and he said, oh, those are phenomenal, we don't have them on the wine list. So they had that little bar area as you walk in, where they would have customers stay before they were seated. And this guy comes out from the kitchen. And he says, are you Dr. Smith? When I said, yeah, he says, I'm going to blow your mind. He turns around and walks out. And he did.

We developed a very close friendship, and we ate at the restaurant about two hundred times. I was involved with the charity events he did. For the millennium Charlie wanted to close it to give everybody two weeks off, and we all went to Hawaii together for his fortieth birthday. We went to Europe together, and had dinner at Frédy Girardet's house.

RAY HARRIS: Chicago had a reputation for steak and potatoes. So people go to Charlie's and it's, what do you want to call it, French or new Japanese, and it's tiny portions. Some people didn't understand it. But my wife and I had dined in places like that, Ducasse, Robuchon, Bocuse, Frédy Girardet, Marc Veyrat. And so we knew what he was trying to do. People thought he was expensive, but you know, when he was around $135, comparable Michelin threes in Paris were 300 euros, so call that $350. He was actually a relative bargain versus the high-end, worldwide.

He had more of an Asian aesthetic in the later years—in the early courses he would serve some kind of bento box with seafood appetizers, some raw, some cooked. And then he obviously was big on foam. There's a period where it was foam, foam on everything. It's a pain in the ass to serve foam, because you gotta whip it up with the little handheld Black & Decker thing and if you don't rush it to the table, it dissipates after about forty-five seconds.

DR. LEE SMITH: I think the absolute greatest period of the restaurant was '95 to 2001. That was the food that I loved the most. Charlie got a little more experimental after '01, he started to do a raw food menu and he did the raw food cookbook. He was into raw foods, Japanese influences, and we love Japanese food tremendously. As he went on, Matthias [Merges, chef de cuisine] influenced him more and more, because Matthias loves Japanese cuisine. He eventually opened a Japanese restaurant, Yusho. I think Charlie allowed Matt to put more and more Japanese influence, because he'd cooked in Japan, or spent some time in Japan. But we liked this French fusion, Continental cuisine of '95 to '01 best.

At first there was a French mafia that was against him. I think they saw a guy who opened his restaurant with his father's money, and they didn't think he was serious because he didn't spend ten years under a famous guy getting beat to death. But he was just as serious as they were, and eventually they dissolved and loved him. Like Daniel [Boulud] just loved Charlie. Michel Richard [Citronelle, DC] was one of the old guys who took a long time to warm up with him, but Michel Richard and I were really good friends. And Michel eventually said to me, oh, yeah, Charlie's a phenomenal guy. He did a painting of all the food cooked when he was invited to Charlie's. And then Charlie, when he closed the restaurant, sent me the painting.

Charlie would cook for the wine. Most French chefs would get insulted, they cooked for the food, and then matched the wine. Charlie would like to match the food to the wine.

RAY HARRIS: One night Charlie calls me and says, Julia Child is coming to the restaurant, you've got to be here. I had a trip scheduled to go out west, so I rearranged my flights to stop in Chicago on the way back. This has to be pre 9/11, when you could carry wine on the plane. I have this old canvas bag I could get about ten or twelve bottles in. So I had Chateau d'Yquem and Domaine de la Romanée-Conti. It was Julia and maybe her PR people, some of her publishing people. So there were about eight of us. Julia was a tall woman, easily six feet, and at this point, I think she was approaching eighty. But everything they served, she tried, and she tried all the wines. I asked her, Ms. Child, how do you do it? And she said to me, quote, everything in moderation—a few bites of each course, and a little taste of each wine. And that was just a typical Charlie Trotter experience.

DR. LEE SMITH: I cooked in the restaurant—I mean, not as a bullshit guest chef, I took weeks off and lived in an apartment and worked fourteen-hour days. I always wanted to be a chef. Charlie would say, oh, you're my friend, you don't need to—I said, no Charlie, I need to sweep the floor, clean the toilets, anything you have regular guys do because I need to experience the whole thing.

Michael Jordan came in—there was this *Chicago* magazine article in which Charlie was the second meanest man in Chicago, and Michael came in first. I don't like being second, Charlie said. Let's step it up. Jordan was there with his wife, and he doesn't like wine. The waiter said, oh, Mr. Jordan, it's wonderful to have you, what would you like? He says, I'd like a Bud Light. The guy runs into the kitchen, he's petrified. And Charlie says, go to the goddamn liquor store and get a six-pack of Bud Light. The guy ran down and got one and poured it in the perfect Riedel beer glass. Like we had it in the restaurant all the time.

RAY HARRIS: Frédy Girardet came over for the fifteenth anniversary dinner. Frédy was the guest chef and after the dinner, Frédy took off his chef's jacket and he gave it to Charlie. And Charlie was like a little kid. It was the equivalent of Michael Jordan taking his jersey off and giving it to you. For Charlie, that may have been one of the happiest moments he ever had.

****

*By the 1990s Trotter was an international name—publishing cookbooks, producing a PBS cooking show (*The Kitchen Sessions with Charlie Trotter*) in his own studio next door to the restaurant, and constantly traveling to collaborate with other name-brand chefs.*

SARI ZERNICH WORSHAM: When I started there his first cookbook[9] was in the home stretch, they were doing recipe testing and photography. So I got to test recipes before starting my station. And then I think, for whatever reason, maybe because I wasn't such a trained chef, my recipe testing was a little more thorough. I didn't mind measuring, timing, all that stuff. So then he kept giving me more to do on that.

After the first book got published I was going to go be a food scientist for Quaker Oats. He said, well, I've been thinking about doing this vegetable

9 *Charlie Trotter's*, 1994.

book, why don't you defer that job for six months and do this? And so then I started doing the vegetable book.[10] And then he's like, hey, how about seafood? How about meat and game? It just kept going. I kept saying to him, like, we're plagiarizing ourselves out of the market. These books are coming out so fast, you know?

We were so proud of *Charlie Trotter's Vegetables*, and of course, I was super proud because it was my first one that I really took from start to finish. Sally Schneider was the editor at *Saveur*. She wrote the first review of the book. And she wrote that she wanted to throw the book across the floor, because the recipes had so many components they would take hours to make, you'd have to make a stock for two days. She was just really frustrated with the complexity of the book. And I remember Trotter and I were just devastated at that first review, because we just didn't agree with her.

I think a lot of people collected them, used them as coffee table books, for sure. But chefs all over the place were dying to get these books because Trotter told all his secrets. He didn't keep anything proprietary. Honestly, once he created a dish, he was done with it, he wanted to do something else. But I think those books really had an important part to play in how the culinary world has evolved, especially putting a place like Trotter's and the Midwest on the map, nationally and globally. We got to go on all these road shows and travel with the cookbooks and meet a lot of great people and do dinners in their homes with Chef.

MICHAEL TAUS: He discovered a lot of chefs. Like I did a dinner one time with Dean Fearing [The Mansion on Turtle Creek, Dallas], Norman Van Aken, Emeril Lagasse. Nobody even knew what El Bulli was when Charlie discovered [Ferran Adrià]. I got to meet all these people in the early days just hanging out.

LARRY STONE: In 1991, when we went [to top restaurants in Europe] they didn't know who he was and they didn't always treat him with respect or credibility. Maybe on the second or third trip that he made back to them, it was like, okay, I know you, I've read about you, and some people have gone

10 *Charlie Trotter's Vegetables*, 1996.

to your restaurant in the meantime to see what you're about. Georges Blanc [Village Blanc, Vonnas], whose vegetable book Charlie had memorized, and Marc Meneau [L'Esperance, Vezelay] were dismissive of us. On the other hand, Bernard Loiseau and his wife Dominique [Le Relais Bernard Loiseau, Saulieu] took amazing care of us and treated us like family.

GIUSEPPE TENTORI: Charlie was an interesting leader because he was lucky enough to travel. It was not just research for fun for him. He had the luxury to travel and see what people are doing and taste it and come back and say, we had a Tasmanian ocean trout. Nobody had that. Now you can call your vendors and get these.

For me the hardest week I ever worked at Charlie Trotter's was when he flew in Frédy Girardet. Not just the hours—I don't want to talk about the hours. If I tell everybody how many hours we work, you'd say, was that for real? Yes. Frédy Girardet flew a private jet with his team to Chicago. Charlie also made a cookbook for Frédy Girardet in English. You have like eight or ten of the best chefs in the states cooking for like 110 guests. And Charlie's kitchen is small and we have to do regular service, too. The next day Frédy Girardet cooks for sixty guests and then we have all the chefs cook for him—Gray Kunz [Lespinasse, New York], Günter Seeger, Daniel [Boulud], Norman [Van Aken].

PAUL KAHAN (chef/co-owner, Blackbird): Trotter came in to Blackbird on a regular basis. And whenever he had luminaries in town, he would always bring them and the wheels would come to a halt. The lunch menu had to be accessible, sandwiches and things like that. And I'd be like, Charlie Trotter's coming in with Gordon Ramsay, Tetsuya Wakuda from Australia. We're doing dishes off the dinner menu. And because of that we'd be so behind getting dinner set up, it would be this long ordeal. But we wanted to show them what we were doing.

Charlie always invited the chefs in the city that he liked to come to lunch the day before those dinners that he put on for anniversaries and whatever. So I got to go there, and eat food from chefs that I didn't have the means to go to their restaurants. And that was incredible.

With national fame, Trotter looked for ways to expand his brand into additional restaurants—beginning with C in Cabo San Lucas in 2004, and then Restaurant Charlie in the Palazzo Resort in Las Vegas in 2008.

GUILLERMO TELLEZ-CRUZ: We were hired to do a restaurant for the whales, guys for whom the minimum bet was like one million, two million. So we came in to cater to them. Caviar, all luxury. Well, after they lost their money [in the 2008 market crash], the whales disappeared. So we were like, let's open it to the public. So they were negotiating that, and they brought in this guy from Texas, and he's like, I don't care about fine dining. I don't want fine dining. I'm gonna turn this place into a family style hotel. And they spend tons and tons of money, they build a theme park, a game arcade. Everything was geared towards the family. Then he's like, I don't want to have any restaurants. So they tell Charlie that he needed to make a family style restaurant. And Charlie's like, well, no, this is not our concept.

SARI ZERNICH WORSHAM: Trotter was the first one to do the thing in Vegas. There weren't name brand chefs there back then. And he was a little too early.

BILL KIM: Half of his crew, half of his longtime personnel, he asked them to move to Vegas. At that point I was almost the most senior person in the kitchen, and Charlie asked me if I wanted to run the kitchen. I'd never been a sous chef, I was twenty-six and two years out of culinary school. And I said no, because I was going to go to Korea and wanted to study Asian foods. He was very disappointed. Two weeks after he tried again, and I talked to my parents about it, and they're like, it's the chance of a lifetime. Why don't you do it?

After that just everything changed for me. I was traveling the world with him, doing demos, and I got to go to three-star Michelin restaurants. Went to Frédy Girardet before he closed. My head was spinning, because I did not know what I was in for. It really opened the world to me. And he made sure that I saw things that I wouldn't see for myself. Like, what fine dining was at the greatest level ever. It wasn't even about food. It was about service and culture. As a twenty-six-year-old that just kind of grew up in the Midwest, I wasn't thinking the world was, you know, that close.

It was a bubble because I didn't know the people that I was cooking for. Or the money that was spent on meals—I didn't grow up that way. People spending $2,500 on a bottle of wine. I appreciated that back then, because I was learning. But as I got older, I created my own opinion of what food should be. And I felt like I needed more experience outside of French restaurants and Charlie Trotter's. I felt like I needed the part of the business that showed me what reality was. So after three years I left because I wanted to see what the real world was like.

When I came back, Matthias Merges was the chef de cuisine. Giuseppe Tentori was a sous chef. Matthias eventually elevated into something a little bit greater. I became chef de cuisine, and Giuseppe was still a sous chef. They had chemistry, they'd worked with each other for ten years. So it was competitive, but in a very friendly way. I'd spent ten years working for all these different places. Could I bring something different to the table?

They were traveling a lot more. We used to only travel on weekends, when the restaurant was closed. By the second time, we were going to Brazil, we're going to London, and this is during the weekdays. Back then [his first stint], Charlie was still in the kitchen. And the second time around, it was a machine. It wasn't a small, quaint restaurant, it was a production. I wanted to do something different, and I thought I could bring that to the table. And it just wasn't part of what they were doing.

SARI ZERNICH WORSHAM: When I was working with Bill, he'd always drive me home and say, like, he wanted to open up this ramen place, and I just didn't get it. I'm like, why are you working here? This was way before Urbanbelly happened, but I really didn't get it. You got the foundation, you got the work ethic, but I think we all kind of gravitated to making foods that you'd want to eat every day instead of just laboring. I love cooking something out of one pan from start to finish, instead of needing like eight different pans. I think when you worked at that level for so long, you take the components of where you're at, and see how you can make something that's a lot more casual.

****

Trotter's long hours and "shift pay"—a set payment for the day no matter how many hours cooks actually worked—were just taken for granted by most who worked there, as they were in most fine dining restaurants at the time. But in 2003, a cook named Beverly Kim led a class action suit on behalf of the kitchen staff; a second one on behalf of front of house staff over the distribution of tips followed. Trotter settled them in 2005, but he didn't forget who took his money.

BEVERLY KIM: At the time, that was normalized. It was almost thought of as, *I'm* helping *you*. For your resume.

The first exposure I had to Trotter's was, he had a cookbook demo. And I was attracted to the beauty and the art of it. And looking back, it was the first place that wasn't just French. The techniques were lighter, and with my Korean American palate, I was looking for some of those qualities, like more savory—he would put kimchi in a few dishes. So from an artistic standpoint, I was attracted to it, and from a place of excellence—I always wanted to work for the best. You're young, you're figuring out how the world works, all you know is you're supposed to work hard, to say "Yes Chef." I was told by cooks to never look a chef in the eye—it's like looking a dog in the eye, you'll get your head bitten off. A lot of people told me, don't go there, I don't think you're going to make it because you're too soft. But I was there for a year and a half. It goes back to my parents telling me that because I was a girl, I could never be financially at the top, or support a family. You tell me no, I try harder.

I don't think my experience at Trotter's was all bad. I think that a lot of it, though, was based in a culture that wasn't questioned. If we don't actually look at it, the hazing, the culture, accepting norms that aren't healthy, the mind games . . . feeling like you can't advocate for yourself, feeling like you can't have an honest question, you can't talk about things like your pay without feeling like you're going to lose your job. Those are the kinds of things that are human rights.

There need to be healthy boundaries. I don't want to get to the extreme where we can't have shadows [trainees following behind an employee], but there's systemic taking advantage of people, and retribution if you speak out against it. In professionalizing our industry, those are the things we need to address. We need to look at the industry as a whole.

One of the former Trotter employees who wound up taking the payout from Kim's lawsuit was chef Curtis Duffy—leading to a 2012 incident recorded in a documentary film about Duffy where Duffy and others try to enter Charlie Trotter's and are angrily turned away by Trotter at the door.[11]

CURTIS DUFFY: I'm still in that mindset of, you kind of knew what you were getting into when you signed up for it. That doesn't make it fair, of course. But there's a proud thing of saying that you worked for Charlie Trotter for so long, because everybody knew how hard that kitchen was to work in. And the longer you worked there, you had that respect from your peers like, oh, this guy is gonna be a fucking badass.

I was at Trio when I got a check—a guy showed up at the door and I signed for an envelope, I didn't know what it was. I know he says in the Trotter documentary[12] that it was like fifty grand. I never saw a check for $50,000, I remember it being just shy of $12,000. But for someone who's young, in their twenties, and barely making it by, that was a lot of money.

I didn't sign on to the lawsuit thinking they were suing Charlie. If somebody would have approached me to be a part of the lawsuit, I would have said no. I just thought it was a done deal. But cashing the check was what put the nail in the coffin for me [with Trotter]. Naive me, I didn't think that Charlie would ever find out.

I think I was just young and dumb. I think anybody would have taken it.

****

Though low pay in the kitchen was a widely known part of Trotter's image, people who worked for him also talk about his generosity, displayed in his restaurant and around the world.

BILL KIM: The one thing that I always say, to anybody that wants to listen, is I didn't learn how to cook from him. But I learned how to give from him. I mean, to be able to do so many charity events. A lot of people didn't know, he had the Excellence program for ten years straight. That was out of his pocket. He would invite twelve to fifteen students from underserved neighborhoods, and he would feed them exactly what we were serving that night to our paying

11 *For Grace* (2015), dir: Mark Helenowski, Kevin Pang.

12 *Love, Charlie: The Rise and Fall of Chef Charlie Trotter* (2021), dir: Rebecca Halpern.

guests from, we would do it from four-thirty to six o'clock, and we would give them a five-course meal on Charlie's dime. And we as cooks, we would go and explain what that food was at a level our audience understood. So another thing that he taught me was, a chef should be able to speak in public.

These were kids who live in parts of Chicago that nobody wants to ever go visit. Some kids didn't get it, but some kids, their eyes lit up and they're eating something that they never thought they'd be eating. One kid was eating a fingerling potato, and he said, what do you mean, I thought the potato was a French fry. You as a cook when you're working that environment, you lose perspective. Because you're taking truffles and you're taking day boat scallops and all these things. And when you get to talk to a group of kids who are basically surviving, and they're asking questions about potatoes and French fries, you're getting a true sense of reality.

GUILLERMO TELLEZ-CRUZ: The way we started it is, this accountant, Jack Davis, came in and approached us. He knew that we loved working with farms, and he had this brilliant idea of trying to help inner city kids [working on a garden plot] in Cabrini-Green [public housing project]. In the beginning we were like, it's crazy, it's Cabrini-Green. But they did it, and I told Charlie, I want to commit to buying their whole production.

And Charlie said, every Saturday, why don't we take two students who work on the plot, and they can come over to the restaurant and see what we do with what they planted. They can see everything we do, and how we plate it, and then we feed them and they're on their way. And then he's like, we got to kick it up a notch. So the next step is, if some of these kids can spend two years without missing a day, we will send them to CIA [Culinary Institute of America], we will pay for everything. And so we started a program. And two of them, we did pay everything for them to go to school.

ROBERT HOUDE: There was a family that came in the door and wanted to have lunch. He gave them a tour and sat them at the kitchen table, and gave them lunch. And they walked out and wondered why nobody was here. It's because we're not open.

The most extreme example—we called them the Three Longhairs. These three young chefs from Alaska saved up everything to come there and we kind of knew that. Charlie found out and started sending out special courses to them and we started doing some extra pairings of wines for them. And then at the end, when we went to give them the bill, it was just a note from Charlie, saying thank you for being our guests. And they basically started crying.

RAY HARRIS: I was having dinner upstairs one time and there were these four chefs from Cincinnati. It was a night off and they drove up. I tell Charlie, hey, there's these four guys from Cincinnati, they're probably like twenty-five or twenty-seven. And they came up here because their goal in life was to eat your food. So then, boom, more courses, he goes to the table, more courses. And of course no bill goes to them. He would do this all the time.

PAULA HOUDE: There were random people who saved up their whole year to dine there. Those were the special ones that we all kind of liked more. I know Charlie sometimes catered to those people a little bit, if he found out it was a special anniversary. These people weren't bankers or didn't have a seat on the stock exchange, but he would go above and beyond and make their nights pretty special. And especially if it was a weekend night, Dona-Lee, his mother, came in Fridays and Saturdays and did tours. I mean, she was my favorite person. When people were sitting too long at their table, she'd come in and she'd be like, okay, who do I need to kick out? She was wonderful, she's like a superhero to me to this day.

The chefs that would come in were always blown out of the water. Charlie almost always went above and beyond the ridiculous for these chefs, especially if they traveled from all across the world. Robert and I are friends with lots of chefs. And every single one still talks about their experiences to this day, of dining there and what Charlie did for them.

MICHAEL TAUS: I was the first person who opened a restaurant after they came out of Trotter's. And the first year, Charlie called me up and goes, okay, your first year anniversary is coming up. We're doing a James Beard dinner at your restaurant, I bring you the staff, and this is what you're doing. It was like the sweetest thing ever. My last day of work there, his mom came up to me, and gave me this really nice leather-bound organizer. And she gave me a hug and told me, thanks for believing in my son. You'll always be part of our family.

DONA-LEE TROTTER: I think it meant a lot to him to help people that were less well-off. He had a big heart for people to help them out. My husband helped out students at Northwestern with scholarship money and things. And we were always giving to people, or to establishments, or schools or whatever, things like that. Because we were fortunate, and we wanted to be able to help other people. And I think Charlie really got that message.

****

Just as Trotter's arrival on the scene had dethroned Jean Banchet as the supreme chef in Chicago, the arrival of Grant Achatz, first at Trio in Evanston and then with his restaurant Alinea in 2005, put a new restaurant at the top of the Chicago scene and popularized a new style known as "molecular cuisine." Achatz had worked for Trotter but disliked the atmosphere of the kitchen, going to California where he found his mentor in Thomas Keller of The French Laundry.

Trotter's reputation took a number of blows in the years to follow, particularly when the Michelin Guide came to Chicago in 2011. Trotter was probably more responsible for them coming to Chicago than anyone—but he only got two stars while Achatz got three.

SARI ZERNICH WORSHAM: I remember when Grant Achatz announced that he was going to open a restaurant [Alinea] just a few blocks from Trotter's. I was in the office with Chef Trotter, he wasn't pissed at all. He thought it was going to be great for the neighborhood—that it would bring more people to sleepy Lincoln Park. He wasn't threatened. Now when the Michelin stars came out, that was a different reaction. But I didn't see him feeling threatened or upset at the beginning at all.

RAY HARRIS: When Grant comes along, he's the hottest new thing. So Charlie is then, like, the old guy in town, they're all these young whippersnappers. And then Michelin comes along, and clearly, Grant's said it, clearly Charlie was a Michelin three-star restaurant for the vast majority of his career. So, did the guy come in and have a bad night? Obviously, Charlie got in enough scrapes over time that maybe people started saying, okay, he's a little weakened, let me go after him.

DR. LEE SMITH: Some of the places he wouldn't go to with me because if they were former employees, he was freaking weird about that. I kept telling him, you know, Grant's a good guy. Yeah, I'm sorry he left. But Grant's an okay human being. I could never get him to go. I tried.

MARK CARO (*Tribune* writer): He never actually ate in Grant's restaurants. He made reservations at Trio and didn't show up. He did one of those Beard dinner things where you invite alumni to come back and Grant would cook. It was a month or two before Alinea opened and he made a dish that was going to be an appetizer at Alinea—almost like a shrimp tempura kind of thing on a vanilla bean, in sort of like a champagne flute with preserves at the bottom of it. They passed them out while we were standing around.

And then when everyone sat down Charlie thanked everyone and never mentioned Grant, didn't mention him once. And you know, at some point, Grant was like, I don't know why I keep coming back here, I come back out of respect. And he just does that shit.

RAY HARRIS: Charlie was clearly not as progressive as Grant and guys like that. He did have Wylie Dufresne [WD-50, New York] at some of the anniversary dinners, had him and Paul Liebrandt [Corton, New York] come and do some of the appetizers. So obviously he was aware of, watching the changes in the industry. But he definitely was not molecular, his brain couldn't think of the things these guys would think of. His big experimental thing was the raw cooking with Roxanne Klein, who was a self-taught chef and they did the raw cookbook together. So for a while I think he was doing three menus—the standard, the vegetarian and the raw.

Michelin to me has never gotten it right in the United States. Even today, I mean, if you go to Paris, I'm going to say there's eight three-stars. And there's probably thirty or forty two-stars, and 150 or 200 one stars. Then you come to Chicago which has a population in the metro area equal to Paris. And they give what, one or two three-stars, and maybe three or four two-stars and fifteen one-stars. But clearly it bothered him. Did it kill him? I wouldn't go that far. Did it contribute to him not being in a positive frame of mind? Absolutely.

SARI ZERNICH WORSHAM: Trotter always had four stars in *Chicago* magazine. And one day John Carroll [publisher of *Chicago* magazine] brought a copy over before it hit the newsstands. He brought a copy to Trotter and he said, hey, we knocked it down a half a star.

It was like devastation. Trotter called everyone into the salon for a meeting. And, you know, he read the review and all of us just, pit in your stomach time. Like we had failed, and Trotter, he was devastated. Like someone had died. I mean, obviously this is extreme, right? But this is how we all felt. I can't remember if it was three months or six months, because normally they wait a year to review you again. But they said, we'll come back in six months. And then he got his fourth star back.

****

In 2012 Charlie Trotter announced that his restaurant would close on its twenty-fifth anniversary.

SARI ZERNICH WORSHAM: In later years, he wanted to do more casual stuff. That's why he did Trotter's To Go [prepared foods]. When he was going to reconcept the restaurant before he decided to close it, he was going to do something a lot more casual. I think the world was shifting—we were all there at Trotter's when the market crashed. The people who had those baller expense accounts couldn't come out anymore.

Everyone was congratulating him on closing the restaurant. And he did not see it that way. You know, he saw it as a failure. After closing a restaurant [Bar Biscay, which closed during COVID] I finally understand why he shut down the auction [of the restaurant's effects], where they're putting pennies of value on things that meant so much to him. I now can see how even a little thing like selling a wine bucket for two bucks would make you crazy, right? I remember that night, I was there. And you know, we're all reminiscing. There's a lot of old friends and colleagues and customers out there, and we're all just having a good time. And he did not want to be there. It wasn't a fun time for him.

RAY HARRIS: When people talk about change at the end, I wasn't popping into Chicago that much, though we talked a lot. But when I did go, we were kind of always getting special treatment. So for me, it was always the same experience. He had top-notch people at the end, he had good sommeliers at the end. He wasn't doing as much business, I noticed when I did go there. Most nights, the three dining rooms were not open—maybe one or two.

He just got tired at the end. You're doing 140, 170 covers at the peak, you're doing it for twenty-five years, five nights a week for fifty weeks, plus whatever anniversary dinners and charity things he would do. He never took vacations—his vacations were that he'd be invited to cook with a chef in England or France or Spain.

One of the elements of the pressure on him was, people would go there and say, okay, this is supposed to be the best restaurant in Chicago, one of the best restaurants in America, in the world, and it's so expensive. So he couldn't put a B+ night out, he couldn't serve something on a scale of 100 that was 92 to 94, 95 to 97, he couldn't even do 99. People expected 100 percent perfection.

Tribune writer Mark Caro made national news with Trotter over Chicago's short-lived foie gras ban in 2006, which led to his book The Foie Gras Wars *(2011). He would be the writer covering Trotter's last days most extensively, notably in a five-part series shortly before Trotter's closed which aired much of the kitchen controversy, including the Beverly Kim lawsuit.*

MARK CARO: Phil Vettel said he had a story for me—that Charlie Trotter had quit serving foie gras. I called him up and he gave me his spiel, that it was cruel to the ducks. Now, he had published a game cookbook just a year or two before, which had like fourteen foie gras recipes in it.[13]

So I called a bunch of other chefs, and some of them were like, well, I respect Charlie's position, but I'm not there. Rick Tramonto [Tru] said, it's a little hypocritical. You're raising animals to kill them, I know Charlie serves veal. And so when I called Charlie back and I was giving him the rundown of what these different chefs that said, he's just like, well, Rick's not the smartest guy on the block, maybe we should serve Rick's liver as a treat, he's certainly

13 *Charlie Trotter's Meat and Game*, 2001.

fat enough. And I remember thinking, oh, my God, he's putting a story about duck livers on the front page of the *Tribune*. It had all the makings of something that the editors now would be like, this could go viral. Chef wars.

I talked to Charlie again and he sort of apologized, sort of, in that Charlie Trotter way of saying, well, you know, I might not have used the best words, but sometimes you have to open a can of whoop-ass.

I got to know Jeffrey Steingarten [food critic for *Vogue*] through my foie gras reporting. We had this really crazy meal at Trotter's. Charlie comes out and meets us in the front parlor. And he's like, I've got a special night planned for you—there was no sort of attempted anonymity or anything. Steingarten is like, so, have you called any other chefs fat pigs lately? And Trotter goes, oh, I was baited into that. I'm just standing there and I'm like, you were *not*. You absolutely were not, I have it on tape.

So Charlie takes us to a table for four, where two other people are already sitting—it's Louisa Chu [cook and later *Tribune* reviewer] and Albert Adrià, the brother of Ferran from El Bulli. And he's just decided that we're all going to sit together and have dinner together. They kept bringing out increasingly large wine glasses—the last glasses they brought out were like the size of the Stanley Cup. And at some point he brings out this 1930-something red, and he says to Steingarten, oh, you and Albert are really going to enjoy this. He pours some for Steingarten and some for Albert, and Louisa and I are just sitting there like, well, I guess *we* don't count. They didn't even bother bringing us glasses. They just brought it for the two of them and completely pretended we weren't there.

Trotter comes back a little later and he says to Jeffrey, so what did you think? And he says, you should have poured it through a coffee filter or something first, it's sediment. And Trotter never showed up again, didn't say goodbye. I just sort of thought, there's so much classic Charlie in that one evening—complaining that he was he was baited in the story, and then this whole sort of kissing up to them. If you're four-star hospitality, you don't—it's not like I *needed* to taste this wine. But you just don't. Not to people at the table.

It was a sad way to be for him to be. I felt bad for him, because I felt like he got in his own way. I remember when we were having this last interview on the phone, and I finally said, well Charlie, you're a complicated guy. And he's like, that's good, right? And I'm like, yes, it's good. That's why I'm writing a big series about you. You don't see me writing a big series about any other chef in town. I said, you're an interesting guy, you have a lot of complicated things going on. This is what it's about, I wouldn't think you'd have a problem with that.

Then he threw me out of his auction a few months later.

****

By the time he closed the restaurant in 2012, Trotter's health was declining, in part due to alcohol consumption, and he'd had at least one stroke, something not known publicly at the time. A little over a year after the restaurant closed, his son Dylan found him unconscious in his home.

DONA-LEE TROTTER: I don't know if he was burned out or what, but maybe there wasn't that challenge anymore. Or there's so many people out there kind of doing the same thing, maybe he would have moved on to something else.

MICHAEL TAUS: Two weeks before he passed away, I was working around the corner at Coppervine [wine bar] consulting for my friend, and I stopped at his house because I had some things I wanted to talk about with him. We just sat at the stoop talking, and he was always great. Giving me life advice, personal or about the business.

RAY HARRIS: He calls me on a Friday night, very peculiar. He calls me at home, which he never did, he always called my office. We talked for about forty-five minutes. He was totally sharp, totally lucid. That weekend he was going to Jackson Hole, and I said to him, Charlie, you're not supposed to fly, because of his aneurysm, plus you're going through Denver which is a mile-high city, you know the pressure in the plane. But it was typical Charlie, he had a whatever happens happens attitude. He says to me, I have two doctors, I checked with the one who says it's okay to fly. And that weekend he passed away. So I think, was he calling me because he was planning a new chapter in his life, or was he calling to say goodbye?

GUILLERMO TELLEZ-CRUZ: It was really sad what happened to him. I didn't know because I was still in New York. And I was always in touch with him.

Then one day I received a gift package. One of the things we went to was the last lunch of The Quilted Giraffe [in New York]. It was a plaque that says, thank you for being at The Quilted Giraffe on the last day, blah, blah, blah. And the letter is just, hello, Chef. I thought you might like this memento.

I didn't think anything of it, just, thank you very much, it's very kind of you. And he never responded back. Like, okay, and then I sent him a text and I called him and he didn't answer, that was kind of odd. Then later, I get another package. Just a letter signed by him, like, I thought you might enjoy to have this. Pictures of visiting Singapore, that he personally took and put together in a little book. So I keep getting these little things, you know, and I'm like, this is good, and then boom, I get the news.

****

PHIL VETTEL: When I got my job, Jean Banchet at Le Francais was the beginning and the end. That's where all the conversations were for—what's the best restaurant in Chicago? Where's the best place to go? But about that time, or just a couple of years after, Charlie Trotter had his restaurant. And that really started to change people's perceptions.

For one thing, Charlie was one of us, by which I mean, a Midwestern kid, grew up on the North Shore, went to the University of Wisconsin. And he opened his restaurant and people were just dazzled. I think that was that was the beginning of the end for the far-flung French restaurants—the Le Francaises and Le Titi de Parises, and places like Le Vichyssois that people would drive an hour and a half to get there and have a four-hour meal, and then drive home. It didn't happen overnight, but suddenly there was no compelling reason to leave the city.

MICHAEL TAUS: I think there's two kinds of people that worked at Trotter's: people that left in two or three months and said he was a dick, and people who said, he was my rock.

I don't think it'll ever happen again. It was an anomaly, just the right time in the right place. He was just so fascinating. He was such an intellect. Like it was my third day, he made me a cappuccino. I'm a big coffee fan, so was he, and we were talking about food. He was so excited. Like a scientist or whatever would be so geeked out talking about protons or whatever. We were just so excited about cooking. Every day coming in there, all these different cooks are talking about different people they worked for, different techniques. Because there was no Google then, right. So to get ideas we had to travel to New York and eat at five or six restaurants in three days.

TOM CORNILLE: Trotter was unique because he was bringing global standards to the United States, which was a difficult thing. Because the Europeans were smug. Especially in those days, very smug. So even the French expatriates who came to America, they were recognized, but not duly esteemed. But Charlie had a lot of money, a lot of influence, good PR, and made Europe come down to its knees and recognize the US. And even more so his little empire, his domain, because you couldn't help but love Charlie Trotter's. He was personable beyond belief.

ROBERT HOUDE: I remember he actually told me once that fine dining was going away. That this was a dying art.

PAULA HOUDE: Charlie could do some crazy things, you hear these wild stories about some of that. In the end, he always picks kindness and he picks family, and he cared about his people, even though sometimes he didn't go about it the right way. He did a lot of good, a lot more good than he did bad. And I think that's one of the things that Robert and I focus on now [with The Trotter Project]. Because everybody's got a story. And I don't want to share the bad ones because he's gone. Why? Why talk bad about someone who's dead? There's no doubt in my mind or anyone else's mind that I know, he changed the entire culinary world. I mean, there isn't anybody that works in this industry that doesn't go, oh yeah, he influenced me, in one way or the other.

SARI ZERNICH WORSHAM: As someone who's had restaurants now, you *can't* treat your team the way we were treated. You cannot. There were a lot of great traits that I consider great traits, some people may think they aren't. But the make-it-happen attitude is definitely something we all got out of those doors.

CURTIS DUFFY: I think Trotter's was by far the hardest restaurant I've ever worked. Even after opening a few of my own, and being the chef and being the owner, and now having multiple restaurants. It was probably the most rewarding restaurant that I ever worked at, before opening my own, of course. It just was fulfilling in every way. Personally and professionally. It was challenging on a daily basis. There was never a level of comfort there. And I liked that because it was you always had to be on. And how long can you maintain that mental focus? That was a constant fight. But me, as a young cook, I loved that.

LESLIE TELLEZ: Everything that Charlie taught me, I pretty much pass on to my people here. And that's just to respect the food and the flavors that it gives you and to let the food speak for itself. That's what he taught, and it took a while to figure that out. Because there's a lot of cheats, like, hide it with a sauce. The hardest part is to find the true beauty of the food and let it speak for itself.

There was so much that he taught us, just how to be people out in the world. He would take us out across the world and do events, and the interaction we had with other chefs from around the world was amazing. And as a person himself, he was great. His family was always there at the restaurant. His mother gave tours, you know? Yeah, it was hard. It was really, really hard. But like I said, I would never give it up. I learned so much and respect the gentleman so much for what he did, and what he gave us.

PATRICK CRANE: I definitely learned the pursuit of excellence, which has followed me throughout my life. It's in every task that I do. I cut the lawn, I cut the lawn on an angle. I clean a refrigerator, I only go up and down. That decision to perform at a high level runs throughout my life.

GUILLERMO TELLEZ-CRUZ: We're never going to be perfect. But if we don't strive for perfection, we're never gonna get anywhere.

JOHN WINTERMAN: There were obviously some negatives of working there. But I took away an overwhelmingly positive experience, and there's certain things I apply to my current restaurant—and certain things I don't.

8: MAKING HEADLINES

Culture was not a priority for the people who ran Chicago in the '50s and '60s. Mayor Richard J. Daley's cultural high point was commissioning a big outdoor sculpture from Pablo Picasso—reportedly the figure of a woman, but mocked by many as looking like a baboon.

By the time his son, Richard M. Daley, became mayor in 1989, Chicago was a different town—and culture, including food culture, had become essential to Chicago's image as a world-class city attracting creative-class workers. How local media covered food culture was one of the key drivers of that change—but only one; the city's own promotional efforts increasingly focused on food as a selling point, and together, the city and the media would work in parallel to make important expressions of Chicago's food culture, like the farmers market Green City Market, a key attraction for what was, by then, recognized as one of the world's great restaurant cities.

CHICAGO MAGAZINE

If a publication and its restaurant reviewers were ever in the right place at the right time, it was Chicago *magazine and its editors and lead critics, Allen and Carla Kelson. Beginning in 1968, they took the program guide for a classical music radio station and turned it into a glossy lifestyle magazine—and did so right at the moment when Chicagoans were starting to embrace dining as culture and recreation. As the* Tribune *wrote in 1993, "For more than 20 years, Allen and Carla Kelson were the most powerful restaurant critics Chicago has ever seen. Through their reviews and columns in* Chicago *magazine, the husband-and-wife team were reputed to be able to make or break restaurants and send chefs into despair if a dish was deemed overseasoned or sloppily presented."*

Allen Kelson was working as a catalog copywriter for Sears—which he called "the easiest job in the world"—and also writing radio ads for Sears that aired on classical station WFMT, which in 1968 offered him a side gig doing their program guide. Among the content that fleshed out the broadcast listings for its "select" audience: restaurant reviews.

ALLEN KELSON: The program guide turned out to be a full-time job, because I had to set all the type on an IBM electric typewriter. And then when the thing got printed somewhere in Iowa, I had to take it around to all the record shops. And in my spare time, I was supposed to sell advertising for the radio station—which I never did.

At first I wrote under my own name. Eventually, we started using Carla's name as well, because I knew I was gonna lose her because I was spending so much time on the magazine that she was starting to resent my listening to WFMT.

She had majored in art in college. By this time we had typesetters, but it had to be cut apart and pasted together. And so she got a group of her friends together, I'd come home at night, give her all the layouts and the type. And they'd put it together overnight. That was when Carla was pregnant with our second child, our daughter. And she got labor pains the night we were finishing up the magazine. I called my assistant and I said we're going to be swinging by, we're on our way to Michael Reese Hospital. And you stay out on the curb. I'll call you when we get onto Michigan Avenue, and I'll give you the pages.

The restaurant reviews soon became the program guide's main draw for readers and advertisers. WFMT spun it into a full-fledged glossy magazine in late 1970, with Allen as its editor and Carla, ultimately, as dining editor, jointly writing a monthly column including reviews, and overseeing a section of capsule reviews in the back of the magazine—the first publication to offer such a comprehensive guide to the Chicago restaurant scene.

It was a very fortuitous time for restaurants. We were just starting to get jet travel from Europe into Chicago. Julia Child was just coming on to public TV. And people were going to restaurants for entertainment, and to taste real foreign food, not Chicago's imitation foreign food. Eating became a major pastime.

There was nobody doing legitimate restaurant reviews in Chicago then. The *Sun-Times* had a paid page of restaurant advertising. The *Tribune*, which had had some great restaurant critics in the past, just had one woman who did kind of sketchy restaurant reviews. She knew what she was talking about, but she did it in a very superficial way.

The nice thing about Chicago was that the neighborhoods were not as homogenized as they are now. And you could go into a Czech neighborhood, there'd be four or five tables and for three and a half bucks, you could get a complete dinner, with a duck. The husband would tend to be the waiter, and the wife was in the kitchen, working at a four-top stove. And she was making homemade food. It was really exciting to discover all of these cuisines that we were really unaware of. Only the people who lived in those neighborhoods where it was the food of their childhood ate that food.

The first restaurant I reviewed was the Parthenon [in Greektown]. I didn't know what the hell I was doing. I talked to the owner of the restaurant [Chris Liakouras], and he was explaining everything to me. And the restaurant became an immediate success, because we had a lot of readers in Hyde Park [home to the University of Chicago]. He wanted to take Carla and me to Greece.

I learned not to identify myself to restaurateurs pretty quickly. But I didn't realize until I stopped reviewing restaurants, nineteen years later, that everybody knew who I was. And they didn't let on. They had pictures of me in the kitchen. And they always made sure I got the hot food hot, and the cold food cold.

We tried to be as fair as we could. If a restaurant was taking out an ad, and they were going to get slammed in that issue, I would call the restaurant and say, I suggest you not run your ad this month. It just seemed fair to me. And if a place seemed good to me, but I suspected others weren't having the same experience I was, we'd send another couple of reviewers the same night we were going back to make sure everything was as it was the first time. We would meet in the johns and exchange information. Eventually, we had, I think, eight teams of critics. Mostly they were married couples. If it was an Asian restaurant, we would automatically send six people, so they could try a wider variety of dishes.

I remember the last year's budget I did, I allotted $50,000 for food. Not counting what we paid the reviewers—just for food bills. I'm sure none of the newspapers could come close to that. So we'd encourage people to go to a restaurant three, four times, or we'd have two parties go the same night.

PENNY POLLACK (assistant to Carla Kelson): I knew the Kelsons because we lived in Highland Park—our daughters were friends. And my second husband and I became the fairly constant dinner companions, because when you go on a review, you need more mouths. So I was already in the culture of what reviewing was about and how it was handled. We would pass the plates around. It was very cloak-and-dagger, looking back on it. We were literally like, is anybody looking, and then we would pass our plates to the right. I can't believe a smart waitstaff didn't figure that out. But small plates had not been invented yet, so we had to do that to try everything.

We didn't write about a place unless it had been visited. And it had to be open at least six weeks before a visit; today the reviews are out as soon as it's open. And then there had to be at least three visits, all anonymous. My worst nightmare was when a restaurant was in our main column, and it closed before we were on the newsstand.

I kept track of how many months it had been since a restaurant had been visited. It would go on assignment again. And it would be re-reviewed and there would be a piece of new copy that said "another helping," which would be longish. And then the next month the "another helping" symbol would go away and it would be edited down. In those thick pages there must have been two hundred-plus reviews.

I called every restaurant every single month and confirmed that they were still in business. I'd go over their hours and we'd list whether they served breakfast, lunch, dinner, all the nuts-and-bolts information. But I would talk to someone every month. Oh, do you still have lunch? Which credit cards they took, all this granular information. And I think that over the years without understanding why or how, the public just became totally dependent on us for information, in addition to the critique.

I absorbed what it was about, and I would read every review, and pretty soon I knew how to write a review, because there's a formula. So from a divorced mom whose only skill was typing, I evolved into this person. And because I made all those calls all those years, and because I opened all the mail, and because I read all the press releases, and because I followed up on anything that seemed like a lead, I developed an amazing relationship with the entire restaurant community. Because they know me. Oh, it's Penny. And I am proud to say that I'm in good standing with the restaurant community today.

ALLEN KELSON: We rated them on ambience, service, menu variation, food quality and value. Carla and I, when we were driving home from a restaurant and it was still fresh in our minds, we'd leave the recorder running and I'd take down her scores. And I would average them with mine, fifty-fifty. And any other reviewers who went we would add theirs, fifty-fifty.

But it was hell finding reviewers. We probably had to audition a dozen people for every one we would take, because if somebody gave a place all ones, they were out. All fives they were out. If they said anything was tasteless, they were out. Because everything has a taste.

We liked to introduce readers to new places and new ideas, and chefs that they didn't know about. People saved up a lot of money to go to these restaurants, and we owed it to them to find good places for them. We didn't write a lot of negative reviews. We ran a listing of recommended restaurants. And all of us who had written up a restaurant and gone to it agreed on the listing for the restaurant and decided how many stars to give it. Four stars was the best you could give a restaurant. And then we used our pen names at the end so people could decide whose tastes they agreed with. Carla and I wrote under the pen name Archy. I picked Archy because Archy was a cockroach [in poems by Don Marquis] and he knew a restaurant kitchen better than anybody.

ANNE SPISELMAN (reviewer for *Chicago*, as "Pip"): I got involved because my then-boyfriend, David Novick, wanted to write for *Chicago* magazine. He wrote a letter to *Chicago* magazine full of terrible food puns—like, "you'll never roux the day you hired us." So Allen Kelson sent us on some trial reviews. This is so long ago that I did everything on an electric typewriter—'78 or '79.

We wrote capsule reviews, and we also did the budget beat for a while. We would get a list of assigned restaurants, to go to in any order we wanted. In most cases, it would be a visit with two people. So we go and have the dining experience and come back. And if we were not recommending that it should be listed, we just turned in a set of notes. And if we did recommend it, we would turn in the set of notes plus a brief review for the back of the magazine—actually two versions, one for the first time it was listed and a shorter one for subsequent appearances in the magazine. And for this rather considerable amount of work, we got paid sixty bucks.

Various people did this various ways—Allen recorded his notes into a microphone hidden in his tie. In our case, I just remembered everything and wrote it up the next morning. I have a pretty good memory, and I figured that anything that I didn't include in my notes didn't matter that much.

One of the first things that happened when we started as reviewers was, David was invited to an event at a restaurant. And they informed us that they would send a car to pick us up. And I told Allen about this, because I wasn't sure about the ethics. And he explained very clearly, that no one working for the magazine accepted anything free from anybody. When we were there, they had very rigorous standards about everything. And we always adhered to them, in terms of the anonymity, and always paying.

I remember one occasion when we were sent to—I think it was Jacques, on the same night as the Kelsons, and it was a vastly different experience. We both ordered the same shrimp appetizer. In theirs, they got nine shrimp, and we got four. And then at the end of the meal, they ordered cappuccinos and got them fine. I think we ordered espresso. And we were told the machine was broken. I guess they didn't feel like making it.

In 1986 the magazine was sold to a group out of Detroit, and Allen Kelson was replaced as editor and reviewer; Carla remained dining editor. He started consulting for restaurants as well as freelancing for other publications—a throwback to his early days making several different gigs into a living. But the world of reviewing had become more rigorous about potential conflicts of interest, and in 1992, when Carla edited a Top 25 restaurant list which omitted the most famous restaurant in town—Le Francais, in the Roland and Mary Beth Liccioni era—there was talk that it was because Le Francais had not hired Allen as a consultant, which he strongly disputed.

ALLEN KELSON: I was doing freelance for restaurants, coaching them on what they were telling their customers to expect, by the way they describe things on their menu, by the typefaces they were using, and by what they were saying and spelling wrong. And I would only go to restaurants that were ready to say they needed fixing. And anytime I was going to work with a restaurant, I would tell them that there is no connection between my work and their coverage.

There was a guy whose restaurants I was criticizing. And when we decided who was going to be honored as one of the best restaurants, all the restaurant critics would sit down and discuss. And his wasn't good enough. So he sent a letter to the magazine saying that there was a cancer growing in the restaurant department. And that's because he didn't win the award. Well, if anything that proved to me that there *wasn't* a cancer growing.

ANNE SPISELMAN: That was patently untrue. I don't think the reviewing decisions had anything to do with his consulting work, in terms of what to review.

ALLEN KELSON: Carla, at that time, was the restaurant editor, and she made the assignments. And if she didn't assign me to a restaurant that I was working with, that was just fine—I preferred that. But the editor decided that she had a bias, and he had Penny Pollack, who was her assistant, take over her job. We sued, but we just gave up on it because we didn't want to fight it in court. That would have been too expensive.

In 1993 Penny Pollack became dining editor, a job she held until 2017.

PENNY POLLACK: The dining department was like an island. It just ran by itself. And no one knew how stuff got done. Richard Babcock [editor in chief] called me into his office and asked, can we just run the listings the way they are? And I'm like, no, no, no, they change every month. "They do?"

But I got the next issue out, with some help from another editor. And a few months went by, and my sister-in-law said, you should ask for the job. So I did, and I think Dick's cheeks got rosier, he was so relieved. So Dick is my hero, because he gave me my chance and I was there for thirty years.

Penny Pollack would remain dining editor until 2017—and a very different media environment. Allen Kelson continued working with restaurants, including for Lettuce Entertain You, and taught at culinary schools; Carla worked for the Chefs Catalog retail chain and for the Chicago Fund on Aging and Disability. She died in 2021; he died in 2023.

Chicago *magazine is still one of the leading sources for restaurant reviews in Chicago, though the world has returned to what it was like when Allen Kelson first started reviewing for the WFMT program guide—most reviewers are freelance, often supporting themselves with other food-related gigs . . . and nobody much worries about it.*

CHICAGO TRIBUNE

The Chicago Tribune *had had food coverage as long as grocery stores existed to advertise in the paper, but dining out was often a secondary aspect of it. As food became more important culturally in Chicago in the 1970s and '80s, the* Tribune *paid it more attention—in different ways in different sections of the paper.*

Carol Mighton Haddix was a writer and food editor at the Tribune *for thirty-four years, from 1977 to 2011. Her Thursday food section was primarily cooking-focused, but it did include one popular restaurant review section—Cheap Eats.*

CAROL MIGHTON HADDIX: I went to Michigan State and majored in home economics, with a minor in journalism. I was very interested in design, interior design, and not food so much. But when I got to the *Detroit Free Press*, and started working in the fashion department of all things—entry-level job—I made friends with the food editor there, and she started me on testing recipes for her. And we would throw these wonderful parties, inviting all the staff members to partake in these recipe tests. It was really fun. And I decided that the people in the fashion world were just not people I wanted to know, compared to the people in the food world, who are for the most part pretty darn friendly and easygoing. Totally different scene.

At the *Free Press*, I made friends with all the editors at the *Tribune*. So when I heard about this job in '77, I called them up. It was the easiest job process in the world.

Cheap Eats really was one of the most popular things that we did. People would call and recommend places and it was fun. Wherever people lived, these were the restaurants they went out to and enjoyed. And the staff and I, we would just cruise the neighborhoods looking for places. Something would look good, and you'd stop and try it. I mean, I had a lot of bad food, because you're going in cold. You didn't know.

So that's all I did, was occasionally run out to a different ethnic restaurant here or there in the neighborhoods. The main reviews were in the Friday section, totally separate. But we would do stories, you know, dealing with all kinds of food issues, from consumer stories to just talking to chefs and getting their recipes and how they do certain dishes. So we had contact with a lot of the chefs in town.

JUDY HEVRDEJS (*Tribune* writer): The Thursday food section, traditionally, was how to cook. So that's where those stories kind of went. The fine dining would go into the weekend section, as opposed to being in the cooking section.

I'd known there were quite a few ethnic communities around the city that had good food, and I thought, for the fifty dollars they're charging some places, you could get really good eats for much less than that. There's also the cultural piece. I thought it was important that we celebrate Chicago's multicultural immigration patterns that have come here and brought different tastes to the table. Because my parents grew up in Pilsen [Slavic turned Mexican neighborhood], we knew a lot of different foods.

The Cheap Eats column was not only about hey, this would taste good. Nothing against the critic with a palate who goes out there and really make a statement about how a restaurant tastes. But I thought it was a way for people who might not have the cash to lay out for a fancy meal, to enjoy food from a different culture. I love the diversity of Chicago, and helping to open up people's eyes.

CAROL MIGHTON HADDIX: I always enjoyed trying to find the odd cuisine, which wasn't always easy. Obviously there was Italian food everywhere, and pizza, and the Chicago classics. But I always enjoyed going out to places like Himalayan [Nepalese restaurant in a strip mall in Niles, in the near northwest suburbs]. We were trying to get a wide wide range of cuisines. Personally I like telling people about new things, new dishes, here's what this is made out of. And how it tasted. There's plenty of different neighborhoods and cuisines out there. I mean, it seems like Italian is never-ending, right?

Paula Camp, as Paul Camp, was brought in when food culture started taking off in the early 1980s, as the editor for Taste, yet another food section—in the Sunday magazine. Camp would become the lead reviewer through the '80s.

PAULA CAMP: The *Tribune* was taking food very seriously. It was considered one of the best food sections in the country, and they had a kind of food lifestyle section called Taste, which was very innovative. They sold eighty thousand more copies of the paper on food day, Thursday. We'd love to take credit for that with the wonderful content that Carol was putting in there—but it was probably the coupons and the circulars.

They brought me from New York to revive Taste, which was dying. And by the time I got here, it had died. So I was a food editor looking for a job, and not wanting to take Carol's, because I had and still have great respect for her. Eventually, I went to my boss and said, look, you don't have a restaurant critic, let me be the restaurant critic. I didn't mention to him that I'd been fired from a restaurant critic job earlier in my career.

I tried my best to be anonymous, I had credit cards in the names of several other people. But I was made at Gordon early on. His publicist knew what I looked like, and I knew it. So the second time I went, I sent in a group of people to order for me, and then I timed my entrance to about the time of the appetizers. So they couldn't change a lot by then. They seated my party right next to a busing station. And immediately after getting there, they tried to move the busing station and dropped the whole Rubbermaid thing full of dishes. It was quite comical, and I think I wrote about this.

As a restaurant critic, I lived to find the little Mexican place or the little Polish place, or the Lithuanian place that was doing fabulous food in their neighborhood location and cost ten bucks for the whole deal. While that still exists, it's no longer the big calling card that it was back in the late '70s and early '80s. Chicago could say, I think rightly, that it was one of the most diverse ethnic restaurant cities in America. There was influence from the west, influence from the east, influence from south of the border, influence from Europe, and each ethnic group had its own restaurants, many of them very modest.

I think the emphasis on it and the delight of discovery is not what it used to be. There were almost no chain restaurants that were successful in Chicago then, because there was such a strong and chauvinistic following for Chicago restaurants. There's less feeling now that we have to support our local restaurants before we go to the chain restaurants. I think that's a real loss.

I got more hate mail for sending people to Lem's [BBQ stand in a majority Black neighborhood on the South Side] than I got for any other review I ever wrote. People didn't want to know about it—I thought, egotistically I guess, that they *needed* to know about it. We literally would rent a van and take 6, 7, 8 people and we would spend an entire afternoon and evening tasting ribs, or pizza, or hamburgers, and sometimes it was really rough work. We'd gather all the opinions—it wasn't just based on mine. But the idea that there is good food on the deep South Side, or that there is a Chicago rib tradition, and it's worth knowing that that tradition exists and tastes a little different from Carson's [rib chain on the whiter North Side], was, I think, worth doing.

I've forgotten when my first review ran, but it was Avanzare, so if we find out when that opened [1982], we'll have an idea. So it was from the early '80s until 1990. By that time, I was one of the features editors, I was doing the food section. Carol nominally worked for me—but she did her own thing. And several of the other features sections were my responsibility. I'd started a new fashion section for the *Tribune* at that point. And I was writing three columns a week and it seemed like a little bit much. So we appointed Phil Vettel as the new restaurant critic.

PHIL VETTEL: I started out at the suburban *Tribune*. They let me do their restaurant reviews, based on the fact that I had once worked as a busboy. Then when I got downtown, I would do work for the critic at the time, pinch-hitting every now and then. We used to do these dining guides, where we'd have little capsule reviews of everything, divided by styles of food. The editors would go through it and say, wow, we're a little light on, say, German food. And they'd give me a hundred bucks and I'd go eat German food for a week.

And then at some point, they just offered me the full-time job. And luckily, there was the kind of funding available then that if I were going to take on, say, the first time I wrote about a Thai restaurant, the first thing I did was eat at five other Thai restaurants. To get some kind of taste memory going, some sort of base of what the state of the art was in Chicago. And I'd work off that. I don't know how I'd do it these days, because that money's not available anymore.

In the suburbs, if you could recommend a place, fine, and if you couldn't recommend a place you'd just tear up your notes and not say anything. They were acutely aware of how devastating a bad review could be, and they weren't about to let you just run free that way. [At the *Chicago Tribune*] you didn't want to bring the hammer down on some out of the way place on Webster Avenue, and it sucks. You don't want to bully them—the market's going to take care of that sad sack in no time. But Rich Melman kind of took the Spaghetti Factory model and opened it in Aurora. And it was terrible, so I didn't feel bad saying, you want to give Rich your money, by all means, but here are eighteen other restaurants he has that are all better than this one.

Vettel's best-known competition during much of his run was Pat Bruno at the Sun-Times.

PHIL VETTEL: Probably about five or six times over the years, we found ourselves in the same restaurant, when we would sort of acknowledge each other without acknowledging each other, one little furtive nod. Never spoke a word.

He didn't have the responsibility of covering any of the chef news like I did. He wasn't full time, ever. He was on a freelance basis. But he was very thorough and a passionate defender of Italian foods. And it used to drive him nuts whenever any national group would list, like, the best restaurants in America, and Italian restaurants would be underrepresented. That would infuriate him. He would write a letter or work it into a column or something like that. He was as fierce a defender of Italian cuisine as there ever was.

****

The seriousness with which the Tribune *approached food by the 1980s was demonstrated in 1986 when they recruited William Rice, a graduate of Le Cordon Bleu in France who had been food editor for the* Washington Post *and an editor of* Food & Wine. *His influence was not only on how the* Tribune *covered food, but how the* Tribune *advocated for a certain idea of what a food-cultured city should be—an idea which included farmers markets for chefs and shoppers.*

MARGARET SHERIDAN (*Tribune* writer): Bill Rice and Jill Van Cleave [cookbook author] met at some event out west. They started dating, and commuting because Bill was in DC and Jill was in Chicago. So somehow [*Tribune* management] were talking to Bill and Bill agreed to come to Chicago. And that was mind-blowing for everyone in our food department. We were just beside ourselves because we so admired his work at the *Washington Post.*

He brought expertise and he had amazing resources. He knew people—if you needed to talk to someone about shellfish or something, try this guy, he's a good friend. He was very, very generous in that.

JUDY HEVRDEJS: Bill was wonderful. He was a man of the world, and he brought a kind of international flair to Chicago. Everybody really admired him a lot. I really admired how he looked at things. With Bill, I felt it was a different view of the world on a culinary level. Yes, we can read cookbooks. And we can meet a French person for five minutes or a chef for twenty minutes. But he would make suggestions. He was a terrific co-worker in the sense that he was able to help you and kind of knock it out of your brain.

He also had a great sense of humor, and it was great to have a glass of wine with him. And Jill, she adored him. Both of them were great.

MICHAEL FOLEY: Bill was a master of trying to get people together. Whatever he wrote, for the *Tribune* or *Food & Wine*, he was very passionate about exposing people to each other and to good food. And he really had such a great talent for helping people get known.

Monique Hooker [chef, Monique's] and I told Bill, we want to collectivize the [wholesale] market and get more purveyors in here. So we worked with the mayor at the time, Harold Washington, and said we're very interested in creating these farmers markets. And [Richard M.] Daley in his terms pushed us even further, he was very much into food and beverage—the cosmetics of the city. This is the very early stages of when Arnie Morton and everybody was trying to put together the Taste of Chicago [summer food and music festival in Grant Park]. So we got them to do the farmers market at Navy Pier, on Saturday mornings.

INA PINKNEY (breakfast restaurant owner): When Bill Rice contacted me about doing a story, I knew who he was because he was married to my friend Jill. He chose the pasta frittata and the whole wheat oatmeal pancakes and the scrapple with chorizo and eggs. I watched from behind the bakery case as he ate and took notes.

When he was finished, he asked me to sit down and give him the backstory of how and why I decided on a fine dining breakfast restaurant with unusual food and superb coffee. I told him that I loved hotel dining rooms and diners, and there was nothing in the middle, so I decided to create that niche and make it my own.

He asked if we had gotten any press and I said he was the first. I told him that I wasn't being taken seriously because I was just an old lady making breakfast. He replied, ha, just you wait! Everyone will take you seriously because you just changed the landscape of breakfast in Chicago! He wrote a glowing two-page story with photos and recipes for the *Chicago Tribune* Sunday Magazine. I cried.

Bill Rice retired from the Tribune *in 2003; he died in 2016.*

FARMERS MARKETS

Farmers markets—offering a mix of produce, baked goods and crafts—were common enough in the '80s, though any relation to actual farmers was often coinci-

dental. In 1989 the Tribune *sponsored a new kind of farmers market, the Best of the Midwest market at Navy Pier, bringing in produce and products from all over the Midwest. The reporter who wrote it up for the* Tribune *was Abby Mandel—who also happened to be the person who had organized it. Mandel was a writer and a consultant for food brands, who went to cooking school in Paris and would become the founder of the city's most influential and longest-lasting market, Green City Market, which she launched in Garland Court, better known as the alley next to the Chicago Theater, in 1999.*

PAT DAILEY (*Tribune* writer): My first job was at Don Roth's Blackhawk Lodge [a popular restaurant downtown, 1920s–1980s]. I did wine education for the waiters—wonderful waiters, but not really wine savvy. One night they sent me to this one table and told me to give them some special attention. Party of six, some people only spoke French, I mainly spoke with this big rotund guy. Toward the end he asks me if I have a Cuisinart—they were the hottest thing that ever happened then. I said no, not until I can afford one. Well, he says, I'm Carl Sontheimer, the president of Cuisinart, I'm going to send you one. And a couple of weeks later I've got a $250 Cuisinart at my door.

Well, it turns out the woman at the table was Abby Mandel, who was a big consultant for Cuisinart. Carl called me up and asked me if I would come work for Cuisinart. I said I didn't want to move to Connecticut, which is where it was based. So he had me work for Abby and he paid me. At the time, she was writing for the *Sun-Times*.

DAVID CLEVERDON (farmer, Kinnikinnick Farms): Abby went to Smith. And she told me how she started writing about food. She was a scholarship student from Chicago—not from the preppy world on the East Coast. She planned to be a social worker. And they wanted to have a small fundraiser with alumni in Chicago. There was another Smith graduate at this fundraiser, named Julia Child. And she brought this contraption, which was the first Cuisinart.

So Abby and Julia spent a weekend just messing around with it. And later, Cuisinart asked Julia to do a cookbook. And she said, I'm too busy to do that right now. But there is a great person in Chicago, who knows the machine and is very good, talk to her.[14]

PAT DAILEY: We eventually got into the *Tribune* with her column. And I was doing all of her ghostwriting. I was writing cookbooks. It was wonderful experience. The *Tribune*, while I was still working for Abby, called me up and said, hey, we know who's really doing the writing. Could you do a freelance column for us? And I'm like, over the moon, and I didn't really think it through because Abby, she had an ego, and I'm not saying that in any negative way. But I say, hey Abby, I have a column in the *Tribune*—well, the end was near for me with Abby.

I wrote about food for them for eight years. That's when there was that first farmers market that Abby organized at Navy Pier, or maybe it was the one on the alley off Garland Court. But she was hell bent on doing a California-type farmers market.

SARAH STEGNER (executive chef, the Dining Room at the Ritz-Carlton): As a young chef, when you think, what's going to distinguish my style? What's going to help my career? Is it something I need to study, or bring in? [Chef Fernand Gutierrez] sent me to France, and when I came back, he asked me, what did you learn? And I said, well, the thing that struck me was the overwhelming attention to the product. They were buying stuff every day, and they were selling it that night. And he's like, yes, you get it. So then it was a search for farms. And where I could get the best tomatoes and what's in season, and I started to infuse seasonality into my cooking, and it was the driving force for the menu.

I had done a series of cooking classes with Abby Mandel, and we were promoting these gorgeous copper pots. And I remember I made this just amazing spinach dish. And the way you make it is, you make an intense chicken stock, but very clean. And then you take the spinach, you give it a quick sauté, and you blend, and add a little bit of butter. And when you do that, it's like it explodes in your mouth. And there's some sweetness if you're using the right spinach at the right time of year, like a fall crop when the stems get really sweet.

14 *Abby Mandel's Cuisinart Classroom*, 1982.

So I'm explaining it to people, and then I say, but you guys can't make it because you don't have access to the best spinach. And it really dawned on me, this is ridiculous. This is really good, clean, healthy food. The farmers need income. And we're keeping this information, you know, out of the hands of the people that need it.

PORTIA BELLOC LOWNDES (co-founder, Slow Food Chicago): Abby came back from visiting Seattle and places like that, and truly believed that we needed a chef's market. That we needed a chef-driven market, because farmers needed to get their products in the restaurants. She knew we needed that to get consumers to buy into some of these new products when organic and sustainable weren't even in people's vocabulary, twenty-some years ago. Getting the products to the chefs and on menus can educate people, and then it's a win-win all around.

And the other thing too, that Abby felt very strongly about is that, up until Green City Market, somebody could be getting the stuff off of a truck on Maxwell Street, and there was a sticker on it and they were selling a watermelon in May. And she's like, that's not a farmers market.

So she felt the importance of farmers being present. The rules aren't as strict now, but in the beginning, the farmer had to be there. It was know your food, know your farmer. The idea is that you connect with the person—it isn't just that you walk up to the stand and buy the product. And so that person selling needs to understand how it's planted, what are the cycles, what's coming up next? What are the things that a farmer is dealing with? And convey that, because that part of our culture where our food comes from, is very tenuous. People really don't know, they're not connected.

DAVID CLEVERDON: Of everyone I've known on the Chicago food scene, Abby was the most farmer-centric. She'd be in a meeting, and finally she'd say, well, what about the farmers?

She organized the market in a typical Abby way, which was that she somehow got hold of some City of Chicago letterhead, and put, for the return address, her address in Glencoe. And with that piece of stationery, she organized the market. They were pissed off at that. The market existed at the sufferance of the police department, the park district, the Chicago Health Department, and the local alderman. It was, as an institution, always vulnerable. And somehow she managed to defend it on every front. And then it developed a life and a presence of its own, and it became hard to make an assault on it.

That's why it survived. She just was stubborn. She would proceed as if it was a fact. If that hadn't been the case, I don't think the market would have survived. She began on the wrong foot with the city, and Chicago generally destroys people who do that.

RICK BAYLESS (chef-owner, Frontera Grill): We would work with a farmer for a season. And then they would call us, or not, and say it's too much work, we can't do it anymore. And they could hardly supply us anything anyway.

Abby started doing these things that were just like a weekend in the fall, where she would put together all of these local producers. And you could go and buy some stuff there and taste things. So I was a big proponent of that and promoting it, and doing everything that I could to support it. And then she came to us and said she really wanted to turn it into a farmers market. She was really good friends with Alice Waters. And she said, Alice will come and do the kickoff, and we'll build this market. So our first market was where the Chicago Theater is. It was in that alleyway there. And we had six vendors. And I went down there for the first one, and my heart just sank, and I was like, oh, this is nothing.

And then after the first year up there, she said, I'm out. I'm done. It's just too hard. It's just squabbles and nobody's happy. And we're not getting enough people to come to it.

PAUL KAHAN (sous chef, Topolobampo): Nobody went there. And nobody shopped there. And she reached out to myself, Rick and Sarah Stegner and we had meetings with her for, you know, months and months and months.

RICK BAYLESS: We all said we're going to take it over. But we asked Abby to come to all of our meetings and help advise us and everything. And we were terrible. Nobody had enough time to do it. So after that horrible year of us trying to manage the market, Abby came back and said, no, I'll do it. I'll do it.

SARAH STEGNER: Rick Bayless had already started finding farmers, he and Michael Altenberg [chef-owner of Bistro Campagne] pioneered that. Once you were connected to one or two of the farms, you started to say, who else do you know? Where else can I get it from? And the farmers would kind of connect as a network.

Abby Mandel and myself and Linda Calafiore [director of the Cooking and Hospitality Institute of Chicago], we started Green City Market. Rick Bayless, Michael Altenberg and I were the primary chefs who came forward with names and shared them. Abby was the founder and I was one of the founding members, and it's still rockin' now, it's up to fifty farmers, all third-party-certified organic.

PAT DAILEY: There was a wonderful sense for consumers that you could really up your food game. And with focus on ingredients, it was like, wow, I can buy this. Look at these baby leeks, look at these wonderful, fresh strawberries or peas. And it was very exciting for home cooks, but then all of a sudden, it's like, whoa, they're pulling cases of stuff out and handing it directly to a chef. And that's when you realized that these markets were going to have a greater impact than just ensuring that somebody up in Glencoe makes really nice risotto. That the restaurants were getting involved and probably more important, or at least as important to its success as were consumers.

PORTIA BELLOC LOWNDES: Abby was so determined to have this market succeed that at the end of the market, if things hadn't been bought, she'd buy it all. She didn't want the vendors to go away and say, oh, that wasn't successful. She'd buy up inventory and then go hand it out to chefs. She was a force of nature, she could get anybody to do anything. Some people thought she was too much of a force.

DAVID CLEVERDON: She was a ballbuster, a powerful, powerful presence. We weren't participants at Green City when she started it—we were at the Evanston Farmers Market. And Saturday after Saturday, we had a very big stand at

Evanston, and I'd look up and she'd be there and Sarah Stegner would be right behind her staring darts at me, and she'd say, when am I going to see this at my market? She would just strong-arm people to join her market.

PORTIA BELLOC LOWNDES: Abby made farmers kind of like celebrities. Now you can say Nichols, you can say Green Acres to food people, and they know what you're talking about. And she drummed up so much excitement with the chefs. We would have chef's breakfasts in the beginning of the market. So chefs started hanging out at the market, and it became a great place for them to see one another and talk.

It's done nothing but grow. And it's like, one year, we would add more farmers. And they would all be freaked out that maybe there weren't going to be enough customers in the next year. But you'd see a huge increase in people, and it kept growing.

BRUCE SHERMAN (chef, North Pond, longtime Green City Market board member): Abby had started this thing with Sarah. But it was pretty small. And I felt like I could help broaden the market, not because of ego reasons, but to help get more farmers into it or growing more. Selfishly, yeah, sure, because I'm interested in having the product. But it seemed like a win-win for everybody. A lot of stuff that those farms were growing wasn't available, even grown conventionally. So people were attracted to something different, regardless of how it was grown. But that also helped get people over the hump of, I could get those carrots at Jewel for less.

For me, the notion of cooking seasonally was second nature. That's what I believe, that's what I did. I lived in France for a year, and then we moved to India. There weren't supermarkets where you got asparagus in December. You got what was coming from the land. So you just learned to cook that way. When we reopened [North Pond] in 2000, I changed the iconography and had the four icons representing a vegetable for each season. And I put up on the sign, North Pond. Seasonal cuisine. The fucking first question I got asked was oh, what seasons are you open?

DEAN ZANELLA (chef, 312 Chicago): Farmers didn't want to deliver at all.

They were like, this is what we do, you come to us. One farmer didn't want to deliver to me because we were down in the Loop and they delivered at night, and he thought the Loop was too dangerous. We had to work with them not just to get delivery, but on what they were growing. They would be like, oh, we've grown so much kohlrabi, everybody should use kohlrabi. I'm Italian. I'm not gonna use kohlrabi.

We had a long chat with a bunch of the farmers at Green City Market. Abby Mandel was there, Rick Bayless was there, Paul Kahan, myself, Bruce Sherman. We basically said, guys, it's nice that you want to grow X, Y, and Z. And we understand about rotation of crops. But here's what people are asking from us. And we had a long chat about, like, how come so much Swiss chard? I mean, it's nice. And I can use it in Italian cuisine. But, you know, if I do a dish with spinach on it, or dish with Swiss chard, I know how much I'm gonna sell. I can sell a ton of spinach and then sell very little Swiss chard.

DAVID CLEVERDON: You have people in the city whose fundamental view of farmers is that they're there to grow food for us. They don't understand what that entails, and they don't give a crap about the problems that farmers face. You ask a farmer to be at a market, he's going to get up at two or three in the morning, get down there, five to six in the morning, set up, he's got to stay there until one o'clock. He gets back around four or five. He's lost a day. He's lost one seventh of his week.

Once there was a winter market, we could diversify, from just produce to doing produce and livestock. And that changes the farm. It just changed the whole balance of what's possible for a local farm. That was a huge decision for us.

BRUCE SHERMAN: A permanent market just never happened for one reason or the other. But Abby was the proverbial "Get the fuck outta my way" CEO. Who wouldn't have stopped for "No" or "Let's talk about it next time."

DAVID CLEVERDON: She left money in her will for a permanent market, but it didn't happen, I don't know why. A permanent market is really tricky.

SARAH STEGNER: I think Green City Market was a tipping point that pushed

Chicago way, way out front of so many cities. I mean, it made us extremely competitive with San Francisco, LA and New York, because so many of the chefs were using local produce, the flavors and the respect for the product.

It kind of became trendy for a while. And unfortunately, I think that it is still not as mainstream as it should be. I mean, everybody knows farm-to-table, they get the expression. But what that actually means to people is very different. The understanding of the plight of the local farmer—it's not as supportive as it should be across the board. I still think we have a lot of work to do.

The core of it is that the food that's at the market is there to show people, this is what you can eat that's delicious in the Midwest, go home and make it. It's to say, look, we're limitless with how good it can taste. And you don't need to add anything but what is right here in the Midwest, because that's what's sold at this market. That was the message. Any of the food there is a showcase of what the Midwest bounty can be, that was the philosophy.

Abby Mandel died of mantle cell lymphoma in 2008, but Green City Market continues twice a week in season in Lincoln Park; it has spawned satellite markets and served as the model for markets in neighborhoods all over the city.

THE MAYOR OF RESTAURANT CITY

By the 1990s, dining was viewed by Chicago officials as a key selling point for the city—if Wheeling's mayor had once been "the Mayor of Le Francais," Chicago's mayors would be the mayors of an entire, internationally recognized food scene.

Judith Dunbar Hines served as Director of Culinary Arts and Events for Chicago's Department of Cultural Affairs. Her account of how she first started working for the city—and for behind-the-scenes powerhouse Lois Weisberg, appointed the city's first Commissioner of Cultural Affairs by Mayor Richard M. Daley in 1989—shows how the city supported, and made use of, Chicago's hot restaurant culture.

JUDITH DUNBAR HINES: I became the manager of a food conference, the International Association of Culinary Professionals, in the spring of '97. It was huge, and pretty international. We ended up having something like 1,750 attendees, which was the most they'd ever had.

I had attended maybe twenty by that point, And what I remembered about every conference was that I couldn't remember what city they were held in. And I thought, if we're going to do it in Chicago, I want people to leave knowing they'd *been in Chicago.* My focus was going to be that it was about the town and what it had to offer. So as we developed programming, I tried to do as much as I could outside the hotel, and get people into the city so that they would know what was going on here.

Along the way, I thought I should find out about the Chicago Office of Tourism, long before it was Choose Chicago, actually see what they had to say, and whether they had anything to offer me. So I made an appointment at the Cultural Center, and a young woman came down to meet with me. And I started telling her this whole thing, and her eyes kind of lit up and she said, you have to meet Lois. Well, I knew who Lois was.

So I met with Lois Weisberg, and Lois got it right away. I had all these ideas, like I was going to build a little museum in the hotel of all the things that had been invented here, anything food, which meant hard goods as well as food items. And I was going to put a piano in the hospitality suite, and hire a pianist to play blues and jazz and gospel, all that kind of stuff that they've never done at a conference before. So Lois said to this young woman, okay, you help her any way you can to do this. They did help me, they gave me materials, they gave me ideas. So I did the conference.

And you know, you go to those conferences, you're exhausted at the end of them. I didn't even want to take a shower or anything, I just wanted to lay on the couch. And I got a phone call. It was Lois's assistant who said the commissioner wants to see you, can you come down? And I said, sure. And she said, can you come down this afternoon? Oh no, what have I done? I thought I must have done something really horrible. But I roused myself off the couch and got down there, shaking.

She said, you know, I went to your conference. I said, you did? What did you think? Holding my breath. She said it was great. Can you do it again? What? There was a big conference coming the next year, a tourism conference. Had nothing to do with food. But she said, you know, we're going to have two thousand people. And I want to do the kinds of things you did to really focus on Chicago. So can you go to Nashville to their conference this year? See what they do? And then come home and tell me how we can make it better. Okay, I said, I can go to Nashville and do that for you. And she said they're meeting now, can you go there? Yeah, as soon as I wash my hair!

So I did that, and I spent quite a long time writing up a report of how we could blend those two things or other things we could do, blah, blah, blah. And I took that in to her, thinking okay, I've done my little project. She looked it over, and as I was thinking we were done with this meeting, she said, well, you're not done, you know, you have to make this happen. And so I was then hired, and that's the beginning of eighteen years of doing that job of promoting food in Chicago, any way I could.

It wasn't just restaurants—it was packing plants and test kitchens and all of that stuff. But the most visible part was promoting restaurants. And people would come in from other cities, and say, tell me about your job, we want to do that in Tampa, or Vegas. I would tell them what I was doing. But nobody could do it, if they hadn't had the magic combination of Richard M. Daley and Lois Weisberg, because those two people loved the food business. Look through media and every publication was saying Chicago was the place to go and place to eat and that it would not have happened without those two people and their vision about how to promote that aspect.

Mayor Daley, the handlers used to lose him at events and they'd be stirring around going, what happened to the mayor, where's the mayor? I'd say he's in the kitchen, he's with the chef. And they go in and he'd be sitting there at one of the silver tables banging his hands on top of the counter, asking them, what do you need?

9: CHICAGO EATS WORLD

Charlie Trotter's was rightly seen as the pivotal Chicago restaurant of the 1980s and 1990s, forging an American style of high-end cooking that could compare with the best cuisine and service worldwide. But two other Chicago restaurants which opened around the same time as Trotter's, in the mid-1980s, would prove to be of similar influence and importance to Chicago—working not in a French tradition, but with two more humble cuisines, elevating Italian and Mexican food in Chicago from peasant food served in family-owned neighborhood spots to serious artisanal fare downtown.

Both also lasted longer than Trotter's twenty-six years—thirty-seven years for Spiaggia, and thirty-eight and counting, at this writing, for Frontera Grill. Both were deeply dedicated to using products from the Midwest. Each maintained a dialogue with their source of inspiration in their respective countries. And both moved the working atmosphere in their kitchens away from the harshness of the French brigade tradition, pioneering a more supportive environment for young talent, including sending them to learn in the countries that inspired their restaurants.

THE ITALIAN AMERICAN

Italian food spread rapidly in Chicago after World War II. But what Chicago called Italian food was mostly Southern Italian food, from Sicily or provinces like

Calabria in the poorer south, which had seen mass emigration to America before and between the wars. Chicago Italian food was thus heavy on acidic tomatoes and garlic (unless garlicphobe Frank Sinatra was dining tonight, as he often did at favorite Chicago-area spots like Italian Village or Slicker Sam's). It was only in the late '70s and '80s that we started seeing a lighter form of Italian food, inevitably dubbed "Northern Italian"—though few knew what, exactly, that meant.

A number of restaurants appeared that were cooking in this style, but the most ambitious and influential new Italian restaurant in that time would be a flagship restaurant on Michigan Avenue for the Levy Restaurants group: Spiaggia. For the first time in Chicago, Italian food was as carefully crafted as French—and commanded similar prices. The chef behind it was an emigre to Chicago—not from Sicily, but from Kenosha, Wisconsin.

TONY MANTUANO: My family didn't have restaurants. As I got into restaurants, in Milwaukee, my brother bought a little building in Kenosha. And we had a little place there for twenty-some-odd years that my sister ran, but we weren't really a restaurant family prior to that at all.

I was going to University of Wisconsin–Milwaukee as a music major. I started working in restaurants to help put me through college, and I realized that I liked cooking a lot more than I liked playing the trombone. So I started working at a restaurant that was run by this European chef named Kurt Weber. He was an amazing chef, and I was lucky just to stumble into that position and learn from him. In 1975, we were working with products like langoustines, stuff you'd never seen before.

Kurt was Swiss-born, and trained in a lot of cuisines including French and a little bit of Italian. But just working with those ingredients back in 1975, I don't know where else I would have learned that. It was in a hotel called the Astor Hotel, and even doing like, breakfast cooking, where you're the only one cooking and just learning how to time everything, it was quite a learning experience.

I moved up to dinner. Toward the end of my five years there Kurt said, why don't we do an Italian night. We did it once a week and I started cooking some of the dishes I knew, even not having been to Italy yet. And it was a big success, but I knew I had to go somewhere else to grow my career, there wasn't anything else in Milwaukee then. It was a great experience, though. I learned a hell of a lot, and I met my wife there.

Cathy and I moved to Chicago in 1980, and I started working at a restaurant at 200 East Chestnut, called Pronto. The novel thing about that place was that we were making all our pasta, in the front of the restaurant facing the street. We had a full-time pasta person making pasta every day. The uniqueness of working with fresh pasta every single day in 1980 was a really good experience.

When he hired me, the owner had a chef who was an older Italian American gentleman—he was probably the age I am now, heh—and when I got there, it was like, man, he's using so many weird shortcut ingredients, like freeze-dried onions, or cooking off all the veal scalloppini before the shift and rewarming it in the marsala sauce or whatever it was. I worked for him for about two weeks and then the owner pulled me into his office, and said, Dominic's going on vacation for two weeks and when he comes back, I'm going to let him go. And you're going to be the chef.

I'm like, what? Am I ready for this? So that's where I learned to run a kitchen. I sort of started to get my voice. Like, there was a really close friend of Dominic's who was the front of house manager-slash-maître d'. And he just challenged me every single day because I replaced his friend. He kept barking orders to the kitchen crew, ignoring that I'm even there. And finally, one day, and this is not my character at all, but finally one day I just picked up a chef's knife and shook it at him and said, get the fuck out of my kitchen. I don't know where that came from. I've never done that before or since. But he just turned on a dime and left and never bothered me again.

I still hadn't been to Italy yet, but I devoured any publication that was out there, reading the restaurant reviews in *Gourmet* magazine, which were a big deal then. In 1982 I left that restaurant, and I met Larry Levy because Cathy was working at the Chestnut Street Grill, which he owned. He'd come in for lunch almost every day and he was bragging about this building that he was building at the corner of Michigan Avenue and Oak Street, and how he wanted to have the best Italian restaurant in town. And Cathy's like, you should meet my husband.

So Larry's like, well, why don't you do a dinner, I'm gonna invite a lot of people. I'm gonna invite like twelve to fourteen people, you cook dinner,

Cathy can do the wines and we'll get you the support you need. There were all these early '80s Chicago celebrities, [like] Gene Siskel. But it was sort of a test. And after that Larry's like, okay, that was incredible. My guests loved it. And I want to send you to Italy. We're going to open this restaurant in 1984. So go to Italy now, spend a year in Italy, come back and we'll open Spiaggia.

On the outside of 900 North Michigan, there's a lot of granite, and there's marble inside Spiaggia, and it all came from Forte dei Marmi on the Tuscan coast. The same marble that Michelangelo used to carve David. So Larry had a connection for us, the head of the Federation of Italian Chefs. He set us up in a restaurant just north of Milan. Well, it was one of those places where you learn what *not* to do. So we didn't stay there long.

We worked in some of the most incredible places in Italy, though. The one place that I think influenced us the most was a place called Dal Pescatore [in Mantua], still has three Michelin stars today. And they told us, whenever somebody in the States wants to open a really good Italian restaurant, they usually call and we send them a chef. But you guys are the first ones to come over here. Working in the kitchens, before the word "stage" meant something. We worked in six different restaurants, and I don't remember ever seeing any other Americans. I saw Japanese, but they'd always say, you guys seem to be the first Americans.

We became really good friends to this day. Nadia [Santini] is the chef, she was a chef back then. But she was pregnant at the time, and now that child, Giovanni, is her executive chef. When we go back, they treat us like royalty, and they're really good friends of ours. When I sent Joe Flamm there to cook, he came back and said, okay, I get it. I know what we're trying to do here.

There's such an elegance there, and that place influenced Spiaggia a lot. Because when we came back, an Italian restaurant at this level? Unheard of in Chicago. Only French.

We broke the menu down like a traditional Italian menu, where there was the first course or antipasto followed by the premium pasta, and then main courses. It was a lot of education in the beginning, at that point in 1984 you had to sort of explain why the menu was set the way it was. Marcella Hazan said the most important ingredient in Italian cooking is the one you leave out. So it was simple, but it was beautiful ingredients. Which was hard, because in

1984 there was no fresh basil. So we set up a grow light system in one of the back rooms of the building.

Unless you grew your own shit, you couldn't find it. Back then, if you ordered radicchio, they'd send you red cabbage. Tom Cornille was great, I'd tell him what I was looking for and he'd find it. Our meat supplier helped us too because he was born in Lucca. Richard's Packing, I don't think it exists anymore. I would tell him what I wanted to do, and he would help me decide on what cut, and he was really very helpful if ever I needed advice, or if he knew the product, he would talk me through it.

The farmer network wasn't as strong. You had Lee [Jones] from Chef's Garden who would grow things for you. He was definitely one of the first, and was super-expensive because he had to ship it from Ohio. But we got a lot of stuff from him as well.

It was hard to find great Italian cheeses, or olive oil that wasn't seven years old and rancid. Getting real balsamic vinegar was tough. I don't think FedEx existed and we had to rely on importers. And if I remember correctly, one that got a lot of stuff for us was European Imports, which I don't think exists anymore either.[15]

SARAH GRUENEBERG (line cook): I think Tony's vision for Spiaggia was to run a real Italian restaurant—super-devoted to Italian cuisine and mimicking the Michelin restaurants in Italy. With the first cheese cave in Chicago, the first wood burning oven.

TONY MANTUANO: George Badonsky, who had George's on Kinzie and other restaurants, he was doing Italian, but really more Italian American food. He said to me, sit down, kid, this restaurant will never make it until you put a meatball on the menu. Meatballs are back, now, but at the time, that was a symbol of the Italian American cooking we were trying to get away from. So he'd say that but the next night, Jean Banchet would come in and tell me how great everything is. And he had that circle of influencers that were from Europe and knew what we're doing or trying to do, and were very supportive.

15 Acquired by Sysco in 2012.

SARAH GRUENEBERG: I went to Tony's house once to watch the Super Bowl or something, and he made these meatballs that were like his grandmother's recipe, and I was like, what are you doing? Meatballs? He put pork neck in his meatballs and braised the sauce and it was insanely delicious. We put them on the menu and ultimately, they were the basis of our meatball at [her restaurant] Monteverde.

I think that Tony's childhood Italian wasn't the Italian American of many of our lives, so he doesn't have this deep connection with, like, chicken parm. He has a deep connection with his grandmother's chicken livers Calabrese. When he made that for me it was like, one of the best dishes I had ever had, and honestly, it was an opening dish on our menu at Monteverde.

Mantuano's first stint at Spiaggia lasted from 1984 to 1990. After that, he opened two restaurants of his own, Tuttaposto and Mantuano's Italian Table.

TONY MANTUANO: You want to continue to learn, I think when you're doing something for a long time you want to do other things. And I just had this desire to do pan-Mediterranean cooking at Tuttaposto—Tunisian rice, smoked chicken wings or Moroccan vegetable tagine, or Greek salad, taramosalata. That's something I don't think people saw before, in one place, so that was always fun for us.

Mantuano's was in NBC Tower, and the partners I had in that project, we weren't seeing the same things, and it got to the point where I just couldn't be in the same room with them. Of course, when that happens, it ends up in a courtroom, which sucked. That is one word of advice to the young chefs who want to own their own joint: pick partners and make sure you like them. Once that happened, Larry Levy reached back out to me again when Paul [Bartolotta, Mantuano's successor] was leaving Spiaggia.

I think we started it off and then Paul took it to another level. And it sort of became the center for Italians in this country, a place they wanted to go eat, because they knew that the dishes were going to be in the spirit of and what they were used to. So I think over those nine years I was gone, it solidified itself under Paul as a real Italian place. And so I think what changed is just, there were more people coming for great Italian food. More people had been to Italy and more people wanted to eat that way when they got back.

It also became well known in Italy, like to this day in Italy, people always ask about Spiaggia. About the wine program too, under the late great Henry Bishop. Henry would bring in the craziest wines that only he could sell. Like a Pinot Grigio from Madonna's dad that was grown in Michigan, and wasn't distributed. So Henry would get in his car and drive up to Northern Michigan to buy cases of it. I remember when Madonna came in one time, I greeted her and she says, is Henry here? I'm like, how do *you* know Henry? But then I realized why she knew him. One of his great jokes that I remember to this day was when a table was asking him what squab was—you know, Spiaggia had those really big windows. And he would tell them, with a straight face, well, it's squab on this side of the windows, and on that side of the windows, it's pigeon.

What really helped is that when Italian winemakers were in Chicago, they came here. And they invite you to see what they're doing when you're over there. That relationship that we have is pretty special. Joe and I did a state dinner at the State Department, this was in the October before Obama left office, and it was 250 people in the State Department ballroom for Matteo Renzi, who was the prime minister of Italy at the time. And they're like, right before we eat lunch, we'd like you to meet the prime minister in a little side room. Fantastic.

So I walk in the room, and Matteo Renzi is in the room with Joe Biden and John Kerry. And he sees me and he starts waving to me, get over here, come on! I go over there, and he's telling Biden and Kerry, "Have you guys ever eaten at Spiaggia in Chicago? You gotta go there! It's unbelievable!" And I'm thinking, this is the prime minister of Italy, selling my restaurant.

That validates it, right there. This restaurant has a great reputation in Italy, and I'm humbled by that. It's pretty cool. I mean, they loved the idea of Obama, and they loved that when he won the election, they celebrated here, at an Italian restaurant. Every television station, everybody in Italy wanted to interview us.

****

Spiaggia had long been successful, but it reached a new level of celebrity thanks to food TV—Mantuano appeared on Top Chef Masters, *and executive chef Sarah Grueneberg came in second on* Top Chef *season 9 in 2012, while her successor Joe*

Flamm won Top Chef *season 15 in 2018. Behind this was Mantuano's emphasis on Spiaggia being a training ground for younger cooks in Italian cuisine.*

SARAH GRUENEBERG: My experience of Italian food was very little, much more Italian American growing up. It started on kind of a whim and a dream, living in Houston and wanting to cook differently. And my chefs said, you should really push yourself outside of the city, so I flew up to Chicago and did a few stages and ended up interviewing with Missy Robbins [Spiaggia's executive chef, 2003–08], and did a two-day stage and just fell in love. I remember the first time I tasted the agnolotti and the gnocchi here, and I said, I have to learn how to make this.

It was really hard. Like the first six months, I didn't know if I was gonna make it. It was so simple and so elevated. The things they had us doing were not easy if you hadn't—I'd never *seen* a langoustine before. How do you clean that? My first day at Spiaggia I learned how to make a tuna rotolo. Things I had never seen before.

And it was so simple, but like, if you didn't cook it right, you couldn't hide behind anything on that dish. You couldn't put a sauce on it, or do anything. You really had to learn the skills.

TONY MANTUANO: I would look for someone who had an open mind and an aptitude to learn, but had never been to Italy. Once we got comfortable with a person, and they understood our style and what we were trying to do, we would slowly give them more and more slots on the menu. It was just a level of encouragement. There was never any yelling in our restaurant, it was all very positive. And it produced a lot of great chefs.

Missy Robbins came on board, and now she's so incredibly successful in New York [Lilia and Misi in Brooklyn]. We're still great friends. And then Sarah Grueneberg, still great friends. I mean, we hired Sarah and she was the steward, the person who does the ordering and receiving. It was such an important part of what we did, you had to have someone who was foraging in a sense, and finding these products, and so it was a great learning platform. And then we sent her to Dal Pescatore.

But you know, it's up to them, if they want to learn and they want to grow, and they have the passion for Italian cuisine, they're gonna find that this is a really good place to be. It's one of those places that you'd go to if you wanted to learn to cook Italian.

SARAH GRUENEBERG: I never really saw Tony that much. Missy was really hands-on in the kitchen, Tony would come around. And you know, as a line cook, I really didn't have any business talking to Tony. But as I grew, I was on the pasta station. Tony and Cathy were going to Pebble Beach Food & Wine [festival], and Missy was going to go until they decided to send me as a line cook. And so there I was going to California with Tony and Cathy and that was the first time I really spent time with them. And it was pretty cool. After that I really felt like I was in the right place, like I could really grow in the company and the kitchen. And then I got promoted in '08, when Missy left.

TONY MANTUANO: We worked so hard to try and stay current, and I think the young talent we put through there was part of it. The menu changed all the time, and I'm very collaborative—I don't think it's my way or the highway. I want to develop talent, and when I can take the training wheels off, I let them go. I tasted everything, everything came through me, but I wanted the restaurant to evolve. I don't want it to stay the same. But people are going to leave, and you have to accept that, you can't hold on to people. There's times that I told people after two years, you need to move on. You're only twenty-six years old, you've learned as much as you can learn here, you need to go learn something else. And I would help them find a place.

Joe [Flamm] was a great example of someone who worked his way from being the Cafe Spiaggia sous chef to running the entire joint. And everyone loved working with him. A lot of restaurants will tell you, it's so hard to find people, it's so hard to hire people. We didn't have that problem. People wanted to work for Joe. And he focused on teaching them how to sharpen their knives, how to butcher, all the things that you should be learning as a young chef. They like that, and there's some discipline, but there's also fun.

I always say we had two chefs to make the top two on *Top Chef.* But Joe winning *Top Chef* brought in a whole different crowd. A lot of nights it was fan night, and they knew their food, too, it's not like they're out of their element. But they were fans of the show. They weren't just from Chicago, either. They were from *everywhere.* The only thing we'd never really had before, was a bar crowd. And then we had a bar crowd, and people eating at the bar. Every night that bar was full.

JOE FLAMM: Tony never asked me. Tony *told* me to take a meeting. He goes, I just got a call from the producer at *Top Chef,* they were casting over at Monteverde and they didn't find anybody they liked. You got any interest in it? I said, I don't know if I want to do that. He said, well, I told them they should meet you. They're on their way.

So these two producers are chatting me up, and I'm like, they're not gonna pick me. They've already had someone from here. I'm not interesting. "So you're a fucking South Side Chicago white dude, no crazy trauma?" I'm like the most regular-ass Chicago person. I'm like every other fucking dude I know in my neighborhood.

We talk for a while, it goes good, and at the end of it the lady says, you gotta do this. It's a long road that you should go down. So I talk to my wife and she's like, yeah, it's good timing, you should do it.

So I'm doing all the process, I have a lot of friends who have done it and got to a certain point, and I'm thinking I'm probably gonna get to that certain point. But finally, the last thing they do is you have to fly out to LA, and you do an in-person meeting with the producers, and you do an in-person physical. So they wanted me to do that. But I was going to Italy to stage around Florence and Mantua. And they're like, well, can you Zoom? So I did a physical here and then I did my Zoom in my friend's parents' backyard in the suburbs of Florence. And it was a disaster, because Wi-Fi in Italy is more like an idea than a thing.

I get back to Chicago and I hear the producers want one more interview. Yeah, the last one didn't go so good. I had a call three weeks later and then they're like, you're gonna be in Denver in two weeks. So it's like all right, I gotta figure out how to leave this restaurant in two weeks. Yeah. And so it's the same year we were cooking at the James Beard Awards, doing all the food for the opera boxes [at the Civic Opera Building]. That was the night before I left for *Top Chef,* so I have like the most stressful dinner in my life a night before I leave for this crazy stressful thing.

Day one, you show up and they come into your hotel room, they take your phone, they take your wallet, take all your stuff. Two months later, everybody gets their phone back on the same day. You sign a million-dollar NDA and you have to make up a cover story. Tony had a restaurant in Disney Springs, and I had to tell all my cooks, all my servers, I'm going to Orlando to redo this restaurant. I told that to my siblings, my grandma, everybody. You're off the grid, you're off email, you're off social, you're off text. You get a ten-minute phone call every few days, on a producer's phone, in front of a camera on speakerphone. We set up a code before I left. "I'm gonna ask you how the Sox are doing. That means I'm still on the show."

The shooting was super intense. Immediate, super-long hours. And you're cut off from the outside world. You have no outlets. You're only with the people you're with. It's really hard. But it's really cool. I mean, I was going spectacular places, we shot all around Colorado. So it's beautiful. And I had access to things I never thought I'd have access to, getting to cook for chefs that were unbelievable.

We're such homers in this city. [While it was airing] I'd be walking the streets and people were like hey, we're rooting for you, Joe. I go to the Whole Foods in Lincoln Park and people are like yo, let's go Joe! Twenty people start cheering and going nuts. It's like *Friday Night Lights.* I've never been the starting quarterback before. Just this city fucking ruling.

So I get back, and you're not allowed to tell anyone. So I take Tony and Cathy out to dinner at Proxi. He says, how did it go? And I said . . . well, I did better than anybody else who's worked for you. And he was like, wait, what? He starts crying and gives me a big hug. As much as I loved the ride of it, I think Tony had the best time of that season, he was so proud of me. He's like, this is your moment, he had my back so hard on it. It was like mentorship at its finest.

****

Spiaggia lasted thirty-seven years, but by 2021, as the restaurant scene spread to hot new neighborhoods like the West Loop, its stretch of north Michigan Avenue ceased being a dining and shopping destination. Hit, like every restaurant, by the loss of traffic due to COVID, Spiaggia closed in 2021. Tony and Cathy Mantuano moved to Nashville, where they opened Yolan in The Joseph, a boutique hotel, returning to Chicago in 2025 to open a second Purple Pig (in which he had been a partner) in Oak Brook.

SARAH GRUENEBERG: We were the crown jewel of the Levy restaurants, and Tony protected Spiaggia a lot. But where we had to play the game was, we had to abide by all of the corporate rules. We had to go in and say, we really want to buy from this vendor, I know, they only supply bottarga and one cheese, but that's the only vendor you can get it from. What was challenging was just keeping up with a lot of that stuff, where I think their other restaurants that weren't making scratch food, could focus more on the systems. But when you're Spiaggia and you're making everything from scratch, like half of your day is focused on food production.

TONY MANTUANO: For Levy, Spiaggia was the card they played when they were negotiating to, say, get the concessions at Dodger Stadium. They would bring the owners in, and be like, look, if we can do this, we can do that. But they sold the company in like, 2007, I don't remember when exactly. And Larry got out over the next ten years, and the culture changed without him. The new regime just didn't see. Or maybe they saw it, but they weren't as supportive as Larry.

It absolutely changed dining in Chicago, and I say even Italian dining in America. It was a really influential place, and the amount of celebrities that would come through or the amount of Italians that would come through—you were expediting on the line and you'd see Elton John walk past you. Or Paul McCartney coming in and saying, oh, you know, I'm vegan, and I want to do a tasting menu. And talking to him, well, just tell me what ingredients you like. "I like porcini mushrooms, I like arugula." At the end of the meal, Paul comes up and thanks every single person in the kitchen. It really felt like you're a part of the world community there. Like, if you traveled abroad, people knew it. So an important place, an important place.

THE MEXICAN AMERICANS

Italian food history in Chicago has been explored, but the prehistory of Mexican food in Chicago remains largely unknown. It changed—from a fine dining perspective, basically began—with a chef from Oklahoma City by way of a master's program in linguistics at the University of Michigan, who had grown up in a family that owned a barbecue restaurant, and who would teach Chicagoans to treat Mexican food not just as drinking food, but as a serious cuisine worthy of study and respect. Where other chefs publish a cookbook a few years after opening their restaurants, Rick Bayless and his Michigan-born wife Deann Groen Bayless started with a book in 1987, followed immediately by their first restaurant, Frontera Grill, the same year.

RICK BAYLESS: Growing up, we had a whole bunch of Texas chains in our area. But there was one that was Oklahoma City-owned called El Charrito. They had three of them in the city and that's what I grew up on. It was really classic Tex-Mex food—Central Texas food is what I would call it.

Guacamole was never a dip, that came later, guacamole was a salad. And it always came on a lettuce leaf. You could get the combination plate, which had an enchilada, which is what I always loved, and a hard-shell taco on it. Although at this place it wasn't really the U-shaped hard-shell tacos like you could buy in the grocery store—they were actually tacos that were folded and they had a toothpick through them and they were fried. So it was a little more homestyle. And you could get tamales. And that's kind of it, for what I remember—the menus were really tiny, they didn't have much on them.

I had been to Mexico several times, during high school, and that's where I was really introduced to the food of Mexico, which doesn't really bear that much resemblance to that Tex-Mex food. I started when I was 14 and I went back every year, pretty much, until I got to college, and my undergrad degree is in Spanish language, literature and Latin American studies.

After that I went to graduate school in anthropology and linguistics. I was really interested in the relationship between language and culture, how a culture is expressed uniquely in the language. Or the dialect—like the Spanish of Mexico is different from the Spanish of Spain. And how the Spanish of Mexico reflects who the people of Mexico are. So I was really interested in that.

But I'd always cooked, so when I got to Ann Arbor for graduate school, I had jobs cooking all the time. And I got really interested in teaching cooking and writing about cooking during that time, and I eventually opened a small catering company with a friend of mine.

Then when I was finished with all my graduate stuff, I'd passed my prelims for my PhD and I was starting to work on my dissertation, I got super into food. And I was spending most of my time just doing food stuff. So I decided to take a year off from my dissertation work and just explore food. And I never went back.

I just decided that food was going to be my thing. So I was really interested in the relationship between food and culture. At the beginning I really wasn't focusing on Mexico. But that sort of came back to me as I realized I had all this background in Mexico, and I had spent a lot of time there, and I spoke the language and I would be able to really research it. And so I began to do a lot of my teaching and writing and thinking and cooking in Mexican food.

We did that for five years. We traveled to every state in Mexico, cooked with local cooks, really delved deeply into the history of Mexican food and what the regionality is like. I mean, we did it the grass roots way.

The person that was writing the most at that time, obviously, was Diana Kennedy, and she would go into a community and say, who's the best cook here? I want to learn from them. I would go the opposite direction—I would go into the marketplace and just eat the food that everyone was serving there. Because in the marketplaces they serve food that is absolutely traditional. They're serving working-class people that want to eat the food of their moms, basically. Moms or wives, because they have to be away from home, and they go into the marketplace, and it's cheap food but it always tastes super traditional.

That's where I really learned to cook, was in the marketplaces. Plus we didn't have any money, so that's what I could afford to do. I wanted to really understand what the food of the people was. Because I came up through anthropology.

We did it like graduate school research—we didn't just go, oh, that tastes good. We were super rigorous in our studies.

DEANN BAYLESS: We had a big library, books published in Mexico, so I did all this research in the books, and created all these charts, comparing one recipe to how many recipes I could find of it, and how they differed. We catalogued markets, and it was very rigorous. We'd stay somewhere for three, five days, and then we'd move on to another city. It was hard travel. We just worked a lot.

RICK BAYLESS: And we walked a lot, too, because we would just walk everywhere. Up and down streets, just looking for things, and making notes about, this looks like a very traditional-style family restaurant, what do they have on the menu, and we'd write down what was on the menu so we could really understand what people were eating in that town.

And if we found something that we thought was the dish of the town, we always ate it three times by three different cooks, so that we could see the variations in it. Because that's what you do in anthropology, you don't take one person's word on anything. And that's why *Authentic Mexican* is written the way that it is.

So that was my first book,[16] and it came out the day we opened our restaurant.

Before the Baylesses came to Chicago, however, they got their start in both Mexican restaurants and food television elsewhere, the beginning of a food television career that ran to twelve seasons by 2018 of their PBS series Mexico: One Plate at a Time, *as well as a vast amount of online video content.*

RICK BAYLESS: [Doing TV] was a quirk of fate. There was a PBS television station in Bowling Green, Ohio, at the university there, and they were interested in doing a show—there's a lot of migrant workers that had settled in that area there. And they had found this really vivacious woman who had moved there as a migrant worker, and then she'd become known as this really excellent cook in the community. And they were going to do a PBS show with her just for the local community. Just sort of a way of saying, these are our neighbors here, here's what they cook.

And at the last moment, she sort of pulled out. And they put an ad in the paper in Toledo at that point, looking for a host for a cooking show. And some friends of mine who had been taking my cooking classes sent me the contact information. I contacted them, and we did two seasons of that show *[Cooking Mexican].*

DEANN BAYLESS: So actually the TV shows, in a lot of ways, are our continu-

16 *Authentic Mexican: Regional Cooking from the Heart of Mexico*, 1987.

ing education. We don't make any money from it, but we get to go to Mexico, we get to research it for one area intensely for ten days, then we get to be back there again filming it. So that's feeding us at the same time it's pushing the image forward.

Plus another role became clear, mostly for [Rick]—which was maintaining a vibrant national image, to keep the restaurants full.

RICK BAYLESS: That, plus in that image is all this knowledge that I'm spreading out there.

Anyway, I took all the money I made off of doing *Cooking Mexican,* and invested it in going back to Mexico and just doing research trips so I could deepen my knowledge.

I had done some restaurant consulting after that, and these people in Cleveland asked me, would I consult on a project. So I helped them with their menu development, and as happens often, the chef they hired that I trained just couldn't do it and he departed after a week. So they said, is there any way you could come be the chef for us? So we said, we'll live there for a year and save every penny we can, Deann got a good job there and we just lived on nothing for a year.

And as we were packing our bags for Mexico, this fellow called from California and said, I saw your cooking show and you're who we need here. He had, what, eleven restaurants—

DEANN BAYLESS: Six.

RICK BAYLESS: Six?

DEANN BAYLESS: They were small. It grew.

RICK BAYLESS: It grew while we were working with them, yeah. He said, I want you to be our culinary consultant, I want you to help us change the menu. They still did that '60s style Mexican chain fare—what Chi-Chi's came out of. Created food to be "Mexican!" which could play everywhere in America. He said, we need you to bring us up to date.

And we thought wow, that could be kind of cool, because we realized that the project we wanted to do was to write a book on regional foods of Mexico. And it was going to take us more than a year to write it. So this guy offered us a job where we could work for three months and be off for three months.

We finished *[Authentic Mexican]*, turned in the manuscript—and then we had to figure out what we were going to do. I didn't know if I could find a way to make a living being a food writer, and what I did know how to do was cook professionally, but I hadn't been to a school that could teach me how to do the kind of food that I was writing about.

So we opened Frontera in 1987. We spent about a year developing it—Deann was really working, like, temp jobs and all that sort of stuff. We were doing a little bit of consulting work during that time, and we opened in the spring of 1987.

We were very lucky that there were not a lot of chain Mexican American places in Chicago. In fact, when we opened up, the closest thing that you could find to that was a couple of Taco Bells. There weren't any of the other national chains that were popular at the time. Really the only thing that people knew about Mexican food in Chicago—if they were not Mexican—was the little corner places, the mom-and-pop places. Which were not offering a variety of food, they just usually offered whatever their town that they came from had, plus a few other things that people told them, if you're going to open a Mexican restaurant, you have to have this thing on your menu.

So there was a little bit of that. But it was definitely not high profile. Or maybe it was considered to be, let's just say, not any kind of food that people talked about, when people ask, oh, where did you go out to eat? But the cool thing was that most people did know something about Mexican hospitality. Which tends to be very gracious compared to a lot of other cultures.

And so we wanted to take that notion of Mexican hospitality, and then build a place that would be very clearly identified by our guests as being sort of upscale casual, not fine dining, but just upscale casual, because our belief was that the food deserves really careful scrutiny. And if you made it with the great products that you would find in Mexico, then it was worth something. And so that's where we entered the market.

DEANN BAYLESS: Also at the time, not just in Chicago, but around the country, there was a strong sense of the Southwest, Southwestern food and border foods, so to speak. And that was one of the things we very consciously chose to use. It was the time of the fajitas craze, and tacos. Tacos *al carbon* are sort of the precursor to fajitas. So we chose to make that connection for people, so they would feel comfortable coming and trying our food. Even the word "frontera" means border. We were trying to bridge the border, to reference the border, all those things.

RICK BAYLESS: We opened this place on a very tight budget. And almost all of our money came from our mothers, each of our mothers' retirement funds. So we couldn't lose anything. And we had to pay them back as quickly as we possibly could. We couldn't fail. Deann and I figured out what kind of jobs we would have to get if this didn't work out, and how long it would take to pay back our moms. So we opened with this idea that we had to do a bunch of border stuff that people recognized.

So I chose to put chili on the menu, really a dish called *carne con chile colorado* that they do in Northern Mexico, which is the precursor to [Texas] chili. And we had it on the menu for probably about, I'm gonna say, five or six months. And then we took that and every reference to the American Southwest off of the menu, and took the sign offering chili out of the window.

Nobody knew who we were. I had never worked in the restaurant business in Chicago, so I was really learning it from the ground up. So I would ask people, like, who's a good vegetable purveyor here? And somebody would say oh, you should talk to these people.

We really knew nothing when we came here. I just fell in love with Chicago and said, this is the place where I want to be, because I really loved the fact that we were in the Midwest. We'd been living half-time in LA—and LA is super trendy. And so after about three or four years, you kind of had to close your restaurant up and reconcept it. And I didn't really want to do that.

Remember, I grew up in a restaurant that was open for thirty-seven years. That taught me that longevity's a good thing. I loved the fact that in Chicago, if you offered good value, and you kind of kept up with the times, but were not super trendy—you could actually have a really long run here.

DEANN BAYLESS: We decided to settle in Chicago because we knew we needed to be in a major metropolitan area to open our restaurant. Because we needed to live somewhere that people traveled and understood the distinction between the chain version of a restaurant—Mexican, Italian, whatever it is—versus something you might find in that country.

So we needed to be where people were sophisticated enough, and then my memory is that when we opened this restaurant—well, first we debated putting things like margaritas on the menu. Because they aren't really Mexican. But we also knew that we needed money to stay in business. We weren't quite *that* naive. But then people criticized us because they weren't made with sweet and sour mix, they were made with lime juice and sugar. It was at that basic level.

But there was this whole other thing where people who understood about Mexico, they came out of the woodwork. Not that we were packed, right away, necessarily, but there were people who understood that it was something special.

JEANMARIE BROWNSON (*Tribune* writer): From the beginning Rick was willing to say, we have a huge Mexican population and many, many good Mexican restaurants, but they're not really bringing the full breadth of Mexican food to Chicago, the different regional specialties. *Sopes* and real enchiladas, not just cheese enchiladas, carnitas made the real way, some of the fish recipes that Rick was doing from coastal Mexico. All these different sort of in-depth flavors that you weren't necessarily seeing at neighborhood Mexican restaurants in Chicago at that time.

It was right at a time—1987—that food was really starting to open up in this country. We were really seeking out authentic, regional Italian foods. Not just meatballs, but we're saying, oh, my gosh, what about risotto? What about polenta? That was all sort of happening nationwide, and certainly in Chicago.

RICK BAYLESS: It was really lucky that our book came out the same day that we opened. We couldn't do any publicity on it—I remember that I had an interview with JeanMarie Brownson, who now works with us and has for twenty years, from the *Tribune* about how we wrote it and that sort of stuff. And that review of the book really helped to launch the restaurant, too.

Because the food was really different from what you would find in most Mexican restaurants in this town. And we wanted to do the real food of Mexico, and just having the *Tribune* review the book was super cool, because they said that these people have done their research. They spent all these years doing this research, so you can trust them.

Now, we could have done the research and still not been good cooks. But we, thankfully, were good cooks.

Paula Camp, the Tribune*'s reviewer, reviewed Frontera Grill just four weeks after it opened.*

RICK BAYLESS: Four weeks! I was shaking in my boots.

PAULA CAMP: It was being talked about in the food world. Even before it opened, it was an eyeopener in the sense that what Rick was doing, of course, was elevating the cuisine from the typical taqueria in Pilsen to something that was much different. And of course, the regional approach opened everyone's eyes to the fact that Mexican cuisine was much more diverse than we thought. Of course, Diana Kennedy and others had already mined the territory of regional differences and influences for Mexican cuisine. But this was the first restaurant, perhaps in the country. You think of New York City as having everything, but there wasn't a decent Mexican restaurant in New York City, period, in the early 1980s. Rick was creating the first really serious Mexican restaurant of the time, yet it was not too serious, in the sense that it was a grill, it was about having a good time.

This would have been a seminal restaurant in Chicago whether I'd written about it or not. But it was exciting, and at this time Frontera, and a couple of other restaurants were the first restaurants where lines were formed outside to wait for a table. Common in New York, common in other cities, but not in Chicago. In Chicago, the attitude was, I'm not sure there's any food *that* good. So that was another thing that made it unique, and I think desirable.

DEANN BAYLESS: We thought really carefully when we opened about how we would bridge a gap and gain people's trust. And Rick, being a live fire guy, said I want the grill to be the touchstone, because everybody loves grilled food. So that'll make everything taste good. And this whole thing of tacos, because we weren't serving ground beef in U-shaped shells, everything had to be super-delicious grilled meats. And the tortillas, of course, were the bedrock of everything, so they had to be handmade from fresh masa.

So we were really calculated in that. And for a long time—maybe not a long time, but for half a year—those tacos were a big part of our sales. And then we started putting on some specials, that were the regional specialties, and then over the period of a couple of years we saw the menu make a shift as people gained trust in what we were doing.

But we thought about those dishes for a long time. What will just be so delicious that people *can't* not come back for it? What will make them feel comfortable even though this food is so different? How can we say, this is Mexican, but it's not what you're expecting, but it's going to be wonderful.

And then, even in the decor, we didn't have anything that marked of stereotypical Mexico. Like mariachis. Even though mariachis are wonderful, we didn't do anything with that.

RICK BAYLESS: Right now you can occasionally hear mariachi music, but there was a moratorium on any mariachi music in this restaurant for twenty years. I wouldn't allow any of it to be played, and nothing on the walls that would smack of stuff that you would expect to see in a stereotypical Mexican restaurant.

DEANN BAYLESS: We wanted people to walk in and say, this isn't what I was expecting Mexican to look like, and then taste it and go, this isn't what I was expecting, but be open to it.

RICK BAYLESS: From day one we had two very, very clear missions. One was to shine a light on the traditional foods of Mexico so that people would respect it at the level that we felt it deserved. And then the second thing was that we wanted to build Chicago into a great restaurant town. And so we did and supported anything that we could do to make that happen. Because in 1987 there were about, what, four or five chef-owned restaurants in the city. That's all. It was a kind of an unheard-of thing. We wanted Chicago to become more of a chef-owned-restaurant town. But we knew that was not going to happen unless a lot of changes happened in Chicago.

We had learned in Mexico that great cuisine came with great local agriculture. So we knew that had to be the foundation of what we did. But we also, and I think that this has stood us in good stead, we also went to all the other chef-owned restaurants in town, on our days off, and we'd get to know them and say let's do some stuff together. And we would band together to support different causes. We got to know each other and we became really tight. I think in some ways, that's the reason that the chef community in Chicago has quite a different feel than the chef community in a lot of other towns, other big towns, certainly than in New York where a lot of chefs don't even know each other and are not supportive of one another. They're much more competitive. And LA's just kind of spread out. There's not a whole lot of camaraderie there.

But Chicago—we're not terribly spread out. And what Deann and I tried to do in those early years and continued all the way through was to always be supporting the other restaurants, we would be talking about them and visiting them. Now we put it out on social media, what a great time we had there.

[The choice of location] was very simple: it was as close to Michigan Avenue as we could afford, as close to the action as we could afford. And it was a place where we thought we could be open for five days a week, and busy for lunch and dinner. So that's what we did. We were only open for four lunches for the first year, almost. And then we added a Saturday brunch—back in those days, the idea of a Saturday brunch was just never, nobody had ever heard of anything like that. Now everybody does it.

DEANN BAYLESS: I would say that River North has always been known as the art center, galleries and stuff like that, and that we wanted to associate with that side. Because we're both totally into artists, and are artists more than business people. So we chose that because we thought people who are into the arts are more open to things that are different, maybe, and they might be more open to us.

And we were kitty-corner from Gordon. He was the pioneer. We knew that people who were interested in interesting things would know Gordon. He was avant-garde, and he put his restaurant in a very sleazy area, because he knew he had all destination diners. They were going to get out of their taxis or limos or whatever, and go right in.

But they also found it fun—it was sort of slumming.

RICK BAYLESS: When people called up and said, exactly where are you? We would say kitty-corner from Gordon and they would go, Oh, well, then it's okay. But we still had people ask if it was safe to walk across the street from the parking lot. That's how sketchy the neighborhood was.

There's a wall by the fire station that separates it from the building where Topolobampo is now. And when Al Friedman bought it, there was really nothing to save in the building except the roof. So he basically demolished the building down to the basement. And when he did that, they found out that the basement was just totally rat-infested. And it dumped all these rats out onto the back alley. During that period, it was slightly traumatic, you couldn't go out the back door unless you had something to scare the rats away. We would go out there with broom handles, bang bang bang, because we parked our car out there.

And it got so bad, that Friedman paid a bounty, I'm gonna say it was five dollars, at least five dollars. And so you would walk out the back door, not only with the rats scurrying around, but you would have the firemen with their BB guns or whatever, sitting on that wall, pointing right at you. The neighborhood was rough! But we lived through it. We not only drew a lot of local attention, but a lot of national attention, because we were doing something that people had never seen before. So we didn't pay a lot of attention to our neighborhood, because we were just trying to keep up with what was going on inside of our four walls.

****

TRACEY VOWELL (managing chef, Frontera): I saw an ad in the newspaper—"The Frontera Grill is looking for careful cooks." I don't think I'll ever forget that, because to me it was the most intelligent help wanted ad I had ever seen. It was like, let's just get this out in the beginning, we're not just looking for a warm body, we're looking for somebody with some focus.

I didn't have all that much experience—a brief stint at Excalibur [nightclub]. I really didn't know what I was doing. I did not go to culinary school or any of that. But I grew up in South Louisiana. I'm accustomed to food that has guts. And the typical Midwestern fare does not have that—there's no heat, there's very little seafood, there's no big draw for somebody that literally grew up eating Creole food. Then I ate at Frontera. And it was like, oh, this is the place, and I started watching the newspaper.

I went and talked to Rick and I said, I don't know a whole lot. But I know that I really like food with flavor. And I know that I'm very motivated about working here. I'm a customer here. And I know what you're doing. Three hours into the interview, Rick finally said, okay, well, let's give this a run.

He hired me to work the grill, which is not a position that a woman typically has. I spent five years on that grill, and to be perfectly honest, when the promotion came, and he said, okay, it's time for you to be a sous chef, let's move you somewhere else, I said, can't I be a sous chef from the grill? Because there's more to it than just cooking dinner. You've got to keep that fire going. You've got a pace, you've got a whole separate dance that you're doing. Apart from what you're cooking on top, if you miss your cue to throw in a piece of wood, you're gonna bring the whole restaurant down. I really liked that pressure. I really functioned on that.

Every night, we knew what was going to happen to us. We had a system in place. And at some point, no matter how high your level of organization, you were still stepping out onto a wire, and any little disruption in that process of the first turn [of tables] is going to throw all the rest of the night off.

I wanted to see that Frontera grill line, standing outside taking care of whatever addictions they might have—you gotta have a boatload of espresso before service starts, go get it. Do you need to smoke, go to the bathroom, do whatever. And then I want you calm, smiling, collected, because in a minute, the whole world's gonna flip upside down. That first turn, and watching the ticket times grow, and keeping up with the food, whatever position I was in, that was why I was there. We were going to watch that wait rise to three hours, and then we were going to beat it back down into the ground.

Once I graduated from work on the line, I really didn't know what to do with myself. I didn't have a line position to get ready for anymore, so what am I? What am I supposed to do?

DEANN BAYLESS: I come from a family of professionals, and I love to eat, my father had loved to eat. He died when I was young. But my family was sort of surprised when I hooked up into this world.

RICK BAYLESS: Even my own family, and I came from a restaurant family, when I said I wanted to be a chef, they were like, oh no, you're better than that.

DEANN BAYLESS: But one of the things I also come from is a very religious Christian background, and I was taught to give to people all my life, that that was the highest value. And one of the things that I thought as a restaurateur, it's a profession that doesn't garner a lot of respect for how it treats people. And I wanted to demystify that and say that that's ridiculous. I wanted to create an environment that respected people at the core, no matter what level they were working at, all equally, that paid fairly, that understood when people needed a day off to go be with their sick kid or, or whatever. I wanted to make an environment in a restaurant that was a good one. And I wanted to say it doesn't have to be—it was the height of [Anthony Bourdain's] *Kitchen Confidential*—

RICK BAYLESS: The bad boy chef, and restaurants were just filled with drugs and sex—

DEANN BAYLESS: I wanted to say, no, there's people that want to make a living here that are respectable people. I was really into our employees, I knew everybody and I knew their stories. And then in one of our spurts of growth, we went from sixty to ninety employees, and I got really depressed, I thought I can't do this for ninety people. And then slowly I learned, I can do it for my small group of managers, and they can feed it out.

RICK BAYLESS: I grew up in a family restaurant where nobody yelled and screamed, and everybody helped everybody. So this whole thing about, restaurant kitchens are just horrible places and everybody's mean and they hurt each other and they're screaming and yelling all the time. I never have worked in a restaurant that was like that, and so I wouldn't say yes, we have to reform the restaurant culture—because I've never been in one like that.

It's one of the reasons we have all open kitchens. I think it's really important for the guests to see the chefs working, and for the chefs to see the guests enjoying their food. We make beautiful food and we give it to you and you eat it, and we can watch you eat it. And so it was really important for me to have open kitchens. All that stuff about people screaming and yelling and throwing things in kitchens—do you see that? It's not happening here.

Maybe the first year we were open here, I opened the restaurant and Deann closed the restaurant, and she was talking to the dishwasher at the end of the night. And he's talking about how he was going to go get a payday loan. And she asked him how much interest they charge, and it's some whopping 40 percent or something that you can't even imagine anybody doing. But she realized that he didn't have any other choices. So she started a no-interest loan program here, which goes to this very day.

DEANN BAYLESS: That first year, I learned about the culture of poverty and I hadn't known it. I come from an upper-middle-class family, I had many privileges. And honestly, in thirty-some years we have been stiffed on my loan program just once.

We're huge into education. And the people that want to work here, either they love it, because education is exciting and makes your job less boring. Or they don't last here, because they have to learn a lot.

RICK BAYLESS: We got our entire opening kitchen crew except for two people from St. Augustine college in Chicago, a bilingual education program where they taught them some basic culinary skills so they could get a job in a deli someplace, that kind of stuff. But I took everybody from that program, because at least they had been introduced to culinary, and they were all trying to learn to speak English. So our kitchen was a Spanish-speaking kitchen. But they had to be able to talk to the service staff that was not all Spanish-speaking, though most of it was when we first opened.

A lot of the kitchens in the United States just speak English, with Chinese words or Spanish words or Italian words thrown in. But we really try to speak Spanish, Mexican Spanish in our kitchen. Sort of metaphorically as well as literally what we speak.

RICHARD JAMES (managing chef, Frontera, Topolobampo and Xoco): I think we push really hard to maintain our Mexican culture here. Particularly through the language. And I find myself correcting some of the younger generation, speaking their Spanglish.

RICK BAYLESS: Because they're all Mexican Americans, raised here. And they really speak Spanglish a lot. There's radio stations that speak Spanglish here. And it's really funny because, when you get a lot of these young, immigrant kids, that came here at seventeen, say. They come here because there's no place for them to work in Mexico. They get jobs, but they've never learned the vocabulary for much beyond their home and their school. They would come to me, because I have a degree in Spanish literature, and say, what's the right way to say this, what's the proper way to say this in Spanish? What's the real word for this?

We have a Mexican American kid who's one of our sous chefs, and he speaks really good Spanish. And he grew up going back and forth to Mexico, because in the summers, he would spend it with his grandparents in Veracruz. And when we go down to Mexico for events, he hates to go down there because, he says, they're all going to call me a *pocho* [a Mexican American with limited Spanish]. Because I speak differently from them.

And he's probably the most rooted of all of our chefs in Mexico, and still they make fun of him. I think he speaks perfect Spanish, but he says no, no, no, because of some of the expressions I use, they say you're not one of us, you're not Mexican.

RICHARD JAMES: I've been working in kitchens for a very long time, so I'd been learning kitchen Spanish at my previous job, and then, when I started working here, I decided that I wasn't going to be teased behind my—well, in front of my face, in Spanish. So I worked really hard, I spent two weeks walking around rolling my R's, so I could make sure I made my R's correctly. And then I fell in love with my wife, who's Mexican.

RICK BAYLESS: He had to go and ask for the young lady's hand, to her mother, in Spanish, because her mother doesn't speak any English.

RICHARD JAMES: And I would have to watch television, with my now-wife, in Spanish, because she didn't speak a lot of English, so that helped me to grasp Mexican Spanish. *Sábado Gigante, El Gordo y La Flaca,* watching novelas . . .

RICK BAYLESS: *El Chavo del Ocho,* did you watch that?

RICHARD JAMES: *El Chavo del Ocho,* oh yeah.

RICK BAYLESS: When I lived in Mexico, I used to watch all the *telenovelas,* because they speak *Really! Dramatically!* and slowly. They enunciate, so you can really understand what they're saying.

An important part of education in Bayless's restaurants is staff trips to Mexico. Andres Padilla, who would become chef de cuisine at Topolobampo and later culinary director for the group, talks about the training and travel:

ANDRES PADILLA: The thing you'd constantly hear was, he just goes to Mexico and he takes their recipes. No, he doesn't. He gets inspired. He goes because he's inspired by the ingredients, he's inspired by the hospitality. He's inspired by the history. He's inspired by the local culture, and all of those things come together. And then that becomes inspiration, not only for him, but then he brings his staff along to be inspired. For me, it was a lot of learning and understanding the cuisine and a lot of traveling with him. I was so thrilled to be a part of these trips, and I tried to soak up as much as I could.

People always ask about authenticity. The authenticity is where you are [on staff trips], and he cooks and inspires with a Mexican soul.

The trips were done with the same idea in mind. You're going to this restaurant, you're going to this person's house to learn this. Or you might go to the World Heritage site, it was always tied in with the history and the culture of where you were. And then there was always, always a market visit, totally inspired by those ingredients. Those of us that were lucky enough to be on those trips, we'd do a dinner, and he'd invite all his friends. Like in Oaxaca, we ended up cooking for fifty people, we'd set up the whole thing just like we would do at the restaurant, but everything was sourced locally. So how amazing of a learning experience is that to connect with a region, actually go into the market interacting with the people selling you the ingredients, and asking them what they use it for? How do they use it? How do they cook it?

It's about servant leadership for Rick, it's providing training and the tools that everybody needs to be successful. And that's from the very lowest level all the way to the top. And he was always very accessible, he was always very easy to talk to. At first I thought he was like, super serious. He communicated through the right channels, he would never go directly into a dishwasher at all, you're doing it wrong. He respected the hierarchy and how it worked. But it wasn't a militant style at all. Especially when he wanted to implement a big change here, he had the vision of how to get there. And he included everybody in it and asked their opinions.

****

TRACEY VOWELL: By the time I was [executive chef at Frontera], we had a big reputation for serving people with allergies and that kind of stuff. If you walked into that restaurant and you said, I'm allergic to cilantro, the next person you saw was me.

I would go out to the table, I would pick up their menu off of the place setting in front of them. I would pull the printed paper sheets out of the cover, take my Sharpie out of my pocket and say okay, so you say you're allergic to cilantro. Is that what we're going with? And I would be a little bit smart-alecky about it because people would show up and they'd say they're allergic to this or that, and it's really I'm afraid of it, or I think I don't like it, or whatever. It's not like I didn't have any understanding of that. But, you know, people would show up, and they would say the wildest things, like I don't eat onions. Oh, honey, you bellied up to the wrong bar now. Good luck getting around here. I suggest you have some of the fried appetizers and leave it at that.

Celiac disease was really growing, and gluten intolerance was becoming more and more of a thing while I was at Frontera. And we were written up in magazines, because we're not a wheat-based cuisine, and the food was really good. We made accommodations for people that were allergic, and I was the accommodation. So Sharpies out, here's the menu, you say you can't eat cilantro. And that Sharpie would start knocking dishes off, left and right. If you came in and you said you couldn't have flour, I'd say I want you to stay away from things that are in the fryer. And you can't have this dish right here, because it does have a little bit of flour in it. But everything else on the menu you can eat. And these people would be in tears at the fact that they had a choice.

But somewhere in there, as they're watching things get knocked off the menu, and one of them was the dish that they had decided that they wanted already, then the truth would come out. Well, I really just try to do, not too much gluten. And the Sharpie would go back to that dish, because now it had been identified that you're toying with me, and the second scratch through would go through that dish. And I would say, I'm sorry, I can't take the responsibility of us making this for you. The Baylesses didn't know what to do about that in the beginning, because I'm a bit more forceful than the two of them are. And I would just say, no, you can't have that.

They get to dessert, and I've been defending them from all of these ingredients that they say they can't have. And then they say, I want the devil's food cake. No, no, no, no, you're not having that. I didn't save your life with savory food for you to make yourself sick with the sweet. We have these ices over here, this dish doesn't have any flour, this dish doesn't have any flour, choose one of these. You may not know what *crepas de cajeta* has, but you know cake has flour.

That part used to drive me crazy, but the people that truly, truly had a problem, you would walk up to the table and as soon as you get there, they're like, oh, I'm so happy to see you. Don't worry, we'll figure it out. But this is Frontera and we're packed, a special order could mess up the machine. If it turned into a special order, I went and raided what I could get off the line and I made the rest of their meal in the back kitchen, because special orders were crippling.

RICK BAYLESS: As I said, one thing that I had learned very clearly in Mexico was, you don't ever have a great cuisine in a place that doesn't have great local agriculture. It just doesn't happen. Charlie Trotter opened six months after we did, and he had come out in the press and said, I would never buy anything local, I get my stuff flown in from other places. And so I said, no, I really want Chicago to become a great restaurant town, and the only way we're going to do that is by developing local agriculture.

I said, there's nothing more iconic as a local product than our local strawberries. So we opened in March. And in the end of May, when local strawberries come, I went down to the wholesale market and I would ask around who's going to carry local strawberries, and they'd all laugh at me and say those things are horrible. They're tiny. They have no shelf life. No, we only carry the great big ones. So Deann and I would get in the car and drive an hour away from here to buy strawberries to bring back to put on our menu.

JEANMARIE BROWNSON: Rick was at Green City Market every Saturday, buying all the produce that he could for the restaurant, from Mick Klug and all these guys, and now those guys supply all kinds of restaurants. Partly because he was supporting them and then calling out their names on every restaurant menu and saying, it matters who grew this. You should know their name. He wasn't the only one doing that, but he was right at the beginning of it.

RICK BAYLESS: We were a high-volume restaurant. Somebody would bring us ten pounds or something. And it's like, that won't even make it through one service for us. So it was really hard for us to be able to work with anybody that wasn't a fairly high-volume farmer. And so we worked with, and still do work with, a fewer number of farms, because they can produce what we need and then we can really rely on them for that. But we struggled with that. Tracey Vowell was the managing chef for Frontera and Topolobampo. She really developed the group that we still work with to this day.

TRACEY VOWELL: When Rick first told me, I want you to start gathering up local producers for as many different things as you can, it took me a week or so to get past, this man is out of his mind. There's no way that we are going to be able to manage food cost and deal with all of these farmers. My life is about to become extraordinarily more complicated.

But it was a wonderful thing. We collected some farms, and the Home Grown Wisconsin [farmer collective] thing back in the day was really cool because they were thirty or forty farms all together. And it was one of the only organizations at the time that could keep up with the demand, because I'd say I need butternut squashes. And he'd say how many you want? I'd say, I don't know, six cases, eight cases. And he'd say, okay, that's gonna have to come from a couple of different farms, but they will all be labeled, where they came from. So that you can trace back if some are better than others, or if you have a quality problem, whatever, then you let me know, and we'll work that out.

I became that person that the farmers all talked to. As I collected more and more of them, a substantial part of my week started to become hanging out in that alley, hot, cold, whatever, visiting with farmers. I didn't care about certification, I care about this relationship that you and I are going to develop while we're standing here. I want to know your children's names, I want to know where you live, I want to meet your wife. I want us to become so familiar with each other, that something like certification really doesn't matter. And we did that. And it was a great experience. But the more exposure I got, the more I realized that this was a road that maybe I could explore, you know, and perhaps becoming a farmer was my next step, after Frontera.

RICK BAYLESS: One of our farmers brought us spinach from Wisconsin, in the middle of winter. And I said, how in the world did you do this in the middle of the winter? He says, well, I know a variety of spinach that's frost-tolerant, and I have this great big high tunnel. And I've planted it with spinach, knowing that I'd be the only one [to offer it in winter]. And, I in my way said, please don't tell another chef about this. I want all of this. And I want twice more than that.

And he said, I can't. This is the max I could ever give you. And it really wasn't enough for us to work with. I said, well, what would it take? And he said another high tunnel. And I said, well, put in another high tunnel! And he goes, oh, it would take me years to save up enough to put in another high tunnel. So I said, what if we lent you the money for the high tunnel, and you could pay us back in spinach next year. And that started the Frontera Farmer Foundation, which is just a no-interest loan program. We had $10,000 that we put away and any farmer could borrow from that.

It taught us something about how little money farmers make. And what they needed was infrastructure stuff. Starting the Foundation was a long story, but a very hard one of getting a 501(c)(3) status for something that gives to for-profit organizations. Even Farm Aid can't give to a for-profit farm, they have to go through another not-for-profit that is spent doing something that's like disaster relief. We're like, no, these people are doing fine. We just want them to do better. So we're going to invest in their farms. We even changed lawyers in the middle to have somebody else go argue our case to the IRS, because we were being turned down over and over for this 501(c)(3) status.

But since then we have given away almost $3.5 million in small increments, because we give around $12,000 average grants. We're just going up this next year to $15,000 grants. But that is like a lifesaver for a lot of these farms. We're kicking them ahead five years in their growth. And it all grew out of this no-interest loan program that we started—it was actually Tracey who had the idea, because we get inundated to give to this charity and that charity and be involved in all these fundraisers and all that sort of stuff. And she actually said one day, what if we took all of this money and just put it back in the farming community here?

TRACEY VOWELL: Rick was very kind, he let me taper off [as a chef] over an extremely long period of time. I bought the farm [Three Sisters Garden, in Kankakee, Illinois] in 2000 and we planted that year, not a lot but we planted, and I didn't leave Frontera until late in '07. Towards the end my biggest responsibility when I was in the building was that I had to do the four o'clock staff meeting. And truly, I loved doing that, because that was my time to say, this is who we get this from, and this is why we love it.

I'm far from getting rich doing this. But I sure do go outside a lot. And I see a great deal of daylight. Which is something that did not happen while I worked at Frontera.

****

Two and a half years after opening Frontera, the Baylesses opened their second restaurant next door: the "modern Mexican" fine dining restaurant Topolobampo. They've continued to grow in the three decades since, including in places like Orlando and Las Vegas—but they remain primarily focused on Chicago, largely on the same block of Clark Street where Frontera started.

RICK BAYLESS: I'm very multifaceted. I'm not just a restaurant chef. And if you have places spread all over the country, then all you can do is have restaurants. You could hire people to write books for you, I guess. But I wrote all my own books, and still am writing books. And I wanted to do television stuff. I wanted to be involved in the non-profit world. And you can't do that if you're just running everywhere. Plus, I had a family and I didn't want to just be gone all the time. So yeah, we've kind of kept close by here. Intentionally.

I knew what I wanted Topolobampo to be when we opened it but there was no way I could achieve it then. At first, it was just like a fancier version of Frontera.

DEANN BAYLESS: And it took reservations. That was a big deal.

RICK BAYLESS: Right. But the prices on the menu were not that different. It was ten bucks more for an entree, that kind of thing. It wasn't a huge jump, so we could sell unreserved tables just off the name Frontera. We have a two hour wait at Frontera, but in twenty minutes we're going to have a table at Topolo, you want to take it?—that's how we got people going over to Topolo.

It's a quieter atmosphere in Topolo, so people would taste the food differently. I remember right after we started, one night we had a problem with the sauce and I said, let's just grab the sauce from Frontera that's the most like this one, and we'll just put it on the menu. So we served it all night long, and a table called me out and said, oh, we really liked our meal. And we eat at Frontera all the time, and I just want to tell you, there is so much more nuance and sophistication to the sauces in this dining room than there is at Frontera.

What she had of course was the sauce that we pulled off the Frontera line. But because it's a quieter atmosphere, people could pay more attention to it. They could perceive nuances in that sauce, that you could have gotten at Frontera.

JEANMARIE BROWNSON: In 1987, when he opened Frontera, in Mexico if you wanted a fancy meal, you would get French food, "Continental" food. Wealthy people for special occasions did not go out for Mexican food in Mexico. But Rick really changed Mexican food, not just in the United States, but in Mexico. He started to have people in their own country say, this is restaurant-worthy food. And so now the restaurants in Mexico are so good. Just working on our TV show, I could see from season 1 to season 10 the change in Mexican food—in Mexico.

DEANN BAYLESS: Some people complained [about what they were charging for Mexican food]. But it was very few. I can see their faces, the people who complained in those early years. They were grumpy people to begin with.

RICK BAYLESS: They were grumpy people. And there's also those people who say Mexican food is cheap food. And that the prices we charge at Frontera are just horrible. Because, if it's Mexican food, it's supposed to be cheap. And I said, oh, yeah, and you're supposed to use really crappy ingredients and never pay the staff, right? So that's what you're looking for? Places where people are treated really poorly and you get really crappy ingredients. That's what you really want?

Well, they don't think that far ahead. You get what you pay for, basically.

We have never liked saying oh, Topolobampo's more sophisticated. Right now, we have *blazing* hot dishes in Topolo, we have really gutsy things on the menu in Topolo. It's because that represents the cuisine. We are trying our best to channel the real cuisine of Mexico. Because now Mexico is just filled with young chef-owned restaurants that are doing amazing things.

Surprisingly, their next restaurant wasn't a Mexican concept: in 1993 they opened Zinfandel with two other Chicago restaurateurs, Susan and Drew Goss.

RICK BAYLESS: We had two people on our staff who we knew we were going to lose if we didn't do another project. One of them was Paul Kahan, and the other was a guy named Sam McGee. When that space [59 W. Grand] became available we decided to take it. But towards the end Sam had major health issues, and he bowed out, and that kind of destabilized that partnership, and Paul backed out and went to work for Erwin Drechsler [Metropolis].

We had met the Gosses and they were really interested in regional American food. And I thought, well, I grew up in that. So we launched into that, and named it Zinfandel, which is the iconic American grape. But it didn't particularly go well, we were very systems-oriented and want to change things and keep things growing, and they were more sort of hanging out and figure out what's the next right moment to put something on the menu. So it never really gelled, and after a year, we just quietly backed out of the whole thing and they ran it for a long time.

Instead of opening other full-scale restaurants, in the next several years the Baylesses created a line of Frontera-branded supermarket products, from salsas and tortilla chips to cooking sauces and frozen foods. They used them as the basis for concessions inside Chicago department stores and other buildings, which led to what many road warriors undoubtedly consider their greatest achievement—creating quality food offerings for Chicago's O'Hare airport.

RICK BAYLESS: When we started doing these licensed agreement things, one of the reasons that I was comfortable doing it was that it was all based on the fact that we now had a prepared foods company that could do shelf-stable product that we were really happy with. And that was going to be the base of the flavors of what we worked with. And so all of those licensed places were part of Frontera Foods, and they've since spun off from that [as Tortazo].

DEANN BAYLESS: For the airport, the city came to us—

RICK BAYLESS: I didn't want to do it.

DEANN BAYLESS: He turned it down for two years. And then finally they came again. And he said, Okay, here's the deal. We can do it, if we can have our own purveyors. Yeah. And that was unheard of at the time at the airport, because you've got to get badged and all this stuff. So we figured out how to do it. I mean, we found one person who would be the aggregator, get everything here and drive. And that was the one person that was badged. But he would take it from all our purveyors, and he brought it to the airport. So that was the thing we did that nobody had ever done. We said, we want really high-quality ingredients and local out there. So we had to figure out the supply chain.

RICK BAYLESS: Number one, I look up to our customers at the airport and everybody else looks down at them. They all say that they don't have any taste and they don't know anything. They really think of their customers as the bottom of the barrel, and I said that I fly, and I know lots of other very sophisticated people who fly. So what if we actually did something that had great integrity? The airport concession operators will tell you, give us a recipe, we'll make it, it will be just fine. And I said, no, that's not the case. You can give them the recipes, but then you have to go out there and you have to train them. And you have to have staff to go out there every week, and look at your unit, spend time in the unit, develop serious quality assurance testing, mystery shoppers, that kind of thing.

HMS [the airport concessionaire] told us we would fail, but the city told them they had to take us.

DEANN BAYLESS: They said nothing spicy, nothing you have to wait for, and nothing aromatic, because nobody wants to get on a plane with aromatic food.

RICK BAYLESS: So we gave them spicy food that they had to wait for that was incredibly aromatic.

10: THE WILD WEST LOOP

Restaurants change neighborhoods, but perhaps no part of Chicago has flip-flopped in character so completely in such a comparatively short span of time as what we now call the West Loop, just over the expressway from the main downtown area (the Loop).

Until the 1980s, it was an important area for the restaurant industry—but not because people went there to eat. Its streets were lined with Greek, Italian and Mexican meat packers, vegetable sellers, equipment suppliers and wholesalers of every kind. To diners, it was with few exceptions largely invisible and to be avoided, an early morning blue-collar community of truckers and butchers, meat juices literally flowing down the sidewalks. The idea that this could ever become a trendy restaurant neighborhood, home to hot tickets like Marché, Blackbird, Girl & the Goat and Next, would have seemed unimaginable . . . let alone that it would rise more than once. This transformation began as the work of a restaurant group called KDK, driven by the vision of a Russian-born interior designer and furniture maker, Jerry Kleiner.

Jim Graziano's great-grandfather started J.P. Graziano & Sons, a wholesaler and importer among many such on Randolph Street, in 1937; today it's an Italian sub shop and a living tribute to Randolph Street's past and heritage. Jim started working in the family business in 1988, when he was eight, making him one of the last to come up in the old Randolph Street.

JIM GRAZIANO: To say it was a different universe back then might be putting it lightly—it was as dirty as it could possibly get. Food was just thrown out everywhere, before everybody had their own dumpsters. On Fulton Market they were doing live kills, and you would see, you know, cows walk in and steaks walk out. The smells that would come off Fulton Market were indescribable, especially if you caught the day where the inedibles truck would come to pick up everybody's inedibles, a specific box of stuff that can't be used in butchering, and that gets filled up and put out on the sidewalk, and with the summer heat it's just baking in there.

But I never felt like it was a dangerous area. By four in the afternoon it was a ghost town. The guys that were down here were, we called them pallet guys. Because you had the extra wide sidewalks. And the boulevard had the service drives, because everybody had a truck. Everybody would park their trucks in front of their own establishments, and would line up the pallets full of products on the sidewalk. So inevitably, there were empty pallets on the sidewalk. And if you didn't bring them in quick enough the street guys would snatch them up.

They would go cash them in, and go buy some beer, or wine or whatever, and go on the corner and drink until they passed out. And then they'd wake up at five o'clock in the morning when the neighborhood started getting going again. Those pallet guys would wait at the exits of the expressway, and they would jump on the side of the semi and help the guy unload. A trucker from Indiana, who doesn't know the neighborhood or where he can drive, the pallet guys knew the neighborhood like the back of their hand, they would shout out where to go. Those guys were busy all day long. So even though it was gritty and dirty, and you had to keep your eyes open, it was a community and it worked.

Where the La Colombe [upscale coffee shop] is now, I'd have to get four Sanka coffees, for my dad and my grandpa and my Uncle Paul and my Uncle Larry. When I got a little bit older and started smoking I would buy my cigarettes down there because I thought I was far enough away, right? That happened for like a week. And then my dad gave me a little crack to the back of the head and he's like, don't you realize I know everybody in this neighborhood? The Greek guys that owned it would sell to me to make the money, but then they'd immediately tell my father what was going on.

The butchers and the vegetable guys would start at three o'clock in the morning. So by the time we would get down here, we opened up at seven or eight, these guys were done for the day. And they were drinking and smoking and playing pool. You couldn't even see from the front door to the counter with the amount of smoke that was in there.

It was just like something out of a book. But to me, this was Randolph Street. I thought most eight-year-olds knew how to drive a forklift, and unload a semi.

Ina Pinkney had opened her breakfast restaurant Ina's—made famous by Bill Rice in the Tribune—*in Lincoln Park, then moved it to Streeterville. After that partnership ended, she was looking for a new place to launch it again and found it in the early '90s at the forlorn west end of Randolph Street.*

INA PINKNEY: People kept saying you really should open again. And I started to believe them after about a year and a half of being out of the business. I sat down with a map of Chicago, and I looked around at this map, and I said, okay, I can't go east, it's the lake. I can't go north, it's Evanston. South, Bronzeville is not going to happen. The only place to go is west, I wonder what's west.

So I drove over there. And once you go over the river, all the buildings were very low profile. So I started to research it. The Randolph Market District was the original place for trading—there were push carts, and then there were stalls, and there were one- and two-story buildings, because nobody could schlep fifty pound bags of potatoes up those rickety ladders. So that's what they had.

A friend of mine had a food distribution company, where City Winery is now, and one day she said to me, I think you should come and look at this place. It's not for sale, not for rent, but the guy needs to retire, the place is really a mess.

So we get in the car, I pick her up. She goes, make a left, make a left and make a right into the parking lot. I went, it has a parking lot? Yes. We walk in the door of this bar, full of union guys, and the first thing I see are these giant pictures of the 1955 Brooklyn Dodgers. So I'm looking at Duke Snider and

I'm looking at Carl Furillo, and I'm going, this is my home. These are my boys. This is where I live, now. When I told people that I was going to the West Loop, they all said to me, what, are you crazy? I would never go *there.* I said, I have free parking. They would immediately say, I'll be there!

I went and introduced myself to the vendors. And I told them who I was, and that I had had a restaurant up north. And I said, you'll never see a Sysco or US Foods truck in front of my place, ever. I'm committed to the street, I'm committed to you—and I hope to God you are committed to me and give me some decent prices. And then we'll be okay.

JIM GRAZIANO: You'd spend an hour at a customer's location, whoever the customer was, and for forty-five minutes you would talk about what's going on in the world. How are the kids, your mom was sick last time I was here, how's she doing? Somebody had a baby, somebody got married, forty-five minutes, and the last fifteen minutes was to put in your order. That's how we stuck around as long as we did, purely based on the personal relationships that were built over generations.

Our sign said wholesale to the public, which was a lie. It should have said wholesale to the public—*if* you're going to buy as much as a restaurant. When artists started living in lofts, they'd walk in and ask for a pound of pasta and a quarter pound of cheese. And my Uncle Paul would chase them out. He'd be like, what are you gonna do with a *quarter* pound of cheese? What about *tomorrow?* But the families that shopped here, three sisters or a brother-in-law, cousins, whatever, they would come and buy two full forms of cheese, and four cases of pasta and three cases of tomatoes and five pounds of oregano, and split it all up among themselves.

INA PINKNEY: Where Girl & the Goat is now, was Central Supply. Greek, of course, and he wouldn't let you in. He would walk over to the door. And he'd look at you. And I'd smile. I had a plate that I needed, and I went, do you have any of these? He opened the door and you'd have to follow him, he walked with canes, to the back. He'd need to talk with you for a little while, so when I went over there I'd tell Seana, my manager, I'm going over to Central Supply, so give me an hour.

JIM GRAZIANO: Nick, the old Greek guy. I'd walk into that place and he would be reading Greek philosophy books. And he pulled me in the back of the store and I'd be gone for an hour over there, my dad wouldn't come hunting for me because he knew where I was and what I was doing. Central Supply, old man Nick. I don't know if I *ever* saw a customer walk into that place.

INA PINKNEY: The place was filled with stuff, piles and piles of stuff. And you couldn't browse—I mean, you didn't know what was in there, it was all in boxes. Eventually I'd say I gotta get back, almost lunchtime. And then he'd say, okay, come with me, and he would open the door [to the warehouse]. "No, you stay here." He would go into this walkway between the cartons and pull one down, and come back and it was *always* the right dish. The whole thing was like a dance, we had to do this dance.

I don't even know how many tractor trailers it must have taken to empty that place out when the Boka boys bought it.

JIM GRAZIANO: Jerry Kleiner, who is the absolute pioneer of Randolph Street without question, when he told people he was going to open up Marché, they told him he was nuts. People do not go down to Randolph Street unless they have to. They don't go at night. And they absolutely don't go for a fancy dining experience. And as Jerry does, he didn't listen to anybody. So he planted the first three flags here, and they all lasted a wildly long time.

****

JERRY KLEINER: I was born in Russia. We lived in Poland. My parents were custom tailors. I've always had a flair for custom clothes and, and things like that. Self-taught, I never went to school for any of that stuff, but I worked at Bonwit Teller—a very high-end store in the John Hancock Building. So I was always around fabric and clothes. I was always interested in design.

I started just sort of manufacturing and putting things together. I opened up my own design studio, in front of Shelter [bar], called Kleiner Design. I started working with guys like Frank Vivo [upholsterer] and other metal guys. And so I learned about the pitch of a chair, the width, the depth, tied springs, all that other stuff. I didn't know about the construction of anything. I started playing around with designs, and Frank would work with me and say, well, we have to have this pitch on this, we've got to do this to that. So he helped me understand how to make furniture that was comfortable.

It was fascinating. Just the people I was meeting and the hospitality aspect of creating a space. When you build something for somebody's house, a lot of people don't get to see it. But I love the fact of creating a space where people could also feel it, you could see it and feel it and engage with all these different bodies of people coming together.

I had Cairo nightclub at 720 N. Wells, '85, '86, and then Shelter at 564 W. Fulton in '89 or '90. Everybody still talks about Shelter. On Fulton Market, in the old Sears and Roebuck Company's original distribution facility. Back then there was really nothing around it, it was really industrial and still a mixed bag of tricks down there. Nobody was living there at that time, everybody remembers how seedy it was. It reminded me of the markets down in New York, in the Meatpacking District—all these cool, seedy, seductive places, where you never knew what was around the corner. There was prostitution, there was all this crazy stuff going on. That was the chicness, the coolness, the hipness of those areas.

But I got tired of counting money. I couldn't take it anymore! You're there at five o'clock in the morning and you have a checkout, by the time you're done it's nine, ten in the morning. I'm a creative guy, and I wanted the feel, the sense of doing something. I loved Randolph Street, and I found this location to do a restaurant and called it Vivo. I was working for Frank Vivo, and his wife Lena was like a master presenter of incredible flavors and tastes in Italian cuisine, very upscale. She sort of helped me with a direction, this really incredible cooking that she did.

HOWARD DAVIS: I was a corporate lawyer who had an entrepreneurial streak, and distant members of my family had some restaurants, but I was not really exposed to it directly.

I met my friend Jerry Kleiner. He was building nightclubs in Chicago. One was called Cairo, on Wells and Superior. And the other was called Shelter, which was just like a cutting-edge, underground place on Fulton Market that just was fantastic. So he and I became friends. We were hanging out, and he said, hey, do you wanna open a restaurant?

We went to 838 W. Randolph—this is like '91, early '91. There's no one over there when we go to look at the place. There was really nothing in the West Loop except Greektown and [an old steak house called] Barney's Market Club—"Yes Sir, Senator!" It was like SoHo in New York, before it developed, when it was still an active food market. And I said okay, let's do it.

Jerry, he was the designer who creates these things. I'm a lawyer and a CPA, so I can help with some of those things, but otherwise, not so much. But I brought in a third guy, a friend of mine, Dan Krasny, who was the day-to-day operating partner.

I saw Jerry do these nightclubs that became very popular, and they weren't in busy areas—they pioneered those areas. But I remember being in the empty space and asking Jerry, what if we open and nobody comes? "Don't worry. They'll come." And sure enough, from the moment we opened we were *so* popular.

JERRY KLEINER: Nobody's ever seen anything like that in a place that industrial. Generally in those times, people were on Lincoln Avenue, they were on Rush Street, those kinds of destination areas. That was the first time anybody's gone off the beaten path. And it just created such a buzz. I don't remember when Michael Jordan started coming into that restaurant, I've forgotten, but you couldn't believe the calls, the lines, everybody wanted to be part of this seventy-five-seat restaurant. The numbers we were doing then were just incredible, astronomical.

So from there I go, hey, let's tighten up this street. Like, if you go to a mall, you've got hundreds of places, let's throw another one across the street, same price point, same affluent customer, a little more sizzle, different look, different feel, different environments. Rent's cheap, we were paying like $800 a month at Vivo. All these buildings are down there, waiting to be taken over. And people went, are you crazy? I'm not going down there. I couldn't convince anybody else to even come in there.

It was like a blank canvas. You could paint your own pictures. And we couldn't build places fast enough. We built three restaurants before anybody even blinked. Rich Melman and everybody was always like scratching their heads, like what the hell are they doing? I remember Rich called me one time, and he was like, is that a good street? What do you think about it?

HOWARD DAVIS: Vivo was loosely modeled on a place in SoHo called I Tre Merli—"the three ravens." There was a look that both places had that was very striking. And I remember one time the owners came over to Vivo and they go, we hate you guys. Everybody goes there and says, are you guys affiliated with Vivo?

From a cuisine standpoint, you still had the classical French restaurants, and then Charlie Trotter was on the scene doing his thing. There wasn't really a ton of what I'd call New American—Blackbird opened up after we opened Marché and Red Light. But during those years, there really wasn't.

JERRY KLEINER: We did Marché [on Randolph Street]. Marché was like a French-American bistro, with chicken frites and steak frites and salmon. Understandable food. I never wanted to get into food that you had to explain to somebody. It's like, what is this? And they sort of look at you, what do you mean, you don't get this? Like, no, I don't get it. Just give me something that I can understand.

SIMON LAMB (manager for KDK Restaurants): When I got to Chicago, I kept asking people, when I do eventually get a day off, where should I go eat? And they were like, you have to go eat at this Marché place.

So when I finally got there, I pushed open the big velvet curtains and went through the giant revolving door and walk into *Alice in Wonderland*, and I vowed that at some point, I would work there.

HOWARD DAVIS: Marché was big and bold. We brought Michael Kornick into our partnership as our chef partner. And just from the day it opened, it was so busy and so successful and so popular. People loved the food and the ambiance and what Jerry created visually there. You walk in, and the first thing you see is the open kitchen. Nobody had ever seen that before. A much bigger, bolder restaurant than Vivo.

Michael Kornick was a very well-known chef and people came because of his food. The food was French brasserie—so we had fantastic steak fries,

French onion soup. We had a woodburning rotisserie grill, which I don't even think you can do now and open. But it made frickin' fantastic rotisserie chicken.

LYNN BUZZA (pastry cook): It felt fresh to us in that it wasn't anything crazy, but it was so simple it felt new. I remember doing a lot of the coriander-crusted tuna loin that we would then slice. I remember the chicken—my husband absolutely loved this pounded chicken breast that they did, that was like seared and smothered with oyster mushrooms and fresh herbs, it was really, really good. And then Audrey Craig's desserts, I just loved the simplicity. She used a lot of fruit, we always used a lot of fruit in the desserts, made sure that there was a balance between chocolate and fruit.

MICHAEL KORNICK: Jerry's a brilliant visionary. When he had Shelter nightclub, I was introduced to him, because he wanted to do like, late-night food adjacent to Shelter. Then in '90, '91, he decided to open up a restaurant that was going to be like I Tre Merli in New York, a very dark, narrow, rectilinear restaurant. And that became Vivo, which I was a consulting chef for. He'd come up to New York, and I would come down from Boston, and we kept spending time together.

Kornick had left Lettuce Entertain You after plans to open an authentic French brasserie fell through. He worked for the Four Seasons hotel chain in Chicago and then in Boston.

When the recession hit [in 1993], and things were challenging for me, Jerry said, look, I want to do another restaurant, you still want to do a French brasserie, and I said, yeah. He said, well, if you move back to Chicago, we'll double your income. And he did. We went into partnership, we opened up Marché in September of '93. And, you know, in a year, I had doubled my income, and had an equity stake in a restaurant.

JERRY KLEINER: The kitchen was right in front, like a showplace. I wanted people to see the place like a piece of artwork. It was designed with all this art on the columns—I had different artists each paint a column. I had this little competition and it's like, fifteen columns by fifteen different artists. You just walked in and it was just a big wow, you walk in and this thing is larger than life. This stylish, fashionable restaurant before everything was like cookie cutter, Rich Melman kind of stuff.

There was a movie, *The Cook, The Thief, His Wife and Her Lover.*[17] Jean Paul Gaultier did the costumes. The way they went into the kitchen, and all this over-the-top design, decor, that's what I wanted for Marché. I wanted you to walk through the kitchen. It was almost like Cirque de Soleil and *The Cook, The Thief, His Wife and Her Lover* created this environment.

SIMON LAMB: The West Loop at that point was still a scary place at night. When I started at Marché, the cab wouldn't go all the way to Marché, it would drop me on the bridge. And we still had off-duty police there at closing time to walk all the servers to their cars. One of the manager's jobs at Marché was to get the hookers cleared off the corner. You would bring them family meal and say, can you go down a block or two? And they'd be like, okay, thank you, honey.

IVAR JOHNSON (server): I used to live over there. I lived on Lake Street like at Ada, and I would just be on my bike or walking home from work or whatever, and I'd get followed by some very well-meaning, wildly intoxicated prostitutes—hey, why are you walking so fast? Just going home, lady. But yeah, that was an interesting neighborhood, for sure.

MICHAEL KORNICK: Marché was a French brasserie that went back to my time with Jeremiah Tower. There was no wood-burning rotisserie in Chicago at the time. The only wood-burning grill that came to Chicago early on was in Larry and Mark Levy's restaurant Chestnut Street Grill, which was modeled after what they had seen in San Francisco. So I brought in the same grill that I had used when I staged at Spago, which was a Montague open top, roll top grill. We put in a rotisserie that Kleiner built in his metal shop. We did rotisserie chicken with frites, the kind of frites that they had at [Lettuce's] Un

17 (1989) Dir: Peter Greenaway

Grand Café, French thin-cut frites, although I did them in beef fat.

I opened up the kitchen to mirror some of the bistros and brasseries that I had experienced in France. So things like salade Lyonnaise, frisée salad, poached egg and lardons, properly done confit of duck with a ton of turnips and port wine, lots of different variations of foie gras. But the staple of the restaurant was spit-roasted chicken with pommes frites, and steak frites where we used flank steak off the woodburning grill. Then we had an *entrecôte*, a double cut bone-in ribeye for two, which a lot of the French steak houses do. And we had all sorts of French-influenced fish dishes. Back in the '80s and '90s you didn't see a rare tuna steak. Seared rare tuna came to Chicago at Avanzare, Melman's place with Dennis Terczak.

It was important to sell to the middle of the market—I knew that from working with Melman, you can't open up a 200-seat restaurant and not hit the middle of the market. And then you can take them where you want to go. But you better have some things that, you know, Chicagoans would recognize and stand behind, like garlic mashed potatoes. The thing about Kleiner that's great is, he always wants to make a lot of money in what he did, whether it was nightclubs or furniture or restaurants, but never at the expense of squelching someone's creative impulses.

MINDY SEGAL (pastry chef): I worked there at a very exciting time, during the time of peak Bulls, Michael Jordan. That neighborhood was not the neighborhood it is now, there were like two restaurants and then hookers and drug addicts. I loved working in that neighborhood. It was artsy, very artsy. It was a great time to be there. It was risqué and kooky and fun, drugs and models and stars.

I loved working for Michael Kornick. I loved his energy, I loved his knowledge. He knew how to run a restaurant and he knew about wine. He knew about service. And he knew about the importance of the presence of a chef in the dining room. He taught me the business, taught me how to read a P&L statement, taught me how to work with vendors and cost out recipes, even though I learned that in culinary school. As a pastry chef, if you don't love working for a chef and following their food and making desserts that complement their food, then you shouldn't be a pastry chef. I loved working for Michael, I loved collaborating. It was like my favorite thing. I still love it.

LYNN BUZZA: Kornick really strove to make it be and feel like one team. We always had family meal and everyone sat down in the same area of the restaurant—front of the house, back of the house. Sometimes, it might be all cooks at this area and all servers in that area, but everyone eating together at the same time and socializing. Towards the end of family meal, either Michael or John [Bubala, sous chef] would stand up and start talking about the specials, so everyone was on the same page. I thought that was really smart, and really appreciated it.

If you remember the big windows up front, people would just be standing there watching what we were doing. Everything being so open was the opposite of Everest, where we were behind the wall, sort of secret. Having Michael Jordan and a lot of the Bulls come in, Oprah Winfrey coming in, David Byrne coming in—we just felt like rock stars.

ERICK WILLIAMS (executive chef at Kornick's restaurant mk): Working for Michael was an incredible experience. I learned so much, from menu design structure to technique in the kitchen. I learned how to open restaurants, and I learned how to close restaurants. I learned a lot about customer engagement. Chefs are as awkward as awkward gets, but Michael taught me how important it was to be engaging and to create a following in the dining room. And for people to feel like they were not just connected to the food, but connected to the person and connected to the team. On a lot of levels, he didn't want his servers to be the only entryway into the brand. It was a very familial relationship that I established, working under his tutelage.

CARYN BOBROWSKI (manager, Marché): Marché was one of the most fun places that you could possibly be in that time frame. It was a party every night. It was packed every night.

It had really caring service. Attention to detail a must. We did a front waiter/back waiter system, but you could come in in jeans and a polo, like, that was the energy that we put out, we didn't want to turn someone away. Everyone was made to feel comfortable, we never wanted to be stuffy. Hiring really warm individuals that are eager to learn, like I didn't know how to pronounce Chateauneuf-du-Pape, but I was eager. And I really wanted to learn.

JERRY KLEINER: Everyone was dressed up to the minute, people were just coming in from all over the place, the energy level. The age groups, the suburban kids, the city kids, people with money, people without money, the artsy people—everybody went in that place. And then people would leave the restaurant and go to my nightclub Shelter. I'd have to call the door guys and tell them to let in these people, they just spent $500 with us. The numbers we did were just incredible.

Marché was beyond legendary. This was the height of Michael Jordan and the Bulls, and people from all over the world wanted to see those games. And everybody wanted to get into Marché and Vivo, it was a who's who globally that came down that street. And then in 1996, we had the Democratic Convention. Mayor Daley asked me to design Randolph Street, the flower boxes, the lights, the whole deal. I was the only guy from the outside that helped to design that street.

HOWARD DAVIS: If you look at the design of Vivo, what you'd primarily see was the spotlights on the wall of wine stacked up on the wood, and the old elevator shaft [private dining room] and kind of a long, narrow place. If that was Vivo, then Marché I always said was like an Impressionistic painting, because there were all these colors. He got these artists to paint the columns right at Marché like they do at La Coupole in Paris.

When he got to Red Light it felt like it was a more cohesive overall design for everything. It was inspired by [Barcelona architect] Antoni Gaudí and his places there, where it's hard to find the straight line. That's what Jerry went for, details like a wavy ceiling or the storefront that he handmade, because he had his own metal fabricating shop. But he said that the design was inspired by Asian cuisine, and it took them a long time to do that restaurant because the level and the depth of all the design was much greater than in the other places.

JERRY KLEINER: Red Light started when I went to China, we went to the opera. We go to the opera and everybody's coming in with bags, because they've got all this food they're bringing in. They're talking, the curtain goes up, and they're still talking and eating. So we open up at Red Light, and it's just like an opera, the energy field. We wanted to create, sort of, Asian-inspired good food, some of it Americanized, but stuff that could be understandable with an Asian influence.

DONNIE MADIA (bartender): At the time I was coming up Jerry Kleiner was opening his third restaurant, Red Light. I was working across the street, at a place called Paladino's. So I'm watching him build the restaurant and he's on all three corners. And I'm thinking, wow, this is really interesting that he puts a concentrated effort into one area. So he's controlling the environment. He's controlling the real estate. And he's also controlling competition, because he's his only competition. Right? With the exception of Paladino's, which didn't last more than two years, I believe.

SIMON LAMB: I got to work closely with Kleiner on opening Red Light, which was eye-opening. People dismiss him a lot of the time, because of the way he speaks and what he's speaking about. Howard was a good counterpoint to that. Howard was always the calm, rational guy, but working with Jerry was one of the greatest things ever.

Every Saturday, he used to come by and drop his kids off in the afternoon, so I could babysit them. And then he'd go and hit golf balls down Randolph Street. Because at that point, it wasn't built up.

We really prided ourselves on being ahead of the curve, like, I would go to New York with Jerry and normally take a chef or two to with me. Jerry knew New York like nobody. And he still had Shelter cash, when he went out of town he would bring a duffel bag to go in the walk-in safe in the corporate office.

And it was all about looking at menus, looking at menu design, looking at dishes. Three days, we'd be in and out and we'd do like 100 to 150 restaurants. Mainly it was buying fabrics and raw materials for the design side of things. But then he would find these crazy little restaurants did one thing amazingly well. He'd be like, we're going to this place for meatballs. And I mean, I remember he was getting upset because he didn't like the foie gras preps that we were doing at Marché, so he booked a flight to go to New York. And one day all we did was eat foie. I seriously thought I was gonna die, I've never felt so ill in my entire life.

Jerry has a passion for creating the scene, and he's got some operational insight, but he doesn't want to be bothered with the day to day. So operationally I had a strong team, I had really great managers, it was a place where you could be yourself. It was super attractive to slightly off-center but true professionals, who didn't really fit in with a corporate thing. They had great chefs, we had great service, great wine programs and booze programs. But underneath that, it was not a regular place to work.

MICHAEL KORNICK: When we did Red Light, I had been to Southeast Asia and I loved the concept of doing a Southeast Asian street restaurant. I think menu-wise, it was a little ahead of its time. The restaurant was doing okay, it cost a lot to build. But it was a weird business because we had three guys, each were 30 percent owners, and I was a 10 percent owner, and Jerry and Howard Davis were in conflict with Dan Krasny. And they got into a lawsuit and it froze up all the assets of the company.

I had my first kid in 1995, and my second kid in '97 and that January, I just bought my first home. And I was in the middle as a minority shareholder of two restaurants that were seizing assets. It was nothing personal that I had with Jerry or Howard or Dan. But it was time for me to do my own thing and not have that kind of situation. So in 1998 I found a site and left KDK in September of '98 and opened up mk that November.

SIMON LAMB: Red Light was amazing. It was Jerry's interpretation of everything that he'd seen. And at that point, we had a fabrication shop because nobody was making anything that we needed. Every single thing in Red Light was custom built in the shop. It was Kleiner-designed to the *n*th degree.

And the thing that I always loved about it was, it's a pan-Asian restaurant and everything in there was totally anti-*feng shui.* So this whole idea of, let's work with the Japanese Tourist Bureau and the Chinese Tourist Bureau. And they were like, oh, no, no, no, we can't come in there. You've got these triangles hanging upside down on the ceiling. And that's incredibly bad *feng shui.*

HOWARD DAVIS: Michael Kornick said he wanted to do the Chinese food. But Red Light did not have a good opening. Because I think the expectations were so high, based on Vivo and Marché. Kornick was obviously very qualified but I think he was out of his comfort zone with Chinese food. It didn't take and he wound up leaving our company.

People were not as open to authentic Asian food. They were like, where's the egg foo young, the egg rolls? And it's like, well, we're trying to do authentic pan-Asian food here. So this dish is from China, this dish is from Indonesia, this dish is from Thailand. And they didn't like it.

JERRY KLEINER: Kornick's food didn't go over. I think some of this stuff was just really too far out, it wasn't understandable enough. It wasn't New York, you can't go too far off the beaten path in Chicago. It was too avant-garde.

So we pulled him out and I don't remember if it was Paul Wildermuth at that time—Jackie Shen came in for the last seven years.

MICHAEL KORNICK: Paul Wildermuth came on board with me to open it, and he ended up being the chef. He had worked in the Mandarin in LA. And he had opened up Ben Pao, which was Chinese comfort food, with Lettuce. He was really the person who was able to shift to kung pao chicken and some of those items that were more middle of the market.

HOWARD DAVIS: We brought in this guy Paul Wildermuth who worked with Arun [Sampanthavivat, of Arun's, an upscale Thai restaurant]. Arun mentored him and they changed the menu and then Red Light became one of the most popular restaurants in the city. There were many signature dishes there. They had these barbecue fried ribs, five-spice ribs, that were spectacular. Paul helped us open up Opera in the South Loop, and Saiko, but at some point he left and Jackie Shen came in to run Red Light.

When Jackie came, she put her stamp on it with her famous chocolate bag dessert and other dishes.

JACKIE SHEN: I read they had an opening for a chef. But I really seriously didn't know Asian, except what my mom cooked. And when we went to

Chinatown to eat. I knew the ingredients from cookbooks, but never how to properly use those ingredients.

So first week, I just kind of do whatever people needed help with. And there's a cook there. His name was Heinie, and he had worked there for seven years. And Arun was the consulting chef. So they sent me to a room for a lecture about Thai food. So one week of writing notes and all that kind of stuff. And then Heinie was the main person in the kitchen that taught me how to cook Asian. He told me all the thing about curries and stuff like that. And then I took a week off to go to Thailand. We infused the French sauces with all the Asian products, and then tweak, tweak it and work with it.

I didn't deal with Jerry Kleiner or Howard Davis. I was in my own world. And as long as the restaurant's making money, they don't bother me and I don't bother them. I did my thing and I did my cooking and that's all I care about.

****

JERRY KLEINER: You had the height of the Bulls games. People were coming in from all over the world. You had Michael Jordan coming in with all of his posses and his crews. And the bands that would come into the nightclubs—I had dinner with Jerry Mickelson from Jam Productions [concert promoter] and Bono on his fortieth birthday on the second floor of Vivo, a little private party. The Jordan days, and the band days where you have these groupie girls following all these guys around—we saw stuff you couldn't even believe.

SIMON LAMB: One of our bartenders just happened to be dating one of the major people in Jam, so whenever there was a band in town they went to Marché or they were in the back room at Red Light. That kind of grew and spread and so people were coming and hanging out and just looking for who was going to be there.

CARYN BOBROWSKI: Part of my training was, if Michael Jordan was coming in, his security is going to call you. And if they call you, you have to have a table for Michael, and you have to have a table for the security and you cannot just say, oh, sure, we'll take care of it. Like you have to have them in close proximity.

So I took care of them for however many months and then one day, finally I got to know security very well. One day, I thought, I'm gonna go introduce myself to Michael Jordan. It's time. I've taken care of him and his group many times. So I asked the security guard and he said yeah, absolutely, come on Caryn. And Michael was sitting at a table with Ahmad Rashad and Charles Barkley and some other people. I walked up to the table, and I'm five-three, and I said, excuse me, Mr. Jordan. And he stands up from the table. And he grabbed me, wrapped his arms around my waist, and he picked me up like a doll. And he just hugged me. And as he was putting me down, I said [timidly] oh, you're going to hug me? Oh-kay. I couldn't get away from the table fast enough.

MICHAEL KORNICK: First of all, at Marché you had this hot young staff. It was a chic audience, it was a cool see-and-be-seen place. One of our biggest customers, the first three years, was Michael Jordan. He came in after games, and then in '97 he opened his own place, one sixtyblue, with [chef] Martial Noguier. Then he had his own dining room, and his own place to go on Randolph.

We had lots of business people because at that time, they all had tickets to the Bulls, and there was nowhere to eat on Madison Street, there was nowhere on Lake Street or Fulton Market. We were the gateway. So Vivo, Marché and Red Light were all busy with that Bulls and Hawks kind of clientele.

Jerry had a great relationship with Mayor Daley, and because of that *we* had a great relationship with him. I ended up doing Maggie [Daley, the mayor's wife]'s birthday, for many many years at mk. I have a drawing that Jerry had done in 1989 that he took to the mayor's Office of Development to show the potential of Randolph Street if they would repair the center, put in old-style lights and create storefronts out of the produce and the wholesale places. And it's exactly what happened.

It was just so much fun. That's the only way to explain it. Just such a great time to be on Randolph Street. The Bulls were in their heyday, and we had the Democratic Convention come to town in '96, which changed Randolph Street. We had so much opportunity to be who we wanted it to be—a casual French brasserie that had four hundred wines on the list. We also had a huge California representation, because those were the people who I knew from my days at Gordon, and, and so it was just a great restaurant to be a part of.

HOWARD DAVIS: During the week, we got more city people and more hip, urban people. Saturday nights, we'd get more suburbanites coming down and wanting to try it, but still a lot of business people because we were kind of close to downtown but off the beaten path. So we were kind of cool, we were an edgy alternative for like, Goldman Sachs and other big companies. They wanted to be in a hip and trendy restaurant for their corporate event. One of the nice things about my involvement with these restaurants was meeting so many interesting people. A lot of out-of-town people, because they'd hear about it and we were close enough to the downtown area that they could go there.

All that was brand-new for them. And even though nothing else was around there, you look up and you see the skyline from downtown, so you're not totally uncomfortable about where you're at. And then all the media would write about us as being the cutting edge.

A lot of famous people who came into Chicago would come dine with us either at Vivo or Marché. Mostly Vivo, some Marché, not so much at Red Light, but we had Mel Gibson and Billy Crystal at lunch one day.

CARYN BOBROWSKI: We had Dennis Rodman in every hair color. Whenever there was a movie being shot in town, it was just the place to go. One night we had Dan Aykroyd, Linda Hamilton, maybe Jim Belushi. And I remember Dan Aykroyd was like helping pour wine, he was really acting as kind of like the host of this party at Marché. He was walking around the tables and chatting with everyone.

And then he started clearing their plates. And I just about lost my mind. I told the staff, everyone, get over there, right now. You're not letting him clear his own plates. I walked right up to him to take the plate out of his hand. And I said, just give those to me, and he said, where's the bus station? And I said, oh, absolutely not. I will take those. And he looked at me and he said, no, the bus station, and I just went straight over to the bus station, where he proceeded to place all the dishes, and he continues to pour wine and clear plates. So that evening, he walked around to staff and every staff member that was working, he gave them $150. He then proceeded to tip the managers, but he ran out of cash, so he started writing personal checks, so I had a personal check made out to me from Dan Aykroyd from 1995 I don't think I ever cashed.

We were also one of Chris Farley's last nights. That was kind of earth-shattering, when he died, having witnessed the start of that.

MINDY SEGAL: I was actually working the night that Chris Farley died and he came into Marché that night. He was definitely fucked up, but I didn't know he was gonna die that night. I couldn't believe it when I woke up in the morning and they said he was dead.

That was crazy. It was always something crazy going on there. I loved it. It was action packed.

LYNN BUZZA: People would just spend so much money there. And servers, you knew how much money they would make. But they were part of this show. Every one of those servers I remember was some kind of a character.

SIMON LAMB: There were people that had very big personalities, or people who were kind of famous in Chicago, like [server] Joseph LoPresti. And Howard was the one who pulled me aside and said, if you can get Joseph to like you, you're going to be okay. If you can't, there's going to be a problem.

Joseph, to say that he was flamboyant would be a massive, massive understatement. I actually had to create a service crew around him. So he didn't actually have to touch anything because most of the time there was no way his outfits were going to pass any kind of health department inspection. It was bondage gear. It was, did you forget your shirt today? It was very short kilts—could you not bend over unless you'd like to put some underwear on? You know, it was a different time and a different place. We did things there that there's no way you can get away with it now. I mean, you'd all be sued or in jail or both.

CARYN BOBROWSKI: Joseph was this beautiful gay man who was completely sculpted. I mean, absolutely perfectly toned body. He would dress up in costume every single day in his section. So one day, he was a Indian. The next day, he was a pirate. One day, he wore assless chaps and a white shirt. He just bent over the table. He was this larger-than-life personality, he made everyone feel like they were the most special person on the planet.

Sam Zell [real estate billionaire and owner of the *Chicago Tribune*] would have his birthday party there every year. He would rent out Marché and have a surprise party for all of his friends, and famous people as surprise guests. So one year, Jay Leno was the host. You would walk in and the Village People were playing in the main dining room, and then Zell would say, okay, everybody follow me. And everyone would follow Sam Zell out to the back of the restaurant through an alley into an abandoned warehouse that was transformed into a beach with sand and palm trees and the Beach Boys were playing.

HOWARD DAVIS: I remember we had a very wealthy guy throw a birthday party for himself in the back room at Marché. That was quite a wild one—they had really good-looking muscle-bound men walking around half naked carrying bowls of fruit and champagne around. Joseph LoPresti shows up with leather chaps on with no underwear. But he was fantastic. People loved him and he had his clientele. They would show up all the time for him.

We always pushed the edge when it came to, like, sexy parties. Like at Vivo we would have parties where some transgender performers from the Baton Club would come and perform. Every New Year's Eve at Marché we had the Marché De Sade Party and we hired these very creative, artistic S&M people and they would bring a steel cage. People could go in and get hot wax dripped on their back or, you know, be spanked, whipped lightly. I remember after one of these parties, I got a letter from a lawyer saying my client dined at your restaurant New Year's Eve and went in the cage and has [injuries to his] bare buttocks as a result, so we're making a claim for damages. I wrote back, nobody forced them to walk into the cage. He assumed the risk when he walked in there.

SIMON LAMB: There was a dominatrix, and all the staff was outfitted in gear from Paul C Leather. I went to Indiana and got six strippers and put two stripper poles up in the restaurants. I mean, I don't think we even got half of the food out of the kitchen, but nobody cared. After that, there was an understanding, if you want something weird, I'm your guy, let's do it.

JERRY KLEINER: We had some crazy parties, wild times. As you look at things today, maybe I just got older and it's a different perspective, but I don't see things like that. Things were a little freer and easier, [fewer] government restrictions and this and that. It just seemed like life was easier. People say change is good, but sometimes maybe change isn't so good.

****

Being fast and loose—with parties, with business—eventually caught up with KDK.

HOWARD DAVIS: We got into a business dispute with Dan Krasny. And we wound up settling where he would get Vivo and me and Jerry would get Marché and Red Light. So then me and Jerry opened up Gioco in the South Loop. Our opening chef was not crazy about cooking Italian, so he didn't last that long. So then we brought in this guy Corky O'Connor, who was [then-Spiaggia chef] Paul Bartolotta's protégé. Corky really elevated that restaurant, got it three stars.

Jerry was Jerry was Jerry. Jerry would scour the streets, he was trying to replicate what we did in West Randolph in another neighborhood. That's how we did Gioco. He felt Wabash [Avenue], versus Michigan or State, was the best choice to do this. That's why we did three restaurants over there.

JERRY KLEINER: I got into the South Loop with Gioco and some of those other places. I just thought it was another untapped frontier, and then I find a great old building. When we started doing demolition at Gioco, there were three buildings connected. One of the buildings, we broke through a back wall and there was a [secret] room back there. The third building, it was built in 1847—it was the oldest town home in Chicago. I brought this guy in, Tim Samuelson, the cultural historian for the city, and he said that the mobsters and Hinky Dink Kenna [alderman and 1st Ward boss] had their businesses and everything going on in this area.

There's great history in those buildings, I've never gone into a new modern building, like a high-rise where everything looks the same. You're just a piece of it next to a Subway, what's the point of that? There's no soul to it. Even if you want to create a different presence, it's very difficult. I want to go into a seedy alley, where it's like, what the hell's over there? Are you really going down there? That's what I want somebody to feel. Before you get into it, the space should tell a story.

SIMON LAMB: He was sold on the South Loop. He was sure that that was the spot. He fell in love with the [Gioco] spot and found the guy who owned the building and talked to him and signed the lease. And at that point, you couldn't get there. The cabs wouldn't go below Roosevelt Road.

I think in my time Saiko [Japanese restaurant in the South Loop] had the best food, the best beverage program and the best service that any of our places ever had. But that was when Jerry and Howard had their falling out. They were both funding their own restaurant groups outside of KDK. So funding was on, funding was off. And the other thing was at that point, Jerry was really busy with Carnivale [massive Mexican restaurant in the West Loop] and kind of disconnected. So we opened a restaurant that obviously was not finished. You couldn't find it—there's no sign, there's no lights, there's no nothing.

At Opera, I was designing the kitchen, working with Paul and the chefs to make sure that the flow of it was correct. And I had to redesign the kitchen nineteen times to work around Jerry's constant changes, and the final time I said to him, I've got the equipment coming in. We can't change the length, we can't change anything. It's the way way it's got to be. And he's like, oh, yeah, no, that's fine.

All the equipment's been measured, so it slides up underneath perfectly. And I walk in there. And as soon as I walked in, I knew something was wrong. All the lights are on and Jerry's construction crew was there. And they have cut the marble expo top off of the line. And they are currently lowering everything. And I'm like, what are you doing? None of the equipment is going to fit now. And they're like, well, you got to talk to Jerry. So I called Jerry. He comes in and he goes last night, I'm standing there, I'm talking to Paul and he's leaning on the line and I realized that it makes him look short. So I cut off a couple inches to make him look tall.

HOWARD DAVIS: We didn't buy our buildings, we always leased—we barely had enough money to scrape together to do the restaurant. And then Jerry didn't want to be limited or restricted. We always locked into long-term leases, our leases were very good. The question was, why open multiple places across from each other? But they were always different cuisines. Jerry just had a vision of creating his own dining destination.

MICHAEL KORNICK: I think Jerry, and all of us in hindsight, wish we'd have bought more real estate in the '80s and '90s. Yeah. Pick whatever neighborhood you want. If you bought real estate fifteen to twenty years before the housing crisis in Chicago, you won big. Because the city has grown exponentially. And we missed out a lot of opportunities to buy real estate.

JERRY KLEINER: Nobody was selling anywhere. All these Greek guys down there wouldn't sell anything. Naaah, we'll rent it out—I don't know how they figured it out but they were smart enough not to sell. Vivo, the dad died and the kids got it. They're asking like $35,000 a month for the Vivo space. It got so inflated, you see so much turnover there now. But everybody's still trying to jump on the bandwagon. Somebody called me a week or two ago, we got a space you might be interested in. First thing I ask him is how much? Ninety dollars [per square foot], 10,000 square feet. That's a million in rent. Can you imagine? Sometimes the best deals are the ones you don't do.

I was thinking about doing a restaurant in the Garfield Park Conservatory. They were gonna give me a space like 6,000 feet and this old power plant they had there and everything else. But it's too far out or just needed too much work and everything. They were going to give me a no-rent deal, but I would have still had to put the money into fixing it. But those neighborhoods—the West Loop worked because you were only a few blocks away from downtown. You could see those buildings, and you have the stadiums there. You had everything going on. You were close to everything, Rush Street, State Street.

People started moving in [the West Loop], and lofts started developing, but that was years later. In the meantime the storefronts sat empty for—how many years after Red Light? Another five years.

Vivo was there for twenty years, Red Light I think our lease was fifteen or seventeen years, Marché was a fifteen-year lease with a three-year option—and then after those years, they wanted like crazy money. It's just too expensive at the end of those leases. But if you got a twenty-year run, you could do very well. When you're the first guy in, just like we did at Gioco, we're paying $3,300 a month for twenty years. He says, if you want to renew, it's going to $26,000 a month. I go okay, goodbye. We did our thing. It's time to move on.

SIMON LAMB: I've spent a long time working as a consultant and primarily doing openings. And that's the first thing I mean, I look at proposals, and I'm like, you do understand what you're getting into here. Rents are insane. I mean, at Marché we sold an $18 chicken, you know, and that was it. And that paid for Red Light. And then Red Light sold a $10 martini that paid for three restaurants. It was just a different world.

HOWARD DAVIS: I do think that at a certain point. Jerry's designs got a bit repetitive. If you look at Vivo, Marché, Red Light, Gioco and Opera, they're all very different. He started using the same lights, the silk light fixtures, the same colors, the same chairs and stuff. I watched him design and build Vivo, Marché and Red Light, each one of those was very different.

We had a great relationship but when we got a little bigger, we started to fight, because I wanted to try to build a bigger company and impose, like, corporate structure, and he didn't like that. Jerry is the designer guy, independent. And he didn't want to go along with that. So we fought for a while. We made up and we're old pals now. We get together every once in a while, but I always joke with him we're like an old married couple who were with each other for too long. We had to get into some fights before we made up.

MICHAEL KORNICK: I'm the least stylish guy. But I've always worked in hipster, stylish places. Kleiner wore really expensive, beautiful clothes, right? He was very much one of the kind of chic people in Chicago. And he was so much fun. There was nobody more fun.

****

JIM GRAZIANO: When it started to be the place to be, [the old vendors in the neighborhood] didn't have the next generation coming up in their business or their family. They had put thirty, forty years into their business, six days a week, twelve-hour days, just grinding the hell out of themselves. And I would say 95 percent of the people left happy. They got a nice payoff for dedicating a huge portion of their life to running their business here. And they left with a big smile on their face.

Now it's private equity money. It's big international brands that come in. You're not getting your mom-and-pops. But I think that's what helps us be who we are. That dent in the counter I made at nine years old, because I backed the forklift into the office. That's what this place is.

There was a hanging light on the Randolph Street entrance of Red Light. Stained glass with cobalt blue and gold accents on it. When it closed, I wanted to drive down there with a forklift so bad and cut that light off. But I was scared out of my mind to do it. My dad would have killed me, I thought one of the cops would have smacked me around. Then a year after Marché closed, Jerry came in for a sandwich. And I told him about that. And he said, you should have taken it, I would have loved for you to have it.

Jerry Kleiner lives in Los Angeles. Howard Davis owns Bar Roma in Andersonville. Ina's closed in 2013, and the space became a Lou Malnati's pizza parlor. Whatever else changes, everyone in the neighborhood still gets Italian subs at J.P. Graziano's.

11: RICK AND GALE AND HENRY AND RICH (AGAIN)

The 1990s saw Chicago achieve recognition for its place on the national culinary scene, as restaurants drew customers from around the world for fine dining whose inventiveness and showmanship were proudly Midwestern. Some built on the Trotter model of an American version of nouvelle cuisine; others would rebel against haute cuisine, seeking to return to a more down-to-earth, playful style of cooking built on the modest ingredients of the Midwest. Interestingly, if you trace both paths back to the early 1990s, you find the same then-husband-and-wife team: Rick Tramonto and Gale Gand.

Their journey from humble American beginnings to cooking at the highest levels worldwide shows the possibilities that Chicago offered young chefs in the 1980s and 1990s—but also how rough it could be personally for people in the industry trying to balance life and work at the top of the restaurant world.

RICK AND GALE

GALE GAND: My family are musicians, so we didn't eat out. We ate at the Holiday Inn, that was like a big deal. I baked a lot as a kid with my mom and my grandma. My grandma was Hungarian, so she came from a great baking tradition. And my mother was this terrific pie baker, mostly because she had bad circulation. She had cold hands, so she could handle and do elaborate lattice-top pies. The whole neighborhood was like, we can't do what Myrna does, so my mom was the designated pie baker on our street in Deerfield [northwest suburb of Chicago].

The problem was, I have dyslexia. And when I would cook with my mom, I would reverse ingredients with quantities, and read the quantity wrong. And my lovely mother wouldn't be like, oh Gay, you wrecked the recipe. She'd say look, you invented something new. So there was always this affirmation of the value of invention, versus that you screwed up.

I was studying silver- and goldsmithing during high school and I was a diamond setter in Highland Park at a jewelry store. For two years, I worked for this jeweler and I was like, I probably shouldn't go to college. But my parents were still middle class, you know, three goals in life, and one is to have your kids graduate college. So my boyfriend at the time and I decided to go to the Cleveland Institute of Art—a CIA, ironically, but not the one that chefs go to [the Culinary Institute of America].

We're broke—starving art students—so I start waitressing at a vegetarian restaurant and bookstore called The Light of Yoga. There's two good things about working in restaurants. One is that you get paid, and one is that you get fed. So I got $2 worth of food every day, which I split with my boyfriend. I would have a $1.25 salad and he would have a $0.75 carob sundae.

I give great waitress. I love describing the food, and I had to understand what's got sesame oil, what's fried, what's steamed, and I kind of understood the techniques. And one day one of the line cooks didn't show up for work, and my manager comes up to me and she says, Gale, can you cook? And I'm like, no, I'm from the North Shore of Chicago. . . . We didn't have the phrase "white privilege" yet, and my dad was a musician so we didn't have a lot of money. But still, I was from a white privileged family on the North Shore, basically middle class. And she threw an apron at me and said, you can cook now, get in the kitchen.

So basically, I was forced. I didn't choose it, it chose me. For six or seven seconds, I'm just terrified and panicked. And then like second eight, I feel this weird sense of calm come over me. Like I'd found my home.

My dad goes, you know, Gay, it's not a very reliable business. And I said,

Dad, you're a folk singer!

RICK TRAMONTO: I'm originally from Rochester, New York, I grew up there in a very traditional Italian family. My mom was from Abruzzi, my dad was from Napoli. I was an only child, but tons of cousins and aunts.

Then in '76-ish, '77, my dad went to prison for embezzlement—I've written about all of this in my *Scars of a Chef* book.[18] Long story short, it kind of blew our world apart, I quit school in the tenth grade and I just needed to get a job. No high school diploma, no education, but there was a new restaurant opening in the area—new to the area, a place that did square burgers. It was Wendy's. So I started just flipping burgers and doing fries and making Frostys, and I did that for a couple of years.

I got to the point where I was old enough to work in restaurants that served alcohol. I went to a steak house called the Scotch & Sirloin, which was a pretty famous upstate New York steak house chain, Rochester, Buffalo, Syracuse. They did everything—cut meat, did all their own aging. It was kind of extraordinary back in the day what these guys were doing. And then at that point, I knew that this was what I wanted to do, and I could do it without a high school diploma.

GALE GAND: I first went to Europe because I had this year off—I was wait-listed to get into the Rochester Institute of Technology's metals department. And I just thought I needed to go. I'd been reading Escoffier and Jacques Pépin, I'd go to work an hour early and eat my wilted free salad and read cookbooks. I wanted to go to France, and my boyfriend at the time wanted to go to England because he was a Sherlock Holmes nut. So we took two months in 1979 to go to England and France.

We had a lunch reservation at Le Pyramide, but we had nowhere to stay because we were sleeping in our car. So we drove to the restaurant at like seven in the morning, to wait till noon. I knocked on the door at eight in the morning. Is there any way that I could hang out in the kitchen while we wait for our lunch reservation? They slam the door in my face. And then they come back,

18 *Scars of a Chef: The Searing Story of a Top Chef Marked Forever by the Grit and Grace of Life in the Kitchen,* 2011.

well, you know, you're a woman. I'm like, oh, yeah, is that a problem? And then they close the door again. And then they come back. Are you a journalist? No, no, I'm just an American girl just wanting to learn. And they're like, okay, and they let me in the kitchen. But sit in the corner over there and don't touch anything! No problem.

Soon I'm like, I gotta get my hands on—I gotta do something. I can't just sit here. I find like, the kid in the kitchen doing the most menial job. Peeling fifty pounds of carrots. And I go over to him and in my bad French I'm like, I'm sure you have better things to do than that. How about I just peel those for you? And then when one of the other guys saw me doing that, he brought his stuff over next. Suddenly I was in the kitchen, and then they're telling family secrets to me, like putting the truffles under the skin of the chicken, let me show you. They had this secret where you put a tea towel at the bottom of a roasting pan and wet it before you put down crème brûlée or any kind of custard you're baking, because it makes a thin barrier between the ramekin and the metal pan. So they're showing me shit like that. And then when it's time for my lunch reservation, they're sending out all this stuff that's comped and Madame Point comes over and signs my menu.

So I have a lot of time in France, not long periods, I never got fluent, but what it did for me was, it verified that what I'd taught myself from [pastry chef Gaston] Lenôtre books was right. And then also, I just noticed when I would talk to people and they'd ask where did I learn to be a chef, I'd say self-taught, and they'd say, stop talking to me. So that's the wrong answer! But then I went to France and they'd ask where I learned to be a chef, and I'd say France—and they'd say ooh, you're so interesting. Tell me all about it!

Gand went to Rochester, where she would eventually meet Tramonto, taking the ambitious younger chef under her wing.

GALE GAND: I graduated from RIT with a degree in metalsmithing. and took a year and made a living as an artist in my loft space, in an industrial building. It was so lonely. I'm like, trying to discover the meaning of life all by myself. I would chat up the UPS guy.

My chef who I had worked for at the University Club in Rochester came to me and said, Gale, can you come do pastry for me at the Strathallan Hotel? And I'm like, okay, but you know that's where girls always get stuck. So just for six months, right? And he's like, right, six months, and I'll let you out. And after six months, he comes to me and he's like, I know I said I'd let you out. I know you want to move to the line. But then I tell him, give me six more months. I'm just in the middle of this really cool thing I'm discovering. I mean, being a jeweler, you can see how pastry is like that, right? It's identical. So I'd found my thing.

That's where I met Rick. He was just a young whippersnapper line cook. After about three years I moved to New York City, and my girlfriend who was supposed to go with me chickens out. And I'd committed to an apartment and a job. So I asked Rick, hey, you want to be my roommate in New York City? And he's like, well, I need a job. So I set him up with a bunch of interviews. Then my girlfriend decides that she wants to go to New York after all, so it's all three of us in this one-bedroom apartment. We worked at Jams for Jonathan Waxman. Then we all went to the Gotham Bar and Grill and worked for Alfred Portale. And then there was one more jump to work for Richard Krause at Batons.

RICK TRAMONTO: My chef had said, look, if you're going to do this, you can't do it in Rochester, you're gonna have to go to the nearest major metropolitan city, which is Manhattan. And you're going to have to start at the bottom and find some chefs and dig in and take your journey.

We ended up going to Manhattan in like '82. It was an exciting time in New York. Larry Forgione [An American Place] had hit the scene, Alfred Portale hit the scene, Jonathan Waxman hit the scene. Le Cirque was on fire, all the French restaurants, La Grenouille, La Reserve, Lutèce. It was an extraordinary time.

I got a job at the Tavern on the Green and did a year there as just a prep cook—and hated it. I mean, it was just the worst job for me because it was so much volume. I wasn't used to peeling garlic and onions in fifty-five-gallon garbage barrels, it was just so much prep, crazy. But I got to meet Patrick Clark, one of the first Black chefs on the scene. And he said, there's a new guy who's really doing some work. His name is Alfred Portale. Let me hook you up. So I went over to Gotham Bar and Grill and interviewed with Alfred, and he's from Buffalo. So we had a connection—upstate New York and snow. And we talked about food. He was my first real chef. He opened the door and gave me my first real job, took me under his wing. It was a loaded 1980s kitchen with everybody, Tom Valenti and Tom Colicchio and Bobby Flay.

Three years of living in a seven-story walk-up one-bedroom in the West Village. It was brutal living with two people sleeping on the floor, sleeping on the couch. But we all worked in restaurants, and we all were committed to the New York journey. Then Alfred said, look, there's a great opportunity with Chef Joe Baum at Aurora. I think you should go explore it and go do some French kitchens. So he set me up with a bunch of stages at La Grenouille and La Reserve and Aurora.

But I didn't speak French. And I didn't read very well, because like I said, I didn't get a high school education. So for me, reading and spelling was a huge challenge. The chefs would be saying, hey, man, go look at your Escoffier, we're gonna do espagnole tomorrow, or we're gonna do consommé tomorrow. Go read about it. I'd be like, huh? Really, Gale taught me how to read in our little apartment in New York. And thank God there was an incredible library in the West Village, and I could find those books. I can't believe how we just survived on sheer grit.

A few years pass in New York, and eventually Gand and Tramonto get married and move to her hometown, Chicago.

GALE GAND: I'm homesick at that point. I went and applied to Banchet, but he's like, I don't hire women. It's too distracting for the men. I got Rick interviews with Rich Melman and with Banchet, but Banchet wouldn't talk to me.

RICK TRAMONTO: I tried to get a job with Banchet a couple of times, but he would kick me out because I had, like, a blonde mohawk and six earrings. It's interesting that when we actually got to France, all the chefs looked past that.

GALE GAND: I went to work for Roland Liccioni at Carlos', as co-pastry chef with Mary Beth Liccioni. He kind of needed a sous chef, he couldn't keep one. So the idea was that Mary Beth would be his sous, because she understood him. And I would take over pastry, which I did. But I got fired there, and Roland wouldn't tell me why. Roland used to take me to the market, and buy me flowers, and [maybe] Mary Beth wasn't comfortable with that.

Next I worked for David Jarvis at Melange, who is probably the nicest chef there is, he makes us all look bad. Rick is working at Avanzare at that point, so Rich Melman hires me too. They needed a pastry chef at the Pump Room, so I went to work at the Pump Room and Rich sent Rick and Michael Kornick over there too, to give it a facelift and make it new and wonderful. This is in '86 to '88.

Rick did a tasting for Gabino and Rich at Ambria, and he decided to do *truite au bleu,* a famous French dish where you have to have a live trout, and you drop it in court bouillon, and the skin turns blue. The restaurants that do it in France have a little stream out back where they catch the fish. So I found this place in Des Plaines where they had live trout [Fishermen's Dude Ranch], you catch them and they cook them.

And I drove out there and I had a bucket and air pump and a hose and I get like three trout for him. And then I drive them back to Ambria for his tasting. I come in the back door with this five-gallon bucket with these live trout and he fishes one out and throws it in the court bouillon, and it turns blue and he serves the dish to Rich Melman. And Rich takes one taste and he goes, I don't know, it just doesn't taste very fresh.

RICK TRAMONTO: I did a tasting for Russell Bry, Lettuce's corporate chef, who was opening Scoozi!. Rich said, look, we'd love to have you. We love your energy, love your love of cooking, and I think you'd be a great entrepreneur with our group. Come join us as a sous chef. I said, okay, great. And then he starts telling me about Scoozi!—"We're gonna do eight hundred or a thousand covers a day." No, I say, I think I'm good. I'm gonna have to pass. And he's like, what? Yeah, you know, I just experienced that in New York. He goes, hold on. We have a bunch of other restaurants. We've got this Northern Italian restaurant called Avanzare, we'll move some people around, make a spot for you.

I loved Avanzare, I thought it was the greatest restaurant, it was in my wheelhouse in so many ways. Marvin Magid was one of the main partners in Lettuce. He started the Italian division for Lettuce and was super visionary when it comes to Italian food. And the first week I got there, he got married and on his honeymoon, he died in a helicopter crash.

But they're still opening Scoozi!, they pulled a bunch of guys out of the restaurants to take it on. Everybody kind of moved up and they juggled everything around, and I stayed at Avanzare for a number of years and really enjoyed it.

GALE GAND: We had a series of jobs. Rick quit Lettuce and these people hired him to open a place called Bella Luna in the West Loop. That's where we start doing the surfaces, we were sort of famous for serving food on marble. It started at Bella Luna because it was the night of the opening and they forgot to order trays. And there were all these terra-cotta tiles and marble left over from the walls. So that was where that happened.

But after about a year he had a falling out with them and he gets mad and rips the phone off the wall. We went to Bice [upscale Italian chain] and sort of the same thing happens. Rick blows up and marches out. He says, you coming with me? And I think, I'm not quitting my job if my husband just quit his.

He ends up walking to Charlie Trotter's, he's so mad. He walks [three miles] from Streeterville to Lincoln Park and ends up at Charlie's back door. And Charlie gives him a day sous gig. And I'm working at Bice and I'm picking up Rick after work every day at like eight o'clock. And Charlie's like, hey, you want to come in and plate while you wait for Rick? So he'd keep Rick like an extra hour or two so that he'd get free labor out of me to plate it up. And there was a guy who was the pastry chef at the time. And when I met him like ten years later, he's like, you know, I *hated* you. Because Charlie told me you wanted my job. And that's why you were coming in every night. You were trying out for my gig. And if I didn't do whatever, he would fire me and hand it right to you. I'm like, oh my God! He was just milking me for free labor!

RICK TRAMONTO: I always describe my career like, Wendy's was culinary high school, moving to New York was like going to culinary college, Lettuce and Chicago was culinary grad school. But what was missing in grad school for me was Europe. I wanted to work for the guys who the people I'd worked for had worked for. Like Alfred had worked for Jacques Maximin [Le Théâtre, Nice] and Michel Guérard [Les Prés d'Eugénie, Gascony] and Paul Bocuse and all these guys.

So I went to Rich one day and I said, hey, you know, I've been here for years, I really need to go to Europe. Do you know anybody in Europe? Rich says, well, I know this guy.

Bob Payton was a Chicago guy, an advertising exec for J. Walter Thompson advertising. His main account was Coke. When Diet Coke first came on the scene, Bob created it. So Bob made a gazillion dollars doing all this and he was living in England at the time. And his passion was food, Chicago food. So he created a company like Lettuce, called My Kinda Town. And he had The Chicago Pizza Pie Factory, he had Windy City Bar and Grill, Chicago Rib Shack. All these Chicago-themed restaurants all over England and all over Europe.

GALE GAND: Bob was kind of well-ingrained into British society, he learned to hunt and horseback ride. He buys this five-hundred-year-old hunting lodge from Lord and Lady Gretton, who owned Bass beer, to turn it into a hotel. But he wants an American chef. He comes to Chicago and goes to people like Melman and the Kelsons and says, who should I be talking to in Chicago? And all their lists include Rick Tramonto and Gale Gand.

RICK TRAMONTO: Bob wanted somebody who could do contemporary American food, but also had the sensitivity for when American guests would come. They could do a barbecue on Sunday, or they could cook a big American breakfast versus a traditional English breakfast.

It was like my first real chef's position at that point. But it was a boutique hotel, and it was pretty controllable. I felt really comfortable. So we took the gig and we loved it.

GALE GAND: We worked for him for three years. Breakfast, lunch and dinner, vaulted ceilings, everything is four hundred, five hundred years old. Five-hundred-acre estate with a gamekeeper who takes you pheasant hunting, we live in a thatched cottage. It was like living in an episode of *Masterpiece Theatre.*

RICK TRAMONTO: Bob knew all these all the famous British chefs, Raymond Blanc [Le Manoir, Oxfordshire], Michel Roux [Le Gavroche], Nico Ladenis [Chez Nico], Anton Mosimann [Dorchester Hotel], Pierre Koffmann [La Tante Claire], the core of the three-star Michelin chefs in London were best friends with Bob. When he bought this stately home, they all used to come up there to stay and ride with the hunt. And when you cook for them, you're spending four to five days with these people at a very close level, not just like a stage or a dishwasher. You're having dinner with them and having drinks and going hunting with them. And then you know, always at the end you're like, hey, if I can get to France, can I come stay with you? Can I come cook? And that's how that door opened. Bob opened that door. So we got to work anywhere we wanted.

We spent three, four years out there and then Gale's mom died. So we ended up moving back. Sometimes I think, if not for that, we'd still be there. It was a pretty amazing gig.

GALE GAND: Rick hated it because there's no Blockbuster Video or Domino's Pizza. He's got dyslexia worse than me, and he can't drive because it's the other side of the road. So every three or four months, he's like, I need you to compose this resignation letter for me, I'm quitting, I'm sick of it. And he'd quit every four months, and then they'd give us a raise. After two years of this, we actually left and came home and then they called and they're like, please come back. So we go back and live in London and fix what's broken in his other restaurants, and even travel to like Barcelona and Paris, because he's got them there, too.

So we traveled a lot. I always joked, what's the best thing about England? France. If we had a day off, we'd catch a thirty-nine-dollar Virgin Air flight and have lunch in Paris twice and then come back home. So we didn't come back to Chicago until 1993, and then we met Henry Adaniya.

TRIO

HENRY ADANIYA: I was working as a fire protection engineer, in my mid-twenties, and I decided—I don't like this. And there was a place called Cafe Figaro, a few doors down from The Bakery in Lincoln Park. It was owned by my girlfriend's sister, Deb Majic. So the food bug was in me, and I thought, I'm going to go work for her as a cook. I never had any experience. So I took a job there in 1978, and the funny thing was that as I was cooking, I was like, I'm really not that good at this either. I mean, I could cook but I didn't have her abilities as a chef. My engineering brain was too methodical and logical and pretty straight-line. I didn't have the finesse to be a chef.

DEB MAJIC: His hollandaise sauce was perfect. Henry came around in the fall, when people started wanting hot food. So we expanded the kitchen and he came to help out and it was so much fun. He was just charming.

HENRY ADANIYA: I went to the front of the house, and I found that this was really good for me. I got to interact and really started to build my people skills, and I learned some things from more experienced people. I happened to be friends with Jimmy Rohr [Jimmy's Place], and I told him I needed to move. He said there was this place called Ambria that had just opened, and you might want to check that out.

Chef Gabino was there in the kitchen, and I had no idea what chefs were. I said I wanted to talk to the man in charge, and he just gave me this look. Long story short, I eventually met with Rich Melman, and got a job as a back waiter. I thought, wow, I was a manager at the other place and now I'm a back waiter—boy, did I have a lot to learn. I have to thank Ambria and Chef Gabino for really introducing me to haute cuisine. I learned to appreciate food, I learned the fine points of service. I was there for five years and made captain, assistant sommelier.

Then I took a maître d' position at Café Provençal in Evanston, under Leslee Reis. So I got to run my own dining room, and that was my entrance to management. But Leslee passed away in 1990. So I left that place and took a year off, I had eyes on opening a wine bar. But that didn't materialize. I did a consulting gig at Va Pensiero [Italian restaurant in Evanston], a turnaround thing for a couple of years, really learned a lot about Italian food and Italian wine.

And then I heard that Café Provençal was closing. I had been friends with the owner of the hotel, David Reynolds, and that gave me the opportunity to go in there. That was 1993. I started scouting chefs, and I eventually found Rick Tramonto and Gale Gand, I was just really impressed with the fine points of their food.

RICK TRAMONTO: We kind of knew Henry from Lettuce, he had just left Ambria to buy Café Provençal. We met and he said, how about the three of us, and he used the word "trio"—the trio of us in this thing.

GALE GAND: I was working for Trotter, and I told him I might be doing my own place. He's like, that's fine, just give me two weeks' notice. So when we signed the lease, I told him I would be leaving in a couple of weeks. And then the problem was that all my pastry people wanted to go with me. And that's when Charlie got pissed. I always kind of felt like, it's not my fault they don't want to work for you. So the pastry people from Trotter's came with me to do Trio.

Charlie had his own stuff with Rick, from when he worked there as a sous chef. Rick used to take a lot of pictures of the food, and Charlie just always kind of felt like Rick copied him. Charlie drank a lot at times in his life, and we would get drunk calls, angry calls and whatever. But there was a reconciliation, later. I think we were at Pebble Beach, and Charlie was there with his third wife, Rochelle. And we were kind of like, we miss you guys. And he's like, yeah, you should come to the restaurant. So we can kiss and make up. We didn't know at the time that he was dying.

RICK TRAMONTO: Henry didn't have any money. I mean, he had like, maybe forty, fifty grand, and the landlord had maybe forty, fifty grand. The restaurant was beat to shit, it was old and had a decent cellar, but it was pretty beat up. We spent like six months, every day, seven days a week in there, doing most of the work ourselves. We painted it, and he went and bought used equipment and cleaned up all the mouse shit off the floor. And by the time we got to the end of that, we were out of money. We didn't have money for china, we didn't have money for the luxury part of what touched the diner, right?

So we had to be super creative. I remember me and Gale going to Builders Square and we started looking for surfaces. Slabs of kitchen tile and mirrors that were really supposed to be for medicine cabinets, like we'd buy a whole medicine cabinet just to get the mirrors. We had old stuff from Café Provençal, we had mismatched stuff from auctions. So that's how that whole aesthetic happened.

HENRY ADANIYA: Initially, I thought of doing a French bistro, just more accessible. More down to earth. But as I got into it more, I thought, Charlie Trotter's was the only game in town. I was like, why don't we go for the whole show? Looking at chefs, definitely Rick and Gale were doing something different at that time. And I think my own nature is that I liked something unique. I liked something groundbreaking. I wanted to do something more challenging that nobody else was doing.

I met them through a customer friend of mine. He said, hey, you should talk to these guys. So I did a tasting with them. And it was like, hey, this is definitely exciting food. The presentations were what got me into it. No staid white plates—we're doing granite and going to Home Depot to buy stuff to serve on. That kind of creativity really, really attracted me, this avant-garde way of saying hey, we can serve on anything.

Some of the visual presentations blew people away—like the Caesar salad. It was a bowl that was eighteen inches in circumference. And the inner bowl in the middle, where the salad would sit, was only about four inches. And there was a breadstick that Gale made. But literally, you had to clear everything off the table. If everybody had one of those, it was crazy.

And Gale offering a root beer float for dessert—it's like, okay, we have strong technique, but we have this playfulness. Some of it was very rustic—like an Italian sausage with greens, that was a very Italian thing. And then *kataifi*-wrapped tuna, that's so different. So there was a nice fusion of different types of foods. They weren't afraid to go there. A lot of fine dining just has that kind of feel, that this is a real serious thing. Well, this was serious food, but done in a playful way.

GALE GAND: I think part of that was my refusal to grow up. So that was sort of retaining my childlike qualities. I just decided, no, I'm not going to have the affectations of a white-collar businessman. I'm going to be myself.

The root beer thing, though, was because we lived in England. There's no root beer there, right? Because it was used for medicinal purposes during the war. It'd be like trying to sell Listerine soda pop. So there's no root beer anywhere in England, except at McDonald's in London. And I can't be seen going into McDonald's, right? So I would stand out front and hand people a pound coin and be like, can you get me a root beer but like in a brown paper bag, like a kid outside a liquor store? I don't know what it is, it just like, calms me and I can focus. So to be without that for three years was a disaster.

SHAWN MCCLAIN (sous chef): I was going to Kendall College [culinary school] and working at a great restaurant called Les Plumes, owned by two guys who were Banchet protégés—it was a great, formidable, serious food-focused French restaurant. I mean, these are Banchet guys, they were there at the crack of dawn, they were there cleaning up at the end of the night, and they only had two other people helping them. At the time, I just thought it was hard, but it was very satisfying. It made me more serious about school and made me a better student in the eyes of my teachers.

[A few years later] I was the sous chef at a French brasserie on Wilmette Avenue [North Shore suburbs]. I enjoyed doing the food and the volume, but the food itself just wasn't as precise as I liked, and ultimately I just felt like I needed to go back to kind of where I felt my roots were, in fine dining. By chance, somebody said, hey, my friend Henry's going to be opening a fine dining restaurant in Evanston, you should talk, the chefs are coming back from Europe. And it was just super intriguing that a new restaurant was going for that high-end market. So I met Rick Tramonto in a parking lot and had coffee and I think I was offered $18,000 a year. Which, at the time, I was probably making $45,000, and I just thought, boy, this is going to be a big change. But I just kind of believed in it, and decided this was my way back in, and ultimately it was going to be good for me.

It was approaching dining with a little bit of whimsy, a little bit of, hey, let's use a granite tile as a food vessel versus a white porcelain plate. How can we make this different? How can we have fun? I really liked that, and I think, honestly, they were incredibly good marketing people way before marketing was a thing. They were focused on getting attention for the restaurant, they were focused on making relationships and becoming a buzzworthy restaurant.

GALE GAND: Trio was really when we first started to get national attention. *Food & Wine* recognized us in the ten best new chefs—though there were eleven that year because we were a couple.

I think the first press was *Wine Spectator* calling us out, and we were also in *Art Culinaire* that year because our food was really visual. Some of that was my art school background, so as much as my dad felt like he wasted his money, I would be like, no, Dad, I use my design background all the time. My visuals are probably somewhat different than most chefs' because I look at the plate and I'm looking at contrast and line and how the eye travels and negative space. Rick picked that up—he's sort of a street-smart kid, he dropped out of high school but he kind of picked it up from me, how to make things visually interesting.

So we got known for our stuff looking super cool—the surfaces, and we had bought all the silverware in England when we lived there, seconds from the Sheffield Silver Company at the local flea market. Every weekend was the Sheffield Silver Company selling their silverware that had nicks. Over the course of two years, we bought a restaurant's worth of flatware not knowing why exactly. But when we met Henry, we're like, don't buy any flatware because we've already got it. We were collecting for a restaurant that didn't exist yet.

RICK TRAMONTO: Phil Vettel gave us our first four stars, and everything started to snowball—*Chicago* magazine, the *Sun-Times*, all that.

PHIL VETTEL: I remember going the first time. This is long before you could look stuff up online. So I dialed 411, and I blanked on the name, the operator answered, and I said, Jesus, sorry, I was trying to get the name of a new restaurant that just opened in Evanston. And she said, oh, Trio. Even directory assistance was getting an idea that there was something big going on, probably because of all the requests.

So I went and I remember just being wowed at what Rick and Gale were producing, that we had never seen in Chicago before. I think I wrote something along the lines of, I've seen the future of fine dining, and its name is Trio. Which was a line I'd cribbed from Jon Landau's famous Bruce Springsteen review.

Bill Rice knew I was writing it up, and he asked me with a slightly worried tone what I had thought of it. And I realized in that moment that he thought the place was amazing, and he was afraid that I might have missed it. I wanted to screw with him and say, yeah, I'm thinking two stars. It was really solid. A lot of potential there. But I said oh, Jesus, Bill, this is a four-star restaurant. And he audibly exhaled with relief.

GALE GAND: A lot of famous people came there—we had Michael Jordan and Carol Burnett and John Malkovich, Keith Richards, Mel Brooks and Anne Bancroft, Robin Williams. I mean, the list goes on. Trio was a little neighborhood place in Evanston. And it was shabby, it was run-down. But we did a lot with it and we turned the lights down low. That's sort of what you do, when you don't have a lot of money. But we were making some good food—important food.

Julia Child never came there. But she came to Brasserie T, though I think that was after I'd filmed with her. So I was in her *Baking with Julia* book in '96.[19] I got to film two episodes of the PBS series *Baking with Julia.* And she gave us our *Food & Wine* magazine awards at the Food & Wine Classic in Aspen. So we're kind of playing with the big kids at that point—we were becoming big kids, I guess.

I got Julia's madeleine pans after she died. They gave all her stuff to the Smithsonian, but they gave some of it back to Les Dames d'Escoffier. They had an auction to raise money, and Rick—we were divorced by this point—bought them for me as a birthday gift, and he bought himself her truffle slicer.

HENRY ADANIYA: I did most of the interviewing for staff. To me it's about really trying to find the nature of the person, why are they there, and the waitstaff industry back then was all, hey, it's good money. There wasn't a lot of refined professionalism in the art of waiting tables. What I looked for was the person who had the passion to be able to convey the food that we were serving, not

19 *Baking with Julia: Savor the Joys of Baking with America's Best Bakers,* 1996.

just to bring plates to the table. For me, there's a lot of understanding the psychological nature of service. We had to know the food as much as the chef does, we had to understand his mind about where that food came from. That's very important to me, because when I eat out, how can I feel the creator of the meal through the food? Through the best dishes, I know who this person is.

DAVE LIGON (manager): Henry had lost his maître d', and we're old buds, going back to Ambria. So he asked me if I would do it. What I thought was going to be temporary ended up being a five-year experience. And it was wonderful. It was like Ambria again, only different atmosphere, totally different type of cuisine. When you look back on what we were doing at Ambria and compare it to what was happening in Trio, it was the cuisine of Ambria, in terms of presentations and things, simplified. It was like getting back in touch with what I had loved to do before.

PAULA HANEY (pastry cook): I remember being in Indiana, after I graduated college, and I could not get a job in my chosen profession, which was journalism, because there weren't a lot of jobs, and I wasn't very good at it. But I was reading *Food Arts* magazine, and there were all these articles about Trio. I moved to Chicago and there was an opening at Trio. I didn't know how desperate restaurants are when they need to hire someone. So I put my resume in at ten thirty and at ten forty-five I get a call from Shawn McClain.

I did the interview and I staged and it was just magical. It was like being led into Willy Wonka's chocolate factory. At that time, we had twenty people on the line for a sixty-seat dining room, which was crazy. And they were all in the full toque, chef coat, matching pants, all the women had their hair up, and all the men had their hair up too—they actually weren't even allowed to have long hair. I just felt like I had walked into the whole dream. And it was really hard and really fun. Henry, honestly, created such a wonderful world for all of us and made us believe that we could do anything. And what we were doing was special.

SHAWN MCCLAIN: Henry was the reason I stayed. There were probably a lot of moments in that first year where I sat on the back steps, and I thought, this isn't for me. Like this is really hard for $18,000 a year. I'm trying to see the forest through the trees. And there were a lot of conversations where he was just—one, he's just a warm human being, just a super awesome person. He's fair. He's a consummate hospitality professional. He can work a floor, he can work a guest. He's funny. He understood the important kind of underpinnings of what he needed to do and make that restaurant successful.

In the 1970s and 1980s much of fine dining was based in the northern suburbs, but by the 1990s it had returned to the city, so when Trio opened in 1993, being in north suburban Evanston made it an outlier.

HENRY ADANIYA: The '80s saw a lot of growth, things were really moving fast. A lot of new ideas coming forward. I think by the time the '90s came around, it softened up a little bit. The recession kind of stopped people from spending the big dollars. Charlie had really captivated the attention of the media, so we entered as this kind of little underdog. We were on a small budget. We weren't flashy. We were just trying to do some great food that was thinking out of the box.

One of our challenges was to capture the city crowds. Going to Evanston seemed like, you've got to go far, though it really wasn't that far. But I don't think there was enough cachet in going to Evanston for dinner to say, this is the place to be. Until we were able to build up enough critical reviews on us, then it was worth the travel.

RICK TRAMONTO: We were at Trio for three years. Meanwhile, Gale wanted to have a family, and she had gotten her first offer from the Food Network, and an offer to do a book. We wanted to do a second restaurant. We tried to convince Henry. At that time, Shawn McClain was our sous chef. And we said, look, Shawn can take over as the chef, we want to go do this brasserie, but we want you to be a part of it, but he didn't want to do it. So we went and did the brasserie and you know, after a couple of years, our relationship [with Henry] kind of fizzled, because we wanted to grow and we had our first child, and everything was changing at that point. So we left Trio and did Brasserie T [in north suburban Northfield].

GALE GAND: Rick put this rigatoni dish on the menu at Trio. I'm like, honey, that's a whole other restaurant that doesn't belong here. He's like this blue-collar Italian guy. Like, you need another restaurant where you can do like your greens and beans with sausage and your simple stuff. So we decided to open Brasserie T. Henry was supposed to be part of it, but he backed out.

HENRY ADANIYA: They already had visions of doing a bistro, which is what became Brasserie T. I said I wasn't interested in that. So it was totally amicable. Shawn McClain had already been chef de cuisine during the transition. He was a cook, and then he became sous chef, and then chef de cuisine.

GALE GAND: What happened was, Rick and I were invited to do a pop-up of Trio, with all our surfaces, in New Zealand. This guy had a restaurant in Auckland, and he turned it over to us for two weeks. We cooked for two weeks, but we were there a month. And we left Shawn in charge. You know, handsome, nice, even-tempered Shawn McClain. And when we get back Henry says, Shawn's really easy to work with and he's like thirty grand cheaper than you and Rick, I think I'm just gonna go with Shawn. So we went and did this thing and lost our jobs. Rich Melman is feeling so bad about this restaurant breakup that's about to happen that he tries to fix the relationship for us, but Henry's like, no, I'm done.

SHAWN MCCLAIN: They were kind of moving on to new projects. And Henry was just like, hey, guys, this is really important. This is my restaurant. We've got to stay focused on this. I'm sure it's something that's played out in a lot of partnerships.

Henry came to me and said, hey, I'm thinking about kind of severing ties, and I want to promote you to take over the kitchen. And I was twenty-six. Really, at the time, I really hadn't thought through wanting to be a lead chef yet, I was still figuring my way and trying to absorb and get better, but it was one of those opportunities presented that I just thought of course I have to do this, I have to prove personally what I can do without them, not in their shadow. New reviews will come out and my name is going to be on them, for better or worse.

[Rick] being volatile—you know, I'd like to say passionate, but at some point, passion just isn't an excuse. And I was the opposite. I just wasn't that kind of personality. I was the calming force for the kitchen. I kept the guys from walking out the door. I was the conduit between the crew and Rick, and ultimately, Henry was observing this daily.

There was a *Chicago* magazine article about the split, by Ted Allen.[20] It was drama. It was page 6 news.

HENRY ADANIYA: I had so much admiration for Shawn's temperament and his style of food. It was different than Rick and Gale's, it was less of the show and more finesse. His food to me has this delicacy of flavors that blend so well without being aggressive. I loved both types of food, but his was more like a ballet of flavors to me. His was a little more Asian than Rick and Gale's, so I related to it more, and gone were the big show plates. He was less theatrical; it was about the food.

I offered him the position and he said to me, I'm not going to do their food. I said, okay, let's go with your food. Which was kind of scary, changing in midstream. We'd had a lot of press with Rick and Gale. It's difficult to make that kind of shift because the restaurant was identified with the chefs, not with me. I didn't really want that attention; it was about the chefs for me. But we went for it with Shawn, and within six months Phil Vettel gave us another four-star review.

SHAWN MCCLAIN: Rick is Italian, he had a natural Italian affinity. So, I took that, I still enjoyed doing handmade pasta, I still enjoyed a risotto on the menu or gnocchi. But it became kind of a complement to something else. I think of a gnocchi dish I did with this pesto, but it had a toasted Madras curry in it. And so it really kind of went in a very different direction, although the gnocchi is kind of the vessel, and that and pesto would be a traditional combination.

I came up with a lot of foie gras dishes. At that time, we used to do a trio of foie gras nightly, three different preparations. And that's where my foie brûlée was born. I was bringing in a lot of fish from the East Coast, trying to

20 "Going Solo at Trio," November 1996.

diversify the proteins a little bit, especially on the seafood side.

I had books from Europe, I had books from New York chefs. But I just think there was something about the Midwest, camaraderie, the friendships, the support in this town that made me succeed. And I don't know if I would have succeeded without them, whether it was a friendship, whether it was help, whether it was just support. It's kind of a little bit intangible. But I owe a huge debt of gratitude to guys like Takashi Yagihashi, Paul Kahan, John Hogan, Roland Liccioni.

HENRY ADANIYA: Shawn was there a long time, at least five years. Eventually he wanted to open his own restaurant—every chef wants his own restaurant. That's cool. And he opened Spring, which was fabulous. But Trio was kind of in limbo. It's like, okay, what am I going to do? I started to interview chefs, and nothing was really captivating. It was good food, but it just didn't have the thing that made me excited. Then along the way, I got an email from this kid named Grant Achatz.

The then-unknown Achatz coming to Trio as its third chef would be the beginning of a new era of avant-garde food in Chicago—but that's a story for another chapter. Meanwhile, Rick Tramonto and Gale Gand returned to Lettuce Entertain You to open a new restaurant in the Avanzare space.

TRU

RICK TRAMONTO: We were four years into Brasserie T when we had a fire. We were still really close with Rich Melman, because he lived out that way. He would come and eat the food and give us feedback, he was still very much a part of our lives. And I'll never forget, right after the firemen left, he came right over. I remember sitting there on the patio with him, and just crying with him, we'd just lost everything. It was horrible.

And he said, why don't you come back with me. I'm about to close Avanzare, I have a fifteen-year lease with a fifteen-year option, and I want to take the option but do a different concept. And I really loved what you were doing at Trio. Would you ever be interested in doing fine dining again? Maybe we'll do a Charlie Trotter's kind of thing. I know that you learned all that stuff in

Europe and worked with all those guys and did all this work. You want to put it to use? I said, yeah! So that's how Tru started.

And it was probably a year from then—Lettuce has this great R&D kitchen, and Rich is really big on tastings, so we went into the Lettuce kitchen while they were in design and construction, and we would just cook, every day. But we also built our team and Rich was gracious enough and generous enough to let us travel as a team. Okay, we're going to Paris next week for four days to go eat at Robuchon, we're gonna go eat at like, eight of the top three-star Michelin restaurants, because our mission statement was to be three-star Michelin, to be Relais & Châteaux. Most of the guys on our team had not had the opportunities that Gale and me had had. We had this frame of reference that most of the other guys around the table didn't have.

GALE GAND: Rich bankrolls the space, it's like $3.3 million. It's the nicest kitchen I've ever worked in. I tell him, it's gonna be hard for me to work anywhere else after this. Because it's such a nice kitchen. He's like, I know. Aha! You *rascal*, you.

RICK TRAMONTO: That everybody in our core group got that opportunity to experience that . . . *craziness* is the best way to describe it; to have that level of being neurotic and insane about what you were trying to achieve. We brought that culture and people just embraced it. I mean, we were still with Lettuce, so there was a level of HR-ness going on, you had to be very HR, in a way that didn't exist at Charlie's, I think. But we had the power of a company like Lettuce, with the ability to say, if you can dream it we can build it.

The signature dish, the caviar staircase at Tru—that actually came out of Trio. At Trio I didn't have the money to make custom plates and have custom pottery. And we were doing a degustation. That's what you were expected to have, a prix fixe and an à la carte menu. You had to have two menus to be respected by the fine dining community at that point, because Charlie was just crushing it with that. So me and Gale are walking around downtown Evanston. And I'm like, I gotta come up with this caviar presentation that's going to set the tone, blow people away as soon as it hits the table. So we're racking our brains, and of course we have no money.

And we just happened to walk by an art store in Evanston. And in the window, there's a painter's palette that had all these colorful dabs of paint. And I immediately looked at her and said, that's it. Let's grab a bunch of these, and we'll do dabs of caviar. So we did it, and it was a huge hit, everybody loved it.

Well, at Tru we're thinking, no more seven-dollar plastic pieces. We've got to build something. We found a company called Glass Artistry, and we went crazy. We did our face plates, glass with our logo etched in them. They weren't china, we wanted non-traditional surfaces—not as far as Grant eventually took it, but it was next-level for its time.

So for caviar we said let's make a staircase, or something that is elevated and sharable. I think it was important because it set the tone. It was very contemporary, and we wanted the room to be like an art museum. Rich has this incredible art collection—we had a million dollars' worth of art in that dining room, original Warhols and Peter Halleys and so on. Rich said it's going to be white with splashes of color, and everything else is about the food. And we're going to pin-spot each table, very dramatic. It was like going into the studio to cut an album, and just jamming. But you have as much money and as much studio time as you want to cut the album.

GALE GAND: We had worked for Charlie, we had breathed that rare air, and had the anxiety from it. We had to go through detox or deprogramming or whatever. Charlie wrecked people.

So it was like, there's got to be a way to do this that you don't make people crazy or suicidal. Our goal was to do fine dining, but with a sense of humor, and Rich bought into it, which was really nice. We could do like, mac and cheese, but in a Versace cup.

****

GREG BIGGERS (cook): I think I was the sous chef at McCrady's in South Carolina at the time. And Tru had just opened, and Rick's book on *amuse-bouches* came out,[21] and it was one of the hottest restaurants in the country. Being a young chef, that was one of the places I wanted to go. I ended up doing an event at EPCOT with Rick and getting the stage while I was there,

21 *Amuse-Bouche: Little Bites Of Delight Before the Meal Begins,* Rick Tramonto and Mary Goodbody, 2002.

and packed up my stuff and ended up getting the job.

That place was so crazy, it was all smoke and mirrors, but holy crap, to a kid from Alabama, seeing like Versace cups in a copper pot that you can't even use because they're just decoration, and all the chefs are wearing toques—it was fucking crazy. Master tins of beluga caviar. Because at the time Rick's big thing was the caviar staircase. I remember one night on the line, we're getting ready for service and I just stopped and started counting toques. And there were twenty-eight toques! And I'm like, where the hell am I at? That was my Bocuse, that was my place of old-school flair, but it was modern at the same time. The dining room having all that artwork in there, and, you know, Saturday night, Mick Jagger coming through and eating dinner, that was my first experience with any of that kind of level of . . . *bourgeois* living.

And the food was crazy too. So over-the-top in every way. Each station had like forty different dishes that you had to know. The diners were very high-class, upper end. In today's day and age, you see a lot of a younger crowd not only being able to afford it, but that's what they spend their money on. But back then, it was still the social elite. It was a dining destination.

One of the most amazing things I've ever seen was watching service at Tru. It was like watching a ballet. Coming from a chef's perspective, if there was ever a restaurant that I've worked in where I could honestly say the front of the house is better than the back of the house, it was Tru.

DAVE BERAN (cook): Tru was awesome. It felt so refined, and so high-end and thoughtful. It felt like a world-class restaurant. If you look at like, the legacy of Tru, it was not a better restaurant than Trotter's, flat out. It just wasn't. But there was a moment in time where Tru was better at that moment than Trotter's was at that moment. And I think that's the moment that I caught Tru.

CHRIS PANDEL (intern/sous chef): As a kid I was overwhelmed. It was my first real brigade kitchen—well, I'd worked at the Breakers hotel in West Palm Beach, in their fine dining restaurant, which had a brigade system. So I was familiar with it, but I didn't know how to cook. I was a young kid and there were a lot of very good cooks there. And the place was immaculate, and the food was fun. And the plateware was expensive and beautiful. It was extremely serious and a very quiet, organized kitchen, very disciplined, so I just kind of kept my mouth shut and kept my head down.

As an intern, I got to bounce around to a handful of stations and, you know, found some confidence in my cooking ability, based upon the feedback of not just my sous chefs and chefs, but of the cooks that were older than me and had been around. But it was intense. I enjoyed the intensity and the environment. You're working long hours, and grinding all the time, but you were responsible for your own station and all of your own mise en place. And that was the first time that I ever worked in a kitchen of that caliber that acted like that.

It definitely tested me, you know, but I didn't feel it was a negative kind of test. It was, can you keep up? Are you cooking to a level that is within the realm of the folks around you? Are you learning on a daily basis, and is your station clean? Are you organized? I picked up a lot of things there that I still use to this day and try to train into my cooks. Mostly discipline, really.

GREG BIGGERS: It was a pressure cooker. If you spent more than a year and a half in that place, it felt like you had done something measurable in your career. The reason for that wasn't so much the chefs, it was the people that you worked next to. The level of perfection that came from each other as chefs was through the roof. The worst thing wasn't getting yelled at, but getting slighted upon, like them looking down at you because you tournée a carrot wrong or burn a sauce or something. It was hard days—if you were there by 10 a.m., everyone looked at you like you didn't even show up to work.

Many people didn't make it. There was a dude who caught his beard on fire. He was working next to me and I look over and his beard's on fire. And I'm like, well, you're not gonna work out.

SCOTT TYREE (sommelier): I basically had autonomy—nobody told me what to buy. I had a budget, a starting budget which I used as wisely as I could. And after the first week, I had gone through so much wine that I said, we have to double the budget right now. My wine program started out with about two hundred selections, and three years into it, we had about fifteen hundred, with two full-time sommeliers on the floor.

There was always a tasting of every single dish. And if I had ideas of something that I thought might work with a dish, or if I'd read about it, something I hadn't tasted, I would try to get samples in—one thing about having a wine program of that size, and selling that much wine, I pretty much enjoyed access to anything I wanted. I might suggest, could you maybe tweak this dish a little this way, to go with a wine I liked. And of course, that doesn't always go over. They could say yes, or they could say no.

The guests at Tru were very open to suggestions, wanting to try new things, very adventurous. I would say 90 percent of the time they left it in my or my team's hands. Then there were some who were very traditional, so we had the verticals of Bordeaux and Burgundy. But overall it allowed me to be creative and ask a lot of questions and find out what people liked and what they were afraid of. And then try to blow their minds by bringing them something they thought they were afraid of, but it was actually really good.

There was a lot of flash and some gimmickry, but most people were into it. They understood that there was some flash going on. I think when people came in they expected an elegant, fun, maybe more relaxed, fine dining experience than they might get at a place that was a little bit more somber or traditional like Ambria or Charlie Trotter's or Everest. And they responded to the kind of goofiness of some of the dishes. Do you really need to have caviar on a glass staircase? No, you don't. But why not?

RICK TRAMONTO: Every time you went to Charlie's, you were so inspired by eating in the kitchen or walking away from a menu. He was doing all the celebrity dinners and the chef dinners, it couldn't help but be contagious. So the thing we came up with was, let's do signature courses throughout our degustation. What does that mean? Well, everybody's going to get four *amuse-bouches*, but they're going to be the same four *amuses*, everybody's going to get the caviar staircase. That's great.

But up to a six-top—if you're a deuce, a four-top, up to five or six, for ten years at Tru, at least, you each got something different. That was my craziness.

My craziness was that I wanted everybody to want to pass and share their plates. I wanted it to feel like we were doing custom menus for every single person, every single table.

So your six-top would get six different cold apps, six different hot apps, six soups, six courses of foie gras—maybe two were terrines, two were torchons, three were hot, whatever. Six different fish courses, six different meat courses. Everybody got the same dessert *amuse*, you'd get a cheese cart and then Gale would do six different desserts. When I run into people that say, I had the best meal of my life at Tru and they start to describe it, the thing they always say, even beyond the staircase, what they always remember the most is, everybody got something different at our table. To use a music analogy, it's like going to see Rush and you want to see the deep cuts, you don't want to just hear "Tom Sawyer." I think that was a very special, thoughtful, aggressive, really hard thing to do.

Tru was just met with an extraordinary amount of embrace. I always joked, I did a restaurant for under a million and then I did a restaurant for $6 million. And we had the same result with both. To be able to do both was extraordinary.

At the beginning, the first three years [Tru opened in 1999], it was like 100 percent, twenty-four hours a day, seven days a week. Me and Gale were there sleeping on blankets. It was so much pressure, not only because someone wrote us a multimillion-dollar check, but it was my whole reputation I threw on the table and rolled the dice. After that, it was keeping up with the Joneses. We always used to say, it's easy to get four stars, but it's hard to keep them. After we got all the accolades in the first eighteen months, then the pressure was on.

So at the beginning, I think I was much more short, crazy with people, not so nice. And then once the team was gelling, and there were other people who cared as much as we did, and we were building this culture in our team, I wasn't going up to people and saying yeah, you know, you didn't cut this *brunoise* perfect, I'm throwing all your shit away, like Charlie would. I could be a mentor.

GALE GAND: We open and Rick and I are actually going through marital problems at this time. But we gotta get this restaurant open. And by the fall, we're not doing well. And we go to Rich, and we're like, I think we're getting divorced. And he's like, well, who's gonna leave the restaurant? And I said, I'm not leaving, I just built this pastry kitchen. It's phenomenal.

So we decide, we're gonna stay working together. We're going to split up, but we're not even going to tell our staff. Like we're gonna keep it a secret. We have a kid at that point, a three-year-old. So we just cruised along. And we're getting our four-star reviews from *Chicago* magazine and the *Tribune* and the *Sun-Times* and like, we don't want to ruin a good thing. So we kept it a secret.

RICK TRAMONTO: The day that me and Gale announced our divorce was interesting, because when we decided to split, we went and told our lawyer and we told Rich Melman and it was like, okay, it's time to tell the staff. We got the whole staff together, on an off day, it was mandatory to come in. And they all thought, we're either going to announce we're going to have another baby, or we're going to quit.

GALE GAND: They thought we were saying we were pregnant with another kid. And we revealed to them that not only are we splitting up, we split up months ago and they couldn't believe it. We just didn't want people to think the restaurant was gonna close, and we didn't want to screw Rich out of his money.

RICK TRAMONTO: We said, look, guys, me and Gale have been separated for almost a year, and we're gonna get divorced. And the reason why we didn't tell you guys is because it's like anything, it's like mom and dad, right? Going to the kids and saying, hey, you know, we're going to split up, but everything's gonna be fine. And you know that that's bullshit. So we kind of had to show everybody before we told everybody, that we're going to be able to still work together and keep this thing going. Even though we're not, you know, going home together. So that was big stuff, that's big life shit, for me anyways, that was. That was my whole life, personal and professional all wrapped together.

GALE GAND: We could keep the secret because I was pastry. So I came in in the morning and Rick stayed late and I left before him and they just never caught on.

And we did love working together, we still do. We were just doing a Mexican concept for Parker Hospitality, my tastings were last week and Rick's there now. Anyway, Phil Vettel at the end of the year, he usually had a column that was like openings and closings and births. And at the bottom of that column that year, he put Rick Tramonto and Gale Gand getting quietly divorced this year. And I remember thinking, well, it *was* quiet, till now.

I was just afraid it was going to affect our careers. And actually, by that point, I had gotten a show on the Food Network *[Sweet Dreams]*. And I remember going to my producer at the Food Network and saying, you know, I hope this doesn't impact whether you still want to continue working with me, but I'm going through a divorce. And this is like 2000, and he goes Gale, Donna Hanover is one of our talent. She was married to Rudy Giuliani at the time. And Giuliani was having this famous public affair. He said to me, we've got enough to worry about with Donna Hanover, you're *nothing*. I'm like, okay, thank you.

RICK TRAMONTO: I think I was going through my personal demons at the time, as far as going back to church and getting rid of any alcohol and drugs that were in my world, but I was also losing my marriage. People have to realize that it cost me and Gale everything. We just had a son, we had a three-year-old. And so there was days I would come in and I'd be really dark. But when I got dark, I got quiet. And people knew that. And then when I was having better days, I would come in and I was much more of a cheerleader, and would bury myself in my work and stuff. So I think that was a positive thing.

GALE GAND: I thought we should write the book on *The Amicable Divorce For Dummies*. Because we figured it out. What it was was, I got a show on the Food Network, right at the time that we got divorced, and it paid me exactly what Rick's income was. Most couples fight about money. And I never lost his income and got scared about money. It allowed us to just focus on what mattered, like our kid—what's best for Gio? We could both kind of go on with our lives without like, you owe me this. We never had any of that.

RICK TRAMONTO: It's not like me and Gale had this, you know, "I hate you" divorce. It wasn't like that. We had a very good divorce. We knew that, we had to choose, you choose your family or your work, and we chose the work. That's what we were more suited to. And you know, we got married very young.

I hope I treated people most days with love and respect. I hope. But not always, not always. None of them knew what we were going through. Nobody was asking me, hey, Chef, how you doin' at home? How's your life?

****

Tramonto stayed at Tru until 2010; Gand left it in 2011. One path from Rick and Gale's careers, playful desserts and quirky serving pieces, leads through Trio to Grant Achatz and Alinea. But another reaches back to Rick's Italian heritage and his early days working at the Scotch & Sirloin: dedication to in-house butchering and simple, rustic cooking.

CHRIS PANDEL: I went with Tramonto to open Osteria via Stato [for Lettuce], and then I went with Rick to start his restaurant company as kind of his right-hand man. He tapped me and said, hey, you want to come work on some rustic Italian food? And you know, I had a little bit of Italian training with Andrew Carmellini in New York. So I was interested in moving to a new restaurant, I was interested in a little more responsibility.

What I learned at Osteria via Stato was organization and systems, how to really be in charge of a kitchen from a managerial standpoint, and how it wasn't all about the cooking. It was about making sure that the cooks were organized, that the food was consistent, that our standards were there. It was a volume restaurant, so it changed my perspective completely, going from cooking, you know, a half-pound of fingerling potatoes for a day's service and throwing them out at the end of the night to cooking five hundred pounds of something a day.

So going from fine dining, we're using little iced tea spoons to plate, and now we're cooking pasta for families to share. It was a very eye-opening experience for me—having Rich Melman teach me how to do inventory, basically. It definitely helped me as far as being okay with rusticity and being okay with food being simple and less ingredients and less manipulation. Less contrived food, across the board.

GREG BIGGERS: I was exec sous at Morimoto in Philadelphia, and I get a call from Chris Pandel. And he's like, hey, Uncle Ricky—to this day we call him Uncle Ricky—wants you on a plane tomorrow. I'm like, okay, what's up? He's like, we're going to open six restaurants in the burbs. Okay, I'll be there. It was Rick, and Gale, and Chris as corporate chef. So I came on as the corporate chef for the steak and sushi division, and ended up working closely with Rick and Gale for about three years. It was like this pressure cooker of talent, all living and working in Wheeling, opening six restaurants in six months, with an unlimited budget. Which, you know, giving an unlimited checkbook to anybody is not a great idea.

CHRIS PANDEL: It was a pretty intense handful of years, because we *ran* to open all those restaurants. It was a tough area to cook in, because your timeline of when diners are out is not five o'clock to midnight. It's seven to eight-fifteen, which changes a lot of things about your restaurant. You have to figure out a way to execute high-end delicious food in a very fast manner.

It was my first jump into a Chicago-style steak house [Tramonto's Steak & Seafood]. And learning the likes and dislikes of what people expect out of something that is so Chicago. It's definitely a service-focused restaurant, where people expect to be taken care of a certain way. I learned a lot about what the expectations were, and it made me understand why you should do service a certain way in that kind of restaurant. Not the kiss-ass version of that, but, you know, things were proper.

JOE FRILLMAN (cook): Rick Tramonto was opening up Osteria di Tramonto in a hotel in Wheeling. A steak house, an osteria, a sushi lounge, Gale Gand's pastry place. I got a job there, and that's where I met Chris Pandel.

After I got back from [staging at] The Fat Duck, I started tugging on Pandel's sleeve. He was nine-to-fiving it at that point, corporate executive chef, he made sure everything went well. At that time, you'd show up at five o'clock and work a station that was already set up for you, because there was breakfast, lunch and dinner. And I thought, this is great, but I need to know how to prep this stuff myself.

So every day, he'd be like, hey, if you want to learn stuff, come here tomorrow at 11:30 a.m., and I'll show you whatever you want. Butchering salmon, and breaking down lobsters, and cooking mushrooms, you name it. And then afterwards, Jared Van Camp came in and they went out to a farm, Chris and I think Michael Ponzio, and they shot a pig and they brought it back and said, we're going to make charcuterie. That wasn't going on at all then, not in Chicago.

Building on that, Pandel and a manager from Tramonto's, John Ross, would soon open a new kind of restaurant, a farm-to-table, nose-to-tail gastropub called The Bristol—but that, too, is a story for another chapter.

12: THE RETURN OF THE WEST LOOP

"Why are you guys moving over there?" Kevin Boehm, co-founder of the Boka Restaurant Group, says he was asked when Girl & the Goat was getting ready to open in 2010. The Jerry Kleiner restaurants that had made the West Loop hotter than hot in the 1990s and early 2000s—the likes of Marché and Red Light—weren't quite gone, but the neighborhood's moment as an enclave of edgy restaurants surrounded by urban grit seemed to have passed. Boehm says that when he visited the construction site, "I got knocked over by a tumbleweed . . . Literally everything was going out of business. Every single building was for lease around here."

Within the year, Girl & the Goat would be Marché all over again, the buzziest, hardest-to-get reservation in town, kicking off a hot restaurant scene on Randolph Street that has shown no signs of slowing down. When did this second revival start? Really, it begins closer to downtown, at a time when the Kleiner restaurants were still thriving. On a sliver of the city between downtown and the expressway, Blackbird opened in late 1997. Those two restaurant groups—One Off Hospitality and Boka Restaurant Group—would create the models for the horde of trendsetter restaurants marching westward along Randolph. One Off chef-partner Paul Kahan, in particular, would be hugely influential in making food in Chicago more seasonal and less formal in how it was made and presented, and sending a generation of cooks forth from Blackbird and avec to open their own hip, farm-to-table restaurants.

ONE OFF HOSPITALITY

PAUL KAHAN: When I was a wee lad, my dad was involved in the restaurant business. He had a series of failed businesses—he had a deli on Devon Avenue called Fan's Fishery in the late '60s, early '70s. I spent a little time there as a kid, and then he opened up a place called the Village Fishery in Rogers Park, a little deli and smokehouse. That was really cool. I got the food bug then even though I didn't know it. And then those failed. He became the manager of a restaurant called Mel Markon's, on Belden and Lincoln Park West. It was open, I think, twenty-two hours a day, and it was busy the whole time. I think it was a precursor to what Melman was doing, before R.J. Grunts.

This was when there were still chubs in the Great Lakes. They would mostly come from Port Washington, Wisconsin. A truck would drive up there and literally pick up barrels of chubs for the Village Fishery. They would put them in these big stainless steel tanks and brine them, and then put them up on these giant rolling racks. You lit a fire inside the ovens, and then you'd close the door and the fire would smolder out and they would smoke in there overnight. I was probably six or seven years old, I would go there with my dad and he'd open up the door, smoke billowing out, and peel the skin back and shovel the flesh in my mouth. There is nothing like smoked fish right out of the oven, warm. Because once you refrigerate, all those proteins and everything seizes up and the quality of the fat changes. And so it's like an ethereal experience when you have it for the first time.

I cooked at home; my family was a big food family. As a young kid I just started experimenting with recipes. The original bug was that show *Great Chefs of Chicago* on PBS. I watched Jacques Pépin, and made omelets and made bread and just had fun with it. My parents got divorced when I was thirteen, and my dad and I would go out to eat, as our relationship builder, we ate a lot of sushi and tried restaurants. That was fun.

In college I started working at an organic co-op, and really just fell in love with product. I was studying Applied Math and Computer Science, got my degrees, took a job in that field, and hated, hated it. Kind of knew halfway through—I was cooking for my roommates in college and baking bread, my whole life revolved around food. I actually had this hippie girl do a reading for me at a party, and everything was about how I was going to end up in food. To this day, my job has changed a lot, but I still really love food, I love product, I love gardening.

I'm also a huge music freak, and my [future] wife Mary introduced me to this guy, Marc Delphonse, who owned a rock and roll bar on the corner of Clybourn and Webster called Batteries Not Included. He was a French-trained chef from Barbados. And he kind of advised me to get a job in a good kitchen. Mary also had a friend named Stephanie Samuels, who was the pastry chef at Metropolis Cafe on the corner of North and Wells—this is probably 1985. And I just interviewed as an entry level, dishwasher-slash-prep cook. And the owner, Erwin Drechsler, gave me the job. He was like, you know, I didn't go to culinary school either.

It was sort of the precursor to high-end carry out. We were making amazing scratch food for sale. It was such nice food, but you couldn't be like fifty bucks a pound for breast of capon salad that we were making—we kind of priced ourselves out. But we made pâtés, we made sausage, we made coulibiac of salmon and we made risotto. And it was just the perfect place to be enthusiastic and say, every day, can you teach me something new? Can I make that? Can I make the meatloaf tomorrow? It's where I got my chops, I learned about the farmers markets from Erwin, we went to the markets every week, or there was only one at the time, the Lincoln Park farmers market, way before Green City.

And then he opened up Metropolis 1800, and I went over there as a sous chef and worked there for a bit and kind of learned everything I thought I could there.

MINDY SEGAL (pastry chef, Metropolis 1800): Erwin was one of the first chefs to use the produce from the farmers market. When I went with him to the Lincoln Park farmers market every Saturday, the only other chef there was Rick Bayless—none of the French chefs were going. Erwin was very instrumental in bringing it to the mainstream.

PAUL KAHAN: As it turned out, Rick and Deann Bayless were regular customers at Metropolis Cafe, they would come on Monday afternoon at like, three o'clock and have lunch. I waited on Rick and Deann every Monday and would recommend what to eat. Erwin had taken me to Frontera as a thank you early on, when it opened and was the hot new place. And I thought it was really cool. I was not so interested, really, in Mexican food. I just wanted to learn how to run a great restaurant. And I went there with my resume, which was not very extensive, and handed it to the hostess. And I saw Rick in the distance, and I kind of waited, I kind of lingered. She handed it to him and he was like, I want to talk to this guy. So I waved, and we had the interview right then and he hired me on the spot.

I told him, I have lofty goals. I want to be sous chef here within six months. He's like, oh? But sure enough I was one of the two opening sous chefs for Topolobampo, and worked there with him very closely. Long story short, he and I are still friends and he's a great mentor. Two things about Rick—when he's in the restaurant, he tastes the whole line, end to end, every night. Tastes everything, sauces, pickles, smells everything, which is a feat. And man, that guy can eat more than anyone I know. So he does that every night and then most nights he and Deann sit down. There's a little area in front of the kitchens, and they sit down and have dinner.

We were really fortunate that all these farmers were bringing us all this great stuff. People don't really give Rick the credit, but he really is the foundation for the farm-to-table movement in Chicago, period. And he's still the biggest supporter, with his Frontera Farmer Foundation.

Anyway, there'd be like a pheasant in the walk-in from this farmer in Indiana named Rudy Pluschke that we didn't have on the menu and I would say, hey, can I cook this pheasant? Can I try a new dish for you? And so they would sit down, and I would present them with new dishes two, three times a week. I was looking at all these French cookbooks and doing, you know, Mexican food. I was putting the pheasants on the rotisserie and breaking them down and doing this and doing that, and just trying everything that I could, and they loved it.

He and Deann approached me and said they wanted to open a restaurant with me. And so we started working on this project. He said to me, what kind of restaurant do you want to open? I said, I'd really like to open up a restaurant that's like the Chez Panisse [influential farm-to-table restaurant in Berkeley] of Chicago. So we started working on the restaurant and I worked on menus, but at a certain point, I realized it wasn't really going to be *my* restaurant, it was going to be Rick's restaurant, even though, full partner, the whole nine yards. But you don't know the name of anyone, any chef at his restaurants except for him.

Which is probably a better business model, but I'm the exact opposite. I want everyone to know who Greg Wade [manager at Publican Quality Bread] is. I want everyone to know who Dylan Patel [chef de cuisine at avec] is and Joe Spain [then-chef de cuisine for the group] is and all the chefs who work for me. Even if it's something that I did, I would rather not take credit for it. I just want to further their careers.

So I decided at that point to sow some wild oats. I had done it one time before with a college buddy, rode freight trains around the country. We went from Naperville, which is where the big yard is in the Chicago area, to Minneapolis to the Northern Rockies to Spokane. We basically got kicked off, arrested, extorted for money in Spokane, and then hitchhiked from there to Olympic National Park, and then down the coast all the way to San Francisco and camped and fucked around. And then I came back, and decided I was going to stay in the business.

****

DONNIE MADIA: I was searching for a career. My cousin was trading commodities at the Mercantile Exchange, so he invited me down, and I took an interest in it. I made a switch to the Board of Trade because I liked the energy. And I also liked commodities, in the sense of the intrinsic understanding of grain, and that lineage, soybeans, wheat, corn. I just enjoyed that a little bit more. So I worked my way up the ladder, runner to clerk to trading independently. But throughout those three years, I always had a bartending gig, to supplement my income. And I worked at really good restaurants and some really good bars. And I felt that my evenings made me happier than my days because I wasn't that great of a trader.

I liked the camaraderie of my colleagues in bars, as well as the entertainment portion of that career. So after a couple of gigs in restaurants, I worked at Tufano's [long-running Italian restaurant in the Taylor Street "Little Italy" area] for almost ten years, and I had a short stint at Vivo for Jerry Kleiner, and a couple of other operators in the '90s. Just having the opportunity to work for other operators who were opening restaurants and bars, I felt that my trajectory was to own my own place. I thought that I would take a shot because I've had a hard time with authority my entire life, and that made me understand that it was time for me to go out on my own. Even though the climb was almost ten years, it gave me not just the basic fundamentals of the guest experience, but I was creating a clientele as well, and people were coming to see me and liking my drinks and liking my atmosphere.

Then I worked for the guys who owned Vinyl [nightclub], the Big Time Production guys—they owned Crobar [club], Angelina and Ooh-La-La! Taking in information about what they were doing, and what I would do different. Just tweaking their business model to fit my ideas. A crucial part of that development was, the people I worked for hired chefs. And I thought that it would be interesting, or more important, to have a culinary partner, not just a hired gun.

I don't think anybody wanted to open a restaurant, especially back in those days, where the success rate was, restaurants wouldn't last a year. I wanted to see if we could put something together that would last longer than a year. I also believed in the real estate deal. In my business plan for Blackbird, there's a page on purchasing real estate, not just leasing it. That was also something that I thought very, very long and hard about, that the real estate deal would be as important as the chef, the fit and finish of the restaurant, and where the restaurant would be located.

Ricky [Diarmit, partner] and I were considering another chef, and because of living in the Midwest, we felt that seasonality was really special. That our menu would change spring, summer, fall, winter. But that partnership didn't work out, and I was introduced to Paul Kahan—and he took it to another level.

PAUL KAHAN: Erwin had offered me another job. He had closed his places and he was opening Erwin [in the former L'Escargot space in Lakeview].

My buddy Mike and I were sort of co-chefs there. He was the sous chef. But it didn't feel like Erwin was willing to—I learned all this stuff from Rick that I wanted to implement there. So I was very frustrated. Not to sound arrogant, but I tried out for five chef jobs and I got offered every job. But they weren't what I wanted to do. I wanted ownership. So I did a bunch of consulting work for a bunch of different companies in the city and started saving money and buying equipment. I started by buying All-Clad sauté pans when they were a new company, and I had like fifty in my room, and I bought French copper and all this stuff and I was just sort of waiting for the opportunity.

And then through a cook that had worked for me, I met Donnie. He was the manager of this little club on Clark Street. And he and Ricky had found a space and they knew an architect—funny thing is I knew the same guy, Thomas Schlesser, we used to hang out at the Rainbo Club at the bar.

DONNIE MADIA: Paul was a big fan of Chez Panisse and Alice Waters. He gave me the Chez Panisse cookbook to read and I read it and we were just inspired from there. With his leadership and the guidance of some of the farmers that he had already contacted, we got the menu, the name, and how we were going to bring in great farmers and great produce. And that it wouldn't just change quarterly, it would change biweekly, which if you remember, didn't really exist in Chicago then. Because in wintertime we have no produce. We had no great experience with purchasing produce from California, because of the price point of bringing it in, but we did it anyways.

PAUL KAHAN: I'll never forget when we first met, I met Donnie and then I met Ricky and we went to Uncommon Ground coffee shop. It's where Erwin always took me. And they showed me their plans. I rode my bike there. Ricky pulled up in a '67 Buick Wildcat with a leather jacket, a cigarette hanging out of his mouth and black wraparound sunglasses. Donnie pulled up, I didn't see the car, but he was dressed to the nines, as usual. And I think I said to them at that meeting, okay, I'll go in business with you guys, but I'm not going to hang out with you. I rode my bicycle there in the winter. You know, tree hugger guy.

BLACKBIRD

DONNIE MADIA: Knowing Jerry Kleiner, I gravitated to that gritty Vivo vibe. But when I looked at real estate on the west side of Halsted [where Kleiner's restaurants were], the cost doubled. So that's why Ricky and I looked on the east side, which was broken streets and more empty storefronts than occupied ones. So we were able to control our destiny with a really low lease amount per month, and then we ended up purchasing the real estate six years later.

You have to make a choice, whether you want to open your dream restaurant, or you want to deplete the funds that you have for your dream restaurant and purchase a building. I went to banks, I put a list together of friends and family that I would ask to invest in Blackbird. And they would look at me and go, is this a one-way street? East of the expressway? They were thinking I'm a scam artist, that it was a horrible location.

PAUL KAHAN: It took us a year from the start of construction to get that place finished. We didn't know what the hell we were doing and just sort of fought our way through it and made it happen. I knew a lot of really great servers and we hired this team that knew what they were doing. Donnie sort of learned management and hospitality as we went.

We were way short of money, we needed like $100,000. So Ricky worked at Club Lucky [retro-themed Italian restaurant in Wicker Park] with this guy named Eduard Seitan. Eduard is like the embodiment of the American dream—moved here from Romania, got a job as a server, made a lot of money and saved a lot of money. So Eduard put in some money and his dad put in some money and we ran up our credit cards.

EDUARD SEITAN: I was in my first year of law school in Romania. And my parents wanted to visit some old friends of theirs who had moved to North Dakota maybe a decade earlier. For whatever reason we met them here, in Chicago, but before that, we were staying with some friends of friends. And this guy worked in construction. So he says to me, hey, one of my guys got injured, do you want to help me for a day or two until your friends from North Dakota get here? So I help them and at the end of the day, I get paid like $50 in cash. And I'm like, hell yeah!

After three months, my parents are like, you gotta get out of the construction business, you need to do something cleaner. How about waiting tables? I didn't speak any English. I spoke some Italian. I had zero experience in the restaurant business. I was lying to everyone. I was making up fancy restaurants in like Rome and Bucharest.

I got fired from probably forty restaurants, because no experience, no English. But I got hired at Club Lucky. I started as a food runner, and then I went into being a server. I was there for four years as the lead server. That's where I met Ricky. And one day he comes up to me, hey, my buddy and I want to open a restaurant. We need some help, we need some cash. Do you want to be partners? Yeah, absolutely. I always say we each had our own quarter of the restaurant business—Paul was cooking, Donnie was hosting, Ricky was bartending and I was serving.

Two things struck the first-time visitor to Blackbird when it opened in December of 1997: the minimalist white interior and the tightly packed seating, at a time when high-end restaurants tended to be luxe, and luxuriously spread out.

PAUL KAHAN: There was no restaurant that really had a design like that. There was no restaurant that wanted to do everything that a great fine dining restaurant does, but wanted to have high energy. As it turned out, it was super high energy. It was like cram them in, don't care how loud it is, don't care if the kitchen can handle it or not, let's fucking go. And that's what it was, and it was fun.

DONNIE MADIA: You've got the fabulous design by Thomas Schlesser, that nobody ever saw before. Floating ceilings, white gypsum board box, gray mohair banquettes. And a seating arrangement with a white Corian bar.

If you look at Thomas's previous designs, you see that he's not only a Francophile, he studied under a protégé of [Italian architect and designer] Gio Ponti. Those restaurants in Italy and France have tight quarters, they're small. And they have a certain way of designing a dining room where everybody is on top of one another, because number one, that's the way the French eat. In 2000, Ricky and I ate at Benoit, which was an eighty-five-year-old one-star Michelin restaurant [in Paris]. I was enamored with how close the tables were. That was the eureka moment, when the light bulb came on. Wow, it does work. Blackbird's supposed to be like this.

A lot of people didn't like that it was close quarters, they didn't like that the music was loud. In those early years we would play great rock and roll music. And that would make the voice levels go up. And then the music would go up. There would be this competition between voices in the room and music and then we just figured, man, we've got to lower the music a little bit because our older clientele is not digging it.

PAUL KAHAN: It was like a fishbowl, those lights were on every day and people would drive by it and it was so stark. It looked like *Nighthawks*, and people I think were like, what the heck is that? And then when they started to drive by and there were people crammed in there, it added color to this really black-and-white palette and it just worked. If it had been one-way traffic going the other way, people wouldn't have sat in traffic there to get on the expressway and seen the place.

We weren't the first [to open in that area] but it felt like we were. On the other side of the expressway on Randolph were Jerry Kleiner's places. It was only like four blocks, but they felt much further away. And then on Fulton Market, there was nothing at all. It was the meat markets—my dad had had his fish factory there.

DONNIE MADIA: Winston Mardis was the liquor commissioner. He did not like restaurants opening with light appetizers, and being more of a bar. You would have to meet with him, and bring your menus. And if your menu wasn't 70-30—70 percent of your business was driven by food, and 30 percent liquor—then you would have a really difficult time getting him to approve your liquor license. He would sit on liquor licenses for months and months, when you put your heart and soul in and you beg, borrow and steal every penny that you have in the world, and you're on the hook for your lease.

We went an entire month without a liquor license, and we would just buy wine and give it away. And people were bringing in wine, the first month was

BYOB. And then through a friend of mine, and this is an old-school move, he reached out to a guy that was in the insurance business and was really powerful, and knew Mayor Daley. And he made a call to Winston Mardis and asked him politely to move the Blackbird license up the pile. And so on New Year's Eve, the last night of 1997, we received our liquor license. And Ricky had everybody in the wings, ready. Like we're gonna get it, we're gonna get it, it's gonna be this week, it's gonna be this week. And finally it came that night. And Ricky called all the orders in.

That was the first push [that drove business]. And then when Pat Bruno gave us three stars in the *Sun-Times*, we got a second push. And then I think the true credibility came when Phil Vettel gave us three stars, and we also got three stars from Penny Pollack in *Chicago* magazine. And then a year and a half in, Paul wins one of the ten best new chefs from *Food & Wine*—you couldn't ask for anything more.

Those days, waiting months for *Chicago* magazine to find you, are gone now—I'll quote Penny, who said critics don't have two or three months to get to a restaurant, you've got a week because the bloggers are already there. But I loved the anticipation, the nail biting. We'd wait outside the *Tribune* or the *Sun-Times* and ask for an advance copy and sit in our car and read it at, like, three or four in the morning. And it was like holy shit. It's fucking *on.* We were going to make it. We can pay Eduard's dad back. We can pay Paul's family back. We can pay our credit card debt. We're really good.

****

PAUL KAHAN: There's just something different about an independent restaurant as opposed to, you know, Lettuce Entertain You or whatever. I'm not sure exactly what it is. But I guess you could feel it.

To this day, I don't care about food cost. I mean, as long as we could get a paycheck, and we're bringing some money to the bottom line. I don't think we even knew. I was just like, every farmer, everything that people brought me that I was excited about, I bought and I cooked with and I put it on the menu. I was inspired by this interview of Alice Waters that I heard on NPR when I was a young cook, talking about how food, for her, is more about the person sitting across the table and the experience of dining and the energy and the conversation and all that stuff. And I really took that to heart.

DONNIE MADIA: I think the first two years we were probably making, each, like two hundred and fifty dollars a week. But we were making a living and we were feeding diners who wanted to change their perspective on dining in Chicago.

EDUARD SEITAN: I had learned a little bit about wine at Club Lucky, although at the time Pinot Grigio was the thing. Paul has a great palate for wine, so I learned a lot working for Ricky and for Paul.

It was Ricky's passion too, but I took over the program at Blackbird and took my first somm level. Then I started judging wine contests. I started with the Michigan state wine competition and then I judged some other international, Pacific Rim wine competitions. I think for me, learning about wine was the biggest thing. When you're judging with three or four other judges, tasting three hundred wines in two days—I mean, it's bam, bam, bam, that was the best for me.

PAUL KAHAN: For me, a tasting menu is like a study of the chef's ego—let me show you what I can do. That was just never the way that I wanted to cook, little precious bites of things. I just wanted to put something in front of you, a complete thought on a plate that you'd eat and go, wow, this is delicious. Or I've never eaten anything like this. Or wow, I've never heard of these farms, I've never eaten this product.

I think it comes from my love of gardening. Just that experience when you pull green garlic out of your garden and take it in the house and cook with it. I have different farmers in the city that I trade with and like, Nichols Farm uses our butcher shop for a drop off point for their CSAs. And so every spring I call Nick up and I say, whaddaya got? And he says, well, we have three different kinds of radicchio, we have this, that, whatever. They drop the plants off at the side of my house at the proper planting time and I just grow a ton of shit. I grow so much that I bring it in in garbage bags to the restaurants, because my wife and I can't eat it all.

Actually on one of those freight-hopping trips I went to Chez Panisse, I knew of it from Erwin, we cooked out of her books at Metropolis Cafe. And so I kind of made a pilgrimage there and I had lunch at Chez Panisse while

I was doing my laundry in Berkeley. It just blew me away. I just remember a plate of the tiniest tomatoes that I've ever seen with beautiful snipped herbs and olive oil. And that was perfect for me. I think the better the product is, the better the food is.

Alice is a pretty good friend at this point. And I get emails from her all the time, and we talk whenever she's in town, or we go for lunch, which is like a dream. I mean, she's, for me, as important as anyone in food in this country.

DONNIE MADIA: I associate the word "clean" with Paul's food. The space was very clean. I wouldn't call it minimalist, but it was minimal. Our direction came from Paul's food; it was simply on a white plate, white tablecloth, white napkin, white backdrop. And so the food looked really, really interesting on the table, more interesting than other food that we were seeing at that time. The visuals were so important to that restaurant—the bouillabaisse that we poured out of a copper pot tableside, the hand-strung basket [for the Lyonnaise salad] that we broke apart tableside.

It was our own departure into French classics, with a modern spin. It wasn't a big Chicago plate of food. I gravitated to the idea that we didn't have to eat in abundance. Doggie bags didn't make sense to us. We're gonna give you enough food to enjoy what you ate. But guests are paying a little bit more, and they're getting a little bit less on the plate. We're very proud that we had the fortitude to think intentionally about what was on the plate, how much was on the plate, and still serve a great meal. We thought of different ways of letting people go home with a little gift. Like we would make cookies and wrap them up with a nice bow and it would be presented at the end of the meal after coffee.

DAVID BARRIBALL (wine director/general manager of Blackbird): In Chicago in the '90s, before Blackbird opened, what were the big restaurants? Like Avanzare. And you had a 32 oz. veal chop—at lunch! I always thought that Blackbird was a restaurant that really changed the landscape. Culinary simplicity, I say it was simple elegance, Paul's ability to take flavors and techniques and make them very approachable was always inspiring.

DONNIE MADIA: In the winter we'd concentrate on root vegetables that were grown and harvested for us through Paul's relationships with farmers. He created a menu through root vegetables and he was the first one, to give him so much credit. The first one to start with an *amuse-bouche*—with the exception of the French guys, nobody was doing that. The first one to put pork belly on the menu, and also sturgeon. Nobody was doing sturgeon, a prehistoric fish that's been around for millions of years.

PAUL KAHAN: Jewish cooking, Jewish cultural food, really stuck in my mind. In my dad's place they'd smoke sturgeon. I remember walking in there as a young kid and seeing something the size of a shark wrapped up in burlap on the ground. And I'm like, what's this, Dad? And he cut the strings and opened it up. And it was a giant sturgeon that they were going to smoke and I was like, holy cow.

So that was always in my mind. The sturgeon dish [at Blackbird] evolved from cooking sturgeon with Erwin—another Jewish guy, he always had sturgeon on the menu. And then my wife was getting a master's degree in social administration from the Jane Addams School and she was in DC for a couple months for an internship, and I went to Jean-Louis Palladin's restaurant [Jean-Louis at the Watergate]. And one of the dishes I ate there was a combination of scallop and oxtail. And I was like, wow, this is amazing. So I started working on a sturgeon and oxtail dish. And there were like five different variations over the years of that dish, but it was pretty iconic, and no one else ever did a dish like that and has not done it since.

So, is that from my Jewish heritage? I mean, I am my history. My family lineage is Jewish, but never that religious. But I just think a lot of it rubbed off on me by osmosis. After my parents were divorced, I went to high school in Skokie, and my sister worked at Kaufman's Deli—so lox and bagels are still to this day one of my favorite foods in the whole world. I guess it's in my genes, I fucking love all that stuff. Like, gefilte fish is so delicious. I like all of it.

But I was a big pork belly guy for a long time. I was the pork chef. For me it was like an obsession with what were lesser cuts, more than what was cheap. It's so interesting to see that all those other cuts are more expensive than pork chops now. I think in that same year, Thomas Keller—before his book came out—he was cooking pork belly, and maybe I had heard about it. I think Tom

Colicchio when he was the chef at Gramercy Tavern was doing pork belly. And so, whether I read about it or whatever, I just became kind of obsessed with it. I've always been a trial and error guy, like if it's the first time I braised pork belly—nobody was braising pork belly, I tried it like thirty times, thirty different ways. And you learn all these little tricks as you go, like let it cool in the braising liquid. It'll soak up all that flavor and all that juice, and it won't dry out, it sort of finishes cooking like confit in its own rendered fat.

We also bought suckling pigs from George Rasmussen, and Greg Gunthorp, when they used to come into town together. I did an event with Suzanne Goin [Lucques, Los Angeles] around the time she won Best New Chef from *Food & Wine* [1999, the same year as Kahan], she had worked in France and so I kind of picked her brain and just fell in love with the idea of treating a small pig kind of like a duck leg. So we would cure the quarters of the suckling pig with salt and black pepper and bay leaves, and sear them all around, and then cover them with duck fat and simmer them in the oven. I'd read that somebody was doing something that I thought was really cool, and kind of went at it in my ass-backwards way, through trial and error and figuring out how to make something delicious.

That's kind of what made me the pork guy. I wish it was a more romantic story—when I did The Publican cookbook,[22] the pork belly recipe, there's sort of a faint X through it, like I'm doing this under protest. Because everybody, at a certain point, was serving pork belly and people who didn't know how to cook it were doing the wrong pork. They were using the wrong pig and it was just like a mouthful of fat, disgusting.

I think another big thing I got when I was doing pork belly in the early days, I did some work with the National Pork Board, and they asked me if I would do a dish at this Research Chefs Association convention in San Diego. So I did pork belly for eight hundred. I got Niman Ranch pork bellies that I had to process for eight hundred portions, and I did this dish that was very simple, braised pork belly with fresh shell beans. And it was terrific. And for years, even to this day, people are like, I had pork belly at this event in San Diego in like 1998 or '99.

22 *Cheers to the Publican, Repast and Present: Recipes and Ramblings from an American Beer Hall,* 2017.

PAUL VIRANT (private events chef): Working with Paul was the first time I was working with my boss, not for him. He respected me for the kind of experience that I had, in more sort of European cooking and French cooking, sauces and that kind of stuff. And so he would lean on me for that stuff. But at the end of the day, what I was super impressed by was, he was really tapped into all these farmers. Just being there and seeing Dave Cleverdon from Kinnikinnick Farm showing up, like, in the middle of the winter, with these incredible beets and different things that he was doing. I was like, man, this *can* be done, it exists, there's enough of the stuff around. Paul sealed the deal for me that you could have a restaurant in the Chicago area and support local farmers, and it can be very seasonal.

PAUL KAHAN: Paul Virant was the private events chef at Blackbird. When we built the second-floor dining room, he had worked for Joho, and was working on his own restaurant, and needed a way to make a living. And so we worked together more as contemporaries. He's a great cook. And I learned so much from him, and I think vice versa. Talk about honest simple food. That's his shtick, and he does a great job with it. And acidity, you know, he's the jar star. He's the pickle guy. So talk about acidity, I would say that I think he's as responsible for that [in Blackbird's food] as anyone. He came from a little more technical background than I did. But we just gelled together, we had a lot of fun.

JUSTIN LARGE (cook): When I was looking to do my externship from CIA, I saw this blurb about Blackbird in *Food & Wine*. And I was like, oh man, that looks cool. What Paul was doing at the time, that's what I want to do. So I literally rang up the restaurant and forced my way into a stage for an externship. I just basically went to Chicago on a whim.

At that time the Chicago restaurant scene was changing quite a bit, getting away from like, the expense account steak house. Doing something that was way more focused, and ingredient driven, and at least attempting to be local, making relationships with farmers, but also doing a modern take on those things. That's what intrigued me, Paul and the guys were doing fine dining, like, Blackbird definitely felt sleek and cool. But we also tried to be very welcoming to just about anybody that would want to walk in and eat.

Anna and David Posey met while working for One Off.

ANNA POSEY (pastry cook, The Publican): I think they saw people who were inspired and wanted to grow. I think they took a chance on us. That's so big to offer somebody that. We worked hard. But they provided everything that let us grow as chefs, like the best food. Food costs were always a thing but they encouraged us to go to the farmers market, explore these books, talk to other chefs. They were just so instrumental in helping with that and guiding us.

I think that's really rare, to learn how to run departments and have that much responsibility. Like, I'd be the one to call people when things were broken, you're almost given the role of the owner when you're not the owner. They gave you so much responsibility—entrusted it to you.

DAVID POSEY (cook, Blackbird): Especially when I started, it was a scrappy little company—it was only Blackbird and avec. But it was a very vision-driven company and it was really inspiring to be around that, and then getting to work with Donnie and Paul and all the owners directly, they were always there, was such a great learning experience.

ANNA POSEY: I think when I took over [pastry at The Publican] it was like, pie with whipped cream on top. And I was just itching to be so creative. So I kind of turned it into something that we could do large quantities of, but still thoughtful. Elevated pub food, I guess, but with a twist. I used vinegars, which back then I feel like not a lot of people did. Just trying to bring it up a notch, more than just a piece of cake or a piece of pie.

PAUL KAHAN: Seasonality was just sort of the roadmap that Erwin instilled in me as a young cook, and through travel, it just got reinforced. And now it's a challenge to the different chefs in the company. Some really embrace the market and others don't. And so it's a challenge to keep them on track and keep pushing it. Brian Huston, who's one of our culinary directors, and I are continually going to the market and bringing them stuff.

I mean, honestly, in this day and age, if you have a dedicated employee, that works hard, that's a good leader, that maybe struggles with that aspect of the business, you can't just be like, you're out. You have to embrace them and teach them. I mean, there's people that just will be like, no, I'm not doing that. And that's not allowed. But a couple of the chefs are a work in progress as far as that goes. And it's always a challenge in Chicago—five months a year, there's nothing, right? You have to embrace what's in season in California and you have to cook with it. Otherwise, your plates will be all brown.

DAVID POSEY: I had no idea what grew in what season when I started at Blackbird. I had no idea that grapes were late summer, early fall. No idea. I would bring a dish to Paul to taste and it would be so out-of-season it was insane. And it was a very humbling learning curve for me. But then when you learn that things that grow together, go together, it gets a little easier. And that's when I kind of started forming my own style.

JUSTIN LARGE: Paul taught me a lot about charcuterie and sausage-making—Blackbird had a house-made charcuterie plate on the lunch menu, which in the early 2000s was very cutting-edge, ahead of its time.

The other big piece that Paul was super impactful on my career was that he allowed us all, every cook in that kitchen, to have a place on that menu if you pushed yourself hard enough to have it. Which made the team drive really hard because the menu was really a reflection not just of him, but you could pull it up and say, that's Jeremy's [Kittelson], that's Jared's [Van Camp], that's mine. You're not just stamping out license plates—you're an owner of that menu.

PAUL KAHAN: For me, the Chicago style, and it's certainly changed with time, is honesty and being genuine. It's not trying to—there's a whole smoke and mirrors thing, science food. At one point we had a chef de cuisine who came to Blackbird from WD-50 in New York. A great guy, a great cook, but it was a painful experience for me, because he was very strong-willed as well. And you know, the way they did it at WD-50, the way they did it in New York, was the way that he knew and thought was right, and he couldn't understand why I wanted to do things the way I wanted to do them.

DAVID POSEY: I really wanted to work at WD-50. So when Mike Sheerin took over, he had been chef de cuisine at WD-50, I thought, this is perfect. It's a good way to see if I like what he was doing at WD 50.

I think Mike pushed it a little further than Paul was comfortable with. Like, there was one dish, where I just didn't know what he was thinking. It was trout, bananas, and anchovy, and it was brutal, it was not good. But then he also did some really great things, like there was a sepia [cuttlefish], lime and chocolate dish that was really good, but it definitely pushed the boundary. It was very satisfying for me to see these dishes where we mixed tapioca and savory food and all these modern techniques, but Paul also grounding it in seasonality and going to the market. It was a perfect mix of the two worlds for me.

PAUL KAHAN: I was, and I still am, very insecure about everything that I do. It's sort of an obsession with every aspect of a dish. I teach the chefs in the company that it's all about how food eats on a plate. It's easy with a tasting menu, because it's one bite or two bites. But when you're doing a complete thought on a plate, there has to be structure to it. And there has to be acidity, and all the right flavors. And so I never was satisfied with the menu being where it should be, with things being in the appropriate season with pretty much anything. So it was always a work in progress.

It's nice to hear feedback that people really enjoyed something, or love something. But sorry, my attitude was like, what do *you* know? It was very self-centric, about me wanting things to be soulful and clean at the same time and to hit every point that my brain goes to when it comes to food, or the way that food should be prepared. Accolades are great, but I never really believed them or paid attention to them. I still don't.

****

JUSTIN LARGE: When I got there, Paul had won *Food & Wine* Best New Chef, but this was before his James Beard awards[23] or anything like that. But you know what those guys were great about? No matter how successful they got, they always acted like the restaurant was going to close the next day, and managed the business accordingly. As stressful as that sounds, it means every

23 Restaurant and Chef, 2004, among others.

guest is important, every meal is important. They never got swayed by the accolades.

DONNIE MADIA: So Paul won the *Food & Wine* Best New Chefs award, and he got the invite to go to New York to be photographed, the whole thing. And one of the nights we ate at Daniel. And I see the way the dining room moves, the way people are served. It energized me to change the philosophy of the dining room.

We couldn't be Daniel, because we didn't have a dining room where each table was five feet apart. Because of the space characteristics, we had to do things better, because we were in a tighter space. And so not every dish could be served from the left and pulled from the right. But we concentrated more on service and hospitality. I think we turned it up a notch, more hospitality. We had more hospitality than service after that.

The *amuse-bouche* would set the tone for the evening, and we started taking wine more seriously as well. It was still kind of close encounters with the guests next to you, but we took it a little more seriously—while still playing rock and roll music. It was really just learning lessons from my mom and my aunt, who were incredible hosts and incredible bakers and cooks in the home. They just cared for people.

IVAR JOHNSON (server): First of all, there was no uniform. For a long time, everyone would just wear their own clothes. So sometimes you'd walk up to the table and customers would be like, do you work here?

There was very little management—the owners were around, but they weren't in your face. If you wanted to, say, delete something off a check, you just did it. It wasn't like I had to go get a manager.

I was working at Tru when they hired me, and I hated it. It was just so stuck up, it was so cold in there. Basically all you'd do is just run food, and call food. And because they would do this thing where every person would have a different course at the table, it would take so long to call the food. It was ridiculous. I was very excited to come on board at Blackbird, because it seemed like the kind of place that I would actually eat at, which is rare for high-end restaurants.

I've worked in restaurants where you feel like you're just ripping people off. Or underperforming for the cost and stuff like that. At Blackbird, I always thought that we were giving people an experience of value and something that couldn't find somewhere else. Even if it was loud. When Blackbird wasn't Blackbird yet, when it was still just like a regular restaurant, people's expectations were always exceeded, because people didn't expect that much. It's just a West Loop restaurant, you know? Then we started getting people who weren't Chicago people, who were just like, oh yeah, I saw this in *Gourmet* magazine. So you're one of the best restaurants in the country? Oh boy, we better overperform.

DONNIE MADIA: What's fucked up is that for the last twenty years, I walk into a dining room during service, and I see all the things that are wrong. I should really be looking at all the things that are right, that we're doing right. That's something obsessive, like, you have everything that's going right, but I don't look at the right stuff. I look at the wrong stuff. And that wrong stuff drives me absolutely bonkers. And I know that's the same for Paul in the kitchen.

AVEC

A few years after Blackbird opened, in 2003, the team opened avec on the next block, initially planning it as a bar to hold patrons waiting for their table at Blackbird. But under executive chef Koren Grieveson, it soon took on a life—and a crowd—of its own.

KOREN GRIEVESON: I was in the army for eight years. I joined when I was seventeen, because I wanted to drive Jeeps. The year I joined they changed to Humvees, which was a bummer.

I would hang out with the cooks, Army cooks in the kitchen, and obviously that kind of piqued my interest. And then I started doing catering in my early twenties, doing rock and roll bands and big shows and Lollapalooza, all that fun stuff. I went to the Culinary Institute of America in '94, I think, and when I graduated I went to Chicago. I actually got my first restaurant gig with Keith Luce, who was the chef of Spruce at the time, and was the White

House chef for the Clintons. He was really kind of instrumental in teaching me how to actually cook vegetables, and meat, the proper way of doing it that you don't really get in culinary school.

I ended up interviewing for a sous chef job at Blackbird, which I got, and Paul's been my mentor ever since. Ricky, Donnie, Paul and I all went to France to do some research for avec and just came back and started conceptualizing what the food would look like. They sent me for a month to New York. I stayed with Gabrielle Hamilton at her house. I worked with Wade Moses at one of Mario Batali's restaurants, I learned to make salumi there. I came back and we started a salumi program for avec early in 2003, and we opened in September 2003.

DONNIE MADIA: The idea was that we're going to create a wine bar. And that wine bar is going to just hold people. So they can wait for their table at Blackbird, because there's no waiting. We also worked very hard in this market to make sure that it's okay to sit at the bar. Because nobody was eating at the bar in the city, especially at a white tablecloth restaurant. So we made sure if you ate at the bar at Blackbird, you had the same dining experience, that you had cotton napkins that were quartered, if you had dark clothes on you'd have a black napkin, same dining experience, same Riedel crystal, same Bormioli water glasses.

So it was just to hold people for Blackbird, but fortunately, the food was so delicious.

PAUL KAHAN: We were trying to block another restaurant from coming in there, like when Grace[24] opened next door. They had a lease on the space, and when they gave it up, we jumped on it. Because it pissed us off that they were going to be on both sides of us. Fuck those guys!

The idea was a wine bar with some great snacks, and it was also an opportunity to open a place for Koren, who was my second sous chef at Blackbird, and work very closely with her on the menu. We worked on all these signature dishes together, I'm like, we need this on the menu, we need that on the menu, and we just sort of pieced together this menu of small plates and large plates.

24 Not the Curtis Duffy restaurant further west on Randolph, but an early 2000s spot led by chef-partner Ted Cizma, later chef for SpaceX.

KOREN GRIEVESON: "Avec" is French, of course. And I feel like Europeans always do it better. They always have that *je ne sais quoi* about food and dining and that kind of hospitality that we wanted to bring to avec. And, you know, there are just certain things, you go there and have, like, a bowl of sardines with crackers. Of course you do, and why not? So you try and translate that back to Chicago. I think people were open to it, embracing it. Where I could never serve that at Blackbird, because people expected a whole dish.

I'm trying to remember our research trip—obviously a lot of game and pâtés. We were looking to make small plates, which was a new thing then. It turned out everybody wanted to eat that way. You don't want a sit-down dinner—I mean, not always. You want three to five or however many courses, you want to nibble and have options. You want to do dessert first? Go for it. You want to do cheese first, great. You want to do the chorizo-stuffed dates first, great, and then jump around and do some fish. I think the openness of the dining experience is what we were definitely looking to accomplish.

EDUARD SEITAN: Koren was just such an incredible chef and always changing the menu, every day something new, and she was just such a creative force. She was fierce and not the easiest person to work with. Or to be friends with or to collaborate with. She was just so serious and so focused, and that came across as rude at times, but she was incredibly talented. She *is* incredibly talented.

JUSTIN LARGE: She had been my sous chef at Blackbird, so I had worked under her for years. And she took no shit in the kitchen. She pushed us really hard. There were no shortcuts, and we created a culture where if she even perceived that you were hacking something out, you'd get called on it.

Paul was maybe good cop, she was probably bad cop in that relationship. You didn't want to piss off the good cop either. But you definitely did not want to piss off the bad cop because bad cop would make your life miserable.

PAUL KAHAN: Donnie was really instrumental in communal seating. Our thoughts were, all these people over the years had tried communal seating in Chicago and it never worked. But it was always that the food sucked, so let's really focus on great ingredients and really incredible, simple food.

JUSTIN LARGE: Oh, we're gonna sit down at a table with people we don't know, we're gonna eat with strangers? I think that shook things up for Chicago a little bit. In the beginning, it was communal dining, but you'd just have these two separate parties at the table, that would not talk to one another. A couple years in, finally, people were starting to break through, and to share food with each other and have a great conversation. For me that was the heartbeat of that restaurant.

PAUL KAHAN: Koren had this way of cooking with a super high level of acidity, which we strive for in all of our restaurants. She was really instrumental in that, like always lemon juice, always vinegar, always real bright flavors that popped.

I'd be remiss if I didn't mention Eduard. His sound bite is, I want to focus on sundrenched regions of the Mediterranean. Which is like the weirdest places that no one was paying attention to. So you might have like, Croatian wine or something, Greek wine, island wine from all these islands that grow amazing wine. And he's a complete nut when it comes to his palate and locations and what he focuses on.

EDUARD SEITAN: When we opened avec I spent a little more time with it because I was doing the wine program and it was something new for me. I really wanted the wine program to go with the food. The concept was rustic Mediterranean-inspired food. Spain, Portugal, Southern Italy, southern France. This was twenty years ago, you could find Bordeaux and Burgundy and Tuscan reds, some Spanish reds, but man, finding Portuguese wines was hard, to find Languedoc, Provence, not easy. So that was my thing. And every time someone would bring me something from the Rhone Valley. I would be like, oh, no, I'm gonna stay right there. Right around the Mediterranean. The Rhone Valley is just like a stone's throw up north. But I wanted to stay focused on that.

DONNIE MADIA: It was a beautiful wine menu. We had twenty bottles by the glass, nobody was doing that. We were buying wine that nobody else was buying. So we thought that was the concept, but Paul and Koren's food was exceptional, hand-sliced meats that we were curing in-house—nobody else was doing that back then. So that place became its own restaurant and its own success.

And we've still got two small little restaurants, and there's no holding space for anybody.

****

PAUL KAHAN: Having everything come out of, essentially, one wood-burning hearth is pretty unique, six burners and a wood hearth, that's the kitchen. It makes you cook things in a different way. And I was really adamant about serving things in the dishes that they're cooked in. If you go to Spain, or you go to Europe, you see a lot of that, and people just don't do that here, or they didn't at the time. And so the food's always really hot there, which is different for people. It was out of necessity, the place is so small, and there's no room in the window. So you put plates up, they gotta go.

JUSTIN LARGE: The way that restaurant was designed forced you to think a lot about the technical aspects of cooking and the actual execution on a line, more than any restaurant I've ever worked in. You had this giant wood oven. And then you've got a four-burner stove, basically. What you're able to put out of that kitchen is pretty amazing. It's still amazing to me. You've got this thirteen-foot line in what appears to be a pretty small dining room, but when you run a service that goes from three thirty in the afternoon to twelve, almost one in the morning, you're going to do a serious number of covers. And all of it was homemade—if we could make it, we would. We would be like, we're gonna do everything on this dish, even the things that may have been mundane or brought into restaurants, like ketchup.

KOREN GRIEVESON: It was such a small space in terms of dining space, cooking space, that you had to figure out how many items we can really put out of this kitchen. Paul's obviously very knowledgeable on what the kitchen should look like. And obviously, you design the kitchen but you don't know what you're going to really end up preparing.

When we first opened we had this pork shoulder on the menu. And, you know, we were still figuring it out so we weren't changing the menu very often. And it's midsummer, hot as hell, and we were selling so much braised pork shoulder. Are you kidding me? It is *so* hot outside and I'm just selling thirty, forty pork shoulders a night. And I'm like, okay, cool. I'm gonna keep doing it.

PAUL KAHAN: The combination of that way of cooking, and high acidity, and just all those variables coming together, I think, made avec. Donnie would slap me on the side of the head, but I think it's more important than Blackbird. When you shake all the change out of the pockets in the laundry, it's just such a unique and important restaurant.

There was a time when Anthony Bourdain dined there. The first time with us was at the bar at Blackbird, and he just went crazy. He loved it. But the second time was at avec, and the restaurant was full, he stood up, commanded the attention of the room, and said, welcome to the fucking future of dining in America. He was so excited.

KOREN GRIEVESON: The whole gastropub thing, I definitely saw that [being inspired in Chicago by avec]. I mean, I had my head down, working, when was I going to go out? But I was aware of it, and it was a compliment, sure.

Grieveson was named a Food & Wine *best new chef in 2008, and won a James Beard award for Best Chef Great Lakes in 2010. She also scored a rare tie on* Iron Chef America *in 2009, against Cat Cora.*

KOREN GRIEVESON: I did not want to do it. My sous chef at the time, Justin, wanted to do it. I'm not good on TV. It's not my jam.

I did it because it's good for business. People watch TV and they want it. I also wanted to just get over my fear of—it's a competition, which, again, not my jam. So I'm happy I did it. You'd kind of train, so to speak, for a couple of months and then get on TV and you cook for an hour and then you get judged.

I was done ten minutes before Cat Cora was done. And they had to, you know, bring it down, make it this climax between us—it's TV, I get it. At the end of the day, it was a fun experience. Once the cooking gets going, your nerves soften a little bit, but it's still not my thing. Save it for the Bobby Flays.

Grieveson moved to New York in 2012; there was talk of opening a New York branch of avec, but ultimately the partners decided to stick to Chicago.

DAVID BARRIBALL: We're constantly bombarded with opportunities in New York City and other major markets. But there's a thoughtfulness about growth—there's so many other people who took their show on the road, and they're in, say, Miami, and it's not the same experience. Avec Miami would not have the same kind of warmth, and thoughtfulness and hospitality that we have here. To be able to grow like that, you need to build the infrastructure first, and that's expensive. I don't think, say, avec Nashville is what we'll do right now, but you could certainly name five towns around the Chicagoland area that are bustling communities that would love to have an avec right in the middle of them.

KOREN GRIEVESON: What I think was interesting and incredible about avec, especially early on, is what the owners and we all created in such a small space, with all its weird little intricacies.

And the staff was so wonderful—Justin was my sous chef, Sam Kass from the White House [chef for the Obamas] was my sous chef, and Erling [Wu-Bower] was my sous chef. I've been blessed to have really amazing guys who've gone on to do incredible things. One Off Hospitality has been a big part of my life. I was there from '98 to 2012, I think that was a good part of my life. And, you know, to this day, Paul is my mentor and he's been such a cool cat. Actually, he did adopt my cat, which is a long story.

THE PUBLICAN

In 2008 One Off opened The Publican—on Fulton Market, where Kahan's father had had a wholesale fish business. It would be one of the first new businesses on that industrial strip that would help make it a rival to Randolph a couple of blocks south. It would also spawn side businesses for the group, beginning with Publican Quality Meats—and it would be part of a new partnership with another Chicago food and beverage veteran, Terry Alexander.

PAUL KAHAN: I was hanging out a lot with Greg Hall, from Goose Island

[Brewery]. We were drinking a lot of beer together, getting in a lot of trouble. And the next big thing was brewpubs. We were supposed to brew beer there, but ultimately, there just was no room.

TERRY ALEXANDER: It was Paul's idea. He said the three greatest things were oysters, pork and beer.

PAUL KAHAN: I came up with the sound bite "oysters, pork and beer." I would run that by friends, chef buddies, people. Because the question for everyone is, what are you doing next? And I wish it would have been like, we're not doing anything next, man, just go to our restaurants. When Blackbird and avec were open, we had this idea. We wanted to open up a French truck stop, like on the freeways in Europe.

We were walking up Fulton Market. We walked from Blackbird, across was all the meat packers. And like I said, my dad's place was right around the corner, so I grew up in that neighborhood. I spent a lot of time at my dad's fish factory working, and it was a rough neighborhood, really rough. A lot of prostitutes up and down Lake Street. A lot of crime.

So we walk by this building and a guy is in there operating a backhoe. It was Bob Kowalski, the guy who owned the building. He was a really interesting guy who, like, nothing came out of his mouth that was honest, ever. I think he went to prison.[25] The building is stunning, and a lot of people tried to cut a deal with him for that corner space. Before there was anything there. We have more patience, or we're not as smart as the other guys. Eventually we just had to finance it on our own, you know, scraping and scratching.

DONNIE MADIA: Our reaction was, this block is like New York, this is all New York. You know, nothing happened in the Meatpacking District [in New York] until Pastis opened in 2000, 2001 on Gansevoort. We loved that place. The bar at avec is inspired by the one at Pastis, it was long and the pass made its way into the kitchen and that's where the food came out of. So seven or eight years later, we're looking at this space with Bob Kowalski, before any-

25 Convicted in 2023 in a case involving a Daley-connected Bridgeport bank, Washington Federal Bank for Savings.

body else did, and there were trucks parked on the street, semis coming down the street. We had New York on our minds, no question.

PAUL KAHAN: We found all these connections to France and to Belgium in the idea. One of the things on [designer Thomas Schlesser's mood board] was the Last Supper. We were going with the communal table idea, the beer hall idea. We just had these meetings where it would be Donnie and Ricky and Eduard and myself, and we'd sit in a room with Thomas and Jason Pickleman, our graphic designer, and we would just talk about stuff. Tons of great ideas came through these collaborations. And we just came up with something that's really unique and different. And again, that's another one where is it comfortable? No, is it ear-bleeding? Really loud? Yes. Did we even care about acoustics in those days? No. It was all about the food and beer.

TERRY ALEXANDER: It was before beer was such a big thing. Now you can get incredible beer at 7-Eleven. But back then, you'd know there were only like two places where you could get a certain beer, or stuff like that.

Paul and Brian Huston were the opening chefs, and the first eight or nine years, they would change the menu every day, just depending on what came in the door that day, what the farmers were bringing in. And then at about one o'clock, the chef, sous chef, and a couple of the guys would sit down and literally discuss what they were going to make. Put the menu together. That's how they did it every day.

PAUL KAHAN: It was rough on cooks. New product came in the door all day, mounds of stuff from the farmers market. That's why we opened [Publican Quality Meats], because we needed a place to butcher. That shop is a labor of love. You might go in there and be like, man, thirty-nine dollars a pound for steak is a lot. We're doing a 50 percent markup—that's what you need to do to run your business. But we're buying really expensive meat, and we're aging it. And you know, when you have a steak that you buy there versus a supposedly great steak that you buy from Whole Foods, there's a huge difference in flavor, and where it comes from and how good or bad it is for you, how you feel after you eat it.

DONNIE MADIA: Oysters, pork and beer. It sounds good. That was the sound bite that Paul came up with on the R&D trip was Belgium, Montreal, London. This was the One Off idea—we're going to do one thing and do it good.

****

Not every restaurant they've had has succeeded, but the One Off partners have a remarkable track record that includes staying together as a team for a quarter century—save for Rick Diarmit, who died in 2018.

PAUL KAHAN: A couple of weeks after we first met, Ricky and I went out for a beer, and then went to his house, and we're sitting around the kitchen table. And Ricky goes, I've got to tell you something. I did hard time. Ricky was in a gang when he was a kid. And I was like, I don't care.

DONNIE MADIA: Ricky was working at Club Lucky when I was working at Tufano's. We were both bartenders and I would go to Club Lucky and he would go to Tufano's. I knew his uncle Bud who's similar in age to me, and his mom and his brother. In about '94 we went to New York together, and we had our aspirations of opening our own place and what that place was going to be. So we decided to save some money and work on a business plan and put that plan into action.

A lovely man, with a beautiful mom who worked in the pastry kitchen for ten years, and rolled thousands of *mignardises*. Thousands. And he was just as sweet and kind as his mom. So a nice, really beautiful friendship.

PAUL KAHAN: Ricky was a joy, he had the biggest heart. He was really the heart of our company. Ricky was like a man of the people, a shot and a beer guy. Loved smoking cigarettes until he quit. The nicest man ever. He put himself in giant debt with credit cards to open up Blackbird. He was our lunch manager, and always had a bunch of tradesmen coming in sitting at the bar having a beer in the afternoon—his friends that helped us with the project. So I would just say, one of the kindest, gentlest people that I've ever met and, you know, obviously sorely missed.

DONNIE MADIA: It's taken me a long time to understand our relationships [as partners] and how we work together. I mean, twenty-five years, twenty-six years, it's a long time. It's a marriage. Do we each have our own territory? I don't know if we need to. We make suggestions. I believe we all can contribute. I believe greatly in the art of collaboration.

Terry gave me a sound bite years ago that I think about all the time. And that's, no one person is bigger than the whole. I hope that Paul respects my opinion, I respect his opinion. I could be wrong, sometimes he could be wrong. We try not to flare up in conversations about what color blue the sky is. Because that in itself is ego.

TERRY ALEXANDER: I think Paul is one of those people that started so many things that we take for granted now in kitchens and in restaurants. Paul was always so far ahead of his time with farmers, instead of just buying in bulk. He was always looking for the best product, the best oysters, the best everything. He wanted to know where it came from, where it was fed, what it was fed. He was one of the chefs that really started all those things.

EDUARD SEITAN: The culinary talent that Paul is—what's the word, when you're a benefactor, when you give back, philanthropy? Such a low-key incredible talent, not pompous in any way, down to work. Donnie, just, like, so driven. I remember one time where Paul, Donnie, Ricky and myself are flying somewhere, maybe New York, just to do R&D. We were at Midway, and we were delayed. And Donnie really wanted us to get out of there. He was pushing, he was going from ticket counter to ticket counter. Donnie is just like, he pushes and pushes and pushes, he wants to get things done. And then Ricky was just such an incredibly good person and like, good with people. So generous. People would come and sit at his bar just because of who he was.

We all have our extracurricular activities. I like to fly animals [as a transport pilot]. Donnie likes to teach kids about business, about entrepreneurship. Paul likes to teach kids about cooking.

PAUL KAHAN: Donnie and I are like brothers. We're both very opinionated. Most of the time when we fight—which we don't really fight any more, well, a little bit—but most of the time, we realized we're fighting, and we both shared the same opinion. So it's been a journey of learning. I mean, we're both stubborn. But really, most importantly, I think Donnie is as responsible for the success of our company as anyone. He's got a very unique eye and incredible style, and is a really hardworking man. I'll just say that he's incredibly dedicated to hospitality. And he wants to make people happy, always has.

And I would also say he is the most loyal person that I've ever met. There's never been a single second where I didn't trust him or think that he had the best interest of me in his decision-making process. So that's a real rare group of qualities. We're both like very, super detail-oriented. A little crazy, a little obsessive-compulsive. And I think that's why we get along so well.

DONNIE MADIA: In today's game, young restaurateurs and young chefs, they're thinking about the first restaurant, but they're also thinking about the next one, and the next one after that. And with all due respect to everyone's capabilities in real estate, and how many restaurants they want to open, I think you lose focus on the main idea of opening one restaurant and digging in, and making it the best that can possibly be. That's all we wanted to do with Blackbird. We wanted to make a little living, but we wanted this sixty-five-seat restaurant to be the best sixty-five-seat restaurant. And that's in the business plan. It says that what we care about is having the best sixty-five-seat restaurant and being the best.

BOKA RESTAURANT GROUP

KEVIN BOEHM: I had restaurants in Florida and I sold them, then I opened a restaurant in my hometown, Springfield [Illinois], and I sold it. The goal was to get to Chicago, but I kept coming to Chicago and saying, I'm not ready yet. So I went to Nashville—and I got the shit kicked out of me. I was part of a very new development in Nashville at the time, I was the first person to open in the Gulch in Nashville, and I went in undercapitalized, and it was right around the time of September 11.

I had dropped out of college with five hundred bucks in my pocket, and saved up enough money to open my first restaurant, and was successful. But to go from those small restaurants to opening a ten-thousand-square-foot restaurant in Nashville, having to deal with big time developers and signing big contracts and stuff like that, I was out of my depth. I was still in my twenties at that point. And it became a very expensive lesson for me. I learned the hard way that you can lose it as fast as you make it.

I had opportunities to go back to Florida, and I could have gone back to Springfield, but my mom was like, you always wanted to go to Chicago. If there's anything I know about you, you can make things happen. Don't go backwards. You'll always regret it, at least go try.

ROB KATZ: I was an options trader. Somewhat numerically inclined. And I came here from Vancouver in 1987, bypassed the college thing and went to work for two market makers. So my boss put me in an apartment in Lincoln Park with two other traders. I didn't know either of them. One of them had made a ton of money by that point, but he was content living with two other guys, he didn't care. So he bought a bar, basically so he could meet girls. It was a rounding error for him to buy a bar. I'm twenty-one, it's the greatest thing in the world for me to have a roommate with a bar where I can drink for free.

Well, one day he came into my trading pit and he said, I just fired every single human being that worked for us. They're all dealing drugs and stealing my money. You have to bartend tonight. I said, Billy, I'll do it, but I don't know how bartending goes for shit. He says, you can open a Bud Light, you can do it. That night changed my life forever. I was hit with a thunderbolt of excitement by hospitality. I loved it, the attention, the action, the speed, everything I loved. So I said to Billy, I will watch this bar for you every Friday night and I will tend bar forever.

I brought in a ton of young guys from the Board of Trade, the CBOE, the Merc, and that bar flourished. Then he sold it, and they let everyone go but they wanted me to stay. They said, we've been watching you, you're not here to steal. You're here to have fun. So I ended up continuing to bartend and became a non-equity partner with those guys. And eventually in 1993 I opened my own place, Waterloo Tavern, which became Elbo Room. I had four bars—frankly, all wildly successful places. I worked with bands from Freddie Jones to Smashing Pumpkins to Dave Matthews.

But my girlfriend at the time, soon to be my wife, and I wanted children, and I wanted to pivot. I wanted to do a restaurant. So friends of mine knew

Kevin, and they said, these guys have to get together. So we met over a cup of coffee and cookies. That cup of coffee turned into a four-hour meeting. And by the end of it, we shook hands and said, well, what the fuck? Let's open a restaurant together.

KEVIN BOEHM: We had both had four places before each other. And he had done very well. And so he had investors that he'd worked with before, that were willing to put up the money for Boka. We opened on a shoestring budget. It was really sort of a gut job that we did for like, less than four hundred grand. Which is insane. Sometimes now you can't do a bathroom for that.

ROB KATZ: So Kevin is, you know, slightly my junior. At our age now, it doesn't matter, but at that point, four and a half years was a big deal. He was very single. He was a brilliant front of house operator, truly, to this day, one of the best front of house operators, I think, in America. It was time for me to be a dad, to be a businessman, to get behind the scenes, and do everything that I do—negotiate the lease, come up with concepts that we would end up doing together, pick designers, work with contractors, deal with the architect, deal with the city. Kevin could do that, too, but he just didn't have any experience in Chicago at all.

It took about a year to find the right spot. It was Don Juan, the former location of Blue Mesa on Halsted, which became Boka. Blue Mesa had a twenty-something year career, Don Juan, maybe five, but it has now been three restaurants for almost fifty years. That's uncommon.

KEVIN BOEHM: I was more like a fine dining guy. Rob was more like a bartender scene guy. And it took us like six months to find our footing. I would come by and I would turn the lights up and turn the music down. And then Rob would do the opposite. And we didn't even realize that it was a running joke between the bartenders. It took us like six months to find middle ground.

ROB KATZ: We would play this dance, lights up, lights down, music up, music down. Until we finally found the happy middle. Which happened last year—no, I'm kidding, it happened very quickly. And we've had what I would consider the second most successful relationship of my life. I've been with my wife for thirty-three years, and with Kevin for almost twenty-two now.

We hired Giuseppe Scurato, which at the time was a hell of a pull for us, coming out of [Michael Kornick's] mk.

KEVIN BOEHM: So we were like, let's find a great chef, who can do really great progressive food, but still be accessible enough that we get everybody. You look at what was going on in Chicago, the three-star restaurants then were the one sixtyblues and Blackbirds of the world. That was kind of generally what I was interested in. Okay, and my palate got broadened, because Rob's taste was a little louder, a little bigger.

If you look at Scurato's lineage, he was from Postrio [San Francisco] and Spago, and then mk. There was always, because he was the hardcore Italian guy, this undercurrent of Italian in his cooking. So if you look at that original menu, it's grouper with oxtail raviolini, it was scallops of cauliflower puree, he was an Italian chef marrying that with American contemporary food. And, you know, he didn't have tweezers out. He did bigger portions on big white Homer Laughlin plates, really beautiful flavor-forward food with relatively large portions.

There was no tasting menu, and it had a little bit of a vibe, a little bit of energy to it. Gordon Sinclair was one of those pioneers who said, I'm still going to do beautiful, chef-driven food, but it's not going to be a church service. It's going to be a fun night out. There was a place in New York called Mad61 that had this incredible wine list. But their big thing was a burger. And I was like, oh, it can be this kind of interesting juxtaposition. There's not just tablecloth restaurants and bars, you can do a little bit of both. When Rob and I got together, I think that we were the exact right two people to put those two kind of opposing forces together and make it work.

I think we and Scurato had different ideas about what we wanted to do. And I think he really wanted to have his own restaurant. And he didn't necessarily want to listen to us. We were thinking more like this for the menu and he'd say, no, I think it's going to be this way. And we needed somebody who really was interested in sitting around a table and collaborating and having spirited conversations to get to where we were going.

ROB KATZ: We had a chef and we were determined to be a great restaurant. But I think maybe he didn't trust us completely, because of past experiences with owners.

****

In 2007 Giuseppe Scurato left Boka. His replacement would be another Giuseppe—Tentori, a veteran of Charlie Trotter's. This was the beginning of Boka becoming a group whose concepts were built around star chefs.

ROB KATZ: Giuseppe was the chef de cuisine at Trotter's. Kevin and I had sort of come to the conclusion that we really needed to find a chef who could take us to the next level, we felt like we were outpacing the back of the house. We met with him at a Starbucks on Clybourn. He was skeptical, that's my recollection. He didn't know who either of us were. I think he was getting a lot of offers to branch out on his own. He was quite thorough in checking us out.

We set up a tasting at Landmark. The only people there were me, Kevin and Giuseppe. And each dish that he brought out just blew our minds. At that point we became a little more convincing, that this was going to be a great opportunity for him. That our goal truly was to make him a culinary name, not only in Chicago, but abroad. Our goal was to get him nominated for *Food & Wine*'s Best New Chef award. And it was pretty amazing that we actually got it done.

Back in those days you were basically praying that *Chicago* magazine, the *Tribune* and the *Sun-Times*, and the *Chicago Reader* would come out and review you. So we knew that a new chef of Giuseppe's caliber, and a facelift for the restaurant, would get all of those publications to come out. It did; they all gave us glowing reviews. So we hired PR to get our name out there [nationally]. The *New York Times* wrote about something, and we were in *USA Today*, and the *Boston Globe* if I'm not mistaken. And we won *Food & Wine* that year, 2008.

GIUSEPPE TENTORI: When it was time for me to leave [Trotter's], there were a few options. I chose Boka and even Charlie was like, who are those guys? It was not the most prestigious restaurant at the time. You go from a pristine, customized kitchen to . . . a shithole, pretty much. A hole in the wall, when it rained it was crazy. But Kevin and Rob taught me a lot from a business point of view. And I was on my own, no sous chef, no pastry chef.

I had never done sides before. So I needed to figure out side dishes, appetizers, what guests wanted to eat. The budget was really low, and also 2007, 2008 was not a great time for the economy. And with a lot of our diners coming for Steppenwolf [Theatre], we had to do things for people who were only going to be here for forty-five, fifty minutes and then go to the show. So salads, or dishes that were quick pick up.

KEVIN BOEHM: Tentori was, interestingly enough, a lot more malleable. His first menu comes out and he says, I think I'm going to have this forty-six-dollar turbot on the menu. And I'm like, you know, this isn't Trotter's. . . . And he's like, okay, well, I'll try the whitefish. So he was able to pivot. From a decade at Trotter's.

GIUSEPPE TENTORI: One day some delivery truck blocked the alley, and our neighbor was trying to get out and he's yelling at him. I go out and I start yelling at everybody, some unique words were said. Rob and Kevin came out and they need to talk to me. We go in the office and they say, Phil Vettel gave us three stars. Which, we were a small restaurant so everything helped, we were excited.

KEVIN BOEHM: By then we had two other restaurants, Perennial and Landmark, all in Lincoln Park. Boka needed to separate from the others. And so you saw Landmark becoming more of a bar, you saw Boka becoming more of a serious restaurant, getting a Michelin star, Giuseppe getting *Food & Wine* Best New Chef. And in really doing stuff that was pretty progressive, he did the tapioca with a stuffed squid, the tapioca with squid ink. Stark black and yellow. Stuff that looks really beautiful on a plate, so we upgraded our china game big time. That was Tentori saying, china is as important as the design of the restaurant, because this is what frames all our food.

The evolution of Boka was what I did not foresee. It became a more serious restaurant as the years went by. It just kind of kept getting upgraded. As we got to be a bigger company, it made more sense for Boka to become the most, in quotes, "serious" restaurant of the company. And I think people kind of dug the evolution—the people that lived in the neighborhood saw it in many different forms, and that kept it interesting for them. Both Giuseppe and Lee [Wolen, current chef] being the kind of people that wanted to change it all the time, you would show up and all of a sudden, there wouldn't be three tables in that middle row in the main dining room anymore. There'd be this beautiful marble service piece. They're the kind of people that push you as an owner-operator to do better, to be better.

And so I walk into it now, and it still has this great nostalgia for me, but when I look at the pictures of what it looked like, in 2003, it's nowhere near the same. Knowing that we've been able to evolve a restaurant over twenty years—of all the stuff that we've done as a company, I think that's probably the thing that I'm most proud of.

GIRL & THE GOAT

KEVIN BOEHM: Rob and I sat down and had a conversation in the Boka bar, where we talked about how it was hard to build a company around one chef. Because if you lose that chef or something happens, you're kind of effed, right? And not every chef was perfect for every spot. So by the time we got to Ryan [Poli at Perennial], and to Giuseppe and then when we started talking to Stephanie, we're like, maybe, maybe this is the angle. But with Stephanie it was an explosion.

STEPHANIE IZARD: I went to University of Michigan for business school, and I just wasn't loving it. And my dad said, well, you've always loved cooking. My mom was an amazing cook, she cooked from all over the world. And as I grew up, we would set up fake restaurants. I would cook with my mom all the time. All these kinds of signs that I was meant to be a chef, as a kid I used to garnish my snacks, things like that.

But when I graduated high school in '94, nobody really talked about being a chef the way they do now. And then when I was trying to pick my major, my dad suggested hey, why don't you go to culinary school? So I graduated Michigan, but then I went to culinary school right afterwards. And the first day I walked in, it was that feeling of, oh my gosh, it's my people.

She was working for a resort in Arizona when she came for a visit to Chicago. She worked at Lettuce's Vong's Thai Kitchen and then under Shawn McClain at Spring.

STEPHANIE IZARD: I went to Chicago to visit some friends and I never went back. I had my stuff shipped up here, because I just fell in love with Chicago.

I was on the opening team at Spring. I always tell cooks, if you get the opportunity to be part of the opening team in a restaurant, helping set up the kitchen and decide where things are gonna go, do it. Shawn was really great to learn from—a lot of Asian influence in his food, which I've always been very drawn to.

Next I worked at La Tache [French restaurant in Andersonville]. A tiny kitchen, I was a sous chef. I got to create specials and, you know, have some influence on the menu. And I was working one day, my chef had gone out of town, so I was running the kitchen. And one of the cooks said to me, hey, you're really good at this, you should just open your own restaurant. And so the next week, I quit my job and started to search for a space. And almost a year to the day that I quit my job, I opened Scylla, which was a little Mediterranean-inspired seafood restaurant in Bucktown.

I was only twenty-seven when we opened, which is just kind of crazy looking back. I had twenty people on my staff, which was mind-blowing to me, oh my gosh, I'm in charge of all these people. In this little sixty-seat, cool restaurant.

After running the place for a few years, running the kitchen, running myself a bit tired, we decided to sell the restaurant to Takashi Yagihashi. A week after I signed the paperwork with him, I get a call from *Top Chef* and they said, hey, do you want to come interview to be on *Top Chef?*

KEVIN BOEHM: I had gone to Scylla. We talked to her and said, hey, maybe this is something. We're like, hey, we should get together. And she's like, well, let me do the TV show, and then we'll get back together and talk again. And then she wins the whole freaking thing, right? So we meet at Perennial. And we just very quickly started looking at buildings.

And then it was like, okay, this is interesting. Because at the same time, we're like, let's become partners with chefs, so we don't lose them. Let's do a really great vetting process as best as we can. Let's get into business with people we want to get into business with. And see if that works.

STEPHANIE IZARD: *Top Chef* was awesome. It was a wonderful experience. They wanted to make sure you can cook but also that you're entertaining and crazy—but not *too* crazy, because you have knives! You're living in a house, I lived in a bedroom with eight women in bunk beds. I always tried to wake up as soon as I could hear someone approaching the house. They wanted to try to catch you waking up which I was like, no thanks.

And each day is like you have no idea what's going to happen. They don't tell you anything of what the next day's adventures will be, so it was just this mind game while pushing yourself through this crazy world of challenges. Everybody was very competitive. But we all got along and supported each other. I think I tend to just get along with people pretty easily.

Izard won season 4 of Top Chef *in 2008—the first woman to win and the first Chicago winner.*

STEPHANIE IZARD: My friends helped me put together a viewing party. My parents are watching it and of course it's edited to make it look like I'm not going to win, right before the last commercial break. My mom says, I'm sorry, do you want a drink? And then I win, and I'm like, Mom, do you think I would have had a party if I wasn't going to win?

Chicago has always been so supportive. I remember that night going into a bar after the party and I walked in and it was everyone cheering like I just won the Super Bowl or something. And then I woke up the next morning, and I had like five thousand people that want to be my friends on Facebook and I was like, what is happening? It wasn't like now, when people who go on may already have an agent. I didn't know what to do, so I just turned off my Facebook.

I went out to dinner with my friend Jessie Oloroso [Black Dog Gelato] at Boka and Rob and Kevin came over to our table. When I tell this story in person, I put a little swagger in my walk, because they have such swagger in life in general. They're like hey, do you want to come next door and have a drink with us? Okay. So we went and they proposed opening a restaurant together. But at the time I had already started working with a friend of mine who wanted to get into the restaurant business. He had not been in it before. So I said no to Kevin and Rob, but one morning I woke up and I was like, you know what? I want to learn from people who know more than I do. I don't want to be the one in the group that supposedly knows everything about running a restaurant.

They picked me up in one of their BMWs, I'm sitting in the back seat. They always finish each other's sentences—they're like this little married couple that's not married. They said, we never asked you what kind of restaurant you want to open. And I just said, The Drunken Goat [a Spanish cheese]. And Kevin just goes, fuck yeah!

ROB KATZ: Stephanie called us, I think. She said she'd gotten two hundred calls a day after *Top Chef*, and she wanted to do a restaurant with us. She liked how we were a chef-driven company. She was pretty adamant to stay away from certain neighborhoods, the preppy, yuppie kind of neighborhoods.

We looked on Milwaukee Avenue, but Logan Square wasn't quite ready yet. I started to focus my attention on the West Loop and the corridor on Randolph that years before had shown extraordinary success with Jerry Kleiner. When it was still a really downtrodden, kind of sketchy neighborhood. Those restaurants in the early '90s were doing really big numbers. But then nothing else ever really materialized, and those restaurants faded away.

Now [in 2008] it's a time when, you're down the street from the United Center, there was a resurgence with the Bulls with Derrick Rose, the Blackhawks were on the doorstep of a dynasty, and even though the recession was happening, all these condos were going up. Also, it was super easy to get to, from anywhere, with all the on-ramps to the expressway.

So I found a space for lease at twenty-two dollars a foot. It was an old import/export sort of storage facility.[26] There was no electricity, there was chicken wire at the back where the kitchen is now, that's sort of how some of the things were stored, there was no lighting, there was no air conditioning, and it was a completely beat-up building. But we loved the location and

26 The former Central Supply (see chapter 10).

decided to take a gamble, we told the owner we would only put that kind of money into it if we could buy the ground floor and the basement, like a condo. It was the recession, so I actually bought the property personally.

KEVIN BOEHM: What we saw in her was, Stephanie was the hardest-working person I've ever met in my life. She's like an eighteen-hour-a-day person. She wanted to be involved with everything. Her food did not taste like anyone else's. She was mixing proteins. And it was layered, but everything still had great balance to it. And every bite was interesting, super flavor-forward. Lots of texture, temperature contrasts. It was just fucking fun. And she wanted stuff to have a middle-class sensibility to it. She wanted it to be fun and a party. And we were just like, this is the perfect time. Because fine dining, on the other side of 2008, '09, we knew it was going to have a rough road. And she was super, obviously marketable. She was great on TV. She just won *Top Chef.* People really responded to her.

Eventually named Girl & the Goat (Izard is the French name for a type of wild mountain goat found in the Pyrenees), the restaurant took more than a year to build out. In the meantime she did pop-up dinners as the Wandering Goat. They sold out almost instantly, each time one was announced.

STEPHANIE IZARD: My partners expected me to want to do a more upscale restaurant, but that's never been my vibe. So the first Wandering Goat dinner, you were greeted by a mannequin with a goat skull, just to give people that the idea was funky and fun and not taking itself too seriously.

ROB KATZ: We tried to raise money, but because of the recession it was the first time we couldn't find investors. We overspent on opening it, we raised a million-two and we spent a million-four. But it was instantly successful, we paid it back in nine months.

The returns to investors were out of this world. At that point, we started getting more confident in our abilities. The way we'd raised money before was just passing the hat to friends and family, people we knew from my trading days. But we started to realize it was time to invest in ourselves, why are we giving away 20, 30, 40 percent annually. We can go to a bank and finance it ourselves.

KEVIN BOEHM: Obviously we had absolutely no clue that it was going to do what it did. I mean, we opened the books up the first day, and we were completely sold out for ninety days. We've never seen that.

STEPHANIE IZARD: It was just a whole 'nother world of trying to keep up with the prep and having to have much more dialed-in recipes because we had so many more people on the team. Just everything about it was such a huge learning curve for us.

The pig face has been on the menu since day two. Because day one, friends and family, we had the same thing with the pig face where we take all the meat off [the skull]. And we fill it with a bunch of spices and stuff and roll it up and freeze it, but we breaded it and had like a green herb-y sauce. And my aunt Marian came in and she was like, you know, I just didn't like that, it was kind of dry. And so that night after a little freakout, like *oh my gosh, we're opening tomorrow,* I took some and I came up with the dish that we've had on the menu for the last fourteen years, which is the seared pig face with three different sauces, on top of the potato sticks. And it's definitely become one of the dishes we're known for.

I've always believed in trying to get your whole mouth happy. A little bit of heat, I feel like having something either sweet and acidic. So we use a lot of pickled red onions, pickled mango, pickled blueberries. We do a lot of things pickled to add sort of sweet and acidic elements at the same time. If you go in our kitchen there's a whole section of containers of crunchy things. I get really excited when we think of a new crunchy thing.

ROB KATZ: With Girl & the Goat's success, developers started to do cool shit in the West Loop, bringing the right clientele here. The restaurants refreshed. Google wasn't here yet, none of the hotels were here. But people came in droves and developers were incredibly smart to jump on it. We did buy three great properties here. And then some great leases with great developers on the ones that we couldn't afford anymore. Because pretty soon we all got priced out of it. It's gonna happen again, when these leases turn over, and leases that were signed for twenty-five, thirty, forty, fifty dollars a foot will be well over a hundred dollars a foot and those people will not be able to re-sign them.

I'll say it again. Great neighborhoods are built on the backs of great restaurants. And Girl & the Goat definitely at least started lighting that fuse. The fuse was lit with that absolute phenomenon.

BEYOND THE WEST LOOP OF THE GOATS

As the West Loop became hot again, Boka Group expanded with new restaurants. For Izard it was a more casual diner, Little Goat Diner, and then a Chinese restaurant, Duck Duck Goat. Izard's account of how both came to be captures the manic frenzy of West Loop development—and her own indefatigability.

STEPHANIE IZARD: Back when we first opened Girl & the Goat, I used to make three goat specials a day, which was insane. My assistant was like, why don't you try making three specials and leaving them on for a month? And I was like, this is genius!

But I was always at my table, prepping. And we had bakers down there baking all our fresh bread in the same kitchen. And we had our butchers, and there'd be like twenty-five people in the basement. It was so crowded. And so we were joking one day, and I was like, we should just get these bakers out of here, we should just find another space in the neighborhood, we can have it be this cute little breakfast place called Little Goat and we can have the bakery there. Eventually, we started looking into that space. And of course, little was not little whatsoever. We ended up finding a giant space. And so Rob and Kevin and I kind of were trying to figure out, yeah, let's put the bakery there. But then what can we do on the main part of it? So first we're gonna go down the path of doing like a meat and three [cafeteria] and we went on a couple of trips to a couple of southern towns and then we were like, wait a minute, I don't know if this idea is widespread enough.

And I was like, well, I grew up on the East Coast and diners were such a thing. We went to New York and went to a few diners, and when Little Goat opened we had ninety-five menu items, and there was like not a single sauce repeated on the whole menu. So my prep team *loved* it. It was insane. I don't know what I was thinking. We had an upstairs private dining room and we did catering, and then we thought how about on Sundays we do these Sunday suppers, to give me another menu to play around with, and we'd pick a different country each time. And the first one we did I was like, why don't we just do Chinese food—I grew up on the East Coast eating Chinese takeout all the time.

So I got to work that Sunday morning and I was like, I think I'll try to make some dumpling wrappers. So I threw together a menu, made this whole dinner. We're like maybe we should open a Chinese restaurant. So I told Kevin and Rob I kind of want to open a Chinese inspired-restaurant and I didn't know what they were gonna say, but they're like heck yeah, they got so excited. So I decided, instead of just being inspired by childhood memories, I should go to China. So we went to China for a couple of weeks and then we went to Taiwan for a couple of weeks. We make our own spring roll wrappers, we make every noodle and I taught myself how to do all that.

And I was eight months pregnant, too.

****

Meanwhile Boehm and Katz found another white whale to pursue in the West Loop: a Chicago steak house, Swift & Sons.

KEVIN BOEHM: If you played baseball long enough, you would want to play for either the Cubs, the Red Sox, or the Yankees, right? There's so much tradition there. I thought about, and I know Rob did too, what our steak house would be like, from the moment I opened up my first restaurant. There are so many comparables, from, what are your core competencies that are on your menu? What do you have to have that makes you a steak house? What do your steak knives look like? What's your bread service? And it was just fun to think about.

I loved putting Swift & Sons together. I think that the first meeting that we had was, let's decide what you have to have on the menu to be a steak house. And then we said, what can we do to bend it? So the bends were cart service for cocktails, chocolate trolley for desserts, beef Wellington cart. It's a wide enough dining room, there's enough space between the tables that we can do cart service. And then, let's do hospitality. Let's have an actual concierge in the restaurant. Let's do really cool fun stuff. And then let's have a fricking magician working the floor. You can go to the table and do fun stuff. And hearken to a different age, like the 1920s. But the food is not old school. On the wine list, let's have a vintage for everybody on their birthday year. We just sat around a room and tried to think of cool shit to do.

Steak houses appeal to a certain type of business traveler. The guys visiting from State Farm corporate. There's one night that they're going to go out, and they're going to go to a steak house. Now you hit a home run when the locals embrace you at the same time as *their* steak house. It's more about familiarity than fine dining. It's about Tom who waits on me because Tom has been there for twenty-two years. That's one of the things Gibsons is so great at. They're super consistent. I'm a big Lombardo family fan. They're successful for a reason.

To run the kitchen at Swift & Sons, they brought in a partner who we've met before: Chris Pandel, last seen at Rick Tramonto's hotel restaurants.

KEVIN BOEHM: I fucking love Chris Pandel. I love Chris Pandel the human, I love Chris Pandel the chef. He's just a great guy. He's so well respected by all our other chef partners. Pandel's a great systems guy, he can cook a lot of different stuff. He's an intellectual. Chris is one of my all-time favorite people to do a restaurant project with because his temperament is so spectacular. No matter what's going on, I never see him lose his shit. He always has people who want to work with him. And they all stay a long time. He would have been a great army general.

ROB KATZ: If you do not like Chris Pandel, it's you, I can assure you.

To tell a story: when we opened Landmark in 2005, it was a smash hit. We wanted it to be a very busy bar with a very busy pre-theater scene, because Steppenwolf Theatre was across the street. We had lines down the block. And I remember one time in like, February, quite literally it was one degree above zero. And the line had a hundred people in it.

And I grabbed Kevin and I said, Kevin, we are fucked. It's over. This place is done. He says, what are you talking about? There's a line down the fucking block! I go, the crowd that we have built our business around soon enough will be gone to the next hot spot that opens. We let it get too far to one side. We became too clubby and it's pissing the restaurant people off, we could already see our restaurant numbers dropping as our bar business kept growing. So even though we're still really busy, we better start thinking what is going to be the next thing because trust me, in a year this is over.

So The Bristol was a hot restaurant, run by two very smart young guys, John Ross and Phil Walters, and they had a great chef who was beloved, Chris Pandel. They approached us and said, we want to do something with you guys. We thought, why don't we change Landmark into a great Italian restaurant, which became Balena. We're gonna give each of you guys some equity, John, Phil and Chris. Balena was a very big success with Chris in the kitchen. Until it had a fire, and never reopened.

CHRIS PANDEL: I'm not Italian and didn't study in Italy. I'm Midwestern Italian. That's a giant question mark at the end of it, but yeah.

So you could take some liberties now and again. We were doing pizza and leaning on almost like New York style, but not New York style. Big pizzas with a fluffy crust that cooks quickly. But not Neapolitan. And honestly, it's the food that I wanted to eat. Like, pizza and pasta and simple grilled meats.

Rob and Kevin had figured out a space in the Google building, or what was going to become the Google building. And they knew they wanted to put a steak house there. And they knew that I had previously run a steak house. So they tapped me—there wasn't a ton of discussion about it. It was like, you in? Of course. Not that I was dying to open a steak house, but it was an opportunity. And I enjoyed working with them, I enjoyed their environments, and it seemed appropriate.

I think that I came to terms with the fact that 90 percent of the guests who walk into that restaurant know what they want before they even walk in. And to provide that level of comfort for people is worth its weight in gold. If I get, you know, 20 percent of the menu to mess around with and be seasonal, and creative and fun, I'm okay with that. I have other outlets, I can do other stuff. I'm here to provide for our guests, period. There's still pasta on the menu, there's the seasonal salads, the sides, there's all the vegetable matter—

all that exists in the conversation. In the summertime the lobster bisque is not rich, creamy soup when it's ninety degrees out, it's a chilled Thai-style lobster soup. It's light and refreshing.

But, you know, we're not taking steaks off the menu. I'm not an artist, I enjoy the craft of cooking. And I do like to cook to make beautiful food and present it as elegantly as I can. But I'm definitely not Curtis Duffy. I'm okay with my, like I said, 20 percent corner of the menu that gets to be interesting and different and fun and allows us to sneak past other steak houses that don't have that opportunity.

****

If you're getting dizzy keeping track of all of Boka's projects by this point . . . well, so were they.

KEVIN BOEHM: I barely remember those years [after opening Girl & the Goat]. We opened eight restaurants in three years. There were four people in our corporate office, doing everything.

It was the hardest time of my life. It was a fucking disaster. There was just momentum and things kept happening and opportunities would happen. Then the chefs want to do other restaurants, Stephanie wants to do a second restaurant, and how can you say no after Girl & the Goat was such a huge success? It was getting to be a twenty-four-hour a day job. There was a moment where Rob put his hands on my shoulders, and I said, what are we doing to ourselves? We had to start looking at it and saying, we need accountants, we need a director of operations for every couple of restaurants.

ROB KATZ: It was 2011. We were sitting in what was going to become Balena. There was a beer cooler, just sitting on the floor. But I knew it didn't belong in Balena, because every cooler was already in its place. I just kind of snapped. What the fuck is this cooler doing in here? Where does it go?

And Kevin just looks at me. At the same time we were doing Little Goat Diner, Momotaro—we had like four places in production at once. And that was this realization of, what the fuck are we doing? Our whole entire infrastructure was Kevin and me, and a very young Ian Goldberg who had just been named director of operations over three or four restaurants. But we were exploding, and we were just trying to do it on our own. And it was basically driving us to a nervous breakdown. I mean, we're young, and we're miserable. We decided we had to step back, slow down, and build a proper infrastructure, basically putting a C-suite together. And then we were ready for phase two of our career.

KEVIN BOEHM: I give Ian [COO] and Abby [Kritzler, chief culture officer] a lot of credit for basically taking all the stuff from our brand and then downloading it into something that was repeatable. So every time we opened up a restaurant, different restaurants didn't have different systems. We have a critical path that we do to open up a restaurant, like, here's the 855 things you need to do to open a restaurant. But we weren't interested in taking everything that we had done for twenty years, and just doing a photocopy of it. And so it was a lot of years of like, changing it again. And now, the worry is, are you middle management? You have all these people working in all these places, and you might not know every single procedure that's going on in every single restaurant.

When you're an ambitious person, you try to build a current for yourself. You're pushing the current, but at a certain point the current will take you. If I could go back in time, which, you know, hindsight is always 20/20, I probably would have gone a little slower.

Boka Group would open more restaurants in the West Loop and elsewhere in Chicago, and has continued to expand—at this writing, with a Girl & the Goat in Los Angeles, Laser Wolf in Brooklyn, and projects in Nashville and other markets.

ROB KATZ: We're doing it because they're friendlier to hospitality. I think our company is going to be much bigger outside of Chicago than it is in Chicago. Chicago now is one of the most competitive dining cities in North America.

In the old days, when we started, we were bringing a level of design to restaurants that people had not really seen yet. And now, there just seems to be so many beautiful restaurants in this town, that are run really well and that are really popular. What does that mean to all the other competition? Does a restaurant have to fail for another restaurant to be successful? We want to be careful not to cannibalize ourselves.

But we are still going to headquarter in Chicago. We are Chicago guys. And it's always going to be a Chicago company.

13: EXILE IN GRUBVILLE

Chicago's hot food scene made international news on April 26, 2006—but not in a way that pleased Mayor Daley. On that day, the Chicago City Council passed an ordinance outlawing the serving of foie gras in the city. Though Charlie Trotter, for one, had made noise about no longer serving it (or serving Rick Tramonto's liver in its place), it was common on menus throughout the posher end of the dining world (probably one of the reasons Trotter no longer cared about serving it). Mayor Daley strongly opposed the ban, calling it "the silliest law that they've ever passed," while the best-known food figure of the day, Anthony Bourdain, said it made Chicago look like "some stupid cow town." Several restaurants openly defied the ban, and one chef, French-born Didier Durand, found a way around it at his restaurant, Cyrano's Bistrot: he sold diners a plated dish, and gave away the foie gras that went with it.

The ban lasted just two years before being repealed in May 2008. In those two years only one restaurant wound up getting ticketed and paying the $250 fine: not a French restaurant or a fancy steak house, but a quirky hot dog stand, Hot Doug's.

In the end Chicago's foie gras ban was just a blip in the news, but the fact of who was ticketed for serving it would prove symbolic of how the food scene was changing in the early 2000s. If the 1980s and 1990s had seen plenty of glitzy upscale restaurants, the 2000s saw the wall between high and low break down.

Blackbird serving pork belly and playing rock and roll, high-end chefs slinging food out of food trucks or at Lollapalooza, casual restaurants creating new food neighborhoods like Wicker Park and Logan Square—here's the new world in which high and low met. And in one case, got busted together.

STAR TOP CAFE

Little-remembered today, this restaurant on Lincoln Avenue in Lakeview, which opened in 1983, now looks prophetic of Chicago dining's future, with its funky thrift store decor, loud rock music and irreverent attitude—owner Bill Ammons was fond of saying that he and his longest-running chef-partner, Michael Short, "aren't alcoholics—we're alcoholists."

BILL AMMONS: My first couple of college degrees were Masters of Fine Arts. So I was working in restaurants, I liked cooking and waiting tables. [Michael Foley's] Printer's Row was pretty close to the first job I had here. And through people I knew there, and the other little job I had, we solicited for investors. And after my first chef and I got to a point where we couldn't stand each other, I had the luck to run into Michael Short, who was working in a restaurant that was cheffed by Jean-Claude Poilevey, who later had Le Bouchon.

Michael was a phenomenon, he was a hard-drinking bon vivant. He was a South Side, Beverly guy who worked in places where he didn't get paid very well, he'd work in Thai restaurants, just to learn what they did. He'd been all over. He had a lot of his own ideas and was super creative and, you know, kind of a force, in a culinary sense. He came in and revitalized the place completely. We got a *Tribune* review, and we were busy from then on.

People that liked the place really liked the place. People who came in and didn't get it, you know, they didn't like it—there was a little bit of edge. We played music loud. People would ask us to turn it down, we'd say no. I don't quite remember who it was but somebody from WTTW came in who was a prominent broadcaster at that point. And he just basically came in, and his eyes turned into saucers, and he walked right out. I mean, we liked having fun. We drank a lot. And we made sure that other people drank a lot, too.

The food was good. I'm not saying that *I* say the food was good. I mean, it was fantastic. Michael was really talented and cared a lot about it. There was definitely that Michael Foley influence from Printer's Row, and it worked pretty well with the character of the place. Because after all, it was just a crummy little storefront with thrift store furnishings. It wasn't so much intentional, but it had an inherent vibe.

It was a post-punk era, people were moving back into the city, things were happening. We had a pretty lively art crowd, we had a strong connection with the music industry. Michael happened to be really, really good friends with Joe Shanahan [music promoter]. So we got music people in all the time and that generated a little bit of a vibe itself. We were really, really good friends with Paul Barker of Ministry, because we all rode Italian motorcycles. A lot of the people who worked for us were involved with those kinds of bands, you know, Revolting Cocks and Pigface and so on. It wasn't exactly a hangout for those guys, but we knew them pretty well. All the people from Wax Trax! [record store and label], and then, at some point, the XRT [rock radio station] people found us too, and were coming in all the time.

We had all the members of the Grateful Dead in once, and they made me promise not to tell anyone. But five minutes before they left, I told my wife they were here, because she was a Deadhead and if I hadn't, it would have been the end of my relationship. I remember Al Jourgensen [of Ministry] brought Eddie Vedder [Pearl Jam] in and I was talking to Al and ignoring Vedder, because I didn't know who he was.

ELLEN FAIREY (server): I was in art school and I did not have a ton of restaurant experience. But I went in and started talking to Michael Short and we just hit it off. I think I worked there for eight or nine years, wow. When I started it was just me, Michael, Bill and some busboys. I would write the menus every night—Michael would dictate it to me. So it was a new menu every night. I would take it to the Kinko's next to Wax Trax! So analog.

I really think Michael was a visionary. Like, his food, I now understand that he was so ahead of his time. And you know, he never studied cooking. I know he lived in New York for a while in the early '80s. And he would go into mom-and-pop ethnic restaurants and offered to work for free for a couple weeks just to learn about their cuisine. He also read voraciously. Like he had *Larousse Gastronomique* sitting around the house, so he had this really amazing mix of cutting-edge ethnic stuff that no one had heard of, at that time. And then hardcore classic French, and California stuff like Alice Waters. When Anthony Bourdain came around, and I started reading him, I'm like, oh, my God, that's Michael, he was so of the same ilk.

Shrimp and sweetbreads with Chinese mustard and fresh rosemary was an appetizer. That was like 1988. Soft shell crab BLT with chipotle mayo. No one had heard of the word chipotle. He would do fun things, like there would be an entree, Surf Surf and Surf, which was whatever three seafood things he did. I remember one time he said okay, we're gonna put a new dish on called Bivalve Jamboree, which was clams, mussels and some third thing.

Bill was an artist, you know, he was a painter. He had an MFA in painting. But he also made these elegant, gorgeous desserts. Like charlottes and trifles, where Michael was making these wild entrees and appetizers. They were just so unique. I never have known anyone like them, before or since. It was kind of European in that way where there was such a mix of clientele, so you'd have an older couple from Lincoln Park, and they're sitting next to Bryan Ferry or the Red Hot Chili Peppers.

I realized, working there, that I learned so much about food but also so much about music. Because we had like an old-school stereo up front with albums and customers could go up and put on whatever they wanted. So many bands would come in. I mean, Joe Shanahan from Metro or the guys from Jam Productions would bring their bands that were playing into our restaurant, because they would be comfortable there. The whole thing was fine dining without the fine dining atmosphere. I have to write about it someday, because it was just such a special, wild place.

BILL AMMONS: After seven or eight years, Michael started seeming a little restless. He left town to go sailing with his father for a little while. We kept the restaurant going until a couple of years after that, using his recipes. Then Michael passed away. But at the same time, I was going to engineering school. And I got my degree, which coincided pretty closely with when the landlord who had bought the building decided to triple the rent. And it just made sense to close [in 1996]. There were a couple of other restaurants that came after it that you could kind of tell had looked over our shoulder. One of them

[Soul Kitchen in Wicker Park] co-opted one of the slogans that we had—Spicy Music, Loud Food.

WICKER PARK

In the early twentieth century, Wicker Park, on the near Northwest Side, was the upscale Polish neighborhood, culturally best known as home to the writer Nelson Algren (who set his novel The Man with the Golden Arm *there). By the 1980s it was all rough edges, known for blue collar diners like the Busy Bee, or the blue collar-crossed-with-hipster Leo's Lunchroom. The new chronicler of its culture was the musician Liz Phair, who immortalized the modern relationship scene in Wicker Park in her 1993 album,* Exile in Guyville.

Terry Alexander, who would eventually become a partner in One Off Hospitality, helped launch many of the new wave of bars and restaurants in the neighborhood, including the hottest Italian chain of 1990s Chicago, Francesca's.

TERRY ALEXANDER: I'm from Omaha, Nebraska, came here to go to graduate school at Northwestern and got a journalism degree. I wanted to be a copywriter, but the advertising industry was not doing so well when I graduated. So I had bar and restaurant jobs. It wasn't my life's dream to work in a restaurant or bar, it just kind of happened. I was working at Berlin [nightclub] four nights a week, Elbo Room when it was a rock club Friday and Saturday, and I worked day shift in a collegiate bar over by DePaul. I was saving money for my big plan, which was to open a coffee shop in Omaha.

One of my friends, Michael Noone, was friends with a man who had opened Danny's Tavern, in about '83 or '84. And he wanted out of the bar business. I was a little hesitant because, you know, opening a bar with all that free liquor right there kind of worried me. My mom and dad were like, we don't know if that's the best thing for you when you're twenty-six years old. But that was my first business in the neighborhood.

Wicker Park to me seemed like the coolest thing in the world. It was desolate, a little bit dangerous. There were not a lot of people. You never saw female joggers, you didn't see anything—except burned-out cars. The Puerto Rican gangs were in one half, and the Mexican gangs were in the other half. There'd be little bodegas, we ate Mexican food probably six days a week. Back then it was cheap. It was everywhere. And it stayed open late, and they didn't care. They would give you a beer at five in the morning. They would put it in a red plastic glass, stick a straw in it. I thought that was the greatest thing.

I went to Danny's a lot before we bought it, when it was kind of a rockabilly club with the jukebox in the main room. So I knew it had something special, just being in a house in the middle of a street. I thought that was super cool.

CAROL WATSON (one of Alexander's roommates): I actually worked at Danny's on the Saturday night shift. Terry and Michael kind of ran into it a little bit with the old crowd at Danny's, because it had been kind of an old man dive bar. They got some flack from people who didn't like the fact that it was changing.

TERRY ALEXANDER: Michael and I physically lived at Danny's, because we spent every penny we had on the bar. Even when I got another apartment with some friends, we still slept there probably six nights, just because you had to get up. You had to mop the floors, every day you stocked the cooler. You had time to take a shower and then you were behind the bar, because you worked every day. And that was your social life. And then when you close the bar, you would go to a four o'clock bar, and then do it all again the next day. We were saving money, Michael and I, because we thought we were going to do a little live music club. But one of my roommates, Carol Watson, I went to undergrad with her in Lincoln, Nebraska, was working with a chef named Scott Harris, and she said, you know, Scott is looking to do something. And so that's how Scott, Carol, Michael and I started Mia Francesca in, like, '92.

CAROL WATSON: I was working at a trattoria called L'Angolo di Roma [in Lincoln Park], and Scott Harris was the chef there. I knew he wanted to do his own restaurant, and Terry and Michael had had Danny's for about a year, and they were looking to do something else. So I kind of introduced them to Scott, and we literally drove around the first day they met, and that's how they found the location on Clark.

TERRY ALEXANDER: Scott's food was great. It was incredibly inexpensive. Back then there were a lot of Italian restaurants, and they were all really pricey.

So we just said, we're going to undercut the shit out of everybody. We're going to go low. I think the wine list topped off at sixty dollars.

We thought we knew how to run a business. But we were young, we really didn't know. The perfect example is, every Sunday we would have a line waiting outside to get in at five o'clock. Nowadays, any intelligent person would go, if there's a line, let's open it at three or let's open for brunch. But of course, we weren't smart enough, we weren't seasoned entrepreneurs.

BILL AMMONS: I was always amazed at how phenomenally successful they were. I mean, sure, it's a good place. But to have people waiting for you to open the door every day of the week, for *years.*

CAROL WATSON: You walked in and you felt like you were in an Italian restaurant, and I think the vibe was a lot of energy. The opening staff was crazy good. Sometimes when you work in restaurants, you get a staff that really clicks and it's a ton of fun and you want to come in and work. I think everybody has fond memories of that opening staff, how crazy it was in a good way, and I think they just kind of instantly built up a following.

TERRY ALEXANDER: Scott was from the suburbs, and he thought it would be a good idea to go, not into a different neighborhood in Chicago, but into the suburbs. So we would get in cars and drive around and just look during the day. Really kind of clueless again. One day we stopped and got a cup of coffee in Naperville. And we're sitting there, in kind of a Mexican restaurant, and we saw the old City Hall for sale. And that became La Sorella di Francesca, our second project. Carol was going to become a partner, and so she moved out there. I had a little scooter, a Lambretta. I would ride it to the train station and take the train out there. Everybody was basically working nonstop.

CAROL WATSON: I was out in Naperville, as a partner, for seven years. I had always just done the front of the house, and you know, wasn't feeling particularly challenged. So I sold out my shares and then I went to San Francisco and went to a culinary program there for like eight months.

I came back and wasn't sure what I was going to do.

A friend of mine, Heidi, got married and her father-in-law had a development company. They were developing buildings in Wicker Park way back, too. They had just bought this building on Division Street and I wasn't sure what I was gonna do, and my friend is like, do you want to open up a café? And I'm like, sure. So that became Milk & Honey Cafe, which is still there.

There would eventually be Francesca's Forno in Wicker Park, but before that, the space—right at Damen, North and Milwaukee—was a hip little café called Soul Kitchen, which Alexander took over from its original owners and moved from Ukrainian Village.

TERRY ALEXANDER: Our chef was Monique King, she was doing this funky fusion of soul food and Caribbean and all kinds of really eclectic things. We had a very eclectic staff. The music was loud, it was great. It was such a great vibe in there. In '95, there wasn't much in Wicker Park or Bucktown, I think the Poileveys' Le Bouchon had just opened, and Debbie Sharpe [cook for touring rock bands] had Confusion.

CAROL WATSON: Everybody loved Soul Kitchen. I think it was just one of those combinations of the right concept at the right time. The right vibe. The music was great. Monique, who was the chef, was amazing. I didn't work there that long. But I always went there.

LYNN BUZZA (pastry chef): Monique King and Michael Clark were co-chefs at the time that I was hired. A lot of talent there. And a lot of drama there, but good, good food. They gave me complete freedom—I would do periodic tastings for the owners and the chefs, but basically it was like, all right, you got this, keep it fresh and keep it changing. People bought dessert there—I really moved some dessert.

It was just a place that was getting a lot of attention—Monique was getting a lot of attention as a female chef, and she was very good at self-promotion and kind of working her audience. So we did a lot of fun events, used to love doing the Bread and Roses event for a women's shelter and we did a lot of charity stuff.

ELLEN FAIREY: After Star Top I was like, oh God, where else can I work? So I went to Soul Kitchen and it was kind of the denouement of my restaurant career—like, okay, I get it, I can't do this anymore. But it was lovely, it was like a more refined version of Star Top. Soul Kitchen was more professional, like a real restaurant with lots of people involved. Monique King and Katherine August both had done little stints cooking at Star Top. Working for Michael wasn't easy, but they picked up some stuff, some flavors, that turned up on the menu.

TERRY ALEXANDER: Scott was doing more Mia Francescas in the suburbs, which were super successful. I didn't know if that was what I wanted to do. It was great to learn the business end, but for me it was more interesting to do different venues or different ideas. We opened Okno down Milwaukee Avenue, and that was our big mistake—because Milwaukee kind of stops, and there's this zone where nothing really happens.

We were going to New York a lot then, and DJ culture was starting to really grow. So my fiancée, then wife, Kristin, was booking DJs. The funniest thing, and I think one of our proudest moments, was when Phil Vettel reviewed it. And at the time he was reviewing noise in restaurants. And his list was a plane leaving O'Hare, a speaker at a Who concert, and Okno was number three. We wore that like a badge of honor.

****

Alexander acquired another property, just down Damen Avenue, which would be two restaurants in succession designed by Suhail, the hot restaurant designer of the '90s—MOD, which was straight out of Austin Powers, and Del Toro, covered floor to ceiling with Spanish tile mosaics. It would become the defining nightspot of modern Wicker Park, the Violet Hour.

TERRY ALEXANDER: We had another partner who had some problems, and the hole he dug us was really hard to get out of. At the time, one of the waiters at Soul Kitchen was a guy named Toby Maloney. He moved up to New York—I was not close friends with him, but whenever I would go to New York, I would somehow run into him. Eventually I would give him a call and say, I'm coming, where should I go? He always knew what places to check out.

Toby was one of the first people to work at Milk & Honey in New York.[27] They chipped their own ice, they squeezed their own juice, a cocktail took them five or six minutes. There was no standing room. It was such a cool place. Unmarked, you had to know where it was.

TOBY MALONEY: I grew up in Colorado, on top of a mountain with no running water or electricity. I started washing dishes and bussing tables really early in my life, because that was the only way to make money other than hauling firewood.

I decided to go to culinary school in San Francisco, spent a couple of years poking around there and cooking, and then went on a trip around the world to cook and eat and drink. I showed up in Chicago—my girlfriend that I was traveling with, her parents lived in Aurora—and I think I had $60 in my pocket. We found an apartment between Division and Thomas on Wolcott. A three-bedroom was $465 a month. And I got a job cooking at Blue Mesa, where Boka is now.

I don't know how I met Monique King, but I got on at Soul Kitchen as an oyster shucker, which I'd never done. And will never do again, ever, for any fucking reason. Oh my God, I mean, I've worked in clubs, done everything, I have cleaned up puke, but I would rather do that than fucking shuck oysters. You're constantly cold, because you're dealing with ice, and you just barely cut yourself and you're instantly infected, because oysters are just little suitcases of bacteria. But it got me in the door, and pretty soon I was waiting tables and bartending at Soul Kitchen.

I met a girl at Soul Kitchen and wound up following her to New York. I was the first bartender hired at Milk & Honey. I first walked in and said, make me whatever you want to Sasha [Petraske, owner]—I didn't know who he was. He made me a daiquiri, and the angels sang and a shaft of light shone down on Eldridge Street. Like, holy shit, there is so much I don't know.

I started going in there on my days off and chatting with Sasha—there was no one in there because he changed the number, like, weekly. He didn't want just anybody in there. So we would just experiment with stuff, taking the temperature of martinis and all that geeky stuff. Finally I said to him, you've

27 No relation to Carol Watson's Chicago breakfast spot.

been working six days a week, why don't you go do some laundry, have a date, whatever, and I'll take Wednesdays for a month. And that way you can have a little break. And I worked there five and a half years.

I worked at Pegu Club, I worked at Flatiron. Terry would come to New York every year, and he started to show up at the bars I was working at. We had the same taste in terms of what was cool and interesting.

TERRY ALEXANDER: We met up at an Italian restaurant in Chinatown. Toby and his partner, Jason Cott, wanted to open their own bar in New York. I said, let's do it in Chicago. There's no competition, you guys would be the only ones doing it. We've got a great space. And so I talked them into it. At that time, I was working with Donnie Madia over at a club called Sonotheque. And so we all hooked up for the Violet Hour.

TOBY MALONEY: I was still dressing in a three-piece suit. With a double-breasted chalk overcoat. I carried my shakers in a violin case. I was so fucking pretentious.

TERRY ALEXANDER: I think it was the start of cocktails in Chicago. I mean, no one was doing what Toby was doing. It was all who could make the biggest Belvedere or Grey Goose martini. Blue cheese stuffed olives. There was cranberry and Ketel. I swear to God, any place you went in had the same exact back bar.

Toby took that and threw it out the window. We debated having no vodka, finally settled on one vodka. All small producers—nobody had ever heard of any of the rums we had. The Violet Hour did not start out busy—it was slow. But every person in there was from the restaurant or bar industry. Because they knew we were doing something different. And they wanted to check it out.

TOBY MALONEY: Nobody has palates like sommeliers and chefs, and also they drink like goddamned fish. We immediately got every bartender, server, cook in there, and they were all like, fuck yeah.

I knew it was going to be a fight [with customers]. I opened up with no cranberry juice and no olives, in 2007. The first five minutes of the interaction was just the staff saying no, we don't have that, no, we don't have that. But I knew that Terry and Peter [Garfield, partner] and Donnie would have my back. We had little five-and-a-half-ounce coupes, here in the land of sixteen-ounce baby bassinets down at Morton's for your martinis. It was so different from everything else, we had people lose their goddamn minds. The confirmed Jack and Coke drinkers, the Bud Light drinkers, they fucking hated us with the passion of a thousand suns.

I think we had one vodka drink on the menu. Six gin drinks like we do. We took a fucking stand. And the other cool thing was that of our opening staff, nobody had ever made a drink. Not one single person that we hired had ever worked behind a bar. We hired baristas and waiters and cooks. Because there was no such thing as a cocktail bartender in Chicago in 2007. Which was great, because I didn't have to untrain them.

The other great thing about having the service industry on your side is they are in contact with all the cool foodies. So they only tell the cool people, they don't tell the assholes because they don't want to bump into table 13 who were a bunch of fucking assholes.

TERRY ALEXANDER: We got so many [customers] who were mad at us because they couldn't stand, they couldn't just walk around and talk to people. It scared the shit out of us, but we hung in there. When we do stuff, I mean, we put all the money up ourselves. So it's like, do or die with us.

I think it was important for us to be slow for those first six months, just for us to figure out how to do all the stuff we were doing. I mean, the bars in New York that started the cocktail revolution had forty seats, and we were ninety-nine seats, we had four bartenders plus barbacks, but it was a completely new way of running a bar. And it was funny. The resumes we looked at, no one had made a cocktail. And now when I look at resumes, every person that applied for a bar job will tell you how many cocktail bars they've worked at, and it really all started from Toby and the Violet Hour.

TOBY MALONEY: On LTHForum [food chat site], some restaurateur, I don't know who it was, did this post and he was like, "So you love going to the Violet Hour, but it's so expensive. I sent one of my bartenders in there, to reverse engineer all of these drinks, so you can make them at home for a quarter of the price." Now, we gave the recipes out to anyone who asked for them, but he reverse engineered them and just fucked every one of them up. And so I got on and was like, thanks for your interest. I'm going to give anyone who reads this the actual recipes I give to our bartenders. This went on for like a year and a half, kind of open-source cocktails. But there was so much interest. The other part was, people would come in and ask if they could get married there. They're like, we've already done the proposal here. . . . People had such a strong attachment. The people who loved it, loved it—and the people who hated it, hated it.

I think one of the reasons why we've endured is because we don't chase trends. Yeah, if something intrigues us, we'll fuck around with it. We had a couple of seasons where we had carrot juice on the menu. It was interesting, and I'm glad we did it, but we were like, well, that's really not for us. And we moved on. We never tried to embrace the molecular or decide that the world is changing and we're going to make the Violet Hour more casual. We stuck to our guns. And we lucked out, and we got a lot of things right, I guess.

The Violet Hour never had a sign, or even an obvious door, but visitors soon learned to look for the succession of murals painted over the building's front.

TERRY ALEXANDER: My wife and I went to Berlin, I can't remember what year. And what the kids were doing over there, they would go into empty spaces. And they would tag the outside or put up advertising. And they would run a bar illegally for as long as they could. And our idea with the facade was, when an artist comes by with a new idea, we're going to keep changing it up as often as we can, just to kind of keep doing different things and get some notoriety for that.

The Violet Hour's success, and presence on Damen, would lead directly to another of One Off's Wicker Park hits: the taco bar Big Star.

TERRY ALEXANDER: After we would get off work at the Violet Hour, Peter and I would go up on the roof. It's kind of a weird-shaped building, but our office is on the second floor and we could go out on the roof from there and drink a beer or whatever. Ricky Diarmit's uncle Buddy had the Pontiac Cafe across the street. I've known Buddy since like 1995. And we'd look down on it and be like, wouldn't it be great to have that gigantic outdoor space? Carol Watson had the space next to it, and she found out that her landlord owned the Pontiac Cafe space, too. And they offered it to her. She said no, it's way too big for me, but I think my friend Terry would like that.

PAUL KAHAN: The landlord kicked Ricky's uncle Buddy out because he wasn't paying his bills. Terry says that it was my idea to open a taqueria and I say that it was his idea. I wanted to open up a greasy burger place.

TERRY ALEXANDER: I'm like, everybody's playing rock music. I want to do alt country, something like that. We're going to do whiskey, we're going to do bourbon. And we're going to do barbecue. And Paul's like, I don't cook barbecue. Okay. I don't know how we came up with Mexican food and whiskey. And tequila. Michael Rubel, who was one of the Violet Hour's managers who came from New York with Toby and Jason, came up with the Bakersfield [1960s California country scene] theme.

PAUL KAHAN: It just happened. And it was popular. It's evolved—this year, we're actually doing demolition over there. It'll be off the grid electricity-wise, we're building a structure next to it. And then we're doing a solar array on top of that and the original structure. We're going for energy neutral with all of our projects, we're exploring making the bakery [Publican Quality Bakery] energy neutral eventually, and just trying to do things right, with a good, clear conscience and trying to make a difference.

Nobody uses more energy [than the food industry]. You know, the beef industry, tons of pollutants. And so how do we do things and actually move the needle and maybe allow future generations to be in the same business? I don't know if we can save it, but I think we gotta try and at least operate with a clear conscience and know that we're moving in the right direction.

****

CAROL WATSON: It's only two decades [since Milk & Honey Cafe opened], but even Division Street has changed drastically. When we opened, there was the Russian bathhouse, Leo's Lunchroom was still open. None of the sports bars were there, I think there was still a little dive bar by what used to be the Shell station. That whole street is completely changed. Now, I feel like Wicker Park's veering into the chains, like Lululemon and Yeti and things like that.

ELLEN FAIREY: I think by the time I got to Wicker Park it was already changing. I've been to Terry's place, Big Star, and it just seems super young there now, and a little bit frat boy. It kind of feels like the same thing that's happened to the East Village in New York.

CAROL WATSON: I don't know if Terry would tell you this, but I think that when Danny's had to close [in 2020], that was probably the saddest thing he's had to go through in business. Because he's opened and closed restaurants, like Okno. But I think Danny's for him was very emotional.

TERRY ALEXANDER: You know, I've always lived in this neighborhood and now I'm in Bucktown [just to the north of Wicker Park], kind of down the street from Danny's, I will probably stay here. Did it turn out exactly how I had hoped? Probably not.

But, you know, probably some of the things we put into this neighborhood helped change it. Some people would say change it for the good, other people would say change it for the worse. I wish there were more independent businesses, I wish the landlords wouldn't price boutiques out of here. But I think with the rents now, you get Nike and Starbucks, and two Walgreens within walking distance from one another. Still, to me, it still seems pretty independent. You know the game plan. First the artists move in, because it's cheap. And you get some cool bars, a couple of cool restaurants. And then gentrification rolls in. It's like that. Every city in every country across the world.

The Violet Hour closed in 2025 following a dispute with its landlord over repairs.

LOGAN SQUARE

A little northwest of Wicker Park, Logan Square has passed through many differ-

ent phases as an ethnic community—Scandinavian giving way to Russian and Polish, to Latino, to an eclectic, artistic community. One of the centers of this evolution—and the employer of many artists in the neighborhood—has been Lula Cafe, which opened in 1999.

JASON HAMMEL (owner): I was a graduate student at Illinois State University in Normal. I went there to study with David Foster Wallace. And I needed money, so I worked in a pizza restaurant, kind of like California Pizza Kitchen. That was my only restaurant experience.

Where Lula is used to be Logan Beach Cafe. It was your typical '90s coffee shop with a lot of bagels and sandwiches and stuff. I remember the owner said she opposed the alderman once and the health department visited her five times that week. But there were some interesting things that happened there. There were folks in the kitchen who would do unusual things, like Indonesian dishes, and they'd do multi-course, extremely casual BYOB dinners.

Logan Square was very different then—I have so many memories of, like, the cigar shop [a space Lula took over]. The name Logan Beach came from the old Cuban guys who would set up lawn chairs on the median and basically hold court, hanging out and smoking or playing cards, and sunbathing on the median. There were a lot of characters on the street in those days, and you certainly didn't see people playing hacky sack, or having picnics on the square. There were a lot of artists, because it was cheap to live there. My apartment was $300, heat included. Friends I knew were making films, or making music or writing books.

Logan Beach Cafe was a major part of my life as soon as I moved to Chicago. The community had a lot of early twentysomethings. It was where I met my wife Lea. It was a really important space for us, and [when they took it over] we were committed to keeping that space going for the community—friends and artists would have music shows and art shows.

There were a couple of other cafés that were also our models for Lula, like Leo's Lunchroom. They usually had a set menu and then they would do all these specials. We didn't know much about the food industry, we were buying produce at Stanley's [a wholesale market] or the Polish grocery stores. It was mostly about hanging out. But pretty quickly we learned about the farmers markets and got interested in cooking. The first one I went to was Green City, probably in 2000.

And then Kelly Courtney, who was the chef at MOD in Wicker Park, she'd been hanging out at Lula and she said, you gotta check out the South Water Market [wholesale market for restaurants]. She took us to Green City and introduced us to Greg Gunthorp and Swan Creek, Mick Klug, all the farmers. But she mostly just told us to buy Alice Waters's books, and *Complete Techniques* by Jacques Pepin, and also all the Trotter books. The Trotter books were soon dog-eared, and written in, and had batter spilled on them. Trotter had like a carrot-cardamom cake, and we'd make that and come up with a dish for breakfast. We read about Tom Cornille in the Trotter books, and we would go down to his warehouse and just poke around. They were so cool—we couldn't afford a case of something, and they would just give us some to experiment with.

We met a lot of people that first year, even with that small kitchen. Like, we met Paul Kahan that first year, and he quickly became kind of an avuncular figure to us. We learned about how professional kitchens work, and where people bought things. Having Paul invite us to dinners at Blackbird and things like that made us more ambitious, as we got to know people like him.

For our first anniversary, Lea and I were so fascinated with the books that someone gave us a gift certificate for Charlie Trotter's. Neither one of us had ever been to a restaurant like that, and we had a great experience. On the way out we met Charlie, and we told him that we were young cooks, and we had a restaurant in Logan Square. He thought we were from London. Then he said, well, you need to be here for lunch tomorrow. We didn't have any employees, we had one other cook, and we worked the line every single shift. So we said, we'd love to come for lunch, but we have to work. And the guy next to us, a busser or something, says, no one says no to Charlie. So we figured it out, and showed up for lunch the next day.

There was a cocktail hour upstairs, in that private wine area. We were standing in the corner, and this woman came up to us and said "Hi! Are you in the industry?" And we told her we had a café in Logan Square, but we're way over our heads, we don't even know what we're doing here. What about you, are you in the industry? She said, yeah, I'm an editor at *Food & Wine*—it was Dana Cowin [editor in chief].

When we got to the dining room there was a solo two-top against the wall, and I said to Lea, we gotta grab that table. But when Charlie came in, he demanded that we stand up and he had people lift the table up and sat us next to Bill Rice [*Tribune* dining editor].

We met a lot of people that day. Like Matthias [Merges] was cooking in the kitchen that day, I didn't know he would become, like, my best friend. We started Pilot Light [food education nonprofit] together. Paul Kahan is one of my great friends and he was also a Pilot Light founder. I just had no idea what was going to happen.

We started doing things like buying whole lambs, and learning how to butcher and cook them. We would change the menu all the time. We started the [weekly] farm dinners around that time. We got a lot of our ingredients through Home Grown Wisconsin, which kind of aggregated different farms. You could have a three-course meal in the café from an early point, but the idea pretty quickly was to make sure we did new dishes every week—I would do one and Lea would do one. Lea would also do the desserts, because we didn't have a pastry chef yet. Eventually we hired two chefs. Jason Vincent was our first chef, and he would do a course and I would do a course.

I think it helped that we weren't reviewed. Obviously people were coming, but we didn't get a *Chicago Tribune* review until, I think, 2015. We got busy because of the *New York Times,* right around September 11. But the Chicago media kind of left us alone for a long time.

One unusual bit of media attention that Lula Cafe got was to be featured on a 2003 episode of the public radio show This American Life,[28] *which focused on service—including testing whether mean servers got better tips than nice ones.*

We don't love that at all. But it happened. The truth is that Ira Glass [host] was a regular, we catered his wedding. We would go out for drinks with him, he was just a really great person to know. There were a lot of interesting people who came in back then. Andrew Bird [musician] was at Lula a lot. Anyway, Ira just said, I want to wire your servers up and see if being mean or nice makes any difference. And we agreed because we were game back then. It wasn't our idea.

28 *This American Life,* "Allure of the Mean Friend," September 5, 2003.

I think we've had a lot of learning to do. We had a small and inexperienced staff, we had to learn how to lead and figure out how to become what we wanted to be. People were forgiving a lot. It's a life's work getting to the point where you understand what the value of hospitality is.

We grew into this space of being restaurant owners and chefs—and parents—pretty slowly. We see a lot of restaurants open as what they're going to be, and close as what they've been. Lula seems to constantly change. I mean, this is going to sound hokey, but in the last couple of years I've been really thinking about how to define values as a business in our restaurant. And one of the values we have defined is the youthfulness of just trying something, to learn and experience it. That is something we want to preserve, now that we're older. We were young and we didn't know what we were doing, and that was part of the charm, and part of the ethos of the space that has never left. I feel like we hire people who have that I-want-to-try-something attitude. I really like having that energy in the space.

Clearly Logan Square has become gentrified, and property values have gone up, and a lot of people have been displaced. A lot of Mexican restaurants then—Reno [pizza parlor] was a Mexican grill, and Dunlays on the Square was Casa de España. But I would say Logan Square is still a place where we have independent owners and operators. We have people who work in their business. We've got Cellar Door Provisions and Giant and Four Letter Word Coffee, so many places that are operated by people who I really respect, who are in their places, working. Not that other neighborhoods don't have that. But it's still a sort of crafts and artists and dreamers place.

Despite its onetime public radio notoriety for service, Lula Cafe won a James Beard Award for Hospitality in 2024.

GASTROPUBS

The term "gastropub" originated in England in the 1990s, but it was the late aughts when it was suddenly everywhere in America—basically meaning a place mixing craft beer with more artful bar food than the usual burgers and wings, the menu frequently scrawled on a chalkboard because of how often it changed. One of Chicago's most influential gastropubs of the era was The Bristol, located in

Bucktown less than a mile north of the Violet Hour and Big Star, and launched in 2008 by John Ross and Phil Walters with chef Chris Pandel.

CHRIS PANDEL: John Ross was the GM at Tramonto's Steak & Seafood [in Wheeling]. And he had left and was looking to open his own restaurant. He and his friend, Phil Walters, were looking for a chef and, you know, obviously we already got along. And I was looking to see if I could still cook, after a few years of learning how to run something way larger than a single restaurant. I was looking to find some creative inspiration again. I felt like I had something to prove to myself. And John and Phil trusted me to create a menu for that neighborhood.

JOHN ROSS: Originally we were going to go down the path of something like Four Corners Group [owner of neighborhood bar and grills]. And I said, I think we really need a *chef* chef. I became very close to Chris at Tramonto's, and just in awe of his talents. I've always said that if he wanted to, he could have won any of those *Chopped* TV battles—you just give him a mass of ingredients and he's going to make it work.

We ended up going to Chris's house for dinner. And he served us the apple salad, the duck raviolo, and some version of roast chicken [all Bristol menu staples]. And we were just blown away. We had way too many bottles of wine, and we basically decided at his house that we were going to do something together, and we started looking for a space.

CHRIS PANDEL: We had a giant beer list at first. But we quickly realized that our guests were coming in more for wine and cocktails. It wasn't a beer hall, but we had the selection available if folks were into it, and if they weren't, the wine program was fantastic.

JOHN ROSS: We wanted to have beer because we thought it was the most accessible thing. And the cocktail movement was happening, and we wanted to have great cocktails. We loved to go to the Violet Hour. And we wanted a nice wine list. We had no idea what the breakdown of those sales would be. I think we sold 60 percent wine, 40 percent cocktails, and beer was like 1 or 2 percent.

We had communal seating, but we didn't do it to be cool. We've never been cool. It was merely about getting more seats in a small space, and having that flexibility of having large parties. Until the pandemic made us break them up. I have seared into my brain a woman who brought in all her kids, from eighteen down to ten, say, and they're the only ones at the communal table, it's not even like anyone else is there. But she absolutely freaked out and stood up and screamed at us, this is not Europe! This is not Europe! We joked about that all the time—*this is not Europe!*

CHRIS PANDEL: It definitely leaned into some of the influences of the gastropub movement, and took a casual riff on, you know, how do you cook delicious, refined, fun food in a casual atmosphere? How do you source better products? And how can you change the menu based on availability from the smaller farms in the area? Those relationships started to get established then, for me, at least. I just did the legwork to find out who grows what and what's good. I met Marty Travis of Spence Farm and got to know him that first summer. I knew that he was really tight with Rick Bayless, and that they had something kind of figured out where he would bring products to the restaurant and they would use it.

It seemed very simple to me to just have them deliver stuff to us, and we would figure out what to cook based on what they had just pulled out of the ground. That's kind of the impetus of where things started. It was like, what makes a good cook? Good roast chicken, some homemade pasta, the skills to butcher whole animals, the waste not, want not mentality.

When Green City Market opened that first season, I went around introducing myself and tasting their food and finding what fit for me and for the restaurant. A lot of my friends by then had cooked within Blackbird and North Pond and places like that, and they had the insight [into how to source from the market] that I didn't. They knew who was doing what the right way, and Beth [Eccles] from Green Acres Farm in Indiana was amazing in helping me get going. You could just walk up to those folks and start a conversation. Just by trying the food they put out in their stalls, you could learn a lot.

You're looking at stuff sometimes, and you're like, okay. They sell you the beets with all the tops on or the turnips with all the tops on and nobody's going to eat that as a salad. Nobody wants wilted greens. So what do you do with it? Well, it turns into pasta filling or something like that. It forces you to become creative no matter what. And maybe not inventive as far as creating a brand-new dish, but finding the utility in items for sure. Because you don't want to throw it away.

JOHN ROSS: Chris keeps everything inside. He would be really good at poker. So you're going along, having these conversations, and then out of nowhere he suddenly does veal brain ravioli.

He's one of those guys that you're like, I just don't know how he does it. It's food where some of it is familiar, but you've never had quite that pop of flavor and that deliciousness. I'm from small-town Iowa, I had a lot of parts growing up, but not in the way that Chris did things.

The big difference between the French and the Italians is, every grandmother in Italy has a different recipe for something. There could be seven thousand different Bologneses. In France, it has to be the exact same coq au vin. I think with Chris it was always, what's it taste like? Do I have to do much to it? Do I have to do way more to it? Do I have to pickle it? So I would always say that he is a seventy-five-year-old Sicilian grandmother wrapped in a thirty-year-old Polish kid.

CHRIS PANDEL: The homemade pasta—that was something that I always kind of gravitated toward, after learning it at Osteria via Stato. I just never really let it go, and I wanted to see if I could be creative with it and learn a few things along the way. And there were some dishes like the duck egg raviolo, that's a dish from San Domenico in Imola, Italy, that I was taught by a chef of mine a long time ago. And I just thought it was one of the most brilliant things I'd ever had my entire life. So why not serve that to the folks at this restaurant? If they've never had it before, they'll be as blown away as I was. And it became a staple.

You've got some simple pastas and good roast chicken and delicious desserts and warm bread, freshly baked for you. So you throw in some stuff that's a little bit left of center, like duck testicles. It's all food. It's delicious. A farmer has them. It's not like we had *fifty* orders of duck testicles. If people were interested in trying them, they would try them, and if they weren't we'd eat them ourselves. People were into both the staples and the weird stuff. So we had a good neighborhood following. It was a busy restaurant.

JOHN ROSS: It's all about hospitality, but we had pig tail and pig head and bone marrow and all those things in 2010. They weren't necessarily new to the United States, or dining in general, but they were new to Chicago. It was kind of a selfish concept for the three of us, but it worked. Chris was making the food that he wanted to cook. Phil and I were working in T-shirts and jeans, but we were doing what we felt at the time was a very high level of service. You would get clean plates, clean silverware [for every course], but we were very much about that high level of service in a really casual place.

CHRIS PANDEL: It was a learning kitchen, so we'd have normal things on the menu, and then we'd have a couple of things that were bits and pieces and odds and ends. It was a fun restaurant at the right time in a city that—I think we were part of a growing dining scene that had some well-established chefs and restaurateurs, but also a smaller pack of independents that were starting to pop up all over the city. We were all young and trying to enjoy what we did.

JOE FRILLMAN (cook): The Bristol was like, holy shit man, boot camp and a half. It was no prep cooks, four cooks, Pandel worked the line on a daily basis with us, expedited the line on a daily basis with us, and we just cranked, man.

It was very intricate food. The chicken wings that we opened the restaurant with took *seven* days to make. Are you nuts, dude? Because they were boneless stuffed chicken wings, but we would make every aspect of the product.

It was a nose-to-tail restaurant, so we did a lot of charcuterie, a lot of pickling, preserving, anything we could possibly get our hands on. It was very meat-centric, pork-centric, and they had one pasta on the menu when we opened, the raviolo. And every single day, whoever worked that station was in the shit, because you're making raviolos, and you have to make every part of it with no prep cooks. Dough, farce, crack the eggs, roll the doughs—we'd make thirty of them a night, we'd sell out pretty much every night. And so every single day, you knew you were making thirty of those things.

Chris pushed me on a daily basis, every single day. He would always come up and say, hey man, I know you've got four pastas on your menu, plus three other items, do you want to run another pasta? And it'd be like two in the afternoon, and in my head I'm like, I'm going to kill you. But you're not going to say no, it was always yes, so we would just have to figure out how to get it done. We had no extruders, we just had to figure out how to do it. It was brutal, but that trained us how to go, and run, and make the best of the bullshit you're handed. That carried over to working for Chris at Balena, because he said, you want to just make crazy amounts of pasta?

We worked with farms hand in hand, and that was the first time we got to really get involved with farms like Klug Farms and Spence Farm. We would get a whole animal in every week, and the menu would be driven around that animal. We did a 230-pound pig each week, and every once in a while we did a goat or a lamb. All fish was whole, everything was broken down by ourselves, because that's the cheapest way to get it.

JOHN ROSS: When we were in it, we didn't even know [how it was being received], it was just like—wow, Charlie Trotter's here. Grant Achatz is here. Rick Bayless is here. It really became an off-duty chef sort of restaurant. We catered Charlie Trotter's wedding. We obviously did a lot of book events with Thomas Keller and René Redzepi and people like that. It really spiraled out of control for what was a little gastropub place to begin with.

JOE FRILLMAN: It kind of wasn't sustainable. We didn't take reservations, and people would come and we'd tell them it was a four-hour wait, and they'd say fine. So they'd go and drink for four hours and come back hammered. And by that point everything on the menu would be 86'd except salad. So we had to get enough of the prime cuts to feed all these people, and that created the problem, we had all these hams left over and stuff like that. Even being nose-to-tail, we had a constant struggle with waste. Nose-to-tail made the restaurant cost-effective, but it also taught us, *Chris* also taught us, how to turn trash into, honestly, some of the best food I've ever had in my life.

****

Another influential gastropub was Longman & Eagle, a restaurant and inn started in Logan Square in 2010 by a group called 16" on Center. It was led by developer Bruce Finkelman, who owned the music bar the Empty Bottle in Ukrainian Village, and Jared Wentworth was its chef. When Michelin came to Chicago in 2011, Longman would be the first Chicago bar and one of only two restaurants in Logan Square to get a culinary star. Other than Joe Frillman's Daisies winning a green star for sustainability, no one in Logan Square has gotten one since.

BRUCE FINKELMAN: My little slice of Ukrainian Village life kind of started at Leo's Lunchroom on Division Street. We had opened up the Bottle in 1992. And Leo's had been around forever. Donna Knezek, who ran it, and those guys were like the first people I knew who were doing the farm-to-table thing. She had an open kitchen, so if you didn't like something you could just walk back and tell Donna you didn't like it. She might throw something at you, but you could do it. And you know, the servers would come to your table and turn a chair around and sit at your table to take your order.

It was my introduction to this whole kind of chef-driven, casual, farm-to-table thing. I don't know if it was just that I wasn't aware of it, or I hadn't put the pieces together that, well, you grow food on a farm. And then you buy that food and you bring it and you put it on the table. Like I didn't really understand the simpleness of that.

When we opened up the Bottle, we'd have these tour buses show up in front of the bar, and these musicians who were playing our bar would pile out and stay in the bar from eleven o'clock to six in the morning. There wasn't anybody who really lived over here, but the artists were starting to move in. And you know, there was really nowhere to eat except Leo's.

We lived on Polish food from across the street. Donna decided to partner with me and another guy to start Bite Cafe. What people wanted back then was grilled cheese and hamburgers, and all of a sudden, here came this whole new arena of home-cooked, real homey, real comfortable food, but made with fresh ingredients. Coq au vin, stroganoff, peasant dishes from around the world. A lot of the vegetarian fare also came from Leo's. I had no knowledge of vegetarian food—my dad worked at a meatpacking company when I was growing up.

We started doing concerts over at the Logan Square auditorium. We drove past this one place, that was a Caribbean restaurant where Longman is today. As we started to get a little bit older, and we started to learn about food a little bit more, and about bourbon, we wanted to do something that was like an exploration of our tastes changing. You build places that you want to go to, that you hope other people will like as well. That was the whole idea behind it. We had another chef, and we were working on the project. We had bought this building, and we weren't really sure what we were going to do with it. But then, at the last minute, I got a resume from this dude in Seattle. Didn't know very much about him at all. But he came in and we talked and he did a tasting for us. And it wasn't much after he put the food on the table, that we said, well, how are we going to tell the other guy that he's not the chef anymore?

JARED WENTWORTH: I kind of had two choices as a teenager—be a dishwasher or be a lifeguard. And I wasn't the strongest swimmer. I was lucky enough to have my first real job being working for Bob Kinkead at 21 Federal on Nantucket, I just sort of blindly walked into that. The first chef I ever worked for is a legend.

I came to Chicago, because I decided I wanted to work professionally for a living and my other job then was as a musician. I went to Kendall College and me and another classmate went to work at Gordon. So I got to spend two years working for Keith Korn, and it was kind of magical.

Keith was super-charismatic, and at the same point super old-school. He was like the first intimidating, psychopathic, artistic chef I ever worked for. It's funny, you look back and you go, wow, that was a whole shitload of abuse that I put up with. I still show up fifteen minutes early to work, and a lot of stuff like that, work ethic-wise.

The comparison of cooks then and now, it's just not comparable. Because there wasn't a thousand restaurants, you had ten to fifteen restaurants that were your four-star *Chicago Tribune* places, and if you wanted to step your foot through that door, you better commit 100 percent. Because all the chefs knew each other, so if you burned a bridge, you were really screwed. But as a young cook, it was great, because I got to witness some of the bigger shots of my time in the process of creating the new cuisine that would carry forward into the 2000s. No one was stuck in pure French, no one was stuck in pure Asian. So it was really kind of interesting to watch, this time period of a melting pot of cooking styles.

And it was the time that the Food Network was kind of launching. For kids of my generation, being a cook was not really the most practical profession, and it turned into that rock star-y, Emeril Lagasse, "Bam!" kind of era, where it was something to get excited about. At first that was kind of great, I mean, anything that puts more spotlight on what you're doing is great. But then it got fucking silly, with vending machine challenges on TV.

I left Gordon because I had a falling out with Keith on a Saturday night. So I just got up and left. I worked for David Burke in San Jose. I was in the northwest, Seattle, for about seven years, and then I came back to open Longman.

My idea for Longman was, I've always loved Blue Ribbon Brasserie in SoHo, which was the quintessential late night, interesting people hanging out, killer food place that I wanted at that point in my career. My partners had a lot of background in bourbon tastings and in music and really wanted to do a classic Chicago tavern. By the time we opened it was the real peak of the [2008] recession, so we really weren't charging a ton of money for anything over there. We wanted it to have a price point where people could come two or three times a week, and not really think twice about it. I mean, I'm a complete Japanese seafood fanatic, but we had people going through half a case of bourbon. I wasn't going to have a light menu. We used to joke with the barbacks that we'd pay them $25 for each person who threw up. I had one of the barbacks leave with $450 one night.

BRUCE FINKELMAN: Jared has got one of the best palates of anybody that I know of. You could be sitting at a table with Jared and you say, we want to do something about Thanksgiving, can you throw a recipe together for that? You talk to most chefs and they would be like, yeah, I have it for you on Monday, Jared would go, it has fucking beets in it, it has roulade on it. And he was just doing the dish in his head, and it wasn't a throwaway. You could tell it was amazing.

He had the pork shank, that became a culinary staple around the world or around the country, I think. It was a fried pork shank, it was really huge, it was on the bone. But to have that sweet sauce that was on there, it was something that I had never tried before. He did the steak dish where he did the succotash that was on it. These were flavor combinations that were that were complex. But yet, there was always something that was very homestyle about it, very common, very approachable. The idea of Longman was, why shouldn't people be surprised with the level of food or the level of service they get when they come in here?

JARED WENTWORTH: It was kind of a downscale sensibility, but at the same time with really great ingredients. One of the things I got out of working for David Burke was making fine dining accessible and not scary for the average person. Not that I want to cook cheeseburgers all the time, but sometimes a four-top will go by and they'll say, want to get a bite? And that one guy says, nah, I don't want that. That's why we ranged from highbrow food to something down and dirty.

Living in the northwest was kind of magical, things grow almost twelve months out of the year there. So people had been getting all their produce from farmers for at least a decade longer than here. Coming back to Chicago, there was a catch-up time for me in going to Green City Market, figuring out who had the best stuff. But I think a lot of chefs feel that connection with where their food is grown. It's too bad that it's become kind of a giant cliché. But really in the 2020s, it's just implied that you buy from farmers. Where in 2010, you really were making kind of a statement.

In 2011, the first year Michelin came to Chicago, Longman & Eagle won a star.

JARED WENTWORTH: I had no delusions about our odds of winning one, but at the same time I eat enough in New York City, I had been to The Spotted Pig half a dozen times, and I thought the food we were doing at Longman compared with what they were doing. I don't want to come off with too much bravado or ego, but I put confidence in our abilities and our product sourcing to think, yeah, we have a shot at this.

BRUCE FINKELMAN: Our original idea was that we were gonna have a huge party when they finally realized that they gave it to the wrong place.

JARED WENTWORTH: Remember the Snowpocalypse of 2014? We were extremely busy, and we had just opened the inn but no one was staying in it. A lot of the kitchen staff were worried about getting home because they had to come back for brunch the next morning, so I just said, you know what, we're just going to stay here. The crowd is starting to get out of control. And then a guy comes in in a gorilla suit at about 10 p.m. At that point, it works.

I'm imbibing whiskey and having a burger, and the gorilla is just tossing them back, I don't know how with a mask on, but he is. I go out for a cigarette, the gorilla guy kind of follows me out. Super cordial, but then he tries to throw our cigarette butt hut through the front window. One of my guys starts chasing him, and they run for like half a mile. I'm just really impressed that this guy in the gorilla suit can move that much. The guy loses us, and we go back in to sleep. The next morning the snow is over the windows, and we are the only restaurant in Logan Square that's open—the Starbucks is closed, everything's closed. By 11 a.m. people are piling in, and a guy tries to drive a Land Cruiser up the snowbank to get in on the second floor. I just think, we have to be the only Michelin-starred restaurant in the world that has served somebody in a gorilla suit.

HIGH AND LOW

In the 1960s, as all America was eating a new hamburger called a Big Mac (which looks tiny in today's supersized world), a few South Side Chicago hamburger stands introduced something called a Big Baby—a double-decker burger with grilled onions. It remained obscure for decades, but suddenly in the 2010s, not only were people talking about it online, it even turned up on the menus of a few upscale restaurants—that were run by chefs who had grown up eating them.

The cross between high and low food hit some kind of peak at that moment, but it's by no means the only example. Two restaurants in particular that showed how the food scene was changing were places serving an everybody food—but in a way that showed unexpected sophistication, or at least luxury ingredients. One was a pizza restaurant, Spacca Napoli, named for the main street in Naples and serving authentic Neapolitan pizza rather than Chicago deep dish or tavern cut; in the years since its opening in 2006 a whole renaissance of artisanally-crafted pizza emerged in Chicago. The other was a hot dog stand, Hot Doug's, serving duck, elk and rattlesnake sausages, topped with things like manchego cheese and truffle aioli . . . and, as would soon become infamous, foie gras.

JONATHAN GOLDSMITH: I was doing real estate at that time, while doing social work, which is my profession. So I was rich with time, and I made the decision to open up a pizzeria. This is around 2003, 2004. Over eighteen months, I was staying in a particular hostel in Naples, most of my visits were in Spacca Napoli, and pretty much all the pizzerias I went to, you just saw one type of flour, Mulino Caputo. I was clueless about flour, but I thought, this is the flour I have to have.

When I came back I learned that Greco & Sons [Italian food distributor] carried Mulino Caputo flour. This is 2005, so we're already in construction for the restaurant, I had my guys over from Italy building the oven. I had already spent three weeks in Naples studying with Enzo Coccia, who was my first teacher there. So I go to Greco in Carol Stream [western suburb] and sit down with a salesman. I later hear from a colleague that when I went in there, a Jewish guy from Scarsdale, New York who says he's going to open a Neapolitan pizzeria in Chicago, they thought I was crazy. Listen, my wife thought I was crazy, too. People thought, what is this guy doing?

Tony Mantuano from Spiaggia was the one who recommended that if I can bring the guys over from Naples to build the oven, that would be something nobody's done. But building the restaurant, you know, that was a lot of money. I could have maybe bought something in America for half the price. I could have bought a mixer for half the price. But we were spending money to do the things that were key to making this pizza.

Nella Grassano [his opening pizzaiolo] was making pies in a nightclub, some kind of club. There was Trattoria Roma on Wells, they were doing an artisanal pie at the time, but in a deck oven, not a wood-burning oven. There was an Italian restaurant called La Bocca della Verita, and Pizzeria D.O.C. on Lawrence doing Roman-style pizza. And of course, we had all the other styles of pizza—the bar pizzas and the slice pizzas and so on. So there were a few people doing something a little different. But it was a small community next to what we see today, which is amazing, all the different branches from people more courageous than I. Because I was taking a tradition that was three hundred years old and trying to be faithful to that tradition. I didn't have the wherewithal to take something and reinvent it and take it in another direction.

When people ask me, did you ever think this would be so successful, my first response was, I didn't realize how stupid I was. I was so tunnel-visioned I wasn't even thinking about whether we would be successful or not. Thankfully, we were embraced—not by everybody. I still remember somebody in the early years at table number one standing up and announcing to the room that it was the worst pizza they'd ever had. Sir, that's not necessary, will you please sit down. . . . Most of our reviews on Yelp are really wonderful. Most people [who don't like it] are very gracious and lovely to say, I understand that people love it, it's not for me. One of my first customers, which was great, was Alessandro Molta, who was the consul general at the Italian consulate. He and his family would come in probably every other Sunday, and to have someone like him come in was truly a stamp of approval that meant a lot to me.

If I look at images from when we first opened to where we are now, we've grown. I've grown a lot. And I've learned a lot over the years. And we're still learning and still practicing and still making errors. But now getting closer and when I can be focused on managing the dough, it can be really wonderful. So we're just very lucky that it caught on so quickly.

With lines from the start, Goldsmith had to learn quickly how to keep a crowd happy.

When we first moved to Chicago, our pizzeria was Leona's [local chain] on Sheffield. I remember that when you were waiting outside, they would go around and give you a plastic cup of wine. But we had that same experience in Italy, whether it was the beginning or the end of the meal, there'd be something. Limoncello, grappa, two or three different cakes, but it was that generosity that was so central to the whole experience.

I'm really happy that the progression went from being this big, famous person [in the pizza world]. My friend said to me, be careful, you can tell somebody once you're a big guy, you can have a second celebrity conversation, but it becomes boring the third time. And I really like how I've gone through this sort of progression with the pizzeria, and really, right now I'm so over in some ways. We benefited so much from social media and all that attention, that I wanted to just be a pizzeria again, and just be present with the people there and work with the kids. Because there's so much fascination with the fire in the oven and the handling of the dough. And that teaching process is really, really important stuff.

****

DOUG SOHN: I sort of felt like hot dogs in Chicago were like bagels in New York, they've got a great reputation but there's three places doing it well and a thousand that are mediocre or not good. And so many places are doing like seventeen other things as well, chicken sandwiches and gyros and so forth. So the hot dog slips down the menu and to do it to make money at that point, when it's not a volume thing, you have to cheap out. It sits in the water for a day and a half. That was just sort of the state of it, so few places dedicated to just doing a really good dog, because to make money at it, you have to sell a lot of hot dogs.

When I was a vendor at the ballparks in 1982, my first real experience was in the commissary taking the giant mesh bag of hot dogs out of the water, cutting it open all over the metal table and then people just grabbing them and putting them into buns and wrapping them up. That's when you don't want to see the sausage being made. I always joked that they steam all the hotdogs in February and there's a hot box under second base. And that's the inventory for the year.

I opened up, the first place was two blocks from where I lived [in Roscoe Village]. The first eight months I was walking to work thinking, okay, if I closed up today, what kind of financial straits would I be in? Could I sell it? What else could I do? And then we get going and it was like, we got through the day, and then we start over the next day. The most weight I've ever lost in a short period of time was opening up the restaurant because it's just misery and stress. If anyone thinks it started off gangbusters, not even close.

If it wasn't for Lane Tech [magnet high school a few blocks away], I would have closed in six months. They were like a large fry and two cups for four kids, but they were great. They were funny, it was almost the same kids every day. They were hysterical, and I knew that they're giving me money, they get treated like customers.

It really changed when we started to get a little press. WTTW [PBS affiliate] had a paper, and we got a nice writeup in the *Reader*. It was all of a sudden, because there was no Yelp yet—I think there was CitySearch and Metromix. And then Pat Bruno, in the *Sun-Times*, every other summer he would write about [the best] hot dog joints. And we were number one. I remember we had to close early that day, because we ran out of food. I wasn't prepared for that. The good thing was we had all those months to work out a lot of the kinks, where now you gotta be great the moment you open the doors. We got a great article from R.W. Apple in the *New York Times*, which I've always joked about, at some point I'll be wearing like three trench coats on a park bench with a tattered copy of that article. I'm Hot Doug, you son of a bitch, I was in the *New York Times*!

And then the place burned down.

It reopened several months later in a location about a half mile west. Hot Doug's offered hot dogs, but the real attraction was its range of sausage specials commanding a higher-than-hot dog price.

DOUG SOHN: We used an eight-to-the-pound, natural casing dog. Which used to be the standard, but now it's nine or ten, and a lot of places you can tell. Eight-to-the-pound are a little more expensive, but the point was to charge enough to make a living while serving a better product. And to buy good mustard, cut the onions fresh every day, slice the tomatoes. The hot dog was still really inexpensive, because I had this other menu, and specials, that was what subsidized them. Because if you really go by food cost, a hot dog should be five dollars. Too expensive, because people come in and say, I remember when hot dogs were a nickel. Yeah, in 1967. I'm not saying they were a loss leader. But if I just sold hot dogs, at that price I couldn't survive.

You'd see an Italian sausage or a Polish here and there, or other kinds of sausages. But there was no single place to get all of them. For me, I didn't want to do burgers, and it gave me something else to put on the menu. I did some research and started with basics like chorizo, the chicken sausages, a veggie dog, etc. Pretty soon the nice thing was that people were seeking me out—sure, I'll take some samples. Let's see what you got. It wasn't so much the different meats as, can we do a bacon sausage? I had a guy who was basically, well, let's find out. He'd send me samples and I'd always be, more garlic. Can we have more of this flavor?

When I first did blood sausage, I sold two. Later, I'd sell hundreds. Some of that was obviously trust in the restaurant, but also, the food culture, especially in Chicago, was changing drastically. You had Food Network, food writing people, seeking that out. Alligator did really well. It's kind of just unusual enough. Maybe it's because they're not cute. The corned beef sausage we did with Russian dressing and sauerkraut would blow out. Anything with bacon. But towards the end [when Doug's announced closing, and the line would wrap around the building for hours] it was rare that anything wouldn't sell.

The other part of the game plan, was personality. A friend of mine said, as much as you say you hate people, you do a great job with crowds. That interaction was what I enjoyed. I didn't want to hire someone else to do that, while I'm sitting there doing paperwork. Or franchising. People would suggest that and I'd say, why would I take away the part of the job I like, and then I get to be the district manager in charge of people. If I'm going to own ten of something, it's not going to be restaurants. No thank you.

I kinda miss the smart answers. Like, people would say, is this one good? No, that one's horrible, I wouldn't get that one. Or people would come in—like from Texas—and say, can I get a chili dog? You're in Chicago, get one with everything. You're going to wait for an hour to get a chili dog and it isn't as good as the one back home. I would talk people out of stuff. Don't get that.

Then there's the Great Foie Gras Caper of 2007.

DOUG SOHN: I had a duck sausage with Sauternes and foie gras in it, topped with a truffle aioli and slices of foie gras mousse. It was kind of for entertainment—I thought it would be cool to have this hot dog stand serving foie gras and truffles. And also because, here are two ingredients that are out of the reach of most people, so here's an opportunity to try them for, I think it was

$8 at first, either $9 or $10 by the time we were done. As I've always said, if there's a lily to be gilded, I'm the guy. And it was a huge seller.

It had been on the menu for a while. It had sort of become a permanent special. When they passed the ban, I first thought about it taking it off because, is this an argument I want to take on? I have a business, I have employees who rely on this business to pay their bills. And then I just thought, we're a hot dog stand on the Northwest Side of Chicago. What are they going to do? It just seemed so absurd. I figured they'd probably go after restaurants downtown, because they're closer to their office.

The health department came in and they said, are you serving this? I pointed to the sign and said, yeah, there it is. So I got a warning letter, which I immediately framed and put on the counter. I was thinking, let's be smartasses and see what happens. The alderman behind the ban was Joe Moore, so I made the celebrity sausage of the week a sausage with lots of foie gras on it, and called it the Joe Moore.

The health department comes in again—on a Friday at noon, of course—and they're basically, you think you're funny? Well, laugh now, hot dog boy. In some ways I felt bad for the health department because the city council passes this, and dumps it on them to deal with. I had to take it off the specials board, with a full restaurant, and we went down into the basement, I opened up a chest freezer and they put this tape over the sausages and tied up the bag and marked it do not use, must dispose, something like that. And they issued me the $250 ticket.

I was about to leave on vacation the next day—ironically, I was going to Alsace to eat foie gras every day. I'm at the airport the next day watching CNN, and I notice my name is on the crawl. I was away for a couple of weeks, so I missed a lot of the immediate furor. When I got back I took it off the menu for a little bit—my feeling was, the anti–foie gras argument is kind of ridiculous, therefore, the pro–foie gras argument is kind of ridiculous, too. And I have a business to run. But then I got to the point of, let's put it back on the menu and see what happens.

ABC's *Nightline* was doing a story, cameras set up in front by the stools. And I look up and I see the two health department people who gave me the ticket coming into the restaurant. And I see them stop in the vestibule. They look to their left. They see the cameras, they look at each other—and they turn around and leave. And one of the servers is like, did I just see. . . . Yeah. You did.

The amount of publicity I got was hysterical. I had friends send me clippings from all over the world, like, I made the front page of the *International Herald Tribune* from Tokyo. Then one day I got a call on my cell. So what are your thoughts about the overturning of the foie gras ban? I didn't know what they were talking about.

About a month later, a guy I knew from high school called me, who worked for the city. He goes, so do you know who really turned you in? And I said, I'm going to guess it was the pro-foie gras people. He's like, you're exactly right. I was like, yeah, to show that this law doesn't just affect the fine dining restaurants that no one can afford to go to. It can be anybody. An iconic Chicago institution like a hot dog stand, they can be affected. That's the route I would have gone, absolutely.

Finally, what is Doug's position on the ketchup on Chicago hot dogs controversy?

DOUG SOHN: You know, you're paying for it. I don't care. My girlfriend puts ketchup on her hot dog.

RENEGADE CHEFS

The model of the tasting menu in Chicago was surely Charlie Trotter's—including that the restaurants offering them tended to be very posh, and well-funded and -staffed. In the early 2000s, that meant restaurants like Alinea, Lettuce's L2O, or Sixteen, in a hotel owned by a guy named Trump.

But as a chef serving an underground tasting menu in his apartment told this author, "With a credit card and FedEx, I can get the same ingredients as any chef." Truffles, foie gras, caviar—not to mention the best of the farmers markets. The result has been a movement of independent chefs setting up in quirky spaces with open kitchens and cooking to the beat of their own inspiration, while playing the music they wanted and often serving the food themselves.

Three who show the rise of these personal fine dining restaurants: Michael Carlson of hard-rocking, molecular Schwa in Wicker Park; Lane (then Iliana) Regan of whimsical, farm-to-table Elizabeth in Lincoln Square; and Phillip

Foss of playful, jokey EL Ideas, in a nowhere industrial strip on the South Side. Did anyone take these DIY fine dining restaurants, the food equivalent of a garage band or storefront theater, seriously? Well, Michelin did, for one: It came to Chicago in 2011, and by 2014, all three of them had stars.

Michael Carlson was set to be on Grant Achatz's opening team at Alinea, as he had been at Trio, when he found a small space in Wicker Park available.

GRANT ACHATZ: Michael is a real talent, and a very strong personality. He was rebellious. But we had a strong mutual respect at Trio, which is why I invited him to be an opening sous chef at Alinea. And he considered it, but then he had this opportunity with his father, to help him open Schwa. And I knew that it would be his own, because he's fiercely original. I didn't know that it was going to be the Nirvana of garage band restaurants, which it was, almost scarily so. Because they misbehaved in that restaurant. But what they were putting out was great, and it was shoestring, which was the charm.

MICHAEL CARLSON: I'd be lying if I said there was a whole lot of thought behind it—to be honest, the opportunity fell into my lap. I'd just come back from Europe, planning on working with Grant at Alinea, and I happened to stumble across the people who owned [the building] prior. A friend I had cooked with the first time I was ever in a restaurant—I hadn't seen him for almost a decade, and I stumbled across him walking down the street. And he's like, I got this little place. You should check it out. And man, when I walked in the door I was like, yeah, I'll take this over.

I came across this style often in Europe, in all of the smaller towns and cities—maybe not to the extent of all the chefs bringing [the food] out, but it was definitely more intimate. It was the chef and his wife and his brother or whatever, out of necessity, because of the financial aspect of it. You can pay your wife cheaper, I guess.

Phillip Foss's EL Ideas—a shortened version of "elevated ideas," with a nod to Chicago's "L" train—grew out of his food truck, Meatyballs, during the 2000s trend for such things. Which in turn grew out of him working at one of Chicago's most historic hotels, the Palmer House—but not for long.

PHILLIP FOSS: I finished at Le Cirque [New York] in '98 and I went to Europe for about a year. I came back from Europe and I landed here because my brother was living here. I applied for a sous chef position at Spiaggia when Paul Bartolotta was the chef, and at Tru. With Tru it was the first year they had opened up, and it was a complete I-do-not-fit-in-with-Lettuce-Entertain-You. I came in with this awful bravado, and it did not go well. I remember my brother dropped me off and I was thinking, I just hope I can get through the day. And that was the day I got fired.

I was already planning on moving to Hawaii, but after September 11th I was like, I've got to go big. So I decided to go to Brazil. My visa ran out but I was not ready to come back to America, and my brother was in Israel, so I went there and saw this beautiful Jewish girl and married her. I was working at the King David Hotel, I got to cook for Bibi Netanyahu, actually knew him on a first name basis.

It was the beginning of posting jobs on the internet. My wife was pregnant and we had no health insurance. I saw an ad for a job at the Palmer House. I went down there and we met for two hours and I got the position. And then they're putting fucking posters all up and down Wabash and State Street about this big arrival who's their new chef. Like, I haven't done anything. So much of it is how you manufacture your own reality. I latched onto the Asian carp thing [an invasive species, which at one point the government tried to develop a market for, to encourage fishing] and I was the Asian carp chef in newspaper articles and on TV news shows. I made sure to get noticed. I was pushing forty, I had a kid and another on the way. And the restaurant in the hotel was not exactly a swanky, pizzazz-y place that people were going to flock to. I needed to make a splash.

You get that little bit of attention and it feels so gratifying. But it rolls into this monster that all of a sudden, you don't even know where you are and who you are. I took on a whole persona in a way that really wound up backfiring on me when I had to calm down and see what was underneath that, what were the insecurities that were behind it?

Lane Regan grew up (as Iliana) in a farm family in northwest Indiana—a story told in their two acclaimed memoirs about growing up queer in a dysfunctional family nevertheless rooted in the land.[29]

LANE REGAN: It was important to my dad to always be cooking, like he had his own garden, and he had the restaurant—Jennie's Cafe in Gary, Indiana—and my mom was a chef in the restaurant. And then when she didn't have that anymore, she was preserving things from our garden or making homemade meals. It was always from scratch. It was definitely a very special occasion where we ordered a pizza. It was rare to get pizza delivered where we were, because we were kind of in a rural area. Most of the time, the easiest thing you could do was to be making homemade meals.

I was going through my first book recently and I picked up on something that was maybe a connection underneath. I realized that a lot of the chaos [in their family life], there's points where I bring it back to food and the food ends up calming that down. It quiets the storms. I think that's the food culture that I learned when I was young; food is the thing that brings people back together.

Often what they cooked was Slavic things, like stuffed cabbage, stuffed peppers, sauerkraut and sausage, goulash. My dad always had this beet and horseradish spread. Lots of pickled items, from pickled pigs' feet to whatever could be pickled from the garden. Occasionally there were steak and potato dinners, or pasta dinners, but that wasn't very often. I think with my mom having all of us in and out of the house, she was always feeding at least me and my dad, she made a lot of one-pot meals and a lot of the things she made at the restaurant.

I worked in restaurants from when I was fifteen. Italian restaurants, Chinese restaurants, pizza places, all those kind of basics. I worked at a French-Vietnamese restaurant in Chicago called Julie Mai's Le Bistro. But my first exposure to fine dining was through Alinea [as a server]. I think, though, that a lot of the things that my mom and dad did, in a way, kind of have the backbone of haute cuisine, like making sure that the ingredients are really fresh and local. Because most of the time if my mom was going to make like fried zucchini, it came from the garden that day, it never went into the fridge because it was still warm from the sun when she was slicing it

29 *Burn the Place,* Agate, 2019; and *Fieldwork,* Agate, 2022.

up. And I think those kinds of things, when you end up eating them, leave big imprints in your memory.

****

The decor at Schwa had a distinct dorm room feel, and so did the music, often punk or heavy metal. One of the most distinctive aspects of the room was the open window into the kitchen—the first step toward all of these restaurants breaking down the barrier between the cooks and the diners.

MICHAEL CARLSON: We had people who would just park there with a glass of wine while I was cooking, half the time dumping it over the station onto my mise en place. They'd just barge in, with the best intentions, but it's easy to get pulled aside and sidetracked. You try to remain respectful of what people are saying and you're listening while you're trying to cook.

WILSON BAUER (chef de cuisine, 2010s): They had to interact if they came back [to the kitchen]—the bathroom's through there. Even if they didn't want to, they still had to come back. Usually we got people who wanted to interact, it was good, I liked it, I guess. Sometimes it can be weird.

This part was still the kitchen. In our eyes. And if I went to a table, I wanted to see that the glasses were a certain way. We organized it like a station. That's how I view the dining room, and that's the only way I could get out here, if I viewed that as, that's also my station, it's part of the kitchen too. Otherwise, it's just weird going out there.

MICHAEL CARLSON: At the same time, that is what makes the experience the experience. It was something I wasn't used to. It took a while to be less introverted. It goes in cycles: you get used to it and then you get a little more shy. It keeps evolving that way. I think there's a point after years of doing it where you become a little reclusive and like, I'm gonna hide in the basement for a minute.

Part of the Schwa experience as a guest quickly became bringing the kitchen a bottle of something, and—if you were lucky—being invited afterwards to do shots with the cooks, or indulge in some other substance.

WILSON BAUER: We did shots. We shared a glass of wine. That's a part of the restaurant that I cherished. We got rowdy sometimes. Which can be taxing. That's maybe the hardest part, like on a Friday, Saturday when we've just been going at it all week, and then people come in and it's like—it's Friday! Let's keep going! Uh, it's twelve thirty, I gotta go. I'm not doing this four nights in a row.

MICHAEL CARLSON: There's always someone in the kitchen who's younger than us, that can handle the guy on table 6 who wants to do a shot with every course. That works itself out real fucking quick, when their head's on the table and their wife is kicking them under the table like, you asshole! We're also not dumb, either. We've been through this drill before.

GARRETT RUSSELL (cook): I think I came in at the end of it being as absurd it was. It was a little more tame, but still, it was nuts. It was such extreme anxiety, you had an impossible amount of work to do, in the amount of time given, in a space that's the size of most people's home kitchen. You couldn't get there any earlier. It was like, this is what time we show up. It's like, well, can I come in early? You can stand outside, but I'm not opening the door.

So you know, you get anxiety, so you just start drinking beer at ten o'clock in the morning. But I would say we only had two or three nights where—I wouldn't say we crashed and burned. But, like, one time the sous chef found some fireworks in the basement. And we were throwing firecrackers into the dining room. And it was all fun and games until somebody found an M-80 and threw that in the dining room. And it was like a bomb went off. Everyone got up and ran out, and this one dude was going to try to fight us, but it was him and five of us. So then he's calling the police. We got everybody out and locked the gate. We all hid in the basement and drank until the cops stopped knocking on the door.

There were times it was like, Carlson would come in and we'd all start drinking, and he'd be like, let's go to lunch. There's no way you're going to have everything ready if you leave for two and a half hours and get all messed up and come back. And so we'd just put a note on the door, we're closed because the icemaker broke or something. But we didn't have an icemaker. We bought all the ice from the Guatemalan lotto down the street.

Phillip Foss clashed with union bureaucracy at the hotel, and when he made a pot joke inspired by Rodney King on Twitter ["Can't we all just get a bong?"] they seized the chance to get rid of him. His response was to hop on the then-hot trend for food trucks.

PHILLIP FOSS: I already had the idea for Meatyballs, as a restaurant. And it occurred to me that it would be so much less trouble and money to do it as a food truck. So I went to the Office of Business Affairs, and they were like, nope, these are the rules, you can't cook on the truck, you have to be two hundred feet away from any other restaurant, and basically you can't do it. If you really look at the map of downtown Chicago, there's almost no place [you can legally operate your food truck]. Or if there's two hundred feet where there's not a restaurant, there's a really good reason for it. It's a shitty area.

People are always excited for something new and exciting, and some of the first days of the food truck, you'd send out one tweet and when you'd get to the location there'd be a line of twenty people, excited that you're a new option for them to have for lunch. It's pure exhilaration, and people are awesome in many ways, especially the first people who figure it out. But a business like that, it's not just "what is your idea?" but "what is going to attach to people about it besides the food?" You've got to be aggressive in your pitch to the public.

Lane Regan worked at restaurants including Trio and Alinea, but started selling homemade goods at farmers markets, then did underground dinners in their condo. In 2012 they opened their restaurant Elizabeth, named for their late sister, which offered whimsical fine dining built in part on foraged foods, a kind of "forest-to-table" cooking that seemed like Alinea crossed with Alice in Wonderland*.*

LANE REGAN: I was working at Alinea when I started my farmers market thing where I was selling pierogis, because I wanted to have a restaurant, I wanted to be a chef. So how can I get my name out there but go in a less-traditional route than working myself up through the backs of kitchens? Because at the time I was already twenty-eight, and going back into the kitchen and working the amount that they worked for the money they made, I was like, I can't do this.

I already owned a condo. So I had to do it where it was more financially stable. And at the time, there hadn't been this kind of cultural reckoning within kitchens, it was still very much the brigade system.

With the farmers markets my intention was just to make yummy food, whatever it might be. So I started out with biscuits and jams. Then other homemade things that people would like, and one time I made pierogi, and that really won people over. I had a whole lot of people waiting for them. And then *Chicago* magazine picked me up as doing pierogi. People would ask, so you want to do a Polish restaurant? No, I'm just trying to do my own fine dining restaurant, but I'm making a name for myself.

When I started doing the underground dinners is when I started trying my hand at haute cuisine, because I had seen Grant [Achatz] do it. And I was really inspired by Michael Carlson of Schwa because I had known him through Trio and we had been friends while we were both there. Schwa was one of the first kind of little chef-run fine dining establishments, at least in Chicago. He told me he opened that place with maybe $80,000. So that was huge to think about that going from like these multi-million dollar restaurant establishments to see somebody kind of be able to do it on their own, or with just a tiny bit of help. And that made me realize, like, wow, I could do this too.

SCOTT NOORMAN (sommelier at Alinea): [Lane] asked me to work in their apartment one night. And I'm like, oh, I heard about you doing these little pop-ups, I'd love to do that. They said, it's gonna be me, you and a dishwasher. I do sixteen people a night. And I just want somebody to pour wine, I've never had a professional waiter like you or a sommelier. I want to take it to the next level and show people what we can do.

****

The best-known course on the menu at Schwa was a dish Carlson made by the hundreds when he was at Trio: Black Truffle Explosion, a raviolo filled with truffle liquid, which you were strongly advised to eat in one bite.

MICHAEL CARLSON: People become suicidal when you don't serve it. Like, people get so angry, it's amazing. There was a point where we wouldn't do it if you asked for it. If you just kept your mouth shut, we would serve it to you at some point. But if you started talking about it, asking for it, wondering why the table next to you got it—then you're not seeing it, man. That was an asshole move for sure.

GARRETT RUSSELL: Developing dishes was just kind of an open-ended conversation. When you were working we would just talk about it out loud. It was a great environment for it because you could just spitball ideas, and no one was going to be like, that's stupid, you're dumb.

If you were standing there, just watching us, you would think that we were all having a great time. But really everyone I think internally was like, there's no fucking way I'm going to finish this. Like, this is an impossible task. But we all had the air of, we were just friends. It really was like a family. But with the understanding that like, if you fuck up one thing, you know, you're gonna hear about it. You do everything perfectly—well, not like Alinea perfect. But perfect for our standards.

Phillip Foss started serving a multicourse dinner in his Meatyballs prep kitchen. It was hard to get a cab there—hell, it was hard to get mainstream reviewers to go there—but he opened EL Ideas in 2011, a BYO dinner space in which guests could wander into the open kitchen and chat with the chefs, and which served dishes like an opening course which does not include silverware—you have to lick your plate clean. Another was inspired by his young daughters' tendency to dip their Wendy's French fries in their Frosty.

PHILLIP FOSS: I wanted to be fun and approachable. I don't just like to cook—I think that's part of why the hotel liked me from the beginning, I can cook good food but I also liked the public game. One of the first nights we opened, Andrew [Brochu, co-chef] was like, we have no walls in our kitchen, and you have to go kind of past the kitchen to get to the restroom. And he's like, so are we just gonna let people come into the kitchen? Well, how can you not? That became a huge niche for us, that people could actually come back and talk to us, and I could actually cook and talk at the same time, no problem. And I loved making people laugh. Give me an opportunity to say something outrageous, and I will.

A lot of times you go to a fine dining restaurant, you feel like you're a corpse in rigor mortis. You can't touch anything, everything's so perfect. You hardly feel comfortable, you feel like you're in a funeral home. So I wanted to make sure that people can get up, walk around, talk to each other, we're just doing the food, you bring the wine, and we'll listen to our music, let's just meet in the middle and have fun. It's like we were the Dave and Buster's of fine dining, in a way.

Being able to come in the kitchen and talk with us, I think people responded to that. You have to give people a reason to want to come back. You have to give them a reason to want to tell their friends about it, I tried something that you're not going to believe. I remember Michelin gave us a hard time the first year they were out. We didn't get a star, and they said something about how we made guests lick their plates on the first course. I used that as a weapon against them. Like, it's just because you don't like our way of having fun. But the other reality is, I don't know that we'd still be here if we hadn't gotten ours [in 2014].

ANDREW BROCHU: Phillip is such a go-getter. When I worked at Kith & Kin [in Lincoln Park], he was always popping in to drop off Meatyballs. Then when it closed, which was kind of abrupt, Phillip reached out to me and said, I'm working on this project, I don't know if you're interested, but it's just going to be one six-foot table. And my question was, what do you need chefs for? And he was like, I thought it would be fun [to work with another chef]. We couldn't really get these small amounts of stuff from purveyors, so we would go to Green City, and Whole Foods, and we basically split up the menu and each of us would find half. And we would do these little twelve- to fifteen-course dinners. It was super awkward. Phillip's kind of an awkward guy, I'm a little quiet. And the kitchen's, I guess, quiet or loud, however you look at it. But it was very interesting.

So it was basically three chefs and Bill [Drewett, server], every night. And that was it. And we slowly just kept expanding like, okay, well, let's just put another table over in this corner. And I think we ended up at about like sixteen or eighteen seats or something like that. So we expanded it from like, eight seats when we open to another ten or twelve. And to be honest with you, it works really well.

The first few weeks were kind of rough. I think people were like, what is this? I don't get it. Schwa was already doing it, but Schwa was this special diamond in the rough, like, a weird, beautiful place. We weren't trying to be that at all, but people couldn't figure out what to compare it to.

LANE REGAN: I contacted the people who had written about my pierogi, I think it was Popsugar that was really popular then, and a couple of blogs because that was when blogs were huge. I said, you guys want to come to the launch of this underground thing I'm doing? And so I had like a little press dinner. And then they all went and wrote about it afterwards. And then somebody came from LTHForum and took pictures. That was huge to get the word out. That filled me up for four or five months, because I think people were really clamoring for those kinds of experiences.

When I started I thought, we're going to do these communal tables because that's how I did it at my house and people loved it. But people would just show up to a restaurant, and not everyone wanted to do that. And sometimes if you got one bad seed, it could spoil the whole bunch. So within six months we decided to do separate tables, and went to one menu instead of three menus.

SCOTT NOORMAN: [Lane] had a couple of customers that offered to invest and that's when they got that little space in Lincoln Square. They asked if I would come on board and I said, I would love to do your wine and be in charge of service. I hired two guys, and we took care of it. It was just a nice little family. And we worked well, I had fun until my health took such a dive that I couldn't do it anymore. I was doing dialysis four hours a day, and then going into twelve- or fifteen-hour shifts. I went back to Grand Rapids, I didn't have the stamina to do Chicago anymore.

WILSON BAUER: The diners [at Schwa] are definitely fun. I think people come here to have more fun, the food's great, we want to have fun too.

I think it's had to become that way. Diners, it seems, aren't putting so much importance on just being waited on, being served. They don't care if all their dishes are cleared at the same time. Some people do, and there's places for them. I like when you see everybody come out at the same time, and it's like, holy shit. Such coordination, it's nice to see that. But I don't think most people care so much for that any more, and I don't think they're willing to pay $500 for that any more. Food's become more expensive, service has become more expensive, so you gotta start cutting something somewhere.

As he hit his forties, Carlson shifted his focus to raising his daughter—and mentoring the next generation of rock and roll cooks.

MICHAEL CARLSON: I don't think my body could take much more, to be honest. I'm surprised I've lived this long. I'm on my 122nd step, at this point, of all the different step programs. People go out to party. We party here—we party at work. And when you spend sixty-plus hours a week at work, it's pretty hard to maintain that for a long amount of time. But we usually have a good, eclectic mix of random people.

I'm here every morning. I answer phones a lot in the mornings, or I'll go get these guys [in the kitchen] whatever they need, do a lot of shopping. We're also starting to grow our own stuff now. We have a huge space sort of close to here that we're utilizing to grow our own shit. We've got a lot of space to play with. Right now, we cruise around on hoverboards and skateboards. But it's just a great evolution of a restaurant in a little space, because what more can we do?

WILSON BAUER: We're still the same people, but . . . we have kids now. It's more stabilized, it's more consistent now. We plan our closures a little more often. It's still the same Schwa.

It's funny seeing all the places that are opening up now. There's so many more options to go to. And that I think can make it more difficult, but it also educates the diner better, so they're more open to try new things. Oh, I saw that ingredient over there, so I know it's going to be okay. It's not like, wait, you're serving barnacles? There's more education out there with more of this caliber of restaurants, which is awesome.

MICHAEL CARLSON: Working at a place like this is an education. If this is the end goal of what you want, and you want to open a small restaurant, you better fucking work in a small restaurant, man, and see what it's like to wake up and not only receive orders, but shit . . . you're your own PR person, writing the bills, paying stuff. It's a lot to do, man. If that's your endgame, it's stupid not to spend some significant time doing it.

Obviously you're trying to give every diner an experience that they're going to remember, that's your main objective. But you have a responsibility to the kids that are working for low pay to learn, and what they do learn is how to be taken out of their element in the middle of service and be able to speak to people, be knowledgeable about all dishes, knowledgeable about wine.

I mean, the shit that people bring in here [to drink]—the majority of the people always share it. You have the potential of trying eight, ten wines a night. And if you have the capacity to maintain that information or to write that shit down, that's an education in itself, at the cost of the people who come in—their generosity of sharing with you.

There's a lot going on back there. To see the kids, the younger kids who haven't been acclimated to dealing with people, it's fucking amazing. It's amazing people-watching. I could just watch that half the time.

When Alinea co-founder Nick Kokonas launched the reservation/ticketing service Tock, Regan was one of the few using it innovatively.

LANE REGAN: With Elizabeth, we experimented and we tested and we were learning a lot along the way. I was certainly learning a lot along the way. And I think people saw that like us just trying to be earnest and for the most part trying to be humble about it.

We went along with that Tock thing of dynamic pricing, to get the volume that we wanted on weekdays. [Tock let you charge more for, say, Friday at seven o'clock than Wednesday at five thirty—a feature many were afraid to try.] We knew what all of our costs are. We knew what our electricity was in the summer, and we knew what it was in the winter. We knew our bottom line, and so we knew how to vary our prices and how many people we need to get in.

That was sometimes why we adjusted the ticket prices, but if it was something that we were really experimenting on, I would say, let's make this inexpensive and play around. People might not love every single course that comes out, but they love that we were pushing ourselves and things like that. And I think we were often very honest with people about that, too. Like, this is a brand-new dish. We've never put it together before. And you're having it right now. How is it?

PHILLIP FOSS: Go big or go home. If you don't have that attitude as an entrepreneur, you're not going to make it. But it's about a lot more than that. You have to make decisions on the fly as a business owner, which is harrowing. Trying to direct anything right is hard . . . whether it's kids, a relationship, or a business.

14: EVERYBODY'S A CRITIC

By the 1970s, restaurant criticism nationwide had become almost a kind of priesthood, with strict rules for participation—like anonymity or requiring multiple visits—that barred ordinary diners from the right to have a public opinion. In reality, not all paid reviewers followed these "rules" to the letter either, but there was plenty of outrage from the professionals when the New York-based Zagat guides first gave the hoi polloi a chance to talk back to critical darlings in print. It was a step toward democracy for food opinions—but a small one; at most you might hope to get a single adjective, your "festive" or "formulaic," into the maroon-covered guide. And in Chicago, the editor of your amateur opinions was none other than Tribune *reviewer Phil Vettel.*

But as internet usage took off in the 2000s, more and more amateur opinions on food found audiences on blogs, chat sites like Chowhound and Chicago's LTHForum, and on television (like Chicago's hugely popular Check, Please!*). Along with giving regular diners a platform, these new outlets shifted the focus of food attention from downtown fine dining to the neighborhoods and the varieties of international cuisine to be found throughout the city. Here's how writing and talking about food changed in the new millennium.*

BLOGGERS AND FREELANCERS

MICHAEL MOROWITZ (technology professional): This was before anybody cheffy was doing anything downscale—hot dog places were hot dog places, and if you went down to Hyde Park there were like three restaurants. About 2002, Hot Doug's was a few blocks from our condo. And he was empty all the time. No one knew about him, not a soul. Lane Tech students *kind* of knew about it.

So I would go in there for lunch, and I learned when the Lane Tech lunch periods were, so I knew how to navigate around them. And he'd have no one else in there. And I remember sitting in there, eating good stuff and wondering why the place was empty. I was reading the *Reader*, and it might have been either a Mike Sula or a Laura Levy Shatkin article about Moto.

Doug saw what I was reading and he shouted to me, read the story about that restaurant in Fulton Market. He just couldn't stop laughing about edible menus and food in syringes, he thought it was the funniest thing ever, just ridiculous. He had nothing to do, so we sat and joked about Moto.

And I went home and talked to my wife about what a great place it is, and how it was like he was the host of the place. And I thought, someone needs to help publicize this guy a little more. And she's like, why don't you start a blog. I was all, *eh*, I don't wanna be the guy . . . she said, well, just don't put your name on it, pick another name. So I just started Eatchicago.net basically overnight. And if Hot Doug's wasn't my first post, he was my second.

NICK KINDELSPERGER (blogger/freelance writer): I have an English writing degree, and I worked at newspapers when I was in high school. My high school cut the newspaper because they ran out of money, and then they were like, oh Nick, do you want to work at the local newspaper? Madison, Indiana, which is like thirteen thousand people, has the *Madison Courier*, so I worked there for a summer and I thought oh, I like this. So I thought, I'll just work in newspapers.

And then by 2006, no newspapers were hiring. People like me thought, well, I'm just never going to get a job in a newspaper. I moved to New York after college, with no plans. I became obsessed with this book by Ed Levine called *A Slice of Heaven,* where he just visits different pizzerias in New York. So my roommates and I did that. We looked in the book and we're like, oh my God, you can go to this one in the Bronx, and this one on Staten Island. And that sort of led us to start a food blog called The Paupered Chef. Which was about restaurant food, but then also cooking at home, because we were broke.

MICHAEL NAGRANT (IT consultant): When I first moved here, I contacted *NewCity* [an alt-weekly]. And I pitched them on me going to the 'NSync show. Because, you know, I was in my early twenties, and I'm a guy, so why would I be interested in 'NSync? It was really anthropological. And I thought I would start writing in earnest, but I had a real job at the time. Another couple of years passed, and then I contacted *RedEye* [free commuter tabloid published by the *Chicago Tribune*], and I wrote this essay about *The Real World.* And how I'd never missed an episode of *The Real World,* which is still true. So then I thought, I should start writing. Shortly thereafter, I quit my job.

This job that I quit, I started it in Cleveland. When I was still in Cleveland, one night I was in a Borders and I see this guy, sitting alone by himself in front of an empty group of chairs—a.k.a. an author who had a reading, and had almost no crowd. And I'm looking at the guy and sort of feeling vaguely sad for him, but also I'm intrigued, like, who's this guy? What's he doing? So I just grabbed a seat in the back.

And it turns out, the author was Michael Ruhlman. This is when he had released *The Soul of a Chef,* or whichever the first one was. So I just listened to him read. And I was like, oh, my God, this is amazing. This is at a point where I'm going to Michael Symon restaurants and teaching myself to cook because it's literally a year out of college.

I moved here partly for the job, but also partly because like everybody else, I was super entranced by Charlie Trotter. This guy was elevating cuisine in America in a way that no other American chef was, and I needed to see that, I needed to be part of that.

Somewhere in the third month after quitting, I read about Butter opening up in the West Loop, literally two blocks from my house. And about this guy named Ryan Poli who'd worked in Spain, nobody knew who he was then. I don't know why I said to myself, you should go down there and tell a story about it. But I did. I think I walked down and knocked on the door—hey, is Ryan here? And they're like, who are you? And I'm like, I'm a journalist. Even though I didn't write for anybody or anything. So Ryan comes out and I'm like, dude, listen, I'd like to do a profile of you and your new restaurant. I'd really like to tell your story. He says, come back tomorrow, we'll sit down.

I had a little Canon or Olympus recorder. I don't even know why I knew I needed a recorder, I probably should have just brought a notebook. And I put it down between us. And we talked for probably like five hours. I start writing a five-thousand-word profile, and I pitched the *Chicago Journal*, which was a pink broadside in the West Loop. I think they paid me like a hundred bucks, two hundred bucks, which was good money for those days. I think maybe I can do this. And so then I started pitching people, and as you can imagine, I got like four hundred Nos.

NICK KINDELSPERGER: The Paupered Chef was one of those things that just kept getting us other jobs. I would write and then someone would link to it—I don't know how that happened—and then Gothamist was looking for new food reporters, so I worked for Gothamist for a year doing stories.

I was doing The Paupered Chef in New York for a few years, and then Ed Levine started Serious Eats. I recognized Adam Kuban in line at the Shake Shack, back when there was only one Shake Shack. He was with Ed Levine, and Ed said to me, you should write for Serious Eats. In New York, Serious Eats was really on the forefront of that style of, we'll eat anything. We'll go anywhere and try anything. And that was really exciting, especially for a kid from a town of two thousand people in Indiana. To be in New York, and to be like, well, let's go to Brooklyn and go to Sunset Park, which is their Chinatown which is bigger than the other Chinatown, in Manhattan, and eat all the food.

MICHAEL NAGRANT: Even though I had written that piece, nobody knew who I was. So I decided I'm going to start a website. And that's when I started Hungry Magazine. I treated it like a blog when I was already hyper-aware that blogs were accelerating and I didn't just want to be like a *blog* blog. I had four hours of Ryan Poli, so I thought, I'll publish this as a podcast. At this point nobody knows what a podcast is. I edited it down and it's like the first podcast I ran on my website. And I got pretty good response. So I'm gonna do podcasts, like hour-long NPR-style interviews with chefs.

Probably my fourth one was Paul Kahan. Because to me, Paul Kahan was the Velvet Underground and all that shit. And Paul's like, hey, I'm working on a new project. And I say, is that this oyster-pork-beer thing? And he goes, yeah, yeah. How do you know about this? I'm like, there's rumors.

Now Paul doesn't know what a podcast is. I barely know what a podcast is. He doesn't think anybody's gonna hear this, I don't think anybody's gonna hear this. He's completely unguarded.

An hour [after the podcast goes live] I get a call from Penny Pollack. I have no idea who Penny Pollack is. Because again, I'm not a food journalist. I'm not really following anybody yet. She says, who *are* you? Literally her first question. I go, who are *you?* And she goes, I'm the editor of the *Chicago* magazine food section. I was like, oh, cool. She's like, why did Paul tell you about this new restaurant? And I literally say, no guile or nothing, I guess 'cause I asked. And she's like, okay, well, nice job. So, Dish newsletter, like later that week, Paul Kahan's opening this place, he mentioned it in this podcast called, blah, blah, blah.

Eventually Jeff Ruby [assistant to Penny Pollack] calls me and he goes, hey, come in to *Chicago* magazine. Dick Babcock, the editor in chief, wants to meet with you. Babcock asks me what the podcast is, and I explain it and tell him what I envision is, I could do one podcast a month for the magazine, you'd excerpt the best Q and A's, publish the podcast on the *Chicago* magazine website, but I would retain simultaneous rights, I'd still put it on Hungry. What do you guys think about that?

Three weeks later, the *New York Times* had a piece about podcasting. Jeff says Babcock called him in and goes, hey, isn't that the thing that guy was talking about? And so that's how I ended up getting the *Chicago* magazine gig.

MICHAEL MOROWITZ: Something that happened between like 2003, when there was almost nobody writing, blogging, digitally about Chicago food, everything was happening either in the *Tribune* or the *Reader*, or their sites like Metromix. And by the time you hit, like, 2008, it became a business. Five short years. And once your expertise becomes marketable, things start looking different.

HEATHER SHOUSE (freelancer): I went to Columbia College in Chicago for journalism. My goal and the reason I went to journalism school was I wanted to be a music writer. Like every music writer, I thought I was Lester Bangs.

And this is kind of when food writing was getting a little bit less stuffy. At the time, the food critic for *Chicago Social* was retiring, so the editor in chief said to me, don't you work in restaurants? And I said, yeah, I've worked in restaurants since I was fifteen. And she said, well, we want somebody to start writing about food the way that they would write about music. I didn't even honestly know that food writing was a possibility or an option or a career. They wanted to start a recurring column, and I wanted to do stuff on places that have been around forever. So they called it "Old Favorites"—I think the first one I did was on Jean-Claude Poilevey at Le Bouchon.

I think the walls were kind of coming down between this *Ratatouille* idea of the snobby food critic who's in disguise and just waiting to rip a restaurant apart, and a little bit more focus on immersive reporting, like getting to know who's behind the restaurant. There was more credit being given to mom-and-pop restaurants and ethnic food in Chicago because of exposure on national TV.

ARI BENDERSKY (music writer): I was writing about music, for *RedEye* and Metromix. And working at Vivo, and still doing writing for the gay press. And I started building more interest in other things. I didn't want to just write about music and gay issues and gay topics. So that's when I started my blog, SomethingGlorious.com. Where my tagline was "Things that I love that you should love, too." Because people always came to me for recommendations of like, new music or a new restaurant to go to with friends or for a date, or like a bottle of wine.

All that is why Eater came to me [to be editor of a Chicago edition]. They were scrappy. They had attitude. They had like a New York positioning and sensibility and a "we don't care what you think about how we're going to write about you" sort of a perspective. They had a feature in New York, that was called "Death Watch." And it was basically like, reporting on a restaurant's last legs and nailing the last nail in the coffin. And I told them that wasn't gonna fly. I said, I don't want to do that, that's not who I am. I don't want to put somebody out of business. I want to help support restaurants.

If there was something that merited being reported on, like a breakup within a restaurant, somebody's leaving—like when Koren [Grieveson] left avec, and I called One Off to get a statement. And they asked me to hold off and I said, look, I'm running the story, regardless of whether you want to comment or not, I'm just giving you the opportunity. And then they gave me a statement. One of my closest friends worked at Blackbird and was close with David and Anna Posey. David was the executive chef at Blackbird at the time. And when I announced I was leaving Eater, he turned to my friend and goes, how are we going to find out what's going on in our company?

NICK KINDELSPERGER: When I came to Chicago, there were places like LTHForum, and the discussion wasn't necessarily what's the hot restaurant downtown, it was what's going on at all these other places. But that was a forum, and the blogs were more of a newspaper, magazine-y kind of format, which is what I grew up doing. I was always very interested in the writing aspect of it. I grew up with a writing major, and my friend and I would edit each other extensively to try to get it to sound as good as it could be. I always gravitated toward publications where you could tell they were great writers.

The newspapers were playing a different game. Kevin Pang [at the *Tribune*] did a pretty good job of trying to focus on other things [than upscale restaurants], but it felt like he was the only one. Pat Bruno was at the *Sun-Times*, and I've heard people say really nice things about him, but his writing was really poor at that time. It just felt like the newspapers were stuck in time. They were like, oh shit, things are going bad. So we're just going to freeze everyone who's here in place.

Helen Rosner was doing Grub Street Chicago [daily restaurant news and gossip site, competitive with Eater], and I loved what she was doing, and I thought I could do that. So I took it over when she left, and it turned out I couldn't. I just didn't care. It was all restaurant news and not food, and I thought I could be okay at it, but I wasn't interested in, this is what this person said about that thing. Where's the things to eat, that's all I ever cared about.

MICHAEL NAGRANT: The *Chicago Tribune* magazine did an article about molecular gastronomy. And the cover photo was basically like, Grant Achatz sitting at a table with his bow tie askew like some like drunken Rat Packer, and there was this hot model slumped over on the table next to him. And I wrote this scathing column about how Grant's a serious chef, and he looks like he's just gotten a blowjob from this model. And it just doesn't make sense for their brand. It really was me saying, I care about this food, maybe more than you guys do, or as much as you do. I was very earnest.

Nick [Kokonas, co-owner of Alinea] called me and was like, I don't disagree with you. I appreciate what you're saying and we should keep in touch. And I think I said, I'm young, I'm stupid, I don't know any better. And I say, are you guys doing a cookbook? And he goes, well, we've talked about it. And I say, well, if you ever do, keep me in mind.

Three months later, I get another call from Nick. He's like, so we're working on a cookbook. We're working with another writer. And I really liked that you care about our brand the way we do, I like what you're doing, I'd like you to be a part of it. But because we have a short window, we're gonna call in a bunch of other writers.

And I was like, oh, okay, that's cool. Who are the other writers? And he says, well, Michael Ruhlman for one. And so it came full circle.

CHEAP EATS AND FOOD TV

In the 1990s and early 2000s, print coverage of food in Chicago, in the Tribune *and* Sun-Times *and* Chicago *magazine, was focused on fine dining and the downtown scene, though there was a small area carved out for lower-priced ethnic dining—"Cheap Eats," as they were invariably called. Cheap Eats were popular with readers but a bit of a poor relation inside the* Tribune*—as typified by the fact that they didn't get star ratings like upscale restaurants, they got one to four "forks."*

When TV started covering food seriously in the '90s and 2000s, it focused on the whole city—and the so-called cheap eats, with their ethnic variety and roots in neighborhoods all over the city, proved to be naturals for TV.

MONICA ENG (*Chicago Tribune* reporter): When I got to the *Tribune* I was one of the Friday [weekend entertainment and nightlife] section editors. And I already had an interest in food. One of my first assignments was called the "Be There" page. They wanted me to include lots of little fun stories about things to do that weekend that the *Sun-Times* would not have. And I had been at the *Sun-Times* for years before I came to the *Tribune*, and I knew we were all working off the same press releases. So how on earth am I going to come up with different events? I mean, if some festival's happening, we're probably all gonna have it.

But I said, well, how about if I feature a dumpling a week and call it "The Dumpling Zone?" The *Sun-Times* won't have that. And my editor says, ha ha, yeah, that'll last for a couple of weeks. I think I did at least a year of just dumplings. Things wrapped in starch.

Along the way Carol Mighton Haddix [food section editor] said, hey, are you interested in helping us out with the Cheap Eats thing? And I said, sure. I've always been drawn to interesting and new things that I hadn't tried before. And one of the early ones was Fish Pond [Filipino restaurant] on Clark, a friend told me about their *kamayan* dinners on Fridays. It's a seafood-based dinner that you eat on banana leaves. And I proposed it to Carol and she was okay with it. And maybe the second or third paragraph, I was writing about *dinuguan*, which is a pork blood and pork organ dish. She sends the review back to me and she said, nobody is going to keep reading this thing if it's so disgusting in the first few graphs. You have to move it down. She wasn't against it being in there, it just needed to be where it couldn't kill the readership.

I thought wow, okay. I guess *Tribune* readers don't have the strongest stomachs when it comes to weird ethnic foods. But I remember Bill [Rice] writing to me, saying, Monica, you're bringing in a whole bunch of restaurants that the reviewers never really went to, or never cared about. I love this breath of fresh air. I thought, cool. I'll take that lane if nobody else is taking it.

STEVE DOLINSKY (TV reporter): CLTV [regional cable news network from Tribune Media] started in 1993, and I was one of the first reporters they hired, based in the Drake Hotel a block away from our studio in Oak Brook. They were hiring young reporters with a year or two of experience under their belts, who they could afford, cheap. I was one of the only ones that lived in the city, because I was so hooked on food by then. I purposely lived above The King Crab on Halsted.

A year and a half later, my bosses announced that we were going to do a TV version of the *Tribune*'s food section, which they're going to change from a Thursday edition, they're gonna have it come out on a Wednesday and call it "Good Eating," and they wanted to launch a cable companion with the launch of the food section. And I came on as a producer. And they said, are you sure you want to be off the air as a reporter? I'm like, yeah, I'm done. News reporting. My heart is not in this. Because like the first week I was at CLTV, I covered the Brown's Chicken massacre in Palatine [a mass murder at a fast food restaurant in 1993]. You gotta have a thick skin for that.

To produce the show, I was going to work with the *Chicago Tribune*'s food staff and learn from them. I never went to culinary school, so this was great experience. If there was a cover story on Vietnamese food, I'd have to go to those same places that were in the story and talk to them and interview them. And spend a couple hours in a restaurant kitchen. So that was my education. Renee Enna was one of the reporters they had and she turned me on to Johnnie's Beef because she was from that part of town [Elmwood Park]. No one was really talking about it and certainly wasn't writing about it in mainstream media, but she'd written a Cheap Eats on it.

I took over as host and producer in '96. My thing was creating a weekly half-hour show based on that food section. So we did a Cheap Eats segment every week, because that was kind of an easy thing for us to do. I would pepper them with questions every week—what are you working on? What's coming up in a month? I'd walk by, sometimes they'd roll their eyes.

In the early 2000s, Dolinsky moved to ABC7, where he became "the Hungry Hound," his headshot pasted up in restaurants all over the city.

STEVE DOLINSKY: They canceled the Good Eating TV show in early '03. They ran out of money. They don't want to pay three people to do a half-hour show every week, that's getting good ratings. I was crushed. What am I ever going to do on television in Chicago? And I just put together my resume tape and figured if I can't get anybody locally to do it, then I'm really done.

I remember I met all the news directors, they all took the time to talk to me about it. And none of them could really see it. But at ABC7, Jennifer Graves saw the need for it.

Food Network had started in like '94, '95. So there were several years of talking about food on television, certainly. Charlie Trotter was at his peak. There was just more talk about food. I think in the early 2000s, people were realizing that it was a viable subject.

They gave me carte blanche, whatever you want to do. I got even more into strip mall food. I remember Mark Giangreco [sports anchor] made fun of me once. He's like, everything with you is strip malls. Hey, that's where the best food is. That's what I took pride in.

But people also want to know what's, like, cool and hot in River North. I just did Rose Mary. I mean, that's a restaurant that's booked two months out. But people want to see what's hot, and why is it hot? And what kind of food are they doing and what's going on in Chicago? It's not always just strip malls. Right? But I'm really cognizant of both. I think what I did really well at 7 over those years was just balance city, suburbs, high-end, low-end. There's a lot to cover here.

When Dolinsky started at ABC7, they had an old-school restaurant reviewer with a loyal following, James Ward.

STEVE DOLINSKY: So I met him a handful of times. We worked in the same building for a number of years. I was kind of persona non grata there with him. His editor was very kind to me, because we worked together at CLTV, but his producer, they felt like I was a threat. I can see that.

He was at ten o'clock on Friday nights. His title was restaurant critic, and I was food reporter. I didn't want to be a critic. I didn't feel comfortable with that title, ever. And so I kept doing my things, you know, interesting place in a strip mall, in a suburb. And he would do his, whatever he did. I always felt like his stories were more about him. And mine were about the food.

I've heard stories, obviously, about him showing up at Gordon and drinking quite a bit, and then packing everything up to go. Because he couldn't sit there for a while, he was too hammered. And giving the place a great review.

He showed up on the air I think a couple of times probably three sheets to the wind. It was another era, it really was.

Ward died in 2009. Steve Dolinsky stayed at ABC7 for seventeen years, winning thirteen James Beard awards for his TV and podcast work, before leaving the station in February 2021. In August 2021, he joined NBC 5 as "The Food Guy."

In 2001, at Chicago's PBS station, WTTW, a new TV show started giving regular diners a voice on television. Check, Please! *featured three ordinary diners, each of whom would recommend a restaurant which the others would try. Then they'd discuss what they thought of them. In nineteen years the show recommended more than six hundred restaurants in every part of the metro area, exposing viewers not just to restaurants but to parts of town they'd never visited—and to Chicagoans from all walks of life.*

DAVID MANILOW (TV producer): I always produced sports. I worked for a thing called Sportsvision, which is now NBC Sports Chicago. But I always loved restaurants, like I was the kid that would explore, tell the family, let's go here.

So one day, I'm in the shower. And I came up with the idea for the show. *Everything,* literally, about the show. To this day nothing has changed, I had the name, I had the whole concept of people recommending a restaurant, because I thought if I went to a restaurant and said, I'm doing a show where I have three regular people reviewing them, that they wouldn't want to participate. But I figured if I called them up and said, well, you've been *recommended*...

What I tried to do is curate a diverse group. So you got different perspectives. You can relate to them, you can not relate to them. And that's fine either way. And I think what ended up happening is we expanded people's comfort zones a little bit. There's people that only would eat in their own little neighborhood. But once you see a place, and you hear from somebody who you can maybe relate to, you're kind of like, oh, I'll try the Ecuadorian place. I'll go try that. I've never had Vietnamese food, but I know what the chef looks like, I know what to order. That guy ordered the so-and-so and he liked it, and I liked him.

We didn't have much in the way of instructions for them. Right before they'd go out, we'd tell them, you're the passionate recommender, defender, that's it—go have a good time. People in Chicago *are* passionate. They're passionate about their neighborhoods and passionate about the type of food they like. And I think for the most part, what I tried to do is show and explore and love the city in the show.

I never did a lot of follow-up with the restaurants—like, what was your jump in business? I just didn't, but they would always tell me, oh my god, we look at the credit card receipts and we see the zip codes where people are coming from, I never had people coming from there before.

The original host was Amanda Puck, then-sister-in-law of chef Wolfgang Puck, who came to Chicago to help open and manage a Chicago outlet of Spago. Beginning with season 3, it was hosted by Alpana Singh, who had been sommelier at Everest and later director of wine and spirits for Lettuce Entertain You.

DAVID MANILOW: Amanda was great. I really liked working with Amanda. She would have a different hairstyle every week. Amanda was very front-of-house, she liked the whole idea of running a restaurant, so she understood customer service. We had a lot of fun.

Alpana got into more depth, I think. She would talk about immigration patterns and how that affected, say, Peruvian food. And obviously she had incredible wine and spirits knowledge. But we always wanted the show to be light and fun, which I think it was.

There was one Check, Please! *episode that didn't air at the time—though it was broadcast years later, after one of the three guests, a state senator from the South Side, had become president of the United States.*

DAVID MANILOW: So that was about the fifth show we did. I believe we taped it before any show had actually aired. The first four shows were magic. Like this is the easiest thing that was ever done, like I don't even have to be here. So then all of a sudden, *he* comes out. The fireman completely freezes, doesn't speak. The store clerk, same. Obama wasn't anybody yet; it was just his charisma.

Now, if we shot that show last week, exact same show, we would know how to make that show work. Even though we had two out of three guests not be great. More B-roll of food, we'd figure it out. But back then we're like, soft.

So just push it to the side, and little did we know, right?

Check, Please! *lasted nineteen seasons, but stopped production during the lockdown in early 2020, and finally announced that it was ending in August 2021.*

DAVID MANILOW: We had the same contract for nineteen years—I barely knew what was in it by then. And I pretty much ran the show and I've worked very closely with a lot of their staff. We had a wonderful relationship that didn't have much to do with their management. And then the management kind of changed, and with that they wanted to change a lot of the texture of the show, who ran the show, and I did not think that the scenario that they were presenting was good for the brand. Good for the show. And they gave me a little bit of my way or the highway. I'm not sure they were prepared for the show going away, but if you give somebody a take it or leave it, you should be prepared for the leave it.

CHICAGO READER

For years the main guide to local restaurants was Chicago magazine's back section listings. Around the turn of the millennium, as the internet became where you went for help picking out a restaurant to go to, the city's longest-lasting alt-weekly, the Chicago Reader, *set out to create a competitor to Chicago's listings. To manage it, in 1998 they recruited freelancer Martha Bayne, who had written a piece for the* Reader *about her visit to Charlie Trotter's—firmly from a pre-foodie point of view of, why would anyone pay this much for dinner?*

MARTHA BAYNE: My work on the Restaurant Finder was directly informed by this Charlie Trotter piece I'd done. When I started working with the *Reader*, I didn't know anything about food. I did not go to what I considered fancy restaurants at all. Completely out of my price range, completely out of the scope of things I was interested in doing. I thought it was pretty ethically dubious in some ways. Yeah, I was young and snotty.

I had contributed some calendar items, and I was hired specifically to help launch the *Reader* Restaurant Finder, which was in development. But for the early months of my time with the *Reader*, all I did was edit those little restaurant capsules. We needed that material to launch and have a body of writing. It's hard to think now, but this was before Yelp and all those things. It was really the first online searchable restaurant finder-type thing in Chicago, where you could put in like, "I'm looking for Italian food near Steppenwolf," and then you plug in the parameters and up pops a couple of restaurants.

In the print edition we would run like thirty or so of these capsule reviews, and there'd be a reported piece about a new restaurant that was opening or an interview with a chef. I think we struggled a little bit with trying to just figure out how much restaurant reviewing in the classical kind of *Tribune*, *Chicago* magazine way we actually wanted to do. That was a little bit of an identity crisis. I don't know if we ever landed on a good place.

There was one writer who was hired to create all this content so we could launch the site, Laura Levy Shatkin, but we also planned to have reader-supplied reviews—it was sort of an early model for that. The idea was that they were not professional writers, although the line between that became really blurry, with contributors from LTHForum [online chat site] and everything. But the idea was, it would be like citizen journalism—that was how we wanted to distinguish it from Phil Vettel or *Chicago* magazine or things like that.

There was this idea among a lot of people at the *Reader* that the whole notion of a critic going into a restaurant anonymously, and writing a review was just sort of like a performative thing that wasn't real. But Mike Sula [reporter] got very interested in that—that's how he got into food writing. He was involved with LTHForum, and really saw a lot of other directions the food section could go, other than the standard restaurant review type things—"try the veal."

We also started to do an annual food issue, in the early '00s. It was really fun when we had the space, in the salad days, to do these really offbeat essays about food and restaurants and restaurant culture. We did a good job of filling in a niche, journalistically, that the *Tribune* and *Chicago* magazine weren't filling, really writing about experiences of eating through literary lenses. We did a piece about the tableware at Alinea. And then because I was the restaurants editor, I got to do things like review Alinea when it opened.

Which was sort of a weird contradiction. But by then we were trying to be comprehensive in our coverage. And so that meant covering fine dining as well as neighborhood joints. I think it strayed sort of from the counterculture ethic of the *Reader* in many ways. But we were also looking at it as, they're interesting business stories. And it was obviously such an important part of Chicago culture, it seemed impossible to ignore. So we just tried to do it in an interesting way. In a *Reader*-y way, however you define that.

I've been thinking about the Trotter essay, or a second one I did for *The Baffler,*[30] a lot lately, because I feel like the conversation about food has come full circle twice since I wrote that piece. I really feel like I should get some credit! Now everybody's turning on foodies. Again. Like the worm turned around 2008, I think, when the recession hit, and now it's happening again—look at [the 2022 movie] *The Menu.*

Bayne, having started the Reader *on that path, left the paper in 2007. The* Reader *hit a high point in food coverage in the late 2000s and early 2010s, winning three James Beard awards between 2010 and 2013—to Mike Sula and to Cliff Doerksen for longform pieces, and to Julia Thiel and this author for a print/video multimedia series, "Key Ingredient." But it also faced the decline in advertising that afflicted all alt-weeklies, as well as the cuts that came with a succession of corporate owners. The* Reader *continues today as a non-profit, but its days of rich dining budgets are past.*

CHOWHOUND AND LTHFORUM

The first notable online food discussion forum for amateurs in Chicago was a Usenet group in the days of 9600 baud dial-up, Chi.eats. A few who participated there would go on to form a core group at the Chicago board of Chowhound.com, a site founded by a New York musician named Jim Leff. Leff's vision for the site was that diners would dine secretly and individually, and report their experiences online.

But Chicago users of the site soon made it more sociable, planning group dinners at obscure ethnic restaurants on the board, and spreading word of their discoveries to attract new members—and media attention. Authentic Chinese food in Chinatown, regional Mexican food from carts at the Maxwell Street Market, African American barbecue stands doing true woodsmoke barbecue,

30 "Charles the Excellent," *The Baffler*, November 2002

Thai dishes previously available only to Thai customers via "secret" menus—these were some of the neighborhood offerings, modestly priced but deeply rooted in immigrant cultures, that would be prized—and publicized—by these Chicago "Chowhounds," soon to be known as "LTHers" once LTHForum was founded in the early 2000s.

PETER ENGLER (biology researcher at the University of Chicago; screen name "ReneG"): Back then, I was using the internet for science—imagine that. And a colleague, who was working in the same room that I was, had been posting on Chi.eats, and he mentioned it to me and sort of showed me how to get started.

I started doing it because I was writing grants at the time. And writing grants is not fun. Some days, I would sit in my office and produce four sentences after sweating and struggling all day. So I decided to start posting to Chi.eats, just as a way to prove to myself that I could write and get something done. And I also emphasized South Side things, because at the time I was working ridiculous hours in the lab, you know, sixteen-hour days were not at all uncommon. But every now and then I'd have a few hours where I had nothing to do so I'd just go out and wander around, get something to eat. And it dawned on me that there was interesting food culture on the South Side that nobody was writing about.

This was when Monica Eng's "Dumpling Zone" started. She covered places that would not get covered. Her column started out with just a specific type of dumpling, focusing on one, usually Asian restaurant, every week. She was doing stuff that nobody else in Chicago was doing. That was an influence, I think.

ROB GARDNER (legal researcher; screen name "Vital Information"): I was on Chi.eats briefly, real briefly. The problem with that era online, and that sensibility, was that it was computer user first, eater second. And I came to it as someone interested in food. When Chi.eats started, you needed special software just to access it, but then you could get on with your AOL account. And to me, it was like, look at all the new stuff, and to them, it was, ugh, the barbarians are here. So I never really felt that welcome, that there was anything interesting going on or any sense of community there.

I found out about Chowhound because I think there was a *New Yorker* article, pre-9/11.[31] I responded to some post on Hugo's Frog Bar. And there was no response, so it didn't seem like it was really worthwhile. I wasn't really following it, but maybe I was looking at it occasionally. And then there was some post on, like, the Clark Street area in Rogers Park, up where Taste of Peru is. And I changed my screen name, which was originally just RG—we had to be anonymous, I don't know why, but back then, it's the internet, you had to be anonymous. So then I switched it to Vital Information, which I had been using online at places like Slate, and it's also my business tagline. I thought, it's catchy, it will draw people's attention to what I'm posting.

So I posted something, "If you like this place, try"—and I rattled off about five places in the stretch. And that post got a lot of play. So all of a sudden I got that validation. That was my first big win, like a gambler—ooh, people liked my recommendations!

DAVID HAMMOND (freelance writer): After 9/11, a lot of us were turning inward a bit, staying at home, warm and cozy, and not going out in a world filled with terrorists. Also, and even more tangibly, a lot of my business, which was writing materials for annual sales meetings, went down the tubes because no one was having annual sales meetings for eight months or so after September 11. I read an article by the *New Yorker* writer Calvin Trillin which talked about Chowhound, and it sounded pretty cool. So I started posting on it and lo and behold, I loved it.

It was thrilling and new to be able to meet people for the first time and have their backstory already, to know where they went to school and what kind of job they had, but more importantly, what they liked to eat, because I had already met them on Chowhound. This is before Facebook, before Twitter, before OKCupid, before all those sites that are designed to get people together in real life. That was *not* the goal on Chowhound—the goal on Chowhound was to keep people talking on Chowhound.

PETER ENGLER: I actively avoided trying to meet people at first. Meeting somebody through the internet was just weird, kind of unsavory in some ways.

31 "New Grub Streets," Calvin Trillin. *The New Yorker*, August 26, 2001.

CHEEKU BIDANI (database developer; screen name "Zim Bida"): In 2000, when I moved back here, I was looking for places to eat, and you could look at *Chicago* magazine. But when I searched for two places, La Pasadita and Harold's Chicken Shack, the only site that popped up with both of them was Chowhound.

SHARON BAUTISTA (technology worker, screen name "Happy Stomach"): I've been a computer geek all my life. And so for me, one of the main things that the rise of the Internet gave me, as a teenager living in the suburbs of Chicago, was that you could find other people who had your interest, even if you had nobody like that around you—*especially* if you had nobody like that around you. I think that I was able to find a community like [the Chicago Chowhound group], because I was just really into finding communities online. Even as a twenty-one-year-old, they were much older than I was and had a very different life context, but we could talk about things that we both geeked out about.

You need other people to connect you to things. There's still very much a human need for human curation and points of view.

The Chicago Chowhound group started inviting strangers from the internet to meet up, beginning with a dinner planned at a Chinatown restaurant, Lao Sze Chuan.

PETER ENGLER: I went to Lao Sze Chuan in its early days, I think I learned a bit about it from a *Tribune* review by Monica Eng. Right away I knew this place was special, and back then a lot of the menu wasn't translated. So I went out and got a copy of James McCawley's[32] *Eater's Guide to Chinese Characters*—at that time it was out of print and going for like $200, so I actually got a copy from the University of Chicago Library, and xeroxed it.

32 University of Chicago linguistics professor (who did *not* speak Chinese) whose xeroxed list of notable ethnic restaurants was circulated among the cognoscenti in pre-internet days. He might have been an important early figure in online food discourse had he not died of a heart attack while bicycling in 1999.

ROB GARDNER: What was so astonishing about that dinner at Lao Sze Chuan, and meeting Cheeku and so on—you think you know all this stuff, but then, what the hell, what are *they* talking about? It was a lot of fun to be exposed to people of similar passions.

CHEEKU BIDANI: Just by virtue of being Indian, I was given a level of authority [on Indian food] that I may or may not have deserved. People would defer to me at events. That doesn't mean they always did, like everyone went to Khan BBQ [a Pakistani restaurant in Rogers Park], but I remember trying to get people to go to this Goan place in the burbs, and I don't think anyone ever went there. But it was kind of cool to get people to realize that Indian food is more than one cuisine, you know, that there are different types of Indian.

DAVID HAMMOND: We had a certain iconoclastic attitude that the current food writers—in 2001, 2002—were really out of touch. And that part of our job was to put people in touch with all the deliciousness that was around them, that was not necessarily in higher-end restaurants, but could be found most readily at little mom-and-pop places which were also better reflectors of the cultures that those foods represented. There was a certain joy in slaughtering sacred cows.

And some of that attitude rubbed off on the general population—that *you* have valid food opinions, and you can go out and try new foods and have opinions about them, even if you don't really know that much about them.

MICHAEL MOROWITZ (screen name "Eatchicago"): There were a number of other things that happened through Chowhound or LTH—Sharon Bautista hosted a Filipino thing in her backyard. She and her sister basically made a Filipino buffet. We did a huge dark chocolate tasting at our house. These are the kinds of things that gourmet clubs all over the country do, but there was a five-year period of just being with people who liked eating things that weren't Cheesecake Factory.

SHARON BAUTISTA: I didn't really know who anyone was, right? In most cases, I really had no idea of someone's race or ethnicity or age or location a lot of the time. And I think that would be true for people perceiving me and how I present in terms of my ethnicity [Filipina]. Part of the reason I joined the community was because I'm interested in ethnic food, which is a weird category. Chowhound and LTHForum were actually much more tolerant and inclusive of people like me, and people outside of the majority, than food cultures elsewhere, or food-centered communities elsewhere.

CATHERINE LAMBRECHT (optical instruments importer; screen name "Cathy2"): It was a lot of information really fast, and you had to learn fast to keep up with everybody. It was very competitive. I mean, I did not know that Italian beef was from Chicago. It was just something we had occasionally, and I didn't think too much about it. I didn't realize that you could go from place to place and make a judgement on how they prepared their meat.

MICHAEL MOROWITZ: We used to do Italian beef tastings. We'd take all day on Saturday, go to like six beef places. It was a complete waste of time, because it was all the same beef, all the same bread.

ROB GARDNER: When we did the first translated menu, that was a big moment. My family and I had been going to Yum Thai, because it was one of the best Thai restaurants in the Oak Park area. And one day I notice that there's a Thai language menu, and I'm like, what's this? They were willing to tell me a couple things on it, but they didn't want to deal with translating it. And somewhere along the way, there was a woman, Robyn Eckhardt, "Food-First," who's since published a book on Turkish cooking.[33] Something came up about how she was learning Thai. Somehow there was communication that if we can get you this menu, could you translate it for us? And she was keen on doing that. That was exciting, because we were like, woo-woo, we've opened up a world that was hidden.

We were able to bring things to the table that regular food media couldn't do. Just by having sheer bodies, we were able to cover so much more stuff. If you're Phil Vettel or Pat Bruno, how much can you cover?

33 *Istanbul & Beyond: Exploring the Cuisines of Turkey,* Houghton Mifflin Harcourt, 2017.

MICHAEL MOROWITZ: The secret Thai menu translations [that followed Eckhardt's], by Erik M. Hill, were really amazing, because without them, to this day I still wouldn't know that what were considered the "secret menus" existed. I always questioned how secret they were, whether it was just hey, if you talk to someone who cooks, they'll tell you about the other things they cook.

The event that brought Chicago Chowhound to wider attention was an all-night dining event called the "24-Hour-a-Thon," which Monica Eng wrote up in the Tribune. *That brought in new participants and led to a series of other "Thons" in which a slice of the city would be picked over for food finds.*

ROB GARDNER: There were threads on the board about twenty-four-hour cabbie restaurants—which raised the question, how do you check out places that are at their best in the middle of the night? We had a sense that there's a whole world out there that you don't experience, and that led to the idea that we could eat for twenty-four hours straight. It was like the line from *Animal House*—"This requires a really stupid and futile gesture on somebody's part, and we're just the ones to do it." It took a while to work out the itinerary, figure out where to go that made sense and to rustle up enough interest. This is before Google Maps on your phone or anything—we did it all by compasses and sextants.

MONICA ENG: I was intrigued by these brainy nerds who had *so* much energy, enthusiasm and curiosity about Chicago food. Who were way more into it than even I was at the time. I asked my editor if I could cover it, and he said I'd need to go at a late hour to make it even more interesting. So I girded myself for a post-midnight meet up at San Soo Gab San [Korean restaurant]. I was not used to being up that late, so I was exhausted but exhilarated at the same time by their passion for Chicago food.

DAVID HAMMOND: When I would tell people we ate around the clock, twenty-four places in twenty-four hours, they'd frequently ask, were you sick afterwards? Hell, no! I was energized after spending a full day, around the clock, with food enthusiasts, talking about nothing but food, and eating a lot of it.

When I got home at noon—one full day after we started eating at Manny's—I nibbled down about a pound of jellybeans and watched *Tampopo*. I was not a bit tired of thinking about and eating food.

PETER ENGLER: We found we could take practically any street that most people don't give a second thought to, like 47th, and if you poke around, there's a lot to be found. The other thing that always makes me happy with showing visitors around, especially on the South Side, is that it's places where they've been told they shouldn't even go. People are always really amazed by the interesting food, and also, almost without fail, just how friendly everybody is. My guess is a lot of people on the 47th-a-Thon in particular had never set foot on those blocks. So for me that was a very conscious motive—helping people to get to know their own city.

As the Chowhound Chicago board became its own community with its own robust schedule of social gatherings, there were clashes with Chowhound founder Jim Leff, who didn't want what he saw as a single clique dominating one of his regional boards. In 2004 about a dozen of them, including this author, launched LTHForum.com, named by co-founder Gary Wiviott for the unofficial name of a Chinatown restaurant, "Little" Three Happiness.

CATHERINE LAMBRECHT: What changed when we went from Chowhound to LTHForum? That's easy—people who used to have their posts pulled were now moderators! That was not fun, figuring out the rules of the road as moderators.

We didn't allow politics, or religion. What we didn't realize was that the religion was how you ate your hot dog growing up, and somebody else thinks that's terrible. So the fun begins.

MICHAEL MOROWITZ: The internet was around, but people hadn't figured out that food was a thing on the internet yet. The idea of taking out your camera in a restaurant was weird. We were at Follia [Italian restaurant on Fulton Market] and Gary Wiviott, who took pictures of everything, just had his camera sitting out, very conspicuous. And the owner came over and demanded to know who we were. And he would not take "nobody" for an answer. It was simultaneously friendly and contentious, like he loved the fact that we loved his food, but seemed like he was a hair's breadth from throwing us out. Because we wouldn't tell him exactly where we were from.

There were stories of people getting kicked out of places, what are you taking pictures of? People coming out of kitchens. It was just considered odd. Which it was, and even with Facebook becoming a thing people still weren't doing it. It wasn't a thing until the more real-time social media like Twitter and Instagram came along, and then it became, look where I am.

Bill Kim, chef-owner of Urbanbelly, was one of the first chefs to object to this wave of food picture-taking publicly, to a Tribune *writer.*

BILL KIM: We had such a small place. And if somebody comes in, they just want to eat. Back in the day, there were flashes. There weren't iPhone cameras then. So some of the customers would say, can we eat in peace?

I don't know how the story got around that I didn't like [bloggers or LTHForum]. It wasn't about that. I just wanted the customers to be happy. It got to the point where it was way too much, it wasn't that I didn't want anybody taking pictures. Come on. Why would I say that? It was that the customers did not want the big flashes, and some people didn't want their pictures taken. So that was what that was about. I don't know how it got misconstrued. But, you know, I'm a cook at heart. I'm not here to position myself or to do anything.

But by then LTHForum *was* the media. And I'm gonna tell you that a lot of the chefs looked at it.

ELLEN MALLOY (public relations professional): LTHForum were huge. I technically was supposed to hate them all. Because I have a fundamental fear of people who identify themselves as foodies. But it was hugely influential. And I was not happy about that. Because I couldn't control them. I didn't even know who the fuck they were.

They were out there, just eating wherever the fuck they wanted to whenever they wanted to. There was no rhyme or reason to it. Nobody got a press release or anything, nobody was ever referencing a press kit or anything like that. They just went in with their own opinion and dug in. And so there couldn't be any kind of a superficial gloss that might influence a reviewer. 'Cause they were fucking *wild-westing* that shit. I felt very much like, do not contact those people, do not try and PR anything with those people. They don't want to talk to you. They want to do their own thing. And if you try and influence them, you might get your ass ripped open. They pushed aside the curtain.

There was another one, eGullet. It was not as influential as far as, like, media or filling up restaurants and shit like that. But LTHForum actually was impactful in terms of customers in seats in a restaurant. It freaked me the fuck out.

CATHERINE LAMBRECHT: We seemed to be very competitive with the outside media world. I don't mind if they grabbed ideas, but man—attribution. If you don't credit them, they're all sore, but that courtesy the other way wasn't recognized. That was sort of eye-opening. We weren't getting the press releases, we stumbled on stuff ourselves.

The first time I met Louisa Chu [later *Tribune* reviewer], years ago, she informed me that I was an influencer. I said, no I'm not. Now that I've read more about it, I probably am, but I don't get sucked into it. I didn't think of it that way and I think I'm better for it.

CHEEKU BIDANI: I think for me the change was when I noticed that Khan BBQ had a lot more white faces. And not just people I knew.

They picked it up from somewhere. It was in the *Reader* and then the Hungry Hound guy [Steve Dolinsky], they were always taking from the [LTHForum] boards. They filtered it into the mainstream. Which, you hope it does that, more so because usually the places to get championed are places where the people behind it really care.

As LTHForum gained local celebrity and influence, clashing egos began to divide the group. There were cliques who wouldn't dine out with other cliques, and users who kept "their" finds secret from the public board, or used them to curry favor with mainstream journalists.

Many of the founding members of LTHForum moved on around this time—often using the voices on food they'd found at LTHForum to pursue other areas of food culture. David Hammond and this author freelanced as food writers for the Reader *and other publications; Catherine Lambrecht put on food talks and seminars at Culinary Historians of Chicago; others started things like the chef's competition Baconfest, and the non-profit Purple Asparagus, which educated schoolchildren about the food system. The latter was part of a general move at this time toward promoting locally grown food.*

MICHAEL MOROWITZ: After eGullet shut down and some of them moved to LTHForum, things got weird. Right around that time, I had started a website, The Local Beet. That was probably 2007, 2008. I had kind of the same feeling I'd had about restaurant blogging, there's a lot of stuff going on, in local growers, local purveyors—people who were doing stuff and really cared about where their food came from, and they weren't getting any publicity for it. I started it with a lot of ambitions, and then my wife got pregnant with twins, which was really bad timing.

ROB GARDNER: There was a period around 2008, where people really wanted local. There was an idea that local itself was the virtue. And I think that turned out to be an extraordinarily misplaced goal, that everybody was going to live like that. At the end of the day, people like those carrots, but they still want a carrot, and if the farmers market doesn't have them, you're going to go to Jewel and get carrots.

DAVID HAMMOND: Because I was writing on Chowhound at the time, Heather Shouse [food and drink editor of *Time Out* Chicago] asked to speak to me and a couple of others. Shortly after that I was recruited by the *Reader*. And I probably did 150 capsule reviews, and some longer things.

Heather said send me some clippings, and I said, I don't have any clippings. I've never written professionally before.

SHARON BAUTISTA: We started these biking and eating tours on LTH. And they were popular enough that we actually turned them into an LLC called

Fork and the Road, and we got some press. So we attracted people, I mean, they're enthusiastic, they're willing to bike fifteen miles to a bunch of neighborhoods. But they don't know to eat local specialties, or at places that we haven't told them about. And we were riding to some restaurant in Humboldt Park, and one of our riders got a flat tire. So the group stops, and it takes us a few minutes to fix the flat tire. And this couple, I think they were visiting from the suburbs, asks, does anyone have a gun in our group?

To my mind, inclusiveness and open-mindedness and tolerance and curiosity about food is usually tied to those same characteristics in regards to other things in the world. And I think that's why a lot of people in a community like LTH form close relationships, because it, I think, oftentimes they share more than an interest in food. And what we found in running a business like Fork and the Road, where we're bringing it to a more general population, was that maybe on the surface, we were attracting people who are interested in food. But their interest is of a different nature, and that curiosity didn't carry over to as many other things as we found in a more specialized community like LTH.

MICHAEL MOROWITZ: LTHForum accomplished our goal. We won. We wanted everyone to care about the little places. There were great restaurants, but no one was lining up. You can go on Reddit today, I saw this the other day, someone was like hey, I'm coming to Chicago, what should we do, where should we eat? And people are saying, go take an architectural boat tour, check out this—oh, and if you can, get in a car and check out Birrieria Zaragoza [one of Peter Engler's finds] out by Midway. The middle of nowhere. If there's a better example of how LTHForum won, I don't know it.

CHEEKU BIDANI: Maybe it's rose-colored glasses, but I think it was really lucky to find that group of people you were comfortable eating with. Who you'd want to spend time with not just exchanging scrawls on a virtual board, but actually eating with.

DAVID HAMMOND: It was a very exciting time. It was almost, if I may use a way overused term, *revolutionary* in that it seemed like it was overturning the traditional authorities about food, and we were exploring foods that were out of the mainstream and presenting a view of dining that was different. It was an upheaval, carried on to this day anywhere that citizen reviewers take it into their own hands to come to judgement about restaurants.

TIME OUT CHICAGO

Time Out *began as a weekly nightlife-and-events publication in London in 1968, noted for its irreverent and cheeky attitude, and expanded to New York (among many other markets) in 1995. A wave of expansions around the world in the early 2000s led to the launch of a Chicago edition in 2005. Food and drink coverage was a key part of the magazine's identity and mission, and while much of that focused on what was new and trendy on the scene,* Time Out *also showed more interest from the beginning in neighborhood and ethnic restaurants than existing print publications did at the time.*

Heather Shouse, then a freelancer for the Tribune *and other publications, joined the opening team as the food and beverage editor.*

HEATHER SHOUSE: The high-end dining experience was becoming super super high-end, and then there was the low end, and there was just this weird gap in the middle. So I think *Time Out* was trying to shoot for the people who were going to [Asian restaurants on] Argyle or going to Chinatown. They wanted readers who were a little more adventurous, which I think skewed to either a younger demographic, or it skewed toward a more well-traveled demographic.

2005, when we launched, was also when Anthony Bourdain's *No Reservations* launched. I think chef culture at that point was just starting to get to be glamorized. And like, people were viewing chefs like rock stars. So I think it sort of just catapulted out of that and we started seeing molecular gastronomy and food as theater and things became all about the wow factor. And if you're going to spend this kind of money, like, where's the smoke and the fire and throwing food on the table?

At the same time, the James Beard Awards were starting to look at Chicago for chefs. It wasn't always New York anymore. It wasn't like we just had the one Chicago guy like Trotter, it was like they're gonna have to create an entire category for us, because we have that many good chefs. And we're not a second-tier city any more. There are chefs coming here to learn from our chefs, you know, and so I think it just became a really interesting and exciting time in food.

On the other end of the spectrum, for budget needs, people were seeking something that was more, I would say, immersive and interactive. And people were definitely wanting to go somewhere where there was a menu translation. I think that was super helpful, because a lot of people up until then may have been interested in that kind of food, but just felt a little intimidated. And so I think the key was getting the younger generation and breaking down the intimidation factor.

Because you might not know the Thai words, you might not understand what you're about to eat. But now you have this menu translation, and you read about it online, and you feel like you can go there with your friends, and you can order and you can have this really cool experience where the whole conversation while you're there is really about food. Who's been to Thailand? And what's this? And who else is doing this? It just became a really cool, energetic time for younger people to really get involved and immersed in food culture.

Food writing had been very PR driven. When I first started freelancing, when I was at *Chicago Social* as an intern, one of my jobs was to open mail. And there were so many press releases. The press releases would come literally by mail, you know, like old school, and you would open them. Eventually, our scene got to be so vibrant and bustling that there was no need for that anymore. If stuff was cool enough that we'd want to cover it at *Time Out,* there's not going to be a press release on it, they're not going to have PR. They're just doing what they're doing. And we were trying to be the one that kickstarted people showing up and finding out about it.

Long before Alan Richman heard of Michael Carlson [Schwa],[34] my apartment was two doors down. And I went over there and was like, what the hell is this place, and talked to Michael for an hour. And I convinced our editor that he was the real deal. He's doing some cool stuff. So we did like a long profile on them and this was just an instance, I think, where things then went off the rails. It became all about glorifying that culture, you know, glori-

34 "Kitchen Savant," Alan Richman, *GQ,* December 2008.

fying chef drug culture. And glorifying, like, Graham Elliot doing corn dogs at Lollapalooza. How cool could you get? We had to really be careful not to become a trope where we were just like, featuring something because it was off-kilter. Somewhere along the line people lost focus on like—*yeah,* but does the food taste good?

As food writing shifted to the web during the early 2000s, the emphasis shifted to restaurant news over longform criticism.

HEATHER SHOUSE: When Penny Pollack started *Dish* [*Chicago* magazine's newsletter], that was the beginning of the end. Once *Dish* became a big thing, around 2010, then our editors started asking us to start coming up with separate web content. They wanted us to have something to compete with *Dish.* It became more about gossip, it became more about scoops, it was like everyone was trying to get a scoop on Penny, because that was what was driving traffic for *Chicago* magazine. I love Penny, she's great, but I think the race to drive traffic to websites was the death of it. That's when I lost interest in the whole thing. I didn't have any interest in trying to call chefs all the time and get scoops on stuff. It just wasn't why I was doing it.

The *Time Out* 100 was always the signature thing for *Time Out* London. But we lost pages during that time, like every magazine did, and when you lose pages, you lose that. So we weren't really able to showcase all of the restaurants we wanted to that week. The idea was to try and drive web traffic, because that was what everyone was saying the future was. So we started really just taking and trying to build this database to compete with Metromix. And I think the listings became less in-depth, and there was less opportunity to do large format, and profiles or in-depth reporting, and it became more about creating a database, a searchable database for traffic.

People are still unfortunately afraid to travel to certain neighborhoods. The South Side is woefully under-supported financially, in all aspects. So going down to Chatham, and trying to write about fried chicken, it was admirable for LTHForum to do that and for us to do that. But at the end of the day, it didn't sell ads. From a journalism standpoint, my bosses and all publishers really didn't care about you getting street credit for knowing where you can get, like, a chana roti, and that you're eating Uncle John's BBQ on the hood of your car. It makes for good TV and sound bites for Dolinsky, but there's no revenue behind it, there's no support from either the Illinois Restaurant Association or the James Beard Foundation, or the city themselves. And once they were also able to track web traffic and track clicks, they saw what was getting clicked on. And that stuff really wasn't a big getter for us.

And with the shift to the web, it opened up a huge, huge conflict of interest for so many people who became so-called influencers and then started blogging and working paid things. It was really difficult to wade through all the noise and the advertorials and the influencers and pay to play and all that. It just became a giant clusterfuck if you ask me, so I couldn't really do it anymore. Everybody trying to get web traffic and not really worrying so much about the print version of food journalism anymore—that was really sad and devastating to me. I mean, I sound like an old bitter—like, the music ain't as good as it was. Well, it's true.

15: SMOKE AND MIREPOIX

It was a brief mention in a Time *magazine article*[35] *referencing Homaro Cantu, chef of Chicago's Moto: a claim that "an avid hunter" had brought raccoon meat into his Fulton Market restaurant Moto, and asked the chef to cook with it. Supposedly Cantu was not appalled by a guest bringing their own meat to his restaurant but amused, and he created a dish that night.*

Well, the story is true but it didn't involve hunters—at least not directly. The person with the Tupperware tub of raccoon meat was Cathy Lambrecht of LTHForum, who had just been to a raccoon feed in Delafield, Wisconsin at the local American Legion hall, benefiting the youth baseball team. While there, she acquired a portion of freshly braised raccoon.

Cantu took the raccoon meat solemnly into his kitchen, and when he returned a few courses later, it was with a dish called "Road Kill," which painted a plate with the yellow lines of a highway—and spread out the raccoon meat with tire tracks straight through it. The idea of a dish resembling something so gruesome might have appalled many diners, but it delighted the LTHForum guests, to the extent that some version of Road Kill was on Moto's menu for years to come.

Moto, and Grant Achatz's more famous and successful Alinea, were two of the most prominent examples of Chicago dining's taste for showmanship in the 2000s—conceptual dining, built around visual jokes, culinary magic tricks and

35 "Food: Even the Menu Tastes Good," March 27, 2005

technology applied to food, and in turn a frequent subject of America's new pastime: sharing photos of what you ate online. Both were sometimes dismissed as stunt food, but that underestimates their roots in the techniques of classic cuisine—not least because both Achatz and Cantu spent time in Charlie Trotter's kitchen. Yet both restaurants would also find their creative invention shadowed by mortality, in ways no one could anticipate.

ALINEA

Grant Achatz grew up in an extended family of restaurateurs in St. Clair, Michigan, across the river from Ontario. From an early age, he worked in his parents' coffee shop.

GRANT ACHATZ: It was an introduction to a sense of urgency, a very fundamental, baseline seasoning, and what hard work does in terms of paying off. And it really reaffirmed the fact that I loved cooking.

More than the food, it was about hospitality making people feel happy, or feel a sense of community, or feel taken care of. It was a social gathering place where people would come sit at the same table at the same time, the same day of the week. It wasn't about emotion, and it wasn't about creativity—it was all of the other things that hospitality kind of embraces. And you know, even at that time, I was very curious. So I was always just kind of playing in the kitchen, going, hey, what is this? What is that?

I think it goes back to my father's restaurant, and my grandfather, all my uncles, they all owned the same kind of restaurant in Michigan. It was never about creativity. It's about hot food coming out fast. And after a while, I got bored, and that curiosity crept in there.

Achatz went to school at the Culinary Institute of America, and got his first job in a kitchen more formal than his family's diner at a hotel in Grand Rapids, the Amway Grand Plaza.

GRANT ACHATZ: It had three restaurants in it, and then a massive banquet program. I was on my internship from the Culinary Institute of America when I first started, and typically interns would work in prep on banquets—

they rarely ever see the fine dining restaurants. It was very serendipitous that the day I started, one of the cooks called out in fine dining. And so they sent me up there, and I got along with the chef. I must have done fairly well, they let me stay up there.

Now for the first time in my life as a cook, presentation was considered, there was composition and play, there was more emphasis on pairing flavors, noticing textures, and a whole different style of service. Like, nobody at the diner would put down a Western omelet and then describe it.

So this was my first exposure to that, and then after culinary school I returned to that restaurant and worked a year. And really, at that point, I was honing a different set of line cook skills—different tastes, and different ingredients that I'd never heard of, but also cooking on the line and plating my own food in an artistic manner. That's where I met Steve Stallard, who now owns Blis, the maple syrup and the sherry vinegars that almost everybody uses. He was the executive chef of that hotel, and he was my mentor and friend.

I had Charlie Trotter's first book,[36] and I would come into the restaurant and show the chef of that fine dining restaurant and say, hey, can we do any of this stuff? This stuff is so cool. And he was very open to it. He was like, yeah, bring the book in. Let's talk about it. Let's talk about why it works. So I started kind of replicating Charlie's style, and really studying his flavor combinations and the way he did sauces and infused oils. And it was fascinating, to the point where Chef Stallard was really wanting me to go to Europe, and either work in France or Scotland, he had a strong connection in Scotland. In the '90s France was still the shit, right? Spain hadn't entered the race yet. And so it was very enticing.

But I was so enamored with Charlie's book and the food that he was doing that I told Steve, I don't want to sound disrespectful, but I'm gonna put Europe as a second choice. I'm excited to get into this restaurant. And he was like, yeah, it looks amazing. And so that's what I did.

Charlie's was the first time I saw someone expressing themselves through food. And it was new, and it was exciting. At that point he was on top of the world. The reason I wanted to go there was that cookbook, but also, I think it was in April of '95, *Wine Spectator* put out their annual top ten restaurants in

36 *Charlie Trotter's*, 1994

the country, and he was front and center. And I was like, that's the best in the country, I have to work there.

And, holy moly, was I out of place. Because I was young, I had tremendous ambition, but I'd never cooked that style of food before. And that place was an animal, it was a beast. But even though we'd get our butts kicked every night, there was something addictive about it. And yeah, it was a very important step in my career, everything is starting to snowball at this point. I'm seeing more opportunities to inject humor and different parts of creativity while maintaining this foundation of French food.

If Achatz thought he'd landed in the right place for his career, life at Trotter's soon proved him wrong. He looks back at it now with the perspective of someone who's been in Trotter's position as a chef-owner for many years.

GRANT ACHATZ: I always say it's like a marriage, or a significant other. There's right partners, and there's not right partners. And that is not a criticism, necessarily, of the restaurant or him. It just wasn't a good fit. My maturity wasn't there. I didn't have enough foresight to really understand what was happening and how it has impacted me.

It was the hardest restaurant I've ever worked in. It was intense. And that level of intensity wouldn't be tolerated now, with the toxicity and everything sort of culturally changing. It was such a stepping stone for me in terms of witnessing an all-out attack, or drive, towards perfection. And obviously, that was my first exposure to that—that didn't happen at the diner, and it didn't happen at the Amway. It was impressive. And again it was contagious. It became very clear to me upon my exit that while I respected everything that was happening there, I didn't feel like I was performing my best because the environment just wasn't suited.

From Trotter's—where Trotter warned him that because he stayed less than a year, he would not be acknowledged as having worked there at all—he went to California to work at the French Laundry under chef Thomas Keller.

GRANT ACHATZ: Again, I don't want to cast shade on Charlie. He just had a different style of management and running a restaurant and creativity. But one thing that I found with Thomas is, he was a working chef, he was a chef's chef. So he led by example, in terms of work ethic. Physically cooking. First one in, last one out. And something interesting happened in there that really catapulted me even further toward the style that Alinea was to become—it was humor. Like, "oysters and pearls" [a famous French Laundry dish of pearl tapioca with oysters and caviar]. Putting a dish in an ice cream cone ["salmon cornets," salmon tartare in a cone]. Dishes that were named as puns, like "tongue in cheek" [beef cheeks with veal tongue] and "peas and carrots" [ginger-carrot emulsion topped with pea shoots].

And I was like, we're putting out some amazing food, and we're intentionally making it kind of funny if you pay attention. And that sort of blew me away. I think this is the other thing that was important. I don't know what Trotter's was like when it opened. But in '95, it had been open for like, eight years or so. With the French Laundry, it had only been around for a year and a half when I landed there. French Laundry wasn't in that issue of *Wine Spectator*—nobody knew about it yet. And so there was a newness, there was an excitement, but more than anything, everybody's hair was on fire, because there was still a lot to accomplish. And I think that that was a big part of the spirit of that restaurant.

Thomas and I formed a bond quickly. Before I even started, he treated me really, really well. I didn't really speak to Charlie that much, so Thomas felt like a father figure to me. He's really such a great teacher, he's calm and articulate. And he really cares about the food, and the people. He was giving me one-on-one demos. That's so important when you're twenty-two years old.

Achatz's next pivotal experience, Ferran Adrià's El Bulli, in Roses, Spain, was the one that would convince him to move on from the French Laundry.

GRANT ACHATZ: I had become a sous chef at the French Laundry. And pre-social media, it was all about *Gourmet* magazine, and the *New York Times*. And I always had my nose in them and read an article in *Gourmet* that Ruth Reichl wrote about El Bulli. And I got really excited, because it didn't sound like anything I've ever been exposed to in terms of food. Thomas had previously sent some of the other sous chefs to wherever they wanted to go for a sabbatical. So he arranged it with Ferran, and that's how I got into El Bulli.

It wasn't what I expected. Because, again, I was twenty-three, something like that. I was a sous chef at the best restaurant in the country. And I had an ego, I absolutely thought if I'm the right-hand man in the best restaurant in the country, what more is there for me to learn, right?

And boy, was I wrong. Ferran ushered me into the dining room and fed me an entire meal before I even started. That was amazing, because I had no reference on how any of it was prepared. And everything that came out, was like it was from outer space. I had no idea how they made it. When the plate drops, I can usually easily identify what's on the plate. And I was just like, humbled and super excited, because this is the thing that's been in the back of my mind since I was at that diner.

I was only there for five days. It was just a week. But that and the French Laundry—massive, massive pivots in my career. The Laundry was like getting my PhD in a known cuisine that was stretching the boundaries of traditional and some highly creative stuff. But El Bulli was like, there's no rules now. There's a lot of rules in French cooking, right? And then all of a sudden there was just nothing, and I was like, man, I have a lot to learn and this is amazing.

I remember that meal really well, even though it was twenty-two years ago. They would take cuttlefish, giant cuttlefish, and freeze it. Slice it paper-thin, because it's raw, and then they would freeze coconut milk into ice cube trays. And lay that coconut ice cube in the middle the sheet of raw cuttlefish, and fold it into a parcel, seam side down. And they would put that parcel under a salamander [broiler]. And when that cuttlefish cooks, it firms up, it made a ravioli essentially, and while that was happening the coconut ice melted.

It was genius. It was on such a high level of understanding the way ingredients behave in a non-traditional sense. And being able to look at a piece of squid and have the idea of turning that into a liquid-filled ravioli—that's some high-level stuff. So it was tremendously exciting. I filed that in the back of my mind, and most definitely it was an impetus for the Black Truffle Explosion [famous Trio/Alinea dish]. The sensation of putting that into your mouth like a soup dumpling and having that liquid shoot out was amazing.

DAVID CARRIER (cook at French Laundry): Grant's culinary vision was growing so fast, faster than anybody else's, that you knew it needed a new home. It outgrew its aquarium. Others did that eventually, too, but Grant was ready to fucking explode. He just needed an army. He needed soldiers to help him facilitate that.

GRANT ACHATZ: When I got back to the Laundry, it became very clear to both Thomas and myself that it was time for me to do my own thing. Obviously it was very respectful. And he reacted like a father—okay, it's your time to leave the nest.

****

In Evanston, Illinois, at Trio, owner Henry Adaniya was looking for his third chef or chef team after Shawn McClain and Rick Tramonto and Gale Gand.

HENRY ADANIYA: I got an email from this kid Grant Achatz. A nice resume, but he was what, twenty-seven? And you claim to be a chef at the top restaurant in America?

I kind of just threw it in the waste basket. I really didn't want a young punk in the kitchen, I wanted somebody with a little more experience. Everybody's a cook, but being a chef takes maturity, you have to be able to understand all the aspects of business as well. And when I look for a chef, I look for someone who has that sense of command and that ability to really convey their food and keep a team together.

GRANT ACHATZ: I think it was an ad from Henry on Monster.com, back in the time of dial-up internet. I did some research and found that Rick Tramonto and Gale Gand had been there. I knew of them, and I knew of Tru. I called Henry and I immediately liked him.

HENRY ADANIYA: Somebody from, I think, Wild Game Distributors, said hey, you should take another look at this guy. So I looked at the resume again, and I said, maybe I should start a dialogue. So I emailed him. And I was really impressed with the way he wrote—wow, this is not just some young buck, trying to get a chef position. He had a lot of knowledge. And of course, he's coming from a great restaurant. But it's the personality that I read in his email that really sparked my attention. So we started a huge dialogue. And I asked him a hundred questions, and he wrote back very thoughtfully, he's a very articulate writer.

Okay, I said, let's bring you in for a tasting. So I flew him in. But he had almost canceled, like, two or three days before he was supposed to fly out. I thought, that's it, he's just pulling my chain. But when he got here, he looked really sick. I later found out he never called in sick, at French Laundry. Due to his nature, he pushes through everything.

He did the tasting. And his tasting was like being in a surgery room. Precise timing of all the dishes. I had said I want the dishes to come out at certain intervals. His timing was perfect. I went through eight courses. And each course was like, whoa, what am I eating here? The one that distinctly sticks out to me was a gelatin ravioli. So it's a precursor of the liquid explosion, but the gelatin ravioli, you could see through it, it was in some type of broth. And I just loved the magic of the visuals, which were studies. But the composition was also highly complex, and well-orchestrated.

GRANT ACHATZ: I definitely gave him Explosion. I gave him about a quarter-sized lozenge of crispy chocolate on the outside, and foie gras in the middle. I gave him a roasted saddle of lamb with a flageolet bean ragu. I made a panna cotta caviar course. I didn't do dessert, because Paula Haney was there as a pastry chef, so that was out of my responsibility. I had to show him I had the foundations, but I also wanted to give him examples of the direction I wanted to go.

HENRY ADANIYA: And then we continued dialogue, and he wants to change everything. His vision of the restaurant—obviously the French Laundry was super well equipped, and we're just some country kitchen. I'm like, I can't do that. You know, I can do so much but his requirements were outside of my budget. So we didn't talk for a few weeks, and a month later, I don't remember why but we revisited it and I said, what can we do here? So we came up with a budget, boom, he came in, and we ripped apart the restaurant anyway, as much as we could. And he established a kitchen that he could work in. We opened in July [2001].

Then 9/11 happened, oh my God. That put the brakes on a lot of things.

GRANT ACHATZ: 9/11, right. So we're in a massive deficit right off the bat. The restaurant had no budget. We're in Evanston, which I didn't even know what that meant. Oh, it's close to Chicago. But it's a pain to get up there. Trio was dying a fast death at that point.

After a couple of long talks with Henry, he's like, look, I want you to do your thing. I said, are you sure, because we're going to be pushing some boundaries here. He said, look, I'm not going to get in the way of the creative, I didn't with Rick and Gale. I let Shawn do whatever he wanted. And I want you to, too. So we started doing the weird stuff. And I was just so blown away by that—that as an owner of a restaurant, he was willing to take that risk with me, was unbelievable.

It was slow at first, but then we started getting some momentum. Phil Vettel reviewed us, Dennis Ray Wheaton [*Chicago* magazine] reviewed us, and they were positive. [Both gave it four stars.] We got Mobil five stars, we had the *New York Times*, Amanda Hesser, come in. Pete Wells was writing for *Food & Wine* at the time, he came in and raved about it. And that's how I ultimately wound up a *Food & Wine* Best New Chef in 2002. And then we're sort of off to the races. I won James Beard Rising Star Chef [in 2003].

PHIL VETTEL: I still remember the very first thing, an ice cream sandwich, except that it was olive oil ice cream and the wafer on either side was like a peppered Parmesan cookie. And as it was about to come out, the server says, the chef recommends a small glass of sherry with that. And he says it's a five-dollar upcharge—like five dollars will make a difference. I'm not second-guessing the guy, not on the first course. So there I was having an olive oil ice cream parmesan sandwich, with a hit of sherry.

As the meal progressed, he was the guy that screwed with your expectations, much more than Rick or Shawn ever did. What you think is going to be a salad is going to be liquid. Here's a pillow, we're doing ham, peas and lavender, but the lavender is coming out of the pillow, so it's the weight of the plate that's pushing lavender air in your face while you're eating, basically fried ham and pea. So everything was an adventure. Of course, Rick and Gale had that great presentation of caviar where it was all arranged on an artist's palette, so each component was like that. But that's about as tricky as they got with presentation. Where right away, Grant was serving stuff in these custom-made bowls and this springy little metallic contraption called the Squid, which just existed to hold a shrimp tempura.

Everything either showed up in a way you would never expect, or it was in a physical condition that you would never expect, and just all these flavor combinations. I could have just floated home if it wasn't so far away.

DAVID CARRIER: It was tough out of the gate. We went from eight to ten people a night to sixty, sixty-five, seventy and everybody doing a fucking twenty-eight-course tasting menu. Henry was an amazing person to work for. He obviously knew what he was doing. There was a good support team there, much of the service staff had stayed, we kept a couple of cooks. Chicago just really has that warm, hospitable Midwest appreciation for food. It has everything that your San Francisco, your LA, your New York has, without the pretension per se. Being in Chicago, Grant was able to become known for what he is today. The money was there, people could afford it. The fluency of people was there, so they can appreciate it. But the cutthroat BS wasn't there, which enabled him to be creative, and people were warm and inviting and accepting of it. So I think Chicago was the perfect spot for him.

HENRY ADANIYA: Some people said, this is just too much for Chicago. And I knew that it was a risk, because trends tend to happen on the coasts. So we were going against the usual way things worked, and to have a twenty-four-course tasting menu—that was insane. The food was challenging, it needed introduction. Because it was an interactive dining experience. It was about eating, thinking, and embodying the whole concept of the food itself.

There was a lot of skepticism. Fellow restaurateurs and chefs were like, this is a little too far out there. This isn't cooking, this is not food, a lot of people just thought it was too contrived. But what I appreciate about Grant's food is, yeah, he can bend it, but it's grounded so firmly in traditional technique, that it could flex, like bamboo in the wind. As soon as we got some prominent people from the coasts reviewing us, I knew we were good.

Initially, there were a lot of classical [ingredients] that were very costly. So I sat down with Grant and said, we have to look at where our costs are. And that's when he started to shift to doing some things that used food product in a different way. So instead of truffles and caviar, which we still used to a degree, we could do other things. We did the vapor [boiling water poured over rosemary, to perfume the air around a lobster dish] to bring different senses into the experience. So it was always an investigation into something different.

One of my concerns was the price point. We were expensive—$125 per person. Nowadays that's peanuts. But I think it began to set a precedent. What could you actually do, that the art of food would be worth paying for?

****

Talk to Achatz's original team at Trio and the attraction of working for this unknown chef quickly becomes obvious:

CURTIS DUFFY (cook): After Trotter's, I thought the French Laundry was going to be my next move. I spent a couple of weeks out there, because Charlie was closed in July. And I really enjoyed it. But my wife at the time didn't see us moving all the way to California for a couple of years, and that's when Grant moved here and took over Trio. So I went up to Trio and had dinner, and I thought, well, if I can't go to California, why not work for the guy who was right there, who was the sous chef for the longest time?

I went up there and did a stage. And Grant's like, I can't hire you. Why not? I can't pay you enough. I'm like, well, what can you pay? I think it was $16,000 a year. And I'm like, well, I'm only making $16,500 a year. So I'll take a $500 pay cut, what is that, like $3 a paycheck. But he's like, no, I still can't. You should have your own restaurant, you should be doing what I'm doing. You should go find a kitchen. And he was very encouraging.

At some point I got in touch with Shawn McClain, who had Spring by then. And he was kind of the same way. You're overqualified. Like, fuck man, all this time I spent at Charlie's was starting to work against me, because I think everybody thought that I was going to bring that style of food or that level to their kitchens. And they weren't looking for that.

Grant finally ended up hiring me. I started as one of the cooks there, and he asked me if I would be willing to do pastry. And everywhere I've worked, I've worked some type of pastry. So I spent the next year and a half doing pastry.

DAVID CARRIER: I went to culinary school, and one of the guys I had worked for in New York while I was going to school moved out to California, Napa Valley specifically, and he met Thomas Keller. TK and his brother [Joseph Keller] were doing a dinner at the Beard House and my buddy got me an opportunity to help out, and at the end Thomas says, hey, if there's anything I can do for you. . . . So I got his phone number.

This is about '99, so I don't think I really understood the magnitude of French Laundry. But I called him up and I got a job. And, I mean, I was a fucking fish out of water. People wouldn't even fucking look at me. I'm like, hey, you know, is there something I can do? Instead of just fucking standing here with my thumb in my ass. There was just so much pressure that was put on these individuals and so much was at stake. And I'm a big son of a bitch, I know they're thinking, who's this big fucking Oompa-Loompa? And I'm thinking, don't let my size fool you. I'll get shit done quicker than you once I figure it out.

Eventually a corner was turned and I was viewed as an asset rather than a liability. For the remainder of my two years there, we built a formidable team. It was like choreography and never was there a beat that was skipped. Then my dad was sick, and Grant presented an opportunity to get closer to the East Coast. So I reached out to him and that was that.

I wanted desperately to maintain what I had learned. I saw leaving with Grant as a phenomenal opportunity where even if it wasn't the same stadium, it was going to be the same culture, the same mentality, the same players on the team.

JEFF PIKUS (cook): It wasn't the weird food, to be honest, that attracted me. It was the fact that Grant was a young chef who had worked with Thomas Keller at the French Laundry. At that stage in my career, I idolized Thomas Keller quite a bit, but I didn't think it was a good choice for me to move out to a small town in Northern California and work for him.

So when the opportunity presented itself to work for someone that was kind of his protégé, that was exciting for me. That's really what attracted me to working at Trio.

Trio was all people about my age and similar kind of upbringing, backgrounds, levels of ambition. It was intense. Quiet. I think I started right after Michael Carlson left to stage at The Fat Duck [Berkshire, England]. It was me and a bunch of young white kids. Grant was the guy that knew everything. And had all the answers. It was very much that kind of culture.

SCOTT NOORMAN (server): One of my friends here in Grand Rapids, who was a chef, told me about working this dinner in Northern Michigan at a place called Tapawingo [Ellsworth, MI], with his friend Steve Stallard, who was Grant's first mentor. My chef friend told me about the forty-four-course menu that Grant did at Tapawingo that just blew everyone away. Like even the vegan food that he was doing looked like the regular food he was doing for everyone else.

And I was like, I need something like this. Something that's progressive, something that fulfills my passion as well. I was starting to learn more about beverages and wine, and I really wanted to kind of steer myself into that instead of just being a waiter for the rest of my life. So I went up there, and I went through, like five interviews with Henry, the Zen master of service.

Paula Haney had recently returned to doing pastry at Trio when Shawn McClain left.

PAULA HANEY: I know Grant did not want me there, he didn't want a pastry chef, you could tell he wanted to do his own thing. But I applaud him for being as gracious as he was to me. It was really hard, and I am so grateful for the experience. We changed the menu every day. Every day something on that menu had to change. And that was really cool. And really exhausting. I think the really great thing about that though, was that instead of things being sweet or savory, he sees it all as a continuum, which it is. We did a menu for a while that started out savory, dipped into sweet, went back to savory, then back to sweet at the end.

Everybody was so focused, and it was a privilege to work in that environment. I would hear people say that, oh, they're just doing it to be outrageous, he can't really cook. But you cannot do what he did without being an amazing cook. As was proved when, after he did it, a lot of people who did not have his experience tried to do it, and it was terrible. Grant would say, you know, we can do all this stuff but the end of the day, the food has to be satisfying. It has to check all the same boxes a hamburger would check.

CHRISTOPHER GERBER (server): My friend Todd, who I had worked with at Italian Village years ago, was a maître d' at Trio. And he said, you've got to come up and eat here, this guy's doing crazy stuff.

So I ate there and of course my mind was blown. Because who was doing food like that at that time in America? Grant comes out to the table and I go, I hate you. He looks hurt and says why? Because I just spent a ton of money eating in New York, and I could have come here four times for the same money and had a better experience. He laughed, and afterwards I tell my girlfriend at the time that I'm going to work with that guy.

DAVID POSEY: I went to Trio on my internship [from Culinary Institute of America]. I was with Curtis in pastry for a month, I was too timid and shy to realize what they wanted me to do on that station, which was go around the pass and plate with Grant. I was terrified of him, because I was just a kid and he was a demigod.

The internship was unpaid, but your payment was that you got to dine at Trio and spend a week with Grant, like being his little commis. I think I was with Grant for like a month of it. It was a pretty surreal experience being a young cook and having Grant Achatz be like, David, what'd you read this weekend? Creating this kind of relationship with a guy that you really looked up to. It was very inspiring, and it was very hard to go back to culinary school with the standards I had learned on my internship.

JEFF PIKUS: I think I learned a lot about discipline, about organization, about accountability, about respect for your employers, your employees, your kitchen, your product. It was more about those things than it was about learning fancy techniques, or how to use hydrocolloids [the chemicals used in many molecular gastronomy techniques]. Like that part wasn't really that interesting. To me, it was more about how to attain the level of discipline that you need to be a successful chef and run your own kitchen. The technique part didn't come in until Alinea. Alinea food was more influenced by that [El Bulli] style, where Trio was like more French Laundry technique, but with different flavor combinations than would be expected at French Laundry. I don't think Trio had the equipment for that stuff.

SCOTT NOORMAN: I'll tell you a story about service at Trio. I had a four-top, and we had it set up through the reservation system that we knew which menu they were interested in. But one of the guys looks like he doesn't know what's going on. So I go to the table, and I say welcome, blah, blah, blah. I understand we're on board for the twelve-course menu, and I just wanted to make sure that was still the plan. And that's when this guy to my right is like oh wait, what are you talking about? I agreed to twelve courses, but I thought I was coming out for a fish or a piece of steak. And I was like, oh boy.

I knew what had happened—the other couple at the table made the reservation and didn't tell their friends what they were getting into. It's not his fault he's angry. I said, we do all degustation menus here. So having just à la carte, isn't something that's gonna happen. But I want you to be happy. And I don't want us to feel uncomfortable with each other all night, that just wouldn't be good for you or me. I said, so hang out. I'll be right back.

I go to the hostess and say, call Oceanique [Mark Grosz's French restaurant in Evanston] and make a reservation for half an hour from now. So I went to the kitchen, and Grant's like, what's with table 32, they haven't started. I explain the situation and I say, I think we need to do something special for them. So let's send them an *amuse-bouche*. He says, when do you want it? In about six or seven minutes. And we'll go from there.

I tell my back waiter, put four champagne glasses on table 32. Don't say anything, if they ask questions tell them Scott will be here in a moment. So I wander over with my champagne. I don't talk—I just let them wonder. I make sure the guy is the last one I pour for—I'm pouring and looking him in the eye. And I say, sir, I understand your reluctance to dine with us tonight. It's not what you were expecting, we understand. But we just want you to see a little inkling of what we do here at Trio. So this is on us. We've made a reservation for you at Oceanique. They'll be ready for you in about twenty minutes, we'll have a cab waiting out front. But here's my card. I said, please think about coming back, and ask for me. And we can try this again.

When they leave, I make sure I'm at the front door to walk them out. He palms me a hundred-dollar bill and apologizes for his actions, he says we will be back in a couple of months and we're completely asking for you. He says, that was one of the best bites of food I've ever put in my mouth.

****

As happens when chefs become the flavor of the month, Achatz started being approached by would-be backers for a restaurant of his own. One of them stood out.

NICK KOKONAS: Before I was born, my dad had a restaurant, James' Lunch, in the West Loop—it was skid row then. Typical Greek diner. He thought that the Loop would go west eventually, but this was the '50s and '60s, so it did not work out for him. All Greeks have cousins of cousins that own restaurants and stuff like that, but I had never spent a single day in a restaurant as an employee or worker until the day Alinea opened.

I grew up a very picky eater, because my mom had a lot of food phobias. She was a great mom but not a good cook. My parents and I would go out to eat once or twice a week, basic things like a steak house or red sauce Italian. I never had pizza till I was thirteen, because my mom didn't like cheese, and I didn't have sushi until my twenties. But when I started dating my wife, her family had Eastern European roots in Latvia, and they were very much into trying good foods and sitting down at dinner as family and having a bottle of wine. It took a while, but what I realized eventually was that anything that's prepared well, that's fresh, and there's thought put into the balance of flavors, is delicious.

So I kind of went holy shit, there's a whole world of food out there, and it should be one of life's great pleasures. We started traveling to France and Spain and places like that, and I started reading all of these classic books—

The Peregrinations of an Epicure,[37] the first [Michael] Ruhlman book[38] when it came out, Ruth Reichl's writing. So I just started cooking—though I had no intention of ever thinking, oh, I'm a good home cook, I should open a restaurant. Not at all.

In 2002, some friends of ours set up a Friday lunch at Trio. I took the day off work to go to this lunch, and then they canceled, and my wife said, we should just go anyway. We had been before and it was kind of Asian fusion, and honestly I didn't love it. But this time we went and everything was spectacularly delicious. And so at the end of that meal, we made a reservation for dinner for the following week, just to see, because lunch was just lunch. So we went to dinner the following week, and we were like, holy hell, this is better than anything we've traveled to eat, and it's ten minutes from our house.

We started telling people the best restaurant in America is in suburban Chicago. And they would laugh, and say that's impossible. I remember we had this one dinner where Grant did the balloon of mozzarella, which was just like a caprese salad, a thin shell of mozzarella stretched out, but when you cut into it both the tomato water and the vinegar came out. It was the simplest thing, but it was done so perfectly and so beautifully that I was like, this guy can elevate the simplest thing into something that's a work of art, and tastes delicious. So we would go there and have the truffle explosion, and the shrimp tempura speared on a vanilla bean, and all those things.

We went to Trio more than I care to admit, because when we would go somewhere else, we would go, well, that wasn't as good as Trio. We would always go on like a Wednesday night, but it was pretty empty. When I say empty, I mean they might do twelve covers.

Kokonas started inviting friends from other cities, and they invited chefs they knew to check out what was happening in Chicago. Pretty soon he was hosting parties of ten or twelve on Wednesday nights.

NICK KOKONAS: Instead of bringing wine to the chef, or beer or whatever, I started bringing some of those culinary books to Grant, and highlighting

37 *Blue Trout & Black Truffles: The Peregrinations of an Epicure,* Joseph Wechsberg, 1954.

38 *The Making of a Chef,* 1997.

some pages in them that I was like, hey, this is, this is what La Pyramide was doing fifty years ago. And it's actually not dissimilar to what you're doing.

And at the same time, he was posting a lot on eGullet. So there'd be, like, a whole post on bread service—what's the point of it? Can you innovate it? Why so much fat with the butter? Is that a good thing or a bad thing? I could tell that he was a thinking person. He was trying really hard to figure this shit out. And, you know, I was a philosophy major in college, and I studied theater, and so I was starting to look at this, going, the reason I like this restaurant isn't just because the food's delicious, it's because there is a very serious reflection on the guest experience as a diner. And I don't mean just service. I mean, how do you interact with food? How do you eat it?

There was that article that Daniel Patterson wrote around this time about the tyranny of Alice Waters.[39] You know, organic, local and fresh whenever possible—that was what everyone was talking about at the time. And for a restaurant like Trio, or any high-end restaurant, those things were given. She already won. But why not do something with them that's unique and engages more of the senses?

CHRISTOPHER GERBER: One time [Kokonas] was in with two other people who eventually became investors as well. And he was sitting there with an odd-looking piece of paper, and I asked what it was. It was a menu from El Bulli—his guests had just gone there. And it was just a bunch of symbols with a Spanish word under them. It was almost like a graph in a way, just full of symbols. And I ask, could I just grab that for a moment? And I went back and I photocopied it, and I take it back to the guy and I take the photocopy to Grant. I go, table 10, they're looking at this right now. "No way, get out of here." I swear to God, Chef. This guy's not just a diner who likes to go out, he's someone interested in cuisine from around the world, and hitting the top restaurants. So I brought Grant to their table, and that's how they met.

And then one time I'm walking him and his wife Dagmara in, and he says, so is Grant under contract? I said, honestly, I can't tell you, but I'll give you his email address, and you can ask him. And that's where their relationship started.

39 "To the Moon, Alice," *The New York Times*, November 6, 2005.

NICK KOKONAS: I started getting this kind of gnawing feeling in the back of my head, like, man, this guy is being underutilized. Here's this world-class person at what he does, and he's young and he's really hungry, and he's in a boarding house in suburban Chicago. And it's probably the best restaurant in America right now, but nobody who visits Chicago is going to drive out to Evanston. I mean, sure, they went to Le Francais in Wheeling, but that was a very different kind of experience, more decadent and over the top. And the city had Trotter, of course, who was kind of at his peak then.

I thought, if you took exactly this and put it in a better setting in Chicago, and really invested in it, it would be the best restaurant in America. And I kept thinking that, but I kept thinking like someone should do this—not that *I* should do this.

We were going for my wife's birthday, January 20, 2004, and I told Grant we wanted the kitchen table, and I told him, she's ethnically Latvian, she speaks Japanese, and she loves Thai food, good fucking luck. Just to mess with him.

The first course was called Flavors of the Sea, and it was like a Japanese-style sashimi course, and it was beautiful and delicious. The next course was Latvian sorrel soup with braised ham hocks. So clearly he had researched what Latvian food was, right? And then the rest was a blend of all three, in a way that was really smart. But more importantly, I got to see the kitchen and how they operated.

The kitchen looked like a Swiss watchmaker shop. And boy was it loaded with talent, you go back and see who was in there—it was Jeff Pikus and Greg Baxtrom and John Shields and John Peters and Curtis Duffy—all these guys that now have Michelin two- or three-star restaurants. And I remember that Dave Carrier, who was, I think, chef de cuisine at the time, he plated something up, and it didn't work the way they thought. But immediately, instead of us having to wait, they adapted some other course that they had. Grant delivered the food to the table, and I said, so what went wrong? He said, not everything works the way you think, but we'll have it ready in a couple of seconds. And I watched him redo that whole course. But it wasn't like yelling or chaos or anything. It was just like, make it smooth. If we'd been in the dining room, we'd never have known that anything had happened.

After the dinner, I said to him, what do you want to do when you're not here anymore? And he's like, what do you mean? I go, well, look, man, I think you have the best restaurant in America right now. But there's like fifteen people here tonight. It's not busy. You must have ambitions. And he was like, yeah, I want to have the best restaurant in America. And I was like, great. I'd like to help you do that. He goes, well, what kind of restaurant do you want to open? I go, how should I know, I never opened a restaurant, but it better be the best restaurant in America. It's the only thing I'm interested in, if we're going to do something like that. And so a couple days later, he emailed me a business plan.

GRANT ACHATZ: I was very cautious. Because he was young, he had no restaurant background, and from my perspective, he was rich. So that worried me—he's going to have all the control, what's he going to make me do? I just didn't know him. So we started talking a bit more. I kept going over to his house, and we would chat. And I knew he was real. He was a straight shooter. He was nice, but intense in the same way that I was. He very clearly had amazing business acumen. And I was just saying, eh, we're going to take a leap here. And he did too. He was putting himself out there. We were both taking an immense amount of risk, and that said something, that he was willing to do that.

SCOTT NOORMAN: Nick sees people that have talent in certain areas, and he pounces on it and helps them. He knew we all knew the restaurant business better than him. So he never once interjected his ideas, Grant was the leader.

CHRISTOPHER GERBER: It was kind of a very interesting whirlwind of wining and dining other potential investors. Nick would fly them in and basically say, listen, if you have a terrible meal, I'll pay for it. And every single person had a great meal and every single person paid for their own meal and eventually signed on to Alinea.

NICK KOKONAS: Our first investor dinner was hosted at my house, on May 4, 2004—here's the concept, here's what we want to do, here's the name. And a year later to the day, we opened Alinea. We spent three or four months just finding the real estate, and decided very quickly that we did not want to be inside someone else's building. In other words, no high-rises, no apartment buildings, no hotels, no any of that stuff. We wanted a standalone building. Why? Because I did a study of the demographics of every high-end, four-star restaurant in every city in America, and the vast majority of them were standalones. And so we're like, okay, that's one of our tenets.

Grant didn't know the city at all, he was not from Chicago. So I literally had to drive him around and be like, this neighborhood, not that neighborhood, this price point, not that price point. We designed the place, and we literally built out a crappy old building into Alinea with a five-and-a-half, six-month build out. We had a general contractor, but essentially, I lived there making sure it got done on time.

GRANT ACHATZ: We printed out this big map that had case studies of all the major restaurants in town, what neighborhoods they were in, what prices they were charging, and how big they were. Just to see a sense of what worked. But in my mind, there was Trotter's and there was French Laundry, and they were about the same size, they both were two stories and had about seventy seats. Two levels was not ideal in terms of operations, but it meant something to the energy in the space. It's grueling. Most people that start here drop fifteen or twenty pounds.

To be honest, I wanted to be close to Charlie. I thought that we were going to pull from the affluent neighborhood of Lincoln Park. If we're going to put it anywhere, we might as well put it in the middle of nice houses and disposable income, right? But I don't think that many people from the neighborhood came in.

NICK KOKONAS: If you're a competitive person, you pick the person sitting on the throne, and you try to knock that person off, right? So when we started building Alinea, I started studying Trotter and his books and his menus and business model, where he traveled and all that stuff, and my attitude was, open up right across the fucking street from the guy and then blow him out of the fucking water. We literally looked at a building across the street, and I was like, great, put it there, because the people already know the fine dining in the neighborhood, put it right there. And Grant was like, we *cannot* open across the street from Trotter's. He was adamant he wouldn't do it. But my code word for Alinea before we had the name was FUCT, and the last two letters were for Charlie Trotter. I didn't know the guy personally. I just was like, that's the guy we need to knock off the throne.

I had my first fine dining experience ever in '96, '95, something like that. I still had a lot of food phobias, and we were invited to go to Trotter's. I loved it. It was delicious. The wines were amazing. We were treated really well, even though we were young. A couple of years later, a friend bought me the chef for the day thing at a charity auction there, as a birthday gift.

So I spent a day there, and they gave me seven liters of fava beans to peel, because that was kind of their weed-out to figure out what kind of person they had. Most people peel a few, and then go, oh, show me this, or give me some wine. Let me watch. And you know, I was a floor trader. If you want me to eat shit, punch me in the face. So I did seven liters of favas, and they brought me another seven liters and I did those, and then they put me on the meat station next to Curtis Duffy, and suddenly I was cooking protein, and he was teaching me how to cook the protein the right way and I'd never seen sous vide before that. I thought everything about it was awesome.

I even liked the fact that Trotter was kind of a tyrant, like it was the standard then, and it was great. And he put Chicago on the map again after Le Francais got tired. So that was part of my learning experience. But when we started building Alinea, I literally said to Grant, we win the day that he closes. And Grant was like, you're out of your fucking mind. I mean, I was young, I would never say shit like that now, but I was thirty-four years old and taking this enormous risk, I had raised a couple million dollars and put in $500,000 of my own money, which was a substantial portion of my net worth, and it felt like an enormous risk. And furthermore, everybody in the world told me it was the dumbest thing I'd ever done—except for my wife.

CURTIS DUFFY: I remember Nick coming in a lot. At that time, Grant and I had formed a pretty close relationship, I think more than anybody else in the kitchen. I was the guy that he could talk to about the restaurants he was interested in, because they were same restaurants that I was interested in, the

Spain movement was just starting. So you know, if he brings up the restaurant Akelarre [San Sebastian], who knows what that is? I'm like, I do. So there were a lot of late nights of just him and I talking about food and Spain and what's going on there and with Ferran and all the team. That's when I traveled to Spain to eat at all those restaurants, because that's what I wanted to do.

So he started to talk to me about this guy, Nick, and what he's doing and how they're starting to form a relationship on maybe doing his own restaurant, then it turned into very, very serious talks. And now we're driving around looking for spaces. I remember doing inventory on nine pans, like how many nine pans does Trio have? How many six pans, how many sheet trays, trying to get an idea as to, what does it take to open a restaurant? How much stuff do we need? I remember us measuring the passes, blue-taping the floor, designing everything the way that we thought it was gonna be. So I learned a great deal doing that. Because we applied it to Alinea, but then I applied that same mentality and thought process of, what do I need for [his future restaurant] Grace. Because by then I'm working in a hotel that has four thousand sheet trays, but how many do I actually use every day?

[In Grant] I saw the drive and I saw the creativity behind it. I loved that it was the drive of wanting to do a great restaurant. I saw that in him even though he's not a talkative guy. So there were a lot of late nights of just conversation of food, food and food. He just thought about food differently. When you're that young, the idea of being different is probably more exciting than it is for me now, where you want every single dish to be a great dish. The menu was large enough where there could be fails, but they were interesting fails.

GRANT ACHATZ: The end of Trio and the beginning of Alinea was right at the moment of popularity for food blogs, eGullet and LTHForum, and those were massively important for us. Pre-social media, that engagement was the best commercial you could have, people talking openly about food.

DAVID POSEY: EGullet was around, but you couldn't really find much stuff about what was happening in other restaurants. I would go to an internet café every Monday or whatever day we were off, and look at the Fat Duck website. So there was nothing really to draw from other than people going on a vacation and coming back and say I ate here, and this is what they were doing.

NICK KOKONAS: I went on eGullet and decided to open source all our plans. If you type in "the Alinea Project," you can see our discussions on there. Here's our test kitchen, here's the logo, here's how we're designing the venue. We were getting feedback from our potential customers, the hardcore food lovers, and seeing what they think of all this. We were getting tens of thousands of views on those posts, that cost nothing but our time.

GRANT ACHATZ: EGullet was a playground for me, because I was so excited about what we were about to do. And people didn't really understand it, so I felt a responsibility, now that this new soapbox was there, to explain myself so that it wouldn't be dismissed as the emperor has no clothes. And so I really enjoyed it, it gave me insight into restaurants I've never been to. It was a kind of a view into the world from a bunch of different people's perspectives. And we listened, it was important to see how people were reacting to this stuff before we even opened.

CURTIS DUFFY: We always loved what we did at Trio, which was working across from one another, and that everything kind of fed into the middle to the pass. But we wanted to create longer serving areas, so that we could put down a lot of plates and do more volume with the same style of food. What was important was how you design the kitchen so that ultimately, we're able to execute the food we want to do. Because most restaurants, they don't start with the menu. Most chefs are walking into kitchens that were already designed. But we had the opportunity to design the kitchen around the style of food that we wanted to do, and that changes everything.

NICK KOKONAS: The day we opened, I literally spent all night laying final kickboards in the basement because the regular ones hadn't come. And we got our final inspection, and we had, maybe, forty covers booked. And so Grant said, bring in a few tables of friends and you eat there tonight, because it's going to take your table, like, eight hours to eat, because we're not organized yet, but we need some bodies in there. Grant gave an awesome talk before we open, about commitment, about striving to be the best in the world and all that sort of stuff.

And then suddenly people were coming in. I remember Chef Sean Brock [Husk, Charleston] was the first guy through the door on the first day. He followed us on eGullet. And then Michael Ruhlman was there, and he pulled me aside and said, holy cow, you know who that is? That's the head dining critic from the *New York Times*, Frank Bruni.

I went down to the kitchen, and I said to Grant, hey, just so you know, table 42 is the dining critic of the *New York Times*. And he was like, oh my God, fuck me. It was like the marketing plan was *too* successful. And I remember eating the food and going, this isn't nearly as good as Trio. Grant says, of course it's not. It's an entirely new menu, and half the kitchen has never worked together before, and we only had, like, five days to practice.

That *New York Times* article came out,[40] and it was a perfectly awesome piece that was on the front page of the food section and two giant open folios in the middle with pictures of mostly Alinea food, a little bit of WD-50, a little bit of Moto. It didn't say anything really bad about Alinea, it didn't say anything really good about Alinea. But Grant was horrified, because in his mind it was critical. And he was like, you never get reviewed twice in the *New York Times*. So that was our shot, and we fucking blew it.

Meanwhile, everybody in America that I knew looked at the picture and went, holy shit, you guys got a three-page spread in the *New York Times*, right? I learned very, very quickly, that the content mattered far less than the spread itself. And so I was trying to explain this to Grant, this is hundreds of thousands of dollars' worth of good publicity.

PHIL VETTEL: It was the most anticipated restaurant, maybe in Chicago history. There were so many pre-opening stories written in so many magazines. I had a line in a story that by that point, Grant Achatz had been featured in every magazine except for *Guns & Knives* and *Barely Legal*. I almost got that by the *Tribune*, but Alan Solomon, former sports writer and former travel writer, knew how to get into the system and read tomorrow's story today. And he walked up to me, and he said, I just want to congratulate you for getting

40 "Sci-Fi Cooking Tries Dealing With Reality," May 11, 2005

Barely Legal into the paper. And just then my editor walked by, and she said, why, is that a legal journal? So now she was on alert. I think I had to change it to *Cat Fancy* instead.

We had the rule then about waiting a month to go to a new restaurant, but we talked it out and I said, we cannot wait. Everybody's talking about it, you got guys in there taking notes while they're still measuring the windows for drapes. The *New York Times* had already weighed in, so I went for a preview, and did not assign stars to it. The question wasn't whether it was going to be good. The question was whether it could possibly be this good, as much as everybody was saying. And so I went, and I don't remember what I said, but more or less, yeah, it really it's this good. If you're going to talk about Chicago dining, and you haven't been, you're not ready to talk about Chicago. You can't ignore what they're doing.

****

JEFF PIKUS: When Grant left Trio, he sat us all down one-on-one and either said thank you for your work, good luck in the future, or, would you like to be part of the opening team at Alinea? I turned it down because honestly, I wanted to see something different. So I was a sous chef at Spiaggia, where I quickly learned that I had no business being a sous chef of anything, especially a restaurant of that size and scale. So I started reconnecting with Grant. He didn't have anything, but things happen fast during an opening. So I was on the opening team, it just took me nine months to get there.

Most of the menu was done. He and Curtis and John [Shields] and Alex Stupak had been developing the menu, using Nick Kokonas' home kitchen to do a lot of the work. So for us, the chefs de partie, we got a packet with all of the items that were on our stations and the recipes that they had worked on, and we just kind of went to work. I think we had maybe a week, maybe less than a week before we started doing live services.

It was a departure from Trio. It was definitely more risk-taking. I thought it was going to be extremely challenging. And it certainly was. And then it just got more and more challenging, the more we explored different techniques. I think Alex Stupak had a profound influence on Grant's direction for the food in the beginning at Alinea, because he was very familiar with sort of advanced molecular techniques. I think even more so than Grant was in a lot of ways in the beginning.

DAVE BERAN: I tried to work at Trio, and I wrote to Achatz, but he never wrote back. So I worked at mk for Todd Stein. I staged at Spring, Boka and Blackbird. It was right when the *Tribune* wrote a piece about Trotter vs. Tru, a ten-point comparison.[41] So I wrote to both of them and I got a job at Tru. So I worked at Tru for a little over a year, until I left for Alinea. I started pretty much exactly at the one-year anniversary.

We all started at Alinea as food runners. That was the waiting line for the kitchen. The food runner position basically allowed you to make a little more money quicker, because it paid more than a cook. It was a tester to see if you were going to be able to cut it, if you had the right attitude and mentality for that restaurant. And it gave you a good opportunity to understand the relationship between front and back of the house. I almost didn't take the job, because I found out I had to start as a food runner. And I happened to be chatting at Landmark with Kevin Boehm, and he said you're stupid if you don't take that job. I think I ran food for about ten weeks before I got into the kitchen. I started as a floater for four months, five months. Basically just helping out. Right after my first-year anniversary, I got promoted to sous chef, and about a year later I became chef de cuisine.

DAVID POSEY: I was the first cook to go straight to the kitchen and not have to run food. Dave Beran had to run food a little longer, because I skirted right around him to get a kitchen spot.

Trio had been fine dining, of course, but Alinea just felt like it was big boy time. Trio was like we were aiming for the big leagues, but Alinea *was* the big leagues. Partly it was that it was a brand-new kitchen that was laid out perfectly, with no quirky corners or anything like that. Like the pastry kitchen at Trio had one of the old stoves from an apartment in the hotel that was brought down, one of the refrigerators was like an old Coca-Cola cooler that had the sliding glass doors. And then you go into Alinea and everything's stainless steel and cut perfectly in 90-degree angles.

41 "Trotter Vs. Tru," May 5, 2005

But the food was the same, you know? Everything went through a high-tech blender into a chinois [strainer] to make sure it was smooth. Those standards were always there, but at Alinea it was just the way to get there was a little more advanced.

SCOTT NOORMAN: When we opened Alinea, Joe Catterson, my wine mentor, and Grant gave me the position of sommelier to start. They said we need guys like you that were at Trio to teach anybody new coming in how we do things. Because it's completely out of the box, we were doing our style of service and doing things that nobody had done before. Like telling guests to put their hands behind their backs and take a piece of food off a wire. How do you do that, and not be a snob or come across as just being stupid? We had to be really conscious of our words, how we approached people, and just reading people, reading their body language as you're coming to the table and understanding what their needs are.

When I became a somm I asked Joe if I should go through the accreditation to became an advanced sommelier. And he said, Scott, you don't need that. You're a sommelier at the restaurant that every other sommelier in the world wants to be at. Why do you need a pin to tell you, you belong here?

CHRISTOPHER GERBER: I hated fine dining, because I felt the service and the style of it engendered a kind of a feeling and attitude from the servers that was maybe condescending and cold. And I like to joke around a lot and make people laugh. I always thought it was a fun juxtaposition of being really technically proficient, and very on your game, but also kind of having like an irreverent attitude. And especially with Grant's food, which is serious, but also could be very whimsical and funny.

There was about nine months between my leaving Trio and Alinea opening, and so I went to Tru. And I remember the Lettuce Entertain You look that I got so many times. I think one of the first things was like, don't ask the guest how they're feeling, how they're feeling is none of our business. And I thought that was like the absolute worst thing to tell somebody who was in service. I felt it should be the opposite. We need to know because that's going to inform you of how you're going to take care of them. Like if they're not having a good day because traffic sucks, maybe you bring them a drink and be like, this is to take the edge off. Or I just got married today, or it's my birthday, or my anniversary, or I just closed on a condo. People will give you little gems while you're talking with them. And you can either do something with it, or, or ignore it.

SCOTT NOORMAN: We changed the scope of dining in America. And now so many restaurants plate like Grant, the swipes and the gels and, and the almost, like, *landscapes* that he would create. He thought outside of the box, and we changed the way chefs think and create food. And that was really special.

****

One of the most striking things about dining at Alinea was the unusual servingware, which seemed to have come from another planet. They were the creations of a Czech-born designer named Martin Kastner.

MARTIN KASTNER: I'm a blacksmith by trade. I worked at an historical castle as a blacksmith for a few years, and kind of realized that I wasn't that interested in the artisanal approach. Blacksmithing, at least in Europe today, you have to work with some kind of historical specialist who supervises you, and you have to follow exactly the tools and trade of the time. So you're always in somebody else's shoes.

I went back to school to study art. I studied, first, natural materials design, which was looking at traditional techniques and materials and technologies, like weaving, carving and ceramics, and trying to find contemporary uses or language for them. And then conceptual art. And I was always interested in the making of things, and in reproduction, and also our interactions with objects. Like, how do we think about objects? What kind of interaction do we want to have with an object? And I had a professor who repeatedly told me, you might be interested in product design. And I said I don't think I'm interested in industrial design. And she's like, well, it's not the same thing.

Kastner met his wife when she was studying in Prague and followed her back to the US.

MARTIN KASTNER: When I got to the States I found that there's no work in

America for a blacksmith with an MFA. So I went around to different fabrication shops and found a couple who would hire me as a contractor to work on things that were too complex for them, but they didn't want to turn the work down. At the same time a friend of ours was getting married, and we didn't have any money. So I started making things at the shop and giving them and then people would call and be like, oh, can I have one of those things? I would make very limited batches of things, like products for the home.

GRANT ACHATZ: At the end of Trio and going into Alinea, the idea was to challenge everything and ask why, and what can we do that's new? At Trio I'd had an idea for a new service piece, it was literally in my head. It was a folded piece of stainless steel with holes that would essentially hold a Tootsie Pop. So the stick would go in the hole, and the guest would pick it up out of that. So I started Googling industrial designers and jewelry makers and all those kinds of people. Stumbled upon Martin and wrote him a full email. Two days later he responded and said this sounds interesting.

He was in San Diego at the time, but his wife worked for Delta so she got free flights. So he would hop on a flight on standby, come to Chicago, we would meet and talk over some ideas, and he would fly back to San Diego and make prototypes. That's how it started. But of course, we had a very limited budget at Trio. So there wasn't a whole lot of room to stretch out. But I knew that he would be a massive part of our identity at Alinea.

MARTIN KASTNER: Grant asked me for a way to present a frozen lollipop, a small sphere of ice as a palate cleanser. He said, we've tried different ways of presenting it, and it's just kind of clumsy and unpleasant. So I just started thinking about the ice itself as a structural material, and the piece ended up being called a Tripod, where it's three pieces of wire that are embedded in a silicone tube. You spread the legs and hold the ice in the middle, and then they collapse when you take the lollipop out of them. That was the first thing and the response to it was super positive, people loved the playful nature of it. So then we started a conversation about other culinary concepts that they were struggling with, or they felt would be better served with a different vehicle.

The next one I think was the Squid, where we were serving a tempura shrimp upright, just kind of hugging it with a cluster of wires. So it would allow airflow so it doesn't get soggy, and it can cool without condensation on a plate. Then there was the Anti-Plate. A spoon on its own is a very good vehicle for a controlled bite, but I was thinking about ways to present the spoon so people could pick it up without having to figure it out. So essentially, it's a plate that doesn't have the center well, so the spoon hooks into it, and you can pick it up naturally.

CHRISTOPHER GERBER: The ones we would have the most fun with were the ones where people didn't know what to do with them, how to eat off them. The Antenna was the one that was the most fun to talk about. Because you basically have to sort of convince people to go get it with just their mouth. That was where you would be like, okay, so just go down and get it with your mouth. And it's like a big phallus with a piece of food on the end of it. You're on the edge of inappropriate, you can go either way with it. And it really quickly separates the people that want to have fun, or are intimidated.

JEFF PIKUS: Martin's pieces were fun for the guests, maybe less fun for the cooks. Grant was very passionate about treating these things with respect. If something wasn't handled properly, or if we weren't using it the right way, he would get upset about it. There was definitely a stress level to using Martin's pieces.

But the collaboration between him and Grant was incredible, because they were coming from completely different sides of the universe. But they both had the exact same end goal in mind, which was to create exciting ways to serve.

When they started working on Alinea, Achatz wanted to have Kastner design the entire restaurant. Kokonas knew they needed an architect experienced in the requirements of restaurant spaces and how the City of Chicago works, but Kastner was still an important influence on aspects of the restaurant from menu design to the deliberately disorienting entrance, designed to mentally separate you from the street outside.

NICK KOKONAS: The conversations between Grant, Martin and I were very first principle thinking, how do we make someone feel uncomfortable so that when they finally feel comfortable, they feel even more comfortable? How do we make something feel more like a magic trick, where it's wondrous and unique? How do we introduce aromas that are not actually on the plate and that flavor the dish and create sense memory? All those things were discussions we had, and Martin was absolutely critical to that, and also had a very different, minimalist, European modernist viewpoint that I very much appreciated. He would strip everything down to the least complicated way of doing it. And it was super elegant. It was really a pleasure at that point to have such an open field that we can play in.

The other critical thing is that certainly, there was talk on the internet about stuff like this, but in those days you wouldn't do a dessert that someone slurps out of a tube, and then it would hit Instagram the next day and be at twenty other restaurants around the world within a week. You could actually create surprise, and so that felt really fertile and wonderful.

MARTIN KASTNER: If you're trying to deliver a holistic experience, you try to control as many aspects as you can. Today, I think this thinking has gone much farther, it goes from before you even interact with the restaurant. But the idea was that we started to look at and think about various aspects of the dining experience. That's kind of where the idea of the entrance being an entryway into the restaurant comes from, and then the menu concept that is kind of little hidden infographics about what you're going to experience.

But at the same time, it's kind of a luxury experience. And it had to work for the clientele that can afford it, you know, it's like refined luxury components that couldn't turn into a completely experimental dinner theater. It was trying to walk that line.

****

*Alinea achieved national acclaim—*Gourmet *magazine named it the best restaurant in America in 2007. Then some terrible news went out to food media—and to staff at Alinea.*

GRANT ACHATZ: This went back to Trio, actually. I started feeling this little white dot on my tongue. And my tongue's bothering me. Multiple dentist visits, and they just said I was biting my tongue at night. And eventually it became such an impediment, it was hard for me to swallow and talk. Nick came in one day, and I looked pretty haggard. He said, what is up with you? I said, I can't eat, it's hard for me to swallow. We went to an oral surgeon and got a biopsy.

The diagnosis: stage 4 squamous cell carcinoma of the mouth. The standard treatment involved surgical removal of most of the tongue; one of the most acclaimed young chefs in America would not be able to taste or speak. His reaction was that it would not be a life worth living for a chef.

NICK KOKONAS: He had been to Rush, and then I got him into Sloan-Kettering in New York, I talked to Roger Ebert, who had had the surgery at Northwestern. And the doctors said to me, you are doing your friend a disservice, he needs to have the surgery. Grant had already decided, I'm not going to have the surgery.

I started researching anti-angiogenesis drugs, and alternative treatments—just to be clear, *not* hocus pocus, because once it got in the newspapers, every bullshit healer in the world wanted a piece of it. After the article came out in the *New York Times*,[42] I'm like, we should write a press release, because it's going to leak out that you have this. He said, you write it, I don't care. But once it was public, Dr. Everett Vokes at the University of Chicago could reach out to me [which he couldn't before] because of the HIPAA laws and because I wasn't related to Grant.

He said, bring him in. We have a clinical trial that we might be able to get him into, but we need to examine him. I told Grant, I'm picking you up and taking you to the University of Chicago. No man, he said, I'm done with doctors. They've all said the same thing. He was in a lot of pain, he'd lost a lot of weight, he was on lidocaine patches. I just drove to his apartment and picked him up and we sat down with the doctors. A few days later, he started chemo there.

In a sense, they had found a doctor as innovative in his field as Achatz was in his. The plan was to treat it with chemotherapy and radiation, but without surgery. Achatz could still be a chef—assuming he survived.

42 "A Chef's Toughest Challenge," Pete Wells, July 23, 2007.

GRANT ACHATZ: Thankfully they had something that, again, was new and innovative. But that was a wild time; we were coming off *Gourmet* ranking us number one in the country. And '07 was the first year that we entered the World's 50 Best list. So the momentum was massive. And then it felt like, shit, we're gonna get chopped off at the knees here.

NICK KOKONAS: We gathered the staff, and I gave the talk. I said to them, there's a very, very good chance that three months from now, he will not be alive. That was a real conversation, and it was super emotional, like people are sobbing, it was right out of a movie. And some people literally stood up. I remember Jeff Pikus stood up and said, I'm not good with shit like this, and just walked out the back door. People did not know how to handle this—nor should they have had to. I mean, they were all a pretty young team, and the guy who was in there twelve hours a day was given a terminal sentence, right? And so it was really tough. It was tough to care about doing service. It was tough to see him when he came in.

DAVE BERAN: Curtis had just left [for an executive chef position at the Peninsula Hotel], there was like this crazy meeting one day over speakerphone. And Achatz basically announced to the whole staff that he had cancer, that Curtis was leaving because that was already in motion, and that they're promoting Jeff Pikus to chef de cuisine, and that myself, Greg Baxtrom and Nathan Klingbail were going to become the sous chefs.

Scott Noorman had lost both his kidneys as a teenager.

SCOTT NOORMAN: I've been through a slew of surgeries, blah, blah, blah. And, you know, Grant knew all that. And he still believed in me. When we heard him on that call, I had to leave the room because I started tearing up. One of the other cooks and I, we went outside and smoked a joint, and just comforted each other.

JEFF PIKUS: It was an enormous challenge. Luckily, I had Dave Beran supporting me. And I had an extremely talented crew. But taking that on was tough.

Me taking on the creative side of it, which I kind of didn't really ever do. I depended on Grant to give me ideas for stuff, and then I would implement it. That part was challenging because, obviously, the style of cooking that I've been doing since I've worked at Alinea is more my style than Alinea food ever was or will be. So I didn't feel comfortable being the creative force there in his absence. That part, I felt like I maybe failed that a little bit. Because we didn't change the menus frequently. We didn't do new things as frequently because he wasn't a part of it. It was still his place, not mine.

GRANT ACHATZ: I was here every day, because it was my safe place. It was the only place I felt comfortable. Even though I was going through chemo and radiation and looked like a mess, it just felt like this is my home. And also, there was so much going on here, it distracted you.

I couldn't taste at some point into the treatment, it just wiped it all out. And at that point, I was such a control freak. The stakes were so high that prior to this, I had my hand on every single thing. And all of a sudden, that ability sort of went away, so I had to lean on like, John Shields, Curtis Duffy, Dave Beran, Alex Stupak, David Posey. Those guys became my surrogate tasters.

And so it was a role reversal. Instead of all of the folks in the kitchen bringing me a pot or something to taste, and I'd say, more salt, more acid, more of this, it was me doing that to them. Ultimately, it was a big shift in terms of management style, trust, collaboration. Long term, it was a net positive, but in the moment, it felt fragile. Very fragile.

I would write new dishes out on paper. Dave Beran and I got really close at that time. We just were comfortable with each other and talking to each other. Curtis had left, so I really relied on Dave. I'd come to him with the piece of paper, and we'd look at the diagram sketch. I'd list out all the ingredients and the components. We'd talk about how we think things would work. And then he would start making it, or both of us would. And when it came time to taste, I would describe how salty, how sweet, how acidic something was with words. I would use examples of levels. Like, this should taste like a pickle, a classic, kosher, Vlasic pickle. Or, this should be as sweet as Häagen-Dazs vanilla. So it became this new way of communicating how food should be seasoned.

I was a chef, I was the owner. And people looked up to me to have the final say. So in that scenario, oftentimes you have a lot of people that don't want to tell you no. So that honesty between Dave and me in particular became invaluable. Like how does a chef in that position feel being criticized? But it was necessary, obviously.

DAVE BERAN: It's a lot of trust, right? You put people into place and you're constantly beating them over the head with this notion of like, taste the food, taste the food, taste the food. And so that's what we did. We just tasted the food. And we all had very similar palates at that point. Because that's all we've been doing for years together.

Everything was a clear path of like, here's photos, here's the concept, here's drawings, here's tasting notes, here's emails. I mean, you were basically handing him a cookbook of a dish. Nothing ever hit the menu at Alinea without Achatz knowing what it was.

NICK KOKONAS: I sat down to eat, which I rarely did at Alinea, because I wanted to make sure that the food wasn't crappy. And I remember I called Grant, and I said, man, that's like the best meal I've ever had at Alinea or Trio ever. He goes, we're doing all the easy stuff. I've got all the tricks up my sleeve, but it's boring. But I'm like, no, dude, this is the best meal for Alinea ever. It's like you're doing better when you can't taste, because you're going to the tried-and-true stuff, but still doing the modern techniques on it. This is fucking great.

GRANT ACHATZ: The most I was away was at the very end of December of '07. I was out for, I think it was nine days. That was the longest stretch. And, honestly, it was such a morale thing here. Like, we were five days a week then. Everybody worked next to each other fourteen hours a day, and it was really genuinely like family. Everybody was genuinely just so freaking excited that the restaurant didn't close. I didn't die. And we could start doing what we set out to do again. We had lost a lot of staff. People had to look out for themselves, it seemed like this was going to end poorly. So we did have a period of having to rebuild.

DAVE BERAN: Pikus ran the kitchen for about a year, and then he walked out. It was a really hard time when Achatz came back from cancer. It was a lot of reasserting himself in the kitchen. I think it just broke Jeff, running that restaurant while Achatz was in treatment, while we were writing a cookbook, worried that the restaurant was going to close. It was like paper-thin staff, the smallest I'd ever seen the restaurant staff, eight cooks and four managers. That was all of Alinea.

JEFF PIKUS: It was just a moment of intense burnout, frustration, anger, that resulted in me leaving. He was healthy enough to be at work. And he wanted to work because that's all he knows how to do, is just keep pushing. And I think he wanted to sort of reassert his control over a place that he hadn't spent as much time in as he had in the previous five years. He's a very quiet person in general. But he can be extremely intense in the kitchen.

And I just, I guess I'd had enough. Because the time that he wasn't there, and the time that he was sick, that was also intense, and I'd been dealing with that. And I decided I didn't want to be a part of it anymore. I think the biggest regret that I have was leaving in a way that was not positive or helpful for him or for the team or for the restaurant.

NICK KOKONAS: When he came back afterwards, he looked terrible, but it was clear that he was on the mend. And, you know, a good chunk of the staff had left like, through no fault of their own. They could see the writing on the wall that this place might not be around, and they needed jobs. So it was really, really challenging to build it back up, but it felt very hopeful again.

The ordeal would, indirectly, provide the inspiration for Achatz's and Kokonas's next restaurant . . . literally called Next.

GRANT ACHATZ: Right when I got diagnosed, Nick was in Michigan at a golf tournament. I called him up and gave him the news. And he kind of freaked out, and he tried to drive five hours straight back from Michigan. And I'm like dude, I'm at work, why are you driving back? Play your golf tournament. And he's like, no, no, no, I'm driving back. I said, if you come back I'll be in the kitchen cooking so, whatever.

So he walked in the back door, he looked like hell, you could tell he hadn't eaten. He'd been golfing all morning and then he got in the car and drove for five hours. So I said, are you hungry? He said, yeah, I'm actually starving. And I'm like, let me cook you something. And I just ripped out this really classical French duck dish. Like, fanned-out duck breast with morels, brussels sprouts, it was like really basic, really French.

NICK KOKONAS: That is the only time I've eaten a bite in the Alinea kitchen for real. And I literally said to him, man, we should open a restaurant like this. And he was just like, nah, that's easy, and we'd get bored of it three months. That's a very telling thing, by the way, like one of the big mistakes I think that restaurants generally make, and ambitious chefs generally make, is that if you come in every day and you have a perfect dish, and you make it the same every day for years, boy, does it get boring? Like, playing the same song if you're a rock band, over and over again, and so instead you go into your experimental jazz phase.

And that's a giant fucking mistake, it's not about you, it's about the customer and the diner and their experience. People might come into Alinea once or twice in their life, and if it happens to be the day that you got bored making Hot Potato, Cold Potato . . .

GRANT ACHATZ: As he was eating it, he was like, damn, why can't we find this anywhere in Chicago? We should open a restaurant like that. And I say, that would be boring. And he said, yeah, but food like this, and what if we did like, really classical tagliatelle, carbonara, and some Sicilian food—and I said, so great, now you want to open a French restaurant *and* an Italian restaurant? All I really want is ramen. He goes, we could do that too! Great, so now we're opening three. We're sitting there thinking about it, and then we go, why not make it all the same restaurant? Why not make it Italian for three months, French for three months, Japanese for three months?

A year or so later we had just put the cookbook to bed.[43] And once they told me the cancer was gone, I felt like I had lost a year. I was energized and

43 *Alinea,* 2008.

I'm on the go, so for me part of that next step was saying hey, I'm alive, I can do this, let's open another restaurant and show everybody that I'm still upright. But the question was really, how do you come up with the next concept, we don't want to cannibalize Alinea. Everybody wanted an Alinea Vegas, Alinea Manhattan, Alinea Tokyo. And it just wasn't right. So Next was born—thematic menus three or four times a year.

DAVE BERAN: We did everything over GChat. So one of them was messaging me late at night. It was like, hey, this is a concept. What do you think of it? Do you think you'd ever be interested in a concept like this? And initially, I didn't want to do it. I was at Alinea. We'd just gotten number seven in the world. By the time Next was under construction, we had just gotten three Michelin stars. And I didn't want to leave Alinea for that. That was my dream. Why would I walk away from that?

Eventually Grant and I talked more about it, and I talked to him about how I was gonna want more, and he knew I was gonna want more. But I didn't know what my identity was. It was a lot like him using Trio to bridge the gap between French Laundry and Alinea. Next could be my Trio for a couple of years.

Eventually through that conversation, we decided that opening with a Paris bistro menu wasn't impactful enough for the caliber of restaurant we wanted to be. And that's when we started talking about the Escoffier menu. Every cook talks about Escoffier, but nobody really knows Escoffier, what his food is. And, frankly, from a sales perspective, you know people will love French food right off the bat, especially in Chicago.

NICK KOKONAS: We were talking French food. And Grant said, what kind of French food? There's eighty different kinds of French food. Is it Parisian bistro? Is it Escoffier, Paris 1906? As soon as he said "Paris 1906," I said we're done. I don't need to explain to you what Paris 1906 is. I like my elevator pitches to be like five words. And until you can clarify something down to that, and people understand what you need, you don't have an idea. If it takes you two pages to understand a restaurant concept, it's not unique or clear. And so once we got down to, "What is Next restaurant? It changes every four months and it's opening with Paris 1906," you can build a place around that.

GRANT ACHATZ: It was [our French roots]. But more importantly, we wanted to do completely the opposite of Alinea. One, because we didn't want to replicate anything or have anyone say oh, they're just slumming it. And we wanted to prove that we could cook real food, and we had range. And who doesn't love French food? And time-travel French food. Now that's pretty popular, I mean, the Carbone guys have thematic restaurants that try to embody New York in the '50s. It felt new, even though it was super-old. I mean, nobody was pressing ducks in the city.

The West Loop had expanded along Randolph, but Fulton Market was still meat processors and just a few pioneering bars and restaurants.

NICK KOKONAS: When we found the West Loop places, the only thing they had going for them was that they were dirt cheap rent-wise. And the bar next to it was kind of a shithole. And we thought, maybe we could get the bar too and do an Alinea for cocktails, at the same time. So our project scope doubled. But you know, when you're building one, building two isn't crazy because it's a lot of redundancy. So that's how that came about.

GRANT ACHATZ: It was a risk, because of my health, and we wanted to get in before a neighborhood gentrified. Back then, there was still blood on the streets from the meatpackers. And so that space was dirt cheap. Even when we first got it the lease was six or seven thousand dollars a month, it was like nothing.

If there was any doubt about an Alinea spinoff doing thematic menu concepts, Next selling out the entire capacity of its first year's three menus within minutes of season tickets—yes, season tickets—going on sale answered that.

DAVE BERAN: The Alinea mentality was exactly the same. Next was just a different medium of food. Like there was still the theatrics, there was still the over-the-top plateware, there's still the caliber of service.

People didn't buy into it as, oh, Alinea is cooking classic French. People bought into it like a theater putting on great shows. And so that was the difference. If it hadn't been Alinea, and it hadn't been Achatz, and it hadn't been that exact moment in time when Facebook was getting crazy, and Twitter was just taking off, and you had Facebook groups and all of a sudden the ticket thing–if any old Joe who happened to have a restaurant announced that he was going to have a French menu, followed by a Thai menu, followed by a menu on the concept of "childhood," it would have failed instantly.

One of the conversations we often had was, are people paying for the [cuisine]? Or are they paying for Next? It was always a concern. I was fortunate enough that I think all the menus I worked on sold out, so I never really had to deal with that. But I do remember having a conversation around, people would pay that for Japanese food. But would they pay it for Thai cuisine? I remember a Yelp review where someone said the menu was $95, and why would I pay that for panang curry when I can get it for $9 on the street? And all I thought about was the two people standing downstairs who for six hours straight, would just juice coconuts every day, so that we could make panang curry sauce with fresh coconut milk. What you really had to do is find an angle, like the one menu I always wanted to do but never got to, was pre and post imperialism India, where you showed the British influence. So it was always a tricky game there.

But you know, the Sicily menu topped out at $85, and we were flying in blood oranges from Sicily and I bought an $8,000 pasta maker to extrude pasta for three courses. If someone were to ever come up to me and say the value wasn't there in those menus, they don't deserve to eat in nice restaurants.

****

"The ticket thing" Beran refers to was another of Kokonas's paradigm-breaking innovations— one that helped whip up the demand for a seat at Next to white-hot levels. (The online phrase "FOMO"—fear of missing out—wasn't widely used yet, but the mania that Next produced was FOMO to a T.) It would also lead to a new business for Kokonas—the reservation platform Tock. It began with something he'd long observed about the way reservations worked at Alinea.

NICK KOKONAS: We had three people answering phones all day and telling people no, and we're doing seventy people on a Wednesday, but we're doing ninety people on a Saturday, but we have more demand than seventy on a Wednesday. Why can't we do ninety on a Wednesday? So I started realizing that there are misaligned incentives. Well, okay, how can we be more efficient? How can we have a better guest experience, pre-booking, before people get to the restaurant?

So we decided we're not going to be answering the phones all the time. We're going to let them go to voicemail and not waste the time. We don't need three people answering phones. We can have one, and we can only answer on certain days of the week, because we're full. There's no point in having the conversation.

I tracked no-shows over the course of a year, and went, holy shit, we're losing $600,000 a year of revenue to no shows. And unlike a busy, two-hundred-seat restaurant with a giant bar, we can't just overbook it. Because we can't have someone show up and wait for an hour to sit down for an Alinea meal.

And so when we started building Next, I was like, look, every other form of entertainment sells tickets. We're going to sell tickets. This won't be hard. I hired one programmer, and he and I built out the rudimentary system for Next in about five months. It was just a two-person operation, but when we turned it on, so many people were trying to book Next that it broke, and then we fixed that. After about an hour, I got onto Facebook at the time to tell everyone, look, stop refreshing, and I'll be able to fix it in a little bit. And then we sold $560,000 of prepaid bookings to Next in a single day.

Even though the system for Next was really rudimentary, it worked in the first year, we sold every single seat at that restaurant. And I don't mean every table, I mean every seat. We only sold in twos, fours, or sixes, and every single one of them sold out. We had perfect revenue, like, when you do the spreadsheet, you go, how much do we discount this by slippage and no shows and seasonality and all that? The answer in our case became zero. And so Next and Aviary were incredibly profitable their first year. That opening menu was eighty-five bucks, right? That was crazy, yeah, and we still made a ton of money. We paid off the investment of nearly $3 million for Next and Aviary combined in nine months.

But other restaurant owners were risk averse. They didn't understand it. They didn't understand that taking a deposit of $5 has no slippage in terms of [fewer people] booking, but even $5 reduces the no-show rate to under 3 percent. So that became the challenge of Tock. I still look at restaurants and small businesses and go, these are being run like they were run when the telephone was invented.

****

Next opened in early April 2011. Just about three weeks later, so did the "Alinea for cocktails" next door: the Aviary.

GRANT ACHATZ: We wanted them side by side, because we knew that we wanted to open a cocktail bar. And that space provided it. When we went in, we were like, we're not going to spend any money on the buildout, we were going to be thrifty and deliberately make it not as luxurious as Alinea. Which it's not, but once we got in there, we couldn't help ourselves, we went way over budget.

I think the Aviary was pure opportunity. We saw a window, where all of this crazy technique was happening at Alinea. And nobody was applying that to cocktails. It was great when the Violet Hour, Barrelhouse Flat, Sable, opened, but they were doing pretty traditional cocktails. We were like, why don't we play with ice, play with the service ware. And use all this stuff that we've developed at Alinea, but put it in a glass. So that's how the Aviary happened.

Andrew Brochu had been on the opening team of Alinea. He was recruited to come back to work on a new project—but first, to improve the Aviary's menu.

ANDREW BROCHU: The Aviary had lost its identity a little bit by then. They were still doing little *amuse-bouches*, little almost sushi bites. I tried to take it in more of a bar food realm. I tried to get the food up just a touch hardier so that people wouldn't get hammered, because that was an issue there every night.

Everything at the Aviary is a tableside presentation, every single thing. And that's such an Alinea thing, everything is about the theatrics, it's got to be over the top theatrics. And I think that that is what makes Alinea so special. But at the same time, I think my hope was that we could do a little bit better job of creating an identity for the Aviary, more than just, this is an offshoot of what we do at Alinea.

I had a great relationship with Grant the whole time. So he definitely let me—in my opinion—go further than most people, because there was a trust there. But it's so hard for Grant to go outside of his style. Because that's what made him who he is, you know? So we would talk about things and he'd be like, okay, cool. So are we still gonna do the Black Truffle Explosion? Which I actually was pushing for the whole time, because I thought that's a great bite for the Aviary.

Besides the main floor Aviary, there was a hidden bar, at first invitation-only, in the basement: the Office. By then, Christopher Gerber was the director of service for all of the Alinea Group's restaurants . . . which meant he was often the one who could give you that much-desired invite to the Office.

GRANT ACHATZ: It was the exact same philosophy as Paris 1906. Bartenders are a different bunch, and often there's not a lot of mutual respect between chefs and bartenders. We were coming out with a bar whose tagline was, chefs for drinks—something like that—and we also wanted to show them that we could do pre-Prohibition drinks, and that's where the Office came in.

CHRISTOPHER GERBER: It depended on the night, whether or not I had the Office phone. It was a beast, doing that was a one-person job because of the amount of requests you would get, the amount of texting back, working out what time they come in, how many people are downstairs, there's only so many seats, obviously you're making sure you're not crushing the bartender and the server down there. But it was a lot of fun though, too, because you got to be sort of mysterious and cheeky with people. And they never knew who had the phone. We made it seem like kind of an accomplishment to get there.

Meanwhile Brochu was working on his other project for them:

ANDREW BROCHU: Grant and Nick had said, hey, we want to do a casual project. You want to come partner with us? And I was like, yeah, absolutely.

We were going to do our version of a British pub, but with higher-end American-style pub food. British pub, but still has a Michelin star.

Nick and I were mainly the ones looking, we really wanted an old corner space that had some cool old Chicago millwork. But we ended up getting the space next door to Aviary. And we all kind of sat down and said, you know what, this space isn't really going to work for the concept that we were looking to do. So let's just create a new concept. And that's where Roister was born. We knew that wood burning was really becoming cool. Started talking about doing a wood-burning oven. Because we knew we wanted it to be casual.

The whole "the kitchen is the dining room" concept came from the dinner party thing that people like Phillip Foss were doing, but everybody was doing it in a small places, like ten or twelve seats. Nick was like, why can't we do that same thing, but with a hundred seats? You walk in and you see the chef, you see the people cooking for you. Well, it worked really well for like the James Beard parties and stuff like that.

GRANT ACHATZ: Roister again was the same 180-degree turn [from Alinea]. What's the opposite of molecular gastronomy? It's primal fire.

****

When Michelin came to Chicago in 2011, Alinea was one of only two restaurants to get three stars—the other being Lettuce's L20, which fell to one star the next year with the departure of chef Laurent Gras. Since then, the only Chicago restaurants to achieve three stars have been Grace, run by former Alinea chef de cuisine Curtis Duffy, and Smyth, run by former Alinea sous chef John Shields.

But everyone noticed which restaurant didn't get three stars: Charlie Trotter's, which held two before closing in 2012.

GRANT ACHATZ: In 2005, when we opened, the *New York Times*'s critic was Frank Bruni, and he came in opening night. And when he was writing his review, he reached out to Charlie for a quote. Charlie said, let's see where they're at in ten or twenty years, I think right now, it's nonsense on stilts. And it's a marathon, not a sprint, so call me back in twenty years. But then, shortly after, I think he realized that we weren't smoke and mirrors, and that we were serious. And we were making an impact. And I think he sort of walked that back a bit, and started being very friendly, very respectful, invited me to his twentieth anniversary celebration.

And he would write me letters, a handwritten letter and be like, congratulations, thank you for doing this for the city. This is tremendous and extraordinary. He would even call me at the very end, not too long before he passed—hey, just wanted to see how you're doing. It took me aback, the first couple of times. I was like, what's the agenda here? But as it continued, it felt more and more genuine. I think he was proud. And if you peel it back to 1995, I would have never thought that that would happen.

I feel like, I've just been so lucky to have these moments, these really monumental moments that somehow turn my way. I guess you could look at it two ways. You weren't very lucky because you got cancer. But the other way is, it was stage 4 everywhere, it was in my neck and everything. So I could easily have been dead in a couple of months. And I found the doctors who could treat it and saved my ability to taste. It's just wild how that works.

Alinea, Next, the Aviary and the Office all continue packing them in. In 2024, Nick Kokonas sold almost all his shares in the Alinea Group with the intention to be disruptive in other industries. With a new partner, Jason Weingarten, Grant Achatz relaunched Roister as Fire ("primal fire") in 2025, but closed it later that year.

MOTO

Homaro Cantu was born in 1976 in Tacoma. A troubled youth, including an extended period of homelessness as a teen, led him to work in fast food and eventually attend culinary school. Interested in science and gadgets as much as food, he went to work at Charlie Trotter's in 1999, finding in the rigorous kitchen and its domineering chef what other kids from similar backgrounds found in the military, and rising to sous chef.

In 2004, a year before Alinea opened, he was hired as the opening chef of Moto on Fulton Market. It was planned as an Asian fusion restaurant; his idea was to showcase molecular gastronomy techniques—and showmanship. It attracted young cooks who similarly wanted to break the rules and dazzle guests. Cantu's restless mind dabbled in experiments from printing his menu on paper you could eat, to cooking your next course in a small "polymer oven" at the table while you ate the previous course, to creating a cuisine based on the miracle berry, the fruit of an African plant that increases perceived sweetness (so a lemon tastes like lemonade).

RICHIE FARINA: I started cooking when I was sixteen, literally as a part-time job because I wanted money to buy clothes. I started at a pizza place, and kind of got bit by the bug there. My uncle had a friend who had a catering business, and every once in a while I would go help them. This is all in Florida and the Tampa Bay and Orlando area. One of the chefs there suggested that if I was serious about it, I should go to culinary school. He suggested Johnson & Wales in Rhode Island.

I did what most young cooks do, work in a place for a year, move to another place for a year. I wanted to learn French bistro food, I went to a French bistro. I wanted to learn Italian so I went to an Italian place.

I saw an *Iron Chef America* episode of Chef Cantu using lasers and edible paper and talking with microphones and liquid nitrogen and all this crazy stuff. And I was kind of into the molecular world already. When I was living in Boston, I used to do little getaways to New York just to eat. I ate at WD-50 one night. and that was my first exposure to that style of cuisine. It wasn't the best tasting food I ever had, but it was definitely the most forward thinking.

All the hydrocolloids weren't available, it was all industrial stuff, but I would call companies that made them and say I'm a line cook at this place, they would send me samples. And I was playing on my own, trying to find a recipe here and there.

My sister moved here in '07, so now I had family here. So I moved here, knocked on the back door of Moto and handed them my resume—"I hope you're hiring." That was in 2008, and I left there in 2015 as the executive chef.

TREVOR ROSE-HAMBLIN: I've been in the kitchen since I was fourteen years old. I really cut my teeth on Italian food at a group called the Bravo Brio Restaurant Group in Columbus, Ohio. I was a line cook for them for a number of years, but I sort of got burned out on corporate cooking, doing seven or eight hundred covers a night. I went back to school and I met a guy there who said he was thinking about going to culinary school in Chicago. He asked if I wanted to come along and I said heck yeah. I went to Kendall and I did my externship at Moto.

My first day of the externship, in 2009 or 2010, I could feel music coming up from downstairs, my feet are rumbling with like hard techno playing. All these cooks are wearing chef whites, but it's fast, there's energy in the air, and they're all getting ready for service. They're doing an amazing amount of covers, twenty-course menus. So everybody's drinking Red Bull, and there's fire in the air.

Walking into the kitchen, it looks like there are these vacuum-sealed bags on the wall with lights over them, and it looks like there's algae inside these bags. And I'm like, what the heck is that? And I start looking at it, and [chef de cuisine] Chris Jones comes up and says, what're you doing, chef? I said, I'm just checking out the stuff. He tells me to follow him into the private dining room and says, sit there for a minute. A minute later he comes back with an NDA.

Some of my chefs at Kendall said, you go to Moto, you're not going to learn classic techniques. When I put my book together for my fine dining teacher there, I think he was a little taken aback by just how many fine dining techniques we were doing. I think people kind of misconstrue the molecular world sometimes, thinking that it's all smoke and mirrors. There was some of that, of course, but there were tons of classic French techniques like confit, and I did more *brunoise* cuts at Moto than I ever did in culinary school. While you think about food differently there, it's really just adding a few new ingredients to the cupboard and understanding how to use them.

The first day I was working with Richie, and he was doing pastry. And I had to make a hundred miniature hamburgers where the buns were macarons, the burger was cocoa nibs and chocolate, there was a slice of cheese that was basically gelatinized banana puree, and the ketchup was like a raspberry sauce and the mustard was banana again. I had never put my face that close to food in my whole life, because it was so teeny. It took me like three hours, because I had to form each beef patty individually before I could do all these things, and it was strange doing this little tiny minutiae of hyper-focused food. But I was really proud of myself afterward. And that was my first day.

HEATHER BUBLICK: I had gotten my degree in non-fiction writing, and then went to culinary school. I thought I'd be a food writer. And then I did my internship at Moto.

I wasn't in love with it during my stage. But then when I got offered my internship, you know, Chris Jones would sit you down and say, we're going to do front of house and we're going to do kitchen, and we're going to do food photography. And there was this wholeness about the entire experience that I really was intrigued by.

D'ANDRE CARTER: I worked at different restaurants around Chicago. I decided I wanted to go to culinary school because I noticed that we weren't actually making food. It was all pre-portioned and we were coming in and heating it up. I really wanted to take being a chef serious, I went to the Cordon Bleu and I did my internship at Moto. I ended up working my way up from intern to Executive Sous Chef.

While I was in culinary school it was time to start looking for internships. I knew I didn't want to do any boring food. They had this spot in the Cordon Bleu where you could use the computers and just see what's available. Moto came up and then I Googled it. I saw like this big laser, and then I went to YouTube. And I was just seeing things set on fire. I was seeing like edible paper, I was seeing like all these different techniques. And I was like, I want to work *there.*

When I first knocked on that back door window, I was just kind of looking at these guys. I'm just a kid coming out of culinary school, I'd seen them on YouTube, and I thought, he's just like you in his kitchen. They were in full throttle prep mode. You could tell like everyone was so concentrated and focused like it's but it was like a good feeling, the energy you got. Everyone was like really focused on a task. That was like my first fine dining atmosphere, so I really didn't know what to compare it to. I just knew that I really had to get in this place.

****

Cantu was at Trotter's for just a few years, but it shaped his approach to cooking—and running a kitchen—indelibly:

RICHIE FARINA: Omar was working the line with Bill Kim and Giuseppe

[Tentori], Matt Merges was the chef de cuisine, all these legends that are still in the city. Omar was known as the science guy, so like if he was working on vegetable station, and they had three different foams on the dish, most people would just hold the hand blender. Matt and Giuseppe used to tease him because he rigged up a way where he had three blenders on a switch. He was always an adventurer, always a tinkerer. And that's always been a big influence on me, the efficiency side of things in the kitchen, how can you still get the same end products, but be clever about it and make it faster. That was the thing that I learned very early on working in the Moto kitchen, using science technology not only to enhance the experience, but also to make it as efficient as possible so that you can get the best service to the guest.

The idea of your dinner being more than just food on a plate is what I got introduced to there. It was kind of my first real introduction to the level of fine dining, with his Charlie Trotter background and having that Charlie Trotter mentality of like, insane focus and creativity and all that stuff. And getting the best possible ingredients and all those things, but not being bound to the traditions of what a fine dining establishment is.

D'ANDRE CARTER: He didn't want to be like Trotter's, as far as like the yelling. He wanted it to be fun.

HEATHER BUBLICK: Moto was always more about loud music and having fun. It was very, like, anti-fine dining restaurants, in terms of the loudness and the talking during service. It wasn't like you're gonna hear a pin drop in the Moto kitchen. Right. And Chris Jones, Darrell Nemeth, Ben Roche, Richie Farina—they all had big personalities.

D'ANDRE CARTER: I think the fine dining community was really tight then. We'd go to a bar, we'd be there with the Tru guys, the Trotter guys, the Alinea guys. But yeah, the stories that I used to hear from Trotter's, it's like crazy, but all the great chefs went through that system. That's what it was about back in those days, you know, working your butt off.

HEATHER BUBLICK: I did my internship and I ended up running *garde-*

manger. I would go to culinary school in the morning and I would come into front of house at night, and that's where I fell in love with working the house. And I never went back into a kitchen again.

D'ANDRE CARTER: Omar really believed in cross-training, and I think that was really good for me. Now I'm learning about wines and I'm learning about where to put the proper utensils or how to fold a napkin. I was seeing the whole dining experience come together. I was seeing how to treat the customer. It makes you have a sense of pride.

****

For Cantu at Moto, even more than for Achatz at Alinea, the appeal of molecular gastronomy was in its magic trick aspect—dishes that looked like one thing but tasted like another, jokes on the guest as they ate.

RICHIE FARINA: There was a time in Moto's heyday, the mid 2000s, that we would see how far can you push the envelope with things that maybe look gross, but taste really good. I guess an example of that would be my raw egg dish. It was an intermezzo between the A5 Wagyu and the desserts on the tasting menu. I turned coconut water into an egg white, and mango and passionfruit juice with a little bit of goji berry to make it look like a yolk, and I found a mold to make an edible shell out of sugar. So it looks like I crack an egg, put it in a little nest and serve it. You have to get it in your mind that this is going to taste nothing like what it looks like. I call it the wide-eye moment, sometimes people would even close their eyes and shoot it.

The cigar was actually the first dish that I put on the menu. I was a line cook three months in. And every Tuesday morning we would have our 10 a.m. meeting. Didn't matter if you're brand new, or if you've been there for years. You had to have some idea to make the restaurant better, whether it be a dish idea or how can service be better. My first couple months I was like, idea, idea, idea. Omar didn't like them. And for the longest time I was Bandana Boy because he didn't even know my name. I wanted to come up with something that's like going to impress him. I grew up in the Tampa area, Ybor City was famous for cigars. And then the Cuban influence in the area, a lot of really good Cuban sandwich places where I grew up. So I'm like, I want to turn [the ingredients of a] sandwich into a cigar. I had no idea how I was going to do it, but as soon as I said that, he's like, make it happen.

So I'm like, if we're gonna do it, it needs to look like someone was playing pool, smoking, and smashed the cigar into an ashtray. Then every single film crew that came in wanted to film it, I had unknowingly created one of the signature dishes of the restaurant. But that was the cool thing, having that opportunity as a young cook. The excitement that I felt, because this famous chef wants to believe in this thing. You're giving them the feeling like they're part of it, that they're working with you rather than for you.

HEATHER BUBLICK: One of my favorites was the garden pot. It was so simple in theory, but it was served in a [ceramic] garden pot. We did a panzanella salad with a squid ink bread crumb on top, and then [planted vegetables in it] like an edible garden. I loved that dish.

People always were wowed. There were a lot of things written about Moto that it was all smoke and mirrors. But the customers were always blown away. We went into service every night with the mentality that we're trying to change people's lives. And people were always so impressed by what they saw on their plate.

Even as an intern, they would make the edible menus behind the curtain and it was shrouded in secrecy until you were in, and then you knew all the secrets and knew all the tricks. But even then they were trying to keep some kind of mystery behind everything.

D'ANDRE CARTER: I remember doing like the roadkill dish with duck—

HEATHER BUBLICK: That was iconic. With the maggots?

D'ANDRE CARTER: It was like a food show. It was a show from the moment you had the edible menu. That's the beginning of it. When you finish the night with the s'mores bomb [a dessert that looked like a bomb in a Warner Bros. cartoon, with a fuse lit at the table], and it explodes in your mouth, it's like a story. The menu was a story.

****

While Grant Achatz was, as he said of his mentor Thomas Keller, a "working chef," by the late 2000s, Cantu followed more in Trotter's path, leaving the cooking to the skilled team he had assembled while he served as a publicist and evangelist for his ideas.

RICHIE FARINA: I joined Moto in 2008. So I missed the heyday when Omar was on the line every day. His job at that point was to spread the word of the restaurant and be more like a chef-owner.

My first interaction with him on the line was during the restaurant show. It was the middle of service. We had a chain-link fence out back around the [liquid] nitrogen tanks. And he wanted to put a basketball hoop in the alley so we could play on our break. So for like an hour at seven o'clock, on a Friday night, I'm in the alley on three milk crates standing holding a basketball hoop above my head, so he can weld it into place. That wasn't as crazy as it sounds to do in the middle of Friday night service. It was a test, entrusting Chris Jones and Darrell Nemeth to run the kitchen for him while he wants to go do this other thing. So there was always like, little tests here and there. Like, the more you kind of piled on at the time, the more it seems you can't get it done. But even if you didn't think you could, you knew you could. I think that he was very, very good at seeing potential in people before we even see it in ourselves and then finding a way to draw it out.

HEATHER BUBLICK: There was nothing like service when Omar was on the line. We always had microphones, we're always communicating with upstairs. If he was on the line, he'd be talking the whole night. He'd be having his own little party on the hotline.

TREVOR ROSE-HAMBLIN: He was kind of a guy who came in for meetings, he wasn't always on the line. At that point we were about to film *Future Food* [a cable series created by Cantu]. So there was a lot of that stuff going on. There were always film crews around. There was a point where the chefs had to get ready for service, but a number of them were on the show. And a lot of times, he was either updating the restaurant, getting ready for the show, or trying to put in new gadgets. He seemed to always be moving and doing something new. He was always exploring.

One of the first times he came in the kitchen, he turned off all the lights and he had this bioluminescent thing that when you added it to milk, would actually make the milk glow, something about the fat or the lactic acid activating the bioluminescence. So you see him suck up this milk with a straw and it's bright green, and then you see him open his mouth and he's got like green teeth.

We collaborated with Mugaritz [San Sebastian] and hung out with Andoni Luis Aduriz during the three months they're closed, while they're doing all their experimentation and they're working in their labs and showing us some of the things they've discovered with food.

So yeah, some of them were hokey and silly—we had an edible menu and we had the doughnut soup at the beginning. But it brought you to a time and place that reminds you of something. And that's important. That's part of what sets fine dining apart from just, regular sitting down and eating, it's an experience beyond just putting food in your mouth.

****

One of Cantu's innovations was called the Matrix—instead of a row of paper tickets spread out on the pass, the Matrix displayed on a screen everything happening in the kitchen and the dining room.

RICHIE FARINA: A lot of the ideas that he had were very far out-there ideas. Some of them worked, some didn't. But a thing that I learned was that true creativity starts when you lose your fear of failure. So you're like, hey, I want to see what happens with this. Yeah, there was someone in there on a headset, where we're doing text-to-speech stuff, but the idea of okay, there's no ticket machine. There's three monitors upstairs, four downstairs. At any point, anyone in the restaurant can look up and see a physical representation of the dining room and know what every table is on. Okay, there's a picture of chicken, they're on the capon dish, there's a picture of beef, they're on A5, there's a salmon picture, we know they're on the salmon course, there's a timer. It was a much easier way to just look up and be okay, I'm out on ten salmon because I see ten pictures of salmon on the board. So there was a lot of like, nonverbal communication that would happen within the restaurant. That again made it very efficient.

TREVOR ROSE-HAMBLIN: You had one person who was operating the pass, and manipulating the system. One person, in a busy restaurant, that's pretty fantastic. And then all of us are responsible for running our own food.

D'ANDRE CARTER: It was basically an Excel program, and someone was manually moving things over. But also, it's twenty courses and keeping track of twenty courses in order, like it would always show you what you were out on. And what you had to do, you could visually see it in front of you. Instead of having an expo just constantly calling it out and having to remember. So that was great.

HEATHER BUBLICK: I actually cut my finger my first day at Moto so I got put on the Matrix when it was brand new. I didn't know the menu, I didn't know anything. And I was the Matrix right off the jump. And he'd be like, come on Matrix. I think they're firing dishes. Aren't they ready to fire yet? And you're like waiting for the front to tell you what to do. And he's getting impatient on the line. He was always like a gentle giant, but he was a character on the line.

TREVOR ROSE-HAMBLIN: The cool thing about the Matrix was that the sisters who directed *The Matrix* [Lana and Lilly Wachowski] actually gave Omar permission to use the name "Matrix," because they were regulars at Moto, because they really loved the futuristic-style dining. I know it could have gone farther if we'd had more time, Omar wanted to take it to the next level and be even more automated.

RICHIE FARINA: We were doing indoor farming before indoor farming became a thing. Like he literally took our office and said, you don't have an office anymore. That's an indoor garden now. Which is, one, a great PR thing, but also you can create the flavor of the green you wanted a certain way if you fed it a certain mixture. I would say the edible [menu] paper, the [miniature tabletop] polymer oven, the indoor farm, and the Matrix were like four really big ideas that I think that seemed very pie-in-the-sky. Weird stuff. But now are common practices.

HEATHER BUBLICK: He would call us up and be like, I was just at SpaceX with Elon Musk, and we're gonna have driverless cars. I'm gonna give you guys one and you're gonna show up and the servers are going to meet the car and you know, we're gonna make donuts. He was always trying to create something. You never stopped.

RICHIE FARINA: I think in the beginning, people were a little weirded out by it. But I think by the time I got there, people knew what it was. It was a well-known restaurant at the time, and people were excited to see what experiment he was working on, or what random thing they were going to get. So let's say 95 percent of them got it. Then there's 5 percent who came because it had a Michelin star and didn't understand what the food was. But the majority of people that came in, came in excited because they had either seen the cigar or something that drew them to the place.

What I really learned from there was, don't be afraid to be who you are. I mean, it was definitely a pirate ship. Like during service, we'd play techno music over the headsets. I definitely learned there that happy cooks make happy food. Yes, there's a lot of pressure there. But also if you take it too seriously then you lose the creative spark.

I think it was about how creating that atmosphere of being able to have fun at work creates the friendships and the relationships with your coworkers. Like we would randomly have LARPing battles in the alley where we would make armor out of like, random things in the kitchen. It's just nice to have that break and then be able to hyper-focus in a situation where it's so stressful that you got taught to kind of cut all the noise out and just focus on what needs to happen. So yeah, thank you, Omar. The biggest thing is creativity, efficiency and always pushing forward.

****

When Charlie Trotter died in 2012, Cantu seemed to seize the role of keeper of Trotter's legacy, as one of the founders of The Trotter Project, which carried on culinary charitable work in Trotter's name.

RICHIE FARINA: We did Trotter's memorial at the restaurant, I think I worked like forty-something hours straight, because it's like, okay, you do service. And then we had to get ready for the thing because we had all these famous chefs coming in and Omar wanted to repaint the kitchen. So after service we had to tarp everything, and literally like me and Chris painted the ceiling. I think Omar working in that situation was like, the same rigidity that Trotter's kitchen was, and taking the chaos from that, but giving it a positive spin. Like, yes, restaurants are always gonna be chaotic and high stress. But how, when you're the most stressed and the most ready to break, you add a little bit of fun in that moment, that breaks that tension and allows you to reset and then get through the rest of service?

HEATHER BUBLICK: He loved and respected Trotter, but he also wanted, in some sense, to prove Trotter wrong. The "I can do this better than you" mentality. But there was always Trotter running through him, for sure.

TREVOR ROSE-HAMBLIN: When Charlie died, I watched a change in my friend. He had nothing but hardcore respect for Charlie. Charlie and Omar had a rough past, he didn't necessarily leave Trotter's in the best state. They butted heads. But in the end, I know right before Trotter's closed, watching him and Trotter together, they were like old friends meeting again. We got to dine in the last days of Trotter's, in a room with an old air conditioning unit, the place was dated. But the food was so damn good, it was one of my favorite dining experiences that I've ever had. And it was great to see Charlie just working the room, pouring wine for everybody.

When Charlie died, Omar was really messed up about it and couldn't get over it. He wanted to help out wherever he could. We actually had the wake at Moto, a celebration of Charlie's life. Emeril Lagasse was there, all his old buddies from Florida—Norman Van Aken was there, all of them sharing stories.

After that he brought me to his office in his home, and I remember he was kind of like pacing, we gotta do something with his house, like he wanted it to be like the next James Beard House. He got all the alumni together. It was awesome watching him work with the family and the kids.

Cantu published a miracle berry cookbook[44] *in 2013 and had plans to open a coffee shop called Berrista, featuring miracle berry–based, low-sugar pastries, as well as a brewery called Crooked Fork.*

44 *The Miracle Berry Diet Cookbook*, 2013.

HEATHER BUBLICK: Chris Jones wanted to create recipes that can be used with the miracle berry, but not have the sugar. And when you cook sugar it's a whole part of the recipe. It's not just like a simple ingredient, it has different textures. So it was hard to replicate that in the recipes, but they worked on it for a long time.

TREVOR ROSE-HAMBLIN: By the end of it I was pretty burned out on the miracle berry, because I had pored over that thing and I had tried so many things over the years to get it to be a little more friendly. It's not something that can be incorporated into something. So it came with its own set of challenges.

RICHIE FARINA: I think the way he was raised, he was always thinking bigger picture. Edible paper? You're cutting back on food waste, printing sixty menus every night and throwing them away. The whole miracle berry thing, yes, it's a parlor trick. It's cool that like, I can eat this lemon, and it tastes like lemonade. But he took that as, to cancer patients, everything tastes metallic. If we do this and develop recipes that taste good by taking this pill from the berry, maybe they can get healthier, because they're going to keep weight on because they're actually going to eat.

If you can bake it into something, or you can use it as an ingredient, now you eat this thing that's got less sugar in it because there's more acid. It was very early exploration of, how can I make junk food healthy? A muffin is a perfect thing already. How can I make that better for people by cutting out the amount of fat and sugar or whatever? There was a lot of failed stuff with the miracle berry, but I think there's still a lot of stuff that can be done with it. I think we got associated with being gimmicky at the restaurant and that might have turned some people off from the miracle berry.

HEATHER BUBLICK: I think in Omar's heart of hearts, what he would have really loved to have seen was, he would talk about coming up with an app that would have all the indigenous plants in your area. And then it would give you recipes and show you videos of how to make things with the indigenous plants. And that's how he was going to solve world hunger, because you can eat the miracle berry and these indigenous plants that are normally bitter, or whatnot, could then be palatable.

****

At the same time as Cantu was building out Berrista and Crooked Fork, he was facing a lawsuit from an investor in Moto and its spinoff, iNG, who charged him with diverting profits from the restaurants to promotion for his miracle berry book. Then came shocking news: on April 14, 2015, Cantu was found dead in the brewery space, a suicide.

RICHIE FARINA: It was technically my last week working there. Talk about a one-eighty for the week. We had all these dinners planned, I had a bunch of chefs that have worked for me that were coming back to run specials certain nights. I distinctly remember Trevor getting the phone call, and him telling us. As the leader in the kitchen, everyone's asking me, what do we do. I said, well, I know we're closed. We're not opening tonight. Other than that, I don't know. We'll figure it out.

HEATHER BUBLICK: D'Andre was on his way when Richie called me and said D'Andre can't come tonight, we're closing. We checked on Katie [McGowan, his widow] first and they wouldn't let us in, so we went over to Richie's and we were with them that night.

RICHIE FARINA: That night, we had a little impromptu thing in my apartment, a bunch of old cooks and people that had worked for him before, they all showed up. And then the good stories start coming out, the happy memories. A few days later, we all went back into the kitchen. We just cooked for the family, anyone that wants to come in and help Katie and the girls, whatever we can do. I had my last service on that Saturday, just to reopen, to get kind of my closure with it.

He was a very . . . close to the heart person. He kept a lot of stuff in. He was troubled, he needed help, but he didn't ask for it. And there were a lot of people who loved him and would have done anything for him. Obviously it's a tragedy to lose him, and that he doesn't get to be with his family anymore. But also his impact on the community, and seeing the impact that he had on people within the city. I think he was bigger than he knew, and if he had asked for help within those situations, there wouldn't have been anyone that wouldn't have helped him.

TREVOR ROSE-HAMBLIN: I think any time someone is going through mental health struggles, there's the stigma. A lot of people don't talk about mental health, they won't talk to the people they love, or to people close to them when they're struggling or hurting.

And I think that's exactly what happened with Omar. I think anyone close to him never would have seen anything coming. I mean, Omar was always on, and he had his ups and downs. But generally a happy-go-lucky guy who was always looking to the future. And the future was always bright.

RICHIE FARINA: I think a lot of his trials and tribulations growing up the way he did left him thinking he wanted to make the world a better place . . . when he left it.

****

Moto reopened after Cantu's death, but in 2016 his widow sold the Fulton Market properties to the Alinea Group. The space that had been iNG became Roister; the Moto space has remained empty ever since.

Several of the staff went to work for a West Coast startup that makes a plant-based egg substitute, Just Egg. Richie Farina worked at Curtis Duffy's Ever and was later chef of the restaurant in the Four Seasons Chicago. You might think that would have a very different approach to cooking from a place like Moto—but then again, maybe not.

RICHIE FARINA: I think probably 50 percent if not more of the R&D chefs that are there [at Just Egg] are ex-Moto employees. Because we all just grew up in that atmosphere of, what crazy shit can we think of to make an actual real thing? We're the few people who actually know how to make it happen.

[In a hotel] there have to be the staples, a chicken dish, a steak dish, whatever. So I have a chicken dish where you get three different preparations of chicken on the plate, but then I render all the chicken skin down and make chicken fat, and then I turn that into a powder with maltodextrin. So okay, now there's four styles of chicken, but when you go to a rotisserie chicken place, there's that smell of roasted chicken fat. So even that's incorporated.

TREVOR ROSE-HAMBLIN: Probably the biggest thing I learned at Moto was that you can figure it out, you know? These huge companies came to us and wanted to utilize our expertise. One of them was a startup, I think it was called Beyond Eggs, originally, and they asked us how we could make an egg that was completely vegan but could work the same way as any egg. We poured a ton of energy into it, but we always did it. And also having a leader who believes you can, that matters a lot when you're molding young culinary minds.

RICHIE FARINA: I always kind of felt like we were the redheaded stepchild—Alinea was Alinea and Moto was Moto, and we didn't have Nick Kokonas's money, we didn't have the backing that we needed. So we would just make things happen.

TREVOR ROSE-HAMBLIN: Alinea and Next do things that are extremely precision-based. They do something, they really take a deep dive. We were more like the kids in the back of the classroom throwing wads of paper.

HEATHER BUBLICK: I think there was a disappointment that like Moto was treated by some people like it was smoke and mirrors and not serious. Even when I went on to Tru, I got told during my interview, well, Moto isn't real fine dining. But Alinea is?

D'ANDRE CARTER: I didn't know what I was getting myself into, I thought I was gonna be going and making cool food, you know. But then I was learning about service and wine. And every Tuesday we had these brainstorming meetings where everybody had to have an idea. It was a cool process. I just knew I wanted to be a part of it. I went in with one idea, and I came out with more than what I thought I was going in for.

RICHIE FARINA: It's by far the craziest and most fun place I've ever worked in my life. I will never be able to recapture the 2009 to 2012 time, when it was like me, then Chris, Darrell, all these kind of big players that were grinding everyday together. Like we would all go home and try to find funny shit on YouTube to play the next day for each other to make you laugh. I met people there that are brothers for life. And I'll never be able to recreate that. I just save it as a memory.

16: COVID CODA

By 2020, Chicago's food scene was at what seemed to be its height. Michelin had come to Chicago in 2011 and rewarded a number of spots with Michelin stars—even if few Chicagoans agreed with everything they chose, or didn't choose. The James Beard Awards started coming to Chicago in 2015, a week of out-of-towners flooding West Loop restaurants, attending the ceremony at Lyric Opera—and then probably going home and writing about how Chicago wasn't as good as in (insert favorite time period here).

Many of the people featured in this book had by now gone on to open their own restaurants, or more of them. In the West Loop, the Baylesses had a microbrewery, Cruz Blanca, and a Baja coastal restaurant, Leña Brava; Curtis Duffy and Michael Muser had had Grace, which won three Michelin stars (but closed after a breakup with their backer), and were in the process of building its successor, Ever; John Ross and Phil Walters had Formento's, a new old-school Italian restaurant; Sarah Grueneberg had her Italian restaurant Monteverde; Bill Kim had Urbanbelly and Bill Kim Ramen Bar in the new Time Out Market; Paul Virant was making okonomiyaki at Gaijin; David and Anna Posey had Elske, a Nordic-inspired restaurant; and Boka Group had more new bars and restaurants than you could count.

Beyond the West Loop, Sari Zernich Worsham and her husband Scott had mfk. and Bar Biscay, Carrie Nahabedian closed Naha, but had Brindille in

River North, Jason Hammel had Marisol, the restaurant in the Museum of Contemporary Art, Kevin Hickey had The Duck Inn on the Bridgeport street he grew up on, Beverly Kim and her husband Johnny Clark had Parachute in Avondale, Erick Williams had Virtue in Hyde Park and Joe Frillman had Daisies, a farm-to-table pasta restaurant in Logan Square. The city's food culture seemed vibrant and healthy.

Little did any of these people, or anyone at all, suspect that it would all come to a screeching halt for two years—because of a virus from a place called Wuhan, in China. Here are some scenes from a pandemic.

Kelly Cheng is a second-generation co-owner of Sun Wah BBQ, a Chinese restaurant in Uptown; it won a James Beard Foundation's America's Classics award in 2018. She was interviewed at the height of the pandemic.

KELLY CHENG (interviewed May 2020): We kind of knew it was coming. We have so many friends all over the world, especially in China. We have extended family, we have friends who have been friends for so long. It was all the ones from China, trying to be careful. "We have masks, you want us to mail you some? We have plenty."

My dad, as soon as he saw the lockdown in Wuhan going for longer than a month, and then the rest of China shutting down, he's like, okay, whatever stuff we get from China, or comes through China, and is already in the US, order it now. We started hoarding early, more for price reasons. And so when everyone closed down, and everyone's asking us, how are you doing? You guys holding up? We're kind of twiddling our thumbs looking up at the sky. Yeah, we're fine. Because we already hoarded all the stuff that we need.

It was just a matter of when and how bad. We didn't think that here in the US we'd actually have to lock down, because we understand the differences between the governments. So if you said to somebody on the street here three months ago, yeah, we're going to lock down, stay in our houses, they're gonna say what? Yeah, right. It doesn't work that way here.

****

GRANT ACHATZ: It was March 13th [2020]. And I was at home on my day off. Everybody knew that we were going to shut down but everybody thought it was going to be two weeks. Nick [Kokonas] called me, and he goes, this is really serious. I'm following the science, I read about what's happening in Asia. It's a disaster. And this is going to last a long time. We're not ready with a vaccine, that will have to be developed. It's going to be a big long thing. I'm like, no way. He says, you need to start working on some to go menus. And I just started laughing. I'm like, dude, first of all, who is going to come to Alinea and pick up a brown paper bag? He says, I just think that we should peel it back. It should be forty dollars. I'm like, *forty* dollars? He says, dude, we have to get ahead of this. They're going to shut everything down. And five days later, or whatever it was, they did.

The question was, what can we produce that would have wide appeal, and relatively low maintenance to produce. And hopefully people will see it as an opportunity to have food from Alinea for forty dollars.

Their answer was high-end comfort foods, like beef short rib Wellington with buttery mashed potatoes and crème brûlée for dessert—plus instructions on how to reheat the parts of the meal that needed it.

GRANT ACHATZ: I remember on that first day, I phoned Nick and said, how many of these do you think we're gonna sell, because I have to order stuff. And he said two hundred. Two hundred? He goes, well, I mean, if we had a *really* good chef, it would be three hundred. Okay asshole, challenge accepted.

So that first day our plan was three hundred. And very quickly, we realized that a *lot* of people wanted Alinea food at a discount. At the most, we were putting out two thousand meals a day. I never thought I was going to put food in a bag to go. But after the ball started rolling, I pulled back and looked at it from a different perspective. We kept three hundred people employed. And emails starting coming in three weeks or a month in, and they were some of the most complimentary emails that we've ever gotten. Like, it was our anniversary, we didn't know what we were going to do. The restaurants are closed. We had this very special bottle of wine that we got twenty-five years ago in France that we were planning on opening. And you gave us that opportunity.

****

The first cases in Chicago were reported on January 24, 2020. On March 15, as a shutdown of at least a few weeks looked more and more likely, Jason Hammel of Lula Cafe and Jason Vincent (former Lula chef and co-owner of Giant in Logan Square) called a meeting of restaurateurs at Vincent's Bucktown restaurant, Chef's Special. While they were meeting, word came that Governor Pritzker had ordered restaurants to be shuttered the next day.

JASON HAMMEL: Everybody was texting each other about what their plans were and what they thought they were going to do. And there was a lot of confusion, obviously, and fear. I had been texting with JV. And we were just sort of in a friendly chat about, what are we going to do? I was planning on shutting down ahead of what was eventually a statewide shutdown. My staff were terrified. We were hearing about it getting worse, and I was going to give them the space to see what was going to happen.

JV actually came over [to Lula]—of course, in those days, we didn't realize getting together was probably not the thing that you wanted to do. And I said, I think we need some kind of consensus, we need to act as a group and share what our needs are. It was Sunday afternoon, so Lula was serving brunch, and I wouldn't be able to host it here. He suggested that we have it at Chef's Special, which had recently opened, who do you want to invite? I said all the people I had been texting.

Very quickly, the room was full of people. It felt like a movie, like the five families around the table in *The Godfather*. It had that kind of energy, obviously an extremely serious feel in the room itself. I am not afraid of public speaking, so I just got up and led the meeting. I said to folks, we need to communicate what our needs are, and what we could use as support from our elected leaders. And we need to come to some sort of consensus about what we're asking for in terms of support, so that our common voice can be heard. What we agreed to was crafting a message that we would all simultaneously record and post at the same time.

We called for some things we needed from Governor Pritzker and the senators and Mayor Lightfoot—interestingly, the mayor had eaten at Lula the night before. And one thing that was really positive was that we got an email list together with roughly a hundred names on it. We started an email chain that lasted through the dark days of the pandemic, when nobody knew what was going to happen or when we were going to reopen. We continue to communicate through that list to this day.

I think there was some discussion of payable sales tax—we pay sales tax on the twentieth of each month for the previous month, and we were talking about [relief from] that. Unemployment insurance was another thing that was top of people's minds, making sure that our employees would be taken care of. Rent and loan abatement.

But the most important thing was the idea of collective action. And when we all posted it at the same time, it did have an impact. I think it showed the power of the industry's collective voice. And many other groups were formed in that time, including the IRC [Independent Restaurant Coalition], which I was a part of, immediately, almost on the same day we got together. And that group eventually lobbied for the Restaurant Act [supporting independent restaurants]. I was contacted by several other city groups, one in New York, one in San Francisco, one in Los Angeles, that were trying to do similar things. So it definitely had an impact on others in the industry.

There was a strong sense of community that we tapped into, made stronger by that moment. And it remains like one of the more profound experiences in my professional life, for sure. Just getting in front of that group of people saying like, hey, what are we going to do? How should we do it? What do we want to say that we need? How do we want to say it? What's our best chance for being heard? It was a seminal moment for us.

****

Erick Williams opened his fine dining soul food restaurant, Virtue, in Hyde Park in 2018. He was among the chefs who attended the meeting at Chef's Special.

ERICK WILLIAMS: We were all standing in that room, meeting and kind of vocalizing our positions, and how this is going to impact us collectively, what steps we can take. Then we dispersed, and after a day or so, I went into doing family meals out of our restaurant. We wanted to make sure our guys had income coming in. We felt like the safest way to execute that was to limit who came into the building.

So the meals were passed out outside, curb service. People would social distance in the line outside, because masks weren't allowed yet, because we were saving the masks for the doctors and nurses so there wouldn't be a shortage. And we all agreed we wouldn't go see our parents or our grandparents until we could get a bit of clarity. Essentially our pod was the group of folks who worked with us, and whoever our mates or roommates were. That actually worked for us—none of our people got COVID during that period.

We got up to about eight hundred meals a day. There was that much demand in the neighborhood, and we had to rethink everything. The kitchen's not set up to serve that kind of volume, and you just don't think about how much room you need to mix mashed potatoes for eight hundred people. It was crazy. And even though we were basically working as a commissary, we still wanted the food to be really delicious—maybe more delicious then than any other time, because people needed a win.

It just became incredibly exhausting, listening to the news every day about the infection rate surging, the death rate surging, not being able to see loved ones outside of FaceTime or Zoom. And so after about three months, we decided to pivot to feeding first responders. We wanted to double down on community, because the community had been so supportive of us.

If we did hospital drops, we could do good, and we could continue to stabilize our team. And we only had to pack the food and then drop it at the front door, because they wouldn't let us in the hospital. But we wanted to do those drops, to remind people who were on the front lines that somebody cared.

We made that decision on a Sunday as we were putting out our last meals, and I shared it with the team on Monday through text. And then Tuesday, we get a text from [the rapper] Common's team, and he, I guess, was having the same idea. He had partnered with [the dating app] Bumble to promote the app, and he was going to announce that he was dating [actress] Tiffany Haddish over Bumble, virtual dates. They would share a meal over Zoom, but he wanted to take the proceeds and donate them to purchase food for a hospital. I knew Common from my mk days—he came in before the premiere of the movie *Barbershop.*

Everybody's PR teams connected, and soon Williams and crew were delivering to John H. Stroger, Jr. Hospital, the leading public hospital and trauma center on the South Side.

ERICK WILLIAMS: It was important that Common was involved, because once the media sunk their teeth into it and spread the story, people at home who wanted to give now had a means to give without leaving home. So now we had a vehicle where the restaurant wouldn't have to shoulder the burden, and the community had come together once again.

We expedited paying our vendors in seven-day turnarounds, because the vendors were having a hard time with drivers and getting product. We started doing three days a week—that would give us one day to physically prep with nobody other than ourselves, so we could rock out in the restaurant like five or six of us, and then the servers that needed to come in would come in and help us pack, organize meal boxes, tape boxes. All we asked people to do is just send us a photo with meals in hand so we could share those photos with the people who were donating.

We ran that for a while, until we had the opportunity to [reopen with] partitions in the dining room. We had no intention of doing al fresco dining, even though we had the equipment. Because it's a long way from a kitchen to the sidewalk if you haven't planned for it. I don't think people really realize that. If you have a vestibule in front of your restaurant, you've got a second set of doors that you got to get through with food. If it's a windy day, then garnishes get blown down the street as you're trying to walk up with the food—all kinds of things we never had to think about.

My days would be filled with phone calls to chef friends to talk. Like, if a picture went out with flowers, they would call, hey, who did your florals? Oh, we actually did that ourselves this morning, and this is where you can get your flowers for a dollar. And that's how we managed for what we thought was going to be six months, and turned into two solid years.

****

"Pivot" became the word of the moment, as restaurants moved from artfully-crafted plates to comfort takeout food like Detroit-style pizza and Nashville hot chicken. Meanwhile, government programs promised relief for restaurants. Matt Sussman, owner of the Alpine gastropub Table, Donkey and Stick in Logan Square, talked about wrestling with both:

MATT SUSSMAN (interviewed May 2020): It was pretty clear there was going to be a devastating effect on restaurants. We all run on pretty tight profit margins and any kind of shock to the business model is something that's going to be hard to adjust to. The last day the restaurants were open [March 15], we actually were closed. I think the day before that we were open for dine-in, and then shut it down, before it got announced.

Obviously, when I was making the decisions, it wasn't known what the stimulus would look like. But it was already clear that they would have to take some action, because whole industries were being shut down overnight. So my intention was to figure out a business model that would support as much of the staff as possible.

Our menu isn't really designed for take-out and delivery—we've never done delivery at all. There are people who live in the neighborhood who pick up a burger now and then. So it seemed like we needed to make some kind of pivot if we were going to be—I don't want to say profitable, but sustainable. And pizza is something that is near and dear to me. Something I had thought a lot about before any of this happened.

We have a guy who comes with a lot of baking experience, and he was doing these pan pizzas for family meal. I think the first day we did it was the Sunday which was our last night allowing people into the restaurant. And then we piloted it the following couple of days and by the end of that week, we had launched more or less at the scale we're at.

The model we moved to with the pizza proved to be sustainable. It doesn't support the level of staffing that we were at before, but it supports more than half of that. As the week went by, we learned more about how the stimulus was going to work and then the PPP [Paycheck Protection Program] thing which is a little bit complicated, and basically took a week and a half of my life from me.

Sussman was handing off pies by night—and trying to sign up for PPP by day.

MATT SUSSMAN: The program was announced. I was keeping a close eye on what was going on with the two banks we work with. That Friday, applications were starting to be accepted. And both those banks don't have any means of accepting applications.

The beginning of the next week, one of them has an online portal. And I tried to use it and I couldn't upload the documents that they required, it was giving me the same error every time. That was literally like twenty hours of trying to upload documents. So it was a pretty frustrating week.

Finally, the money was deposited in our account, and that starts the clock on an eight-week period, when you can use the funds for forgivable purposes, which are primarily payroll expenses. But also rent and utilities, as long as those costs are less than 25 percent of the amount that you asked to be forgiven. And so that was enough to bring back all of our full-time, or full-time-ish employees.

For businesses that are still operating, but are impacted, I think it works pretty well. But there's also been a major personal issue, that my father died a few weeks ago. And that was also happening at the time that I was applying for PPP. Speaking of fuckups, he died of COVID. In New York. Potentially preventable. He had lymphoma, but that's not something that necessarily kills you. But it is something that if you have it, and you get COVID, it's probably not good news. So that happened, and just in the last week, I've gotten back to looking at what we're doing.

You don't open a restaurant to have the easiest path, I guess. And even in good times, there's a lot of responsibility if you employ twenty people. This obviously isn't a scenario that I envisioned. I guess maybe I should have.

****

Real estate had become so expensive for restaurants—and suddenly they weren't bringing revenue in. Al Friedman described how a landlord approached the situation:

AL FRIEDMAN (interviewed April 2021): Every restaurant we worked with we tried to help. Some were completely unreasonable. But anyone who was reasonable, we worked with. Reasonable meaning, if they said when I get back on my feet, I'll repay you, okay. But if they said hell no, I'm not paying anything—it's not a one-way street. We're both in the same predicament here.

****

CARRIE NAHABEDIAN (owner, Brindille, interviewed November 2020): We're losing, bit by bit, Chicago. The fact that so many restaurants are saying, we're going to close till spring [2021]. I look at [her cousin and co-owner]

Michael and say, do you think we should pull a Banchet and close the whole month of June to figure it out? Let the staff go on vacation? And he looks at me and goes, where would they be able to go? I don't know, but I just don't see us sitting around to do seven to-go orders.

We have friends that not only do they have loans on their restaurants, they have mortgages on their houses, and now they've gotten second mortgages, and they've blown through PPP, they've already gotten the small business loans. You get a grant here, you get a grant there and, and then you're boarded up and you're trying to figure it all out.

****

JIMMY BANNOS SR. (owner, Heaven on Seven, interviewed April 2021): We're not even close to being back open. Mostly my employees are either back in Guatemala, or working in factories. It's honestly a joke. So I get a bunch of employees, and nobody's going to be making any money. Not me—I'll be paying everybody's salary.

I was talking to one of my purveyors, it's amazing that in the suburbs, as long as you have a mayor and a police chief on [the side of restaurants], you can go do anything you want. You can open up 100 percent. Here, they're writing tickets. I'm like, really? We're fighting for our life here.

Bannos delivered takeout food, which he cooked himself through much of the pandemic, but after forty years, Heaven on Seven never reopened after closing in March 2020.

****

John Ross's experience at The Bristol, recounted in 2024, shows how hard it was to keep up with the rules—as they frequently changed, and especially for a small restaurant that, even at 50 percent allowable capacity, could not separate tables far enough apart for City Hall.

JOHN ROSS: If you look back at it now, you know a lot of it was just made up in terms of what the standards are. Nobody knew, but everyone's an internet expert.

We didn't want to put our team in harm's way. Secondly, we had to make sure the guests feel like they're good, so they feel like they're having a safe experience for themselves. Because obviously the Maple & Ashes [Rush Street steak house] of the world, the Gibsons of the world, seated all the way through COVID. And made gazillions because they never closed. I went to Maple & Ash one night with my wife, because I was like, I gotta see this. And it was packed. There's tables of fourteen, there's tables with twenty, and you're like, I'm in an alternate universe right now. I can't get anybody to come to my restaurant, because they're scared. I don't have any staff. The government's threatening us with every fine in the world. And this place is like living a year and a half ago. It was unreal.

Among other things, The Bristol put in an elaborate air filtration system—and then the rules changed again. The favored way to separate people was now with clear plastic tents, or "igloos," so they could eat outside even in a Chicago winter.

JOHN ROSS: We did those things, because we felt like it was the right thing to do. Not knowing what was right or wrong, but we wanted to make sure that at least that was there for staff and for the guests. And obviously, it was a tremendous expense to us. I mean, it was great to have PPP and so on, but you spent all that money. You spent all that money on your team. You spent all that money on trying to stay open.

The tents were ridiculous. We did it because it placated the city—if that's what you're going to allow us to do, then that's what we're gonna do. But it was ridiculous. You're gonna put people in a bubble, as opposed to a filtration system that you know is inside with little filters on each and every table? I mean, listen, everyone was scrambling, everyone thought they knew and nobody knew, you know, blah, blah, blah. I'm just glad it's over and I hope it never comes back.

The Bristol reopened fully as the rules were relaxed, but after Ross was shot in the leg during a holdup in the alley behind the restaurant in 2021, he and partner Phil Walters closed it for good at the end of 2022.

****

In the end, fewer restaurants closed due to COVID than anyone expected at the low points, but some of the big ones were still major blows to the food scene. And no closing was bigger than One Off Hospitality's Blackbird, which was made permanent in June 2020.

PAUL KAHAN: COVID was a game changer, an industry changer. What can I say? The hardest time business-wise, or life in general, that I've ever had to endure. Just the unknown, a thousand employees in our company, no road map how to approach things, we made a ton of mistakes. I think fewer than a lot of groups or people, but who knows?

There was one point where we did a GoFundMe for our teams. Number one, we kept people on the payroll, a lot of them the whole time, but a lot as long as we could and we kept their benefits going as long as we could. But there's no money coming in. And at a certain point, either we close the doors of all of our businesses, or we've got to furlough people, just like everyone did. We did a GoFundMe campaign for that, and we raised a fair amount of money and we looked at the most equitable way to share that money with our teams. There's tax implications, and we found out that the best way to do it would be to give them gift certificates to a grocery store. People need food, and it skirted the tax implications. But we got destroyed on social media by our employees for sharing money with them and saving them money in taxes because we gave it in the form of gift certificates.

Every decision you made was under a microscope. Was it right? Was it wrong? Who knows, because no one ever had to go through that before.

DONNIE MADIA: Closing Blackbird was one of the toughest decisions that I've had to make in my life. I went through a long process. I called Danny Meyer and got some advice from him. And the advice that sticks with me today is optionality, when you own a piece of real estate, you don't have to decide to do something detrimental, you can wait. And maybe we should have waited a little longer.

Our cooks work seamlessly in a very close environment. I don't know how somebody can stand six feet away from another. The kitchens aren't built that way. No foodservice is built that way.

But also understand that the survival of the others was really important. And that was weighing heavily on us. There was the possibility of losing more.

So we made a decision to close two restaurants, Blackbird and Café Cancale [in the Soul Kitchen space in Wicker Park], and the other restaurants survived. They're doing well. So I have a great respect for the decision. Even though I miss that place all the time. And it's a part of who I am. I loved working there. I got married there. I have only lovely feelings about everything I did there, and everything that Paul did there and everything that Ricky did. And everybody, every chef that came in there and worked their way up from line cook to sous chef to chef de cuisine.

PAUL KAHAN: Honestly the question for me was, is fine dining gonna survive? That was a big conversation. My thought was, I don't think it will, which was the wrong opinion. But truth be told from my end of it, the restaurant wasn't the same as when I was running the kitchen. Talented people, not doing anything wrong, but I just felt like I was very disconnected from it. Personally, that's just my end of the decision.

DONNIE MADIA: COVID and the other situations that were unfolding were distractions to what one of the main focuses should be, which is understanding what that restaurant meant to us, but also to the city. Maybe there was a better decision, or maybe we should have just waited a little longer, or whatever the next chapter would have been. I don't think there's a day that goes by, that I don't see someone that if I lock eyes with that person, that person might say, man, I really miss Blackbird.

****

Meanwhile, Kevin Boehm and Rob Katz were part of national efforts to get government support for the restaurant industry.

KEVIN BOEHM (interviewed December 2020): Once we went into the winter, and you don't have any outdoor dining, you're only doing takeout. Some landlords are sympathetic, but many of them don't do anything. And you just lose copious amounts of money.

We dug a hole that was in the millions. I don't care who you are, it's fucking painful. I'm grateful it hit me at a point in my career, where Rob and I could take the punches. But it doesn't make it any easier to possibly see thirty years of work going down the drain. And not knowing when there's going to be an end to it.

You see articles that talk about who got PPP and who didn't, it's talked about without context. You look at, like, Rick Bayless, and as soon as the PPP came out, he was paying all his employees, and they weren't even generating any income. Right? You know, PPP only works when you're generating income. It pays for your rent, and it goes to payroll—it doesn't go to the owners' pockets. No one was getting rich off of PPP—in the restaurant business.

The moment we went into this whole thing, we said, hey, we're gonna extend our base health coverage, Rob and I donated personally $100,000 to our employees. We put together a fund for employees, which raised more money for everybody. I think if you talk to people that actually work for our company, they would say that we've tried to do as much as we possibly can, and at the same time, just keep our business solvent, so they have a business to come back to.

Right as the lockdown was set to begin, Boehm's greatest inspiration, his mother, died of pancreatic cancer.

KEVIN BOEHM: Two days after my mom died, I sat in my office, organizing the Independent Restaurant Coalition. The great thing about the IRC has been, it's not just advocacy. It's been a support group. And there's about fifty operators that I'm on the phone with every single morning. Locally, that's Jason Hammel and Donnie Madia and Rick Bayless, and nationally, Bobby Stuckey [Frasca Food and Wine, Boulder], and Adam Saper [Eataly USA] and Sean Feeney [Lilia, Brooklyn] and Ashley Christensen [AC Restaurants, Raleigh] and Kwame Onwauchi [Tatiana, New York City] and Tom Colicchio [Craft, New York City]. I can't tell you how many hours we've spent on the IRC, and we came so close to getting the Restaurant Act passed. Fucking wrote a bill and got it past the House. And then fifty co-sponsors in the Senate, and we couldn't get past the one-yard line. We literally were on the one-yard line.

I've said it so many times. Our country has a long history of bailing out companies that were culpable in their own demise. We gave money to Fannie

Mae and Freddie Mac very easily. When Chrysler couldn't make an economical car in the late 1970s, here's a billion and a half dollars.

ROB KATZ (interviewed 2024): COVID was just such an absolute devastation, not only to our employees, to our industry, to hospitality around, of course, the whole fucking world. But hospitality suffered exponentially to the point of, is our life's work going to be over? Are we going bankrupt? Are we truly gonna just lose everything that we have worked decades for?

I made a call to the bank about two days before the shutdown. I said, I need every possible dollar that you can spare for a line of credit. And I need it now. So we took all that money to protect ourselves, because we knew that we had a massive payroll. And we didn't know if it's gonna be a week, three weeks, or six months or a year, we just didn't know what we didn't know.

Kevin and others from around the country were really working behind the scenes with government, while I'm on the phone with landlords and bankers and lawyers all fucking day. Because we needed money, we needed more money, then we needed more money, then we needed relief from our rent. We needed to renegotiate the best we could. And to put it in perspective, with your children and your wife, how do you separate this to keep them from realizing the severity of what's happening?

We were shut down. Government mandated us closed, [it was] illegal to open to do anything. Then you can open but you've got to be six feet apart. You can only have this much occupancy. Okay, then what happens? They shut you down again in October. You open, you close. In any other industry, how would that even have been possible?

Now that we've gone through COVID and come out of COVID, business is better than it's ever been. The post-COVID reality check was the supply chain and inflation. And a little bit of the millennial malaise. Zero loyalty, we don't give a shit. You know, we tried to build our business around culture and loyalty and longevity. And young people are like, hey man, fuck you, what have you done for us? Not everyone, but it was very difficult to come back. Hiring became impossible. Pricing became impossible. You needed a walk-in cooler, you needed a light fixture—six months. An electrical panel—eight months. I'm grateful for everybody who stuck to it, and are feeling some of the rewards of it now.

****

After a few months, anger seemed to well up at restaurant owners. Social media accounts appeared where restaurant workers could anonymously accuse their bosses of being awful people, or attack them for cooking a cuisine from a culture they don't belong to, or whip up fury against an Asian chicken wing joint for not posting "Black Lives Matter" on their social media the instant an anonymous person online ordered them to.

Joe Frillman had his farm-to-table restaurant Daisies, using produce from the farm run by his brother. He was never a major target of the people on these sites, but he saw it in action:

JOE FRILLMAN (interviewed June 2020): We did takeout for a short time, and then we shut it down. The service staff was kind of exhausted. We started losing staff members for various reasons, it was I'm going home, or I'm gonna go, you know, stay with my parents or hey, I've been in contact with one individual who may have had it. And at that point, there was no testing. And so it was a self-quarantine situation where we would lose somebody for two weeks.

Now we've got the Sunday [Logan Square farmers] market, and we've got this market that we're trying to build in our back room, to see how many different revenue streams that it's going to take for us to get back to even 50 percent of what we were doing. One of the hardest things for us has been getting servers to come off unemployment and giving them enough work, especially if it rains three or four days out of the week. If the weather's bad, how much of that can we afford to keep paying out, to make it worth their while to essentially come off of unemployment.

I've been seeing some crazy shit online. One of our former employees tried to start some shit with us, and it's like he had zero traction whatsoever. Back in February he basically tried to get a staff walk-out because he thought he wasn't treated properly, which is just bullshit. I think what these kids don't realize is sometimes you're just not good at your fucking job. Not everyone can do everything.

People think we're millionaires. The margins in this business, they're just not great, no matter what you're doing. If they're great, you're either doing crazy volume, or your product is probably not the greatest product from a broad liner [large wholesaler]. All I want is to pay my employees as much money as I can pay them. It's not perfect, it's still a restaurant, it's still a job. Not everybody loves going to work on a daily basis. But we try to do everything we can to make it as inclusive, as creative, as stimulating and encouraging as we can. You're canceling people before they even have an opportunity to learn from the lesson to make it right. If we knew everything, we would probably just do it the right way ahead of time, right?

Part of the whole thing is like, we donate and we do charity, and we donate so much of our time and our products. And I don't sit here and yell it from the mountaintops. We do what we do. Because we believe in it. I'm not gonna sit here and misuse it from a marketing standpoint. Like, why do you have to know what I donate? And who I donate to? We do a ton of stuff, but I'm not gonna sit here and go through it, just because you're calling me out on it.

****

Even Alinea had a spell as the online whipping boy, thanks to one dish served outdoors at what was dubbed Alinea In Residence, or AIR:

GRANT ACHATZ: We were scrapping, and we were determined to seize any opportunity to keep people paid. And so when they opened up outdoor dining, we knew the space on the rooftop [at 952 W. Fulton Market, across from Next, Roister and the Aviary] because the owner of 555 Design, he owns that building. And he was the one that built out Roister for us. So we contacted them. It was primarily a wedding space, and obviously there were no weddings happening, so we rented it from him.

The issue was a typically conceptual Alinea dish—a small blue sphere of coconut custard, studded with freeze-dried bits of raspberries. In short, it was an edible coronavirus. A doctor who ate at AIR and was amused by it posted it on Instagram—provoking online outrage.

GRANT ACHATZ: I mean, it *was* too soon. And there was just too much chaos in the world and people were still dying. I thought it was like raising awareness and it just felt right. And I talked to Nick and he's like, yeah, you know, I think this is fine. And it wasn't really fine.

This author expressed admiration for the black humor of it, and the spirit of defiance it showed against the virus that had upended all our lives:

GRANT ACHATZ: Thank you. But you're the only one.

****

There wasn't a single Day of Liberation from COVID. Instead, step by step, it faded from our lives. Restaurants could seat at 50 percent capacity as of March 2021, then 100 percent by June 2021—the guests all eating around their masks. In January 2022 masks were no longer required, but guests had to show proof of vaccination to enter public spaces like restaurants. Then on February 28 that requirement was officially dropped. Just days shy of the original lockdown's second anniversary, Chicago restaurants were free of COVID restrictions.

*The new restaurants that opened in the first year after lockdown were mostly safer bets—steak houses and Italian restaurants. But Chicago chefs were quickly itching to display their creativity and variety—there were Filipino and Indian and Mexican tasting menus, and neighborhood places doing all sorts of artisanal food and drink, drawing on every part of the world. And Chicago's culinary creativity and diversity would be showcased on a hot TV series set in the world of restaurants—*The Bear.

The city's food scene isn't quite back to what it was in the mid-eighties, when Charlie Trotter's and Frontera Grill and Spiaggia opened, or in the mid-2000s, when Alinea and Blackbird and The Bristol and Elizabeth defined the scene. But at this writing, three years from the last time any of us had to show our vaccination cards at the host stand, Chicago seems on its path to the next great era of Chicago dining. It's the Chicago way.

ACKNOWLEDGEMENTS

First thanks must go to my publisher, Doug Seibold of Agate Publishing, who—having published a book on Chicago theater in its most exciting era (*Ensemble*, by Mark Larson, 2019)—went looking for another topic on which Chicago had been a center of creative ferment over pretty much the same time period. And having found one (that wasn't basketball), he proposed it to me, with perfect timing just as a pandemic was about to make the past more active than the present. I'll also thank John Podhoretz, who suggested over dinner at Boka that after a few years of weekly journalism, I should think about writing something more substantial (or at least less ephemeral), thus ensuring I'd be receptive to Doug's idea when it fell in my lap.

Thanks to everyone quoted in this oral history, of course; a list of them with capsule biographies follows. Several in particular went beyond the call of duty to help me track down other interesting people to interview—some, names I knew; others I'd never have known about without help. For offering suggestions and connections, I especially thank Bill Ammons, Laura Windt Collins, Casey Cora, Emily Clark Ehrenberg, Jenn Galdes, Carol Mighton Haddix, Anne Trotter Hinkamp, Janet Isabelli, Ann Johnson, Darcy Jusich, Cindy Kurman, Sarah Kwasinski Evans, Catherine Lambrecht, Michael Muser, Heidi Peckat, Ina Pinkney, Lauren Schumacker, Margaret Sheridan, Liz Lombardo Stark, Jason Stern, Maggie Trboyevic, Jeffrey Ward, and Sari Zernich Worsham.

Particular thanks for assistance in getting me up to speed on the past (if not before I was born, certainly before I was a fine diner) to Penny Pollack, who lent me her notes from many years of covering food for *Chicago* magazine; to my fellow LTHForum co-founder Rob Gardner, who lent me a number of Chicago food books from the 1960s and 1970s; to Anne Spiselman and Michael Nagrant, who I would occasionally quiz about obscure aspects of the dining scene and bounce theories off of; and to Gary Adcock for helping with technical questions related to the planned video capture of my in-person interviews, which came to a screeching halt when COVID happened—but still, thanks!

Especially in the early days of collecting interviews, when I was working out what the overall narrative would be, I talked to a lot of people, and invited industry people on social media to look me up. Some of those people and restaurants ended up not being part of the overarching story I tell here—but still, talking to them was important for my understanding of the scene, especially as it existed forty, fifty or more years ago. So sincere thanks for helping me find my story to people including Dave Bonomi, Michael Boucher, Leigh Bush, Belinda Chang, Aydin Dincer, Didier Durand, Terry Durkin, Melissa Graham, Bruce Kraig, Chris Liakouras, Keith Luce, Michael Nahabedian, Dudley Nieto, Michael Niksic, Jonathan Porter, Peter Regas, Jan Robert Richardson, Bob Schwartz, and Aldo Zaninotto.

NOTES ON CONTRIBUTORS

Grant Achatz worked at Charlie Trotter's and The French Laundry before joining Trio in Evanston as its third chef. In 2006 he opened Alinea, which ranked #7 on the World's 50 Best Restaurant list in 2012. His other restaurants have included Next, The Aviary and Roister.

Henry Adaniya was a server and manager at restaurants including Ambria and Café Provençal before opening Trio in Evanston in 1994. He lives in Honolulu, where he owned Hank's Haute Dogs from 2007 to 2024.

Terry Alexander co-owned Danny's Tavern in Bucktown and helped launch and manage the Mia Francesca chain, also owning Mod, Del Toro and other Wicker Park restaurants. He went into business with Donnie Madia to open the nightclub Sonotheque, and joined One Off Hospitality to open The Violet Hour, Big Star and others.

Bill Ammons owned Star Top Cafe in Lakeview. He's an HVAC engineer.

Stephen Anderson got his MFA from the University of Massachusetts; after that he returned to Chicago, working for Jovan Trboyevic at Le Perroquet and Les Nomades. Retired, he lives in Deerfield.

Doris Banchet met Jean Banchet when he was working in London, and followed her husband to America, opening Le Francais in 1974 and owning it (with some interruptions) with him until 2001. She lives in Florida.

Jimmy Bannos Sr. started serving Cajun recipes at his family's coffee shop on the seventh floor of a Loop office and retail building in the early '80s. It became a sensation as Heaven on Seven, lasting four decades before it closed during the lockdown.

David Barriball joined Blackbird as a server and rose to general manager and wine director; he is now operations director for One Off Hospitality.

Wilson Bauer worked at Elizabeth, Longman & Eagle and Grace, and was chef de cuisine at Schwa. He owns Flour Power, a pasta restaurant and shop.

Sharon Bautista is a researcher, designer, and yoga teacher. For several years, she co-owned and operated Fork and the Road, a small business leading off-the-beaten path culinary bicycle tours around Chicago.

Rick and Deann Bayless researched Mexican foodways for five years before publishing their first book, *Authentic Mexican,* and opening their first restaurant, Frontera Grill, in 1987. They've since opened Michelin-starred Topolobampo and other restaurants, published multiple books, and did twelve seasons of the PBS series *Mexico: One Plate at a Time.*

Martha Bayne was an associate editor and then dining editor of the *Chicago Reader* from 1999 to 2007, and has worked for the *Chicago Tribune*, *Plate* Magazine, *South Side Weekly*, Belt Publishing and the University of Illinois Press. She started Soup and Bread, a fundraising event at Chicago's The Hideout, and is the author and editor of *The Soup and Bread Cookbook* (Agate Publishing).

Portia Belloc Lowndes was a co-founder of Slow Food Chicago and co-author of *The Slow Food Guide to Chicago,* as well as a board member of Green City Market. She was the executive director and chef at Heritage Prairie Farm and runs Project FEAST, a culinary event agency.

Ari Bendersky is a lifestyle journalist specializing in food, wine, spirits and travel. The founding editor of Eater Chicago from 2010 to 2012, Ari's work has appeared in the *New York Times*, *WSJ* magazine, Associated Press, *Men's Journal, Wine Enthusiast, Departures,* RollingStone.com, *Crain's Chicago Business, Time Out* Chicago, liquor.com and many other publications. He writes a Substack newsletter called Something Glorious.

Dave Beran worked at restaurants including mk and Tru before joining Alinea, where he rose to chef de cuisine before becoming opening executive chef for Next. He opened Dialogue in Santa Monica in 2017, and now has Pasjoli.

Cheeku Bidani was an early member of LTHForum. He is a database developer who works with Chicago area non-profits, and a collector of vintage audio equipment and African music of the '60s and '70s.

Greg Biggers worked for chefs including Rick Tramonto (Tru, Tramonto's Steak & Seafood), Sean Brock (McCrady's in Charleston), and Masaharu Morimoto in Philadelphia. He has been executive chef at Café des Architectes in the Sofitel Chicago, and Michael Mina's Margeaux Brasserie at the Waldorf-Astoria Chicago. He is chief operating officer of Stephanie Izard's product line, This Little Goat.

Caryn Bobrowski is a restaurant industry veteran who worked for KDK Restaurants in the West Loop, mk, Boka Restaurant Group and others. She works for Bon Appetit Management Group, which provides food services to corporate and institutional clients.

Kevin Boehm is co-founder with Rob Katz of the Boka Restaurant Group, which includes Boka, the Girl & the Goat empire, Swift & Sons, Alla Vita and many others. He started in Springfield, Illinois, and had restaurants there and in Florida before coming to Chicago.

Juan Boldizsar worked for Louis Szathmary at The Bakery from the age of twelve. He is a mortgage professional and lives in Belleville, Illinois.

Andrew Brochu was a chef at Chicago restaurants including Graham Elliot, Kith & Kin, EL Ideas and Roister. He owns Brochu's Family Tradition in Savannah, Georgia.

Kevin Brown started at Lettuce Entertain You as a manager at R.J. Grunts, and went on to become CEO of the company; he is now executive chairman.

JeanMarie Brownson was a food editor and test kitchen director for the *Chicago Tribune* from 1980 to 1996. She wrote about the opening of Frontera Grill, and went on to co-author several of Rick Bayless's cookbooks, to help launch Frontera Foods, and to collaborate on his PBS series *Mexico: One Plate at a Time.*

Heather Bublick worked at Moto, where she met her husband, D'Andre Carter; they had a catering company, Feast & Imbibe, and then launched a local chain of barbecue restaurants, Soul & Smoke.

Gerald Buster, with his then-wife Carolyn, owned The Cottage restaurant in Calumet City for twenty-one years.

Lynn Buzza is a cook and pastry chef who has worked at restaurants including Everest,

Marché, Soul Kitchen and Wolfgang Puck's Grand Cafe. More recently she's been the kitchen manager for a group of private schools in Chicago.

Paula Camp was a restaurant reviewer and editor for the *Chicago Tribune*, as Paul Camp, from 1984 to 1990. She owns Carriage House Ciders in Benton Harbor, Michigan.

Joe Campagna made a career switch from finance to cooking by going to work for Charlie Trotter. He worked for other restaurants, and now runs a credit card processing business for food and beverage clients.

Michael Carlson worked under Paul Bartolotta at Spiaggia, Heston Blumenthal at The Fat Duck, and Grant Achatz at Trio. He opened Schwa in 2005, and was named one of *Food & Wine's* best new chefs in 2006.

Mark Caro was a staff writer for the *Chicago Tribune* from 1986 to 2015, and is the author of *The Foie Gras Wars* (Simon & Schuster, 2011). He has the music podcast *Caropop*.

David Carrier worked at The French Laundry and went with Grant Achatz to help him take over Trio. Later restaurants in Chicago included (the much-loved but short-lived) Kith & Kin; he owns Certified Burgers and Beverage in St. Simons Island, Georgia.

D'Andre Carter worked at Moto, rising to the position of sous chef. He met his wife, Heather Bublick, there; they had a catering company, Feast & Imbibe, and then launched a chain of barbecue restaurants, Soul & Smoke.

Jason Chan grew up with parents who owned restaurants and bars, and worked for many of the top restaurateurs in Chicago, including Lettuce Entertain You, Jerry Kleiner and Michael Kornick. His restaurants have included Butter (named by John Mariani in *Esquire* as one of the top 20 restaurants in America), Ohba, Urban Union and Gavroche.

Kelly Cheng is, with her brother and sister, a second-generation owner of Sun Wah BBQ, a Hong Kong-style Chinese barbecue restaurant which won a James Beard Foundation America's Classics award in 2018.

David Cleverdon worked in the civil rights movement in the 1960s and in Illinois politics in the 1970s, serving as assistant to Governor Dan Walker. He was a trader at the

Chicago Board of Trade, and started Kinnikinnick Farms in Caledonia, Illinois, serving as a founding board member of the Green City Market.

John Colletti is a native Chicagoan who worked for restaurants including Ditka's City Lights and Shaw's Crab House. He joined the original Gibsons Bar & Steakhouse on Rush Street as general manager in 1992; today he is managing partner of Gibsons Restaurant Group.

Regina Contos was the fourth wife and widow of Bill Contos, owner and proprietor of Chez Paul. She divides her time between Miami and her native Germany.

Tom Cornille, great-grandson of a farmer on what's now the Far North Side of Chicago, is the third-generation head of a boutique produce supplier to chefs, George J. Cornille & Sons.

Patrick Crane is a veteran chef who worked at Charlie Trotter's, 1776 in Crystal Lake, the Drake Hotel and Chicago Cut Steakhouse, among others. He started several Facebook groups devoted to Chicago restaurant history, such as Chicago Restaurants 86 But Not Forgotten.

Michael Curtin was a server and manager at The Bakery, the Mid-America Club and other Chicago restaurants. Retired, he lives in Ennis, Ireland.

Pat Dailey was a feature writer for the *Chicago Tribune* from 1989 to 1997, and a publisher and editorial director for Reed Elsevier, as well as a trustee of the Culinary Institute of America.

Howard Davis is an attorney who was one of the partners in KDK Restaurant Group, co-owning Vivo, Marché and other popular West Loop restaurants. He owns Bar Roma in the Andersonville neighborhood.

François de Mélogue was an executive chef for Louis Szathmary at The Bakery and later ran Chicago restaurants including Bistrot Margot and Pili Pili. He lives in Vermont and is the author of *French Cooking For Beginners* (Rockridge Press, 2020).

Steve Dolinsky covered Chicago food for CLTV and then spent seventeen years as the Hungry Hound at ABC7 in Chicago before joining NBC 5 as The Food Guy from 2021–2025. He also co-hosted the podcast *The Feed* with Rick Bayless and has won thirteen James Beard awards for his broadcast work, while contributing to print publications including the *Chicago Tribune* and Canada's *The Globe and Mail.* He's the author of two books on Chicago pizza, *Pizza City, USA* and *The Ultimate Chicago Pizza Guide.* He works for Levy Restaurants.

Dave Dravenack is a graduate of Second City and worked as a server at Ed Debevic's in the 1990s. He performs stand-up comedy in the Chicago area.

Jennifer Smith Drilon started as a cook and pastry chef for Lettuce Entertain You at Ambria, Cafe Ba-Ba-Reeba! and Corner Bakery, among others. She is executive chef for the Toast Hotel Group in southwestern Michigan.

Curtis Duffy worked for Charlie Trotter and for Grant Achatz at Trio, becoming chef de cuisine at Alinea. He served as chef at Avenues in the Peninsula Hotel before opening his restaurant Grace, which held three Michelin stars from 2015 until its closing in 2017. He has Michelin-starred Ever in the West Loop.

Monica Eng has covered food, food policy and local issues at many Chicago outlets, including the *Chicago Sun-Times,* the *Daily Southtown*, the *Chicago Tribune* from 1996 to 2013, and WBEZ from 2013 to 2021. A six-time James Beard award nominee, she is co-reporter for Axios Chicago, and co-author (with David Hammond) of *Made in Chicago: Stories Behind 30 Great Hometown Bites* (3 Fields Books, 2023).

Peter Engler is a biological researcher and an early participant in LTHForum.

Ellen Fairey worked for Chicago restaurants in the 1990s including Star Top Cafe and Soul Kitchen. Her play *Graceland* got good reviews in Chicago and New York, and she went on to become a writer for TV shows like *Nurse Jackie, Masters of Sex* and *Away.*

Richie Farina worked at Moto, where he rose to the position of executive chef, and appeared on season 9 of *Top Chef.* He worked at Ever and other restaurants, and was the chef of Adorn in the Four Seasons Hotel in Chicago.

Gary Alan Fine taught sociology at Northwestern University for many years. He is the author of a study of restaurant culture, *Kitchens: The Culture of Restaurant Work* (University of California Press, 1996).

Bruce Finkelman is a developer and bar and restaurant owner whose places have included Longman & Eagle, the Empty Bottle, Thalia Hall and the Salt Shed.

Joe Flamm worked in various Chicago kitchens including Bill Kim's BellyQ, Girl

& the Goat and the University Club before joining Spiaggia, becoming its executive chef in 2015. He won *Top Chef* in 2018, and opened his first restaurant, Rose Mary, in 2021; he is culinary director of Day Off Group.

Michael Foley opened Printer's Row in 1981, helping to revitalize the South Loop and pioneer the farmers market movement in the Midwest. He had other restaurants, including First Street wine bar and reopening Le Perroquet in the early '90s; he was named to the Who's Who of Food and Beverage in America in its inaugural year, 1984.

Phillip Foss worked around the world, from Le Cirque in New York to the King David Hotel in Jerusalem, and came to Chicago to work at the Palmer House Hilton. He had the Meatyballs food truck, which evolved into doing fine dining in his prep space with EL Ideas.

Charles D. "Skip" Fox IV is a retired attorney in Charlottesville, Virginia. He taught at Northwestern University School of Law from 1983 to 2005.

Al Friedman inherited some properties in a rundown neighborhood from his father in 1970. Renaming the area River North, he revitalized the area by focusing on restaurants—like Gordon, Frontera Grill and Maggiano's Little Italy—as a draw for others to the neighborhood. He's Chairman and CEO of Friedman Properties.

Joe Frillman worked as a cook at restaurants from Chicago's The Bristol and Balena to The Fat Duck in England. He owns Daisies, a farm-to-table pasta restaurant in Logan Square.

Christian Gaborit was working for Maxim's in Paris when he was sent to Chicago as part of the opening team for Nancy Goldberg's Maxim's. He worked there from 1963 to 1969, and worked in Paris, New York and Los Angeles before returning to Chicago, where he continues to consult for hotels and restaurants.

Gale Gand is a two-time James Beard award-winning pastry chef. With her then-husband, Rick Tramonto, she opened Trio and Tru in Chicago. The author of multiple cookbooks, she hosted the Food Network's *Sweet Dreams* from 2000 to 2008.

Rob Gardner is a legal researcher who blogged at Vital Information, was a founding member of LTHForum and later ran The Local Beet.

Christopher Gerber was the manager of Trio and then maître d'/manager at Alinea, later becoming director of service for the Alinea Group. He also worked at NoMI, the Aviary, and Bavette's Bar & Boeuf, and is general manager/partner at Smyth and the Loyalist.

Jonathan Goldsmith was a social worker and real estate investor when he opened Spacca Napoli, baking authentic Neapolitan pizzas using "00" flour in a woodburning oven, in 2006.

Jim Graziano is a fourth-generation operator of his family's business, J.P. Graziano & Sons, which began as a wholesaler on Randolph Street and today serves Italian subs to the new residents and businesses in the now-hot area.

Koren Grieveson was a sous chef for Blackbird and then chef de cuisine of avec from its opening in 2003 until 2012. She was executive chef of Resto in New York, and now lives in Connecticut and is the executive chef for a group of private schools.

Mark Grosz is a Detroit native who came to Chicago to work for Jean Banchet at Le Francais. He worked in France and Hong Kong before opening Oceanique in Evanston in 1989.

Sarah Grueneberg grew up in Texas and came to Chicago to work at Spiaggia, becoming its executive chef in 2010. She opened her restaurant Monteverde in 2015, and won a James Beard Award for Best Chef Great Lakes in 2017. She is the author of *Listen To Your Vegetables* (Harvest Books, 2022).

Bernard Guinand is a retired chef who was born in St. Chamond, France and worked in Chicago at Le Perroquet, Le Tour in the Park Hyatt, Le Francais and Ambria.

Carol Mighton Haddix was the editor of the food section and supervisor of the test kitchen for the *Chicago Tribune* from 1977 to 2011, and is the author of several cookbooks.

Jason Hammel is the owner of Lula Cafe and the author of *The Lula Cafe Cookbook* (Phaidon, 2023).

David Hammond is a food writer and freelance marketing and corporate writer. He was a founding member of LTHForum and has written for *Time Out* Chicago, the *Chicago Sun-Times*, the *Chicago Tribune* and *NewCity*. He is co-author (with Monica Eng) of *Made in Chicago: Stories Behind 30 Great Hometown Bites* (3 Fields Books, 2023).

Paula Haney worked at Trio under Shawn McClain and Grant Achatz. She is the owner of Hoosier Mama Pie Company, and author of *The Hoosier Mama Book of Pie* (Agate Midway, 2013).

Ray Harris is a retired managing director/vice chairman of Morgan Stanley, who dined approximately four hundred times at Charlie Trotter's.

Philip Hess is a California attorney who, with his late wife Margaret, was a regular patron of Jovan Trboyevic's restaurants during and long after the years he attended college and law school at the University of Chicago.

Judy Hevrdejs worked for the *Chicago Daily News* and then for the *Chicago Tribune* from 1978–82 and 1990–2015, serving as dining editor for Play, including Good Eating, Cheap Eats and The Stew blog.

Kevin Hickey is a Bridgeport neighborhood native who worked all around the world for the Four Seasons and Ritz-Carlton hotel chains, winning a Michelin star at Chicago's Allium. He now owns The Duck Inn on the same block where he grew up.

Judith Dunbar Hines has taught cooking, consulted for food companies and television programs, and was Director of Culinary Arts and Events for the City of Chicago's Department of Cultural Affairs.

Anne Trotter Hinkamp is the sister of Chef Charlie Trotter, and a founding member of The Trotter Project.

John Hogan worked his way up in many Chicago restaurants, including Everest and Kiki's Bistro, before opening the critically acclaimed Savarin in the late 1990s and launching Keefer's in 2001. More recently he ran River Roast and worked for Whittingham Meats.

Robert and Paula Houde met while working at Charlie Trotter's. They run Robert Houde Wines, an importer and distributor in Chicago, and are both founding members of The Trotter Project; he is president of the board and she is the director of operations.

Stephanie Izard made her name with her restaurant Scylla, and achieved national fame as winner of season 4 of *Top Chef.* Joining the Boka Restaurant Group, she opened Girl & the Goat, Little Goat Diner, Duck Duck Goat and Cabra in the West Loop. She now lives primarily in Los Angeles, where she has outposts of Girl & the Goat and Cabra.

Richard James has been a cook and chef for Rick Bayless's restaurants for two decades; he is managing chef of Frontera, Topolobampo and Xoco.

David Jarvis was born in Buffalo and attended Johnson & Wales culinary school. He trained under chefs including Jean Banchet and Wolfgang Puck before opening Melange American Eatery on the North Shore in 1986, later working for Rick Tramonto at Tramonto's Steak & Seafood.

Ivar Johnson was a server at Blackbird for about sixteen years, circa 2000 to 2016. He works at Providence, a Michelin-starred restaurant in Los Angeles.

Jean Joho was born in Alsace and trained under Chef Paul Haeberlin at Auberge de l'Ill beginning at age 13. He came to Chicago to run Maxim's, and soon joined Lettuce Entertain You where his restaurants included Everest, Brasserie Jo, Corner Bakery, and The Eiffel Tower in Las Vegas.

Farmer Lee Jones is a distinctive sight in overalls and red bowtie on his family farm, Chef's Garden, in Huron, Ohio. He provides produce to top restaurants nationwide and is a frequent speaker on regenerative farm practices.

Paul Kahan is the chef partner of One Off Hospitality, which has included Blackbird, avec, The Publican and Big Star, among others. He got his training under Erwin Drechsler (Metropolis, Erwin) and Rick Bayless (Topolobampo); among other honors he won the James Beard Award for Outstanding Chef in 2013.

Sherman Kaplan spent forty-six years as a news anchor for WBBM-AM, the CBS news radio station in Chicago, and served as its restaurant reviewer and theater critic from 1985 to 2010. He retired in 2015.

Martin Kastner is a Czech-born industrial designer and owner of Crucial Detail, who created many of the unique serving pieces used at Grant Achatz's restaurants. He lives in Lyon, France.

Rob Katz is co-founder and the primary financial partner for the Boka Restaurant Group (Girl & the Goat, Boka, Swift & Sons and many more). He owned several bars before switching to restaurants with partner Kevin Boehm.

Allen Kelson started doing writing and paste-up for the WFMT (classical music radio) program guide and evolved it into *Chicago* magazine as its founding editor. With his late wife Carla as dining editor, the Kelsons were the dominant restaurant reviewers on the Chicago dining scene through the 1970s and 1980s. He died in 2023.

Beverly Kim worked at the Ritz-Carlton, Charlie Trotter's and Aria in the Fairmont Chicago before opening Parachute, where she and her husband Johnny Clark won a James Beard award for Best Chef Great Lakes in 2019. They also have Anelya, devoted to his Ukrainian heritage.

Bill Kim went to Kendall College and trained in classic French fine dining under Charlie Trotter, Jean Banchet and Pierre Pollin. On his own, he's explored his native Korean cuisine with restaurants including Urbanbelly, Belly Shack and Dimmi Dimmi.

Nick Kindelsperger co-founded the blog The Paupered Chef and served as editor of Grub Street Chicago and Serious Eats Chicago. He was a writer and restaurant reviewer for the *Chicago Tribune* from 2016 to 2023.

Jerry Kleiner is an interior designer and furniture designer who owned popular bars and restaurants in the West Loop in the 1990s and early 2000s, including Shelter, Vivo, Marché, Red Light and Carnivale. He now lives in Los Angeles.

Nick Kokonas co-founded the Alinea Group with Grant Achatz, opening Alinea, Next, the Aviary and other restaurants. He also founded the reservation platform Tock, and co-wrote Achatz's memoir *Life, on the Line.* He sold the bulk of his shares in the Alinea Group in 2024.

Michael Kornick is a veteran Chicago chef and restaurateur who has worked for everyone from Lettuce Entertain You to Arnie Morton and Jerry Kleiner. He owned the upscale River North restaurant mk for two decades, and with David Morton started DMK restaurant group, owning about twenty restaurants at its peak. He now lives in Golden, Colorado.

Michael Lachowicz started in his family's restaurant, then trained under Jean Banchet and Roland Liccioni at Le Francais, and Maxime Ribera in France. His restaurants have included Les Deux Gros in Glen Ellyn and Restaurant Michael, George Trois and Aboyer in Winnetka.

Simon Lamb has managed a number of top restaurants for Levy Restaurants, KDK (including Marché and Red Light), as well as Le Sud and others.

Catherine Lambrecht was a co-founder of LTHForum, the Greater Midwest Foodways Alliance and Culinary Historians of Chicago's Chicago Foodways Roundtable, among other mostly food-related organizations she is involved with.

Justin Large was a cook for One Off Hospitality's Blackbird and avec, eventually becoming the group's first culinary director. He works as an in-house hospitality operations consultant for PAR Technology.

Bernie Laskowski was a chef at many top restaurants in Chicago including the Four Seasons Hotel, Bin 36 and the Park Grill Chicago. He owns CraftUrban in Aurora, Illinois.

Frank Lee worked as a cook in Chicago for Jovan Trboyevic before becoming opening chef at the acclaimed restaurant S.N.O.B. (Slightly North of Broad) in Charleston, South Carolina in 1993; he is the author of *The S.N.O.B. Experience* (2016).

Mary Beth Liccioni worked at Le Francais as a pastry chef and then at Carlos', where she met her then-husband, Roland Liccioni. They took over Le Francais from the Banchets in 1989, running it until 1999; she also acquired Les Nomades from Jovan Trboyevic in 1993.

Roland Liccioni was born in Saigon and trained and worked in Paris and London before coming to Chicago in the 1980s and working at Carlos' and Le Francais. He and his then-wife Mary Beth Liccioni ran Le Francais from 1989 to 1999, and Les Nomades from 1993-2004. His restaurants have also included Le Lan and Old Town Brasserie; he returned to Les Nomades in 2011 and retired in 2024.

Dave Ligon was a manager at the Pump Room and Ambria for Lettuce Entertain You, and later at Trio.

Steve Lombardo is a Chicago bar and restaurant veteran who got his start in the army, managing officers' clubs. He owned Sweetwater and other bars in the Rush Street area, and co-founded the Gibsons Restaurant Group, which operates several of the top-grossing restaurants in the country.

Michael and Susan Maddox worked for Pierre Pollin at Le Titi de Paris in Arlington Heights, then purchased it from him when he retired and ran it until it closed in 2012. They've taught at Kendall College and College of DuPage Culinary School.

Donnie Madia worked on the hospitality side of many Chicago restaurants including Tufano's Vernon Park Tap and Ooh-La-La! before co-founding Blackbird in

1998, the start of what would become One Off Hospitality.

Alain Maes attended college in Provence before coming to America and working for the French Trade Commission in Chicago, and later as a consultant for international businesses. He has the website French Virtual Cafe, an exhaustively researched resource about French restaurants in the Chicago area.

Deb Majic was chef and co-owner of Cafe Figaro in Lincoln Park in the 1970s and '80s. She is a CPA in Chicago.

Ellen Malloy worked for One Off Hospitality and then had her own PR firm in Chicago.

Toby Maloney worked in Chicago restaurants such as Soul Kitchen before going to New York, where he worked at many of the originators of the modern cocktail scene, including Milk & Honey and Pegu Club. In Chicago, he opened the Violet Hour, and later Mother's Ruin; his book *The Bartender's Manifesto* (with Emma Janzen) won a James Beard award in 2023.

David Manilow is a television producer and creator-producer of the TV program *Check, Please!* which ran in Chicago from 2001 to 2020 and had spinoffs in San Francisco, Seattle and other markets. He is a contributor to *Crain's Chicago Business,* doing the *Dining Table* podcast.

Tony Mantuano was the founding chef of Chicago's Michelin-starred Italian restaurant Spiaggia and ran it for twenty-eight of its thirty-seven years. He and his wife Cathy next went to Nashville, where they ran restaurants, including Yolan, in The Joseph Hotel, from 2021 to 2024. He now operates two outposts of The Purple Pig, in Chicago and Oak Brook.

Shawn McClain was the chef at Trio before opening his Chicago restaurants Spring and the vegetarian restaurant Green Zebra. His group now has restaurants in Las Vegas and in Detroit.

Rich Melman is the founder and chairman of Lettuce Entertain You restaurants, which he launched in 1970 with its first restaurant, R.J. Grunts.

R.J. Melman is the oldest son of Rich Melman and now serves as CEO of Lettuce Entertain You, having been involved with launching Lettuce properties such as Hub 51, Paris Club, and Sushi-San and Ramen-San.

Mary Sue Milliken trained in Chicago before moving to Los Angeles in 1981 where, with Susan Feniger, she opened several restaurants including CITY, Border Grills in LA and Las Vegas and Socalo in Santa Monica. Additionally, she starred in three hundred episodes of *Cooking with Too Hot Tamales,* co-wrote five cookbooks, competed on *Top Chef Masters* season 3, and has won awards from both the James Beard and Julia Child Foundations.

Michael Morowitz is a technology professional in Chicago. He launched the food blogs Eatchicago.net and Localbeet.com, and was a moderator at LTHForum.

Amy Morton is the daughter of Arnie Morton (Playboy Clubs, Morton's). She owned restaurants like Mirador in the 1980s and 1990s; after a break, she returned to the restaurant industry in the 2010s with restaurants including Found and LeTour in Evanston.

Michael Muser worked at Ambria, Avenues in the Peninsula Hotel, and other fine restaurants in Chicago. He was co-owner and manager of Grace and Ever with Chef Curtis Duffy. He is also executive director of The Banchet Awards.

Michael Nagrant is a technology consultant and started the food blog Hungry Magazine. He has been a restaurant reviewer for *Redeye* and the *Chicago Sun-Times* and written for other publications including *Chicago* magazine and the Alinea cookbook. Today he has a Substack newsletter, The Hunger.

Carrie Nahabedian worked at the Ritz-Carlton in Chicago, Le Francais, and for Gordon Sinclair at Sinclair's in Lake Forest before opening Naha with her cousin Michael in the former Gordon location in 2000; they opened Brindille in 2013, and closed Naha in 2018.

Carlos Nieto was born in Mexico and worked in Chicago restaurants including L'Escargot and Le Francais, before opening Carlos' in the northern suburbs in 1981. It ran for three decades as one of the city's top restaurants before evolving into the more casual Nieto's; today he owns The Happ Inn in Northfield.

Scott Noorman was a wine steward at Trio, opening sommelier at Alinea and opening wine director and service coordinator at Elizabeth. He lives in Grand Rapids, Michigan.

Andres Padilla was born in New Mexico and rose at Rick Bayless's restaurants to chef de cuisine of Topolobampo and Leña Brava, and culinary director for the group. He is executive chef at Hotel Paso del Norte in El Paso.

Chris Pandel worked for Rick Tramonto at Tru, Osteria via Stato and other restaurants, before being opening chef for the gastropub The Bristol in Chicago's Bucktown neighborhood. He is executive chef at Boka Group's Swift & Sons and other restaurants.

Jeff Pikus has worked at many Chicago restaurants including Alinea, the Aviary, Spiaggia, Perennial, Rootstock, and Maude's Liquor Bar, and for Marjie's Grill in New Orleans.

Ina Pinkney owned Chicago's beloved breakfast restaurant Ina's from 1991 to 2013. She is the author of *Ina's Kitchen: Memories and Recipes from the Breakfast Queen* (Agate, 2015) and the subject of a 2015 documentary, *Breakfast at Ina's.*

Penny Pollack started at *Chicago* magazine in 1987, and was its dining editor for twenty-four years, from 1994 to 2017.

Pierre Pollin was born in Normandy and trained in French restaurants such as Lucas Carton. He moved to Chicago in 1974 to work at Le Titi de Paris in the northwest suburbs, and bought it in 1978. He sold it to his employees Michael and Susan Maddox in 2004, and taught at Kendall College.

Anna and David Posey met while working for One Off Hospitality; she was pastry chef at The Publican, and he was chef de cuisine at Blackbird. He had previously worked at Alinea. They own Elske, a Nordic restaurant in the West Loop.

Lane Regan, as Iliana, worked in Chicago restaurants including Trio and Alinea before starting their restaurant Elizabeth. They're the author of *Burn the Place: A Memoir* and *Fieldwork: A Forager's Memoir* (Agate, 2019 and 2022). They now have the Milkweed Inn in Michigan's upper peninsula.

Trevor Rose-Hamblin worked at Moto, and was going to be the brewer at Moto's brewery spinoff Crooked Fork. He is the brewer at Old Irving Brewing Co.

John Ross was a manager at restaurants including Tramonto's Steak & Seafood before teaming up with Philip Walters to launch B. Hospitality Co. with The Bristol. Other restaurants have included Balena and Formento's.

Garrett Russell worked at Chicago restaurants including Schwa, Oriole and Kumiko. He lives in Honolulu.

Mindy Segal is a James Beard award-winning pastry chef who worked at restaurants including Gordon, Ambria, Charlie Trotter's, Marché and mk. She owned the restaurant Mindy's Hot Chocolate from 2005 to 2020, and now owns Mindy's Bakery. She is the author of *Cookie Love* (Ten Speed, 2015).

Eduard Seitan was born in Romania and was an opening partner at Blackbird, with an emphasis on the wine programs there and at avec. He is a certified sommelier.

Jackie Shen worked in Chicago hotels before opening Jackie's on Lincoln Avenue, being featured in PBS's *Great Chefs of Chicago* and becoming famous for her chocolate bag dessert. She worked at Red Light and other Chicago restaurants; today she owns Jackie's Cafe in New Buffalo, Michigan.

Margaret Sheridan was a food reporter for the *Chicago Tribune* from 1979 to 1989, and has written for other publications, including as editor of *Restaurants & Institutions.*

Bruce Sherman lived and trained in Paris and India before becoming chef/owner of North Pond in Chicago in 1999, operating it until 2019, and winning the James Beard award for Best Chef Great Lakes in 2012. He has been a board member of the Green City Market since 2000.

Heather Shouse wrote for *Chicago Social* and the *Chicago Tribune*, was the Chicago reporter for *Food & Wine* and was founding food and drink editor of *Time Out* Chicago from its launch in 2005 to 2013. She owns Bottle & Branch, which creates interior and exterior landscape design for the hospitality industry.

Miklos P. Simon was born in Hungary and worked as a server at The Bakery while attending the School of the Art Institute of Chicago. He is a sculptor and teaches at Columbia College and other institutions in the Chicago region.

Gordon Sinclair worked in public relations for the military and the *Chicago Tribune* before opening the popular and trendy River North restaurant Gordon in 1976. He closed it in 1999; in retirement he has lived in Chicago and Mexico.

Dr. Lee Smith is a retired plastic surgeon who lives in West Virginia. He dined at Charlie Trotter's approximately two hundred times.

Doug Sohn worked in publishing before opening his "encased meats superstore," Hot Doug's, in 2001. He's co-author of *Hot Doug's: The Book* (Agate Midway, 2013).

Gabino Sotelino is a Spanish-born chef who was the chef of Le Perroquet, before joining Lettuce Entertain You as a partner and opening restaurants including Ambria, Mon Ami Gabi and Cafe Ba-Ba-Reeba!

Joseph Spellman is a certified master sommelier who worked for many top Chicago restaurants including the Pump Room, Maxim's and Charlie Trotter's, and for Justin Vineyards.

Anne Spiselman has been a restaurant and theater reviewer for publications including *Chicago* magazine from 1979 to 2004, the *Chicago Reader*, and *Crain's Chicago Business* from 1983 to 2004.

Camille Stagg was a food editor at the *Sun-Times* from 1965 to 1977, and wrote or reviewed restaurants for *Cuisine, A Taste of California* and FM 100; she is the author of *The Parthenon Cookbook, The Eclectic Gourmet Guide to Chicago* and other books.

Sarah Stegner was a cook and executive chef at the Dining Room at the Ritz-Carlton from 1984 to 2004, and is chef-owner of Prairie Grass Cafe in suburban Northbrook. She is a co-founder of the Green City Market, and won James Beard awards for Best Rising Chef in 1994 and Best Chef in 1998.

Todd Stein is a veteran Chicago chef who has worked for restaurants including Gordon, David Burke, mk, The Bristol and Formento's, and had his restaurant Cibo Matto.

Larry Stone worked as a wine columnist for the *Chicago Tribune* and for the Four Seasons Hotel before joining Charlie Trotter's as sommelier, building the restaurant's legendary wine program. He later opened Rubicon in Napa with Drew Nieporent and joined Niebaum-Coppola Estate Winery as general manager, before founding Lingua Franca Wines in the Willamette Valley.

Matt Sussman worked in public policy before opening the Logan Square gastropub Table, Donkey and Stick; he also owns Bar Parisette.

Michael Taus worked for Charlie Trotter before opening restaurants of his own including Zealous, Duchamp and Taus Authentic.

Guillermo Tellez-Cruz rose to chef de cuisine at Charlie Trotter's and served as chef for his projects in Las Vegas and Los Cabos, Mexico, where he continues to live and work.

Leslie Tellez was a pastry chef at Charlie Trotter's. With her husband, Guillermo, she works in Los Cabos, Mexico.

Giuseppe Tentori came to the US from Milan to work for chef Gabriel Viti in Highland Park, Illinois. He worked at Charlie Trotter's and then took over the Boka Group's flagship, Boka, in 2007, being named Best New Chef by *Food & Wine* in 2008. He later opened GT Fish & Oyster and GT Prime. He left the Boka group in 2024.

John Terczak was the longest-running chef at Gordon, and later had Chicago restaurants including Terczak's, Tamales and Chameleon. He has lived in Florida and then the Philippines, and had an online cooking school called The Seasoned Cook.

Rick Tramonto is a chef who worked at Chicago restaurants including Avanzare and Charlie Trotter's. With his then wife Gale Gand, he opened Trio, Brasserie T, and Tru, for which he won a James Beard award for Best Chef Midwest in 2002. He now has Restaurant R'evolution in New Orleans, and also serves as director of food and beverage for Parker Hospitality in Chicago.

Maggie Abbott Trboyevic is an artist and interior designer who helped design and manage her late husband Jovan Trboyevic's restaurants, including Le Perroquet and Les Nomades.

Dona-Lee Trotter is the mother of Chef Charlie Trotter, and was the restaurant's hostess for many years.

Scott Tyree was a server and sommelier at Shaw's Crab House before building the wine program at Tru. A certified master sommelier, he worked for the auction house Hart Davis Hart before returning to the floor at Chicago's Sepia. He lives in Freeport, Maine.

Norman Van Aken, owner of Norman's in Coral Gables, is one of the most acclaimed chefs in Florida and an originator of "New World cuisine." He worked for Gordon Sinclair in Jupiter, Florida and at Sinclair's on the North Shore, where he met and became lifelong friends with a young cook named Chuck Trotter.

Phil Vettel joined the *Chicago Tribune* in 1980 and became its dining critic in 1990, holding that position for thirty-one years. He retired in 2021.

Paul Virant owned Vie in Western Springs, and now owns Petite Vie in Western

Springs, Vistro in Hinsdale and Gaijin in the West Loop. He worked for restaurants including March in New York and Everest, Ambria, Charlie Trotter's and Blackbird.

Tracey Vowell rose from grill cook at Frontera Grill to executive chef at Frontera and Topolobampo, also leading the development of the group's network of farmer vendors. She owns Three Sisters Garden in Kankakee, Illinois, where she grows winter spinach, among other things.

Scott Warner is a freelance journalist on food, contributing to publications including the *Chicago Tribune*, the *Chicago Sun-Times*, and the *Oxford Encyclopedia of Food and Drink in America*. He is President and Program Chairman and a founding member of Culinary Historians of Chicago.

Carol Watson co-founded the Francesca chain of Italian restaurants and owns Milk & Honey Cafe in Wicker Park, which also spawned a grocery store brand of granolas.

Jared Wentworth is a chef who's worked in Seattle, San Jose and Chicago, where he has been the chef at Longman & Eagle, Thalia Hall, Moody Tongue Brewery and others.

Erick Williams worked at Michael Kornick's mk, rising to executive chef and partner over nearly two decades. He owns Virtue and Daisy's Po-Boy and Tavern in Hyde Park, and won Best Chef Great Lakes at the James Beard awards in 2022.

John Winterman worked at Charlie Trotter's in Chicago before going on to work for Gary Danko in San Francisco and Daniel Boulud in New York. His restaurant Batard in Tribeca won a James Beard award for Best New Restaurant in 2015; today he runs Michelin-starred Francie in Brooklyn.

Sari Zernich Worsham started as a line cook at Charlie Trotter's, but spent much of her time there as his collaborator on his cookbooks and television programs. She has opened mfk. and Bar Biscay with her husband, Scott.

Jim Wygonski was a server and restaurant manager for Gordon, John Terczak's Tamales, and Ambria, among many other restaurants. He works in the funeral industry in Des Plaines, Illinois.

Don Yamauchi was born in Chicago and attended Kendall College before going to work at Carlos' on the North Shore, training under Roland Liccioni and Gabriel Viti. He took over from Jean Banchet at Le Francais in 2001, and has worked since then in

Detroit, Las Vegas and Sanibel Island. He owns Big City Burrito in Colorado.

Celeste Zaccaro is a pastry chef who has worked for many restaurants, including Sinclair's, Carlos', Le Francais, Bittersweet, The Bristol and Princi.

Dean Zanella is a longtime Chicago chef at restaurants including 312 Chicago, Chicago Cut, Rhapsody, Tripoli Tap and Tutore Italian Cooking School.

CHRONOLOGY OF SELECTED RESTAURANTS

JACQUES FRENCH RESTAURANT 1935 - 1983
J.P. GRAZIANO CO. 1937 -
THE PUMP ROOM 1938 - 2017
CHEZ PAUL 1945 - 1995
LEO'S LUNCHROOM 1951 - 2005
MAXIM'S 1963 - 1986
THE BAKERY 1963 - 1989
JOVAN 1967 - 1986
L'ESCARGOT 1968 - 1993
R.J. GRUNTS 1971 -
LE TITI DE PARIS 1972 - 2012
LE PERROQUET 1973 - 1991
LE FRANCAIS 1973 - 2007
THE COTTAGE 1974 - 1996
GORDON 1976 - 1999
CAFÉ PROVENÇAL 1977 - 1993
THE DINING ROOM AT THE RITZ-CARLTON 1977 - 2007
MORTON'S [STATE STREET ORIGINAL] 1978 - 2020
LES NOMADES 1979 -
AMBRIA 1980 - 2007
INA'S RESTAURANT 1980 - 2013
HEAVEN ON SEVEN 1980 - 2020
CARLOS' 1981 - 2012
PRINTER'S ROW 1981 - 2004
UN GRAND CAFÉ/MON AMI GABI 1981 -
AVANZARE 1982 - 1997
JACKIE'S 1983 - 1995
STAR TOP CAFE 1983 - 1996
SPIAGGIA 1984 - 2021
ED DEBEVIC'S 1984 - 2015, 2021 -
CAFE BA-BA-REEBA! 1985 -
THE EVEREST ROOM/EVEREST 1986 - 2020
SCOOZI! 1986 - 2014
CHARLIE TROTTER'S 1987 - 2012
FRONTERA GRILL 1987 -
SUN WAH BBQ 1987 -
GIBSONS BAR & STEAKHOUSE 1989 -
TOPOLOBAMPO 1989 -
VIVO 1991 - 2015
MAGGIANO'S LITTLE ITALY 1991 -
MIA FRANCESCA 1992 -
SOUL KITCHEN 1993 - 1996
TRIO 1994 - 2006
MARCHÉ 1994 - 2011
BRASSERIE JO 1995 - 2010
RED LIGHT 1996 - 2011
BLACKBIRD 1997 - 2020
NORTH POND 1998 -
TRU 1999 - 2017
MK 1999- 2017
LULA CAFE 1999 -
NAHA 2000 - 2018
SPRING 2001 - 2010
HOT DOUG'S 2001 - 2014
AVEC 2003 -
BOKA 2003 -
MOTO 2004 - 2016
ALINEA 2005 -
SCHWA 2005 -
OSTERIA VIA STATO 2005 -
HOOSIER MAMA PIE CO. 2005 -
TRAMONTO'S STEAK & SEAFOOD 2006 - 2013
SPACCA NAPOLI 2006 -
THE VIOLET HOUR 2007 - 2025
THE BRISTOL 2008 - 2022
HUB 51 2008 - 2024
THE PUBLICAN 2008 -
BIG STAR 2009 -
GIRL & THE GOAT 2010 -
LONGMAN & EAGLE 2010 -
NEXT 2011 -
THE AVIARY 2011 -
EL IDEAS 2011 -
BALENA 2012 - 2017
ELIZABETH 2012 - 2022
LITTLE GOAT DINER 2012 -
TABLE, DONKEY AND STICK 2012 -
SWIFT & SONS 2015 -
DUCK DUCK GOAT 2016 -
ROISTER/FIRE 2016 - 2025
DAISIES 2017 -
VIRTUE 2018 -

ABOUT THE AUTHOR

Michael Gebert is a James Beard Award–winning food writer and video producer. Born and raised in Wichita, Kansas, he came to Chicago to work (and eat) as a copywriter in advertising, working for most of the top advertising agencies in Chicago. When the dot-com crash and then 9/11 brought advertising to a halt for a time, he started writing about food online, co-founding Chicago's food chat site LTHForum and writing for publications including the *Chicago Reader*, *Chicago* magazine, *Time Out* Chicago, Grub Street Chicago, Air Canada's magazine *En Route,* Saveur.com, Serious Eats, Thrillist, *NewCity* and others. He has been nominated for a James Beard award three times, for the *Reader* and his own site, Sky Full of Bacon, and won in 2011 for a chef challenge video series for the *Reader, Key Ingredient.* He also won the Headline Club's Peter Lisagor Award in 2018 for his site Fooditor. His past books include *The Encyclopedia of Movie Awards* (St. Martin's Press, 1996) and an annual Fooditor restaurant guide, *The Fooditor 99.*

INDEX